Third Edition

Gender

Psychological Perspectives

Linda Brannon
McNeese State University

Allyn and Bacon
Boston • London • Toronto • Sydney • Tokyo • Singapore

Executive Editor: Carolyn Merrill
Editorial Assistant: Lara Zeises
Senior Marketing Manager: Caroline Croley
Editorial-Production Service: Omegatype Typography, Inc.
Manufacturing Buyer: Joanne Sweeney
Cover Administrator: Linda Knowles
Electronic Composition: Omegatype Typography, Inc.

A Pearson Education Company
75 Arlington Street
Boston, MA 02116

Internet: www.ablongman.com

Between the time Website information is gathered and published, some sites may have closed. Also, the transcription of URLs can result in typographical errors. The publisher would appreciate notification where these occur so that they may be corrected in subsequent editions.

Library of Congress Cataloging-in-Publication Data
Brannon, Linda
Gender : psychological perspectives / Linda Brannon.—3rd ed.
p. cm.
Includes bibliographical references and index.
ISBN 0-205-32750-8 (alk. paper)
1. Sex differences (Psychology) 2. Gender identity. 3. Sex role. 4. Feminist pyschology. 5. Women—Psychology. I. Title.

BF692.2 .B73 2002
155.3—dc21

2001022424

Printed in the United States of America
10 9 8 7 6 5 4 3 2 1 06 05 04 03 02 01

Contents

Preface

This book examines the topic of gender—the behaviors and attitudes that relate to (but are not entirely congruent with) biological sex. A large and growing body of research on sex, gender, and gender-related behaviors has come from psychology, sociology, biology, biochemistry, neurology, and anthropology. This research and scholarship form the basis for this book, providing the material for a critical review and an attempt to generate an overall picture of gender from a psychological perspective.

The Topic of Gender

A critical review of gender research is important for several reasons. First, gender is currently a hot topic, and almost everyone has an opinion. These opinions are not usually based on research. Most people are not familiar with research findings; they simply know their own opinions. People's opinions are strongly influenced by their own experience and also by what they have seen in the movies, on television, and in other media. Whether these programs are news reports or fiction, both types of presentations make an impact. Based on these portrayals, people create images about how they believe women and men should be, and they attempt to re-create these images in themselves. In *Gender: Psychological Perspectives,* I present what gender researchers have found, although the picture is neither simple nor complete. Research findings are complex and sometimes contradictory, but I believe that it is important to understand this research rather than draw conclusions based only on personal opinions and popular media portrayals.

Second, research is a valuable way to understand gender, despite the bias and controversy that have surrounded the research process. Although scientific research is supposed to be objective and free of personal bias, this idealistic notion often varies from the actual research process. Gender research in particular has been plagued with personal bias. Despite the bias that can enter into the research process, I believe that research is the most productive way to approach the evaluation of a topic. Others disagree with this view, including some who are interested in gender-related topics. A number of scholars, especially feminist scholars, have rejected scientific research as the best way to learn about gender.

Although I agree that science has not treated women equitably, either as researchers or as participants in research, I still believe that science offers the best chance for a fuller understanding of gender (as well as of many other topics). Some scholars disagree with this view, but I want to make my point of view clear. My proscience orientation is the reason I have chosen to concentrate on research throughout the book—to examine what gender researchers have found and how they have interpreted their findings.

In this book the emphasis on gender is similar to another approach to studying gender—examining the psychology of women. The psychology-of-women approach concentrates on women and issues unique to women, whereas the gender approach focuses on the issue of gender as a factor in behavior and in the social context in which behavior occurs. Gender research and theory draw heavily from research on the psychology of women, but the emphasis differs.

By emphasizing women and their experience, the psychology-of-women approach often excludes men, but gender research cannot. Studying both women and men is essential to an understanding of gender. Researchers who are interested in gender issues may concentrate on women or men, but they must consider both, or their research reveals nothing about gender. Therefore, this third edition of *Gender: Psychological Perspectives* examines the research and theory from psychology and related fields in order to evaluate the behavior, biology, and social context in which both women *and* men function.

The gender approach also reflects my personal preferences: I want a psychology of women and men. When I was completing the first edition of this book, I attended a conference session on creating a course in psychology of women. Several instructors who had created such courses led a discussion group about obtaining institutional approval and the problems they had encountered, including resistance from administrators (who were mostly men) concerning a course in which the enrollment would be mostly women. One of the group advised trying for approval of a course on gender if obtaining approval for a psychology-of-women course was not successful. The implication was that the topic of gender included men and would be more acceptable but less desirable. I disagreed. I wanted men to be included—in the research, in my book, and in my classes. This desire comes from the belief that women and men are required in order to consider and discuss gender issues. I prefer the gender approach, and I wanted this book to reflect that attitude.

My interest in gender comes from two sources—my research and my experience as a female psychologist. The research that prompted me to examine gender issues more carefully was on risk perception related to health problems. I was interested in investigating people's perceptions of the health risks they created as a result of their behavior, such as the perceptions of health risks in smokers versus nonsmokers. In this research, I found that women and men saw their behaviors and risks in similar ways, even when the actual level of health risks did differ for men and women. My research showed gender similarities rather than gender differences.

In examining the volume of research on gender-related attitudes and behaviors, I discovered that many other researchers' findings were similar to mine. Among psychologists, exploration of gender seemed to show more similarities than differences, and when differences appeared, many were small. I came to doubt the widespread belief that men and women are opposites, and to consider that this view is, at the very least, overstated—women and men are more similar than different. Gender-related differences exist, but the tendency to concentrate on these differences has obscured the similarities.

As a female psychologist, I was forced to attend to gender issues from the outset of my career. Sexism and discrimination were part of the context in which I received my professional training and in which I have pursued my career as a psychologist. Women were a small minority in the field during my early years in psychology, but the numbers have since increased, so that now women receive over half the doctoral degrees granted each year in psychology. This increase and several antidiscrimination laws have produced some improvements in equitable treatment for women in psychology (as well as in other professions and in society in general).

The psychology-of-women approach came from women working in the field of psychology during the feminist movement that began during the 1960s. Those female psychologists wanted to make psychology more hospitable to women, so they created a field of study devoted to women. Although most of the women working in psychology have not been directly involved in the study of the psychology of women and some are not feminists, the presence of a growing proportion of women has made psychology more inclusive. This spirit of inclusiveness spread to issues of culture and sexual orientation, and made psychology of gender not only possible but, I think, inevitable.

Gendered Voices

Although I believe that research is a good way to understand behavior, including gender-related behavior, this point is controversial. On one side of this controversy are some feminist scholars who believe that traditional science is not the best way to approach the study of women—or perhaps anything—and these scholars have proposed a set of alternative methods.

Rather than collecting quantitative data consisting of numbers, some researchers prefer data consisting of interviews and personal accounts. The latter approach has advantages and disadvantages (discussed more fully in Chapter 2), but Louise Kidder (1994) contends that one of the drawbacks is the vividness of the data generated by accounts of personal experience. Statistical compilations may be more representative, but people are more impressed by personal accounts. Qualitative methods of studying people do not lead to a comfortable blurring of the results. Rather, each person's account is sharply depicted, with no averaging to blunt the edges of the story.

The text of *Gender: Psychological Perspectives* consists of an evaluation of quantitative research findings—exactly the sort of information that people may find difficult to relate to their lives. I decided that I also wanted to include some personal, narrative accounts of gender-relevant aspects of people's lives, and I wanted these accounts to connect to the research studies. The perils of vividness seem small compared to the advantages. I believe that people's personal experiences are distilled in statistical research, but I also know that a lot of the interesting details are lost in the process.

These "Gendered Voices" narratives restore some of the details lost in statistical summaries, allowing men and women to tell about their personal experiences. Telling these stories, separated from the text, was an alternative approach to presenting information about gender and highlighting the relevance of research findings with vivid detail. Some of the stories are funny, showing a lighthearted approach to dealing with the frustrations and annoyances of discrimination and gender bias. Some of the stories are sad, revealing experiences of sexual harassment, violence, and abuse. All of the stories are real accounts, not fictional tales constructed as good examples. When the stories are based on published sources, I name the people who are presenting their experience. For other stories, I have chosen not to name those involved, to protect their privacy. I listened to my friends and students talk about gender issues and wrote down what they told me, trying to report what they said in their own words. I hope that these stories give a different perspective and add a sense of the reality of gender in personal experience to the volume of research reported here.

Headlines

Long before I thought of writing a book about gender, I noticed the popularity of the topic in the media. Not only are the sexes the topic of many private and public debates, but gender differences are also the topic of many newspaper, magazine, and television stories, ranging from sitcoms to scientific reporting. I had read warnings about the tendency in the media to oversimplify research findings and to slant reports to give an incorrect impression about research. I wanted to examine the research on gender to try to understand what the research says, with all of its complexities, and to present the media version along with an analysis of the research findings.

Of particular concern to me was the tendency of the media and of people who hear reports of gender research to want to find a biological basis for the behavioral differences between the sexes, as though evidence of biologically based differences would be more "real" than any other type of evidence. The division of the biological realm from the behavioral realm is a false dichotomy. Even genes can be altered by environment, and experiences can produce changes in behavior as permanent as any produced by physiology. The view that biological differences are real and permanent, whereas experience and culture produce only transient and changeable effects, is a popular myth.

Unlike some other books about gender, this book spends several chapters examining this biological evidence. As Naomi Weisstein (1982) said, "biology has always been used as a curse against women" (p. 41). I want to present and evaluate this research because it is the basis of popular assumptions and media reports about differences between the sexes, and also because people accept these findings without question. I want readers to question the extent to which the biological "curse" should apply.

To further highlight the popular conceptualizations of gender, I decided to use headlines from newspapers and popular magazines as a way to show how gender is presented by the media. Some of the headline stories are examples of responsible journalism that seeks to present research in a way that is easy to understand, whereas other headline stories are more sensational or simplified.

My misgivings about the media were dramatically confirmed by a personal experience. As I was beginning to write about chromosomes, hormones, and sex differences in the brain that relate to mental abilities, a student approached me, wanting to interview me for the student newspaper. She was taking a journalism class in which she had to write a story about the differences between men's and women's brains, so a friend had recommended me as a good interview source. I explained to her that the relationship between brain structures and behavior was complex and difficult to establish, and most of the research was based on rat brains rather than human brains, so making generalizations was tricky. She said she wanted some statistics about differences, and she knew such statistics existed. When I explained that statistics on the frequency of occupations or performance differences between men and women do not necessarily reveal brain differences, she said she was not interested in knowing the truth—she just wanted information for her story!

A journalism student's disregard for the truth does not condemn all journalists; however, the media does sometimes give in to the urge to portray findings in sensational ways because such stories get attention. Such sensationalism distorts research findings and perpetuates stereotypical thinking about the sexes. I believe that Beryl Lieff Benderly (1989), a science reporter, was correct when she warned about media sensationalism of gender research by writing the headline, "Don't believe everything you read..." (p. 67).

According to the Media/According to the Research

In addition to gender in the headlines, I have included a boxed feature called "According to the Media/According to the Research" that concentrates on gender portrayals in the mainstream media. "According to the Media" boxes examine how gender is portrayed in the various media—magazines, television, movies, video games, cartoons, and fiction. "According to the Research" boxes provide research findings related to the media topics, offering a more systematic and unbiased view. The contrast of these two presentations provides an opportunity to examine gender bias and stereotyping in the media. I hope this feature leads students to question the accuracy and fairness of the thousands of gendered images that they experience through the media.

Considering Diversity

The history of psychology is not filled with a concern for diversity or an emphasis on diversity issues, but these topics represent an area of increasing interest and concern within psychology. Indeed, gender research is one of the major fields that represents the growing diversity in psychology. In addition, cross-cultural research has begun to provide a more comprehensive picture of psychological issues in the context of different ethnic groups within the United States as well as comparisons to other countries.

To highlight this developing research and tie it to gender issues, this edition of *Gender: Psychological Perspectives* includes a section in each chapter called "Considering Diversity" that discusses diversity research. Although diversity issues enter the text at other points in the book, the creation of a section to examine diversity ensures that these important issues are considered. In some chapters, the research is sufficiently developed to present a cross-cultural review of the topic. For other topics, cross-cultural research remains sparse, so those diversity sections present a specialized topic that relates to the chapter.

Acknowledgments

At the completion of any book, authors have many people to thank, and I am no exception. Without the assistance, support, and encouragement of many people, I never could have written this book or completed the third edition. I thank all of them, but several people deserve special mention. My colleagues in the psychology department at McNeese State University were supportive and helpful. Jess Feist, my coauthor on the fourth edition of *Health Psychology: An Introduction to Behavior and Health,* provided advice and improved my writing of this book. Patrick Moreno not only acted as librarian to help me obtain material but also surfed the Net on my behalf. Their assistance was very important in completing this edition.

In addition to Patrick Moreno, many other people helped me obtain the materials I needed to complete this revision. The staff at McNeese's Frasier Memorial Library were knowledgeable and supportive in helping me locate information. I would like to thank the entire staff, but especially Adrienne Detwiler, Leslye Quinn, Anne Frohlich, Jan McFarlain, Barbara Royer, Kenneth Awagain, Brantley Cagle, and Jeannie Brock. Their patience and skill continue to astound me.

I would like to thank all the people who told me their personal stories for the "Gendered Voices" feature of the book. To respect their privacy I will not name them, with one exception: Melinda Schaefer deserves special thanks because her story was so good that hearing it made me realize that others had stories to tell. Without her story, I would not have realized how important these accounts are.

Husbands often deserve special thanks, and mine is no exception. My husband, Barry Humphus, did a great deal to hold my life together while I was researching and writing—he kept the computer working and offered me his praise, support, and enthusiasm. I would not have attempted (much less completed) this book without him.

The people at Allyn and Bacon have been helpful and supportive. My editor for the first edition, Susan Badger, deserves special thanks; without her I would not have thought of writing a book on gender. Carolyn Merrill, my current editor, has offered her continued support and assistance.

I would also like to thank reviewers who read parts of the manuscript and offered helpful suggestions, including Luciane A. Berg, Southern Utah University; Christina Byrne, Western Washington University; Linda Heath, Loyola University–Chicago; Marcela Raffaelli, University of Nebraska; and Stephanie Riger, University of Illinois at Chicago.

Chapter 1

The Study of Gender

HEADLINE

The New Gender Wars

Psychology Today, November/December, 2000

> *The latest skirmish in the war between the sexes has flared up between psychologists studying the origins of gender differences. Research has shown that despite feminist advancements, gender differences persist. The question no longer is whether there are differences between the sexes but what to make of them.*
>
> *On one side are those who claim that it is evolution and biology that make us significantly different, and that no amount of feminist agitation will change that. Men will continue to be philandering, non-nurturing and sex-focused, and women will continue to be mothering keepers-of-the-hearth. On the other side are those who claim there's a lot more variation to our gender roles. Society, they say, and not our genes, determines how we react to our biological course. Change, this latter group says, is possible and evident.*
>
> *How willingly does our biology respond to our environment? And even if biology plays a role, how much of the male–female split is nonetheless reinforced by the culture we live in?... Where do these differences come from and where might they go? (Blustain, 2000, p. 43)*

Sarah Blustain's (2000) article presented the two sides of one current version of the "battle between the sexes." This conflict lies within psychology, and, as the title of Blustain's article suggests, this "war" is a new one, only dating back to the mid 1990s. At that time evolutionary psychology began to capture headlines proclaiming that differences between men's and women's behavior can be traced to evolutionary history, and recent changes in society will make little difference in women's and men's behavior.

Evolutionary psychology holds the **essentialist view** that biology is the basis for differences between the sexes. According to most people's views of the relationship between biology and behavior, biological differences determine behavior. Therefore, if the differences between women and men are biological, those differences are perceived as fixed and invariant.

The other side of the battle includes psychologists who believe that social roles rather than biology are the basis for most behavioral differences between women and men. This view holds that strength and reproductive capacity differences between men and women prompt societies to encourage women and men to adopt different gender roles. The existence of such differences creates the need for socialization pressure to ensure that girls and boys learn and adopt the roles associated with their sex. In this biosocial view, biology is an important factor in the creation and maintenance of differences between women and men, but it is not the main determinant of these differences.

Perhaps not by coincidence, many evolutionary psychologists are men, whereas many of the psychologists who believe in the preeminence of social gender roles are women. Thus, this new battle is a conflict not only in theoretical, but also in personal, terms. This battle is not the first for psychology. Since the early years of psychology, women in this field have struggled for acceptance and equitable treatment in a profession dominated by men.

The struggles in psychology mirror those in the larger culture, where women have striven to change laws and attitudes concerning social, professional, and personal opportunities. Questioning the "common knowledge" that women were not capable of making rational choices about political candidates, benefiting from education, or occupying a profession, women in the 1800s pressed for the right to vote, get an education, and pursue a professional career. Those successes led to additional questioning of the capabilities and limitations of men as well as women.

Therefore, the new gender war in psychology is the latest incarnation of conflicts and questions that have also permeated the wider culture: Which is more important, nature (biology) or nurture (culture and society)? What is the extent of these differences? What types of differences exist? What is the basis for these differences? Consistent with the position of evolutionary psychology, many people see the answers to these questions as simple and obvious: Women and men are born with biological differences that dictate the basis for different traits and behaviors. Indeed, they are so different that women are the "opposite sex," suggesting that whatever men are, women are at the other end of the spectrum. Those who hold this view find the differences obvious and important. Those who hold the biosocial view see the answers as more complex. Drawing from research in psychology, sociology, biology, and anthropology, the differences between women and men seem to be a complex puzzle with many pieces.

Thus, the psychologists on the two battle lines look to volumes of research, and both sides see evidence to support their respective view. Some people at some times have believed that differences between males and females are few, whereas others have believed that the two are virtually different species. These two positions can be described as the **minimalist** and the **maximalist views** (Epstein, 1988). The minimalists perceive few important differences between women and men, whereas the maximalists believe that the two have fundamental differences. Many maximalists also hold an essentialist view, believing that the large differences between women and men are part of their essential biological makeup. Although these views have varied over time, today both the maximalist and the minimalists views have vocal supporters.

This lack of agreement coupled with commitment to a position suggests controversy, which is almost too polite a term for these disagreements. Few topics are as filled with emotion as discussions of the sexes and their capabilities. These arguments occur in places as diverse as playgrounds and scientific laboratories. The questions are similar, regardless of the setting: Who is smarter, faster, healthier, sexier, more capable, more emotional? Who makes better physicians, engineers, typists, managers, politicians, artists, teachers, parents, friends? Who is more likely to go crazy, go to jail, commit suicide, have a traffic accident, tell lies, gossip, commit murder? The full range of human possibilities seems to be grounds for discussion, but the issues are unquestionably important. No matter what the conclusions, at least half the human population (and most probably all of it) will be affected. Therefore, not only are questions about the sexes interesting, but the answers are important to individuals and to society. Later chapters explore the research concerning abilities and behaviors, and an examination of this research allows an evaluation of these questions.

Answers to these important questions about differences between women and men are not lacking, but consistency is. Almost everyone has answers, but not the same answers. It is easy to see how people might hold varying opinions about a controversial issue, but some consistency should exist among findings from researchers who have studied men and women. Scientists should be able to investigate the sexes and provide evidence concerning these important questions. Researchers have pursued these questions, obtained results, and published thousands of papers. There is no shortage of investigations—or headlines—about the sexes. Unfortunately, researchers are subject to the same problems as everyone else: They do not all agree on what the results are and what the results mean.

In addition, many research findings on men and women are not consistent with popular opinion, indicating that popular opinion may be an exaggeration or distortion of people's experience. Both the past and the present are filled with examples of exaggerations of differences between women and men. Carol Tavris (1992) discussed the tendency for people to think in terms of opposites when considering only two examples, as with the sexes. If three sexes existed, people might not have the tendency to draw a comparison of such extremes; they might be able to see the similarities as well as the differences in men and women; they might be able to approach the questions with more flexibility in their thinking. The sexual world may not actually be polarized into only two categories (as Chapter 3 explores in more detail), but people do tend to see it that way. This perception of only two sexes influences people to think of the two sexes as polar opposites. To maintain these oppositional categories, people must exaggerate the differences between women and men, which results in stereotypes that do not correspond to real people (Bem, 1993b). Although these stereotypes are not realistic, they are powerful because they affect how women and men think about themselves and how they think about the "opposite" sex.

History of the Study of Sex Differences in Psychology

Speculations about the differences between men and women probably predate history, but these issues were not part of the investigations of early psychology. Wilhelm Wundt is credited with founding modern psychology in 1879 (although there is some debate over the accuracy of this date) at the University of Leipzig (Schultz & Schultz, 1992). Wundt wanted to establish a natural science of the mind to investigate experimentally the nature of human thought processes. Using chemistry as his model, he tried to devise a psychology based on an analytical understanding of the structure of the conscious mind and founded the **structuralist** school of psychology. This structure of interest was based on adult human cognition, and Wundt and his followers believed that psychology could not be applied to children, the feebleminded, or species of nonhuman animals.

Wundt's psychology was concerned with the workings of the mind as unaffected by individual differences among adult humans. The structuralists were interested in investigating the "generalized adult mind" (Shields, 1975a) and therefore any individual differences, including differences between the minds of women and men, were of no concern to the early psychologists who followed Wundt.

This inattention to sex differences did not mean equal treatment of men and women by these early psychologists. Wundt and his followers used a method of investigation called *introspection,* a type of self-observation of one's mental processes (Schultz & Schultz, 1992). Students underwent training to become subjects in the experiments, and these students (and thus the subjects in this early psychology research) were men. The generalized adult mind on which the findings were based was a generalization drawn from data collected from and by men.

Wundt's psychology spread from Germany to the United States, where it changed focus. Although some U.S. psychologists were interested in following Wundt's definition and goals for psychology, many others found Wundt's views too limiting and impractical. As psychology grew in the United States, it developed more of a practical nature. This change is usually described as an evolution to **functionalism,** a school of psychology that emphasized how the mind functions rather than its structure (Schultz & Schultz, 1992). Darwin's theory of evolution was a strong influence for the functionalists in the United States. As these psychologists with a functionalist orientation started to research and theorize, they drew a wider variety of subjects into psychological research and theories, including children, women, and nonhuman animals.

The Study of Individual Differences

Among the areas of interest in functionalist psychology were the issues of adaptability and intelligence. From these interests evolved intelligence testing and the comparison of individual differences in mental abilities and personality traits, including sex differences. The functionalists, influenced by the theory of evolution, tended to look for biologically determined differences, including a biological basis for sex differences. Indeed, as Stephanie Shields (1975a) pointed out, these psychologists were hesitant to acknowledge any possibility of social influence in the sex differences they found, and their findings usually supported the prevailing cultural roles for women and men.

The studies and writings of functionalists of this era tended to demonstrate that women were less intelligent than men, benefited less from education, had strong maternal instincts, and were unlikely to produce examples of success or eminence. Women were not the only group deemed inferior: Nonwhite races were also considered less intelligent and capable.

These findings of the intellectual deficiencies of women did not go uncriticized. As early as 1910, Helen Thompson Woolley contended that the research on sex differences was full of the researchers' personal bias, prejudice, and sentiment (in Shields, 1975a), and Leta Stetter Hollingworth took a stand against the functionalist view of women (Shields, 1975b). These female psychologists argued against the prevailing view. Hollingworth contended that women's potential would never be known until women had the opportunity to choose the lives they would like—career, maternity, or both.

The functionalist view began to wane in the 1920s, and a new school of psychology, **behaviorism,** gained prominence. The behaviorists emphasized observable behavior rather than thought processes or instincts as the subject matter of psychology. With the change from a functionalist to a behaviorist paradigm in U.S. psychology, the interest in research on sex differences sharply decreased. "The functionalists, because of their emphasis on 'nature,' were predictably indifferent to the study of social sex roles and cultural concepts of masculine and feminine. The behaviorists, despite their emphasis on 'nurture,' were slow to recognize those same social forces" (Shields, 1975a, p. 751). Rather, behaviorists were interested in the areas of learning and memory. Research on these topics ignored social factors, including sex roles and sex differences. In ignoring gender, psychologists created what Mary Crawford and Jeanne Marecek (1989) referred to as "womanless" psychology, an approach that either failed to include women as participants or failed to examine gender-related factors when both men and women participated in psychological research. During the time when behaviorism dominated psychology, the only theorists who unquestionably had an interest in sex differences were those with a psychodynamic orientation—the Freudians.

Psychoanalysis

Both Freud's theory of personality development and his psychoanalytic approach to treatment appear in more detail in Chapter 5. However, the history of psychology's involvement in issues of sex and gender necessitates a brief description of Freud's personality theory and his approach to treatment.

Although Sigmund Freud's work did not originate within academic psychology, the two are popularly associated. And unquestionably, Freud's work, and Freudian theory concerning personality differences between women and men, have influenced both psychology and society in general. These influences have made the work of Freud very important for understanding conceptualizations of sex and gender.

In the United States, Freud's work began to gain popular attention in 1909, when Freud came to the United States to give a series of invited lectures at Clark University (Schultz & Schultz, 1992). Immediately after his visit, newspapers started carrying features about Freud and his theory. By 1920, interest in Freudian theory and analysis was evident both in books and in articles in popular magazines. Psychoanalysis gained popular interest, becoming almost a fad. Indeed, popular acceptance of Freud's work preceded its acceptance by academicians.

Freud emphasized the role of instinct and physiology in personality formation, hypothesizing that instincts provide the basic energy for personality and that the child's perception of anatomical differences between boys and girls is a pivotal event in personality formation. Rather than relying on genetic or hormonal explanations for sex differences in personality, Freud looked to early childhood experiences within the family to explain how physiology interacts with experience to influence personality development.

For Freud (1925/1989), the perception of anatomical differences between boys and girls was critical. According to Freud, the knowledge that boys and men have penises and girls and women do not forms the basis for personality differences between boys and girls. The results of this perception lead to conflict in the family, including sexual attraction to the other-sex parent and hostility for the same-sex parent. These incestuous desires cannot persist, and Freud hypothesized that the resolution of these conflicts comes through identification with the same-sex parent. However, Freud believed that boys experience more conflict and trauma during this early development, leading to a more complete rejection of their mother and a more complete identification with their father than girls experience. This difference in strength of identification produces enduring differences in personality between men and women. Consequently, Freud (1925/1989) hypothesized that men typically form a stronger conscience and sense of social values than do women.

Did Freud mean that girls and women were deficient in moral standards compared to men? Did he view women as incomplete (and less admirable) people? It is probably impossible to know what Freud thought and felt, and his writings are sufficiently varied to lead to contradictory interpretations. Thus the question of Freud's view of women has been hotly debated. Some authors have criticized Freud for supporting a male-oriented society and the enslavement of women, whereas others have defended Freud and his work as applied to women. In defense of Freud, Carol Tavris and Carole Wade (1984) pointed out that his view of women was not sufficiently negative to prevent him from accepting them as colleagues. Freud accepted a number of women into psychoanalytic training and encouraged his daughter, Anna, to pursue a career in psychoanalysis. Freud's writings, however, reveal that he held many negative views about women and seemed to feel that they were inferior to men. As Michael Jacobs (1992) concluded, "It is difficult to avoid the impression that Freud saw women as less developed than men, genitally, emotionally and in their moral thinking" (p. 107).

Regardless of Freud's personal beliefs, the popular interpretation of his theory represented women as inferior to men, as being less ethical, more concerned with personal appearance, more self-contemptuous, and jealous of men's accomplishments (and also, literally, of their penises). Accepting the feminine role would always mean settling for inferior status and opportunities, and women who were not able to reconcile themselves to this status were candidates for therapy because they had not accepted their femininity.

Freud's theory also held stringent and inflexible standards for the development of masculinity. For boys to develop normally, they must experience severe anxiety during early childhood and develop hatred for their father. This trauma should lead a boy to identify with his father and to experience the advantages of the male role through becoming like him. Boys who do not make a sufficiently complete break with their mothers are not likely to become fully masculine but to remain somewhat feminine, and thus experience the problems that society accords to nonmasculine men.

The psychoanalytic view of femininity and masculinity has been enormously influential in Western society. Although not immediately accepted in academic departments, the psychoanalytic view of personality and psychopathology was gradually integrated into the research and training of psychologists. Although the theory has prompted continuing controversy, interest continues, in the form of both attacks and defenses. This continuing stream of books and articles speaks to the power of Freud's theory to capture attention and imagination. Despite limited research support, Freudian theory has been and remains a force in conceptions of sex and gender. Table 1.1 summarizes psychological theories and their approaches to gender. In contrast to these male-dominated theories, some investigators have begun to emphasize the study of women.

The Development of Women's Studies

The development of the study of women came as a result of the feminist movement of the 1960s (Ferree & Hess, 1985). This movement was not the first to push for changes in women's roles and legal status. Earlier versions of feminism had pressed for the vote for women, availability of birth control, and other legal changes to improve women's social and

TABLE 1.1 Role of Gender in Psychological Theories throughout the History of Psychology

Theory	Emphasis of Theory	Role of Gender
Structuralism	Understanding the structure of the human mind	Minimal—all minds are equivalent
Functionalism	Understanding the function of the mind	Sex differences are one type of individual difference
Behaviorism	Studying behavior in a scientific way	Minimal—behavior varies with individual experience
Psychoanalysis	Studying normal and abnormal personality development and functioning	Biological sex differences and their recognition is a motivating force

economic status. The feminist movement of the 1960s grew out of the civil rights movement and brought about some of the changes that earlier feminist movements had sought.

Beginning in the 1960s, women entered the workforce in record numbers, producing changes in society that affected the lives of women, men, and children. Although most of these jobs were in clerical or retail sales work, women also entered the professions in increasing numbers. Women in psychology began to change the field, bringing an interest in gender-related behaviors that differed from the earlier focus on individual differences (Walsh, 1985). Blustain's (2000) headline article referred to this new gender war in psychology; the one that began in the 1960s was the predecessor for the current conflict.

In 1968, psychologist Naomi Weisstein presented an influential paper, "'Kinde, Küche, Kirche' as Scientific Law: Psychology Constructs the Female," that influenced a generation of psychologists. In this paper, Weisstein (1970) argued that psychological research had revealed almost nothing about women because the research had been contaminated by the biases, wishes, and fantasies of the male psychologists who conducted the research. Although the criticism was aimed mostly at clinical psychology and the Freudian approach to therapy, Weisstein also charged research psychologists with finding only what they wanted and expected to find about women rather than researching women as they were. She wrote, "Present psychology is less than worthless in contributing to a vision which could truly liberate—men as well as women" (p. 231).

Weisstein's accusations came at a time when the feminist movement in society and a growing number of women in psychology wanted a more prominent place for women in the field and sought to create feminist-oriented research. One of Weisstein's points was that psychological research had neglected to take into account the context of behavior, without which psychologists could understand neither women nor people in general. Twenty years later, this criticism seems to have contained a great deal of foresight (Bem, 1993a); psychological research on women began to change in the ways that Weisstein advocated.

Psychologists held no monopoly on this new orientation to the study of women. Sociologists, anthropologists, ethnologists, and biologists also became involved in questions about biological and behavioral differences and similarities between the sexes (Schiebinger, 1999). Motivated by the feminist movement, women began to assert their view about the inequity of stereotypes of the abilities and roles of men and women.

Although the history of studying gender in psychology is lengthy, psychologists' involvement in feminist research is relatively new; the formation of a division of the American

Psychological Association (APA) devoted to women's issues and studies did not occur until 1973. Women were admitted as students in doctoral programs from the early years of psychology, but they had to struggle for professional acceptance and had a difficult time finding positions as psychologists. In 1941, a group of women who were psychologists formed the National Council of Women Psychologists to further the work of female psychologists in the war effort (Walsh, 1985). This group became the International Council of Women Psychologists in 1944 and attempted to become a division of the APA but was rejected repeatedly.

Another group succeeded in gaining APA division status in 1973. Division 35, Society for the Psychology of Women, can be directly traced to the Association for Women in Psychology, a group that demonstrated against sex discrimination and for an increase in feminist psychological research at the 1969 and 1970 APA national conventions (Walsh, 1985). Unlike the earlier International Council, Division 35 goals included not only the promotion of women in psychology, but also the advancement of research on women and issues related to gender. The great volume of psychological research on sex and gender that has appeared in the past 20 years is consistent with the Division 35 goal of expanding the study of women and encouraging the integration of that research with current psychological thinking. Indeed, Division 35 members have conducted much of that research, but other disciplines have also contributed substantially. Therefore, not only have psychologists participated in the current plethora of research on sex and gender, but the topic is actively investigated in biology, medicine, sociology, communication, and anthropology.

In summary, psychological research that includes women dates back to the early part of the 20th century and the functionalist school of psychology, but this approach emphasized sex differences and searched for the factors that distinguished men and women. When the behaviorist school dominated academic psychology, its lack of interest in sex differences created a virtually "womanless" psychology. During that same time, Freudian psychoanalysts held strong views on the sexes, but this theory proposed that women are physically and morally inferior to men. This belief in the innate inferiority of women influenced research on women. With the feminist movement of the 1960s, a different type of research arose, producing results that questioned the stereotypes and assumptions about innate differences between the sexes. Not only did this research begin to examine sex differences and similarities, but these researchers also expanded ways to study women and men. This more recent orientation has led to voluminous research in the field of psychology, as well as in sociology, anthropology, and biology.

The feminist movement questioned the roles and stereotypes for women, and soon the questioning spread to men, who began to examine how the inflexibility of gender stereotypes might harm them, too.

The Appearance of the Men's Movement

The men's movement mirrors the women's movement, beginning during the 19th-century women's suffrage movement. During this time, the women's suffrage movement was not the only challenge to men's roles. Men felt increasingly constrained in their masculinity by the change from agricultural to industrial society. An early form of the men's movement was the Boy Scouts, with its emphasis on men and boys involved in outdoor activities (Hantover, 1992). The contemporary women's movement has also questioned and challenged men concerning the status quo of legal, social, and personal roles and relationships. Some men have failed to see the problem, but other men have begun to consider how the questions pertain to their lives, too. Table 1.2 lists some important events in both movements and when each event occurred.

During the 1970s, these concerned men sometimes became feminists interested in ending the inequalities in power and privilege accorded to men, because they also saw toxic

TABLE 1.2 Important Events in the Women's and Men's Movements

Women's Movement		Men's Movement	
First women's rights convention, Seneca Falls, New York	1848		
		1870	15th Amendment to U.S. Constitution gives African American men the right to vote
19th Amendment to U.S. Constitution gives women the right to vote	1920		
National Council of Women Psychologists	1941		
Simon de Beauvoir's *The Second Sex* published	1952		
Betty Friedan's *The Feminine Mystique* published	1963		
The Civil Rights Act prohibits discrimination on the basis of sex	1964	1964	The Civil Rights Act prohibits discrimination on the basis of sex
National Organization for Women formed	1966		
Association for Women in Psychology demonstrates against sexism at APA convention	1969		
APA Division 35 formed	1973		
		1983	National Organization for Changing Men founded
		1990	Robert Bly's *Iron John* published
		1995	APA Division 51 formed
		1996	Million Man March, Washington, DC
		1997	Promise Keepers rally, Washington, DC

elements connected to the male sex role. Robert Brannon summarized this view by saying, "I have gradually come to realize that I, with every other man I know, have been limited and diverted from whatever our real potential might have been by the prefabricated mold of the male sex role" (1976, pp. 4–5).

Feminist men formed groups equivalent to the consciousness-raising groups common in the women's movement (Astrachan, 1986). Although these group members discussed their common problems and sought support from each other, their activities usually did not progress to the larger organizations that sought political power, as the women's groups had done. Many of these groups tended to remain small, local-level organizations, but a few became national organizations.

Within psychology, the Society for the Psychological Study of Men and Masculinity succeeded in gaining divisional status in 1995, becoming Division 51 of the American Psychological Association. The goals of this division include (1) promoting the study of how gender roles shape and constrict men's lives, (2) helping men to experience their full human potential, and (3) eroding the definition of masculinity that has inhibited men's development and has contributed to the oppression of others.

But other national groups within the men's movement are not interested in feminist goals; indeed, these men are interested in restoring the traditional gender roles that they believe have been destroyed by the women's movement. One such group is the National Organization for Changing Men, a group that wants to "throw off the shackles of female oppression" (Gallagher, 1987, p. 39). Many of these men's rights groups are organized around specific issues, such as changing divorce laws or promoting joint child custody, but some of the groups offer support to men who feel as though they have experienced discrimination. Rather than joining feminist groups for men, these men join groups that are antifeminist organizations. Their members feel confused and threatened by the changes that have come about during the past 20 years in women's and men's roles and would like to return to well-defined, separate roles for the sexes.

Some participants in men's groups would like to see a less sharply gendered society, in which both women and men have choices not bound by their biological sex, whereas other men would like a more sharply gendered society, in which changes brought about by the women's movement are reversed. Men in both types of groups consider themselves part of the men's movement.

Yet another variation of the men's movement comes from men trying to find a masculine identity. Authors such as Robert Bly (1990) and Sam Keen (1991) contend that modern society has left men with no easy way to form a masculine identity. The culture provides inappropriate models, and fathers are often absent, providing no model at all. This deficit produces men who are inappropriately aggressive and poorly fitted to live in society, to form relationships with women, and to be adequate fathers. Bly proposed explorations of masculinity and ceremonial initiation into manhood as a means of overcoming the failure to establish the missing masculine role. These initiation ceremonies have been the subject of much ridicule (Pittman, 1992). In many ways, these groups echo the scouting movement, with the emphasis on male bonding in an outdoor setting. The need to find and affirm a masculine identity is a need that many men feel. Unfortunately, Bly's recommendations for achieving masculinity can be characterized as antifeminist, relying on devaluing women and forcefully rejecting feminine values to help men achieve masculinity.

GENDERED VOICES

"When you wake up in the morning and look in the mirror, what do you see?" a Black woman asked a White woman (Kimmel & Messner, 1992, p. 2).

"I see a woman," was the White woman's reply.

"That's precisely the issue," the Black woman replied. "I see a Black woman. For me, race is visible every day, because it is how I am not privileged in this culture. Race is invisible to you, which is why our alliance will always seem somewhat false to me" (p. 2).

As Michael Kimmel witnessed this exchange, he was surprised. He examined his own thoughts and realized that when he looked into the mirror, he "saw a human being: universally generalizable. The generic person" (p. 2).

Just as the White woman did not see her ethnicity, the White man saw neither his gender nor his ethnic background. His privileged status as White and male had made him blind to these factors. Rather than thinking of himself as White or male, he considered himself a generic human. The White woman saw femaleness because she was aware of the discrimination she experienced as a woman. The Black woman saw both her skin color and her gender when she looked into the mirror due to her experiences of those factors in her life.

Michael Kimmel and Michael Messner (1992, pp. 2–3) summarized these experiences: "The mechanisms that afford us privilege are very often invisible to us.... Men often think of themselves as genderless, as if gender did not matter in the daily experiences of our lives. Certainly, we can see the biological sex of individuals, but we rarely understand the ways in which gender—that complex of social meanings that is attached to biological sex—is enacted in our daily lives."

The Promise Keepers do not share Bly's vision of how to reclaim masculinity, but reasserting masculinity is an important goal for these men (Messner, 1997; Silverstein, Auerbach, Grieco, & Dunk, 1999). This organization is part of neoconservative, evangelical Christianity, and it urges men to reclaim their position as head of the family, living up to their roles and keeping their commitments to their wives and children. Promise Keepers rejects the racism that is often associated with the evangelical movement, but it does not accept homosexuality or equal partnerships with women. A study of men who have participated in Promise Keepers (Silverstein et al., 1999) revealed that this movement provides men with support for their attempts to become more nurturant, involved fathers.

Another testament to the pull of the men's movement was the Million Man March held in Washington, D.C., on October 16, 1995. Organized by Louis Farrakhan and the Nation of Islam, the march brought African American men from the entire United States to Washington to be together. Five percent of the African American men in the United States attended (Loury, 1996). Farrakhan's agenda includes goals similar to those of the Promise Keepers, with men reclaiming their position as head of the family. His movement also rejects gays, lesbians, and people who are not African American. Even men who disagreed with Farrakhan's religious and political agenda experienced the power of the gathering. The need to be together, as men, brought them to Washington.

The number of men who have participated in the Promise Keepers' weekends and the 400,000 to 1 million men who attended the Million Man March represent a growing interest in some version of the men's movement. However, none of the versions of the men's movement has exerted the impact of the women's movement in influencing public opinion and changing social policy.

Sex or Gender?

Those researchers who have concentrated on the differences between men and women historically have used the term **sex differences** to describe their work. In some investigations, these differences were the main emphasis of the study, but for many more studies, such comparisons were of secondary importance (Unger, 1979). By measuring and analyzing differences between male and female participants, researchers have produced a huge body of information on these differences and similarities. As Rhoda Unger pointed out, this information was not of primary importance to most of these researchers. When the analyses revealed statistically significant differences, the researchers provided a brief discussion; when no significant differences appeared, researchers dismissed their lack of findings with little or no discussion. Thus, the differences between male and female participants' responses have appeared in many studies, but not necessarily as the focus of these studies.

What have researchers meant by *sex differences?* One objection to the term is that it carries implications of a biological basis (McHugh, Koeske, & Frieze, 1986). Another objection is that the term has been used too extensively and with too many meanings, including chromosomal configuration, reproductive physiology, secondary sex characteristics, as well as behaviors or characteristics associated with women or men (Unger, 1979). Rhoda Unger proposed an alternative term—**gender.** She explained that this term describes the traits and behaviors that are regarded by the culture as appropriate to women and men. *Gender* is thus a social label and not a description of biology. This label includes the characteristics that the culture ascribes to each sex and the sex-related characteristics that individuals assign to themselves. Carolyn Sherif (1982) proposed a similar definition of gender as "a scheme for social categorization of individuals" (p. 376). Both Unger and Sherif recognized the socially created differentiations that have arisen from the biological differences associated with sex, and both have proposed that use of the term *gender* should provide a useful distinction.

Unger suggested that use of the term *gender* might reduce the assumed parallels between biological and psychological sex, or at least make explicit those assumptions. If researchers had accepted and used the term consistently, then its use might serve the function Unger proposed. However, no such consistent usage has yet appeared, and confusion remains. Some researchers use the two terms interchangeably, whereas others have substituted the term *gender* for the term *sex* but still fail to make any distinction.

Douglas Gentile (1993) proposed additional terms, including *biologically sex-linked, gender-linked,* and *sex-correlated* to distinguish between biological and social differences, and between differences that are causally linked to sex and those for which a causal link has not been established. Others have objected to the attempt to draw distinctions, saying that distinguishing between the biological and social aspects of sex is not possible (Maccoby, 1988). Still others (Deaux, 1993; Unger & Crawford, 1993) have objected to Gentile's proposed distinctions, pointing out that the knowledge to make these distinctions does not exist. As Rhoda Unger and Mary Crawford (1993, p. 124) wrote, "The problem of distinctions between sex and gender is due to unresolved conflicts within psychology about the causality of various sex-linked phenomena rather than to the terms used."

Therefore, psychologists have attempted to draw distinctions between the concepts of sex and gender to distinguish between those differences that are social and those that are biological. Such distinctions have been elusive, but those who use the term *gender* often intend to emphasize the social nature of differences between women and men. Indeed, the terminology that researchers use can indicate their point of view, with those researchers who are biological essentialists using the term *sex* to refer to *all* differences between men and women, whereas those who use the term *gender* want to emphasize the social nature of such differences.

Should Psychologists Study Gender?

Does the controversy and confusion associated with past research merit further research in the area of gender? Should psychologists continue to study gender? Psychologists have taken both positions, with some advocating that psychologists should do a more objective job of gender research, and some challenging the worth of additional research.

Alice Eagly (1987a) recommended that all psychological research should report on gender if such comparisons were part of the design. Rather than restricting reporting to theoretically meaningful or replicable results, she advocated making gender a routine part of psychological research. Furthermore, Eagly (1997) and Diane Halpern (1994) both have professed a belief that the methods used by psychologists are sufficiently sophisticated to yield credible results.

Both Roy Baumeister (1988) and Bernice Lott (1997) have raised questions about the wisdom of continuing gender research. Baumeister argued that Eagly's strategy would result in virtually all research in psychology becoming gender research. He proposed that psychology should go in the opposite direction—away from reporting on gender comparisons. Both Baumeister and Lott pointed out that by reporting and discussing gender differences, psychological research serves to perpetuate the exaggeration of gender differences. When people believe in large gender differences, they find it easier to categorize and treat women and men differently. Baumeister would like to see a gender-neutral psychology of people, which he proposed would serve society and science better than exaggerating gender differences. Lott advocates that gender research go beyond the simple comparisons of men and women to find similarities and differences so that the complexities of human behavior can be explored.

Although these suggestions about how to proceed with gender research are in opposition, all have similar concerns—that research on gender may be misunderstood and inappropriately used to perpetuate stereotypes and discrimination. This concern was also voiced by female psychologists in Blustain's (2000) headline article. Despite these concerns, the suggestion that gender research should be abandoned is not likely to be implemented. As Eagly (1995) pointed out, the area has gained a momentum that is not likely to stop. Although dangers exist in connection with gender research, it will continue.

Other psychologists (Bem, 1993b; Yoder & Kahn, 1993) have expressed an additional concern in connection with gender differences in psychology. They contend that the comparison of women and men places men as the standard, making women appear deficient if the comparison yields differences. Bem referred to this as an *androcentric bias,* contending that this bias has permeated not only psychology and its research, but also society in general, putting women at a disadvantage. Whenever research finds a gender difference, that finding is interpreted as a disadvantage for women.

Janice Yoder and Arnold Kahn (1993) voiced a concern that the same disadvantage resulting from comparing women and men has occurred in attempting to include women from various ethnic groups in psychology research. White, privileged women have become the standard for research with women, and when women from other ethnic groups are included, they are compared to White, usually middle-class, college women. In such a comparison, the dominant group tends to consider its own experience as the standard, and differences can be interpreted as deficiencies (Unger, 1995). Diversity in psychological research is a desirable goal, but Yoder and Kahn (1993) warned that "just as there is no singular male experience, there is no one experience or characterization that can be applied indiscriminately to all women" (p. 847).

Therefore, the study of gender will certainly continue in psychology, but several concerns exist for this research. Some psychologists have contended that gender research poses dangers in exploring differences, while others have argued that such research can be valuable. Others have pointed out that examining differences has continued discrimination by placing men as the standard in gender comparisons, and yet others have warned against extending this disadvantaged comparison to women from ethnic minorities.

Gender in the Media

Print, broadcast, film, and electronic media are an integral part of daily life for most people in developed countries, and gender portrayals are daily events for those who are exposed to these media. People learn about gender from entertainment programming, advertisements, and news reports. Entertainment programs show men, women, boys, and girls in a wide variety of situations, and these programs transmit messages about what is desirable and attractive in femininity and masculinity. Advertising sends signals about gender as well as sells products. News reports cover gender research, and examining the style of the news report as well as the content reveals the attitude behind the story.

Media portrayals can be so powerful and persuasive that these portrayals become the standard on which people judge what is normal and desirable for their own lives. Indeed, the media can be more important than personal experience in shaping attitudes and behavior. People look at the media and see what they believe they should be; then they attempt to change their behavior to fit the media presentation.

This book uses media portrayals of gender to reflect on and contrast with research on gender. By presenting both the media portrayal and the research, it is possible to debunk the biased view that the media often convey. To allow for this type of evaluation, two features appear throughout the book. One feature, called "According to the Media/According to the Research," gives examples of how various media depict gender, and then presents research results that reveal a fuller picture. The second feature is "Gender in the Headlines." Each chapter starts with a story from a newspaper or magazine that serves as a focal point for the chapter. These two features allow the reader to explore the gender messages from both broadcast and print media.

Media Bias in Portraying Women and Men

Media portrayals of women and men are powerful influences in forming images of acceptable and desirable behavior. Media portrayals of men and women are stereotypical in a number of ways, presenting a systematically biased view. By presenting these stereotypical depictions as attractive, the media perpetuate restrictive roles for both men and women. These biases include not only inaccuracies, but also omissions. That is, television, movies, and magazines not only portray women and men in ways that glorify traditional gender behaviors, but these media also omit important factors that would lead to a more accurate picture.

Although television portrayals of women have changed over the past 30 years, women are underrepresented on television—fewer female than male characters appear (Signorielli & Bacue, 1999). Nor are the portrayals equal in other ways: Female characters are younger, less likely to be employed, and more likely to appear in secondary and comedy roles. Although the number of female characters and their roles have altered since the early 1970s, these alterations have not kept pace with actual changes in women's employment and responsibilities. Thus, women on television are less visible and less significant than men.

Male characters on television are older and occupy more prestigious positions than female characters (Signorielli & Bacue, 1999). Men also are more often the leading characters in drama and adventure programs, activities that take them away from home and family relationships. These characteristics devalue women by making them less visible and credible on television, and limit men by restricting them to aggressive, competitive roles.

The underrepresentation of women also occurs in movies. In top-grossing movies from the 1940s through the 1980s, women appeared less frequently than men (Bazzini, McIntosh, Smith, Cook, & Harris, 1997). This underrepresentation was true for women in both primary and secondary roles, and it applied more strongly to older than younger women. In addition, older women were portrayed in less favorable ways than older men. Thus, the lower visibility for women on television extends to movies.

Some people (including network programmers and studio executives) argue that television and movies furnish entertainment, and people know that the depictions are not accurate. Despite the knowledge that entertainment programming is fictional, the gender messages on those programs have the power to influence people when they experience similar characters in real life (Murphy, 1998). Knowing that a character is fictional does not decrease that character's appeal and may not diminish the character's credibility. Television's tendency to create realistic-looking situations in programming enhances this problem. For example, the popular television series *ER* centers on a hospital emergency room and its personnel. The ethnic diversity and number of women in administrative positions in the show gives the impression that the medical profession is gender equitable and ethnically diverse. This impression is inaccurate—less than 5% of medical professionals are African American, and women tend to occupy lower-status positions within medicine (U.S. Bureau of the Census, 1999).

Advertising on television also conveys stereotypical gender messages similar to those on entertainment programming. Commercial messages on television include more men than women, and the women are younger than the men (Furnham & Mak, 1999). Men are more likely to be the authoritative central figures, whereas women are shown as secondary and often decorative. Men appear as professionals; women are shown at home. The gender of the people in advertising tends to be consistent with the gender stereotyping of the product—women appear in commercials for personal products and men in commercials selling automobiles and sports-related products. These differences apply not only to the United States, but also to television advertising in 14 countries in North and South America, Europe, Asia, and Africa.

Magazines are another medium that sends strong gender messages, both in feature articles and in advertising. Hundreds of different magazines exist, fitting into various specialty niches. However, a wide variety of magazines is aimed at women and another group at men, and the two vary substantially (Rapping, 1994). Women's magazines are filled with information and advice oriented toward making girls and women better versions of themselves, concentrating on appearance and relationships more than on financial advice and careers. Indeed, women's magazines are not very different from their counterparts in the 1950s, with only superficial attention to the enormous changes that have occurred in women's lives. This emphasis on appearance and relationships is similar for magazines aimed at teens, such as *Seventeen* (Schlenker, Caron, & Halteman, 1998), for those oriented toward working women and older women, such as *Working Woman* and *Lear's* (Rapping, 1994), and in the advertising that appears in women's magazines (Kang, 1997).

The stereotyping in teen magazines aimed at boys can be much more subtle. A content analysis of a general-interest magazine aimed at boys (Willemsen, 1998) showed that the topics were similar to those in magazines for girls—fashion and appearance were common topics. However, the language differed in the two, with boys' magazines having more tough words and those for girls having more emotion words. Magazines for men also include articles about appearance and products, but these publications lack the emphasis on relationship maintenance, and they include information (or photos) about sex (Rapping, 1994).

These prominent and persistent biases warrant examination and correction. The feature boxes titled "According to the Media/According to the Research" addresses these biases by presenting some media depiction related to gender side-by-side with an examination of research on this topic.

Gender in the Headlines

Gender has become such a hot research topic that news stories on gender research appear frequently on television, in newspapers, and in magazines. These stories often present less technical versions of research findings than those appearing in research journals, and these popular versions of research results are easier to understand. However, some important details and limitations of research findings can be lost in the simplification process, and the urge to write an eye-catching story can lead to sensationalizing research results. Simplistic, unidimensional, and oppositional ways of thinking about women and men are common in our culture, and media portrayals are part of the process. When people hear about research on gender, the way those findings are reported (in addition to the findings themselves) shapes people's beliefs about the importance of gender in determining behavior.

These reports can be part of the problem of gender stereotyping, presenting a mirror that reflects the cultural climate (Bridge, 1995). Media reports can distort research findings through the lens of sensationalism and, in doing so, promote stereotypical thinking, which in turn entrenches stereotypes in popular belief and can lead men and women to strive to measure up to these portrayals. Thus, popular media not only reflect cultural beliefs, they shape attitudes as well:

> *In a free society such as the United States, the way the media cover the news provides an excellent cultural looking glass. The attitudes, values, biases, strengths, and weaknesses of the society covered by the media are reflected in the media mirror. Simultaneously, the media, by the way they report the news and by the way they define what is newsworthy, influence the society they cover. (Bridge, 1995, p. 19)*

Headlines, along with the images they present and the research on which they are based, form the unifying theme for this book. Each chapter begins with a headline from a story about the sexes, providing a starting point for an evaluation of the theory and research evidence that contributed to the headline story. This evaluation will delve into the research and examine the popular story and the popular stereotypes. By examining how the media present information about women and men, and by contrasting these headlines with the research in psychology, biology, sociology, and anthropology, an evaluation of these popular views of the sexes is possible. Through this evaluation process, readers can develop an understanding of personal and societal beliefs and attitudes, as well as a view of what psychological research has revealed about the sexes.

Considering Diversity

Lack of diversity was the problem that sparked women to protest their exclusion in psychology and in society. Ironically, the diversity that they brought was limited. The women who entered psychology in large numbers and joined women's groups were mostly White, middle-class, college-educated professionals who protested sex discrimination in education and work. Women of color joined the women's movement and entered psychology only in small numbers—their energies often went toward ending racism rather than sexism, and their participation in the civil rights movement was often limited. As the title of one book lamented, *All the Women Were White, All the Blacks Were Men* (Hull, Bell-Scott, & Smith, 1982). This title reflects African American women's exclusion from both the women's movements and the civil rights movement.

During the 1980s, feminists sought to include more diversity in their organizations, theories, and research (Weber, 1998). Recognizing that multiple dimensions of inequality exist, scholars began to explore not only the connection of gender and ethnicity, but also social class and sexual orientation. Scholars sought ways to include these dimensions in their work, bringing diversity to feminism.

The field of psychology is guilty of exclusion similar to that in the women's movement, but diversity also became a goal within psychology (Reid, 1993; Yoder & Kahn, 1993). Scholars used the same critical thinking that had led them to analyze the male bias in psychology to examine the biases within the psychology of women. As Nancy Felipe Russo (1998, p. ii) explained, "Feminist psychology is now beyond simply critiquing yesterday's findings. The challenge now is to build a knowledge base of theories, concepts, and methods to examine women's lives in all of their diversity." With the recognition that cross-cultural comparisons add to the study of women and gender, feminist psychologists value an inclusive psychology. Thus, diversity was not something that came quickly to the women's movement or to psychology, but it is now a major focus for both.

The history of the men's movement is shorter than that of the women's movement (see Table 1.2), and the timing of that movement influenced its composition. Early men's groups tended to include White, privileged men, but the Million Man March drew African American men together, and gay men have been active in pressing for changes in laws and social attitudes.

The men's movement is less united than the women's movement, encompassing more divergent perspectives. For example, the men's movement is composed of both men who are antifeminist and those who are profeminist. Among antifeminist, conservative men's groups, diversity may not be a goal. Those groups that promote a return to traditional masculinity do not strive to include diverse ethnicities, social class, and sexual orientations among their members. Groups that aim to redefine masculinity often seek to promote changes in society to make it more inclusive. Therefore, the men's movement has a history that reflects more diversity than the women's movement, but some factions of the men's movement reject these goals.

Summary

Typically, the first thing that parents learn about their child is the child's sex. This highlights the importance of sex and gender. Beliefs about gender differences are common, but opinions vary, with some people believing in minimal differences and others holding that the differences are maximal and part of essential biological differences.

Gender research in psychology can be traced to the functionalist school of the late 1800s, which held that men and women differ in ability and personality (a view that received criticism at that time). With the transition to the behaviorist school, interest in gender differences faded from academic psychology but persisted in psychoanalysis. Psychoanalysts held that differences in anatomy produce personality differences in women and men, with women being inferior in a number of important ways. The feminist movement of the 1960s produced a resurgence of interest among psychologists concerning questions about gender differences, and research tended to question stereotypes about the sexes.

The traditional terminology—namely, the use of the term *sex differences*—has been criticized. By proposing the use of the term *gender,* psychologists have tried to clarify the difference between socially determined and biologically determined differences. However, both terms continue in use, and the proposed distinction between sex differences, meaning biological differences, and gender differences, meaning socially determined differences, has not yet come into consistent use. Controversy also exists over the emphasis on gender in research. Roy Baumeister and Bernice Lott have argued that gender research should decrease to avoid promoting bias, but Alice Eagly proposed that such research should become even more common to reflect more complete information about gender.

Gender portrayals appear in all the media, and these portrayals have enormous power to shape our beliefs and expectations. Women are depicted in inaccurate and stereotypical ways on television, and magazine stories and advertising emphasize stereotypical femininity. Research on gender often appears in media reports, but these reports are usually simplified and sometimes distorted, thus promoting misconceptions. Evaluations of media portrayals and headlines from stories on gender allow an examination of the media images of women and men, and research provides a counterpoint to these portrayals.

Ethnic and economic diversity did not appear during the early years of the women's movement, but inclusion is now a goal for feminist scholars. The men's movement has always been diverse, but some factions of the men's movement object to gays, profeminists, and various ethnic groups. Therefore, diversity remains an issue in both women's and men's movements.

Glossary

behaviorism the school of psychology that emphasizes the importance of observable behavior as the subject matter of psychology and discounts the utility of unobservable mental events.

essentialist view the view that gender differences are biologically determined.

functionalism a school of psychology arising in the United States in the late 1800s that attempted to understand how the mind functions. Functionalists held a practical, applied orientation, including an interest in mental abilities and in gender differences in those abilities.

gender the term used by some researchers to describe the traits and behaviors that are regarded by the culture as appropriate to men and women.

maximalist view the view that many important differences exist between the sexes.

minimalist view the view that few important differences exist between the sexes.

sex differences the term used by some researchers (and considered to be inclusive by others) to describe the differences between male and female research participants.

structuralist a school of psychology arising in Europe in the 1880s that attempted to understand the workings of the conscious mind by dividing the mind into component parts and analyzing the structure of the mind.

Suggested Readings

Bem, Sandra Lipsitz. (1993). *The lenses of gender.* New Haven, CT: Yale University Press. Bem contends that gender provides a lens, and people view the world through the distortion of this lens. She discusses three lenses of gender: androcentrism, gender polarization, and biological essentialism. Bem argues that viewing the world through these lenses provides the basis (and biases) for organizing gender knowledge.

Eagly, Alice H. (1997). Comparing women and men: Methods, findings, and politics. In Mary Roth Walsh (Ed.), *Women, men, and gender: Ongoing debates* (pp. 24–31). New Haven, CT: Yale University Press. Eagly takes the position that research concerning the study of gender differences is important for creating a more complete picture of gender.

Keller, Teresa. (1999). Lessons in equality: What television teaches us about women. In Carie Forden, Anne E. Hunter, and Beverly Birns (Eds.), *Readings in the psychology of women: Dimensions of the female experience* (pp. 27–35). Boston: Allyn and Bacon. This short article provides a good introduction to the treatment of women in various media, the stereotypical portrayal of media images, and the effects of this stereotyping.

Lott, Bernice. (1997). Cataloging gender differences: Science or politics? In Mary Roth Walsh (Ed.), *Women, men, and gender: Ongoing debates* (pp. 19–23). New Haven, CT: Yale University Press. Lott takes the position that research concerning the study of gender differences is dangerous. Compare the two discrepant views presented by Eagly and Lott reflecting the debate concerning the study of gender differences.

Shields, Stephanie A. (1975). Functionalism, Darwinism, and the psychology of women: A study in social myth. *American Psychologist, 30,* 739–754. This lively article details the history of early psychologists' research on gender differences, with all the biases showing.

Weisstein, Naomi. (1970). "Kinde, küche, kirche" as scientific law: Psychology constructs the female. In Robin Morgan (Ed.), *Sisterhood is powerful: An anthology of writings from the women's liberation movement* (pp. 228–245). New York: Vintage Books. Also reprinted in 1993 in *Feminism & Psychology, 3,* 195–210. Weisstein's article has been reprinted many times and appears in many anthologies, a testimony to its influence. Originally a presentation, this angry criticism details psychologists' tendency to distort the view of women and describes the failure to study women in an unbiased way. Psychological research is no longer as inadequate as Weisstein charged, partly because of changes made in response to her criticism.

Chapter 2

Researching Sex and Gender

HEADLINE

The Science Wars

Newsweek, April 21, 1997

> *Scientists worship at the shrine of objectivity, but even the pious occasionally lapse. A century ago archeologists who discovered the great stone ruins of Zimbabwe went through all sorts of contortions to prove that the magnificent oval palace and other structures were built by the Phoenicians of King Solomon's time—or by anyone other than the ancestors of the Bantus. In the 1960s biologists studying conception described the "whiplashlike motion and strong lurches" of sperm "delivering" genes required to "activate the developmental program of the egg," which "drifted" along passively. The model portrayed sperm as macho adventurers, eggs as coy damsels. And throughout the 1970s and later, ornithologists gathered sheafs of data proving that, in birds, a female's success laying eggs and rearing hatchlings was always enhanced by the presence of a male.*
>
> *These acolytes of scientific objectivity were spectacularly wrong. The Bantus' ancestors did build the great stone complex. The human egg does play an active role in conception. And in some bird species, particularly the eastern bluebird, the father's presence makes little or no difference to the survival of hatchlings. But why did scientists get it wrong in all three cases, and many others? (Begley, 1997, p. 54)*

According to Sharon Begley (1997), this question is the basis of a major battle in contemporary science. The heart of the battle is the question of objectivity in science. The defenders of science see science as a process of discovering the natural principles that govern the functioning of the world. Although objectivity is not easy to attain, this position holds that through careful research design, it is possible to conduct objective scientific research.

The critics claim that science, like all other human activities, is a reflection of the values of the society in which it functions, and these values include biases. These critics argue that science is a process of constructing a view of the world. These **constructionists** believe that "we do not discover reality, we invent it" (Hare-Mustin & Marecek, 1988, p. 455). That is, science does not lead researchers to map a realistic picture of the world, but to construct views of the world in ways that reflect their personal perceptions and biases. In this view, science is a process of invention rather than one of discovery. Bias is inevitable, the constructionists argue, because all humans are tied to their perceptions and actively try to organize and interpret all information, including scientific data. To disconnect perception to the point of objectivity is impossible, so science must always contain the influence of subjective perceptions: "Knowledge bears the mark of its makers" (Schiebinger, 1999, p. 143).

Although the constructionist position may sound like a minor concession to the limitations of human perception, it is a more fundamental criticism of science because it challenges the philosophies that underlie science (Gergen, 1985). According to science, the only way to legitimately gather information is through observing objective facts and rejecting information gathered from other sources. Constructionists argue that objective facts do not exist, and anything presented as fact is personal and subjective perception. Therefore, science cannot be free of values, nor can it be socially or politically neutral (Schiebinger, 1999).

The "science wars" relate to gender research more strongly than to many other scientific fields because gender issues are among the most controversial in science and society. In addition, scientists have a long history, to paraphrase Judith Lorber (1997), of seeing because they believe, rather than believing because they have seen. This criticism applies to research on gender-related topics even more strongly than to many other areas.

Criticisms of science apply to the various disciplines that have explored gender issues, including psychology, sociology, medicine, biochemistry, biology, and anthropology. Researchers in these disciplines may vary in their viewpoints and approaches, but their methods of investigation usually do not—most researchers adhere to a set of methods that are part of traditional science. The alternatives to traditional science offer different ways to approach gender research. An understanding of the traditional approach to research is necessary before we examine the alternatives.

How Science Developed

Modern science arose in the 16th and 17th centuries and came to prominence during the 19th century, bringing about radical changes in ways of knowing and understanding the world (Caplan & Caplan, 1994; Riger, 1992). Instead of looking to religion and the Bible for knowledge and wisdom, the new science looked to knowledge gathered through observation. This view represented a radical departure from ancient and religious thought. This new scientific view assumed that the world works by a set of natural laws and that these laws can be discovered by careful, objective investigation. Humans can understand the laws of nature if they use the correct methods of investigation.

During the 18th and 19th centuries, science proliferated in Europe and spread throughout the Western world. Research in chemistry, physics, biology, and medicine produced findings that changed the world and the lives of most people. New products, medicines, and industries came into existence because of the research of scientists. The success of science created an enthusiasm that fostered the development of more sciences, including the social sciences of psychology, sociology, and anthropology. These social sciences held to the same assumptions and methods as the natural sciences—that is, the laws of human behavior and society were also subject to discovery through **empirical observation** and objective investigation.

Empirical observation requires collecting information through direct observation, and objective investigation necessitates removing personal feelings and biases from the process of research. Critics of science contend that objectivity is not possible, whereas proponents believe that it is necessary for good science. What steps do these proponents believe are necessary to ensure careful and objective investigation? What makes scientific investigation different from other ways of gaining knowledge? What techniques do scientists use to accomplish these goals? The following sections explore these questions.

Methods and What They Reveal

Science is not just a set of methods; it is also a process of gaining information, an activity (Ray, 1993). By performing this activity, researchers gain information, but that information must meet certain criteria. One of those criteria applies to the type of information, which must be open to empirical observation. Scientific information must be observable not only to the person doing the observing, but also to anyone else; that is, it must be publicly observable. By restricting information in this way, the observer's perceptions and biases can be minimized, and scientific observation can attain some level of objectivity.

Another restriction on gathering information in science is that scientific observation must be systematic: Scientists must follow some plan or system to gather information. Everyone makes observations, but most people in most circumstances do so in a nonsystematic, personal way rather than according to a systematic plan. This lack of systematicity can lead people to notice certain things while ignoring others—a selection process that can result in distortion and bias. Scientists strive to be systematic in their observations in order to gather information that more accurately reflects the situations they have observed. This is not to say that scientists are free of personal biases; as humans, they are subject to the same perceptual distortions (and even biases) as other humans. However, acting as scientists, they strive to treat the information fairly, although they cannot avoid personal opinions (Gould, 1996). Working with observable information according to a systematic plan can help researchers to minimize bias.

Thus, science is an activity that is restricted to gathering information through observation and by forming systematic plans. The care such observation requires has led to an erroneous impression about science—namely, that science is precise. The use of numbers for **quantification** of observations further contributes to this mistaken impression. People tend to believe that numbers lend precision, when actually numbers are only one way to summarize certain characteristics of a situation. Scientists collect **data,** which are usually quantifications of their observations. These data are not the same as the observed phenomenon, but rather are representations of some facet of the phenomenon the researcher considered important.

For example, a researcher who is interested in cross-gender interactions in preschool children might choose to study how many times children approached a child of the other gender in play situations. The researcher would observe children of the appropriate age and count the number of such interactions, perhaps both by girls and by boys. The data would consist of the number of times such interactions were initiated by girls versus by boys. These data capture one aspect of the play situation but omit many others. Thus, when this study is finished, the researcher will have a collection of data—in the form of numbers—that can be analyzed to determine the results of the study.

An additional narrowing of the observations in science comes from the specification of a **variable** or several variables in research studies. A variable is the factor of interest in a research study. The term comes from the notion that the factor varies, or potentially has more than one value (as opposed to a constant, which has only one value). Most things vary, so finding a variable of interest is not nearly as difficult as restricting a study to only a few variables. For example, variables include factors such as time of day, family income, level of anxiety, number of hours of practice, gender of participants, and so forth. Thousands of variables are of interest to researchers, yet studies typically include only a few.

The systematic plans and measurements in science include many different specific techniques or methods, each of which has the power to reveal different types of information. In addition, each method has it own advantages and disadvantages. Scientific methods fall (but not neatly) into two types: descriptive and experimental. Different methods exist within each type, but descriptive research techniques have limitations and advantages that experimental techniques do not, and vice versa. Therefore, one approach to understanding research methods is through an examination of these two approaches.

Descriptive Methods

Descriptive research methods help investigators answer "what" questions. That is, descriptive research can tell what types of things exist, including great detail about those things and even the extent of relationships among various things. Descriptive methods include naturalistic observation, surveys, and correlational studies. All of these designs allow researchers to gather information about phenomena that already exist, and none of these methods involves manipulation of existing conditions or the introduction of change by the researcher.

Naturalistic Observation

Naturalistic observation involves just what the name implies—observation of a naturally occurring situation. Like all scientific observation, this gathering of information must be of publicly observable phenomena and according to a systematic plan. In making these observations, the researchers must not change the situation in any way, or it is no longer naturalistic. The phenomenon may change when researchers become part of the situation, so researchers must find ways to gather data without changing the situation. Therefore, naturalistic observation is not a particularly easy method.

For example, if a team of researchers wanted to study the gender-stereotypical versus gender-atypical toy choices of 3-year-old children through naturalistic observation, these investigators would have several tasks. First, they would have to define what they considered gender-stereotypical and gender-atypical toy choices so that observers could classify the toy choices the children make. Researchers might choose to specify an **operational definition,** a definition of a variable in terms of the operations used to obtain data on that variable rather than in terms of the concepts underlying the variable. For the study on toy choices, the researchers would need to specify which choices would count as gender stereotypical and which would count as atypical.

Second, the researchers would have to find a way to observe 3-year-old children playing with toys. The children could not come in contact with or see the investigators lest their presence change the children's behavior. In such a study (Lloyd, Duveen, & Smith, 1988), 3- and 4-year-old children were observed playing with gender-stereotyped toys to examine the different toy choices according to situation and play partner. These young children tended to use gender-stereotyped toys, especially in action play and to a lesser extent in pretend play. This naturalistic observation revealed that the situation was an important factor in children's gender stereotypical toy choices.

What can researchers learn through naturalistic observation? In this example (Lloyd et al., 1988), the researchers determined that the play situation is a factor in how gender-stereotypical children's toy choices were. Other similar studies might investigate toys children bring with them to day care, how long the children play with each type of toy, which toys children are willing to share and which they are not, or many other such questions. Indeed, many possibilities exist for this method, even with this single topic.

This method is limited to descriptions of what occurred, but this information may be exactly what the researchers want, and thus this limitation may not be a disadvantage. An advantage of this method is its lack of artificiality, which is a problem for laboratory research. The specification of the behaviors under observation and the decisions concerning how to collect data narrow the focus of the research to certain aspects of the naturalistic situation. Thus, naturalistic observation is not a recording of a situation but a choice of which data to collect from a complex environment. The complexity of the naturalistic situation results from many factors that make simple interpretations of this type of research nearly impossible. Although researchers may gain some insight into the important variables in a situation, naturalistic observation lacks the power to allow researchers to determine causal relationships.

Surveys

Surveys are a second method of descriptive research. In surveys, researchers construct questionnaires, choose a group of people to respond to the questionnaire, collect the data, and analyze the data to yield results. This method sounds deceptively simple—almost anyone can think of questions to ask. However, the method is filled with choices. For example, researchers using this method must decide about the wording of questions (e.g., "Do you agree...." versus "Do you disagree..."), the answer format (respondents reply versus respondents choose from a set of answers), the appearance of the questionnaire (number of pages, size of type, page layout), the choice of people responding (representative of the entire population versus a select group, such as registered voters or first-time parents), the number of people needed (what number will give a good estimate for accuracy), and the method of administration (face-to-face interview, telephone interview, mailed questionnaire). Unwise choices on any of these decisions may result in a survey that does not allow the researcher to answer the question that prompted the research or, worse, may give the researcher an answer that is misleading.

The main limitation of the survey method is inherent: Surveys pose questions rather than make direct measurements. That is, surveys typically rely on self-reports rather than direct observations of behavior. Researchers ask people to respond to a series of questions either in person or through a mailed questionnaire or telephone survey. In many surveys, participants are asked to share their opinions and attitudes, but in some surveys participants try to report on past behavior. The responses that people give may not accurately reflect their beliefs or behaviors. Even if people are honest about their beliefs, they may not always behave in a way that is consistent with reported attitudes. Indeed, people may lie, withhold the truth, or simply do not know or remember the information.

Replies to survey questions are open to bias due to participants' beliefs about social standards and their tendency to present themselves in a favorable way. This bias can invalidate a question or even an entire survey, and information obtained through self-reports is generally not considered as strong as information obtained by direct observation. Despite the wide variety of information that can be obtained through the survey method, that information is limited not only by its descriptive nature but also by its potential inaccuracy.

Despite the disadvantages, surveys offer the advantages of allowing researchers to ask people about things that the researchers could not easily (or possibly ethically) observe directly. Thus, the method is flexible and useful in a variety of situations. Surveys are a very common method for measuring people's attitudes. Psychologists, sociologists, market researchers, and political pollsters all use this method to help decide how people feel about a wide variety of issues.

For example, survey of over 1,500 college students in the United States, Russia, and Japan questioned students' experience concerning token resistance to sex and consent to unwanted sexual intercourse (Sprecher, Hatfield, Cortese, Potapova, & Levitskaya, 1994). Token resistance to sex is defined as saying "no" when the person actually wants to have, and later consents to have, sex. One focus of the study was the stereotype that only women engage in token resistance, and the survey showed that this stereotype is incorrect—the behavior occurs in both men and women. Consent to unwanted sex occurred in all three cultures, but women in the United States reported higher frequency of this behavior than women in the other countries.

Correlational Studies

If researchers want to know about the relationship between two specific variables rather than information about several variables, they will do a **correlational study,** another type of descriptive method. Correlational studies allow researchers to determine both the strength and types of relationships between the variables under study.

To do a correlational study, researchers must choose two variables for study, operationalize (create an operational definition of) and measure these variables, and then analyze the relationship between them. To perform this analysis, researchers calculate a correlation coefficient, the results of a statistical test that reveals the strength or magnitude of the relationship between two variables. The correlation coefficient is described by a formula, and researchers must apply the formula to their data. A number of variations on the correlation coefficient exist, but the most common is the *Pearson product–moment correlation coefficient,* symbolized by the letter r. The results of the analysis yield a number that varies between $r = +1.00$ and $r = -1.00$. Correlations that are close to $r = +1.00$ indicate a strong, positive relationship: As scores on one variable increase, those on the other also increase. Correlations that are close to $r = -1.00$ indicate a strong, negative relationship: As one measurement increases, the other decreases. Correlations that are close to $r = 0.00$ indicate little or no relationship between the two variables.

For example, one study (Furnham & Rawles, 1999) correlated estimated and measured IQ scores for both women and men. The participants estimated their IQ scores and four months later took a standardized IQ test. The results indicated that only modest correlations existed between the estimated and assessed scores. The correlation was higher for men ($r = .16$) than for women ($r = .09$). Indeed, the correlation between women's estimated and assessed IQ scores indicated no relationship. These results suggest that men are more accurate than women in perceptions of their own intelligence. Additional analyses from this study indicated that women underestimate their IQ scores.

Correlational studies, like other descriptive methods, do not reveal why the relationship exists. That is, correlations do not indicate causality. However, such a deduction may be very tempting. Indeed, a causal relationship may exist between two variables that have a high correlation, but the method does not allow that conclusion. Even a high correlation would not allow a researcher to know the source of the relationship: Did changes in one variable produce changes in the other, or vice versa? Another possibility is that both variables may be causally related to a third variable that was not part of the study. In any case, a conclusion of causality is not legitimate on the basis of the evidence from a correlational study. Thus, the information that researchers obtain and the conclusions that they may draw from correlational studies exclude causality but include information on the existence and strength of relationships.

Experimental Designs

To obtain information about cause and effect, researchers must do **experiments.** This type of design allows researchers to answer "why" questions—questions with answers that involve explanations rather than descriptions. An experiment is a method that involves the manipulation of one factor, called the **independent variable,** the measurement of another factor, called the **dependent variable,** and the requirement of holding all other factors constant. By manipulating the independent variable, the experimenter tries to create a change. Detecting change requires some basis for comparison, so the simplest version of an experiment requires two conditions to provide this comparison. These two conditions consist of two different levels of the independent variable, with all other factors held constant. The manipulation may be more elaborate, consisting of three, four, or more levels of the independent variable, and experiments may include more than one independent variable.

The dependent variable is the one that the experimenter measures. Choosing and quantifying dependent variables can also be complex. In psychological research, dependent variables are always some type of behavior or response. By using such dependent variables, psychology is placed among the sciences that require empirical subject matter—behavior and responses that can be observed and measured.

The logic of experimental design holds that the manipulation of the independent variable should produce a change in the value of the dependent variable if the two are causally related. When the experimenter also holds other factors constant, the only source of change in the dependent variable should be the manipulated change in the independent variable. Thus, in a well-designed experiment, the changes in the value of the dependent variable can be entirely attributed to the manipulation of the independent variable. That is, the changes in the independent variable caused the changes in the dependent variable.

Although the logic of experimental design is simple, creating conditions to effectively manipulate one factor while holding all other factors constant is far from simple. Such a situation would be almost impossible in a naturalistic setting, because any one change would result in many others. Therefore, almost all experiments take place in laboratories. These settings offer the possibility of the necessary control, but they open experiments to the criticism of artificiality. Despite the validity of that criticism, scientists highly value experiments because of their potential to reveal cause-and-effect relationships, a type of information that other methods cannot show.

An example of an experiment was one performed by Margaret Gentry (1998), who explored the sexual double standard. The sexual double standard calls for chastity in women but allows (and even encourages) men to have a variety of sexual partners and experiences. In this study, participants evaluated either a man or a woman who was either involved in a monogamous relationship or who had many sexual partners. Gentry's study combined several independent variables, including the gender and sexual history of the target, that is, the person being evaluated. Different versions of the descriptions portrayed the target as a man or as a woman. Therefore, the description of the person as male or female was part of the manipulation involved in the experiment. The dependent variable was the participants' evaluations of the target on several dimensions, including how good or bad they thought the person was. Gentry was interested in determining if standards of sexual behavior apply differently to men and women, so she presented descriptions that varied only in the factors of interest, holding other elements of the description constant. She found little evidence to support the sexual double standard—descriptions of male and female targets received similar ratings for similar behaviors. The variable that lowered ratings was number of sexual partners: People described as having many sexual partners received lower ratings than those described as monogamous. Therefore, the variable of sexual history showed an effect, but the variable of gender did not.

Gender research such as Gentry's defines gender as a social category. Researchers who use this approach investigate how people use information about gender as part of their beliefs and expectations about behavior, and how people assimilate information about gender into their own behavior. Researchers like Gentry manipulate information about the gender of the target to determine the reaction of participants to this information. This approach allows gender to become an independent variable because researchers can manipulate the gender of a person in a description and yet hold all other factors in the description constant. According to Kay Deaux's (1984) review of this approach, the results indicate that gender is an important piece of information that people use in forming impressions and interacting with people: "The focus is not on how men and women actually differ, but how people *think* that they differ" (Deaux, 1984, p. 110). This approach is especially well suited to investigating stereotypes, attitudes, and conceptions of gender.

Experiments are prized because, carefully designed and conducted, this method allows conclusions concerning causality. If the experiment is not done carefully, however, interpretation of causality can be in error. The participants in the Gentry study were asked about hypothetical people whom they rated based on brief descriptions. These participants may have behaved differently in a more naturalistic situation—evaluating descriptions differs from evaluating actual people. In addition, the laboratory situation may prompt different behavior than would occur in a more realistic context. Because participants in a laboratory setting are always aware that their behavior is of interest to researchers, they may behave differently than they would in a natural setting. This possibility limits the extent to which researchers can generalize their results to other situations. The artificiality of the situation and its limitations in generalizing results to other situations are drawbacks of the experimental method. Researchers have a prejudice in favor of experiments, which leads them to prize experiments above other methods (perhaps inappropriately), and scientists do experiments whenever they can. Table 2.1 presents both descriptive and experimental methods with their advantages and limitations.

TABLE 2.1 Advantages and Limitations of Descriptive and Experimental Methods

Method	Advantage	Limitation
Naturalistic observation	Looks at behavior in a natural setting	Cannot distinguish among many variables that can affect a situation
Survey	Examines a variety of topics without being intrusive	Relies on self-reports rather than direct observation of behavior
Correlational study	Allows determination of strength and direction of relationship between two variables	Cannot reveal any information about causality
Experiments	Allows determination of cause-and effect relationships	Conducted in laboratory situations that are artificial
		Can only investigate a few variables at a time

Ex Post Facto Studies

Researchers cannot always do experiments. Some variables of interest are beyond possible manipulation, either for practical or ethical reasons. For example, researchers might want to know about the effect of brain damage on memory. To do an experiment, researchers would be required to select a group of people and perform the surgery that would cause brain damage in half of them while leaving the other half with undamaged brains. Obviously, this research is unethical, but the question that prompted it—Does brain damage influence memory?—is still of interest.

Researchers interested in the question about brain damage and memory have at least two choices. They might choose to do the experiment with nonhuman subjects (although some would object to the ethics of this research, too), but the problems of generalizing the findings to humans would be a severe limitation. Another choice would be the **ex post facto study.** In this type of study, researchers might select people who have sustained brain damage in the area of interest and enlist these individuals as research participants, contrasting them with a group of people who have not experienced brain damage of any sort, or with those who have damage in some other area of the brain. Both groups would participate in the assessment of memory. Therefore, the presence of brain damage would be the **subject variable**—the characteristic of interest in the subjects—and the scores on the memory test would be the dependent variable.

Such an ex post facto study would not be an experiment, because the researchers did not produce the brain damage while holding all other factors constant. Instead, the researchers entered the picture *after* the manipulation had occurred through accidents (hence the term *ex post facto*, meaning after the fact). With no opportunity for precision in creating the values of the independent variable or in holding other factors constant, the ex post facto study lacks the controls of an experiment that would allow researchers to draw conclusions about cause-and-effect relationships (Christensen, 1997).

The ex post facto study seems very much like an experiment, including the presence of contrast groups and a dependent variable measurement. These similarities can lead to misinterpretations of these studies and incorrect attributions of causality. Researchers are usually careful to use the correct language to interpret their findings from ex post facto studies, but people who read the research may not be appropriately cautious, leading to misunderstandings of research findings.

Gender of participants is a subject variable, a characteristic of the subjects that exists prior to their participation in a study, but one that can be the basis for division of subjects into contrasting groups. This type of research has a long history in psychology and has constituted the traditional approach to gender research. In 1974, two psychologists, Eleanor Maccoby and Carol Jacklin, published *The Psychology of Sex Differences,* a comprehensive review of research-based psychological findings about gender-related differences. These authors collected over 2,000 studies in which gender was a subject variable, and they organized the findings around different topics, such as aggression and verbal ability. Maccoby and Jacklin then evaluated the findings for each topic, determining how many studies failed to find a difference, how many studies supported a difference, and the direction of the differences for those comparisons that showed differences. Maccoby and Jacklin's book was soon accepted as a classic in this type of research review (Deaux, 1984).

Studies with gender as a subject variable remain a common choice in psychology gender research. Susan Sprecher and her colleagues also conducted such a study (Sprecher, Regan, McKinney, Maxwell, & Wazienski, 1997). These researchers were interested in the sexual double standard and how it might apply differently to women and men choosing dating partners and potential marriage partners. Gentry's (1998) experimental study also investigated the sexual double standard, but that study manipulated the gender of a person to determine if sexual behavior was judged differently for a female versus a male target. Sprecher et al. selected women and men to question about their choices in order to determine differences between men's and women's attitudes about sexual experience. The results indicated little difference. Women and men both expressed a preference for chastity in potential partners and rated having many sexual partners more negatively. Sprecher et al. did find gender differences in sexual experience—the men in their study reported more sexual partners than the women, confirming a behavioral version of the double standard for sexual behavior. However, the two did not differ in their preference for sexual experience in either a dating or potential marriage partner. This ex post facto study is consistent with Gentry's experimental study on the same topic. Both studies suggest a decline in the acceptance of a double standard of sexual behavior.

The studies that approach gender as a subject variable are ex post facto studies, with all of the limitations of this method. That is, these studies do not and cannot reveal that gender *causes* differences in any behavior. This caution is difficult for many people to keep in mind, and those who are not familiar with research methods have a tendency to believe that gender-related differences in behavior have biological sex as the underlying cause. This reasoning contains two errors: (1) incorrectly attributing causality to a research method that cannot demonstrate cause-and-effect relationships and (2) reducing the many variables that coexist with biological sex to the subject variable gender. Therefore, an erroneous interpretation of such studies can lead people to conclusions for which there is no research evidence.

Figure 2.1 illustrates some of the differences between experimental and ex post facto designs, using gender as an example. In the experimental design, researchers often randomly divide the participants into groups in order to keep individual differences equal among the groups. Therefore, the groups in an experimental design would not consist of one group of men and another group of women, because random assignment would be very unlikely to yield such a configuration. The ex post facto design, on the other hand, assigns

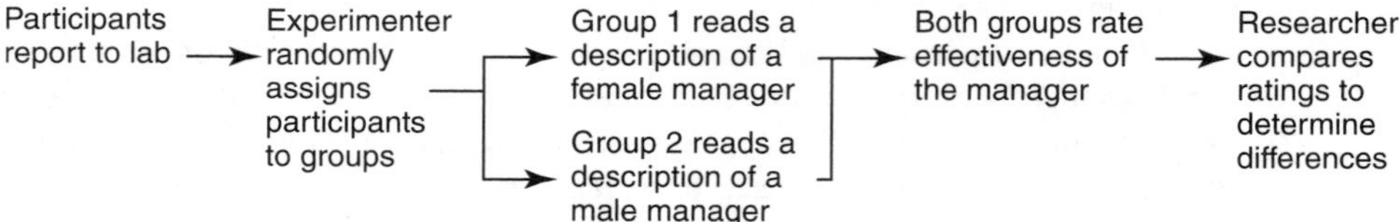

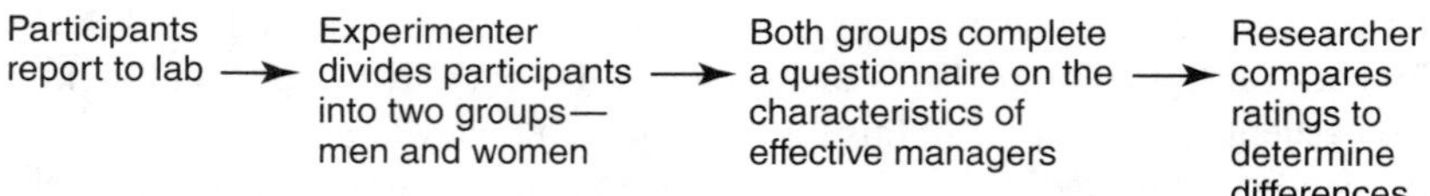

FIGURE 2.1 Two Designs with Gender as a Variable

participants to groups on the basis of some factor that the participants already possess, such as gender. In this type of design, such as the Sprecher et al. (1997) study, the researcher might have one group consisting of women and another of men. Indeed, thousands of studies use this design to study gender-related differences and similarities.

An experimental design, such as the study by Gentry (1998), can use gender as a variable if the researcher manipulates the gender of some target person whom the participants rate, evaluate, or react to. This approach makes gender a social category, not a subject variable. Further, the subject variable of gender can be included in a study that manipulates an independent variable to study each variable as well as the variables in combination. Therefore, ex post facto designs can examine gender as a subject variable, experimental designs can study gender as a social category to which participants react, and studies can use gender as a subject variable combined with additional, manipulated independent variables. These approaches are not equivalent, and each yields information that requires careful interpretation of findings.

In summary, different research methods yield different types of information. Descriptive research methods include naturalistic observation, surveys, and correlational studies. Such studies help to answer questions about *what* occurs; that is, they describe what exists. Experimental research, on the other hand, allows researchers to explain *why* a relationship exists between independent variables and dependent variables. Because it yields information about cause-and-effect relationships, this method is highly prized. A quasi-experimental method, the ex post facto study, is similar to an experiment in the designation of variables (called subject variables) and dependent variables, but these designs differ from true experiments in that they use the existing values of the subject variable rather than create the values of the independent variable through manipulation.

Qualitative Research

Descriptive and experimental research methods are usually quantitative; that is, these research methods involve the process of collecting data in terms of numbers. As previously mentioned, researchers must choose some aspect of the situation to measure, and these measurements almost always result in numbers that can be analyzed by statistics. Some scholars have raised objections to this process, claiming that quantification fails to capture important aspects of the situations under study.

An alternative to the quantitative approach is qualitative research. Qualitative researchers focus on attempting to understand the complexity of the situation rather than trying to manipulate and control different variables. They also reject the notion that researchers should be detached and impartial; instead, they accept the subjectivity of the research process and attempt to form cooperative relationships with those whom they study. By interacting with research participants as equals, they try to understand the meaning and context of what they study. In addition to a different philosophy of research, qualitative studies include a different set of methods.

Qualitative research has been more common in anthropology and sociology than in psychology, but the interest in qualitative methods has grown among psychologists in recent years (Crawford & Kimmel, 1999). **Ethnography,** one of the most common qualitative methods, has a long tradition in anthropology. Researchers using this method spend time becoming immersed in the situation they are studying. For anthropologists, this situation is typically another culture; for psychologists and sociologists, the situation may be a school, company, or hospital. By becoming part of the situation, the researcher can gather and interpret information situated in the context in which it occurs.

Barrie Thorne (1993) conducted an ethnographic study in which she observed students in middle school to understand how children of this age behave with children of the same and the other gender. She sat in their classrooms, ate in the lunchroom, and observed activities on the playground. Although she did not become one of the children, her status was unlike that of the other adults. Her presence for over 8 months allowed her to make in-depth observations and interpretations of the gender interactions among these preadolescents and to describe and classify these interactions.

Case studies and **interviews** are also qualitative methods. A case study is an intensive study of a case—that is, a single person (or a small sample of people). Several different factors determine which case is chosen for study. The person may be typical and thus reflective of many other people, or unusual and thus of interest. Researchers conducting case studies often spend days or months interviewing or observing the person in order to write a case study. Miguel, a gay Mexican American man, was the subject of such a case study (Carrier, 1997). The case study told of Miguel's sexual life history, contrasting the sexual behaviors and cultural attitudes of Mexican American and European American gay men. In addition, the case study described Miguel's relationships with women, his career, and his problems with alcoholism.

Interviews can take many forms, but qualitative interviews differ from interviews conducted as part of survey research in both format and goals. Survey interviews are quantitative, including a specified and uniform set of questions to which all respondents reply. The uniformity of responses allows statistical analysis, but such analysis is not the goal of qualitative interviews. These interviews can take the form of oral or life histories, or the interview may be oriented around a narrower topic. An interview study of convicted and imprisoned rapists helped clarify the rapists' motivations and attitudes toward women (Scully, 1990). The interviews varied in length, with some lasting only a few minutes and others lasting for hours. This procedure did not yield a uniform set of data, but an analysis showed some common patterns of motivation and attitudes among the rapists' responses.

The focus group is another qualitative method that psychologists have borrowed; this method is more common in communications and marketing research than in psychology. A **focus group** is a discussion centered around a specific topic. The individuals in the group can consist either of people brought together for the purpose of the discussion or of people who belong to some existing group, such as a family or sorority. Groups usually consist of 6 to 8 people, and rarely more than 12. Focus groups are similar to interviews in terms of the questions and topics that can be explored. However, this method allows group members to interact with each other as well as with the researcher, making the focus group more similar to naturally occurring situations than the interview method is (Wilkinson, 1999).

Jeanette Norris and her colleagues (Norris, Nurius, & Dimeff, 1996) used the focus group approach to study women's perceptions of risk for sexual victimization. These researchers chose sorority women, who responded to questions and discussed their attitudes and feelings about aspects of Greek life and the social system in which they participated, including unwanted sex. The focus group discussion lasted 90 minutes. Most women felt that they were not vulnerable to situations involving forced sex—an attitude that kept them from planning effective strategies for escaping a coercive situation. Furthermore, their involvement in the Greek system made some women hesitant to report coercive sex or take direct action that would offend or embarrass fraternity men. Therefore, this focus group study allowed Norris et al. to explore some of the attitudes that allow sexual coercion to continue on college campuses.

Qualitative research methods are growing in acceptance and frequency but still constitute a minority of the research, even in the area of gender (Crawford & Kimmel, 1999). An analysis of two leading journals, *Feminism & Psychology* and *Psychology of Women Quarterly,* revealed that the interview method was the most common of the qualitative approaches (Wilkinson, 1999). That method accounted for over half of the research articles in *Feminism & Psychology* but only 17% of research articles in *Psychology of Women Quarterly.* Other qualitative methods accounted for much lower percentages, and no other qualitative method represented more than 2% of the research studies in these journals.

Qualitative research offers alternatives to traditional quantitative research methods. A comparison of the two approaches appears in Table 2.2. The philosophy and practice of

TABLE 2.2 Comparison of Quantitative and Qualitative Research

Quantitative Researchers	Qualitative Researchers
Often work in laboratories	Rarely work in laboratories
Strive to detach themselves from the situation to attain objectivity	Immerse themselves in the situation and accept subjectivity as part of the process
Attempt to study a representative group of individuals to be able to generalize	May seek unusual individuals because they are interesting cases
Create a distinction between researchers and subjects	Treat participants as equals
Collect data in the form of numbers	Collect information that is not reduced to numbers
Attempt to control the influence of variables other than the independent variable(s)	Attempt to understand the complexity of the situation as it exists
Use statistics to analyze their data	Do not use statistics to analyze their information

qualitative research differ from quantitative studies. Qualitative researchers emphasize context and acknowledge that subjectivity is part of the research process; they become involved in the research situation, interacting with participants in order to understand the patterns of their behavior. Researchers who use these methods believe that this approach offers advantages over the traditional quantitative approach.

Gender Bias in Research

Despite the long history and success of science, some modern scholars have questioned its assumptions and procedures. One criticism is that science grew from not only the activities of men but also from a gendered, masculine bias that is inherently part of science. According to this view, this masculine bias affects our modern conception of science, including the thinking of the men and women who do scientific work. Another more concrete criticism of science has come from the constructionists, who contend that science is incapable of revealing an objective picture of the natural world. According to constructionists, this inability stems from the inevitable bias within the perceptions of scientists, who are influenced by their personal and societal prejudices. Scholars who take this view have used the study of gender as a particularly good example of the distortions and misrepresentations of science.

Sources of Bias

Bias can enter research at many levels, beginning with the very framework of science. The philosophers whose work spurred the founding of science were all men, and Evelyn Fox Keller (1985) has argued that these philosophers introjected a masculine bias into the very conceptual foundation of science. She has interpreted the emphasis on rationality and objectivity in science as masculine values, and she has contrasted those masculine elements of science with the feminine elements of nature—feeling and subjectivity. Thus, Keller discussed what she interpreted as the gendering of science and nature: masculine for science and feminine for nature. She also analyzed the interaction of the masculine–feminine dichotomy in the view of one influential philosopher, Francis Bacon, who proposed the metaphor of a marriage between Nature and Science. In Bacon's metaphor, Nature is the bride and Science is the groom. Keller took Bacon's metaphor as particularly significant in its gender and sexual connotations. She argued that this metaphor has influenced contemporary views of science as a masculine activity that strives to bring rationality and to dominate unruly feminine nature. Thus, even at its inception, science carried connotations of maleness, rationality, and dominance. According to Keller, not only have women been discouraged from the pursuit of science as a profession, but the activity of science itself suggests masculinity (see "According to the Media/According to the Research").

Theories are another potential source of bias in science. The study of gender is full of examples of situations in which speculations and theories have attained a status in which they are mistaken for results. Freud's theory is probably the most prominent example, with its emphasis on the importance of biological sex differences in building personality. Research has not supported this theory (see Chapter 5 for more on Freud), and supporters of the theory speak with unearned authority.

ACCORDING TO THE MEDIA…

Scientists Are Men, Often with Evil Motives

In the movies, scientists are most often male and more often evil than good. These depictions go back to the era of silent film and continue to the present. "The movies have always been full of insane chemists, demonic doctors and obsessive inventors who, whether purposely or inadvertently, unleash malevolent forces that neither they nor anyone else can control" (Ribalow, 1998, p. 26). Some scientists in the movies want to do evil, but even with noble motivations, movie scientists often cause serious problems when they fail to understand the implications of their actions. Both evil and well-meaning scientists are portrayed as obsessive, self-centered, personally cold, and removed from society. Movie scientists work in isolated laboratories without the support of the scientific community. Their brilliance is ignored or disdained by the rest of the world, and their innovations are revolutionary.

Women are more often background rather than leading characters in media science. In children's science programming, about 80% of the women were in secondary or supporting roles, and the proportion of male to female scientists was two to one (Steinke & Long, 1996). However, during the 1990s, a new movie scientist appeared: the "brainy babe" (Ribalow, 1998). This female version of the scientist is usually similar to the male versions—either evil or oblivious, obsessive, and also flawed, but she is also more vulnerable. Two examples are Ellie Arroway, Jody Foster's character in *Contact* (1997), and Emma Russell, Elizabeth Shue's character in *The Saint* (1997). Both are brilliant, obsessive, shy, and personally unsure of themselves. Emma's vulnerability is her heart condition. Ellie's is the memory of her dead father. These brainy babes are outcasts because of their role as scientist, just as the male scientists are, but their vulnerability is a departure from the portrayals of male scientists.

Additional bias in research on gender (and many other topics) comes from the procedures involved in planning studies and evaluating results. Researchers' values enter the research process as early as the planning stage of studies, influencing the choice of problem to investigate and the choice of questions to ask (MacCoun, 1998; Wallston, 1981). Publications place too much emphasis on results and too little emphasis on the conceptualization of the questions underlying the research process. The answers that researchers find depend on the questions they ask, so the planning and questioning aspects of the process is critically important.

When researchers formulate their studies, they ask questions and choose methods of gathering information that will allow them to answer their questions. Most researchers know what they expect to find when they ask their questions, so research is not free of the values and expectations of the scientists, even at this stage of the research. These expectations lead to the formulation of a **hypothesis,** a statement about the expected outcome of the study. Researchers test hypotheses by gathering data and analyzing them to obtain results. The researchers can then decide if the results support or fail to support their hypothesis.

To evaluate the data collected from studies, researchers often use statistical tests. Many different statistical tests exist, but all of those used to evaluate research data have a common goal—to allow the researcher to decide whether the results are statistically significant. A **statistically significant result** is one due to events other than chance alone. If researchers

ACCORDING TO THE RESEARCH...

Science Doesn't Play Well at the Cineplex

According to author and director Michael Crichton (1999), the problem with science in the movies is not that the media misunderstand science, but that scientists misunderstand the media. The scientific process does not produce the material for exciting entertainment; the situations in which most scientists do research do not contain enough drama to hold the attention of movie audiences. Thus, science is portrayed in the movies in exaggerated ways or with added plot elements for the purpose of entertainment. The media do not single out scientists for negative portrayals; all professions look bad because the point of presenting a profession is to further the plot, not to present accurate career information.

The daily work of scientists includes too little action and too much thought for good entertainment (except to the scientists). Unlike the screen presentations, most scientists work in university or hospital laboratories with a research group rather than alone in some isolated, secret lab. The majority of scientific research is funded by government grants obtained through a peer review process, not by some malevolent company intent on taking over the world. This funding process creates research that extends current knowledge in small ways and makes it unlikely that large breakthroughs will occur or that any scientist working outside the system would be able to make a substantial contribution. Thus, the process of scientific research allows for too few heroic acts, too few explosions, and too much time and patience for good plots. Real science is not going to be a really interesting movie.

On the other hand, real scientists can be very interesting characters, and presentations of their lives can be entertaining. Depictions of the lives of Marie and Pierre Curie and Thomas Edison have been movies with fairly accurate and entertaining depictions. In addition, a Public Broadcasting System series, *Discovering Women* (1995), showed female scientists conducting their work and living their lives. The series presented a positive portrayal of these women and their work, and such programs can provide encouraging images for women to enter science as a career. These role models are an improvement over the brainy babes of recent movies.

---

are careful in the design of their studies, then they can attribute significant results to the factors they have identified in their studies. The procedure for determining the statistical significance of a result involves choosing the appropriate statistical test and analyzing the data from the study using that statistic. If the analysis indicates significant effects, then the researchers can conclude that their results were not due to chance alone; that is, the study worked as hypothesized. If the analysis does not indicate a significant effect, then the researchers cannot claim that their results are due to anything but chance or that their study worked as hypothesized.

Researchers are constrained from making claims about factors that do not produce significant results, because these results are not considered "real," and researchers have no confidence in the validity of nonsignificant results. When researchers obtain statistically significant results, they have confidence that their research has revealed effects that probably are not due to chance. However, the term *significant* can be misleading, because people who are not sophisticated in the logic of statistical evaluation may believe that statistically significant means *important.*

The concepts of statistical significance and practical significance are not the same. A result is statistically significant when it is unlikely to have occurred solely on the basis of chance. A result has **practical significance** when it is important to everyday life. For example, a low correlation ($r = 0.20$) can indicate a statistically significant relationship if the number of people participating in the study was sufficiently large (what constitutes a large sample varies with the design and statistic), but this magnitude of correlation does not reveal a strong relationship between the two variables in the correlation. That is, this correlation would have little practical significance. People who hear about significant results may believe that the results have practical significance when the researchers have reported statistical significance. Confusion between these two concepts can result: "Reasonable people who are repeatedly exposed to findings reported as significant mean differences or nonchance factors…sometimes begin to think and talk as if those differences were actually true in most individual cases" (Bernstein, 1999, p. x). Such misunderstandings can lead people to believe that results mean more than they actually do and apply to everyone when they actually do not.

For example, one well-publicized gender difference is performance in mathematics (Maccoby & Jacklin, 1974). How much better are boys at math? Do all boys do better than all girls? How much do math scores of boys and girls overlap? Figure 2.2 shows some possibilities for the distributions of math scores for boys and girls. Group A of this figure shows two distributions with no overlap. If this figure represented the mathematics performance of boys and girls, then all boys would do better than all girls. Group B shows the performance of boys and girls overlapping slightly. If this figure represented the performance of boys and girls, then most boys would do better than most girls. A few girls would do better than a few boys, but no girls would do better than boys with the highest performance. Group C shows a lot of overlap between the performance of the two. If this figure represented performance, all boys would not do better at math than all girls, and many girls would do better at math than many boys.

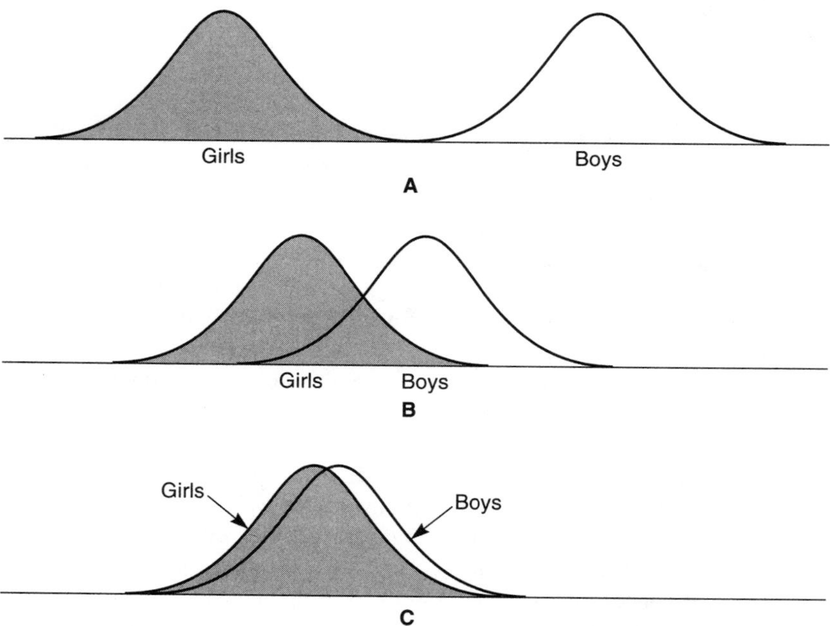

FIGURE 2.2 Distributions with Varying Degrees of Overlap

Hyde (1981, 1986, 1994) contended that the upper range of difference between men and women is no more than 1% in mathematical ability. Only a small percent of the distribution of math scores for boys and girls fails to overlap, and most of the scores for the two are in the same range. Figure 2.2C comes closer to this distribution of math ability than the other parts of Figure 2.2. These gender-related differences in math performance are sufficiently large to show a statistically significant difference, but not large enough to have any practical significance when applied to the performance of most boys and most girls. This magnitude of difference would not lead educators to create different math classes for boys and girls because their abilities were so dissimilar, nor would counselors advise girls to avoid math courses because of their lack of ability.

Finding statistically significant differences is the goal of both experimental and ex post facto designs. When researchers plan studies, they typically look for differences and draw their hypotheses accordingly. Such researchers do not look for similarities. If researchers find the expected differences, they report and discuss these differences. If they fail to find differences, such results do not typically lead to a discussion of the similarity of the groups. Instead, researchers will often dismiss a study (or part of a study) as a failure and gloss over the absence of statistically significant differences as unimportant.

Studies that do not find hypothesized differences in outcomes are less likely to be published than studies that offer support for the hypotheses. Thus, a strong prejudice exists in favor of findings that show differences rather than findings that do not succeed in showing differences; that is, there is a prejudice against findings that show similarities (Greenwald, 1975). This tendency prompts researchers to highlight the differences they find and to dismiss the similarities. Indeed, researchers may omit any mention of failure to find a difference, such as a gender-related difference, but researchers who find statistically significant differences will always mention the differences and the level of statistical significance. Researchers cannot discuss an effect they have failed to find, and they must discuss effects that they have found. However, the omission of some information and the mention of other information can lead to a distorted view of overall findings by magnifying differences and obscuring similarities.

Table 2.3 shows the stages of research and how bias can enter at various points in the process. The possibilities for gender bias listed in the table are only a few examples; the history of gender research is filled with too many other examples.

Ways to Deal with Bias in Science

Begley's headline article, which opened this chapter, pointed out that critics have questioned the notion of objectivity and the view that science shows an orderly progression toward "truth." "Ever since the scientific method became a way of learning about nature, including ourselves, some people have hailed science as the only way to comprehend natural phenomena, while others have questioned whether it is an appropriate road to knowledge" (Hubbard, 1990, p. 9).

Advocating Transformation

The constructionists deny the possibility of objectivity and thus reject the basic tenets of science. The extreme of this position calls for abandoning science as a way to deal with its inevitable bias. That position is unlikely to prevail—science has been too successful and is

TABLE 2.3 Stages of Research and Potential for Bias

Stage	Ways Bias Can Enter	Gender-Related Example
Finding a problem to investigate	Allowing personal and societal values to influence choice of topic	Studying heart disease rather than breast cancer in middle-aged populations
Selecting variables	Using inaccurate, incomplete, or misleading definitions	Defining rape as vaginal penetration accompanied by force or threat of force (excludes other forced sexual acts and excludes men as victims)
Choosing a design	Choosing a design that does not allow for the evaluation of context	Testing participants in a situation that is anxiety-provoking for women but not for men
Formulating a hypothesis	Failing to consider the validity of the null hypothesis	Always hypothesizing gender differences rather than similarities
	Following a theory that is biased	Following Freudian theory to hypothesize that women have weak superegos
Collecting data	Permitting personal bias to influence measurement; using a definition of the behavior that is too narrow	Defining battering as the number of police reports of domestic violence
Analyzing results	Allowing personal values and expectation to guide the choice of which factors to evaluate	Failing to make a comparison of female and male participants
Interpreting results	Failing to report effect sizes	Interpreting a gender difference in a way that makes it seem large when it is not
	Interpreting gender differences as due to biological factors when no biological data exists	Claiming that boys' advantage in math is biological when no biological data have been collected
Publication bias	Publication of findings showing significant gender differences	Publication and media attention for findings of gender differences, but no attention for findings of similarities

too widely accepted. Therefore, some other ways to deal with the bias in science are necessary. A growing group of scholars advocates replacing or supplementing traditional science with alternative methods, whereas others argue that scientists must try harder to do good science.

Scholars who claim that research should center on women advocate *feminist standpoint epistemologies* (Riger, 1992). Scholars who take this view claim that women have a unique point of view and different cognitive processes that have been ignored. These researchers believe that the analytical categories that are appropriate for men may not be appropriate for women, and that research should remedy these shortcomings by devising methods to study the unique experience of womanhood.

Several scholars have argued that feminist research has the power to transform research with women and even the discipline of psychology. Historian Londa Schiebinger (1999) asked a broader question about the influence of feminism in all of science. She evaluated the possibility that feminism and its criticisms of traditional science has changed modern science. Her conclusions were both positive and negative. That is, feminism (and the presence of women) has brought about some changes in science, but not in its basic assumptions or approach. The criticisms concerning masculinist bias in science may be founded, but the women who enter the profession of scientific research must play by the rules of science. In that sense, feminism has not changed science. Women have changed science in terms of what questions researchers ask and possibly how those results are interpreted. Research on issues important to women, such as incest and sexual abuse of children, rape and sexual assault, sexual harassment, spouse abuse, and achievements by women, has increased dramatically within the past 25 years, parallel to the increase in women in psychology (Worell, 1996). In addition, extending research to understudied populations has been a force in expanding psychology research beyond White, middle-class college students (Worell & Etaugh, 1994).

As a way of gaining additional information about women and their experience, the feminist standpoint epistemologies have considerable value and appeal. Some feminist scholars have rejected traditional quantitative research as impoverished in capturing the female experience and have opted for more qualitative approaches. Such methods allow researchers to be subjective and interpretive, which qualitative researchers believe is important in studying behavior.

A demonstration of the value of widening research methods came from a study (Landrine, Klonoff, & Brown-Collins, 1992) that approached the same problem with two methodologies: one quantitative and behavioral, and the other qualitative and based on personal perceptions. The study focused on self-perceptions of African American, Hispanic American, Asian American, and European American women concerning several gender-stereotypical behaviors. The quantitative analysis showed no differences among these groups of women, but the qualitative evaluation revealed ethnic differences by allowing participants to express feelings that the more traditional approach failed to show. This study demonstrated that more diverse methods of investigation have the potential to enrich traditional science.

The feminist standpoint epistemologies have the disadvantage of departing radically from accepted methodology, and such departures are difficult for mainstream science to accept (Riger, 1992). The growing interest in qualitative research and its increasing frequency in psychology journals speak to the possibility of including these changes in research. Less radical changes, however, are easier to accept and enact. Thus, decreasing bias in gender research is a more feasible goal.

Decreasing Bias

Those scholars who advocate a more objective study of gender can be termed *feminist empiricists* (Riger, 1992). These feminist researchers have argued that the development of a feminist methodology will not benefit research on women and gender-related behaviors. "A distinctive set of feminist methods for psychological research are not only futile but dangerous," and "any method can be misused in sexist ways" (Peplau & Conrad, 1989, p. 380). This view rejects the notion that methodology is gendered or that feminist research must be conducted by women or exclusively on women. Instead, it states that the use of diverse and appropriate methods is best for the study of women and gender-related behaviors.

To adequately study gender contrasts, research must include men (or boys) as well as women (or girls). Such comparisons are the subject matter of gender similarities and differences, and this research cannot include only one sex or the other. However, the necessary research must differ from much prior research, because so much of the existing research concerning gender is filled with serious bias. Diane Halpern (1995) contrasted the feminist empiricist position with previous research:

> *The fact that research has been used to justify discrimination and support the prevailing social view is precisely why sound empirical research is needed. If researchers find that society consistently values those traits that are associated with being a man and devalues those traits that are associated with being a woman, then the fault lies in the society in which researchers are participants, not in the research that demonstrates that there are gender differences. (p. 79)*

Several groups of feminist empiricist researchers have alerted researchers to the potential for inadvertently introducing sexist bias into research and have presented some suggestions for conducting nonsexist psychological research. Maureen McHugh and her colleagues (McHugh, Koeske, & Frieze, 1986) acknowledged that psychology research has included biases, some of them unintentional, and an unwarranted confidence in traditional research methods can lead to bias. In addition, bias can come from the theories and explanations researchers use as well as from inappropriate labeling and definitions.

Unwarranted confidence in traditional research methods occurs, for example, when psychologists accept that observations of behavior are objective. Observations are not necessarily free of sexist (or other) biases, because the observer may be biased and the *context* of the observation is rarely included in the analysis of the situation. For example, Paige Hall Smith and her colleagues (Smith, Smith, & Earp, 1999) criticized the process of measure-

---

GENDERED VOICES

Women's Position in Science Is Not Assured

Historian Londa Schiebinger (1999) examined women's influence in science as well as their position in science. She concluded that feminist scholarship and the presence of women in science have affected science, but women's position within science is not assured:

> *The early history of women in science teaches us several things. First, it teaches that scientific institutions have taken many forms over the centuries and that the structure of these institutions can encourage or discourage women's participation. Second, it reveals that in modern industrial societies the division of labor between work and home remains a barrier to women's entering the professions. Third, history teaches that women's success in science depends on a variety of interdependent factors: the prestige of scientific institutions, the fortunes of war and peace, the political climate, the structure of the family vis-à-vis the economy. Many of the problems women face in science today—domestic versus professional responsibilities, the tenure clock versus the biological clock—have deep historical roots. And fourth, history dispels the myth of inevitable progress in respect to women in science. There is a sense that nature takes its course—that, given time, things right themselves. The history of women in science, however, has not been characterized by a march of progress but by cycles of advancement and retrenchment. Women's situation has changed along with social conditions and climates of opinion. (pp. 31–32)*

Advances for women in science do not assure that women will continue to advance; male-dominated labs make women's position difficult and their future uncertain.

ment, arguing that it constituted a "measurement trap" that fails to capture critical aspects of experience. These researchers examined how various measurements fail to capture the experience of women who are battered, and how these failures influence the design and implementation of effective programs for battered women. The researchers suggested a more comprehensive definition of battering that included more information about women's experience of battering.

Gender may be part of the context of research and yet go unmentioned in the study. For example, the gender of the participants may be a subject variable in the study, but the gender of the experimenter usually is not. The gender of the experimenter may affect the behavior of participants, yet researchers rarely consider this factor.

Bias in an explanatory system occurs when researchers use broad terms (such as *hormones* or *modeling*) to explain specific behaviors. Appropriate explanations should take into account many factors, including social, cultural, biological, and situational factors. Inappropriate labeling and definitions occur in gender research when differences exist and one variation is labeled in a derogatory way. For example, women's attention to the context of behavior has been labeled as "dependence," a term that carries negative connotations. Researchers should avoid placing value-laden labels on behaviors before they either have evidence of the value, consider the context of the behavior, include both women and men in research on gender-related behaviors, or give appropriate emphasis to topics of interest to both men and women (McHugh et al., 1986). It may not be possible to eliminate gender bias in research, but such bias can be decreased. Critical thinking can lead to an appropriate skepticism and a reformulation for gender research that includes a step-by-step consideration of how bias can enter the study of gender at any point (Caplan & Caplan, 1994).

Specific analysis techniques can reduce the bias in evaluating research, depending on the technique chosen. The development and use of a statistical technique called **meta-analysis** allows researchers to evaluate results from several experimental studies and thereby determine the overall size of various effects. This information is related to practical significance because it can reveal which results are small and which are large. Janet Hyde (1986) explained that meta-analysis allows "the synthesis or integration of numerous studies on a single topic and a quantitative or statistical approach to that synthesis" (p. 3). She contended that meta-analysis is preferred over evaluations that count the outcomes or combine probabilities from various studies because meta-analysis allows similar studies to be combined and statistically evaluated.

This analysis technique allows researchers to simultaneously combine the results from many studies in order to determine the overall size of the effect of a variable of interest. The size of this effect is called *d,* which represents the mean of one group subtracted from the mean of another group divided by the pooled standard deviation. Combined across studies, *d* values reflect the size of group differences. Effect sizes of .2 or less are considered small, those around .5 are considered medium, and .8 or larger are considered to be large differences (Cohen, 1969). These levels are somewhat arbitrary, but many researchers have accepted them as a metric to evaluate the growing number of meta-analytic studies.

Analysis and reporting results also require changes (Hyde, 1994). Researchers should conduct all appropriate significance tests and report all (even nonsignificant) findings and sizes of effects, exercising caution in interpreting results so as to make appropriate conclusions, and applying appropriate scientific standards to assure that findings are not misused.

All of these suggestions are intended to make the research on sex and gender more scientifically rigorous and thus eliminate the biases that have been so common in this area, creating a feminist empiricism.

Considering Diversity

The activities identified as science arose in 16th- and 17th-century western Europe, and science is filled with the assumptions and biases of that cultural climate. The urge to understand the world is common for all cultures over the world and throughout history, and all have developed some understanding of physical, biological, and social existence. Some of these conceptualizations have been close to the views of modern science, yet many have differed substantially. The cultures that did not develop this type of science took an alternative path due to their view of the world and how it operates. Several prominent cultures have existed within civilizations that have not adopted the positivist, materialist, empiricist traditions that underlie European science.

For example, Chinese culture developed some sophisticated technology and engineering, but not much science. This omission reflected a Chinese outlook (Ronan, 1982) that regarded the entire universe as a vast unified organism, with humans and the physical world as part of this unity. This view prompted the Chinese to develop an understanding of some aspects of the world, but to ignore others. Their understanding of the world was influenced by those who followed either the Confucian or the Taoist philosophy. Followers of Confucius tended to make no division between the physical and social world and to concentrate on promoting social harmony rather than intellectual understanding about the physical world. Taoists had an interest in nature, but their view was not one of domination of humans over nature, a view basic to western science. Rather, the Taoists strove to gain knowledge as a path to inner peace. Neither of these views prompted the development of a science comparable to western science, with its emphasis on objectivity and the separation of the observer to the object observed.

The theme of the unity of nature and humanity was also part of the two religions that dominated India—Hinduism and Buddhism. Neither of these views was conducive to the development of science (Ronan, 1982), so the science that existed in India was largely borrowed from the West.

The dominance-oriented, objective, rational approach that is basic to western science differs from the African view (Harding, 1986). The African conception is one of connection rather than opposition, with a reluctance to divide the world into nonoverlapping categories, including a split between self and nature. Such a split is essential to the type of objectivity for which science strives, but African philosophy found such divisions impossible. Furthermore, the African view is curiously similar to that of Native Americans and many feminist scholars, being one of connection and interrelatedness with an emphasis on relationships to the world rather than an analysis of it.

All of these nonwestern views of the world are similar in their conceptualizations of nature as intertwined with humanity rather than as describing the two in dynamic opposition (Fee, 1986). These views of nature did not prevent these cultures from developing a formal understanding of the world, including engineering, agriculture, medicine, and astronomy. However, none of these cultures developed the kind of science that arose in Europe, and the science that developed in Europe has spread to all countries and dominates modern knowledge, perhaps to the exclusion of other world views.

Summary

A "science war" is currently under way, with critics maintaining that traditional science is not (and cannot be) objective. This criticism has prompted scientists to examine the extent to which societal values are included in the process of research, producing biased and inaccurate results. The history of gender research is filled with examples of scientists' bias in studying gender issues.

Science as a method of gathering information can be traced back to the 16th century and rests on philosophical traditions that assert the advantages of an objective, observation-based understanding of the world. By using descriptive methods such as naturalistic observation, correlational studies, and surveys, researchers gather and evaluate information that leads them to understand the world. By using the experimental method, researchers can develop an understanding of the cause-and-effect relationship between an independent variable and a dependent variable. Although the ex post facto method resembles experimentation, it differs in procedure and in the type of information it yields: Ex post facto studies do not involve the manipulation of independent variables and do not allow the determination of causality.

All studies with gender as a subject variable are ex post facto designs, and none have the ability to reveal the cause of any differences they might show. Gender can be an independent variable in experimental studies when, for example, the researcher manipulates the description of targets, identifying some as male and some as female. This type of approach treats gender as a social category and, like all laboratory research, suffers from artificiality.

Dissatisfaction with traditional quantitative research has led to a growing interest in qualitative research methods among psychologists. These methods include ethnography, case studies, interviews, and focus groups. Researchers using these approaches acknowledge that they are part of the research process, try to treat their participants as equals, and attempt to preserve the complexity of the situations they study.

Bias can enter the research process at any point, and the history of gender studies is filled with examples of bias. Some have argued that science has a masculinist bias, and theories such as Freud's psychodynamic theory have a clear bias against women. Any of the steps in conducting research can be contaminated by personal bias. In addition, studies that reveal gender-related differences may show a difference that is statistically significant—that is, not due to chance. Yet the difference may not have any practical significance; for instance, it may not reveal important differences between women and men.

Solutions to the bias in science include an abandonment of science, which is unlikely. Less drastic measures include recommendations for making researchers more careful. Those researchers who advise taking care to avoid sexist bias in research can be described as feminist empiricists. On the other hand, some researchers advocate abandoning the traditional scientific method and adopting alternatives that center on women and that use different methods of gaining information, especially qualitative research methods such as ethnography and interview studies. The term feminist standpoint epistemologies applies to those who want to create a woman-centered approach to researching the female experience. In psychological research, feminist empiricists are more numerous than feminist standpoint epistemologists, and some psychologists have considered the problems and proposed solutions for carrying out nonsexist research. Feminist standpoint epistemologies can add new dimensions to the study of both women and men, but abandonment of traditional scientific methods is unlikely. Some feminist scholars argue against excluding any method and propose a more objective feminist empiricism.

Science arose in Europe in the 16th century and has spread around the world. All cultures developed a knowledge of the natural world, but many did not develop science because the cultures lacked a world view that is compatible with science. Cultures such as those of ancient China and those of many Native American societies held the view that nature is an integrated whole that cannot be analyzed.

Glossary

case study a qualitative method that focuses on gathering extensive information about a single person or a small group.

constructionists a group of critics of science who argue that reality is constructed through perception and is inevitably subject to bias. Included in this bias is all scientific observation, thus excluding science from its claim of objectivity.

correlational study a descriptive research method that requires researchers to measure two factors known to occur within a group of people to determine the degree of relationship between the two factors.

data representations, usually in numerical form, of some facet of the phenomenon that the researcher observes.

dependent variable the factor in an experiment that the experimenter measures to determine if the manipulation of the independent variable has an effect.

descriptive research methods a group of research methods, including naturalistic observation, surveys, and correlational studies, that yield descriptions of the observed phenomena.

empirical observation collecting information through direct observation.

ethnography a type of qualitative research in which the researcher becomes immersed in a situation in order to make observations and interpretations of that situation.

experiment a type of study in which a researcher manipulates an independent variable and observes the changes in a dependent variable; only through experiments can researchers learn about cause-and-effect relationships.

ex post facto study a type of nonexperimental research design that involves the comparison of subjects, who are placed in contrast groups, on the basis of some preexisting characteristic of the subjects.

focus group a qualitative research method consisting of a discussion involving a group of people centered around a specific topic.

hypothesis a statement about the expected outcome of a study.

independent variable the factor in an experiment that the experimenter manipulates to create a difference that did not previously exist in the participants.

interview a type of qualitative study in which respondents are interviewed in order to determine patterns or commonalities among their responses.

meta-analysis a statistical analysis that allows the evaluation of many studies simultaneously.

naturalistic observation a descriptive research method that requires researchers to collect information about a naturally occurring situation without changing the situation in any way.

operational definition a definition of a variable in terms of operations used to obtain information on that variable, rather than in terms of concepts underlying that variable.

practical significance an important result with practical implications; different from statistical significance.

quantification the process of turning observations into numerical data.

statistically significant result a result obtained by analysis with statistical tests and found unlikely to have been obtained on the basis of chance alone.

subject variable a characteristic of the subjects, such as gender, that allows researchers to form contrast groups in quasi-experimental studies.

survey a descriptive research method involving the measurement of attitudes through the administration and interpretation of questionnaires.

variable a factor of interest to researchers; something that can have more than one value, as opposed to a constant, which has only one constant value.

Suggested Readings

Peplau, Letitia Anne; & Conrad, Eva. (1989). Beyond nonsexist research: The perils of feminist methods in psychology. *Psychology of Women Quarterly, 13,* 379–400. Peplau and Conrad criticize the concept that a feminist methodology is necessary for feminist research in psychology, contending that any method can be sexist or feminist. They instead argue for the use of a variety of methods.

Riger, Stephanie. (1992). Epistemological debates, feminist voices: Science, social values, and the study of women. *American Psychologist, 47,* 730–740. This excellent article outlines the different positions and ongoing debates about the scientific method. Although the article is not easy reading, Riger does a fine job of stating the complex issues in clear terms.

Schiebinger, Londa. (1999). *Has feminism changed science?* Cambridge, MA: Harvard University Press. Schiebinger's book does not concentrate on psychology but covers diverse fields of science. Her book presents not only feminist scholarship and its influence, but also women who are scientists and the influence that these female scientists have exerted on their specific fields. She also offers a sharp critique of the biases that female students encounter in pursuing science careers.

Chapter 3

Hormones and Chromosomes

HEADLINES

Testosterone Rules: It Takes More Than Just a Hormone to Make a Fellow's Trigger Finger Itch

Discover, March, 1997

PMS: Is It for Real?

Cosmopolitan, April, 1995

> *Right before her period, Cheryl, an otherwise bubbly twenty-nine-year-old account executive, gets irritated with her boyfriend. She may throw things at the wall, even threaten to end the relationship. "He just rolls his eyes," she says, "because he knows: It's that time of the month."*
>
> *Jamie feels sad and incompetent for a couple of weeks each month. Negotiating with clients at a business meeting not too long ago, the thirty-four-year-old computer analyst burst into tears, then skipped dinner with colleagues because she couldn't decide what to wear.*
>
> *Both Cheryl and Jamie attribute their behavior to being premenstrual. (Murray, 1995, p. 209)*

The story "PMS: Is It for Real?" (Murray, 1995) evaluated the evidence about premenstrual syndrome (PMS), beginning with the two cases in the preceding extract. These two women described their symptoms in ways that are consistent with popular thought. Although few people question the reality of PMS, this story did, and the conclusions were very different from most popular reports on this subject in the press.

In the article "Testosterone Rules," endocrinologist Robert Sapolsky (1997) works toward refuting the role of testosterone in violent behavior. Unlike most of the media coverage and the dominant popular belief, Sapolsky presented the case that the relationship between testosterone and aggression is complex rather than a simple, straightforward cause and effect.

Both these popular articles evaluated the role of hormones in a variety of behaviors, and both rejected simple views of the role of hormones in behavior. Is the role of hormones in behavior simple or complex? What role do hormones play in physical development and ongoing behavior? Are hormones the key to the differences between males and females? Or are chromosomes the key? To answer these questions, this chapter explores the contribution of chromosomes and the effect of hormones on human development from conception throughout prenatal development and again during puberty. When hormonal or chromosomal abnormalities occur, individuals do not follow the pattern of developing into women or men. Instead, these individuals develop both male and female characteristics, providing revealing examples of the roles of chromosomes and hormones in the development of sex and gender. Finally, this chapter examines the role of hormones in adult behavior, including the relationships mentioned in the headlines between hormone levels and the behaviors associated with premenstrual syndrome and with aggression.

The Endocrine System and Steroid Hormones

Hormones are substances released from **endocrine glands** to circulate throughout the body. Receptors on various organs are sensitive to specific hormones, which produce many different actions at various sites. Although the body contains many endocrine glands that secrete many different hormones, **steroid hormones** relate to differences between the sexes and reproduction. The reproductive organs, the ovaries and testes, are the **gonads.** These organs are obviously among the physical characteristics differentiating the sexes and are also essential to reproduction, but the ovaries and testes are not the only endocrine glands that are important for sexual development and functioning.

The **pituitary gland** is located within the brain and is often referred to as the master gland because its function controls the production of many other hormones. The pituitary produces many **tropic hormones,** which stimulate the release of other hormones. Thus, the action of the pituitary controls many hormones. Gonadotropins are one type of hormone produced by the pituitary. These hormones circulate through the bloodstream and stimulate the ovaries and testes to release their hormones.

The action of the pituitary is affected by a nearby brain structure, the hypothalamus. The complex action of the hypothalamus results in the production of a class of hormones called **releasing hormones.** The action of releasing hormones is necessary for the pituitary to release its tropic hormones. Therefore, the hypothalamus acts to produce releasing hormones such as the gonadotropin-releasing hormone, which stimulates the pituitary to release gonadotropins, which in turn stimulate the gonads to produce their hormones. Figure 3.1 summarizes the action of these glands and hormones.

Gonadal hormones are of the steroid type; that is, all gondal hormones are derived from cholesterol and consist of a structure that includes four carbon rings. The two main classes

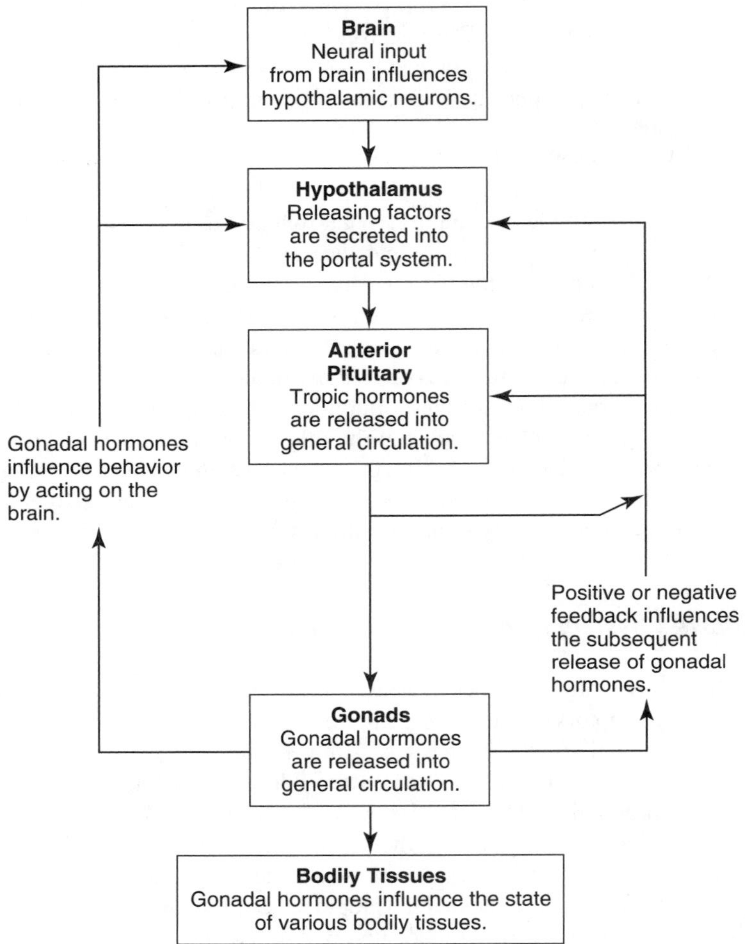

FIGURE 3.1 A Summary Model of the Regulation of Gonadal Hormones

SOURCE: From John P. J. Pinel, *Biopsychology* (2nd ed.). Copyright © 1993 by Allyn and Bacon. Reprinted by permission.

of gonadal hormones are **androgens** and **estrogens.** Although people tend to think of androgens as male hormones and estrogens as female hormones, that belief is inaccurate—each sex produces both types of hormones. The most common of the androgens is **testosterone,** and the most common of the estrogens is **estradiol.** Men typically produce a greater proportion of androgens than estrogens, and women typically produce a greater portion of estrogens than androgens.

The gonads also secrete a third type of hormone, the **progestins.** The most common progestin is progesterone, which plays a role in preparing a woman's body for pregnancy.

Men also secrete progesterone, but its function for the male body is unknown (Pinel, 2000). The chemical structure is similar for the androgens, estrogens, and progestins.

The gonads are not the only glands that produce steroid hormones; the adrenal glands also produce them. Although the amount of hormones produced by the adrenal glands is smaller than the amount produced by the gonads, the types of hormones produced are the same. These hormones are one factor involved in differentiating male and female.

Stages of Differences between the Sexes

Humans (and most other animals) are sexually dimorphic; that is, they come in two different physical versions—female and male. This **sexual dimorphism** is the result of development that begins with conception and ends at puberty, resulting in men and women who are capable of sexual reproduction. Sexual dimorphism can be conceptualized as the product of five stages: genetic, gonadal, hormonal, internal genitalia, and external genitalia (Kaplan, 1980). The *genetic stage* refers to the inheritance of the chromosomes related to sex. The *gonadal stage* includes the development of the gonads. The *hormonal stage* begins prenatally, with the secretion of androgens and estrogens. Hormonal development also occurs at puberty, producing mature, functional gonads. The stage when *internal genitalia,* the internal reproductive organs, develop occurs prenatally and affects not only the ovaries and testes, but also other internal structures relating to reproductive functioning. Therefore, the **internal genitalia** consist of the internal structures related to reproduction: ovaries, Fallopian tubes, uterus, and upper vagina in women; and testes, prostate gland, seminal vesicles, and vas deferens in men. The **external genitalia** are reproductive structures that can be seen without internal examination: clitoris, labia, and vaginal opening in women; and penis and scrotum in men. These developments result in differences that are apparent at birth. The stage of developing *external genitalia* occurs later during the prenatal period than the development of internal genitalia.

In the development of sex characteristics, prenatal development is critically important. For the doctor to be able to pronounce "It's a boy" or "It's a girl," a great many prenatal events must occur in a coordinated sequence. These prenatal events occur within a complex set of stages that result in a girl or a boy, but sometimes things go wrong. When things go wrong, the result is a baby who has some developmental abnormalities as a result of a combination of female and male patterns of development. These mistakes are rare, but these cases are revealing because they provide a means of understanding the necessary elements of normal development.

Sexual Differentiation

The development of sexual differences is a complex process. Physical differences between men and women start at conception—the fertilization of an ovum by a sperm cell. Most cells in the human body contain 23 pairs of chromosomes, but ova and sperm carry half the normal amount of chromosomal material. In the fertilized ovum, the full amount of genetic material is present, with half coming from the mother's ovum and half from the father's sperm.

Of the 23 pairs of human chromosomes, pair number 23 is the one that is critical in determining chromosomal sex. Although most chromosomes are X shaped, only those in pair 23 are called **X chromosomes.** An individual who inherits two of these X chromosomes (one X from their mother and the other X from their father) will have the genetic patterns to develop according to the female pattern. Individuals who inherit one X and one **Y chromosome** (the X from their mother and the Y from their father) will have the genetic information to develop according to the male pattern. Therefore, normal girls and women have the XX pattern of chromosome pair 23, and normal boys and men have the XY pattern.

The presence of the XY chromosome constellation is only the first factor that produces male physiology, and its presence is not sufficient to produce a normal male. Other configurations are possible for pair 23, but those patterns are abnormalities, discussed later in the section titled "When Things Go Wrong."

Development of Male and Female Physiology

After conception, the fertilized ovum starts to grow, first by dividing into two cells, then four, and so on. The ball of cells becomes larger and starts to differentiate; that is, they begin to form the basis for different structures and organs. Within the first 6 weeks of prenatal development, no difference exists between male and female embryos, even in their gonads. Both the embryos with the XX pattern and those with the XY pattern have the same structures, and this replication signifies that both types of embryos have the potential to develop into individuals who look like and have the internal reproductive organs of either boys or girls.

The Reproductive Organs

Both male and female embryos have a **Wolffian system,** which has the capacity to develop into the male internal reproductive system, and a **Müllerian system,** which has the capacity

---

GENDERED VOICES

Beyond Hormones, There's Very Little Room for Movement

A male engineer told me of his belief in a strong biologically deterministic view of behavior: "I don't think that there are any real differences in intelligence between men and women, but I think that both are overwhelmed by hormones. Beyond hormones, there's very little room for movement, very little chance for people to exert any effort toward behavior that is genuinely adaptive. People can't depart from those hormonal influences. It deprives both of any real intelligence, making their behavior restricted to what their hormones allow."

He expressed the belief that men's shorter average life span was due to hormonal influences on their behavior and that they have little choice in actions. He said, "I think that men harm themselves due to the influence of their hormones. Women have many advantages over men, benefiting from men's behavior, but it's not that women force men to do the difficult things while women take it easy. I think that men's choice to do things like go to war is due to their hormones and not to their desire to protect women. Men have little choice, and they are harmed by their hormones. Women's behavior is also fixed by their hormones, but they live longer, so it must not be as much of a disadvantage for them. I don't think that people have much free choice in their behavior. It's all hormones."

to develop into the female internal reproductive system. During the third month of prenatal development, two processes typically begin to occur to fetuses with the XY chromosome pattern to further the developing male pattern.

The first involves the production of androgens, which begin to be produced by the fetal testes during this period. The presence of androgens stimulates the development of the Wolffian system. The growth of the testes further increases production of testosterone, which stimulates development of the male pattern. The second process that prompts male development is the production of Müllerian-inhibiting substance, which causes the Müllerian system to degenerate.

Therefore, one type of secretion prompts the Wolffian system to develop into the male internal reproductive organs, and the other causes the female Müllerian system to degenerate. One action produces a masculinization and the other a defemininization of the developing fetus, and both actions produce male internal reproductive organs in the fetus. Figure 3.2 shows how the male reproductive system develops from the Wolffian system, resulting in testes, vas deferens, and seminal vesicles. This figure also illustrates how both male and female reproductive structures originate from the same prenatal structures.

The fetal ovaries produce few estrogens, but the development of the female reproductive system requires no surge of fetal hormones. In female embryos, the Wolffian system degenerates and the Müllerian system develops, resulting in ovaries, uterus, Fallopian tubes, and the upper part of the vagina. Figure 3.2 also shows how the female reproductive system develops from the Müllerian system.

Six weeks after conception, the external genitalia of male and female fetuses are also identical. The structures that will become the penis and scrotum in males and the clitoris, outer and inner labia, and vaginal opening in females have not yet formed. The fetal structures that exist at this point have the potential to develop into either male or female external genitalia, depending on the presence of androgens, especially testosterone.

Figure 3.3 shows the development of the external genitalia for both the male and female patterns. Notice that the structures are identical at 6 weeks after conception but start to differentiate into the two different patterns after the 7th week of gestation.

Prenatal production of androgens produces the male pattern, and the absence of androgens results in an incomplete version of the female pattern. If few or no hormones of either type are present, a fetus will develop external genitals that appear more like the female than the male structures, suggesting that the basic pattern for development is female (Pinel, 2000). These prenatal hormone effects organize developing fetuses around the female or male pattern, resulting in permanent changes in the ability to produce hormones and also in the existence and function of reproductive organs.

The Nervous System

During prenatal development, the hormones that produce sexual dimorphism in the body also affect the brain, making it possible for the brain structure and function to vary by sex. Sexual dimorphism of the brain is not as obvious as the differences between female and male bodies.

Investigations of structural differences between the brains of women and men have concentrated on several specific structures, but a gender difference exists concerning the entire brain: The brains of men are larger than those of women. Unlike many of the gender differences, this one is present at birth (Breedlove, 1994). The meaning of this difference,

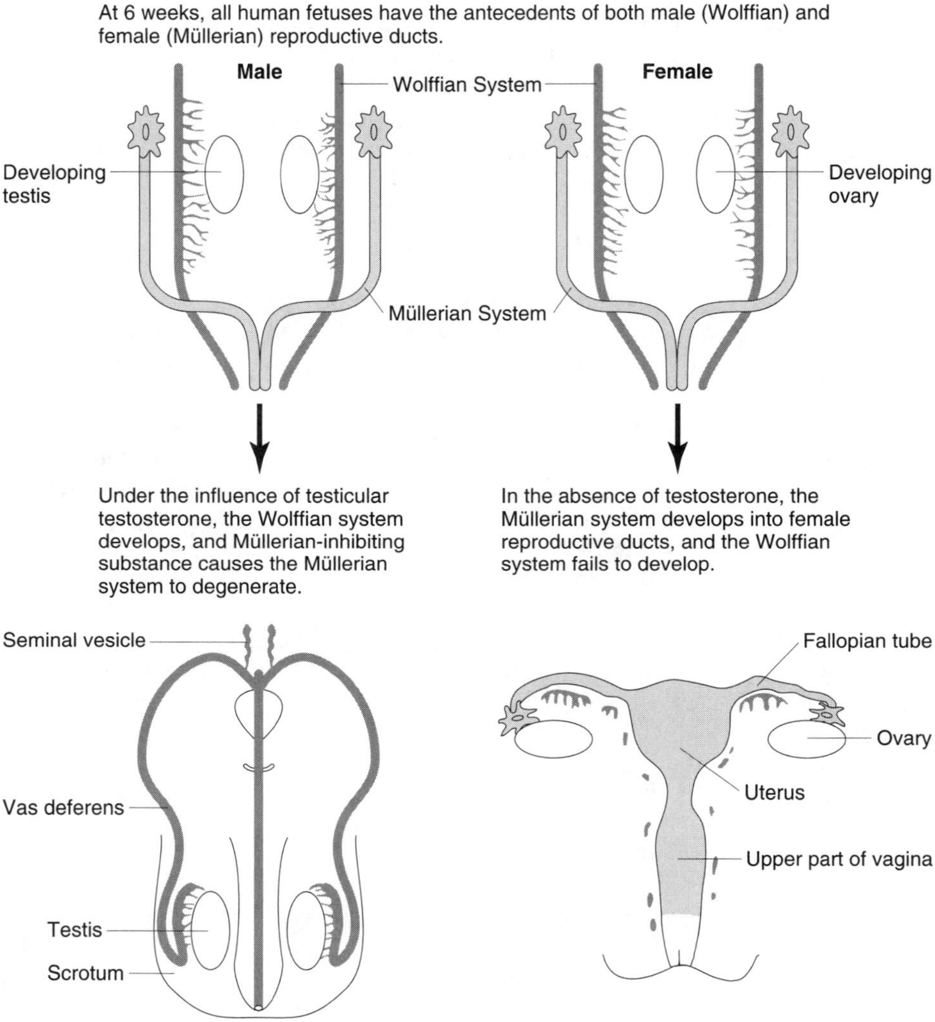

At 6 weeks, all human fetuses have the antecedents of both male (Wolffian) and female (Müllerian) reproductive ducts.

Male

Female

Wolffian System

Developing testis

Developing ovary

Müllerian System

Under the influence of testicular testosterone, the Wolffian system develops, and Müllerian-inhibiting substance causes the Müllerian system to degenerate.

In the absence of testosterone, the Müllerian system develops into female reproductive ducts, and the Wolffian system fails to develop.

Seminal vesicle

Vas deferens

Testis

Scrotum

Fallopian tube

Ovary

Uterus

Upper part of vagina

FIGURE 3.2 Development of Internal Reproductive Systems

SOURCE: From John P. J. Pinel, *Biopsychology* (2nd ed.). Copyright © 1993 by Allyn and Bacon. Reprinted by permission.

however, is unclear, but most (and perhaps all) of the difference can be explained by differing body size. That is, the ratio of brain weight to body size is very similar for women and men.

Except for the difference in brain size, the other structural differences do not exist at birth. Thus, any differences might be influenced by experience rather than the result of biological development. The identified structural differences are small, but some researchers

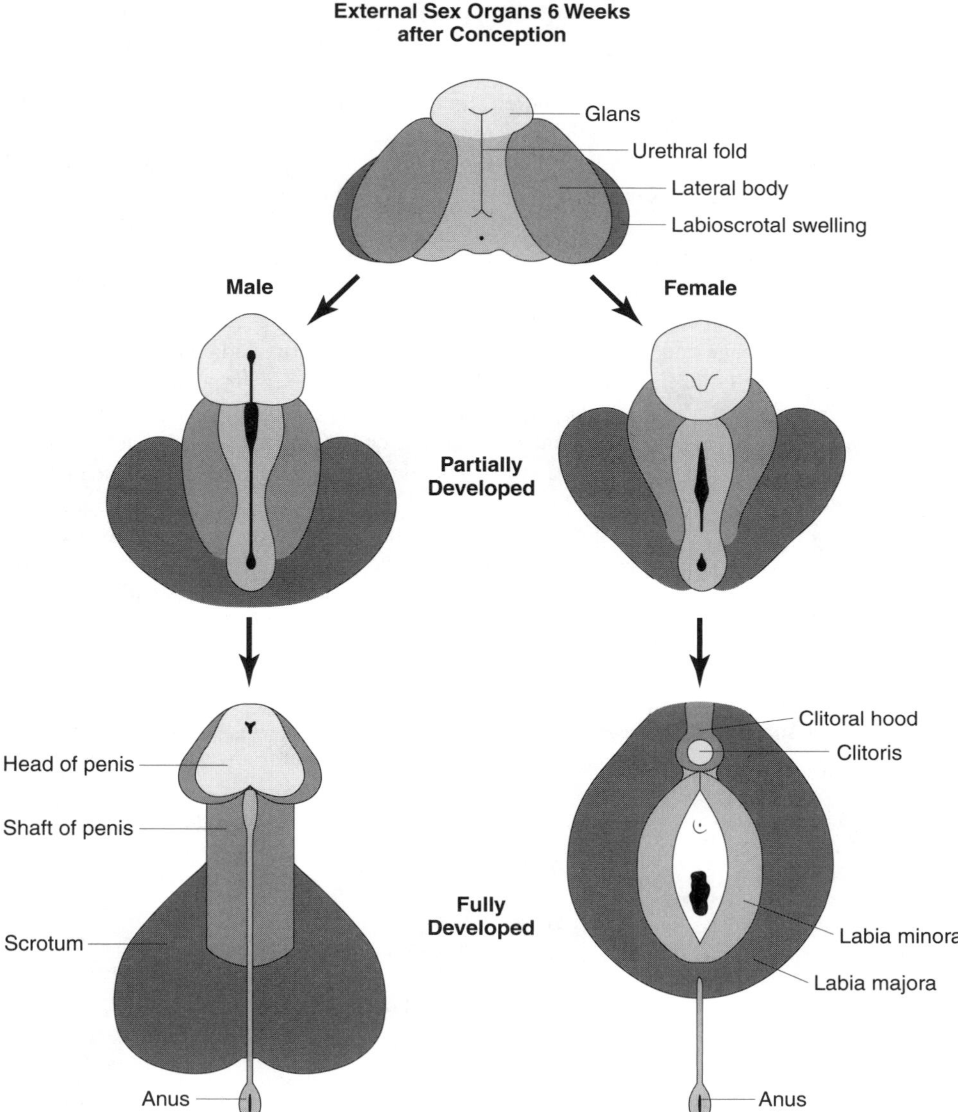

FIGURE 3.3 Development of Male and Female External Genitalia

SOURCE: From John P. J. Pinel, *Biopsychology* (2nd ed.). Copyright © 1993 by Allyn and Bacon. Reprinted by permission.

have interpreted these differences as very meaningful. Figure 3.4 shows two views of the brain, one view as seen from the top, and another view as seen cut down the middle (a cross section). The view of the brain from the top shows that the cerebral cortex is divided down the middle into two halves, or hemispheres. This division forms a left cerebral hemisphere and a right cerebral hemisphere. The view through the midsection shows some of the structures in the brain beneath the cerebral cortex. These structures—the anterior commissure, the massa intermedia, and the corpus callosum—are all structures that, according to some researchers, are sexually dimorphic. In addition, the left and right cerebral hemispheres may also differ in men and women.

Beginning in the 1800s, research indicated that, despite appearances, the cerebral hemispheres are not mirror images of each other (Springer & Deutsch, 1998). Rather, the two hemispheres appeared to direct different mental abilities: The left hemisphere is specialized for language and speech, and the right hemisphere for spatial abilities. The concept of **lateralization** holds that the left and right hemispheres are each specialized for different functions. A great deal of research and theory has explored gender differences in the lateralization of the cerebral hemispheres, and most research is consistent in showing that women have less lateralized cerebral functions than men. That is, women tend to have both the language and spatial functions more equally represented in both hemispheres, whereas men tend to have language represented in the left hemisphere and spatial abilities represented in the right. An evaluation of this research (Hiscock, Inch, Jacek, Hiscock-Kalil, & Kalil, 1994; Hiscock, Israelian, Inch, Jacek, & Hiscock-Kalil, 1995) showed that the gender differences in laterality are small, ac-

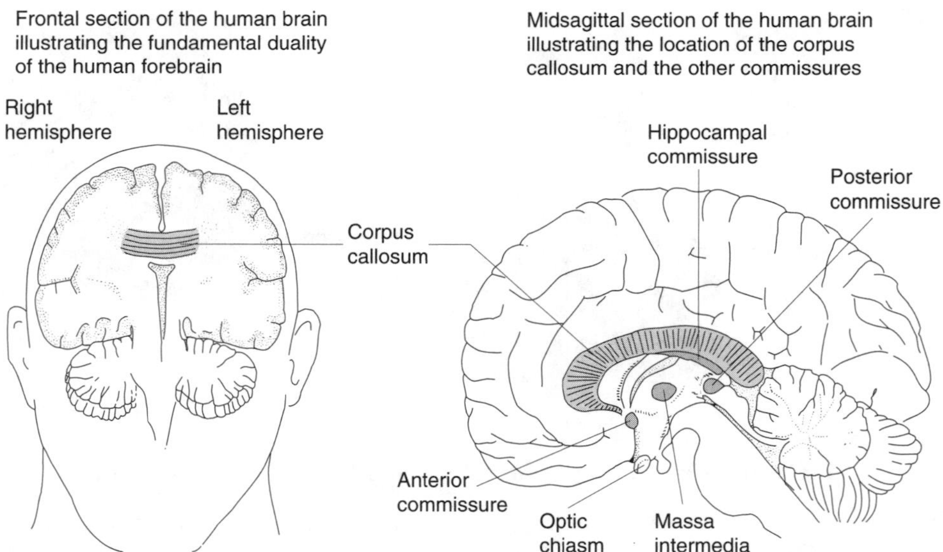

FIGURE 3.4 Cerebral Commissures and the Hemispheres of the Human Brain

SOURCE: From John P. J. Pinel, *Biopsychology* (2nd ed.). Copyright © 1993 Allyn and Bacon. Reprinted with permission.

GENDERED VOICES

Will I Be Smarter?

Male brains are larger than female brains, and this situation has lead to much debate regarding the relative intelligence of women and men. The relationship between brain weight and intelligence is not entirely clear and has been the topic of research and debate for over a century. The initial belief that larger brains make for greater intelligence has been abandoned—under that metric, elephants would be smarter than humans. The measurement of the ratio of brain weight to body size puts humans at the top of the scale, and thus it has been accepted (by humans, at least) as the standard.

Although the ratio of brain weight to body size among species is an index of intelligence, the variations within species are difficult to interpret. The difference in brain weight between men and women falls into this debate. When considering the ratio of brain weight to body size, the interpretation of gender difference varies; some authorities argue that this gender difference is reduced, others contend that it is eliminated, and some even claim that it is reversed (see Breedlove, 1994 for a brief summary of this argument). The division of opinion may reflect a controversy regarding what measurement to use to define body size. Should the measurement be body weight, height, or skin surface? Each of these measurements has both advocates and opponents.

When I explained these arguments and problems to one of my classes, a student listening to this lecture posed a question that frames the problem: "If I lose weight, does that mean that I will be smarter?" She wasn't serious, but her question highlights the obvious absurdity of using individual body weight in the calculation of intelligence.

counting for 1 to 2% of the variation in lateralization. This magnitude of difference means that other individual factors are much more important than gender in understanding variations in lateralization. Chapter 4 includes an exploration of mental abilities that relate to brain lateralization and an evaluation of this gender difference.

Several of the structures in the brain that connect the left and right sides of the brain show gender differences. The anterior commissure, massa intermedia of the thalamus, and corpus callosum all provide such connections, but clear evidence for their sexual dimorphism is sketchy (Breedlove, 1994).

The evidence for sexual dimorphism in the brain is strongest for a small section of the hypothalamus called the **sexually dimorphic nucleus (SDN).** This structure is larger in male rats and in men than in female rats and in women (Gorski, 1987; Swaab & Fliers, 1985). Although not understood, its function may be related to sexual behavior or gender identity. This nucleus is very sensitive to testosterone and estrogen, so the presence or absence of these hormones influences its development. In humans, gender differences in this structure do not exist at birth. Between birth and ages 2 and 4 years, the number of cells in this structure increase rapidly (Swaab, Gooren, & Hofman, 1995). The number of cells begins to decrease in girls but not in boys, creating a sexual dimorphism that peaks in young adulthood to middle age (Breedlove, 1994).

Otherwise, the differences in structure between female and male brains are small. Table 3.1 summarizes the results of studies on structural differences between women's and men's brains.

In addition to brain differences, other nervous system structures show gender differences. For example, one of the nervous system sex differences is in the **spinal nucleus of the bulbocavernosus** (Breedlove, 1994). The spinal nucleus of the bulbocavernosus is 25%

TABLE 3.1 Summary of Brain Differences between Men and Women

Structure	Difference
Cerebral hemispheres	Men may be more lateralized than women for language and spatial functions
Sexually dimorphic nucleus (SDN) of hypothalamus	SDN in men is 2.5 times larger than in women
Splenium of corpus callosum	Early studies indicated larger and more bulbous splenium in women; later studies found an interaction with age and gender
Anterior commissure	Evidence for sexual dimorphism is sketchy
Massa intermedia of the thalamus	Evidence for sexual dimorphism is sketchy

larger in men than in women. These neurons aid in the ejaculation of sperm in men and constrict the opening of the vagina in women. These spinal neurons are present in both male and female rats at birth, but the neurons die in female rats. In male rats, the presence of androgens allows these neurons to survive. Therefore, there is a larger difference between the nervous systems of male and female rats than male and female humans, and a simple generalization from rats to humans would be invalid.

Another caution is related to interpretations for sex and gender differences in understanding hormonal versus social factors. The tendency exists to see a one-way chain of causality in which genetic and hormonal influences produce physiology, which in turn, produces behavior. As S. Marc Breedlove (1994) pointed out, this reasoning is false because it is impossible to separate biological from social influences and because the causality goes both ways. He contended that it is possible to concentrate on either biological or psychological measurements, but because biologists and psychologists are studying the same phenomena, any distinctions they make are illusory. In addition, social influences can affect behavior, which can alter the brain. For example, any change in the number, size, or connection of neurons in the structure of the brain constitutes a biological measurement, but such alterations will have psychological implications in terms of behavioral changes. Conversely, behavior can alter brain chemistry, which can alter brain structure, resulting in biological changes. Breedlove warned against confusing biological measures and biological influences, claiming that psychological and biological influences are impossible to separate.

Gonadal, hormonal, genital, and brain organization are not sufficient to produce sexually interested and sexually active people capable of reproduction. Such changes depend on the activating effects of hormones during puberty.

Changes during Puberty

The levels of circulating hormones are low during infancy and childhood, but these levels increase during puberty, the onset of sexual maturity. The changes that occur during this period include not only fertility but also the characteristic adolescent growth spurt and the development of secondary sex characteristics. These characteristics constitute the differences between male and female bodies other than reproductive ones (see Figure 3.5). Both sexes experience the growth of body and pubic hair and the appearance of acne. Young men experience the growth of facial hair, larynx enlargement, hairline recession, and muscle de-

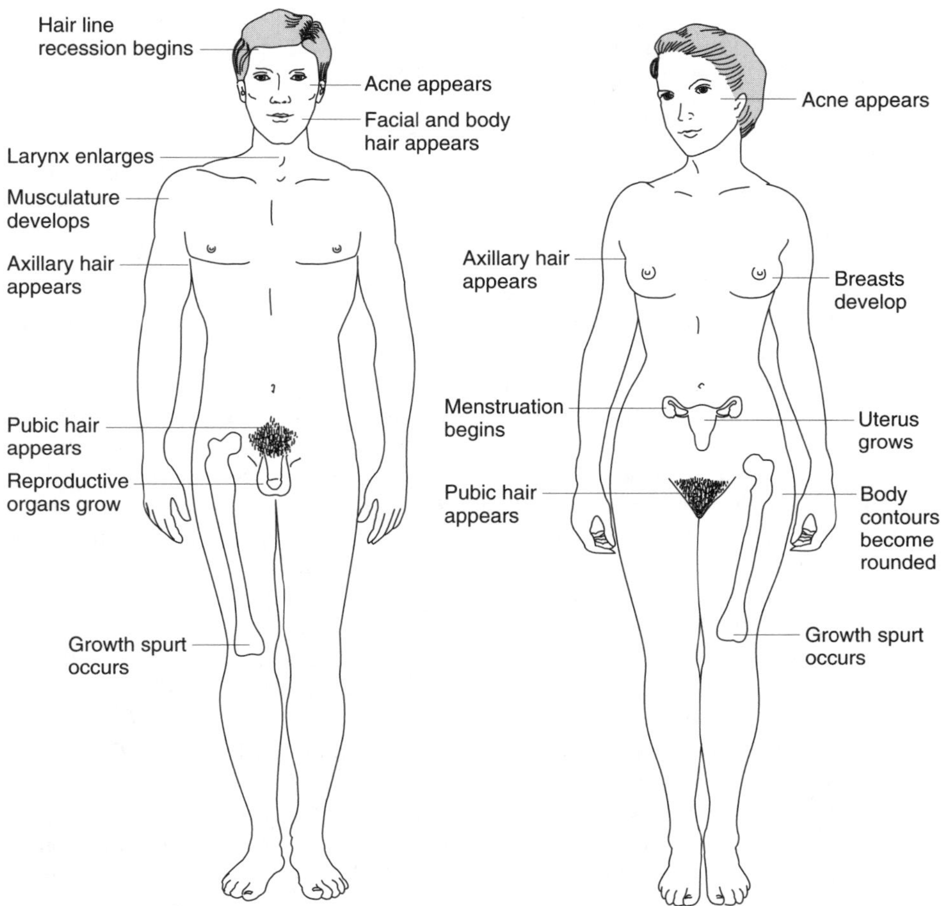

FIGURE 3.5 Changes Occurring in Males and Females during Puberty

SOURCE: From John P. J. Pinel, *Biopsychology* (2nd ed.). Copyright © 1993 by Allyn and Bacon. Reprinted by permission.

velopment, whereas young women experience breast development, rounding of body contours, and menarche—the beginning of menstruation. All of these changes are prompted by changes in the release of hormones.

The adolescent growth spurt is the result of muscle and bone growth in response to increased release of growth hormone by the pituitary. Increased production of tropic hormones by the pituitary act on the adrenal glands and the gonads to increase their production of gonadal and adrenal hormones. As puberty begins, the pituitary starts to release two gonadotropic hormones into the bloodstream—**follicle-stimulating hormone (FSH)** and **luteinizing hormone (LH).** These hormones stimulate the gonads to increase their production of estrogens and androgens. Increased circulation of these gonadal hormones results in maturation of the genitals, that is, the development of fertility as well as the development of secondary sex characteristics.

In adolescent boys and adult men, the production of androgens is proportionately higher than their production of estrogens; in adolescent girls and in women, the production of estrogens is proportionately higher than their production of androgens. Again, it would be inaccurate to think of androgens as "male" hormones and estrogens as "female" hormones. An example of the influence of one hormone on both sexes is the growth of pubic and underarm hair: The same androgen results in the growth of pubic and underarm hair in both boys and girls.

LH and FSH, the hormones that initiate puberty, are also important for reproduction. In girls and women, the production of these two hormones varies cyclically, whereas in boys and men, their production is not cyclic (but neither is it entirely steady). The cyclic variation of LH and FSH produces the menstrual cycle, beginning with an increase in the production of luteinizing hormone releasing factor and follicle-stimulating hormone releasing factor by the hypothalamus. As with other releasing factors, these two cause the pituitary to produce LH and FSH. Follicle-stimulating hormone stimulates follicles, a group of cells within the ovaries, to mature an ovum. Luteinizing hormone causes the follicle to rupture and release the ovum, which begins to travel down the Fallopian tube toward the uterus. The remainder of the follicle starts to produce the hormone progesterone, which prepares the uterus to receive and implant the ovum, if it happens to be fertilized. Then all of these hormone levels begin to decline. If the ovum is fertilized, pregnancy will produce an increase in estradiol and progesterone, but if the ovum is not fertilized, the prepared lining of the uterus is shed in menstruation, and the cycle starts again.

In boys, puberty causes the maturation of internal and external genitalia, including growth of the penis, seminal vesicles, and the prostate. The maturation of seminal vesicles and prostate is necessary for ejaculation of seminal fluid, and sperm production is necessary for fertility. FSH is involved in the production of sperm. LH contributes to the maturation of sperm, but its main function is to stimulate the production of testosterone. Testosterone is controlled by feedback to the hypothalamus, which can inhibit or prompt the production of LH and FSH, which in turn can affect the production of sperm.

The role of hormones is essential in the regulation of fertility, and the role of hormones for sexual activity is very clear in some animals. In rats, for example, the cyclic production of hormones by the females relates to sexual receptivity or level of interest in sexual activity. Female rats are receptive during the time in their cycle that they are fertile, and male rats respond to that receptivity. Hormone levels are also important for the development and maintenance of sexual interest. Rats that have their gonads removed before puberty fail to develop any interest in sexual activity. If their gonads are removed after puberty, their sexual interest fades. In humans, the relationship between hormonal levels and sexual interest is less clear-cut, but some activating effects exist for hormones on sexual interest.

Individuals who do not undergo puberty generally fail to develop much interest in sexual activity (Meyer-Bahlburg, 1980), so hormones seem to be important in the development of sexual interest in humans as well as in other animals. However, the relationship is far from simple, with puberty necessary but not sufficient for development of sexual interest. No single measure of sexual interest or activity correlates very well with the onset of increased hormone levels in humans during puberty, but conditions that prevent this increase seem to result in a failure to develop sexual interest and activity.

The story is even more complex concerning the maintenance of sexual activity in humans who experience a decline of hormone levels. Such declines can occur for a number of reasons, including removal of the gonads or decreased hormone production associated with aging. For men, removal of the testes tends to produce a decrease in sexual activity, but the extent and rate of decrease varies enormously from person to person. Some men experience the significant and rapid loss of either ability to get erections, ability to ejaculate, or both, whereas other men experience a slowly decreasing interest in sexual activity, followed by difficulty in ejaculating, and then by loss of ability to achieve erections. Few men remain unaffected by loss of androgens, though replacement testosterone can reverse the decline in sexual interest and possibly in sexual performance. Testosterone replacement therapy has increased with the creation of the testosterone patch, but its cost and availability only by prescription has limited the widespread use of this treatment (Cowley, 1996).

On the other hand, women's sexual interest seems less affected by the removal of ovaries. Indeed, some women report increased sexual motivation after such surgery. One possibility is that the hormones that are important for the maintenance of sexual interest in women are androgens, and so a decrease in estrogen is not critical. Adrenal androgens may be sufficient to maintain sexual interest. Another possibility is that humans are so little controlled by their hormones that drastic physical changes in sexually mature adults are mediated by experience and expectation. Additionally, some combination of hormones and expectancy may account for the variations of sexual motivation in men and women without gonadal hormones.

In summary, LH and FSH produce the changes in reproductive and secondary sex characteristics associated with puberty. In girls, these changes produce cyclic variations in hormone levels that are associated with the maturation and release of an ovum approximately every month. If this ovum is fertilized by a sperm, the fertilized ovum will implant in the uterus and pregnancy will occur. If no fertilization occurs, the lining of the uterus is shed in menstruation, and the process will reoccur. In boys, the changes during puberty produce growth of the penis and maturation of the internal reproductive system, which will allow them to produce and ejaculate sperm. In addition to the physical changes associated with boys' bodies and reproductive systems, raised levels of gonadal hormones seem to be related to the development of sexual interest. Individuals who do not undergo puberty do not develop motivation to participate in sexual activity. However, the maintenance of sexual interest in humans is not directly related to the levels of hormones but instead depends on experience and expectancy.

When Things Go Wrong

A number of events relating to the development of the reproductive system can, but usually do not, go wrong during prenatal development. Problems can originate at several points, beginning before conception with the formation of the mother's ovum or the father's sperm. Yet other problems can arise when the prenatal hormones are not consistent with the genetic configuration of the developing fetus. These mistakes provide contrasts to normal development and highlight the complexities of defining male and female.

Beginning with the single cell consisting of a fertilized ovum, males differ from females in their chromosomes, but the presence of the normal sex chromosome pattern does not guarantee the development of a normal boy or girl. Abnormalities sometimes occur in the assortment of chromosomes carried by the sperm and ova. Instead of the normal 23, sometimes missing or extra chromosomes appear. Several types of chromosomal abnormalities have direct effects on the development of the internal reproductive system, the external genitalia, or both.

Abnormalities in Number of Sex Chromosomes

Several disorders involve the number of sex chromosomes. All of these disorders result in some problems, often affecting reproductive organs, genitalia, or fertility. In addition, these disorders show what chromosomes contribute to development. **Turner's syndrome** (sometimes identified without the possessive as *Turner syndrome*) occurs when the fertilized ovum has only one chromosome of pair 23—that is, one X. This syndrome is usually described as X0, where the zero stands for the missing chromosome. Individuals with Turner's syndrome appear female at birth, because their external genitals develop according to the female pattern. Their prenatal development begins normally, but their Müllerian systems degenerate, producing individuals with no functioning ovaries. At birth the appearance of the external genitalia prompts identification as females, but without ovaries, they produce no estrogens, so they do not undergo puberty or produce ova. With hormone supplements, they appear female but can never be fertile.

Another mistake in chromosome number is the presence of an extra X chromosome—the XXX pattern. Individuals with the XXX pattern develop prenatally as female, but their development may not be entirely normal. Women with the XXX pattern may have normal intelligence but may have developmental disabilities that affect cognitive ability. They also may have problems that affect their reproductive ability, including menstrual irregularities or amenorrhea (absence of menstrual periods) that results in sterility (Mittwoch, 1973), but they may not. Women with this chromosomal pattern have been known to have children. Individuals with the XXXX pattern and XXXXX pattern have also been identified. These individuals tend to have more severe developmental problems and are very likely to be seriously developmentally disabled as well as sterile.

Klinefelter's syndrome is characterized by the XXY configuration, and this problem is the most common of the sex chromosome abnormalities occurring in 2 cases per 1,000 male births (Mittwoch, 1973). Individuals with Klinefelter's syndrome have male internal and external genitalia, but their testes are small and cannot produce sperm, resulting in sterility. They may also develop breasts and a feminized body shape during puberty. Like other people with extra chromosomal material, individuals with Klinefelter's syndrome have an increased chance of developmental disabilities. Other configurations of chromosomes are similar to Klinefelter's syndrome, including XXXY and XXXXY, which produce more severe problems in the skeletal and reproductive systems as well as severe developmental disabilities.

The XYY chromosome pattern has been the subject of a great deal of publicity. In the early 1960s, articles appeared linking the XYY gene pattern to "aggressive tendencies" and "criminality" (Hubbard & Wald, 1993). These studies were based on the estimate of this gene pattern among men in the general population compared to men in prison, who were more likely to have the XYY pattern than the estimates for men from the general population.

These sensational reports, however, were largely unfounded. When measurements were taken from the general population, the results showed that the large majority of XYY men are not aggressive or criminal. Individuals with the XYY pattern of chromosomes are men who tend to be very tall, and some research (Witkin et al., 1976) indicated that these men were more likely than normal men to be in prison. This further examination of XYY men in prison showed that the XYY inmates were no more likely to be imprisoned for violent crimes than other inmates. They are significantly taller than other men, and like other individuals with extra chromosomal material, XYY individuals are more likely to have lower intelligence test scores. Thus, their height and their lower intelligence, or a combination of the two, may be the reason why a disproportionate number of XYY men are in prison: They are not very adept criminals, and witnesses may find a very tall man easy to identify, making their apprehension more likely than other offenders.

In summary, missing or extra sex chromosomes often affect the development of the sexual organs but more often affect other areas of development, especially intelligence. Both missing chromosomes (Turner's syndrome) and extra chromosomes (Klinefelter's syndrome) result in sterility, but individuals with the XXX pattern and the XYY pattern may be fertile. This extra chromosomal material does not make individuals "hypermasculine" or "superfeminine." Indeed, extra chromosomes produce developmental problems rather than adding anything useful.

Abnormalities in Prenatal Hormones

The presence of the XY chromosome pattern is not necessary (or sufficient) for the development of male internal or external genitalia; the hormone testosterone is the key to these developments. Therefore, a fetus that is genetically female (XX pattern) can be masculinized by the addition of testosterone during the critical period of the third and fourth months of prenatal development. Normally, female fetuses would not produce testosterone during this critical period of developing the genitalia, but prenatal exposure to androgens can occur, either through the action of tumors in the adrenal gland or through the pregnant woman's inadvertent or intentional exposure to androgens.

The **adrenogenital syndrome** occurs when the adrenal gland decreases its production of the hormone cortisol, which produces an increase in production of adrenal androgens. For a male fetus or for a boy, increased androgen production is not a very serious problem, except that it accelerates the onset of puberty. For a developing female fetus, however, the presence of excessive androgens produces masculinization of the external genitalia. Although their internal genitals are usually normal because the excess androgens are produced too late to affect this stage of development, these girls are born with a clitoris that may look very much like a penis. If their genitals appear abnormal at birth, their parents and physicians often recommend surgical correction to produce a more normal female appearance. These girls usually receive oral doses of cortisol, which reduces the levels of circulating androgens and allows them normal physical development.

These girls have also been of interest because their brains were exposed to androgens prenatally, leading researchers to study their behavior and sexual orientation. The early medical and parental attention focused on their genitals makes these girls different from others, so hormone exposure is not their only difference. Adrenogenital syndrome is associated with play activities more typical of boys than girls; that is, these girls are more likely to be "tomboys" (Berenbaum & Snyder, 1995). As adults, most are heterosexual, but bisexuality is somewhat more common among these women than among women with no prenatal androgen exposure (Ehrhardt & Meyer-Bahlburg, 1981).

A more serious problem is **androgen insensitivity syndrome.** This disorder occurs in normal XY male fetuses whose body cells are insensitive to androgens; that is, the androgens produced by their fetal testes will not induce masculinization because the androgen receptors in their bodies do not function normally. These fetuses will develop as though no androgens were present, and at birth the XY baby will appear to be a girl. The internal genitalia are not female, however, because the production of Müllerian-inhibiting substance caused the normal degeneration of the Müllerian system. Thus, these individuals do not have the internal genitalia of either males or females, but their external genitalia appear female.

Individuals with androgen insensitivity syndrome (and their families) can be completely unaware of the disorder until they reach the age at which puberty should occur. Complicating the diagnosis further, their testes produce sufficient estrogen to prompt breast development, increasing their feminine appearance. They have no ovaries, Fallopian tubes, or uterus, so they will not reach **menarche,** the beginning of menstruation. Nor will they grow pubic hair, a characteristic under the control of the androgens, to which they are insensitive. No amount of added androgens will reverse this problem, because their body cells are insensitive to it. Indeed, their levels of circulating androgens are within the normal range for men, but their bodies are "deaf" to these hormones.

Individuals with androgen insensitivity syndrome are identified as girls at birth, raised as girls, and have no reason to doubt their gender identification for years. At puberty they grow breasts and begin to look like young women, giving them no reason to imagine they are anything but women. Typically, few suspicions arise concerning any abnormality until they fail to grow pubic hair and fail to reach menarche. Even then these symptoms may be discounted for several years due to the variability of sexual development.

When gynecological examination reveals the abnormality of their internal genitalia, these individuals and their families learn that they are, in some sense, men. This information contradicts years of gender role development, and these individuals often have a difficult adjustment to their new status. No treatments exist to masculinize these individuals, so no attempt is made to change their gender identification. Individuals with androgen insensitivity syndrome continue in the female gender role, and most seek sexual relationships with men. Although they cannot have children, surgical alteration can lengthen the vagina so that they can have sexual intercourse. Despite their male chromosomes, these individuals are women in terms of gender identification, physical appearance, and behavior.

Through a variety of mechanisms, a person can be born with characteristics of both sexes. The traditional diagnosis for these individuals is **hermaphroditism;** a more modern term is **intersexuality,** but both terms continue in use. Hermaphroditism occurs when an individual has both ovarian and testicular tissue—either an ovary on one side of the body and a testicle on the other side, or both types of tissue combined into a structure called an ovotestis. This condition is extremely rare, with no more than 60 cases being identified in Europe and North America within the last century (Money, 1986). However, pseudohermaphroditism—in which individuals have some of the structures of both sexes—occurs much more frequently. Those with adrenogenital syndrome would be considered pseudohermaphrodites, as would those with androgen insensitivity syndrome.

A provocative example of pseudohermaphroditism comes from individuals with a genetic enzyme (5-alpha-reductase) deficiency that prevents chromosomal males from developing male external genitalia during the prenatal period. Like individuals with androgen insensitivity syndrome, these babies appear more female than male at birth and are often identified as girls. The appearance of their external genitals is ambiguous, not truly female but definitely not male. Unlike people with androgen insensitivity syndrome, these individuals respond to androgens during puberty and develop masculine characteristics. That is, their voice deepens, their muscles develop, their testes descend into the scrotum, and they grow a penis (Herdt, 1990). If these children had been identified as girls, they no longer fit into that category. However, these individuals do not clearly fit into the category of male, either. One early study (Imperato-McGinley, Guerreo, Gautier, & Peterson, 1974) reported that the majority of the intersex individuals had made at least fairly successful transitions to the male role, but a later study (Rubin, Reinisch, & Haskett, 1981) reported that none did so. These individuals may never fit comfortably into either category. Indeed, the New Guinea culture in which this form of intersexuality is relatively common acknowledges the existence of these individuals by devising a third category of sex to describe them (Herdt, 1981).

A third sex or some continuum for sex seems a better choice than the two categories of male and female. The intersex individuals represent cases in which chromosomal, hormonal, gonadal, and genital sex are not consistent and show that the determination of sex does not necessarily require complete consistency. These individuals may identify themselves unambiguously as male or female. On the other hand, they may not. For example, individuals with androgen insensitivity syndrome have a male chromosome configuration and normal levels of androgens, but they may look and feel female—they are female in their own opinion and in the opinion of society. Those individuals with 5-alpha-reductase deficiency may have trouble identifying as either male or female. A dichotomy is not the best conceptualization for the many possibilities of sex.

Hormones and Behavior Instability

In addition to their role in sexual development and activity, hormones are widely considered to affect other behaviors. The concept of premenstrual syndrome (PMS) has received wide publicity, and one of the headline stories for this chapter questioned how real this syndrome is. Another of the possible influences of hormones is the effect of testosterone on aggression; the other headline story for this chapter questioned the validity of the belief that this hormone is the basis for aggression: "Raging hormones" might be one cause of unstable, problem behaviors in both men and women, but popular belief may be mistaken about the role of these hormones in problem behavior.

Premenstrual Syndrome

A pamphlet available in doctors' offices proclaimed, "Every month, millions of women unwillingly ride the emotional roller coaster known as PMS.... Experts suggest 70 to 90 percent of all women undergo a similar crisis each month" (Murray, 1995, p. 210). Are these figures accurate? Is PMS the rule rather than the exception for women? Does PMS lead women on an "emotional roller coaster" over which they have no control?

As one of this chapter's headline articles (Murray, 1995) mentioned, recent, more careful research has suggested that the experience of PMS may be more closely associated with expectation than with hormones. That is, PMS may be a way of labeling some behavior rather than explaining the underlying cause of symptoms, and the concept's overuse has made it inaccurate as a diagnosis.

Recall that the cyclic variation of LH and FSH produces the menstrual cycle by affecting the release of estrogens and progesterone. In the middle of the cycle, the follicles produce larger amounts of one of the estrogens (estradiol) than during other times of the cycle, and this increase produces a surge of LH and FSH. This surge causes the release of the matured ovum, and the remainder of the follicle then starts to produce progesterone. Therefore, during the ovulatory phase of the cycle, estrogen levels are higher than progesterone levels. During the premenstrual phase of the cycle, both estradiol and progesterone are falling, and progesterone is at a higher level than estradiol. During the menstrual phase, the levels of both hormones are relatively low. Figure 3.6 shows the levels of hormones during the different phases of the cycle.

The notion that women's reproductive systems affect their lives is ancient (Fausto-Sterling, 1992), but the concept of the premenstrual syndrome can be traced only to the 1960s. During this time, Katharina Dalton published research (reviewed by Parlee, 1973) suggesting that women experience a wide variety of negative emotional, cognitive, and physical effects due to the hormonal changes that precede menstruation. These effects became known as a *syndrome,* although the list of symptoms extended to over 150, and some of the symptoms were mutually exclusive (such as *elevated mood* and *depression*).

The symptoms associated with the premenstrual phase of the cycle include headache; backache; abdominal bloating and discomfort; breast tenderness; tension or irritability; depression; increased analgesic, alcohol, or sedative use; decreased energy; and disruption in eating, sleeping, sexual behavior, work, and interpersonal relationships (Blechman, Clay, Kipke, & Bickel, 1988). The most common among these symptoms are tension and irritability.

All of the hormonal changes that occur during the menstrual cycle have been candidates for the underlying cause of premenstrual syndrome (Rubin, Reinisch, & Haskett, 1981). Several possibilities have been suggested, including an excess of estrogens, falling progesterone levels, and the ratio of estrogens to progesterone. However, research has failed to show that hormonal differences vary according to the experience of PMS (Rubin et al., 1981). This failure to tie hormonal changes to the experience of PMS is a major problem for the concept of PMS.

Other problems come from the changing pattern of research findings on PMS. Inconsistency is one problem (McFarlane, Martin, & Williams, 1988). Until the mid 1970s, researchers tended to find that mood is highest during the ovulatory phase of the cycle and lowest during the premenstrual and menstrual phases. Beginning in the late 1970s, researchers no longer found this pattern. The earlier menstrual cycle research may have had methodological problems. Such problems include the bias that expectation can introduce into studies in which the participants know that the research is about the menstrual cycle, a reliance on participants' memories of symptoms, and the failure to use appropriate comparison groups. Indeed, a random survey of women (Deuster, Adera, & South-Paul, 1999) indicated that only 8.3% experienced PMS.

Jessica McFarlane and her colleagues (McFarlane et al., 1988; McFarlane & Williams, 1994) have conducted two longitudinal studies that avoided the methodological problems from other studies. Both studies involved instructing women and men to keep records of their daily moods without knowing that the menstrual cycle was the focus of the study. Both studies included women who were cycling normally, women who were taking oral contraceptives and thus not cycling normally, and men.

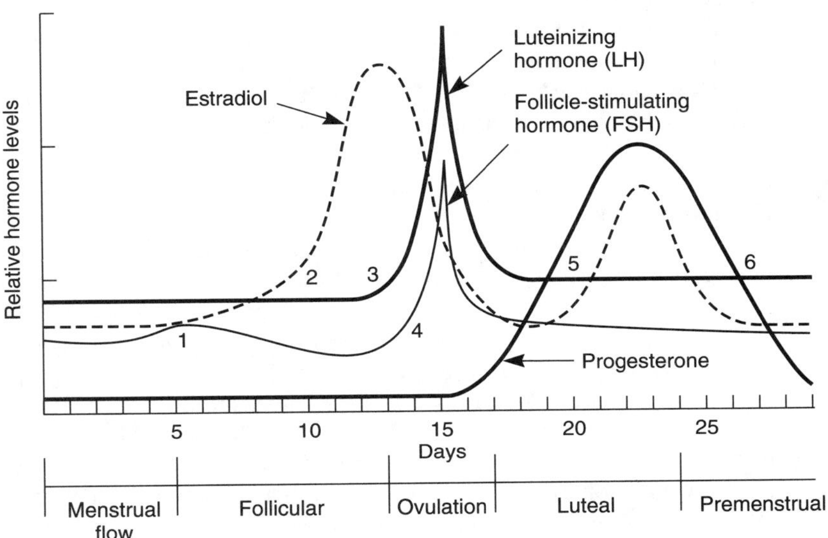

Phases of the Human Menstrual Cycle

1. In response to an increase in FSH, small spheres of cells called ovarian follicles begin to grow around individual egg cells (ova).
2. The follicles begin to release estrogens such as estradiol.
3. The estrogens stimulate the hypothalamus to increase the release of LH and FSH from the anterior pituitary.
4. In response to the LH surge, one of the follicles ruptures and releases its ovum.
5. The ruptured follicle under the influence of LH develops into a corpus luteum (yellow body) and begins to release progesterone, which prepares the lining of the uterus for the implantation of a fertilized ovum.
6. Meanwhile, the ovum is moved into the Fallopian tube by the rowing action of ciliated cells. If the ovum is not fertilized, progesterone and estradiol levels fall and the walls of the uterus are sloughed off as menstrual flow and the cycle begins once again.

FIGURE 3.6 Hormones during the Menstrual Cycle

SOURCE: From John P. J. Pinel, *Biopsychology* (2nd ed.). Copyright © 1993 by Allyn and Bacon. Reprinted by permission.

The main result of the study by McFarlane et al. (1988) was that no differences in mood stability appeared when comparing the young men and the young women who participated in the study. All participants experienced similar mood changes within a day as well as from day to day. Also, the men and women reported similar variability in mood during the 70 days of the study.

A second study (McFarlane & Williams, 1994) recruited participants who were older than the typical college student participants and lasted at least 12 weeks to cover more menstrual cycles. The analysis for this study included an evaluation of each participant's cyclic mood variation over time. This study also revealed that people experienced cyclic mood variations, but that these changes did not conform to the PMS pattern.

In comparing women who were cycling normally to women taking oral contraceptives and to the men, the women who were cycling normally reported *more pleasant moods* during and immediately after their periods than in the ovulatory or premenstrual periods (McFarlane et al., 1988). The male and female participants experienced cyclicity as the norm, but few reported emotional symptoms consistent with PMS (McFarlane & Williams, 1994). Neither of these studies found evidence to support the concept of PMS, but both studies showed that cyclic variations in mood occur for both men and women.

The McFarlane et al. (1988) study included a component that may provide an explanation for the belief in PMS. They asked participants to fill out a questionnaire at the end of the study in which they had to recall their moods. They reasoned that if PMS is influenced by biases in memory, then the memory of moods might conform to PMS, whereas the daily reports would not. Their analysis supported that hypothesis: When the female participants remembered their moods rather than recording their moods as they occurred, they reported symptoms of PMS that, according to their daily reports, they had not experienced. This finding strongly suggests that the mood changes associated with PMS may be a product of expectation and labeling rather than of hormones. However, the physical symptoms associated with the premenstrual part of the cycle have some research support (Slade, 1984).

In the studies by McFarlane and her colleagues, about half the women who met and about half who failed to meet diagnostic criteria consistent with PMS reported that they had it. Another study (Hardie, 1997) also asked women to self-diagnose, and the results showed that 40% of women reported that they had PMS. However, none of them exhibited the pattern of cyclic emotional changes that are part of the diagnostic criteria. That is, regardless of symptoms, some women will believe that they have PMS (see "According to the Media/According to the Research").

Why do people believe in PMS? The syndrome is certainly well accepted, widely publicized, and even medically treated (Tavris, 1992; Murray, 1995), yet the research that has supported the concept is flawed, and placebo treatment is as effective as drug treatment in controlling PMS (Apgar, 2000). Better research has failed either to find a hormonal explanation for PMS or to demonstrate the variety of mood and behavioral symptoms associated with it. A possible explanation comes from the willingness of both women and men to attribute moody behavior to PMS (Koeske & Koeske, 1975). That is, when furnished with information about a woman's cycle, both men and women tended to use this information to partly explain the woman's emotional behavior. The more irrational the behavior, the more willing the participants were to attribute it to PMS. As Murray's (1995) headline story suggested, women who experience problems, stresses, and irritations to which they respond emotionally may explain their reactions by their phase of the menstrual cycle. If they believe that these symptoms are associated with the premenstrual period as well as menstruation, they can apply this explanation about half the time—the week before and the week during menstruation. When they experience the same situations and reactions at other phases of their cycle, they seek other explanations. In this way, premenstrual syndrome can become a self-perpetuating myth for the women who react to problems, stresses, and irritations in their lives as well as for the people who observe the reactions.

Murray (1995) suggested that many women's "PMS" may be other problems that women (and those around them) label and accept as PMS. Unhappy marriages, poor working environments, and depression can produce symptoms on the list for PMS. Research (Hardie, 1997) has shown that the perceived quality and number of personal relationships and stress predicted emotional reactions that women labeled as PMS. Consistent with this research, Jamie, one of the cases in Murray's story, was actually depressed. Her symptoms increased in severity, and she sought treatment for depression. As her treatment for depression became effective, her "PMS" disappeared.

In summary, PMS has received wide publicity and wide acceptance, but much of the research supporting this concept suffers from flaws in methodology. The results from more careful studies have indicated that premenstrual syndrome is difficult to define on a biological level and does not appear as emotional symptoms except as a function of expectation or emotional problems. The moods of both women and men vary cyclically, but not according to the pattern consistent with PMS.

Testosterone and Aggression

The subtitle for Robert Sapolsky's (1997) headline article suggested that "it takes more than just a hormone to make a fellow's trigger finger itch." Sapolsky acknowledged the association between being male and being violent: "We males account for less than 50 percent of the population, yet we generate a huge proportion of the violence" (p. 44). He also admitted that testosterone has behavioral effects, but he argued against the widely accepted belief that testosterone causes aggression. What, then, is the relationship, and how are both women and men affected?

According to research by James Dabbs and his colleagues, hormone levels play a role in aggression in men and in women, but the research indicates that the role is not a simple one. One of these studies (Dabbs, de la Rue, & Williams, 1990) investigated differences in testosterone levels for men in various occupations, including physicians, football players, salesmen, actors, ministers, professors, and firemen as well as unemployed men. Their analysis showed that the only significant difference occurred in a comparison of the actors and the football players, who both had higher testosterone levels than the ministers. Another study (Dabbs, Hopper, & Jurkovic, 1990) confirmed the differences between actors and ministers and explored possible reasons for this difference in testosterone levels that might relate to personality differences. Dabbs and his colleagues reasoned that the factors of competition and antisocial tendencies might differentiate the two groups. Ministers' lives have little competition compared to actors' lives; actors also tend to be more selfish and self-absorbed than ministers. Therefore, competition and selfishness, not aggression, showed a relationship to testosterone in this group of men.

Research on the relationship between testosterone level and occupational achievement (Dabbs, 1992) showed a complex relationship: Men with higher levels of testosterone had lower-status occupations. Dabbs interpreted this finding to indicate that high testosterone levels are related to antisocial behavior, and such behavior makes success in white-collar occupations less likely. An additional study (Heusel & Dabbs, 1996) confirmed that for

ACCORDING TO THE MEDIA...

If You Think You Have PMS, You May Have PMDD and Need Drugs

In July, 2000, Eli Lilly and Company received approval from the U.S. Food and Drug Administration to market a drug to treat premenstrual dysphoric disorder (PMDD). This disorder was a controversial inclusion in the fourth edition of the *Diagnostic and Statistical Manual of Mental Disorders* (American Psychiatric Association, 1994). PMDD is an extreme form of PMS and qualifies as a mental disorder. The symptoms include those associated with PMS—irritability, depression, anxiety, mood swings, fatigue, food cravings, bloating, and breast tenderness. To be diagnosed with PMDD, women must have at least five of these symptoms, and their presence must interference with their work, school, social activities, or relationships. An estimated 3 to 5% of women who menstruate have PMDD.

Before the approval of a drug to treat PMDD, suggestions for treatment had included various vitamin and herb preparations, exercise, salt restriction, caffeine restriction, and other lifestyle changes. Now, the Lilly Company has started a marketing campaign that tells women if they have PMS, they may have PMDD, and a new drug can help them. The television advertisement includes a telephone number that women may call and a website address that gives information about PMDD and the availability of the drug Sarafem as a treatment. The website (www.pmdd.com) leads women to ask if they might have PMDD by saying, "But before you dismiss your symptoms as PMS, or just part of being a woman, you should realize you could be suffering from PMDD (Premenstrual Dysphoric Disorder), the intense mood and physical symptoms right before your period." The website then urges women to talk to their physicians about their symptoms and the possibility of a Sarafem prescription. The large percentage of women who believe that they have PMS (Hardie, 1997) creates a big market for this "new" drug, and the advertising campaign capitalizes on these beliefs and encourages women to seek out this treatment.

engineers working in the same company, those with high testosterone levels were more likely to quit or be fired than those with lower testosterone levels.

The interpretation that antisocial tendencies are positively related to testosterone level is consistent with other research by Dabbs and his colleagues. For example, little relationship appeared between testosterone and personality in the college students, but veterans showed a positive relationship between testosterone level and drug and alcohol abuse, antisocial behavior, and affective disorders (Dabbs, Hopper, & Jurkovic, 1990). Among U.S. military veterans, high testosterone levels were related to problem behaviors (Dabbs & Morris, 1990). Men whose testosterone levels fell within the upper 10% of testosterone had a history of trouble with parents, teachers, and classmates as well as a history of drug use and more instances of going AWOL (absent without leave) while in the military.

A comparison of college students and young men who were delinquents showed higher testosterone levels in the delinquents (Banks & Dabbs, 1996). An assessment of the testosterone levels in two college fraternities showed that men in the "rowdy" fraternity had higher testosterone levels than the men in the fraternity with a reputation for academic success and social responsibility (Dabbs, Hargrove, & Heusel, 1996). These behaviors can create problems, but they are not necessarily examples of aggression or violence.

A more specific example of the relationship between testosterone and violence appeared in a study of male prisoners (Dabbs, Carr, Frady, & Riad, 1995). Those prisoners

ACCORDING TO THE RESEARCH...

The "New" Drug for PMDD is Prozac

The drug Sarafem, approved in July, 2000, by the U.S. Food and Drug Administration as a treatment for premenstrual dysphoric disorder [PMDD] has the same active ingredient as Prozac, the widely used antidepressant drug. Some physicians have prescribed Prozac for their patients with severe symptoms of PMS, but the Lilly company did not seek to include PMDD as one of the conditions for which Prozac is an effective treatment. Rather, it created another brand name for the same drug. According to a Lilly official (CBS News Transcripts, 2000), the company felt that women would get better diagnoses and treatment if the drug had a separate identity from Prozac. They wanted to avoid the connotations of taking an antidepressant drug and publicize the benefits of Sarafem for PMDD. Another way to interpret the creation of a new brand name is that it represents Lilly's attempt to extend the patent for Prozac, which will expire soon. By creating a new drug, Lilly can market Sarafem as a brand name rather than fluoxetine, the soon-to-be available generic form of Prozac.

The marketing of Sarafem differs from that of Prozac. The antidepressant effects of Sarafem are not the focus of the advertising campaign. Depression is one of the symptoms of PMDD, but the disorder includes a host of other symptoms, including mental and physical problems. However, the active ingredient of the two drugs are identical, so differential symptom relief is not a possibility. If Sarafem can relieve symptoms of PMDD, then so can Prozac or its generic form, fluoxetine.

The research on the effectiveness of fluoxetine for symptoms of PMDD (Freeman, Rickels, Sondheimer, & Polansky, 1999; Jermain, 1999) has indicated that it is more effective than a placebo for several of the symptoms. That is, women who have severe symptoms can get relief by taking Sarafem. However, they can also get the same amount of help from any form of fluoxetine. In order to obtain the benefits of this drug, women must take Sarafem as they would Prozac—on a daily basis for at least several months and possibly longer (CBS News Transcripts, 2000). In addition, they may experience side effects from this drug, which ironically include some of the same symptoms as PMS or PMDD, such as anxiety and difficulty in sleeping.

who had committed crimes against individuals involving sex and violence had higher testosterone levels than prisoners who had committed property crimes. The prisoners with higher levels of testosterone also were more likely to be involved with rule violations and personal confrontations while in prison.

Testosterone levels in men seem to be related to a greater variety of behavior problems, but this pattern is not constant over all socioeconomic groups. For example, for men with low socioeconomic status (SES), high testosterone levels heightened their risks for problem behavior, including adult delinquency and drug use (Dabbs & Morris, 1990). Men with high SES and with high testosterone experienced fewer negative consequences than their low-SES counterparts. The effects that appeared in this research were small; despite their statistical significance, these results may be too small to be of practical significance. Table 3.2 summarizes the complex findings from research by Dabbs and his colleagues.

Women also produce testosterone, and some researchers have studied the relationship between this hormone and women's behavior. Dabbs and his colleagues (Dabbs, Ruback, Frady, Hopper, & Sgoutas, 1988) also studied the relationship between testosterone level and antisocial behavior in women by measuring the testosterone levels of inmates in a women's prison and contrasting them with testosterone levels of female college students. Within the prison group, they found some indication that testosterone levels were related to violence: Women with the highest levels of testosterone had the highest incidence of

TABLE 3.2 Relationship of Testosterone to Various Behaviors in Men and Women

Behaviors Associated with Higher Testosterone Levels	
In Men	In Women
Occupations of actor and football player	Professional, managerial, and technical occupations
Lower-status occupations	Unprovoked violence among prisoners
Job loss	
Drug and alcohol abuse among veterans	
Antisocial disorders among veterans	
Affective disorders among veterans	
Trouble getting along with parents, teachers, and classmates among veterans	
Delinquent behaviors while young	
Membership in a "rowdy" fraternity	
Incarceration for crimes involving sex or violence	
Rule violations and personal confrontations among prisoners	
Behaviors Not Associated with Higher Testosterone Levels	
In Men	In Women
Occupations of salesmen, firemen, professors, physicians, or the unemployed	Violent criminal acts
Personality traits among students	Prisoner versus student
	"Butch" role in lesbian relationships

unprovoked violence. They found that testosterone levels differed among inmates convicted of unprovoked violence, defensive violence, theft, drugs, and other crimes. The inmates who had committed acts of unprovoked violence had the highest testosterone levels. For these female inmates, testosterone was related to the number of prior charges and to prior parole board decisions about length of time they should serve before being granted parole. Women who had committed violence in protecting themselves, such as those who had murdered an abusive spouse, had the lowest levels of testosterone in the prison group.

Interestingly, the mean levels of testosterone were similar for the inmates and the college students, and both averages fell within the normal range for women. These results provide some support for the notion that testosterone is related to aggression, as the inmates who had committed the most violent crimes—those involving unprovoked violence—also had the highest testosterone levels. However, the failure to find differences between women convicted of crimes and female students indicates that aggression and violence are influenced by factors other than testosterone level, including SES, which Dabbs and his colleagues found moderated the relationship between testosterone and problem behavior in men.

Other studies have explored the role of testosterone in women's behavior, including some typical and atypical gender role behaviors. For example, one study (Purifoy & Koopmans, 1979) showed that women's levels of androgens varied according to occupation. The mean levels of testosterone were significantly higher in women with professional, technical, or managerial jobs compared to women who had clerical jobs or who were housewives. This study did not demonstrate that high testosterone levels cause women to pursue certain occupations. The possibility exists that levels of androgens might influence career choice and also that career stresses might influence androgen level.

Some research has also explored the role of androgens in the gender role behavior in lesbian couples (Pearcey, Docherty, & Dabbs, 1996). If hormones prompt women to conform to stereotypes, then "butch" lesbians should be higher in testosterone than "femme" lesbians. However, the results showed no pattern of variation according to gender role. Instead, the lesbian couples were similar to each other in testosterone levels, and the variation appeared among couples rather than roles.

The studies by Dabbs and his colleagues show a relationship between high testosterone levels and a variety of antisocial behaviors, but the behaviors are not always within the definition of aggression. Additional complications are highlighted by a finding that testosterone levels do not vary in aggressive versus nonaggressive boys (Constantino et al., 1993). Research (Pope, Kouri, & Hudson, 2000) on responses to anabolic steroids (a synthetic analog of androgens) demonstrated that men's responses were variable—most (84%) showed no increase in activity level or aggression, a few (12%) showed mild increases, and very few (2%) experienced substantial increases.

All of this research shows that the relationship between testosterone and aggression is not a simple cause and effect. In his headline story, Sapolsky (1997) argued that there is a cause-and-effect relationship between testosterone and aggression, but in the other direction—aggression causes increases in testosterone. One line of research supports his contention.

Allan Mazur and his colleagues (Booth, Shelley, Mazur, Tharp, & Kittok, 1989) examined the relationship between testosterone levels and winning versus losing in athletic competition. Participants were the six members of the University of Nebraska varsity tennis team who agreed to provide saliva samples throughout the season so that the researchers could analyze testosterone levels. These players were measured four times in relation to each of the season's six matches—the day before a match, about 15 minutes before each match, immediately after they had finished playing, and one or two days after each match. The researchers predicted that winning players would experience increased testosterone levels compared to losing players. The carryover effects of winning on testosterone level were also a topic of the study.

This study was a test of a biosocial theory of status (Mazur, 1985; Mazur & Booth, 1998), which hypothesizes that testosterone level is part of a feedback loop in which testosterone and assertiveness are interrelated. When an individual's testosterone level rises, that person is more willing to compete in contests for higher status. Winning such competitions produces a rise in testosterone or helps to maintain a high level of testosterone, which will sustain the willingness to compete. Conversely, losing produces a drop in testosterone, which deters the willingness to compete. Thus, "losing streaks" and "winning streaks" in competitions are sustained by the feedback loop's relationship with testosterone level. This theory also holds that testosterone level and behavior influence each other rather than a unidirectional cause-and-effect relationship between the hormone level and behavior.

In the study with tennis players (Booth et al., 1989), the researchers compared the changes in testosterone level before and after matches. They expected winners to have higher testosterone levels than losers, but their findings were more complex. Players showed increases of testosterone on days when they played, but their hormone levels were highest before the game. Winners showed rises in testosterone across the matches and losers showed declines, but no significant differences appeared in the average levels of testosterone when comparing winners and losers before and after the matches.

The tennis players also rated their feelings about their overall performance. The players who felt positively about their performance tended to have higher testosterone levels. Therefore, winning and losing did not appear to be simply related to testosterone levels, but rather, some emotional or mood factors might have mediated the hormonal effects. That is, winning might produce positive moods that in turn might heighten testosterone levels. This research was consistent with the biosocial theory (Mazur, 1985), which would highlight the finding that testosterone levels affected *and* were affected by competition. However, the study suggested that the effects of testosterone on performance and responses of players to high levels of testosterone follow complex, rather than simple, patterns related to competition.

As Sapolsky (1997) contended, the influence of androgens on behavior turns out to be complex, bidirectional, and influenced by a multitude of factors. Rather than testosterone simply producing aggression, competition and aggression can also increase testosterone. There is some evidence that men *and* women with high testosterone levels are more likely to commit violent crimes than people whose testosterone levels are lower, but that correlational evidence does not rule out the possibility of a bidirectional action. People with high testosterone levels are also more likely to commit crimes that do not include violence and to exhibit antisocial but legal behaviors, such as heavy drinking. Conceptualizing all of these behaviors as aggression would be inaccurate. Therefore, hormone levels probably play some role in aggression, but that role is relatively small, and a higher testosterone level is possibly a result, rather than a cause, of aggression. Testosterone is not the main factor that accounts for the violence that is associated with men's behavior.

Considering Diversity

The possibilities for cultural variations in sexual development seem limited: Biological sex is a matter of chromosomes and hormones. Most people develop unambiguously according to the male pattern or the female pattern, and those patterns do not seem subject to cultural variations. The factor that can vary is the way that cultures divide those categories and how the languages of those cultures name the sexes. Although English includes many words to describe variations in sexual interest and behavior, we have no word for people who do not fit either the male or female patterns of sexual development. However, anthropologist Gilbert Herdt (1990) contended that some cultures do; that is, some cultures name a category for a third sex.

These cultures tend to have a factor in common—the relative frequency of the hereditary enzyme disorder that produces one type of intersexuality. This disorder is the result of a deficiency in the enzyme 5-alpha-reductase, which prevents prenatal testosterone from producing a boy with normal external genitals. These individuals are chromosomally normal males with normal internal genitalia, but they are born with external genitals that more closely resemble a girl's than a boy's—a clitoris-like penis, an unfused scrotum that resembles labia, and undescended testes. At birth, these babies are sometimes identified as boys but are more often identified and reared as girls. At puberty they produce testosterone and become "masculinized": Their penis grows, their testes descend, they grow facial hair, and their musculature increases. That is, they change from individuals who look more like girls to ones who look more like boys.

This disorder is very rare but is more common in the Dominican Republic and New Guinea than in most other parts of the world. Herdt contended that these two cultures have a term for a third sex, one that is neither male nor female but that starts out as female and becomes male. In his evaluation of both cultures, Herdt concluded that individuals with this disorder fit into neither the male nor female category and that their cultures acknowledge and respond to these differences. Acknowledgment is not the same as acceptance, however, and neither culture accepts these individuals as normal. Even after these individuals had developed masculine characteristics, the Sambia culture of New Guinea did not grant them full male status.

Several Native American cultures not only designated a category for a third sex, but honored the individuals in this category. More than 130 Native American societies accepted *berdaches*—men or women who adopted the gender-related behaviors of the other gender (Wieringa, 1994). Berdaches were not intersex individuals, but instead individuals who chose to blend masculine and feminine roles. The male berdache tradition was the more common; and male berdaches were not only well accepted but also achieved high spiritual status in their societies. Lakota, Navajo, Crow, and Zuni societies all included berdaches who were not thought of as homosexual but as a merging of feminine and masculine spirits, which they attained through a blessing from the spirits. These departures from the ordinary gender roles, therefore, were not viewed as deviations because they were chosen as special, and there was no connotation of deficiency or pathology. Their behaviors represented a blending of male and female that, to the Zuni and others, constituted a third gender rather than an adoption of the "opposite" gender. Thus, for individuals whose biology has not clearly designated male or female and for those who choose to blend roles, a category for a third sex exists in some cultures.

Summary

Several steroid hormones are important to sexual development and behavior, including the androgens, the estrogens, and the progestins. All normal individuals produce all of these hormones, but women produce proportionately more estrogens and progestins, whereas men produce more androgens. The prenatal production of these hormones prompts the brains of fetuses to organize in either the male or the female pattern. During puberty, these hormones activate the internal genitalia to develop fertility and secondary sex characteristics, such as facial hair for men and breasts for women. The role of hormones in the activation and maintenance of sexual interest and activity is less clear in humans than in other species, but humans who do not experience the pubertal surge of hormones tend not to develop much interest in sex. Testosterone, one of the androgens, plays a role in maintaining sexual activity in men and possibly in women as well.

Sexual development may be conceptualized as consisting of five stages—genetic, gonadal, hormonal, internal genitalia, and external genitalia—all of which usually proceed according to either the male or female pattern. The first stage in sexual development is genetic, the inheritance of either XX or XY chromosomes of pair 23. Although the inheritance of chromosomes is the beginning of the pattern, embryos are not sexually dimorphic until around 6 weeks into gestation. Those with the XY pattern start to produce androgens and Müllerian-inhibiting substance during the 3rd month of gestation. These hormones masculinize the fetus, prompting not only the further development of the testes, but also degeneration of the Müllerian structures and development of the Wolffian structures that form the other internal male genitalia. Shortly thereafter, external male genitalia develop, and this development also depends on androgens.

The female pattern is not as dependent on the presence of estrogens as the male pattern is on androgens, but some estrogen is necessary for the development of normal ovaries and other internal genitalia. During the 3rd month of pregnancy, those individuals with the XX pattern of chromosomes start to develop the Müllerian structures, which become the ovaries, Fallopian tubes, uterus, and upper vagina. In addition, their Wolffian structures start to degenerate. An absence of all steroid hormones will allow the feminization of external genitalia, but the internal reproductive organs do not develop normally.

Prenatal hormones also affect brain development, producing differences in the brains of males versus females. Several brain structures are affected, but the sexually dimorphic nucleus of the hypothalamus shows the biggest difference. Its function is not known. The cerebral hemispheres differ in function between the left and right hemispheres, and this lateralization of function is also hypothesized as a gender difference. Some research indicates that men are more lateralized than women, but this gender-related difference is small.

Things can go wrong at any stage of sexual development, beginning with the inheritance of the chromosomes that determine sex—the X and Y chromosomes. A number of disorders exist that create individuals with too few or too many sex chromosomes, and some of these configurations produce problems with the development of internal or external genitalia. In addition, several of these disorders produce individuals with developmental disorders, especially lowered intelligence. Individuals with Turner's syndrome (X0) appear to be female but lack ovaries; individuals with Klinefelter's syndrome (XXY) appear to be male, often with feminized body contours, but have nonfunctional testes; XXX individuals are female and may be otherwise normal; XYY individuals are tall males who may be reproductively normal but with low intelligence.

Even normal chromosomes do not guarantee normal development in subsequent stages, and several types of intersexuality exist. These cases of individuals who have the physiology of both males and females highlight the complexity of sexual development and suggest that many components contribute to gender identity and functioning.

Media reports tend to indicate a role for hormones in two areas of problem behavior—premenstrual syndrome (PMS) and aggression. Careful research has indicated that the premenstrual phase of the cycle may include some physical symptoms, but it also suggests that expectation, not hormones, is the major cause of the emotional symptoms associated with PMS. Both women and men may attribute behavioral symptoms to PMS, when those symptoms may actually indicate other problems.

Research on the role of testosterone in aggression has revealed that the relationship is not a simple cause-and-effect one. Indeed, the relationship may occur in the direction opposite to what was previously expected: Aggression may cause increases in testosterone, rather than vice versa. For women as well as for men, testosterone levels differ for people who have committed violent crimes, with higher testosterone levels found in the criminally violent. However, testosterone is not a very accurate predictor of criminal violence, as both male and female inmates do not differ in testosterone levels from male and female college students. Men with higher than average testosterone levels tend to engage in a wide variety of antisocial behaviors that include (but are not restricted to) violence. Studies of competition and testosterone show that competition raises testosterone levels, suggesting that the relationship between the two may be causal but in the opposite direction from what people have imagined.

The role of hormones in sexual development is not subject to cultural variation, but how culture deals with the sexes varies enormously. In addition to male and female, some cultures define a third sex. One basis for this third sex has been the frequency of a developmental problem that produces individuals who are born with ambiguous external genitalia that masculinizes at puberty. That is, these individuals seem to be born female but become male. The other basis for a third sex was a belief common among Native American societies that allowed for a melding of the two spirits, male and female, in an individual. These conceptualizations highlight problems for cultures that allow only two categories.

Glossary

adrenogenital syndrome a disorder that results in masculinization, producing premature puberty in boys and masculinization of the external genitalia in girls.

androgen insensitivity syndrome a disorder in which body cells are unable to respond to androgens, resulting in the feminization of chromosomal males.

androgens a class of hormones that includes testosterone and other steroid hormones. Men typically produce a greater proportion of androgens than estrogens.

endocrine glands glands that secrete hormones into the circulatory system.

estradiol the most common of the estrogen hormones.

estrogens a class of hormones that includes estradiol and other steroid hormones. Women typically produce a greater proportion of estrogens than androgens.

external genitalia the reproductive structures that can be seen without internal examination: clitoris, labia, and vaginal opening in women and penis and scrotum in men.

follicle-stimulating hormone (FSH) the gonadotropic hormone that stimulates development of gonads during puberty and development of ova during the years of women's fertility.

gonads reproductive organs.

hermaphroditism a disorder in which individuals have characteristics of both sexes.

hormones chemical substances released from endocrine glands that circulate throughout the body and affect target organs that have receptors sensitive to the specific hormones.

internal genitalia internal reproductive organs, consisting of the ovaries, Fallopian tubes, uterus, and upper vagina in women; and testes, seminal vesicles, vas deferens, and prostate gland in men.

intersexuality a more modern term for hermaphroditism.

Klinefelter's syndrome the disorder that occurs when a chromosomal male has an extra X chromosome, resulting in the XXY pattern of chromosome pair 23. These individuals have the appearance of males, including external genitalia, but they may also develop breasts and a feminized body shape. Their testes are not capable of producing sperm, so they are sterile.

lateralization the concept that the two cerebral hemispheres are not functionally equal but rather that each hemisphere has different abilities.

luteinizing hormone (LH) the gonadotropic hormone that prompts sexual development during puberty and also causes a maturing ovum to be released.

menarche the first menstruation.

Müllerian system a system of ducts occurring in both male and female embryos that forms the basis for the development of the female internal reproductive system—ovaries, fallopian tubes, uterus, and upper vagina.

pituitary gland an endocrine gland within the brain that produces tropic hormones that stimulate other glands to produce yet other hormones.

progestins a group of steroid hormones that prepare the female body for pregnancy; their function for the male body is unknown.

releasing hormones hormones produced by the hypothalamus that act on the pituitary to release tropic hormones.

sexual dimorphism the existence of two sexes—male and female—including differences in genetics, gonads, hormones, internal genitalia, and external genitalia.

sexually dimorphic nucleus (SDN) a brain structure in the hypothalamus, near the optic chiasm, that is larger in male than in female rats and larger in men than in women.

spinal nucleus of the bulbocavernosus a collection of neurons in the lower spinal cord that control muscles at the base of the penis.

steroid hormones hormones related to sexual dimorphism and sexual reproduction that are derived from cholesterol and consist of a structure that includes four carbon rings.

testosterone the most common of the androgen hormones.

tropic hormones hormones produced by the pituitary gland that influence the release of other hormones by other glands, such as the gonads.

Turner's syndrome the disorder that occurs when an individual has only one of chromosome pair 23, one X chromosome. These individuals appear to be female (have the external genitalia of females) but do not have fully developed internal genitalia. They do not produce estrogens, do not undergo puberty, and are not fertile.

Wolffian system a system of ducts occurring in both male and female embryos that forms the basis for the development of the male internal reproductive system—testes, seminal vesicles, and vas deferens.

X chromosomes one of the possible alternatives for chromosome pair 23. Two X chromosomes make a genetic female, whereas genetic males have only one X chromosome in pair 23.

Y chromosome one of the possible alternatives for chromosome pair 23. One X and one Y chromosome make a genetic male, whereas genetic females have two X chromosomes in pair 23.

Suggested Readings

Angier, Natalie. (1999). *Woman: An intimate geography.* Boston: Houghton Mifflin. Angier's readable book delves into female biology. The first three chapters focus on chromosomes and hormones in development, and Chapters 14 and 15 analyze the contribution of testosterone to behavior. Angier's presentation is both readable and provocative.

Breedlove, S. Marc. (1994). Sexual differentiation of the human nervous system. *Annual Review of Psychology, 45,* 389–418. Breedlove's article is not easy reading, but it is a thorough and careful review of the research. Breedlove is also careful to acknowledge the interaction of biology and experience in the development of gender differences in the nervous system.

Fausto-Sterling, Anne. (1992). *Myths of gender: Biological theories about women and men* (2nd ed.). New York: Basic Books. Although this book does not have the most recent research, the chapter titled "Hormonal Hurricanes" contains a readable, critical review of the role of hormones in women's behavior.

Pinel, John P. J. (2000). *Biopsychology* (4th ed.). Boston: Allyn & Bacon. For more details about the action of the endocrine system, the brain's involvement in endocrine function, sexual development, and some of the things that can go wrong, see Chapter 11 of this biological psychology textbook.

Chapter 4

Intelligence and Mental Abilities

HEADLINE

The Great Debate: Gender Differences

Current Health 2, December, 1995

> *"Need help?" Brenda asked. The woman grimaced. "I never could read maps. Where's the Emporium?"*
>
> *John tapped the map. "Turn here. Walk east four blocks, go south and—"*
>
> *Brenda cut in, pointing right. "He means to go right at this intersection, and walk four blocks to the Big Dollar Store on the corner. Go right. It's just past Tucker's Toys, on Mission Street."*
>
> *As the woman crossed the intersection, John asked, "Why did you butt in?"*
>
> *"Maps are confusing. I prefer landmarks like Tucker's Toys."*
>
> *"I'll show you how to read a map," offered John, but Brenda shook her head. (Monroe, 1995, p. 22)*

Judy Monroe (1995) reported this exchange and then wrote that some people believe that men read maps better than women. She contended that determining who is better at finding the way is not so simple because women and men tend to use different strategies. Like Brenda, many women prefer to use landmarks as a strategy to find their way. Like John, many men rely on maps. Monroe's article focused on the research that has related map reading to spatial ability and the findings that men on the average are better at these tasks than women.

The great gender debate to which Monroe's headline referred concerns differences between women's and men's mental abilities. Is the conversation between John and Brenda typical? Do women and men have different mental abilities, do they use different strategies, or both? If such differences exist, are they expressions of hormonal or brain differences between the sexes, or do these differences represent different learning and experience?

Monroe's article mentioned the controversy over mental abilities: Some researchers contend that gender differences do not exist, whereas others have argued that the differences exist and that they have a biological basis. As Monroe discussed, the research in the area of cognitive abilities is filled with complex findings and strongly held (but opposing) views; her article is but one of dozens that has appeared in the popular press. Monroe pointed out the conflicting findings about both the existence and source of gender differences in mental abilities, but other reports have not been so balanced.

The level of controversy reflects the strong feelings that this topic has produced. To what extent do gender differences explain mental abilities? Are differences sufficiently large to explain the distribution of men and women into different areas of study and different occupations, or do these findings represent insignificant differences in how women and men think? Do differences apply only to specific mental abilities, or to overall intelligence?

Mental Abilities

Other than defining intelligence as "how smart a person is" (a trivial and circular definition), an acceptable definition of this concept has been difficult to formulate. Indeed, heated debate over the nature of intelligence has occurred throughout the history of intelligence testing, a controversy not confined to psychology. The prominence of this concern highlights the importance of the issue: Understanding intelligence and the abilities that contribute to intelligence is a basic question for understanding humans.

Psychologists have been concerned with the concept of intelligence since the 1890s (Schultz & Schultz, 1992). However, the current conceptualization of intelligence was most influenced by the creation of the intelligence test in 1905. This test, formulated by Alfred Binet, Victor Henri, and Théodore Simon, measured a variety of mental abilities related to school performance, including memory, attention, comprehension, vocabulary, and imagination. A version of this test—the Stanford-Binet—appeared in the United States in 1916, and the intelligence testing movement became an important part of psychology, especially in the United States.

The prevailing view of intelligence during the 19th and early 20th centuries was that women's intellect was inferior to men's (Lewin, 1984a; Shields, 1975a). Lewis Terman, who adapted the Binet-Simon test into the Stanford-Binet, did not believe in the intellectual inferiority of women. He himself had no trouble accepting the results of this test, which revealed no average differences between the intelligence of men and that of women. Indeed, the scores on the early versions of the Stanford-Binet showed that women scored slightly higher than men, but after some of the items that showed differences were eliminated, the average scores for women and girls were equal to those of men and boys (Terman & Merrill, 1937).

This general gender similarity, however, has not yet gotten through to people on an individual level. Significant differences exist between women and men in their estimates of intelligence (Furnham & Gasson, 1998). Both women and men judge women's intelligence as lower than men's. These differences occur when students estimate their own intelligence, when college students estimate their parents' intelligence, and when people judge children's intelligence. The prejudice of the 19th century has lasted into the 21st century.

With the development of the intelligence testing movement came increased attention to the different abilities that might be included within the tests of intelligence. In the test devised by Binet and his colleagues and adapted by Terman into the Stanford-Binet, most test items could be classified as verbal; that is, most questions require the understanding and use of language. Psychologist David Wechsler created an alternative intelligence test that divided abilities into the categories of verbal and performance skills. The verbal subtests require those being tested to provide verbal answers by performing certain tasks: supplying factual knowledge (information), defining vocabulary items (vocabulary), performing basic arithmetic computation (arithmetic), repeating a series of digits (digit span), understanding similarities between objects (similarities), and properly interpreting social conventions (comprehension).

The performance subtests of Wechsler's test require no verbal responses, but instead people respond by performing some action. The performance subtests include arranging pictures into a sensible story (picture arrangement), duplicating designs with blocks (block design), completing pictures that have some missing part (picture completion), assembling cut-up figures of common objects (object assembly), and learning and rapidly applying digit symbol codes (digit symbols) (Gregory, 1987). Figure 4.1 shows samples of the types of items on the Wechsler tests.

Unlike the Stanford-Binet, Wechsler's test shows differences between the scores of men and women, with women scoring higher on the verbal subtests and men scoring higher on the performance subtests. Wechsler's test includes no item adjustment to equate average performance of women and men on the subtests. Although the combined scores on the Wechsler tests do not show gender differences, the subtest scores always have.

Nor are the Wechsler tests the only assessments that have revealed different performance between male and female participants. Eleanor Maccoby and Carol Jacklin's (1974) review of gender differences in intellectual performance likewise found differences on verbal, mathematical, and spatial tasks. More recent research, however, has revealed that the patterns of gender differences in these mental abilities are smaller and more complex than the early reviews suggested.

Part of the complexity comes from the tests used to assess these various mental abilities. The term *mental abilities* is somewhat inaccurate, because most of the assessments have been tests of performance or achievement, such as the Scholastic Aptitude Test (SAT), a test used for college admissions. Such tests do not measure innate abilities, so findings of gender differences do not necessarily mean that women and men are inherently different in these abilities. Rather, differences imply only different levels of current performance, and any generalizations to innate ability are incorrect. Differences in performance might come from different biological endowment, but could also come from social roles, parental encouragement, school courses, or leisure activities.

Verbal Performance

The tasks that researchers have used to study verbal ability include not only the verbal subtests of the Wechsler tests, but also verbal fluency, anagram tests, reading comprehension tests, synonym and antonym tasks, sentence structure assessments, reading readiness tests, and writing assessments as well as the spelling, punctuation, vocabulary, and reading subtests from various achievement tests. Researchers have defined all of these tasks as verbal despite the wide variation in the tasks themselves (see Table 4.1); this variation may be one reason why research on verbal performance has not yielded entirely consistent results.

Verbal Subtests	**Sample Items**
Information	How many wings does a bird have? Who wrote *Paradise Lost*?
Digit span	Repeat from memory a series of digits, such as 3 1 0 6 7 4 2 5, after hearing it once.
General comprehension	What is the advantage of keeping money in a bank? Why is copper often used in electrical wires?
Arithmetic	Three men divided 18 golf balls equally among themselves. How many golf balls did each man receive? If 2 apples cost 15¢, what will be the cost of a dozen apples?
Similarities	In what way are a lion and a tiger alike? In what way are a saw and a hammer alike?
Vocabulary	This test consists simply of asking, "What is a ______?" or "What does ______ mean?" The words cover a wide range of difficulty or familiarity.

Performance Subtests	**Description of Item**
Picture arrangement	Arrange a series of cartoon panels to make a meaningful story.
Picture completion	What is missing from these pictures?
Block design	Copy designs with blocks (as shown at right).
Object assembly	Put together a jigsaw puzzle.
Digit symbol	

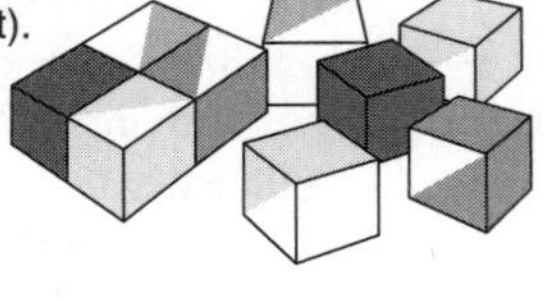

1	2	3	4
X	III	I	O

Fill in the symbols:

3	4	1	3	4	2	1	2

FIGURE 4.1 Sample Test Items Similar to Items on Wechsler's Tests of Intelligence

SOURCE: From Wood & Wood, *The World of Psychology.* Copyright © 1993 by Allyn and Bacon. Reprinted by permission.

Literature reviews (Halpern, 1992, 1994, 1997; Maccoby & Jacklin, 1974) have taken a variety of verbal tasks into account and have come to the conclusion that girls and women have some advantages in verbal performance. These advantages include the rapidity and proficiency with which girls acquire language compared to boys, an advantage that girls maintain throughout elementary school. During middle and high school, the pattern becomes more complex, with girls having certain advantages in spelling, language use, and writing, and boys having an advantage in verbal reasoning (Feingold, 1988). The advantage in writing ability is large and persists throughout college (Willingham, Cole, Lewis, & Leung, 1997).

Meta-analysis is a statistical technique that combines the results from many studies to estimate the size of certain effects, and this technique offers advantages over the literature review approach. Janet Hyde (1981) completed such a meta-analysis of the studies from

TABLE 4.1 Examples of Different Measures of Verbal, Quantitative, and Spatial Abilities

Verbal	Quantitative	Spatial
Vocalizations during infancy	Pointing to a member of a set	Reproducing geometric forms
Visual-motor association	Estimating proportion	Matching geometric shapes
Talking to mother	WISC arithmetic subtest	Reading maps
Verbalization in free play	Digit-processing task	Matching photos for orientation
Parents' reports of speech problems	Digit-symbol subtest of WAIS	Distance perception
Complete sentences	Math achievement	Assembling puzzles
Anagram task	Math reasoning	Rotating shapes
Carrying out simple and complex tasks	Problem solving	Reproducing patterns
Judgment of grammatical sentences	Addition	Disembedding figures
Verbal imitation	Subtraction	Angle matching
Verbal reproduction of story	Arithmetic computation	Maze performance
Reading speed	Number arrangement	Localization of a spatial target
Reading vocabulary	Math subtests for SAT	Discrimination of triangles and mirror-image reversals
Reading comprehension	General Aptitude Test Battery	Distinguishing right from left, east from west, and top from bottom
Errors in similes	ACT	Rod-and-frame task
Spelling		Matching pictures to objects
Punctuation		Seguin Form Board
Synonyms and antonyms		Spatial subtests from: Differential Aptitude Test; General Aptitude Test Battery
Verbal subtests from: Peabody Picture Vocabulary; Illinois Test of Psycholinguistic Ability; Expressive Vocabulary Inventory; WISC		Piaget's water level task
		Making judgments about moving objects
		WISC Block Design

SOURCE: Adapted from *The psychology of sex differences,* by Eleanor Maccoby & Carol Jacklin, 1974, pp. 76–97. Stanford, CA: Stanford University Press.

Maccoby and Jacklin's (1974) literature review and concluded that the gender-related differences in verbal performance are small. About 1% of the difference in verbal ability relates to gender, leaving the other 99% of difference related to other factors.

A later meta-analysis by Janet Hyde and Marcia Linn (1988) examined additional studies, and this analysis indicated that women have the advantage in some verbal abilities, but men have the advantage in others. In addition, this analysis indicated that earlier studies showed gender-related differences, whereas more recent studies have not, indicating a decrease in this gender difference over time.

Mathematical and Quantitative Performance

Most studies with children younger than age 13 show either no gender differences, or certain advantages for girls in mathematical performance, defined as proficiency in arithmetic computation (Fennema, 1980; Hyde, Fennema, & Lamon, 1990). Around age 13, gender differences favoring boys begin to appear in many of the assessments of mathematical performance.

Girls who excel at arithmetic computation do not become women who are poor at such tasks. For example, the numerical ability subtest of the Differential Aptitude Test (DAT) shows no gender differences for students in grades 8 through 12 (Feingold, 1988). Instead, measurements for what constitutes mathematical and quantitative performance change between the middle school and the high school years. Rather than consisting of arithmetic computation, the tests of quantitative ability begin to include tasks that are more abstract, as Table 4.1 shows.

The disadvantage for women is not as large as generally believed. As Hyde's (1981) meta-analysis of quantitative abilities showed, only 1% of the difference in performance was related to gender, which indicates a very small overall gender-related difference in mathematical performance. Later analyses showed no gender difference for a representative group of 12th-grade students (Willingham et al., 1997) and a small, nonsignificant advantage for women in the general population (Hyde, Fennema, & Lamon, 1990). Therefore, these results contradict the stereotype of women's lower performance in mathematics.

Analyzing quantitative abilities into different skills and different ages shows a complex pattern of gender differences (Hyde, Fennema, & Lamon, 1990; Willingham et al., 1997).

GENDERED VOICES

I Was Good at Math and Science

A female chemical engineer said, "I was good at math and science, so my high school counselor suggested engineering. I looked into the various kinds of engineering. I didn't really like physics all that much, so I decided that electrical engineering would not be a good choice. I didn't consider myself very mechanical, so I ruled out mechanical engineering. I liked chemistry, so I thought chemical engineering would be a good choice, but I didn't really know what chemical engineers did. My high school had a cooperative arrangement so I could work for an engineer, but that experience didn't really let me know what the work of a chemical engineer was like. In fact, I didn't really understand the work of chemical engineers until I was a junior in college, and I learned that I didn't find the work all that interesting.

"I went to a technical college that specialized in engineering, and it was definitely male dominated; only about 25% of the students were women. But I never felt any favoritism either for or against the women. Everybody was treated fairly. The courses during the first two years were designed to weed out students, so everybody felt that the curriculum was difficult, but the women did as well as the men, and I never felt that the professors or students showed any bias.

"What was missing on campus were ethnic minorities. The campus was very White. There just weren't any Black students, and there was one Hispanic girl. The geographic area had lots of minorities, but they didn't go into engineering at this school. I noticed the absence of minority students more than the small number of women.

"I didn't feel that being a woman was a factor in school, but it sure was on the job. I didn't necessarily feel discriminated against, but the women were very visible. There were few women, and whatever a woman did stood out. If I did a great job, I got noticed more than a man who did a great job. If I screwed up, I got noticed more than a man who made a mistake. Whatever a woman did—good or bad—came to the attention of everyone."

Girls and women have a small advantage in math computation. Girls' advantage in math concepts changes during high school, and by 12th grade, boys have an advantage (Willingham et al., 1997). During elementary and middle school, no gender difference appears in mathematics problem solving, but boys begin to do better at solving math problems during high school. Changes after high school become more difficult to interpret because individuals who take tests tend to be from selected groups rather than representative of the entire population. Examining mathematics performance for the general population yields no significant difference, but selected groups show substantial differences.

A large gender difference in higher-level mathematics appeared in several studies, showing that, in selected groups, males have a large advantage over females (Benbow & Stanley, 1980, 1983; Willingham & Cole, 1997). Some studies (Benbow & Stanley, 1980, 1983) have shown differences on the SAT mathematics test among intellectually gifted children under 13 years old, before these students had formally studied higher mathematics. These results are confined to mathematically gifted students, but the gender differences represent large gender differences in math performance.

Several tests have consistently revealed gender-related differences in math performance, including the mathematics subtests from the Preliminary Scholastic Aptitude Test (PSAT) and the Scholastic Aptitude Test (SAT), the Graduate Record Examination (GRE) Quantitative section, and the Advanced Placement Program calculus exam (Feingold, 1988; Willingham et al., 1997). The gender-related differences in performance on these tests demonstrate the influence of a progressively selected group of students, more math training for men, characteristics of the test and test format, and greater variability in scores for men. All these factors contribute to the male advantage in math scores in certain groups of students. Table 4.2 summarizes the findings on math performance.

Students who take these tests are a self-selected group taking the test as a part of entrance into college or graduate school. With progressively selected samples, men show dis-

TABLE 4.2 Gender-Related Differences in Mathematics Performance

Group	Advantage	Mathematics Skill
Elementary school students	Girls	Arithmetic computation
Elementary school students	Girls	Math concepts
Middle school students	No difference	Problem solving
13-year-old gifted students	Boys	SAT Mathematics subtest
High school students	Boys	Math concepts
High school students	Boys	Problem solving
College-bound students	Boys	SAT Mathematics subtest
College-bound students	Boys	Advanced Placement Calculus test
Grades 8–12	No difference	Numerical Ability subtest of DAT
Representative group of 12th-grade students	No difference	Math performance
College students	Men	Mathematics subtest of GRE
Adults in general population	Women	Arithmetic computation
Adults in general population	No difference	Math performance

tinct advantages over women in quantitative performance. Part of the reason for the advantage is the selection factor: Men who decide to take these tests have completed more math courses than the women who take the tests, providing a difference in preparation (Fennema, 1980; Willingham et al., 1997). In the late 1990s, that situation changed, and the average number of math classes for girls and boys in high school is now equal. These differences in preparation will probably produce changes in the future.

Test format and bias within the tests are other factors that favor men. Men do better than women on multiple choice format tests and on tests with time limits (Willingham & Cole, 1997), and both characteristics are common to the mathematics tests that show a male advantage. For as long as the Educational Testing Service (ETS) has collected information on gender, the Mathematics section of the SAT has shown substantial differences, even among young women whose math grades are equal to or better than young men's grades (Schiebinger, 1999). In the 1970s, ETS changed the SAT Verbal section in ways that eliminated the female advantage, but it left the Mathematics section with a substantial male advantage. Researchers at ETS (Willingham et al., 1997) have acknowledged that the SAT Mathematics test systematically underpredicts women's college math grades, but they contend that colleges' considering the combination of high school grades and SAT test scores compensates for this problem. The use of SAT scores as the basis for scholarship awards, however, discriminates against women.

Men's performance also varies more on many types of tests, and this trend puts more men in the top (and at the bottom) of the range than women, even when men's and women's average scores are similar. When the averages differ in favor of men, as they do on several mathematics tests, the number of high-scoring men is even higher (Willingham et al., 1997).

The preparation of female and male students in mathematics was a factor that complicated a comparison of the underlying mathematical abilities of women and men. Until the late 1990s, boys took more math classes than girls. That difference highlights an important gender difference: Girls make different choices than boys in their curricula. Regardless of any possible differences in ability, choices made by girls and boys can have far-reaching implications in their lives as men and women. Beginning at age 12, girls start to feel less confident than boys about their ability to do mathematics (Eccles, 1989). As students age, the gender differences in confidence increase, and this trend continues into adulthood. Girls also begin to believe that math is not important to them, starting at the same age that they begin to lose confidence in their ability to do math. Boys, on the other hand, have greater confidence in their mathematical ability and evaluate math as more important to their future. Thus, different perceptions and confidence levels exist as the result of believing that math is a male domain (Kimball, 1995). Both children and parents share this cultural perception, resulting in the differential beliefs concerning boys' and girls' math abilities.

When girls choose to avoid math courses, this decision may stem from their beliefs concerning the likelihood of success and the perceived lack of value of the coursework (Eccles, 1987). The combined lack of confidence and the belief that math is not important to their future form a powerful disincentive for girls during high school, when they have the option to choose elective math courses. Not coincidentally, the differences in math scores begin to appear at this time.

The choice to avoid math courses can have lifelong repercussions (Sells, 1980). The selection of high school mathematics courses can act as a filter, effectively barring female and ethnic minority students from many professions. For example, if a student has only two years of high school math, that student cannot take calculus as a freshman in college, which thereby eliminates some college majors and filters some students out of those majors and out of careers requiring those majors.

A meta-analysis of attitudes toward mathematics showed surprisingly few gender-related differences (Hyde, Fennema, Ryan, Frost, & Hopp, 1990). Contrary to the stereotype, girls and women do not dislike and fear math, but when differences exist, women have more negative attitudes than men. Similar to the findings concerning math performance, the results concerning math attitudes showed no gender differences during elementary school, but some differences emerged during high school. The only dramatic difference revealed by this meta-analysis was in gender stereotyping, with men being most likely to perceive math as a male domain.

Gilah Leder (1990) has proposed that mathematics achievement is influenced by a combination of learner and environmental variables—her model appears in Figure 4.2. In this view, cognitive abilities are only one of the personal factors in achievement; beliefs concerning personal ability and the usefulness of math achievement also contribute to success. Environmental variables also provide a host of factors that can result in differential achievement for boys and girls, including social, home, and school factors.

Social factors in Leder's model include cultural expectations, such as the stereotyping of math as a male domain (Hyde, Fennema, Ryan, Frost, & Hopp, 1990), media emphasis on differences, and peer encouragement for math-related activities. Home factors include family socioeconomic status as well as parental encouragement (or lack of such encouragement) and sibling behavior related to math. School-related factors include teachers' attitudes and behavior, organization of instruction, methods of assessment, and acceptance by peers. Although Leder constructed this model to explain mathematics achievement, the combination of factors could apply to all achievement situations.

Chapter 11 discusses the gender bias that occurs in schools and classrooms. Teachers interact with female and male students in different ways, giving boys more instruction and encouragement than they give girls. These differences are large and should produce differences in achievement:

> *When one considers that females endure remarks from teachers or texts indicating that mathematics is not a female domain, are involved in far fewer interactions with their teachers involving mathematics, are rarely asked high-cognitive-level questions in mathematics, are encouraged to be dependent rather than independent thinkers, spend more time helping their peers and not getting helped in return, and are often not placed in groups that are appropriate to their level, it is amazing that the gap [in mathematics achievement] is not considerably larger. (Koehler, 1990, p. 145)*

In summary, gender-related differences in mathematics performance do not exist in the general population, but differences do appear in selected groups. Among students, girls and boys do not differ in mathematics performance until junior high school. At this time, boys begin to show higher average levels of math performance and confidence, and these differences persist throughout adulthood. Studies of gifted children have shown that

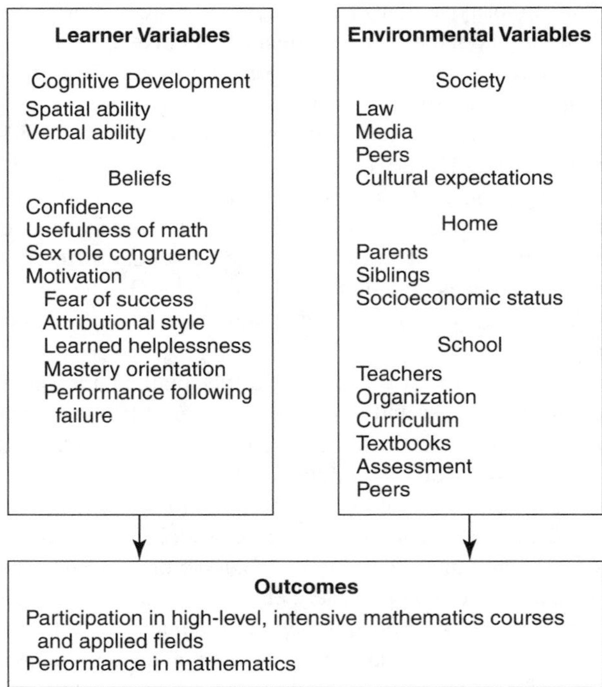

FIGURE 4.2 Variables Studied in Relation to Gender Differences in Mathematics

SOURCE: Reprinted by permission of the publisher from Fennema, Elizabeth & Leder, Gilah, *Mathematics and Gender* (New York: Teachers College Press, © 1990 by Teachers College, Columbia University. All rights reserved.), p. 15.

extraordinary mathematics performance is much more common among boys than girls, although this level of ability is rare even in boys. Differences exist in the number of math courses completed, with boys choosing to enroll in and complete more math courses than girls. Such choices may limit career options. Differences in mathematics performance and attitudes toward mathematics show small gender differences, despite the stereotype that girls and women dislike math and do poorly in the subject. This stereotype may be the underlying basis for the biased treatment, regarding mathematical ability, that girls and women receive from their peers, parents, and teachers.

Spatial Performance

Although the definition of what constitutes spatial ability has varied from study to study (Caplan & Caplan, 1994; Caplan, MacPherson, & Tobin, 1985), this variation has not hindered many people from accepting the notion that men are better at these tasks than women.

Variation has existed in the definitions of verbal ability and quantitative ability, but researchers have defined spatial ability in a wider variety of ways. Table 4.1 includes some of these definitions. Any of these tasks represents a reasonable way to measure the concept of spatial abilities, but they vary sufficiently to yield results that may not be consistent from study to study.

Researchers disagree on the number of spatial abilities that exist. One group (Linn & Petersen, 1986) placed spatial tasks into three groups, but another (Voyer, Voyer, & Bryden, 1995) contended that three categories were too few to capture the complexity of spatial abilities. Another investigator (Stumpf, 1993) argued that there are hundreds of tests of spatial ability that can be classified into 16 groups. This variety of tests illustrates the many ways that researchers have defined and measured spatial ability and substantiates the claim that spatial ability is far from unitary. The complexity of findings relates to this variety of measurement.

The three-category approach (Linn & Petersen, 1986) provides a convenient framework for summarizing (although possibly not for providing a full picture of) these spatial abilities. The three categories include spatial perception, mental rotation, and spatial visualization. **Spatial perception** includes the ability to identify and locate the horizontal or vertical planes in the presence of distracting information. Examples of measures of spatial perception are the rod-and-frame task and Piaget's water-level task, both shown in Figure 4.3. These tasks usually show gender-related differences, with boys and men outperforming girls and women. The magnitude of this difference is small during childhood and adolescence, but fairly large for adults.

Mental rotation includes the ability to visualize objects as they would appear if rotated in space. An example of a measure of this type of ability also appears in Figure 4.3. The gender-related difference for this spatial ability is large, with boys and men scoring substantially higher than girls and women on speed and accuracy of mentally rotating objects (Halpern, 1992; Voyer et al., 1995).

Spatial visualization refers to the ability to process spatial information so as to understand the relationship between objects in space, such as the ability to see a figure embedded in other figures (also shown in Figure 4.3), find hidden figures in a drawing or picture, or imagine the shape produced when a folded piece of paper is cut and then unfolded. Gender differences do not always appear on measures of these tasks. When such differences appear, they are small, and men have this small advantage.

A fourth category of spatial ability is called **spatiotemporal ability** (Halpern, 1992). This ability involves judgments about moving objects in space, such as predicting when a moving object will arrive at a target. The limited research on this ability indicates that men do better than women on such tasks, but more recent research (Law, Pellegrino, & Hunt, 1993) has shown that prior experience was a factor in performance on this type of task. Feedback concerning performance improved the performance of both men and women. Thus, any advantage that boys or men show might be due to their experience with such tasks.

An additional complication in assessing gender differences in spatial ability comes from the possibility that some tasks labeled "spatial" may not constitute clear measures of spatial abilities. Instead, some of these tasks or the situations in which they are measured may include other factors. For example, the rod-and-frame task may include situational factors that affect performance (Sherman, 1978). This testing typically occurs in a darkened room, with a male experimenter testing participants. Perhaps the testing situation may contribute to the

Mental rotation
Which figure on the right is identical to the figure in the box?

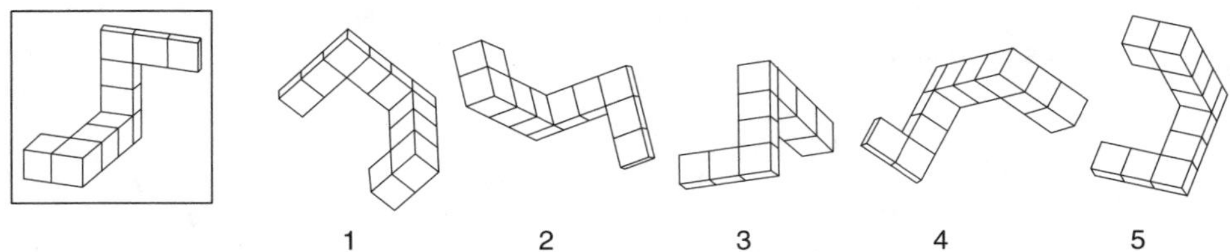

Piaget's water-level problem
This glass is half filled with water. Draw a line across the glass to indicate the top of the water line.

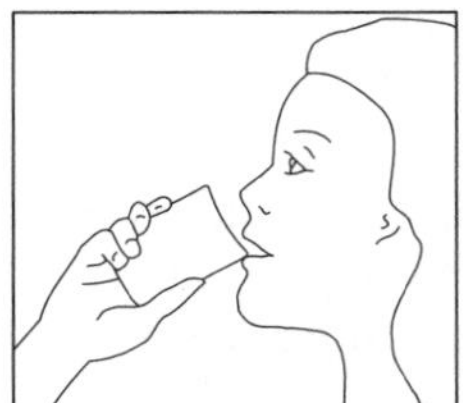

Rod-and-frame test
Ignore the orientation of the frame and adjust the position of the rod so that it is vertical.

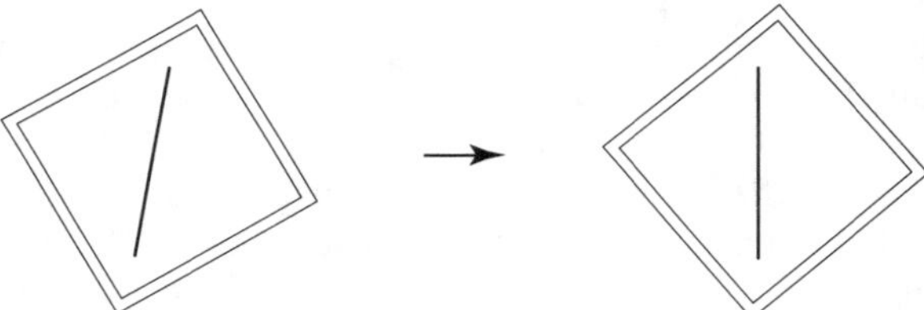

Disembedding
Find the simple figure on the left embedded in one of the four more complex figures on the right.

FIGURE 4.3 Spatial Tasks Favoring Men

gender differences—female participants may feel uncomfortable in this situation and be less likely to persist in asking the male experimenter to continue to adjust the rod. Thus, lack of assertiveness and uneasiness with the testing situation may contribute to the gender differences that often appear on this measure of spatial ability.

The male advantage on the rod-and-frame task disappeared when a human figure replaced the rod and the task was presented as a measure of empathy (Naditch, in Caplan et al., 1985). In this situation, women outperformed men. The task still involved the same spatial factors as the original task—namely, judging relative position in space—but the resulting gender difference was reversed.

The instructions accompanying a spatial task can influence men's and women's performance on one spatial memory and one mental rotation task (Sharps, Price, & Williams, 1994; Sharps, Welton, & Price, 1993). When instructions emphasized the spatial nature of a task, women's performance decreased compared to their performance when instructions de-emphasized the spatial nature of the tasks. Women's (but not men's) performance changed in relation to the instructions. These studies demonstrate the importance of expectation and context: Although the tasks remained the same, performance varied in stereotypical ways with different sets of instructions.

Several research findings provide evidence against a simple conclusion for a male advantage on spatial tasks. A major complication comes from the finding that women show an advantage on some spatial tasks (Kimura, 1992; Montello, Lovelace, Golledge, & Self, 1999). Women tend to do better on tasks of perceptual speed in which people must rapidly identify matching items. Women also outperform men on tasks in which people must remember the placement of a series of objects. Examples of these tasks appear in Figure 4.4. An additional complication comes from the finding that gender differences appear in some age groups but not in others, the differences are subject to change with variations in testing procedure, and gender differences in some spatial abilities seem to be decreasing (Voyer et al., 1995). In addition, these differences do not apply to all cultures. Considering studies from nine different nations (Feingold, 1994), men showed a slight advantage overall, but in some cultures, these differences do not exist.

These various findings raise the question, Do gender differences in spatial abilities really exist? Of the many spatial abilities, men show an advantage in some, and women show an advantage in others. Men in the United States produce reliably better scores than women in spatial perception, such as Piaget's water-level task, and in mental rotation, but training decreases this difference (see "According to the Media/According to the Research").

The embedded figures task has also yielded complex results for gender and ethnic background, suggesting that men have no clear advantage for this measure of spatial ability. Women's advantage in spatial abilities appears on measures of perceptual speed and on memory for the placement of objects. Therefore, of the gender differences in spatial abilities that exist, a number favor men, a few favor women, and some vary by gender, culture, context, expectation, or some combinations thereof.

Other Mental Abilities

Verbal, mathematical, and spatial abilities are important and have been the subjects of extensive research, but other mental abilities exist. Memory, creativity, musical ability, and nonverbal communication are all abilities that have been the focus of research, but within this research, gender has not been the emphasis; likewise, the research has failed to show gender-related differences.

A consideration of these other mental abilities is important for putting comparisons concerning gender-related cognitive abilities in perspective, because these other abilities

ACCORDING TO THE MEDIA...

Video Games Are for Boys

Popular video games are oriented to boys. Both arcade games and home video games contain primarily male characters, lots of action and violence, and games involving plots attractive to boys. Indeed, the video market has been dominated by games for boys, and video games oriented to girls are a more recent development (Goodale, 1999).

The most common portrayal of women in video games consists of nothing—literally. Over 40% of popular video games have no female characters, including 30% of videos that contained human characters (Dietz, 1998). When women appear in video games, sometimes they are helpless and in need of rescuing; sometimes they are evil and in need of conquering. Female characters also appear in the background as supporters of male characters. Occasionally female characters get to be heroes. Regardless of their role, they are often large-breasted and provocatively dressed.

The amount of violence in video games is an area of concern (Dietz, 1998). Early video games tended to depict spaceships and aliens, but human or humanlike characters are now more common. Thus, players have repeated exposure to chasing and doing violence to both male and female characters. In addition, 21% of the game included violence directed specifically toward women. These games give players the opportunity to act within a situation in which women are the designated targets of video violence.

The combination of themes for boys, few female characters, and fewer attractive, powerful female characters makes video games more attractive to boys than to girls. The portrayals of women as victims, targets, or sex objects puts girls in the position of seeing unflattering depictions of female characters, choosing from the limited range of games for girls, or avoiding video games altogether.

have shown that such differences are unusual. As Diane Halpern (1992) pointed out, "It is important to note that the number of areas in which sex differences are even moderate in size is small. Males and females are overwhelmingly alike in their cognitive abilities" (p. 96).

Memory can reflect either verbal or spatial abilities, depending on the material learned and remembered. The majority of tasks that psychologists have studied fall into the category of verbal learning and memory. According to Maccoby and Jacklin's (1974) review of research in this area, few gender-related differences exist in the various types of learning and memory. When studies show differences, girls and women have a small advantage. Subsequent research has indicated similar findings: No gender-related differences exist (Savage & Gouvier, 1992), or only a small female advantage exists for learning verbal material (McGuiness, Olson, & Chapman, 1990).

Women's small advantage in verbal abilities and men's small advantage in spatial abilities lead to the prediction of differential memory performance in these areas. Do these differences hold true, as Brenda's and John's conversation (Monroe, 1995) in the chapter headline suggests? Does men's advantage in spatial orientation lead them to use maps to navigate, whereas women are more inclined to use landmarks?

Studies of route learning have offered some support for the different strategies commented on by John and Brenda. Research shows that women and men may, indeed, use different strategies to navigate (Lawton, 1994; Montello et al., 1999; Schmitz, 1999). As Brenda did, women seem more likely to report that they used the strategy of learning landmarks on a route; men were more likely to report that they used a spatial orientation strat-

ACCORDING TO THE RESEARCH...

Video Games Can Improve Spatial Skills

Video games may be oriented toward and played mostly by boys, but research indicates that both girls and boys can improve their performance on spatial tasks by playing video games. In a study with 10- and 11-year-olds (Subrahmanyam & Greenfield, 1994), boys had more experience in video games and showed better performance on a spatial task, but children who played a video game improved on the spatial task more than children who played a vocabulary game. A study with college students (Okagaki & Frensch, 1994) showed that playing a video game (Tetris) improved performance on mental rotation and spatial visualization tests. The improvements in both studies applied to both genders. These results suggest that playing video games may be a way to improve spatial skills.

Other research also suggests that experience is an important factor in spatial skills, and boys tend to gain more experience in these skills than girls. A meta-analysis (Baenninger & Newcombe, 1989) on the role of experience in spatial test performance confirmed the advantages to both men and women of experience in such tasks. Two studies (Liben & Golbeck, 1984; Vasta, Knott, & Gaze, 1996) reported on two different training procedures that erased the gender differences in performance on Piaget's water-level task.

Therefore, the design and marketing of video games for boys puts girls at a double disadvantage. By appealing to boys, these games are unattractive to many girls, keeping girls away from this type of activity, and girls tend to do more poorly on spatial tasks. The studies that demonstrated improvement in spatial skills used the traditional, male-oriented games, and the benefits of games oriented toward girls remains to be established. Thus, boys have greater incentive to participate in activities that boost skills on which they already have higher performance, whereas girls have lower motivation to play video games that could improve their spatial skills.

egy, as John did. These strategies are not unique with women or men, and some men and women use the strategy more typical of the other gender. In one study (Schmitz, 1999), a combination of the two strategies proved more effective in terms of speed and number of errors than either. Some research (Galea & Kimura, 1993) has found that men made fewer errors in finding their way, but other studies (Crook, Youngjohn, & Larrabee, 1993; Montello et al., 1999) showed gender difference too small to be of any practical consequences. That is, men's advantage in memorizing spatial information may not give them much advantage over women in getting around in the world, especially if the landmarks stay the same. Therefore, Brenda and John will both find the Emporium with comparable ease.

Some of the gender-related differences in memory seem more strongly related to the gender-stereotypical nature of the task than to the gender of the learner. For example, when women and men were asked to memorize a shopping list and directions to a particular place, the differences were in a predictable direction (Herrmann, Crawford, & Holdsworth, 1992). Women were better than men at memorizing the shopping list, and men were better than women at memorizing the directions. Furthermore, the labeling of the task influenced women's and men's memories. When people heard that the shopping list pertained to groceries, women showed an advantage, but when the same list was described as pertaining to hardware, men's memories were better. Similar results appeared in a study involving a memory test of high school students (Halpern, 1985). The procedure involved varying the name of the protagonist in the story and testing for story recall. The participants remembered more about the same-gender than the other-gender protagonist. Furthermore, participants tended to remember the other-gender protagonist as stereotypical, whereas their memory for the

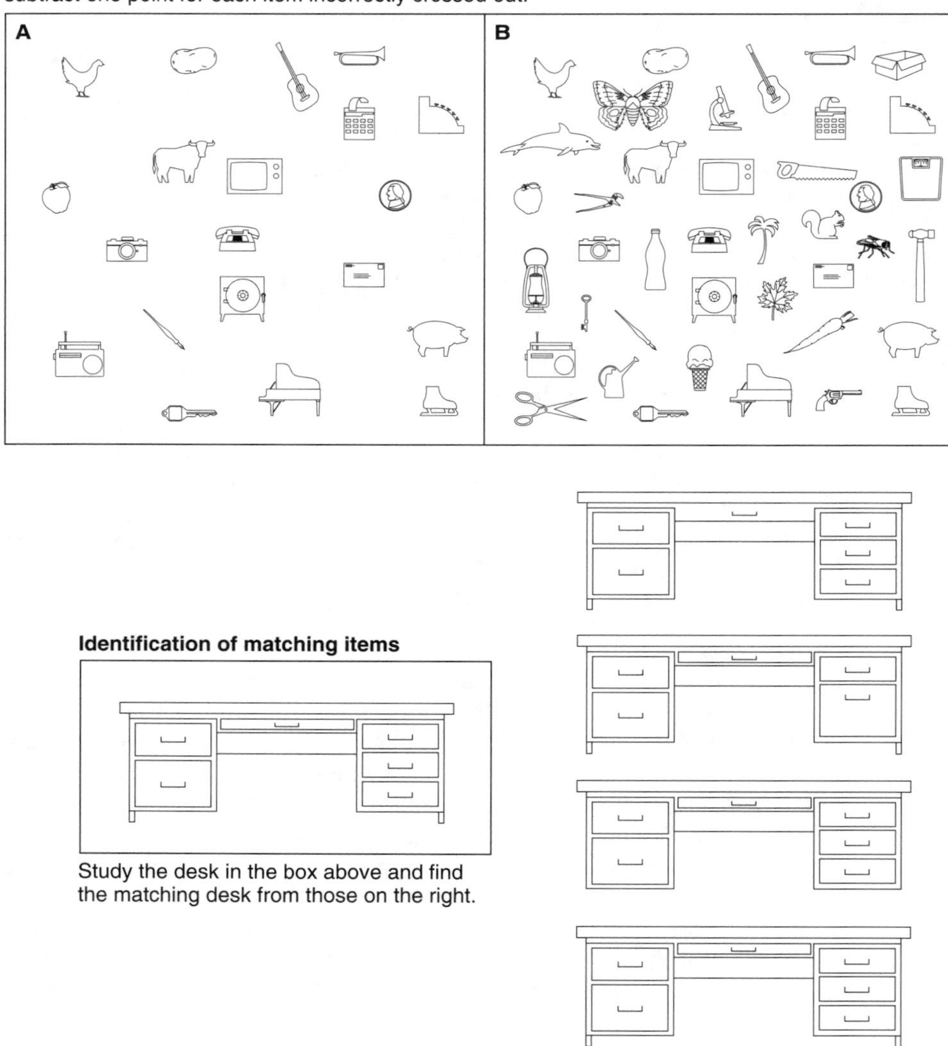

Study the objects in group **A** for one minute and cover it up. Then look at group **B** and put an X through the figures not in the original array. Score one point for each item correctly crossed out, and subtract one point for each item incorrectly crossed out.
A
B
Identification of matching items
Study the desk in the box above and find the matching desk from those on the right.

FIGURE 4.4 Spatial Tasks Favoring Women

same-gender protagonist was more accurate. Thus, memory may depend on factors other than ability, with men and women performing according to their attention, interests, and stereotypes.

Creativity is a term that researchers have defined in a variety of ways, leading to a great diversity of findings. Studies of kindergarten and children in 1st grade (Lewis & Houtz, 1986), children in grades 4 through 8 (Rejskind, Rapagna, & Gold, 1992), and college students

GENDERED VOICES

It's Not Something on the Y Chromosome

"I don't think that it's something on the Y chromosome," a 13-year-old girl said, referring to the ability to play percussion. "But some boys act like it is. The boys in the school band are used to me because I've played percussion all through junior high school with them, but when I go to competitions, the boys act like I shouldn't be playing percussion. Almost like it's an insult that a girl should be playing."

She explained that lots of girls play in the school band. There is generally no prejudice against girls who are musicians, but the band is gender segregated by musical instrument. The instruments toward the front of the band are more "feminine," such as violins, clarinets, and cellos. The instruments toward the back are more "masculine," such as tubas and the percussion instruments: "There are lots more girls toward the front of the band, and the boys dominate the back.

"At the all-city band competition, it was especially bad. The boys who played percussion were especially obnoxious, acting like I shouldn't be trying. They acted like it was their right as boys to be able to play drums or other percussion—like there was something on the Y chromosome that gave them the gift. Well, I guess they were really surprised when I won."

(Goldsmith & Matherly, 1988) have failed to show gender-related differences in creative thinking. In addition, a musical expert rated the compositions of female and male composers equal in possessing musical creativity (Hassler, Nieschlag, & de la Motte, 1990).

When researchers have defined creativity in terms of achievement, men have shown higher levels of creativity. This advantage, however, may not be due to greater creative ability but rather to access to training, parental and societal encouragement, and limited acceptance of women in creative fields. The greater number of prominent musicians who are men is not due to greater musical ability of boys and men; gender differences in tests of musical ability show minimal differences (Halpern, 1992).

The discrepancy between the numbers of male and female visual artists and musicians may be due to encouragement rather than talent (Piirto, 1991). Creatively gifted boys and girls are very similar in personality but differ in level of commitment to their field. The differences in creative accomplishments come from lesser commitment on the part of girls and women, and commitment comes from encouragement. Gifted girls should be encouraged to devote themselves to their talents in the same ways that boys are encouraged.

Nonverbal communication includes a variety of behaviors related to conveying and receiving information through gestures, body position, and facial expressions. According to stereotype, women are able to decipher nonverbal cues better than men. Indeed, women are believed to have "intuition"—the ability to understand social situations, people's motives, feelings, and wishes, all without being told. Sara Snodgrass (1985, 1992) has investigated this facet of gender-related behavior and has found that no gender differences exist in the ability to read such cues. Snodgrass found, instead, that people in subordinate positions are better at reading the nonverbal behaviors of those in dominant positions. That is, women's intuition is really the intuition of subordinate status and is shared by those for whom advantage rests in understanding small nuances in the behavior of those in charge.

Although the gender differences are small in verbal, mathematical, and spatial abilities, differences do not exist in other cognitive abilities such as memory, creativity, musical ability, and nonverbal communication. The studies that have revealed gender-related differences in performance in these areas have shown that the differences come from social stereotypes and expectations rather than from ability.

Source of the Differences

If social stereotypes and expectations shape performance on aptitude and achievement tests, then are these factors the source of differences between men and women? Does biology play no role in the gender differences in cognitive performance? The possibility that cognitive gender differences can be traced to biology appeals to many people, possibly because it offers a simple answer to many complex questions. The tendency to resort to biological essentialism is strong, both in the media and among the general population. This appeal has prompted theories and research.

Biological Evidence for Gender Differences in Mental Abilities

Several theories have proposed a biological basis for gender differences in cognitive abilities. These theories concentrate on differences between the cerebral hemispheres of the brain. One of these theories, by Norman Geschwind and Albert Galaburda (1987), emphasizes the role of prenatal testosterone exposure in cerebral lateralization and the effects on subsequent mental abilities. (Chapter 3 discussed the lateralization of mental abilities.) This theory hypothesizes that boys and men will have better spatial abilities than girls and women because of the pattern of prenatal growth of the right hemisphere. The theory also predicts that this pattern of prenatal development will result in better verbal abilities for girls and women than for boys and men. Geschwind and Galaburda's theory is complex and difficult to test (McManus & Bryden, 1991), but several lines of evidence fail to support their theory.

The Geschwind and Galaburda theory assumes a straightforward division of verbal and spatial tasks lateralized into the left and right hemispheres for both women and men. Some research suggests that men have more lateralized brains than women, which does not fit with this theory. In addition, the theory predicts that gender differences will correspond in a simple way to tasks controlled by the left and right hemispheres, which is not what research has shown. The argument that lateralization improves mental abilities is not supported by the evidence: Men have an advantage in some spatial abilities, but are at some disadvantage in other spatial abilities and in some verbal tasks. If strong lateralization were an advantage, then it would be an advantage for both types of abilities (Springer & Deutsch, 1998). Likewise, if less lateralization were an advantage, it would extend to spatial as well as verbal abilities. Thus, the evidence shows that differences in brain organization at the level of the cerebral hemispheres do not coincide with gender differences in mental abilities.

Another biologically based view has emphasized the role of evolution in gender differences in lateralization (Kimura, 1992; Levy, 1969). Following this explanation, different role demands of men and women in the hunter–gatherer societies of prehistory posed different task demands and resulted in different brain organization. Although the logic of these stories may be appealing, these speculations are impossible to confirm or disconfirm—those early societies are gone and can no longer be observed. Also, alternative stories make as much sense. For example, more remote periods in prehistory when prehumans were tree dwellers would present similar selection pressures for spatial abilities (Benderly, 1987). Such abilities would have been very important for both sexes. For example, poor spatial abilities would result in falling out of trees, which would not be conducive to survival and reproduction. Despite the validity of an evolutionary view, differential evolutionary pressures as a theory to explain cognitive differences has many possible versions, and it is impossible to confirm any of these versions.

Despite the lack of evidence that brain structure differences produce gender differences in mental abilities, other possibilities exist for a biological basis for gender differences in cognitive tasks. These possibilities center around functional differences in the brains of women and men, and recent technology developments have opened new possibilities for this study. Positron emission tomography (PET) and functional magnetic resonance imaging (FMRI) can detect metabolic changes in the brain that accompany heightened neural activity (Raichle, 1994). Although these techniques are so new that the findings have not yet yielded a complete picture, researchers have applied them to study images of the brain as it responds to various types of stimuli and tasks.

The studies usually test fairly small samples of participants and compare the average response of female and male brains. Although some of the studies have found average differences, they have also found that some brains behave more like those for the other gender—not all male brains react in ways that are typical for men, and not all female brains show the responses of the average woman. Individual variation may be as important as gender in understanding differences in brain functioning, and this conclusion is a repeated theme from the research results on performance tests. Individual differences are more important than gender differences in understanding variations in mental abilities.

For example, one research project (Shaywitz et al., 1995) studied women and men by using FMRI as the two groups performed three tasks involving language sounds. The results showed that men used their left cerebral hemisphere, whereas women used both hemispheres, in performing a rhyming task. No gender differences appeared in brain activation for the two other tasks, nor were the patterns of activation divided neatly by gender. Over 40% of the women in the study exhibited the activation pattern more typical of the men. Furthermore, the pattern of brain functioning may be of little or no practical significance because the male and female participants performed comparably. That is, the difference in patterns of brain activation made no behavioral difference. As brain researcher Ruben Gur and his colleagues (1995, p. 531) commented, "the brains of men and women are fundamentally more similar than different."

The search for a biological basis for differences in cognitive performance remains attractive to many, but the evidence is weak. Under some circumstances, men's and women's brains (on the average) function differently. The differences, however, are not clear-cut, with cases of both female and male brains functioning in ways more typical of the other gender. Several of the studies indicate differences in function, but no difference in performance. Men's and women's brains may function differently while trying to solve verbal or mathematical problems, but if their performance is the same, then the differences have no practical importance.

Evidence for Other Sources of Gender Differences

If a cognitive ability has a large biological component, rapid changes or variations across cultures would not occur. However, cognitive abilities vary both over time and culture, pointing to social factors as the source of gender differences in cognitive abilities. For example, some research indicates that changes have occurred over time in the results of cognitive ability tests. Studying the performance of girls and boys on the Differential Aptitude Tests (DAT) administered between 1947 and 1983 revealed that the gender differences that appeared on several subtests of these tests have changed over the years (Feingold, 1988). The gender differences declined significantly from 1947 to 1980 and had disappeared completely on one verbal subtest. Boys' advantage decreased on the DAT subtests of Mechanical Reasoning and Space Relations. Thus, these gender-related cognitive differences seem to be disappearing.

Studies from a variety of cultures demonstrate that the patterns of gender difference found in the United States do not apply to men and women in other cultures (Feingold, 1994; see also the "Considering Diversity" section at the end of this chapter). Alan Feingold's (1994) cross-cultural analysis indicated that women and men vary in performance on verbal ability tests, but these variations show no gender-related pattern. These findings mirror the recent research on U.S. samples, which show few gender differences in most verbal abilities. The analysis for mathematical and spatial abilities, however, differed from those for U.S. samples: The variability of performance did not show the advantages for men that have appeared in the United States. Thus, the patterns of performance on these cognitive abilities differ in other cultures: "The biology of femaleness and maleness is the same the world over, yet the gender differences that are found in cognition are not universal" (Halpern, 1995, p. 84).

Jacquelynne Eccles (1987) proposed an explanation of gender differences in math achievement; an extension of this model might also explain other gender differences in cognitive performance. Her model of achievement focused on choices and their link to expectancies for success and to the values individuals place on the available options. She attempted to anchor the choices an individual makes in the cultural setting, by examining gender roles and different parental and social pressures on boys and girls when they decide to take a course or choose a college major. Therefore, Eccles's model emphasized the social factors that influence achievement rather than the biological factors that might influence cognitive abilities.

Eccles stressed the importance of choices for educational and vocational achievement and how women and men make different choices. She reviewed research that found that women and men have different expectancies for success, as well as different evaluations of difficulty and of the personal relevance of mathematics to future success. Eccles argued that women's lower math achievement fits into this framework. Women choose to take fewer math courses because they believe that they may not succeed in the courses, that they will have to work hard to do well, and that math achievement is not as important for them. Eccles thus presented a theory and additional evidence that could explain why men and women differ in achievement.

Eccles's model emphasizes social context, but it does not exclude the possibility that biological factors contribute to ability and performance. Not only do biological factors influence behavior, but behavior influences biology, forming a complex interaction of these factors (Halpern, 1997). No resolution of the nature–nurture controversy is possible in the case of cognitive gender differences because it is impossible to disentangle these factors. Furthermore, concentrating on the source of gender differences in cognitive abilities obscures the more important consideration: Such differences are small and may have few practical consequences, whereas the choices that women and men make differ a great deal and have enormous practical consequences.

Implications of Gender-Related Differences

As reviewed in previous sections of this chapter, gender-related differences in mental abilities are small and may be decreasing in the areas in which they do exist. These small differences should mean equally small differences in scholastic and occupational achievement for which these abilities are required, as well as small differences in confidence in mental abilities. Instead, there are large differences in the choices that men and women make concerning careers and in their confidence in their abilities. These choices and levels of confidence may be mediated through social beliefs about the abilities of men and women. People's behavior may be more closely related to their images of what men and women can do than to what women and men actually do.

Misunderstandings of gender research have contributed to these images. Hyde (1981) has discussed the ways in which research on gender-related cognitive differences has led to erroneous beliefs about these abilities. Her meta-analyses have been important in demonstrating that the magnitude of these differences is small and possibly decreasing. These small differences mean that a factor, such as gender, that accounts for 1% of the variance in an ability leaves 99% of the difference in that ability due to other factors. Figure 4.5 presents two distributions of scores that have a 99% overlap and a 1% difference. This figure shows how similar the two distributions are. If 1% of the variance in verbal ability is due to gender, we would not know much about any specific person's verbal ability by knowing that person's gender, because too much variation in verbal ability would be due to other factors.

Assumptions about the person's verbal ability would be unfounded if they were based on the knowledge that the person was a woman, because many men have verbal abilities that equal or exceed most women's verbal abilities. Stereotypes based on gender differences in these cognitive abilities will lead to incorrect conclusions about the abilities of men and women, because women and men vary more from one person to another than from one gender to another. With only a small percentage of the variance attributable to gender, individual differences overwhelm any gender difference.

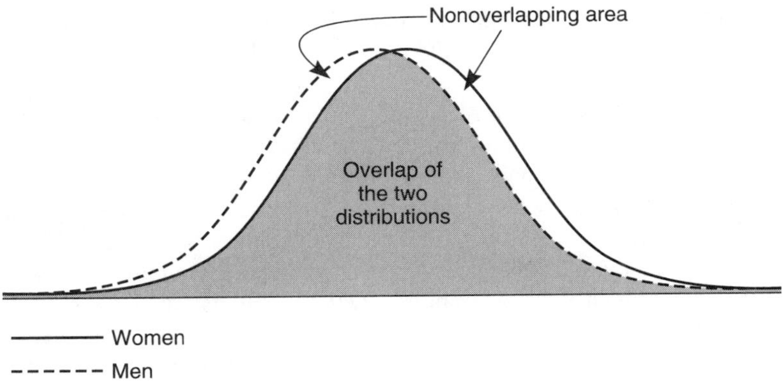

FIGURE 4.5 An Example of Two Distributions with 99% Overlap

NOTE: This distribution represents differences similar to those for verbal ability in men and women.

Hyde (1981) also contended that the term *well-established* should be distinguished from *large*. (At this point, using the term well-established to describe cognitive gender differences may be inaccurate, but this usage persists.) Hyde suggested that people tend to consider the two terms as similar, but in this case they are not the same. When researchers conclude that a difference is well-established, that conclusion does not mean that the difference is also large, merely that it has been found in several studies. Hyde criticized those psychology textbooks that include information about women's advantage in verbal abilities and men's advantage in quantitative and spatial abilities. Although many studies have found these small differences (making them well-established), such differences are by no means large. Describing the differences as well-established in texts and in the media can lead people to misunderstand their own abilities as well as the abilities of others.

Even small differences can have larger implications, as one computer simulation study (Martel, Lane, & Emrich, 1996) showed. Researchers created an organization with eight levels. A computer algorithm then simulated promotion based on ability within this hypothetical organization, with a 5% and a 1% difference in ability (with women having less ability than men). With an initially equal number of women and men in the hypothetical work force, the simulation resulted in 35% of the top-level jobs going to women (for the 1% deficit). When women were given a 5% deficit in ability, they ended up in 29% of the top-level positions.

Does this simulation mirror workplace situations? Probably not. Few specific abilities show as much as a 5% difference between women and men. Mental rotation ability shows about a 9% difference between men and women, which is enough to make a sizable difference for any occupation that relies entirely on mental rotation. However, none does. Indeed, no occupation relies entirely on one mental ability, and social abilities also contribute to workplace success. The simulation also varied from actual employment situations in another respect: An equal number of men and women were hired, which is true of almost no occupation. The selection factors begin years prior to employment and result in a much greater gender inequality in most occupations. For example, the gender gap in engineering has been much larger than the difference in the simulation analysis (Martel et al., 1996). Until the 1970s, about 1% of students receiving engineering degrees were women, and that percentage rose to around 11% in the late 1990s (U.S. Bureau of the Census, 1999). This magnitude of difference would not occur on the basis of the gender differences in mental abilities.

The size of the differences in gender-related cognitive ability is sufficiently small to have limited implications for men's and women's lives, yet people's beliefs allow these small differences to have a large impact. When parents, teachers, and children come to accept that boys are better at math than girls, this acceptance of a gender-related difference leads to differential expectations for math achievement. These expectations influence the level of encouragement that teachers and parents give children, thus affecting how girls and boys feel about their own abilities. These feelings affect the choices that girls and boys make concerning their elective math courses, and these choices have lifelong consequences for careers as well as attitudes toward the subject. Although the gender-related differences in cognitive abilities are small, people throughout society largely accept these differences, which creates additional divergence.

In summary, meta-analysis has shown that the magnitude of gender differences is small for verbal, quantitative, and spatial abilities. Gender differences in these three areas account for between 1% and 5% of the differences, too small a difference to explain or predict most variation from person to person. The gender stereotyping of cognitive domains has magnified small differences, thus perpetuating the belief that gender-related differences exist and that there are large differences in the abilities of women and men.

Considering Diversity

Most of the studies on cognitive abilities have focused on European Americans in the United States, and many imagine that these results apply to other groups. Cross-cultural research indicates otherwise. Studies on various ethnic groups in the United States and research in other countries have indicated that the pattern of cognitive gender differences varies.

Anneliese Pontius (1997) reported on her program of cross-cultural research on gender differences in spatial perception. One result from the Auca Indians, a Stone Age culture living in the Amazon basin, revealed a very different pattern of gender differences in spatial performance from testings in the United States. In this culture, the women outperform the men in block design tasks in which U.S. men have an advantage over women. Her analysis of boys and girls in northwestern Pakistan revealed no gender differences in the spatial abilities she measured. A study with Norwegian sixth-grade students (Manger & Eikeland, 1998) also failed to reveal gender differences in spatial visualization. Therefore, a variety of cultures fail to show the gender differences typical of the United States.

An analysis of various ethnic groups in the United States showed a different pattern of findings than the one obtained by studying European Americans. Ethnic background, gender, and mathematical ability were shown to interact when testing Hispanic American, African American, and European American adolescents enrolled in New York schools (Schratz, 1978). Unlike much previous research, the Hispanic American girls showed better mathematical performance than Hispanic American boys in this study, and African American girls showed the same trend. In contrast, the scores for European American adolescents showed much the same pattern as previous research; that is, boys scored higher than girls.

Spatial ability was also a component of this study (Schratz, 1978), in which spatial ability was measured with the embedded figures task. No difference appeared for preadolescent participants, but there was an interaction between gender and ethnic group for adolescents. These results were comparable to others found for mathematics performance. That is, for adolescent Hispanic Americans and African Americans, the girls did better than the boys, whereas the European American boys did better than the European American girls. However, on this measure of spatial ability, the Hispanic American girls did better than *any other group.*

A cross-cultural analysis of verbal, mathematical, and spatial abilities failed to find in other cultures the pattern of results that appeared in U.S. samples (Feingold, 1994). In some cultures, men score higher in math ability, but in others, women do. The same variability appeared for spatial abilities. In summarizing the meta-analytic studies of mathematical abilities, Janet Hyde (1994) discussed analyses of different ethnic groups in the United States. The gender difference was largest for Whites, showing a small advantage for men. For African Americans, Hispanic Americans, and Asian Americans, no differences appeared. She concluded, "Perhaps the traditional belief of psychologists that men do better at math tests is a result of reliance on mostly White samples in research" (Hyde, 1994, p. 457). Therefore, the patterns discovered by U.S. researchers may be a result based on inadequate comparisons rather than universal advantage.

Summary

The assessment of mental abilities has a long history in psychology, dating from the development of the intelligence test. The Stanford-Binet, an early intelligence test, showed no gender differences, but the Wechsler tests revealed advantages on verbal tasks for women and girls and advantages in performance tasks for men and boys. In addition, some types of mathematics ability tests have shown an advantage for boys and men, starting at junior high school age and persisting into adulthood. These gender differences have become well accepted, but their acceptance may be far greater than their magnitude warrants.

In addition, the verbal advantage that was once associated with women is not only small but also disappearing, except for performance on writing tasks. Differences in some types of mathematics performance continue, but these differences are not clearly attributable to differences in innate ability and may be attributable to differences in the number of math courses completed, the selection of people who take the test, test construction factors, and higher male variability in performance.

Examining the gender differences in spatial ability is even more complex than for either verbal or mathematical abilities because researchers have defined and measured spatial ability in many ways. Men show an advantage in performing spatial visualization and mental rotation tasks and an occasional advantage on spatial perception tasks, but women show advantages on tasks of perceptual speed and memory for placement of objects. Therefore, any conclusion about a male advantage in spatial ability is overly simplistic.

Other cognitive abilities show no gender-related differences. These abilities include learning and memory, creativity, musical ability, and the ability to read nonverbal cues. Some studies have shown gender differences in these abilities, but these studies have fallen along gender-stereotypical lines: Women tend to have better memories for grocery lists, whereas men can better remember how to get to a particular place. Studies on wayfinding have revealed differences in strategies, with women preferring landmarks and men preferring position orientation. These strategy differences do not make significant differences in success in finding one's way. The differential achievement for men and women in creative arts and music reflects variance in social support and access to these careers rather than differences in ability.

One biological theory for cognitive differences relies on gender differences in hemispheric lateralization of the brain to explain cognitive differences. This view is not consistent with results showing that stronger lateralization produces an advantage on spatial tasks and a disadvantage on verbal tasks for men, even though women, who have less lateralized brains, have a slight advantage in verbal tasks and a disadvantage on some (but not all) spatial tasks.

Theories that emphasize the social aspects of gender-related cognitive differences hypothesize that ethnic and cultural variations should exist in cognitive performance, and research confirms this hypothesis. Such variations should not occur if these abilities were biologically determined.

Although gender-related differences in cognitive abilities may be relatively small, the choices that men and women make in taking courses, choosing college majors, and pursuing occupations differ enormously. Differences in occupational achievement are influenced by a large number of social and personal factors, which reflects gender and ethnic differences in achievement. The differences in performance on cognitive tasks are small, and individuals vary from each other a great deal, but men's and women's choices differ a great deal. These choices have huge implications for the lives of men and women.

Studies of other cultures and other ethnic groups have revealed that the advantage for men in mathematics and spatial ability tests may be the result of testing White college students in the United States rather than because of a universal pattern of gender difference.

Glossary

mental rotation a subtype of spatial ability that includes the ability to visualize objects as they would appear if rotated in space.

spatial perception a subtype of spatial ability that includes the ability to identify and locate the horizontal or vertical in the presence of distracting information.

spatial visualization a subtype of spatial ability that refers to the ability to process spatial information so as to understand the relationship between objects in space, such as the ability to see a figure embedded in other figures, find hidden figures in a drawing or picture, or imagine the shape produced when a folded piece of paper is cut and then unfolded.

spatiotemporal ability a subtype of spatial ability that involves judgments about moving objects in space, such as making a judgment about when a moving object will arrive at a target.

Suggested Readings

Baxter, Susan. (1994, March/April). The last word on gender differences. *Psychology Today, 27,* 50–53, 85–86. Baxter's readable article takes a sarcastic and cynical look at research on gender differences in intellectual ability and the connections to hormones and brains. Baxter includes quotations from famous gender researchers that are often more revealing than their more balanced presentations in scholarly journals.

Halpern, Diane F. (1997). Sex differences in intelligence: Implications for education. *American Psychologist, 52,* 1091–1102. Halpern's review of the extensive research and theory on cognitive differences makes it impossible to view this area in overly simplistic terms. Her thorough examination of the literature includes the complications and contradictions in this work.

Hyde, Janet Shibley. (1996). Where are the gender differences? Where are the gender similarities? In David M. Buss & Neil M. Malamuth (Eds.), *Sex, power, conflict: Evolutionary and feminist perspectives* (pp. 107–118). New York: Oxford University Press. This review by one of the leading researchers in the area of gender comparisons provides a brief summary of the history of gender research, an explanation of the technique of meta-analysis, and a summary of cognitive and other gender differences and similarities.

Chapter 5

Gender Development

The Psychoanalytic Approach

HEADLINE

The War against Boys

Atlantic Monthly, May, 2000

> *Carol Gilligan is a much-celebrated figure. Journalists routinely cite her research on the distinctive moral psychology of women....* In a Different Voice *offered the provocative thesis that men and women have distinctly different ways of dealing with moral quandaries. Relying on data from three studies she had conducted, Gilligan found that women tend to be more caring, less competitive, and less abstract than men; they speak "in a different voice." Women approach moral questions by applying an "ethic of care." In contrast, men approach moral issues by applying rules and abstract principles; theirs is an "ethic of justice." Gilligan argued further that women's moral style had been insufficiently studied by professional psychologists. She complained that the entire fields of psychology and moral philosophy had been built on studies that excluded women. (Sommers, 2000, p. 64)*

Gilligan's contention was correct, but Christina Hoff Sommers (2000) argued that Gilligan was biased in her own research methods and conclusions. Sommers argued that Gilligan, in her desire to present women in a positive way, has contributed to a negative view of men. This controversy over gender differences in morality is not the first. Many theories of personality development have included different patterns of development for men and women, but the most influential of the traditional theories, Freud's psychoanalytic theory of personality, viewed the development of women's personalities as problematic. This theory postulated that the course of female personality development is likely to create individuals whose moral judgment is inferior to men's.

Do the personalities of women and men differ? Do these differences produce a different set of moral values for men and women? If so, is one set of values superior, or do the two present valid variations of ways to make judgments?

The Psychoanalytic Approach to Personality

Ironically, psychology's traditional approach to personality theory has come from outside psychology—from Sigmund Freud, a Viennese neurologist who devised a theory of personality development and a method of treatment for psychological problems. Freud developed his theory during the late 19th and early 20th centuries, a time when psychology did not include the study of personality. Only later did theories of personality development and functioning become part of psychology, and Freud's theory became the first to generate great interest.

Differences between the personality development and functioning of men and women were an essential part of Freud's theory, and those differences became a point of contention that led other theorists, including Karen Horney, to propose alternatives. The traditional approach to personality has emphasized not only gender differences but also sex and sexuality, hypothesizing that sex is a basic factor in personality. Therefore, issues of gender and sex have always been factors in these theories.

Freud's Theory of Personality

Although Freud's theory of personality has been the most influential of the traditional approaches, its popularity and acceptance in psychology have varied over the years. During the early years of Freud's theorizing, in the late 1800s and early 1900s, academic psychology did not include theories of personality or treatment for people with mental problems. Freud's background was in neurology, an area that was not well accepted either as part of medicine or of psychology (Schultz & Schultz, 1992).

As Freud's work gained prominence, his treatment became the accepted approach for dealing with people with mental problems. The field of psychology also underwent changes to include both theories of personality and treatment for mental problems. Freudian theory became associated with psychology and strongly influenced many psychologists during the 1930s, 1940s, and 1950s, but it dwindled in popularity as other theories and therapies developed. The decades of interest in and association with Freud's work, however, have led to the popular belief that psychology is Freudian, when actually Freudian concepts are of greater interest in other fields, such as psychiatry and sociology. In addition, psychoanalytic concepts "have been diffused by the mass media into our popular culture," making these concepts part of social context (Buhle, 1999, p. B4).

Basic Concepts

Freud's theory hypothesizes the existence of the **unconscious,** a region of the mind that functions beyond conscious personal awareness. Freud was not the first to consider the existence of something like the unconscious (Ellenberger, 1970), but he was the first to place a great deal of emphasis on the influence of this region of the mind. He described the basic energy for personality development and functioning with a word that is most often translated as "instinct" but might also be translated as "drive" or "impulse" (Feist & Feist, 2002). Freud hypothesized that the life, or sexual instinct, and the death, or aggressive instinct, furnish the dynamic energy for personality development and functioning. That is, these **instincts** are the forces that underlie thought and action.

Freud's medical background led him to consider these instinctive forces to be biologically determined. The role of biology was also important in personality development, which Freud described in terms of **psychosexual stages.** These stages occurred from birth and continued through adulthood in a sequence named according to the regions of the body that were most important for sexual gratification. The early stages were the most important for personality development, emphasizing the importance of early childhood for personality formation.

By hypothesizing that the first psychosexual stage began at birth, Freud described infants as sexual beings and explained many of their actions as sexually oriented. Freud termed the first psychosexual stage the *oral stage,* during which babies receive sexual gratification from putting things into their mouths. Although this interpretation can be difficult to accept, his description of infants' behavior is easy to verify: Babies have a strong tendency to put things into their mouths.

During the next stage, the *anal stage,* the child receives pleasure from excretory functions. The main frustrations at this stage come from toilet training, and unresolved problems in this psychosexual stage appear in adult behavior as concerns with neatness, stubbornness, and retaining possessions.

The *phallic stage* begins in children around 3 or 4 years of age and is the first of Freud's psychosexual stages that describes a different course of personality development for boys and girls (Freud, 1933/1964). During this stage, sexual pleasure shifts from the anal region to the genitals; children begin to focus on their genitals, and they gain pleasure from masturbation. Parents are often disturbed by their children's masturbation and try to discourage or prevent this activity, furnishing one source of frustrated development during this stage.

Freud believed that the focus on genital activity resulted in a sexual attraction to the parent of the other sex and an increasing desire to have sex with this parent. These dynamics occur on an unconscious level, outside of children's awareness, and set the stage for the **Oedipus complex.** Freud used the Greek tragedy *Oedipus Rex* as an analogy for the interactions that occur within families during the phallic stage. According to the story, the oracle prophesied that Oedipus would kill his father and marry his mother, and this prophecy came true. Freud hypothesized that all boys feel jealousy, hatred, and aggression directed toward their fathers and sexual longing for their mothers. In boys, these family interactions result in competition with their fathers for their mothers' affections and growing hostility of the fathers toward their sons.

Boys in the phallic stage concentrate on their genitals and prize their penises. They notice the anatomical differences between girls and boys, which leads them to realize that everyone does not have a penis (Freud, 1925/1989). The realization that girls lack penises is shocking, disturbing, and threatening because, boys reason, penises must be removable. Indeed, boys come to fear that their fathers will remove their penises because of the boys' hostility toward their fathers and affection for their mothers. Thus, boys experience the **castration complex,** the belief that castration will be their punishment. Boys believe that girls have suffered this punishment and are thus mutilated, inferior creatures.

These feelings of anxiety, hostility, and sexual longing are all intense and produce great turmoil for boys. All possibilities seem terrible: To lose their penises, to be the recipient of their fathers' hatred, or to be denied sex with their mothers. To resolve these feelings, boys must end the competition with their fathers and deny their sexual wishes for their mothers. Both goals can be met through identification with their fathers. This identification accomplishes several goals. First, boys no longer feel castration anxiety, as they have given up the sexual competition that originated such feelings. Second, boys no longer feel hostility toward their fathers; they now strive to be like their fathers rather than competing with them. Third, boys no longer desire their mothers sexually, but instead, they receive some vicarious sexual gratification from the identification with their fathers, who have a sexual relationship with the mothers. By identifying with their fathers and becoming masculine, boys develop a sexual identity that includes sexual attraction to women. Therefore, identification with fathers is the mechanism through which boys resolve the Oedipus complex and develop a masculine identity.

Freud hypothesized a slightly different resolution to the Oedipus complex in girls. During the phallic stage, girls also notice the anatomical differences between the sexes. Aware that they do not have penises, girls become envious of boys and experience *penis envy* (Freud, 1925/1989). Freud hypothesized that penis envy is the female version of the castration complex and that girls experience feelings of inferiority concerning their genitals. Their clitorises are so much smaller than penises, and they perceive their vaginas as wounds that result from their castration. Furthermore, girls hold their mothers responsible for their lack of penises and develop feelings of hostility toward them. Fathers become the object of their affection, and girls wish to have sex with their fathers and to have babies. Freud saw both the desire for sex and the wish for a baby as substitutes for penises and as expressions of penis envy.

The feelings that accompany the male Oedipus complex—hostility and competition—are also present in the female version. Girls, however, cannot experience the castration complex in the same way that boys do, as girls have no penises to lose. Thus, girls do not experience the trauma of the phallic stage as strongly as boys. Girls must still surrender their sexual desires for their fathers and identify with their mothers, but the process is not as quick or as complete as it is for boys (Freud, 1933/1964).

After the resolution of the Oedipus complex, children enter the *latency stage,* during which little overt sexual activity occurs. This stage lasts until puberty, when physiological

---

GENDERED VOICES

Big Guns

"I just joined a gun club," a man told me, "and the men in the club do appear to have a relationship with their guns that seems symbolic to me. Of course, guys who own guns are pretty macho, but I have noticed two distinct styles, one of which seems more Freudian than the other.

"One style concentrates on shooting, and those men seem to like weapons that allow accuracy. Those types of guns tend to be rifles and are pretty lightweight. Maybe that's symbolic, but the other style concentrates on the size of the weapon. With some of these guns, it's just not possible to shoot accurately, but they are big guns with lots of firepower. That's all that some of these guys go for, that's all they talk about—how many guns they have and how big they are. They don't really want to shoot targets, but they want to shoot, and they seem to love their big guns. It's pretty embarrassing, in a symbolic sense."

changes bring about a reawakening of sexuality, and children enter the *genital stage.* During the genital stage, individuals will desire a genital relationship with people of the other sex. The regions of the body that have furnished sexual pleasure during childhood are now secondary to genital pleasure obtained through intercourse.

Table 5.1 shows Freud's psychosexual stages and the types of gender-related differences that he hypothesized for these stages. Development is similar for girls and boys in several stages but differs drastically in the phallic stage. Freud also believed that women have a more difficult time achieving a mature sexual relationship than men. He described the sexuality of the phallic stage, with its emphasis on masturbation, as immature sexuality that should be replaced in the genital stage with mature, heterosexual intercourse. For men, such activity involves their penises, but women must redirect their sexual impulses away from their clitorises and toward their vaginas.

Freud believed that girls have little awareness of their vaginas until puberty and that the redirection of their sexual energies is another difficult task for women. Freud saw masturbation as an immature form of sexuality for both men and women, and he believed that women who failed to achieve pleasure from vaginal intercourse had not achieved the mature, genital type of sexuality that signaled adequate personality development.

Moral Development

Freud believed that, until the Oedipus complex is resolved, children are ruled by seeking pleasure and gratification—as controlled by a component of personality Freud called the **id.** This component is part of the unconscious and is ruled by the instincts, even to the point of irrationality. Through development of the **ego,** children learn to moderate their behavior and seek pleasure and gratification in ways that are not irrational or harmful. Nonetheless, Freud believed that the ego is practical, not moral, and that initially children, because they have only an id and ego, are without morals or conscience.

TABLE 5.1 Freud's Psychosexual Stages and Gender-Related Differences in Each Stage

Stage	Gender-Related Difference
Oral	None
Anal	None
Phallic	Boys notice that they have penises and that girls do not
	Girls notice that boys have penises and that they do not
	Oedipus complex
	Boys experience extreme trauma connected with the Oedipus complex, undergo stronger identification with their fathers, and develop a stronger sense of morality
	Girls experience less Oedipal trauma, undergo weaker identification with their mother, and develop a weaker sense of morality
Latency	None
Genital	Women must transfer their sexual pleasure from their clitorises to their vaginas, making mature sexuality more difficult for them
	Men's penises remain the center of their sexuality, making mature sexuality easier for them

Freud hypothesized that children develop a conscience by developing a third personality structure, the **superego,** which reflects the rules of society and is used to control sexual and aggressive impulses. Freud believed that the superego develops as a result of the resolution of the Oedipus complex. However, he imagined that this process happens differently in boys and girls, with unequal results (Freud, 1933/1964).

In boys, identifying with fathers prompts the development of the superego and thus of morality. Through identification with fathers, boys develop a conscience, morals, and a way to incorporate the rules of society into their behavior. Freud believed that such development is essential to maintain society and is dependent on the proper resolution of the Oedipus complex. Because the male Oedipus complex is resolved more completely and more swiftly than the female Oedipus complex, boys and men have stronger superegos than girls and women. The difficulty of resolving the female Oedipus complex results in weaker superegos and thus weaker morals in girls and women (see "According to the Media/According to the Research"). Therefore, Freud contended that women are morally inferior to men, lacking a mature sense of justice and incapable of reaching full psychological maturity:

> *The fact that women must be regarded as having little sense of justice is no doubt related to the predominance of envy in their mental life; for the demand for justice is a modification of envy and lays down the condition subject to which one can put envy aside.... There are no paths open to further development; it is as though the whole process had already run its course and remains thenceforward insusceptible to influence—as though, indeed, the difficult development to femininity had exhausted the possibilities of the person concerned. (Freud, 1933/1964, pp. 134–135)*

Freud and Women

Freud knew that his theory was uncomplimentary to women, because his female associates, such as Karen Horney, told him so (Gay, 1988). He gave the matter a great deal of thought and heard many criticisms but never changed his mind about women being, essentially, failed men. Although Freud may have thought women were inferior in some ways, intelligence was not among them. Freud considered that an intelligent, independent woman deserved credit and praise and might be "virtually as good as a man" (Gay, 1988, p. 507).

Freud seemed to have held contradictory attitudes about women (Feist & Feist, 2002). On the one hand, Freud was a proper Victorian gentleman who wanted women to be sweet, pleasant, and subservient. On the other hand, he admired women who were intelligent and "masculine" in their pursuit of intellectual achievement and careers. Freud acted on both beliefs. His wife, Martha, held the role of wife and mother and shared none of his professional life. Feminists were prominent among the intellectual circles of Vienna and Germany where psychoanalysis gained prominence, and many women participated in these discussions (Kurzweil, 1995). Although Freud contended that the sexes could never be equal and disparaged the efforts of feminists, who argued for the equality of men and women, he also admitted women into the ranks of psychoanalytic training at a time when women were admitted to few professions (Tavris & Wade, 1984). The person who carried on his work was his daughter, Anna, whom he encouraged to become an analyst. However, his most intimate personal friends were all men.

Therefore, Freud's attitudes about women and their personalities showed some inconsistency. Freud undoubtedly held negative attitudes about women, and he expressed his lack

ACCORDING TO THE MEDIA...

Bad Women Are Sexual

During the era of silent films, a portrayal of women appeared that combined evil and sexuality (Dijkstra, 1996). This model coincided with Freud's conceptualization of the dangerous forces from the unconscious and reflected his poor opinion of women as well as his uneasiness with female sexuality. Freud was typical of his time period in imagining that women's sexuality is mysterious and, once released, difficult to control. This popular conceptualization holds that women who give in to sexuality become less than human. Silent screen star Theda Barra was an example of this vampire (vamp) or femme fatale who preys on men, taking them from their loving wives and using her sexuality to enslave and ruin the men she seduces. She exemplifies a particular version of immorality that is consistent with traditional psychoanalytic theory—a woman who is independent, uncaring, and openly sexual.

This early model of the femme fatale has appeared repeatedly in movies: Marlene Dietrich in *The Blue Angel* (1930), Barbara Stanwyck in *Double Indemnity* (1944), Glen Close in *Fatal Attraction* (1980), Sharon Stone in *Basic Instinct* (1992), and Linda Fiorentino in *The Last Seduction* (1994). All of these female characters are bad in a variety of ways, including crimes of property and violence. They are also openly, aggressively sexual, and they use their sexuality to accomplish their goals.

Recently, femmes fatales have become more dangerous because they have become successful (*The Economist,* 1994). That is, these women get away with their evil acts. In the earlier years of movies, evil was punished, and bad women came to bad ends. Currently, crime can pay for these immoral women.

of understanding and lack of certainty about women in several of his papers. One of Freud's last statements about women appeared in his 1933 paper, "Femininity." He concluded with a tentative statement about women, acknowledging his awareness of the criticisms and also his own far-from-complete understanding:

> *That is all I had to say to you about femininity. It is certainly incomplete and fragmentary and does not always sound friendly. But do not forget that I have only been describing women in so far as their nature is determined by their sexual function. It is true that that influence extends very far; but we do not overlook the fact that an individual woman may be a human being in other respects as well. If you want to know more about femininity, inquire from your own experiences of life, or turn to the poets, or wait until science can give you deeper and more coherent information. (Freud, 1933/1964, p. 135)*

Other researchers and theorists have attempted the last alternative rather than the first two. In general, they have sought other information about personality and gender. One of those theorists was Karen Horney, a colleague of Freud.

Horney's Theory of Personality

Like Freud, Horney was also a physician and psychoanalyst, but the two were a generation apart in age, and this difference contributed to their different views of the world and their different theories (Williams, 1983). Horney was one of the first German women to enter medical school, where she specialized in psychiatry. In 1910, Horney began a training anal-

ACCORDING TO THE RESEARCH...

Bad Women Do Not Fit the Femme Fatale Model

Some women exploit and harm others, but the model of the femme fatale is more common in movies than anywhere else. According to arrest records (U.S. Department of Justice, 1999b), sexuality is a common component of women's arrests—60% of the arrests for prostitution are women. However, violence is not, and the combination is quite rare. Women are more likely to commit property crimes, such as larceny, forgery, fraud, and embezzlement than assault, robbery, or murder.

Although women commit a low percentage of violent crimes, that rate has increased in recent years (Yeoman, 1999). For example, 95% of the cases of stranger murder committed by women occurred after 1970, and the number of women arrested for violent crimes increased by 90% between 1985 and 1994.

Even when women commit violent crimes, most fail to fit the femme fatale script. Women may be fatal, but most do not combine sex and violence like the women in the movies do. Susan Smith is more typical of murderous women. Her victims were her two sons, whom she drowned in a lake. Women who kill an abusive husband and those who kill their children are the most common descriptions of female murderers. These crimes are violent, but sexuality is not a factor. However, some examples of female violence are closer to the movie version: Aileen Wuornos, who murdered a series of her sex customers, Amy Fisher, the teenager who attempted to murder her married lover's wife, and Lorena Bobbitt, who retaliated against an abusive husband by amputating his penis. Not surprisingly, these women's stories have been made into movies.

ysis with one of Freud's close associates, and after her treatment was completed, she began to attend seminars on psychoanalysis (Feist & Feist, 2002). By 1917, Horney had written her first paper on psychoanalysis, which reflected the orthodox Freudian view. Her orthodoxy did not last, and Horney became a vocal critic of Freud's theory of personality, especially concerning gender differences in personality development. Horney reexamined Freud's concepts of penis envy, inferiority feelings in women, and the masculinity complex (the expression of masculine behavior and attitudes in women). In addition, Horney's interpretation of feminine **masochism** (deriving pleasure from pain) differed from the Freudian version.

Between 1922 and 1935, Horney wrote a series of papers in which she reexamined some of Freud's concepts and argued for a course of female personality development that differed from the one Freud hypothesized (Quinn, 1987). Horney began to write about the masculine bias in psychoanalysis, and she reinterpreted psychoanalytic theory. However, Horney stayed within the framework of psychoanalysis, as shown by her acceptance of the unconscious as a motivating force in personality, her emphasis on sexual feelings and events in personality development, and her belief in the importance of early childhood experiences for personality formation. She differed from Freud in her interpretation of the significance of the events of early childhood and her growing belief in the importance of social rather than instinctual, biological forces in personality development.

Part of Horney's reinterpretation of psychoanalysis was an alternative view of the notion of penis envy, the feelings of envy that girls have when they discover that boys' penises are larger than their own clitorises. Horney argued that penis envy was a symbolic longing for the social prestige and position that men experience, rather than a literal physical desire for penises. Indeed, she hypothesized that men envy women's capability to reproduce and proposed the concept of *womb envy.* She interpreted the male strivings for achievement as overcompensation for their lack of ability to create by giving birth.

Freud argued that for women, penis envy is such a strong and threatening feeling that it must be rejected by the conscious mind and pushed into the unconscious. Horney suggested that for men, envy of women's breasts and reproductive abilities is equally strong and must also be repressed into the unconscious. Thus, both women and men have unconscious envy and fear concerning each other, and these unconscious feelings can be manifested in attempts to portray the other as inferior. Horney believed that men fear and attribute evil to women because men feel inadequate when comparing themselves to women. To feel more adequate, men must see women as inferior.

Horney postulated that men's assertion of women's inferiority exists to keep men from contending with their own feelings of inferiority. She explained that men still retain the feelings of inferiority that originated with the perception of the small size of their penises during childhood, when they initially noticed them. Therefore, men go through life needing to prove their masculinity, and they do so by having sexual intercourse. Any failure in erection will be perceived as a lack of masculinity, making men constantly vulnerable to feelings of inferiority. Women have no similar problem and do not suffer feelings of inferiority for reasons related to sexual performance. Horney (1932/1967, p. 145) summarized this conflict by writing

> *Now one of the exigencies of the biological differences between the sexes is this: that the man is actually obliged to go on proving his manhood to the woman. There is no analogous necessity for her. Even if she is frigid, she can engage in sexual intercourse and conceive and bear a child. She performs her part by merely* being, *without any* doing*—a fact that has always filled men with admiration and resentment.*

This resentment can lead men to attempt to diminish women, and these attempts can succeed, leaving women with feelings of inferiority. Therefore, female inferiority originates with male insecurities rather than, as Freud hypothesized, with the female perception of inferior genitals. These female feelings of inferiority are perpetuated by men's behavior toward women and by the masculine bias in society.

Horney argued against several Freudian concepts that posit separate courses of personality development for women and men. She disputed the biological basis of penis envy, hypothesizing that women's envy was for men's power and social position. She also argued against the view that women see themselves as inferior because of their genitals, pointing out that men also envy women's ability to give birth and that men have feelings of inferiority about their genitals. Horney again relied on social and cultural factors to explain why women might exhibit the active, achieving behavior associated with masculinity and why both men and women might exhibit masochism.

Table 5.2 shows the points of agreement and disagreement between Freud's and Horney's psychoanalytic theories. As this table shows, both theories are psychoanalytic in that they accept the importance of unconscious forces and early childhood experiences. However, the difference in their interpretations of the importance and cause of other events makes the two theories substantially different.

Feminine psychology was of lesser interest to Horney later in her career, but the issues that she raised, and her theoretical and therapeutic endeavors, contributed to her develop-

TABLE 5.2 Points of Agreement and Disagreement in Horney's and Freud's Psychoanalytic Theories

Concept	Horney's Theory	Freud's Theory
Existence of unconscious	Yes	Yes
Importance of early childhood experiences	Yes	Yes
Gender differences in personality	Yes	Yes
Source of differences	Social	Biological
Feelings of envy for other gender	Men envy women's ability to give birth	Women envy men's penises
Feelings of inferiority	Constant need to perform sexually leads men to feel inferior	Lack of penises leads women to feel inferior
Masculinity complex	Driven by girls' lack of acceptance of femininity and identification with their fathers	Driven by girls' feeling of inferiority
Masochism	Socially determined part of development that is abnormal for women as well as men	Biologically determined, inevitable part of feminine development; abnormal in men

ment of a general theory of personality that retained the emphasis on dynamic, unconscious forces in personality and the importance of early childhood experiences. Unlike Freud, she emphasized social and cultural forces rather than biological factors in shaping and maintaining personality. Her theory applied equally to men and women, but she also saw that society and culture treat women and men differently.

Women, Men, and Psychoanalytic Theory

Freud's theory of personality appeared during the late 19th and early 20th centuries in a Victorian culture that viewed women as passive, dependent, and intellectually inferior to men. This view of women was easy for Freud to accept, not only because it was the view of his culture but also because his female patients reflected these characteristics. Freud built his theory on the basis of observing his patients, many of whom were upper-class, bored, unhappy, mentally unhealthy women who lived in a repressive society that assumed women's inferiority. The extent to which their experience reflects that of contemporary women is questionable, but Freud's female patients and the culture in which they lived influenced his view of women.

During the time that Freud formulated his theory, a feminist movement was active in Europe and the United States (Kurzweil, 1995). Many of these feminists objected to Freud's theory as insulting to women, with its proposal that women experience penis envy, feelings of inferiority, and inadequate superego development. Freud (1933/1964) prefaced his remarks about personality development in women as tentative and speculative, but the majority of psychoanalysts accepted these proposals. Thus, Freud's theory was never popular among those women and men who believed in and worked for fair treatment for women, both by society and in personal relationships.

Psychoanalysis and feminism have a long tradition of interconnection because both are radical movements, and those who adhere to one are sometimes attracted to the other (Kurzweil, 1995). Early feminists argued with Freud, and some, such as Karen Horney, broke with him and formulated alternative theories. Continued interest in psychoanalysis as theory and therapy produced heated controversy within psychoanalytic circles during the 1970s and 1980s. These controversies involved an event in the history of psychoanalysis—Freud's abandonment of the seduction theory—and the appearance of an alternative psychoanalytic theory of personality development—feminist psychoanalytic theory.

Freud rejected the **seduction theory** early in the history of psychoanalysis. He originally proposed that sexual activity between children and adults is the basis for psychological problems when these children become adults. Later, Freud replaced this theory with the idea that children fantasized these seductions by adults—the events were not real. Freud's revision of the seduction theory had important implications for the credibility of psychiatric patients' accounts and for society's beliefs about early childhood sexuality. For many years after Freud's rejection of this theory, psychotherapists, even those who did not have a psychoanalytic orientation, often discounted women's reports of childhood sexual abuse, preferring to view such reports as mere wishful fantasies.

Effects of Freud's Abandonment of the Seduction Theory

Much criticism of traditional Freudian theory has appeared, ranging from the inherent difficulty in testing the theory's hypotheses in a scientific way, to its male-centered point of view. However, beginning in the 1970s, several psychoanalytically trained theorists attacked Freud for rejecting the seduction theory, the view that sexual activity between parent and child is the basis for psychological problems when the child grows to adulthood. These attacks differed from the previous criticisms in their intensity and in their personal nature; not only Freud's theory, but also Freud personally was the object of these criticisms.

Although the seduction theory was part of Freud's early thinking about the source of psychological problems, he rejected this concept and postulated that attraction between the child and an other-sex parent is part of the child's wishful *fantasy,* which has no basis in reality. Freud (1925/1959) continued to recognize that some children had experienced actual sexual abuse, but his adoption of the Oedipus complex in place of the seduction hypothesis changed the way he and many subsequent psychoanalysts viewed the psychology of women. In his final theory, Freud hypothesized that children become attracted to their other-sex parents during the phallic stage. This attraction forms the basis for the Oedipus complex, the unconscious sexual attraction to the other-sex parent combined with feelings of rivalry and hostility for the same-sex parent. Children want sex with their other-sex parents, but this incest never occurs except in the children's fantasies. Indeed, Freud came to believe that societies must develop strong prohibitions against actual incest, making incestuous relationships rare.

Although Freud never completely rejected the seduction theory, several of his critics have taken him to task for his emphasis on children's sexual fantasies. An early critique by Florence Rush (1977/1996) analyzed the changes in Freud's theory and the consequences of these changes. Based on clinical (and personal) experience, Rush argued that sexual abuse of children is common and, similar to Freud's early formulation, does a great deal of harm to the molested children. Rush argued that Freud's abandonment of the seduction theory was based on personal and political criteria rather than on any evidence: "When Freud arrived at the seduction theory, he did so by listening carefully and intently to his female patients; when he arrived at his Oedipal theory, he did so by listening carefully and intently to himself" (Rush, 1977/1996, p. 270).

Marie Balmary (1979/1982) concluded that Freud misinterpreted the Oedipus legend on which he based his entire hypothesis of childhood sexuality and personality development. She contended that Freud overlooked the actions of the father in the Oedipus legend as actions that set the tragedy into motion. According to Balmary, Freud's inability to see the fault of the father in the Oedipus legend came from Freud's difficulty in dealing with his relationship with his own father; he could not consciously acknowledge that his father contributed to the psychological problems exhibited by his children, including Sigmund himself. The result of this failure to acknowledge his own father's faults produced a distortion of the entire direction of psychoanalysis, including the notion that childhood seduction is a fantasy. Balmary argued that Freud incorrectly emphasized the fantasy aspect of children's seduction by a parent.

Another critic was Jeffrey Masson, who held the position of projects director of the Freud Archives, which allowed him access to unpublished documents. In examining letters written by Freud, Masson (1984) came to believe that the official version of how Freud rejected the seduction theory differed from what had really happened: Freud did not quickly and easily reject the notion of childhood seduction. Instead, it was the notion of parental seduction that he relinquished slowly and reluctantly. Masson concluded that Freud rejected the seduction theory because his colleagues found the notion so unacceptable. Freud believed that he would never find acceptance for his theories if he maintained that many children were molested by their parents and that these incestuous relationships produced permanent psychological damage in the children.

Masson argued that Freud had been aware of the rape and murder of children by parents, especially on the part of fathers, from the time of his early interest in "nervous disorders." This knowledge led Freud to believe his patients' stories about childhood seductions. Masson interpreted Freud's rejection of the seduction theory as an act of cowardice; Freud was not willing to endure the poor opinion of his colleagues, so he chose to disbelieve his patients and began interpreting their stories of childhood seduction as fantasy rather than reality.

Rush, Balmary, and Masson have argued that psychoanalysis might have been more useful (and closer to the truth) if Freud had kept his original notion that adult emotional problems can occur as a result of sexual abuse during childhood. By rejecting the notion of parental seduction, Freud portrayed his patients in several negative ways. First, he presented patients as unable to distinguish fantasy from reality. Although they believed the stories of their childhood seductions, these seductions were fantasies rather than reality, and therefore their stories did not need to be taken seriously. By rejecting the seduction theory, Freud cast doubt on information furnished by patients; he diminished their credibility.

Second, by asserting that childhood seduction was a fantasy, Freud suggested that children are the ones who wish this seduction. Children want to commit incest with their parents and, during the phallic stage, may behave seductively toward the other-sex parent. Therefore, if any incest occurs, children and not parents are at fault.

Rush, Balmary, and Masson contended that Freud's influence has been great, but some of that influence has been negative. Freud established a pattern of working with people with psychological problems by attacking the credibility of these patients and by blaming the children for any sexual activity in which they had been involved. As the majority of Freud's patients were women, his rejection of the truth of their stories led to the general belief that women have fantasies about sexual abuse during childhood or rape during adulthood, but these fantasies are not based on reality. According to this view, any story that a child tells about incest is probably not true, but if evidence exists, then the incest was initiated by the child.

Those critics who accused Freud of incorrectly abandoning the seduction theory blame Freud for some contemporary problems. Freudian theory has so influenced our society that its claims about the fantasy nature of childhood sexuality and the prevalence of fantasies of rape are not only popularly accepted, but have also been incorporated into our legal systems. This lack of credibility of children and women who claim to have been sexually abused poses a problem for successful legal action against those who commit rape or childhood sexual abuse. If Freud had not changed his mind about the seduction theory, society might have different views about these problems.

Contemporary Psychoanalytic Theories of Personality Development

Beginning with Horney, feminist personality theorists have worked toward revising psychoanalytic theory. The urge to retain the basic tenets of psychoanalytic theory has led some theorists to either remove the objectionable elements of Freud's theory or to create revisions of his theory that are compatible with a positive view of women.

Some feminist psychoanalysts have attempted to integrate research findings about female personality development into psychoanalytic theory (Chehrazi, 1986). The resulting view is an update of psychoanalytic theory, with only minor modifications. Other theorists have departed from the Freudian tradition in more radical ways. Sociologist Nancy Chodorow (1978, 1979, 1994) and psychologist Ellyn Kaschak (1992) have formulated psychoanalytic theories that are significant departures from Freud's view. Chodorow's theory proposes a progression of development that gives women advantages, and Kaschak's theory replaces the emphasis on male psychological development with a woman-centered view of personality. Both theories are examples of feminist psychoanalytic theory.

Chodorow's Emphasis on Mothering. Like Freud, Chodorow (1979) expressed pessimism about any potential equality between men and women. Unlike Freud (who concentrated on the perception of anatomical differences), Chodorow's reasons for believing in the continuation of inequality focused on the early experiences of children in relation to their mother. Chodorow described a psychoanalytic theory of development that concentrates on the **pre-Oedipal period** during early childhood, before the Oedipus complex, and centers on the process of being mothered by a woman.

Although Chodorow (1978) acknowledged that women are not unique in their capacity to care for infants, she also granted that mothers (or other women) provide most nurturing, and fathers (or other men) do little caregiving. Thus, Chodorow explained how this early relationship between mother and infant makes a permanent imprint on personality development—an imprint that differs for boys and girls.

Chodorow (1978) described early infant development in terms similar to traditional psychoanalytic theory. Babies have no sense of self versus other people or the world; infants are one with the world, and most of their world is their mother. The early mother–daughter relationship is closer than the mother–son relationship, because mothers and daughters are of the same sex. Infants have no initial perception of their sex or gender, but mothers always know about the sex of their infants and treat girls and boys differently.

Chodorow (1978) hypothesized that when children start to develop a sense of self and to separate from their mothers, events differ for girls and boys. Girls have an easier task in developing a sense of self because they have already identified with their mothers. This identification gives them an advantage in developing a separate identity, because this identity will likely be feminine and much like their mothers. Boys, on the other hand, have a more difficult time in developing separate identities because they have already identified with their mothers. To become masculine, boys must reject the femininity of their mothers and develop an identity that is different as well as separate. Thus, boys have a more difficult task than girls in accomplishing these developmental goals of separation and identity.

But according to Chodorow, girls never separate from their mothers as boys do. The gender similarity is something that both mothers and daughters know, and this similarity between the two influences each. One study (Benenson, Morash, & Petrakos, 1998) confirmed the difference in emotional closeness between daughters and sons, as Chodorow's theory hypothesizes. Boys must work to accomplish their separation, even with the aid of their mothers. This effort extracts a price. Chodorow (1978) described the aftermath of boys' separation in terms of their rejection of all femininity and the development of fear and mistrust of the feminine. Chodorow thus explained the almost worldwide denigration of women by men as a by-product of boys' efforts to distinguish and separate themselves from their mothers. On the other hand, girls have no such need, and they accept their mothers and the feminine role without the turbulence that boys experience. Girls grow into women and reproduce their early relationships with their mothers in their own mothering.

Table 5.3 shows the differences between traditional psychoanalytic theory and Chodorow's feminist psychoanalytic theory. Notice that the differences lie not only in the outcomes but also in the stage of development that each theory hypothesizes to be important in personality development and in gender-related differences.

Thus, Chodorow's psychoanalytic theory represents an alternative to Freud's theory. Although she retained the emphasis on early childhood, Chodorow concentrated on the pre-Oedipal period and on the early infant–mother relationship. She hypothesized a different course of personality development for boys and girls, with girls having an easier time than

TABLE 5.3 Differences between Chodorow's Feminist Psychoanalytic Theory and Traditional Freudian Theory

	Stages	Gender-Related Outcome
Chodorow's Theory	Pre-Oedipal stages	Boys work toward separation from mother, rejecting femininity. Girls retain connectedness with mother, becoming feminine.
	Oedipus conflict	Gender differences have already emerged.
Freud's Theory	Pre-Oedipal stages	No gender-related differences emerge.
	Oedipus conflict	Family dynamics and perception of differences in genitals prompt personality differences.

boys of accomplishing the goal of separation from their mothers. In their incomplete separation from their mothers, girls develop a feminine identity and the ability to mother. In the more complete separation from their mothers, boys reject femininity to develop masculinity. The difficulty of this separation leads them to reject and denigrate the feminine. In this way, Chodorow explained the personality development of women and men, plus men's common tendency to believe that women are inferior.

Kaschak's Antigone Phase. Ellyn Kaschak (1992) revised psychoanalytic theory by making an analogy in personality development to Antigone who, like Oedipus, is a character from Greek plays by Sophocles. Kaschak argued that the Oedipus legend was useful in Freud's theory of male personality development, but that the minor changes Freud made to accommodate women in his female Oedipus complex were inadequate. Instead, Kaschak casts female personality development in terms of Antigone, Oedipus's daughter (and half-sister).

In Sophocles' plays, Antigone was the daughter of Oedipus and Jocasta (who was Oedipus's mother). After Oedipus learned of his incest with Jocasta, he destroyed his eyes, and Antigone then became her blind father's guide and caretaker. Antigone sacrificed an independent life to care for her blind father, and he considered it his right to have this devotion. Kaschak interpreted personality development of men and women in similar terms: "As Oedipus' dilemma became a symbol for the dilemma of the son, so might that of Antigone be considered representative of the inevitable fate of the good daughter in the patriarchal family" (p. 60).

Men grow and develop in societies that allow them power in those societies and in their families, and in taking this power, men come to consider women their possessions. Men experience relationships with women that are an extension of men's needs rather than a genuinely mutual interaction. Kaschak hypothesized that mothers, wives, and daughters are all extensions of men and their needs. Women grow and develop in positions of subservience in which they are possessions of men, and women's lives and personalities reflect this status.

Kaschak hypothesized that many men and women never resolve these complexes because the social structure perpetuates differential power for women and men, encouraging both to adhere to these different roles. For men, an unresolved Oedipus complex results in treating women as extensions of themselves rather than as independent people. With this sense of entitlement, men tend to seek power and sex in self-centered ways that may be destructive to others, such as via incest and rape. For example, Kaschak explained father–daughter incest in terms of fathers' feelings of owning their daughters (and, to some extent, all women) and being able to do as they wish. Consistent with Kaschak's formulation, Michael Johnson (1995) researched family violence and proposed that some men engage in systematic violence within their families because they feel that they have the right to do so. He called this form of family violence *patriarchal terrorism.*

Kaschak considered the resolution of the Oedipus complex unlikely in a patriarchal society. Those men who do resolve these feelings will relinquish their grandiosity and drive for power, will see women as whole persons rather than possessions, and will come to see themselves as individuals who act within boundaries and limits, rather than as kings.

When women fail to resolve the Antigone phase, they allow themselves to be extensions of others rather than striving for independence. Girls learn that men are important and their own wishes are less so, thus limiting their lives with this knowledge. Among those limits are restrictions on what women may do in the world and conforming to a limited sexuality, all defined and controlled by men. In addition, women learn to deny their physicality and try to make their bodies invisible, and this denial can be expressed in terms of eating disorders. These limits can lead to feelings of self-hatred and shame and the need to form relationships with others to feel self-worth.

Women who successfully resolve the Antigone phase achieve separation from their fathers and other men to become independent people. This independence allows them to form relationships with women, which Kaschak believes to be a problem for women who have not resolved the Antigone phase. In their relationships with men, women who have resolved these issues are able to stop making men central to their lives and can form interdependent, flexible relationships. Table 5.4 shows the four possibilities in Kaschak's view of personality development—men and women who have and have not resolved major developmental issues.

Is feminist psychoanalytic theory an improvement over traditional psychoanalytic theory? Any theory that relies heavily on unconscious mental processes will rely on events that are not directly observable, which is a problem for scientific testability. All versions of psychoanalytic theory have this shortcoming. Proponents of these psychoanalytic theories tend to accept the evidence of patients and their own interpretations of what patients say, evidence that some researchers would not accept as objective. Therefore, any psychoanalytic theory shares the problem of providing adequately objective, observable research evidence.

Feminist psychoanalytic theory shares all of the drawbacks of traditional psychoanalytic theory. The feminist revisions offer a more favorable view of women, but these advantages occur at the expense of their views about men. Chodorow's theory hypothesizes that women have an easier course of personality development than men, whereas Freud's theory holds the opposite view. Kaschak's theory views men as proprietary and demanding, ignoring women except as extensions of themselves. Some women have found that these feminist theories validate their personal experiences and as such these theories are attractive. Understandably, fewer men than women consider these feminist theories relevant to them.

Therefore, both traditional and modern psychoanalytic theory emphasize the importance and inevitability of gender differences. Whereas Freud's psychoanalytic theory has a masculine bias, newer psychoanalytic theories, like the ones proposed by Chodorow and

TABLE 5.4 Possible Outcomes of Personality Development According to Kaschak

	Not Resolved	Resolved
Men (Oedipal phase)	Patriarchical Gaining power a major goal See women as extensions of self—they have the right to have women serve them Sexually self-centered	Nonpatriarchical Gaining power not a major issue See women as independent Sexually unselfish
Women (Antigone phase)	Accept subservience Passive and dependent Accept male-defined sexuality Deny their own needs, including physical needs Cannot form friendships with other women	Reject subservient role Assertive and independent Define their own sexuality Accept and express their own needs Form friendships with other women

Kaschak, are part of a view of personality from a feminist standpoint, a view that emphasizes and values the unique qualities and special experiences of women.

Feminist Standpoint Theory: A Different Voice

Chodorow's (1978, 1979, 1994) and Kaschak's (1992) feminist psychoanalytic theories are only two of several theories that have concentrated on women. The feminist theorists claim their interest in women is an attempt to remedy past exclusion; women have been secondary in theories of personality development and have been excluded as participants in many research studies. This neglect has led to theories that explain men's personality development and behavior and assume that women's will be similar. Feminist theories have attempted to consider women and their unique experiences in an attempt to enlarge personality theory to include women: "Giving voice to women's perspective means identifying the ways in which women create meaning and experience life from their particular position in the social hierarchy" (Riger, 1992, p. 734).

In their attempts to include women, feminist standpoint theorists often exclude or denigrate men, as Sommers's (2000) headline article asserted. Their reasoning is that men have long been the center of existing theories, and that women need special consideration or else their exclusion will continue. However, feminist standpoint theory is as exclusionary as traditional psychoanalytic personality theory, the difference lying only in who is excluded. Although both approaches can make contributions to research and theory, neither excluding men nor excluding women will lead to a theory of personality that captures gender development; studying gender requires the inclusion of both sexes. Although feminist standpoint theory will not lead to a complete investigation of gender, this approach provides a different and valuable point of view.

One feminist standpoint theorist whose work made a significant contribution to psychology is Carol Gilligan. When she questioned women and men about moral judgments, Gilligan (1982) "began to hear a distinction in these voices, two ways of speaking about moral problems, two models of describing the relationship between other and self" (p. 1). She concluded that these two voices belonged distinctively to men and women. Her observation led to the publication of her research in the book *In a Different Voice: Psychological Theory and Women's Development,* which detailed the characteristics of the different voice Gilligan heard from women.

Gilligan's Theory of Moral Development

Gilligan began her research because of an interest in moral development and a belief about how women's moral development had been neglected and slighted by research in psychology. Two important influences on her work were Chodorow's (1978) feminist psychoanalytic personality theory and Lawrence Kohlberg's (1981) cognitive developmental theory of morality. Chodorow's theory explained how girls develop personalities that are influenced by similarities to their mothers, thus promoting a feeling of interpersonal connection, whereas boys must work hard to separate themselves from their mothers, thereby promoting a feeling of personal separation. In Gilligan's theory, these two orientations form the psychological basis for gender differences in moral reasoning.

Kohlberg's theory of moral development took a cognitive developmental approach rather than a psychoanalytic approach to moral development, explaining that children go through a series of stages in understanding and making moral decisions. These stages relate to cognitive capabilities, with younger children unable to make moral decisions based on abstract, rule-governed principles. Instead, young children make moral choices based first on their own needs, and later on their relationships with others. Only as they mature cognitively do adolescents and adults make moral choices based on their knowledge of abstract principles of justice.

Much of Kohlberg's theory used data from a longitudinal study, a project in which he repeatedly tested a group of boys from their years in late elementary school through young adulthood. These boys answered questions about moral dilemmas, hypothetical situations involving a moral problem such as "Do you think a man should steal an expensive drug to save his dying wife if he is too poor to pay for it?" On the basis of the responses, Kohlberg formulated a theory with three levels of moral reasoning: preconventional, conventional, and postconventional. The preconventional level involves responses based on fear of getting caught, the conventional level involves a respect for the existence of rules and laws, and the postconventional level involves an acknowledgment that moral rules should be sufficiently flexible to put human life over all other values.

Kohlberg's stages of moral development came from research on boys and men, and their answers formed the basis for his theory. But does his theory apply to girls and women? Of course, the stages can be applied to the responses of girls or women and analyzed in the same terms as responses from boys and men. Gilligan was familiar with research that indicated that, on the average, girls and women tended to fall into a lower stage than boys and men. Kohlberg's cognitive developmental theory of moral development, like the psychoanalytic theories, seemed to indicate a female moral inferiority.

Gilligan (1982) maintained that girls and women develop a different moral sense from boys and men. Whereas the male moral sense is based on abstract principles of justice, the female moral sense is based on the value of human relationships. Men are oriented toward "separateness," whereas women are oriented toward "connectedness" and "care." In Kohlberg's system of classification, the emphasis on human relationships results in a score indicating a lower level of moral development than does reasoning based on abstract principles of justice. Therefore, Gilligan argued that Kohlberg's system is biased against the type of moral reasoning that girls and women tend to use, which leads to the misclassification of girls and women as morally less developed than boys and men.

Gilligan contended that women were capable of the type of abstract reasoning that would lead them to make moral judgments like men; thus, the differences were not due to cognitive deficiencies. But women value human relationships and feelings and make their moral judgments on the basis of potential damage to those relationships. Women have different priorities from men in making moral decisions, but they are not inferior in their moral reasoning.

Indeed, valuing human relationships over abstract principles might be considered superior, and many women embraced Gilligan's work for this reason (Sommers, 2000). Women's orientation to care for others could be considered a better value system than the abstract and impersonal one that men tend to use. Indeed, both men and women acknowledge that women tend to be more truthful (Robinson et al., 1998). The variation in possible approaches to moral decision making also brings up the possibility that, contrary to Kohlberg's position, no one universal set of moral principles exists.

Gilligan's theory qualifies as a feminist standpoint theory—it turns a traditional female "deficit" into a female "asset" by taking the position that women have a unique contribution to make and that society should acknowledge and value this contribution. As is true for other feminist standpoint theories, the female advantage comes at the expense of men.

As Sommers's headline article suggested, a variety of critics have expressed misgivings. Some of those criticisms have been aimed at the methodology of Gilligan's studies, other researchers have failed to find the magnitude of gender differences that Gilligan proposed, and, like Sommers (2000), a few have offered personal attacks. One line of criticism focused on Gilligan's data collection, which resembled clinical case studies more than objective data gathering (Colby & Damon, 1983), and on her selective citation of illustrative examples, which differed from characteristics of a more representative analysis (Davis, 1994). Thus, Gilligan's methods of data collection and analysis differed from the usual research procedures, making her conclusions more difficult for research psychologists to accept.

Sommers (2000) focused on the problems with Gilligan's research, contending that Gilligan's research lacks validity. Although that contention is incorrect, some studies have failed to find the sharp distinctions in moral reasoning that Gilligan initially found. Several studies (Crandall, Tsang, Goldman, & Pennington, 1999; Johnson, 1988; Lyons, 1988) found evidence for the justice orientation and the care orientation in moral reasoning and the tendency for a gender difference in their use. However, these studies showed that neither orientation was uniquely associated with men or women. Women more frequently expressed the care orientation, and men more frequently expressed the justice orientation, but both were capable of using either orientation. Studies of moral reasoning would be incomplete without considering both orientations (Gilligan & Attanucci, 1988).

Therefore, Gilligan's original contention that women have a unique moral orientation is not a position she continued to support, a situation that Sommers (2000) ignored in her critique. Instead, Gilligan and her colleagues have provided evidence that the different voice, the moral orientation characterized by concern for people and relationships, is not unique to women. They proposed that it is more likely to be held by women than men, but other research (Davis, 1994; Wark & Krebs, 1996) has found that moral reasoning is more complex. Both the care and the justice orientations are types of reasoning that both men and women can and do use, and both are desirable for mature moral reasoning. The "different voice" is different, but not unique to women.

Gilligan's altered position has not received the publicity that her original work did. As is often the case in media coverage of gender issues, the findings of a complex relationship between gender and morality failed to gain the media attention that the simpler, more sensational findings generated. When Sommers (2000) criticized Gilligan's methodology and conclusions, she focused on Gilligan's early research and the publicity that research generated. Sommers wanted to make the point that Gilligan was biased in her approach, but Sommers herself came to the discussion with biases that she wanted to support. She accused Gilligan of being selective in choosing examples to support her point, but Sommers was also guilty of similar tactics.

The Maximalist Approach and Its Implications

Gilligan's *In a Different Voice* (1982) represents an approach to gender differences that highlights the differences between men and women. This concentration on differences typifies the **maximalist** view—the view that the differences between the sexes are more important than the similarities. Although Gilligan later modified her position about women having a different voice in making moral judgments (Gilligan & Attanucci, 1988), her work still inspired others and promoted the maximalist view that women and men operate on a different moral basis.

The maximalist view highlights differences, searching for the points of divergence rather than commonality. Concentrating on differences has several implications for the study of gender: perpetuating the notion that men and women are at opposite ends of a continuum, a tendency toward ignoring individual differences within genders, and concentrating on one gender or the other rather than studying both. Although some contemporary theorists take a feminist orientation to the maximalist view, this position can also reflect the opposite stance—namely, that the differences between men and women give men the advantage and put women at a disadvantage. The maximalist view, regardless of position, perpetuates polarities.

Feminist researchers and theorists who promote the maximalist view (Belenky, Clinchy, Goldberger, & Tarule, 1986; Brown & Gilligan, 1992, 1993; Chodorow, 1978, 1979; Gilligan, 1982) believe that emphasizing differences between women and men will allow researchers to concentrate on the strengths of the overlooked point of view and bring it to attention and acknowledgment. Chodorow (1979) wrote, "In this view, women are intrinsically better than men, and their virtues are not available to men" (p. 43). For example, in researching the care orientation to moral judgments, Gilligan hoped to validate women's special perspective. Those researchers and theorists who object to the maximalist view (Crawford, 1989; Epstein, 1988; Tavris, 1992, 1994) believe that highlighting differences perpetuates stereotyping based on overgeneralization. For example, if the care orientation is unique to women, then women should be well suited to certain jobs (like elementary school teachers, who must care) and poorly suited to other jobs (like judges, who must be detached and objective).

In addition to encouraging stereotyping, the maximalist view tends to overlook individual differences. Dividing people into oppositional categories obscures the differences of individuals within these categories. Therefore, the individual differences among women and among men are of less interest to the maximalists than differences between the two groups. By ignoring individual differences, this view also minimizes the important influences of factors such as age, ethnicity, and social class. These factors have a long research history; hundreds of studies have shown that each can contribute to many facets of behavior. In overlooking these factors or assuming the influences to be small, the maximalists endanger the credibility of their research (Crawford, 1989).

Maximalists have tended to concentrate on either men or women, but not both. The traditional maximalist theories, such as Freud's psychoanalytic theory of personality, have detailed the development of men but neglected women. The modern maximalist theories, put forward by feminist scholars such as Gilligan, have concentrated on the unique aspects of women's experience and neglected men's experience. These feminist scholars argue that women deserve special attention to compensate for the long history of neglect, but they cannot claim that their research and theories reveal anything definite about gender unless they study both men and women. Neither can these researchers rely on existing research that uses only male participants to furnish valid comparisons for the female subjects they have studied, as some researchers (Belenky et al., 1986; Gilligan, 1982) have done. Men who participated in research during the 1950s would not be an appropriate comparison for women who participated in research during the 1980s (Crawford, 1989). Therefore, singling out either women or men as subjects tends to endanger the scientific validity of a study.

"If masculinist values have undermined the validity of past sex difference research, do feminist values lead to more valid research, or merely substitute a different set of biases?" (Crawford, 1989, p. 128). Some scholars believe that the substitution of feminist values would bring about desirable changes in research. Other scholars believe that substituting one set of biases for another offers no improvement. Both opinions have produced valuable research and have raised important questions, so this controversy shows no sign of disappearing.

Considering Diversity

What role does culture play in moral development? Do people with different cultural backgrounds vary in the factors they take into account in making moral judgments? Do people take others' cultural backgrounds into account in judging behavior?

A male African American student from a southern African American community expressed his disagreement with Carol Gilligan's division of the care and the justice orientations by saying,

> *If Carol Gilligan is right, my brothers and I were raised to be girls as much as boys, and the opposite goes for my sisters. We were raised in a large family with a morality of care as well as injustices at an early age. Sisters, brothers, it doesn't make a difference. Carol Gilligan should come visit my home town! (Stack, 1997, p. 51)*

This opinion led to an investigation of moral reasoning among African American working-class adolescents and adults who had migrated to the North but returned to the rural South (Stack, 1997). The data from this investigation failed to support universal gender differences in moral judgments. Women and men were equal in using both care and justice reasoning, indicating that the situation, ethnicity, and social class of the respondents influenced their choices in moral reasoning.

People can also vary their moral judgment according to the beliefs of other cultures. Children, adolescents, and young adults all showed their willingness to adjust their beliefs about what was right or wrong according to another culture's belief system (Wainryb, 1993). Participants received information about beliefs in a hypothetical culture and judged whether a particular action was right or wrong. The results indicated that people of all ages were able to assimilate information about another culture's set of moral values in judging the actions of people in that culture. No gender differences appeared in these judgments. In the situations in which the information concerning the moral beliefs of another culture varied from their own, two-thirds of participants took this information into account in making their judgments; they said that it was right to act in ways that are consistent with each culture's values.

However, some types of information did not prompt people to modify their moral judgments concerning discrimination. Regardless of information about how a culture considered women inferior, 60% of U.S. children, adolescents, and young adults believed that it was not acceptable to discriminate against women in hiring, even in a culture that believes women are made to serve men (Wainryb, 1993). Therefore, people in the United States have a limited willingness to modify their moral judgments when cultures clash in values.

These findings highlight a conflict between cultural sensitivity and moral universals: How do people accept the beliefs from other cultures when those beliefs are morally offensive to them? This dilemma is very complex (Hatfield & Rapson, 1996). On the one hand, acceptance of cultural diversity has been lacking in U.S. psychology, so inclusion of a variety of ethnic and cultural groups is a positive change. Part of that inclusion is learning to accept these diverse cultures. On the other hand, some cultures have beliefs and practices that go against the values of many people in North America. For example, in parts of India and southeast Asia, infant girls are killed whereas infant boys are prized; in Thailand, very young girls are coerced into prostitution; in Africa and both the far and middle East, genital mutilation of girls (and, to a lesser extent, boys) is a part of the cultural heritage. These cultural differences are difficult for many people in Europe and North America to accept, despite their long traditions in these other societies. How do we accept other cultures and celebrate their diversity when we find some of their practices morally repulsive?

This unwillingness to accept discrimination and unfair treatment may be part of a worldwide trend toward accepting principles of equality. Perhaps a "Westernization" of values is occurring that includes an increasing value for democracy, human rights, and gender equality (Hatfield & Rapson, 1996). As these values gain wider influence, people will be increasingly likely to disagree with some cultures' practices. But the wider acceptance of equality should also lead to a decrease in reprehensible practices and a growing acceptance of values that emphasize human rights. That is, the world may be moving toward a universal morality.

Summary

Psychoanalytic theory, originated by Freud, is the traditional approach to personality theory and relies on the concepts of unconscious forces and biologically determined instincts to explain personality development and functioning. Freud's theory hypothesized a series of psychosexual stages—oral, anal, phallic, latency, and genital—to account for the influence of childhood experiences on adult personality. Gender differences appear during the phallic stage, with its Oedipus complex in which children are attracted to their other-sex parent and feel fear and hostility toward their same-sex parent. Boys experience a more traumatic and a more complete resolution of the Oedipus complex than girls, resulting in a stronger superego and thus a stronger morality for boys.

Horney disputed Freud's view that women inevitably experience inferiority by arguing that social, not biological, forces form the basis for personality differences between the sexes. Her analysis of the differences in personality development between men and women showed that men have feelings of inferiority compared to women, especially regarding women's ability to give birth. Horney hypothesized that men try to feel more adequate by disparaging women.

Although the popularity of psychoanalytic theory within psychology and psychiatry has declined over the years, its influence has never disappeared. During the 1970s and 1980s, Freudian theory was once again brought to prominence and became controversial because of accusations that Freud acted improperly in abandoning the seduction theory. Freud abandoned the seduction theory, the hypothesis that seduction by an adult (usually a parent) is the basis for adult emotional problems, in favor of the view that most of these seductions were children's fantasies rather than realities. This change created credibility problems for victims of sexual abuse, and several psychoanalytic scholars have proposed that psychoanalysis would have been more accurate and more useful if Freud had retained this element of the theory. Controversies in psychoanalytic theory were fueled by the appearance of feminist psychoanalytic theory.

Feminist psychoanalytic theories include those originated by Nancy Chodorow and Ellyn Kaschak. Chodorow's theory emphasizes the primacy of the early relationship with mothers and hypothesizes that boys have a more difficult time separating themselves from the feminine than do girls. Men's success in forming a masculine identity results in a denial of all that is feminine, including a rejection of female values. Kaschak's theory relies on the Oedipus legend, hypothesizing that Oedipus personifies men's drives for power and feelings of entitlement, whereas Antigone, the faithful daughter, personifies women's self-sacrifice. She maintained that patriarchal culture perpetuates these roles and makes resolving these complexes difficult for men and women.

These feminist psychoanalytic theories are some of the feminist standpoint theories that approach personality from the point of view of women and their unique experiences. Gilligan's research on moral development is a feminist standpoint theory that originated in Gilligan's hearing a "different voice" in women's moral decisions. She studied moral development and decided that women are more likely to make moral decisions based on care for relationships than on abstract principles of justice. Criticisms of her method of study and conclusions resulted in additional research, indicating that the types of moral reasoning Gilligan found in women are not unique to women. Both men and women accept the care orientation and the justice orientation in their moral reasoning, and moral judgments vary according to situational factors more than by gender.

Traditional psychoanalytic theory and feminist standpoint theories both take a maximalist approach to personality, which holds that men and women show large gender differences in personal styles. Such theories tend to encourage stereotyping, obscure individual differences, and exclude one sex or the other from research. Although maximalist theories may provide interesting and valuable information about women or men, this approach does not work when applied to a study of gender, because both men and women must be included in such studies for the results to be valid.

Moral values show some differences among cultures, and people are able to take these differences into account when they judge people from other cultures. However, some behaviors are judged as unacceptable, even when those behaviors are accepted by the other culture. This standard of moral judgment suggests that a Westernized universal morality may be developing throughout the world.

Glossary

castration complex in Freudian theory, the unconscious fear that the father will castrate his son as a punishment for the son's sexual longings for his mother.

ego in Freudian theory, the structure of personality that is rational and practical, and allows individuals to moderate their behavior to seek gratification in ways that are rational and do not harm others.

id in Freudian theory, the structure of personality that is the repository for instincts and urges to seek pleasure and avoid pain at any cost, even to the point of irrationality.

instincts in Freudian theory, the drives or impulses that underlie action, thought, and other aspects of personality functioning, which include the life, or sexual, instinct and the death, or aggressive, instinct.

masochism feelings of pleasure as a result of painful or humiliating experiences.

maximalist a person who holds the view that many important differences exist between the sexes and that women and men are more different than similar.

Oedipus complex in Freudian theory, the situation that exists during the phallic stage in which the child feels unconscious hostility toward the same-sex parent and unconscious sexual feelings for the opposite-sex parent. Freud used the story of Oedipus as an analogy for the family dynamics that occur during the phallic stage of personality development.

pre-Oedipal period time during early childhood, before the phallic stage and the Oedipus complex. Some feminist psychoanalytic theorists, including Chodorow, have emphasized the importance of this period for personality development.

psychosexual stages in Freudian theory, the series of stages ranging from birth to maturity through which the individual's personality develops. These stages are the oral, anal, phallic, latency, and genital stages.

seduction theory in Freudian theory, the view that sexual activity between parent and child is the basis for psychological problems when the child grows to adulthood. Freud held this view for only a short time, replacing it with the notion that the seduction was fantasized by the child rather than real.

superego in Freudian theory, the structure of the personality that incorporates the moral rules of parents and society, and functions to control sexual and aggressive impulses.

unconscious in Freudian theory, a region of the mind functioning beyond a person's conscious awareness.

Suggested Readings

Buhle, Mari Jo. (1999, February 5). Feminism, Freud, and popular culture. *Chronicle of Higher Education,* p. B4. Buhle discusses the resurgence of psychoanalytic theory in feminist studies and how Freudian theory has had an important impact on popular culture as well as on academic theory.

Chodorow, Nancy. (1978). *The reproduction of mothering: Psychoanalysis and the sociology of gender.* Berkeley, CA: University of California Press. Chodorow's book is difficult reading, with its psychoanalytic terminology, but it offers a compelling alternative to Freud's theory and has influenced many of the scholars who take the feminist standpoint on personality development.

Freud, Sigmund. (1964). Femininity. In James Strachey (Ed. and Trans.), *New introductory lectures on psychoanalysis* (pp. 112–135). New York: Norton. (Original work published in 1933.) Freud's last lengthy statement about the psychology of women is interesting to read rather than read about, because Freud seems much more tentative on some issues, but completely convinced on other issues, of gender differences.

Kaschak, Ellyn. (1992). *Engendered lives.* New York: Basic Books. Kaschak's book is not easy reading, but she offers an interesting, radical alternative to traditional psychoanalytic theory. Chapter 3, "Oedipus and Antigone Revisited: The Family Drama," presents her revision of Freudian theory, but the entire book is worth reading for its different view of gender and the impact of gender on all facets of psychology and culture.

Pollitt, Katha. (1995). Marooned on Gilligan's island: Are women morally superior to men? In Katha Pollitt, *Reasonable creatures: Essays on women and feminism* (pp. 42–62). New York: Knopf. Katha Pollitt criticizes Gilligan and feminist standpoint theory in this witty essay that examines theory, research, social policy, and personal moral dilemmas.

Chapter 6

Gender Development

Social Theories

HEADLINE

Singing the Pink Blues

Mothers Who Think, www.salon.com, December 13, 1999

> *Thirty years of feminism notwithstanding, the mass-market toy industry has either slept through the women's movement or woefully misunderstood it. Nowhere is this more apparent than at the annual American International Toy Fair, where gender apartheid flowers freely in a hothouse of go-go commerce: girls get dolls, kitchen sets and makeup packaged in Pepto-Bismol pink; boys get weapons, action figures and vehicles in everything but pink. Color-coding starts at birth, and the role assignments kick in when children are still toddlers, barely able to keep their balance, much less process the demands of their gender role. (Mifflin, 1999, p. 1)*

Margot Mifflin (1999) wrote about her distress over the gender typing of toys and the inflexibility of the roles that these toys promote. She bought a Little Tikes Wee Waffle farm set hoping it would be much better, but she discovered gender typing there, too: "the father plugged into a round role in the driver's seat of the tractor but the mother—literally a square peg in a round hole—didn't" (Mifflin, 1999, p. 1).

Her 4-year-old daughter was being pushed into a pink world, and Mifflin decided that the answer to the toy problem was to urge her daughter to play with boys' toys. She discovered that the realm of boys' toys was not pink, but it was a realm without girls. All of the action figures were male (except for Princess Leia, an action figure that didn't actually do anything). Even the computer games were gender-segregated into stereotypical divisions of action and aggression for boys and fashion and crafts for girls. This situation was annoying for Mifflin, but was her daughter as affected? How influential are toys in learning gender roles?

A **gender role** consists of socially significant activities that men and women engage in with different frequencies. Robert Brannon (1976) discussed the origin of the concept of *role,* tracing its adoption in the field of social science back to the terminology of the theater. The word *role* was French for "roll," referring to the roll of paper on which an actor's part was printed. This usage is particularly meaningful, if we consider that the role, or the part a person plays, differs from the person. Therefore, the male gender role or the female gender role is like a script that men and women follow to fulfill their appropriate masculine or feminine parts. Social scientists use the term *role* to mean expected, socially encouraged patterns of behavior exhibited by individuals in specific situations. Thus, a person acts to fulfill a role by behaving in the expected way in the appropriate situation.

Chapter 5 examined the development of gender from the perspective of psychoanalytic personality theory, a view suggesting that unconscious forces and early childhood experiences form personality. The psychoanalytic view is not the only explanation for the development of personality, including gender differences. Mifflin's story about gender typing in toys concentrated on the social factors that children experience as they play with the toys that adults choose for them. The influence of such factors forms the foundation for social learning theory, cognitive developmental theory, gender schema theory, and gender script theory.

Social Learning Theory

Social learning theory explains gender development in the same way that it explains other types of learned behaviors, by placing gender development with behaviors that are learned. This theory takes a stand on the nature–nurture controversy by describing the influence of nurture in the social environment. Biological sex differences are the basis for gender roles, but social learning theorists contend that a great many other characteristics and behaviors that have no relation to sex have been tied to gender roles. In this view, gender role development is the result of social factors (Bandura, 1986; Bussey & Bandura, 1999).

The social learning approach is a variation of traditional learning theory, which includes the principles of operant conditioning developed by B. F. Skinner. **Operant conditioning** is a form of learning based on applying **reinforcement** and **punishment.** To understand the relationship between social learning theory and traditional learning theory, a consideration of traditional learning theory and the concept of operant conditioning is in order.

In this traditional view, learning is defined as a change in behavior that is the result of experience or practice. Operant conditioning is one type of learning. In operant conditioning, a person (or other animal) changes behavior after receiving either reinforcement or punishment. The behavior is more likely to be repeated in the future if that person (or animal) has received a reinforcer after performing the behavior in the past. That is, a reinforcer is any stimulus that increases the probability that a behavior will recur. On the other hand, a person is less likely to repeat a behavior in the future if that person has been punished after performing the behavior in the past. That is, punishment is any stimulus that decreases the probability that a behavior will recur. The previous consequences of a behavior thus influence the resulting behavior, with reinforcers making the behavior more likely and punishments making it less likely. Patterns of reinforcement or punishment produce change in behavior, which is the definition of learning. Table 6.1 gives an example of how reinforcements and punishments can work to mold gender-related behaviors.

TABLE 6.1 Results of Reinforcement and Punishment for Gender-Related Behaviors

Behavior	Consequences	Result
Little girl plays with doll	*Reinforcement:* Her mother praises her toy choice	Girl plays with doll again
Little girl plays with truck	*Punishment:* Her mother scolds her for choosing a truck	Girl does not play with truck again
Little boy plays with doll	*Punishment:* His mother scolds him for choosing a doll	Boy does not play with doll again
Little boy plays with truck	*Reinforcement:* His mother praises his toy choice	Boy plays with truck again

Traditional learning theorists attempted to avoid mentalistic concepts and terminology in their explanations of behavior. That is, they rejected all concepts of internal mental processes that might underlie learning, and concentrated instead on objectively observable behaviors. This approach emphasized the importance of the conditions under which learning occurs and the factors that affect performance, especially reinforcements and punishments received, rather than the cognitive factors within the learner.

The experiences of reinforcement and punishment furnish each individual with a unique learning history: No other person has exactly the same experiences. The reinforcements and punishments in each individual's history contribute to present and future behavior. Thus, future behavior can be predicted from past experience.

Social learning theory also includes the concepts of reinforcement and punishment, but it extends learning theory to include cognitive processes. This addition changes the emphasis of learning, by increasing the importance of observation. Social learning theorists consider observation more important to the process of learning than reinforcement. To these theorists, learning is cognitive, whereas performance is behavioral. The social learning approach thus separates learning from performing learned behaviors, and it investigates factors that affect both.

According to social learning theory, learning is produced by observation rather than by directly experiencing reinforcement or punishment (Mischel, 1966, 1993). Observation provides many opportunities for learning, including the learning of gender-related behaviors among children. The social environment provides children with examples of male and female models who perform different behaviors, including gender-related ones. The models who influence children include mothers and fathers, but also many others, both real people and media images of boys, girls, men, women, and cartoon characters. In observing these many male and female models, children have abundant opportunities to learn. However, not all models have the same influence for all children, and not all behaviors are equally likely to be imitated.

The differential influence of models relates to their power or prestige as well as to the observer's attention and perception of the similarity between model and observer. Children tend to be more influenced by powerful models than by models with less power (Bussey & Bandura, 1984), but children are also more influenced by models who are similar to them. This similarity extends to gender, with children more likely to imitate same-sex models than other-sex models.

Another important factor in performing a learned behavior is observing the consequences of that behavior. If people observe a behavior being rewarded, then they are more likely to perform that behavior than if they see the same behavior punished or unrewarded. Social learning theorists believe that reinforcement and punishment are not essential for learning, which occurs through observation. Instead, reinforcement and punishment are more important to performance, affecting the likelihood that a learned behavior will be performed in circumstances similar to those observed.

Children develop in an atmosphere in which they are exposed to models of gender-stereotypic behaviors "in the home, in schools, on playgrounds, in readers and storybooks, and in representations of society on the television screens of every household" (Bandura, 1986, p. 93). These presentations do two things. First, all children are exposed to both female and male models, so all children learn the gender-related behaviors associated with *both* genders. Second, children learn which behaviors are gender-appropriate for them. Children learn that certain behaviors are rewarded for girls but not for boys; for other behaviors, the rewards come to boys and not to girls.

For example, children see girls rewarded for playing with dolls, whereas they see boys discouraged and ridiculed for this same behavior. Children see boys rewarded for playing with toy trucks, but they may see girls discouraged from that behavior. Both boys and girls learn how to play with dolls and trucks, but they are not equally likely to do so due to the differential rewards they have seen others receive. Their learning is not based on observation of merely a few models; the world is filled with examples of men and women who are rewarded and punished for gender-related behaviors. The portrayals of gender-related behavior are especially stereotypical in the media (Lont, 1995) and offer a multitude of sexist examples for children to model (see "According to the Media/According to the Research"). Therefore, children may behave in ways different from their parents, including expressing sexist views that their parents do not endorse.

Not all observed consequences are consistent with each other; some people are rewarded and others punished for the same behavior. Consistency is not necessary for children to learn gender-related behaviors (Bandura, 1986). Children observe many models; they notice the consistencies among the behaviors of some models and start to overlook the exceptions. As more same-sex models exhibit a behavior, the more likely children are to connect that behavior with one or the other sex. Through this process, behaviors come to be gender related, although these behaviors may have no direct relationship to sex. Children learn to pay attention to sex and the activities associated with each, and thus they become selective in their modeling.

Children experience many sources of modeling and reinforcement, and these sources influence the development of gender-related behaviors (Beal, 1994). Beginning before birth, parents often have some preference for a boy or a girl—more often for a boy. When their children are infants, parents interact differently with their sons and daughters. For example, children accept and show equal enthusiasm for toys typically considered girls' and boys' toys (Idle, Wood, & Desmarais, 1993), but *parents* use some gender-typical preferences in selecting activities and toys for their children. Parents are not alone in these preferences; in one study (Campenni, 1999), adults who were not parents showed even more stereotypical toy choices than parents did.

Studies that observe parental interactions with children have confirmed gender differences in treatment. Mothers gave more instructions and directions than fathers did while

ACCORDING TO THE MEDIA...

Cartoons Put Girls in the Background

Children's television programming has always been oriented toward boys. The programming executives believe that boys are more numerous in the Saturday morning audience, and that boys will not watch programs with female lead characters (Thompson & Zerbinos, 1995). The early analyses of cartoon programming indicated few female characters. Overall, female characters were less visible, important, active, and responsible; they were also younger and more in need of rescuing or help. All of these characteristics are stereotypically feminine and cast girls and women in traditional roles.

Between the 1970s and 1990s, gender portrayals in cartoons changed (Thompson & Zerbinos, 1995). Gender stereotyping persisted, but at lower levels, and the presentation of female characters changed more than for male characters. One of the factors in these changes was the nature of cartoon programming. Many of the cartoons in the earlier decades involved chases and pratfalls, and the main and secondary characters in such cartoons tended to be male. Such cartoons have declined in popularity, and thus the typical characters in cartoons have changed.

Continuing adventures have become the most common format for cartoons (Thompson & Zerbinos, 1995). Female characters are now more independent, assertive, intelligent, competent, and responsible and less emotional, sensitive, and tentative. In the continuing adventure, female characters are most independent and least domestic. The male characters in continuing adventures still behave in stereotypical ways for men, giving orders and being brave and aggressive.

The changes in the ways male and female characters are portrayed do not imply that gender stereotyping has disappeared from cartoons. Male characters still appear more often, talk more often, and are more active and assertive than female characters. Female characters still ask for and need more help, care for others, and show more affection than male characters. That is, male and female gender role traits and behaviors remain prominent in children's cartoons.

playing with their 18-month-old children, but fathers spent more time playing with them than mothers did (Fagot & Hagan, 1991). Their different treatment of the toddlers was shown by fathers giving fewer positive responses to sons who chose to play with "girls' toys" and mothers giving more instructions to daughters who tried an activity commonly associated with girls—communication. During the preschool years, boys come to believe that their fathers disapprove of cross-gender toy choices and behave accordingly, rejecting these toys (Raag & Rackliff, 1998). Thus, parents both encourage and discourage gender-related behaviors.

Social learning theory hypothesizes that these forces affect gender-related thinking, and children come to develop gender knowledge and gender standards for their own behavior. In children age 2 to 4 years, behavior typical of the same sex was more common than behavior typical of the other sex for all ages of children (Bussey & Bandura, 1992). The younger children in the study reacted to their peers in gender-stereotypical ways but did not regulate their own behavior by these same standards, whereas the older children did both. These results indicate that these 4-year-olds had begun to develop a coherent set of cognitive strategies for controlling their gender-related behaviors.

ACCORDING TO THE RESEARCH...

Gender Depictions of Cartoon Characters Convey a Message

Children must notice and be influenced by the disparity in presentations of female and male cartoon characters for this stereotyping to be a factor in children's behavior. According to a review of research on gender development and social learning theory (Bussey & Bandura, 1999), the media offer many more opportunities for children to observe stereotypical gender behaviors than actual experience does. The extent to which children are influenced by these presentations depends on a number of factors, including how similar the media characters are to the children's perceptions of themselves. Thus, gender is one of the salient characteristics that influence whether a child will model a particular behavior.

Children who identify with television characters tend to choose gender-stereotypical characteristics as the basis for their identification (Hoffner, 1996). When asked to identify their favorite television characters, nearly all the boys and about half of girls chose a same-gender character. For the children who identified with male characters, intelligence was the most important characteristic, regardless of the gender of the child, but for boys, strength was also important. For the children who identified with female characters (all of whom were girls), attractiveness was the only significant factor. These choices reflect stereotypical criteria used by the 7- to 12-year-olds in the study.

Research indicates that children not only notice but are also influenced by gender portrayals in cartoons. Interviews with children between ages 4 and 9 years (Thompson & Zerbinos, 1997) showed that 78% noticed that cartoons contained more male than female characters, and 68% noticed that boys talked more in cartoons. When asked what cartoon characters did, the children named behaviors stereotypically associated with men (being violent) and women (being considerate). In addition, the children who noticed the gender differences in the cartoon characters tended to be more likely to envision themselves in a gender stereotypical job than children who were less aware of the gender portrayals in cartoons. This tendency was stronger for boys than for girls. In contrast, the children who noticed characters behaving in nonstereotypical ways were the ones who were more likely to see themselves in a nontraditional job. This tendency applied to both girls and boys.

Therefore, the gendered presentation of characters in cartoons has the power to do harm. Children notice and are influenced by these stereotypical presentations, and young children take this information into account when they imagine themselves in an occupation.

When children start interacting with peers outside the home, these other children become a major source of both modeling and approval. Children's play groups tend to be gender segregated, especially in school settings. Children often put a great deal of effort into maintaining this segregation and even begin to use insults and severe prohibitions aimed at those who attempt to join an other-sex group (Thorne, 1993). The formation of relationships, including the gender composition of play groups, is a topic explored in Chapter 9.

The differential treatment of boys and girls is enhanced by parents' and teachers' expectations and encouragement during the school years. Both parents and teachers are more likely to urge boys to persist in solving problems than they urge girls. By the time children reach adolescence, their models and reinforcements tend to encourage boys toward careers and sexual expression and girls toward domesticity and physical attractiveness (Lips, 1989). Therefore, children develop in environments that contain many sources of social learning that will lead to differences in the gender-related behaviors of boys and girls.

In summary, social learning theory views the development of gender-related behaviors as part of the overall development of many behaviors that children learn through observation and modeling. This theory emphasizes the contribution of the social environment to learning and behavior. Social learning theory sees learning, which occurs through observation, as cognitive and separate from performance, which is behavioral. Whether a learned behavior is performed or not depends on the observed consequences of the behavior and the observers' beliefs about the appropriateness of the behavior. Thus, children have many opportunities to observe gender-related behaviors and to develop beliefs about the consequences of those behaviors. Children observe many gender-related behaviors from a wide variety of models and learn to exhibit appropriate gender-related behaviors as a result of their observation of these models.

Sandra Bem (1985) criticized social learning theory, arguing that the theory portrays children as too passive. Bem pointed out that children's behavior shows signs of more active involvement than social learning theory hypothesizes. Children do not exhibit a gradual increase in gender-related behaviors, but rather seem to form cognitive categories for gender and then acquire gender-related knowledge around these categories. In addition, research evidence suggests that children may develop stronger gender stereotypes than their parents convey, which implies that children actively organize information about gender. Other social theories of gender development place a stronger emphasis on cognitive organization than does social learning theory.

Cognitive Developmental Theory

The cognitive developmental theorist Lawrence Kohlberg (1966) described this theory by saying, "Our approach to the problems of sexual development starts directly with neither biology nor culture, but with cognition" (p. 82). Cognitive developmental theory views the acquisition of gender-related behaviors as part of children's general cognitive development. This development occurs as children mature and interact with the world, forming an increasingly complex and accurate understanding of their bodies and the world.

GENDERED VOICES

I Wouldn't Know How to Be a Man

"I never thought of myself as very feminine, but I wouldn't begin to know how to be a man," said a woman in her 30s. "There are thousands of things about being a man or being a woman that the other doesn't know. It takes years to learn all those things. I have been struck several times by the differences in women's and men's experience, by small things.

"During college one of my roommate's boyfriends decided to paint one of his fingernails. It was an odd thing to do, but he said that it was an experience he hadn't had, and he just wanted to try it. What was interesting was that he didn't know how to go about it—didn't know how to hold the brush, which direction to apply the polish. It was interesting to watch him. That was the first time that I really thought, 'Men and women have some unique experiences that the other does not know.' I've had that thought several times since then, usually about small experiences or skills that women have and men don't.

"I'm sure that it works the other way, too. There's a world of little experiences that are part of men's lives that women don't have a clue about. For example, I wouldn't know how to go about shaving my face. In some sense, these experiences are trivial, but they made me think about the differences between the worlds of women and men."

This approach follows Jean Piaget's theory of cognitive development, which places the development of gender-related concepts into the category of growth of cognitive abilities, and which emphasizes children's active role in organizing their own thoughts (see Ginsburg & Opper, 1969). Piaget described four stages of cognitive development, beginning at birth and ending during preadolescence, throughout which children achieve cognitive maturity. During childhood, limitations in cognitive abilities lead children to have problems in classifying objects according to any given physical characteristic such as size or color. During their elementary school years, children gain in cognitive abilities but may still have difficulty in dealing with abstractions, such as the ability to imagine hypothetical situations—"what if." Piaget believed that once children reach cognitive maturity, at around age 11 or 12 years, they no longer have any cognitive limitations on their understanding. (Although lack of information may be a limitation at this or any age, this problem is different from the limits on cognitive ability that appear during childhood.) Thus, Piaget explained cognitive development as a series of stages leading to an increasing ability to understand physical reality and deal with abstract, complex problems. Infants are capable of almost no abstract thought, but by preadolescence, children have fewer limitations on their cognitive abilities.

Cognitive developmental theorists see the development of gender-related behaviors as part of the task of cognitive development. Very young children, lacking a concept of self, can have no concept of their gender. Most 2½-year-olds are unable to consistently apply the words *boy* or *girl* to self or others; thus they fail at **gender labeling.** Kohlberg (1966) hypothesized that children acquire some preliminary category information about gender during early childhood, but **gender constancy,** the belief that their genders will remain the same throughout life, is a cognitively more complex concept that may not appear until between ages 4 and 7 years.

By age 3 years, children are more often successful at gender self-labeling; over half of children at this age are able to correctly use the words *boy* or *girl* to describe themselves. This word usage does not signal development of **gender identity,** the process of identifying oneself as female or male. Three-year-olds apply these words incorrectly in many cases. For example, a child may label all people she likes or all members of her family as "girls" and all others as "boys."

When children can consistently apply gender labels, they may still do so on the basis of some external and irrelevant physical characteristic, such as clothing or hairstyle. In addition, children of this age do not see gender as a permanent feature; they believe that a boy can become a girl if he wishes or that a girl might become a boy if she dressed in boys' clothing (Kohlberg, 1966). Between ages 5 and 6 years, most children develop a gender identity that is based on a classification of self and others as irreversibly belonging to one gender or the other. This gender constancy is part of children's growing ability to classify objects based on physical criteria. Thus, in the development of gender identity, children younger than age 5 or 6 years make mistakes in understanding gender and using gender-related words, but by age 6 years, children have a developed sense of gender identity that includes correct gender labeling of self and others as well as gender constancy.

These cognitive developments in conceptualizing gender parallel other cognitive changes in children. Below ages 5 or 6 years, children have an incomplete understanding of the qualities of physical objects, and their misunderstanding of gender is part of this limitation. By around age 6 years, children have developed a correct, if concrete, understanding of physical reality, including gender identity. Cognitive developmental theory sees changes that occur in gender identity as part of cognitive development, and the mistakes that children make concerning gender identity are seen as part of their general cognitive limitations during the course of development.

The cognitive developmental approach is similar to the social learning approach in its emphasis on the role of cognition. However, the two approaches differ in several ways. Cognitive developmental theory hypothesizes that development moves through a series of stages, whereas social learning theory does not rely on the concept of stages in development. That is, cognitive developmental theory sees gender role development as proceeding through discrete stages. Each stage has internal consistency and a set of differences that delineate it from successive stages. Social learning theory sees development as more continuous and not bounded by stages. Figure 6.1 illustrates the difference between development as a continuous process and as a series of stages.

Cognitive developmental theory views the acquisition of gender-related behaviors as a by-product of the cognitive development of gender identity. Children begin to adopt and exhibit gender-related behaviors because they adopt a gender identity and strive to be consistent with this identity. On the other hand, social learning theory hypothesizes that children come to have a gender identity because they model gender-related behaviors. Through the performance of these behaviors, children conform to either the masculine or feminine social roles of their culture. In summary, social learning theory sees gender identity as coming from performance of gender-related behaviors, whereas cognitive developmental theory sees gender-related behaviors as coming from the cognitive adoption of a gender identity.

When children develop an understanding of categories, including gender categories, they tend to concentrate on the classification rules and show a great reluctance to make exceptions. Applied to gender, this strategy leads to classifying all women and all men by invariant phys-

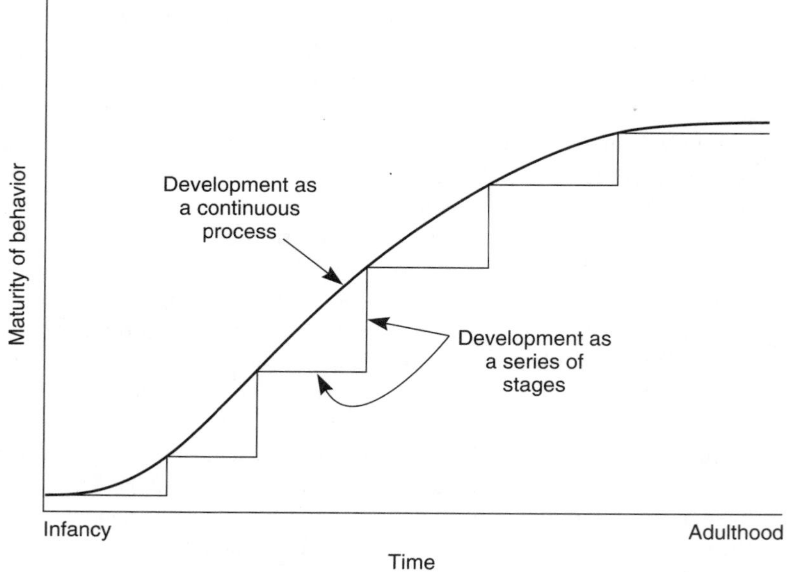

FIGURE 6.1 Two Views of Development

ical or behavioral characteristics. That is, cognitive developmental theory predicts that children will develop gender stereotypes as part of their process of developing gender identity. A great deal of research evidence substantiates the notion that children form stereotypical gender concepts beginning early in their lives. Children as young as 2 years old exhibit stereotypical gender-related knowledge, and this level of knowledge relates to their comprehension of gender identity and gender constancy (Kuhn, Nash, & Brucken, 1978). The process of acquiring gender stereotypes is related to the development of gender constancy (Warin, 2000). However, stereotype development is complex, and Chapter 7 explores this process more fully.

One problem with cognitive developmental theory comes from its emphasis on gender constancy as the primary force underlying the development of gender identity. Although Kohlberg's predictions are not completely clear on this point (Stangor & Ruble, 1987), he hypothesized that gender constancy is the most important component of cognitive developmental theory, and that all other facets of gender identity stem from establishing gender constancy. Research has failed to substantiate this contention (Martin & Little, 1990), leaving a major component of this theory in doubt.

Another problem with cognitive developmental theory comes from the need to treat gender the same as any other cognitive category. As Sandra Bem (1985) put it, "The theory fails to explicate why sex has primacy over other potential categories of the self such as race, religion, or even eye color" (p. 184). This theory fails to explain why children choose gender as a primary domain around which to organize information. This problem has been addressed in gender schema theory, which extends the concepts in cognitive developmental theory.

Gender Schema Theory

Gender schema theory is an extension of the cognitive developmental theory. A **schema** is "a cognitive structure, a network of associations that organizes and guides an individual's perceptions" (Bem, 1981, p. 355). Piaget used the term *schema* (plural, *schemata* or *schemas*) to describe how cognitions are internalized around various topics; gender schema theory hypothesizes that children develop gender-related behaviors because they develop schemata that guide them to adopt such behaviors. In this view, gender-related behaviors appear not only as a result of general cognitive development, but also because children develop special schemata related to gender.

According to gender schema theory, the culture also plays a role in gender development, providing the reference for the formation of gender schemata. Not only are children ready to encode and organize information about gender, but they do so in a social environment that defines maleness and femaleness (Bem, 1985). As children develop, they acquire schemata that guide their cognitions related to gender. These schemata influence information processing and problem solving in memory and also regulate behavior (Martin & Halverson, 1981). Gender schema theorists believe that children use these schemata to develop a concept of self versus others, and each child's gender schema is included in that child's self-schema, or self-concept. In addition, gender schemata can provide a guide for concepts of personal masculinity and femininity, including personal judgments about how people personally fit, or fail to fit, these schemata (Janoff-Bulman & Frieze, 1987). Thus, gender schema theory provides an explanation for the concepts of masculinity and femininity and how people apply these concepts to themselves.

Bem (1985) emphasized the process rather than the content of gender schemata. The information in the schemata is not as important as the process of forming schemata and acting in ways that are consistent with them. Gender schema theory predicts that the cognitive changes that accompany schema formation lead to the ways that children process gender-related information, which changes the ways in which they behave. Research (Levy, Barth, & Zimmerman, 1998) confirmed these predictions, showing that gender-schematic preschoolers behaved in more gender-typical ways than less schematic children.

Gender schema theory also predicts that developing gender schemata increases accuracy and memory for gender-consistent information compared to gender-inconsistent information. A number of studies have demonstrated such memory effects in both children and adults. Gender-typed college students tended to remember words in clusters related to gender—for example, the women's proper names in a cluster and the men's names in another (Bem, 1981). This schematicity did not affect the number of words remembered, but the organization of memory differed according to participants' gender schemata. In addition, participants with strong gender schemata were faster at making gender-related judgments that were consistent with their gender schemata than they were at making judgments inconsistent with their schemata.

The types of differences found among gender-schematic college students prompted further research using a similar approach, but with participants of various ages. A review of the research on gender schema and information processing (Stangor & Ruble, 1987) indicated that children with well-defined gender schemata tend to remember gender-consistent information better than gender-inconsistent information. For example, when children see drawings, photos, or videotapes in which men and women perform activities such as cooking and sewing or driving a truck and repairing appliances, gender-schematic children remember the gender-typical pairings (women cooking and sewing and men driving trucks and repairing appliances) better than the gender-atypical pairings (women driving trucks and repairing appliances and men cooking and sewing). In addition, children tend to change their memories to fit the gender-typical activities, such as remembering a man driving a truck when he was pictured as cooking. This tendency to distort memory in ways consistent with gender schemata suggests that the development of gender schemata influences the way that people interpret information.

In developing gender schemata, children become increasingly ready to interpret information in terms of gender. A tendency to interpret information in gender schematic terms may lead to gender stereotyping—exaggerated and narrow concepts of what is appropriate and acceptable for each gender.

The formation of gender stereotypes can be understood as a natural reflection of the use of gender schemata (Martin & Halverson, 1981). Some of the effects of gender stereotyping are positive, such as increased ease in classifying behaviors and objects, which can give children the feeling that the environment is manageable and predictable. But stereotyping can also have negative effects, leading to inaccurate perceptions and failures to accept information that does not fit the stereotype. Thus, the existence of gender schemata prompts the formation of gender stereotypes, with both positive and negative consequences.

Is schematic processing and the accompanying stereotyping inevitable in children? Gender stereotyping may be a typical outcome, but it is an avoidable one (Bem, 1985, 1987). Parents, however, must take measures to raise "gender-aschematic children in a gender-schematic world" (Bem, 1985, p. 213). Those measures do not include ignoring gender, because society does not. Rather, parents can attempt to eliminate gender differentiation that has nothing to do with gender, they can concentrate on the biological rather than social correlates of sex, and they can substitute some alternative schema.

Bem advised parents to eliminate the multitude of cultural messages concerning gender that have no relation with sex except by association. For example, occupations, household chores, leisure activities, and even color preferences are gender typed by their association with either men or women, and none of these need to be so. Bem advised parents to eliminate gender-related differences from their own activities and to teach their children about the culture's biased messages about gender. She also recommended that parents emphasize the biological rather than social correlates of sex. By teaching children about anatomy and reproduction, Bem argued that parents can limit gender-related associations to biological sex, thus minimizing the pervasive associations of gender with so many aspects of life. Bem also suggested that parents substitute alternative schemata, such as the individual differences schema, for the gender-related differences schema that is the basis of traditional gender stereotyping.

Do Bem's suggestions help to alter the development of gender schemata and lessen the strength of gender stereotyping? Research (Fagot & Leinbach, 1995) suggests that Bem's recommendations can be effective. This study of a group of parents who had sought to establish egalitarian child care routines showed that these efforts were successful, not only in involving both parents in their children's lives, but also in altering the development of their children's gender knowledge.

Some family patterns are more likely to produce nonsexist children than others (Weisner & Wilson-Mitchell, 1990). Traditional families, of course, are likely to have children with strong gender schemata, but some nonconventional families also produce gender-schematic children. The families that followed Bem's suggestions—by using egalitarian behavior patterns combined with questioning of societal norms—produced children with less gender-typed knowledge than other family patterns. Table 6.2 summarizes the factors that relate to children with and without strong gender schemata and shows the combination of factors that tends to make children sexist. Regardless of family attitudes and behavior, all children displayed gender-related information that went far beyond the knowledge that genitals determine a person's sex. That is, no family attitudes or behavior can completely counteract the influence of society's pervasive gender associations.

In summary, gender schema theory extends the cognitive developmental theory by hypothesizing the existence of gender schemata, cognitive structures that internally represent gender-related information and guide perception and behavior. Children internalize their schemata for masculinity or femininity to form a self-concept, or self-schema, for gender-related behaviors. Research has indicated that gender schemata can affect the processing of gender-related information and can lead to gender stereotyping. Parents can attempt to circumvent gender-related messages by concentrating on the biological rather than the social correlates of gender, but all children come to understand their culture's messages about gender.

Gender Script Theory

Gender script theory is an extension of gender schema theory, proposing that the social knowledge that children acquire concerning gender is organized in sequential form. Schemata

TABLE 6.2 Factors in the Development of Gender-Related Attitudes in Children

Children Who Exhibit Inflexible Attitudes about Gender	Children Who Exhibit More Flexible Attitudes about Gender
Have parents who exhibit traditional attitudes concerning gender-related behaviors	Have parents who question traditional attitudes concerning gender-related behaviors
(Weisner & Wilson-Mitchell, 1990)	
Have parents who concentrate on the social correlates of gender	Have parents who concentrate on the physical determinants of sex
(Bem, 1989)	
Interact more with parents	Interact less with parents
(Levy, 1989)	
Have same-gender siblings who are gender-inflexible	Have same-gender siblings who are gender-flexible
(Katz & Ksansnak, 1994)	
Have same-gender peers who are gender-inflexible	Have same-gender peers who are gender-flexible
(Katz & Ksansnak, 1994)	
Are more likely to have mothers who are homemakers	Are more likely to have mothers who work outside the home
(Levy, 1989)	
Are high school boys who are seniors and who are contemplating careers and marriage	Are high school girls who have mothers who work outside the home
(Jackson & Tein, 1998)	

are representations of knowledge, whereas scripts depict an organized sequence of events. That is, the concept of a script enlarges on the notion of schema by adding the component of sequential order. The script allows for the understanding of social relations and can be described as "an ordered sequence of actions appropriate to a particular spatial-temporal context, organized around a goal" (Nelson, 1981, p. 101).

Children as young as 3 years of age show evidence of the type of generalized sequential event knowledge that may be considered a script. Children can describe how to get ready to go out, how to eat lunch at day care, and many such sequences. If young children have well-organized knowledge of events, perhaps they use this organization to acquire information about gender.

Applied to gender role acquisition, gender scripts are "temporally organized event sequences. But in addition, gender scripts possess a gender role stereotype component which defines which sex stereotypically performs a given sequence of events" (Levy & Fivush, 1993, p. 113). For scripts such as eating lunch, the gender of the actor is not important, but the script for cooking lunch is likely to be gender specific.

Researchers have investigated the existence of gender scripts in information processing and memory, using tests that are similar to the ones used to test gender schema theory. Children of varying ages were given colored line drawings representing several gender scripts, such as building with tools and cooking dinner, and were asked to arrange the drawings in the order that these events would happen (Boston & Levy, 1991). The results indicated that older children were more accurate than younger children in doing so, but also that children (especially boys) were more accurate in ordering own-gender rather than other-gender sequences.

Gender scripts also influence memory. One study (Levy & Boston, 1994) presented children with two own-gender and two other-gender scripts and asked them to recall as many parts of the scripts as they could. The children were more accurate in recalling own-sex scripts, a similar memory effect to findings from research on gender schema theory. Another similarity in the cognitive difficulty with schemata is the tendency of younger children to be more strict in their adherence to the script than older children are (Levy & Fivush, 1993).

Therefore, the sequencing component of gender script theory seems to broaden the concept of gender schemata. The research on gender script theory is less complete than the other theories of gender role development, but this theory is a promising addition to the other social theories of gender development.

Social learning theory, cognitive developmental theory, gender schema theory, and gender script theory all attempt to explain how children come to exhibit gender-related behaviors and choose personal concepts of masculinity and femininity. These theories all emphasize children's surroundings in the family and in society, but each theory has a different view of how children come to understand gender. Table 6.3 compares these theories. Each of these theories hypothesizes a course of development of gender-related knowledge and

TABLE 6.3 A Comparison of Social Theories of Gender Development

	Social Learning Theory	Cognitive Developmental Theory	Gender Schema Theory	Gender Script Theory
Gender differences develop through...	reinforcement and observation of models	general cognitive development, especially gender constancy	development of gender-specific schemata	learning gender scripts
Children's participation involves...	choosing which models to imitate	organizing information about the physical world	developing schemata specific to gender	developing scripts through social interaction
Gender development begins...	as soon as the culture emphasizes it, usually during infancy	during preschool years	during preschool years	during early preschool years
Gender development proceeds...	gradually, becoming more like adult knowledge	through a series of stages	through development of schemata	through learning script components
Gender development finishes...	during adulthood, if at all	during late childhood or preadolescence	during late childhood	when all scripts are learned
Girls and boys...	may develop different gender knowledge as well as different gender-related behaviors	develop similar cognitive understanding of gender	may develop different structures and schemata, depending on parents and family patterns	develop different scripts, guided through learning stereotypes

behavior, but what does the research on this topic indicate? How do children come to understand gender and develop gender typing, and how does the research fit with the theories?

Developing Gender Identity

Traditionally, a child's sex was announced at birth, but now many parents know their child's sex prenatally; this knowledge now allows for gender differentiation even before a child is born. In either event, the pinks and blues appear early in children's lives, as Mifflin's (1999) headline story about toys described. All social theories of gender development rate this type of differential treatment as important in causing children to attend to and adopt the appropriate gender role. Thus, the process of developing gender identity might start early in infancy.

Some research indicates that infants possess the ability to begin gender typing—they can tell the difference between male and female faces. Although infants' thoughts are difficult to study, one approach involves showing the infant such objects as photos of faces and measuring how long these objects hold the infant's attention. When infants see something new, they tend to gaze at the novel object; when they grow bored, they begin looking around rather than at the object. The process of becoming accustomed to an object is called *habituation.* By noting when infants attend to an object and when they grow bored (habituate), researchers can deduce which stimuli infants can distinguish and which they cannot.

Results using such a procedure showed that infants had the ability to distinguish between women and men (Fagot & Leinbach, 1994; Leinbach & Fagot, 1993). Infants 7, 9, and 12 months old could distinguish male from female faces, mainly by using hair length as the cue. This ability gives infants some basis to begin to make gender distinctions.

Factors influential in the development of gender identity include not only the ability to distinguish between the sexes, but also the ability to label each, know about gender roles, adopt gender roles, recognize gender constancy, and be flexible in applying gender roles to self and others. Research indicates that these elements of gender identity are separable and that they develop at different times.

Childhood

The ability to make a distinction between the category of men and women is far from possessing a gender concept or identity (Fagot & Leinbach, 1993). Infants may be able to distinguish between men and women, but they use hair length to signal gender, thus missing the true basis of the distinction. However, when children begin to talk, they soon start to use words that denote gender. That is, they use gender labels to refer to women (or girls) and men (or boys).

The Sequence of Development

When children begin to attach words to gender, they may not do so correctly. In one study (Fagot & Leinbach, 1989), none of the toddlers passed the gender-labeling task before age 18 months, and these children also showed no differences in gender-typed behaviors. By age 27 months, half could apply gender labels correctly. The children who succeeded in this task, like those in another study (Fagot, Leinbach, & O'Boyle, 1992), had parents who showed more traditional gender role behavior and provided their toddlers with positive and negative feedback for playing with gender-typed toys. These studies showed not only that children start to develop the ability to label gender at around 2 years of age, but also—as social learning theory predicts—that parents' attention to gender plays a role in this development.

Children's gender knowledge has several different dimensions and develops in a pattern, with older children showing more complete and complex knowledge concerning gender roles and stereotypes than younger children (Martin & Little, 1990; Ruble & Martin, 1998). Three-year-old participants were able to label the sexes, form groupings based on gender, and exhibit some knowledge of the behaviors typically associated with women and men. They did not show evidence of gender constancy at age 3, nor did they show extensive knowledge of gender-typical clothing or toy choices. Around age 4, the majority of these children could complete the tests of gender discrimination and gender stability, and their understanding of gender-typical clothes and toys was closer to the stereotypes.

The patterns of gender knowledge for the children in this study seem to fall into a sequence of development. Young children may not exhibit a great understanding of gender-related knowledge or preferences, even in the ability to label and show preferences for gender-typical toys. Toddlers between 20 and 28 months old have some gender knowledge, and some can label according to gender (Levy, 1999). However, children who succeeded in gender labeling did not always exhibit other gender knowledge or preferences; labeling is a necessary step in developing gender knowledge. Those children whose gender knowledge is complete will likely be able to succeed on all the tasks. Table 6.4 shows these four stages of development. An analysis of the children's responses showed that 98% of them fell into one of these categories. Their findings revealed that, contrary to Kohlberg's conceptualization, gender constancy was not a critical component in the development of gender knowledge.

Gender constancy may not be an all-or-nothing development. Two components are separable: *gender stability,* the knowledge that gender is a stable personal characteristic, and *gender consistency,* the belief that people retain their gender even when they adopt behaviors or superficial physical features associated with the other gender. For example, a child who shows gender stability will say that she was a girl when she was a baby and will be a woman when she grows up. A child who shows gender consistency will say that a boy will remain a boy even if he grows long hair or puts on a dress. Some children showed gender stability without gender consistency, but never the other way around (Martin & Little, 1990). Thus, gender constancy might consist of these two separable cognitive components, which would explain why researchers have found age variation in this aspect of development.

Motivation may be an additional factor in gender role development. Children who develop gender constancy become motivated to adopt gender-role behaviors, causing them to

TABLE 6.4 Stages of Developing Gender-Related Knowledge

	Gender Labeling	Gender Preferences or Knowledge	Gender Constancy
Stage 1	No	No	No
Stage 2	Yes	No	No
Stage 3	Yes	Yes	Possibly
Stage 4	Yes	Yes	Yes

SOURCE: Based on The relation of gender understanding to children's sex-typed preferences and gender stereotypes (pp. 1434–1435) by C. L. Martin & J. Little, 1990, *Child Development, 61.*

GENDERED VOICES

You Could Be a Boy One Day and a Girl the Next

"When my daughter was 2 or 3 years old, she clearly had no concept of gender or the permanence of gender," a man told me. "She would say that she was a girl or a boy pretty much randomly, as far as I could tell. One day, she would say one, and maybe even later the same day, the other—for both herself and others. You could be a boy one day and a girl the next. This lack of permanence also extended to skin color. She would say that your skin was the color of your clothes, so that changed from day to day, too. One day, you were blue, the next day, your skin was red. I thought that was very odd, even more odd than being a boy one day and being a girl the next.

"She's 5 years old now, and gender is a very salient characteristic for her. She seems to realize that she is a girl, and I think that she knows that she will always be a girl, but she is very concerned with gender and gender-related things—as though she is working on sorting out all this information and making sense of it."

avoid some activities and engage in others (Newman, Cooper, & Ruble, 1995). Children who are gender constant, therefore, have the motivation to adopt gender-typical behaviors.

Preschoolers, 1st graders, 2nd graders, and even some 4th graders can be misled into making mistakes about gender consistency, which is the more advanced of the two components of gender constancy. Changes in appearance and name of a character can produce this confusion (Beal & Lockhart, 1989). For example, changing the appearance of a target child to make the target look more like the other sex, or changing the name and pronoun used to refer to this target child can lead children to make mistakes. Children were more likely to say that the target was the same sex, even with a changed appearance, when the target kept the same proper name throughout the transformations. This finding suggests that children whose understanding of gender constancy was not solid could be misled by changes in superficial characteristics, such as appearance or proper names. The age of the participants and their difficulties in demonstrating this facet of gender constancy are clear indications of how difficult this concept is for children and how long it takes children to develop gender constancy.

In summary, children begin to acquire knowledge concerning gender at an early age. Although infants show some signs of being able to differentiate between women and men, this ability does not constitute cognitive knowledge about gender. Between ages 2 and 3 years of age, children succeed at gender labeling but have usually not developed other aspects of gender knowledge, such as gender preferences, gender stability, gender consistency, or knowledge of gender stereotypes. These aspects of gender knowledge develop between the ages of 3 and 6 for most children and do so in a regular pattern: first gender labeling, then gender stereotype knowledge and gender preferences, and then the two components of gender constancy—gender stability and gender consistency. Even during the first few grades of elementary school, children can be misled into making mistakes of gender consistency by changes in physical appearance or proper name, which indicates how difficult this aspect of gender knowledge is for children to acquire.

Differences between Girls and Boys

The course of gender development shows some differences between boys and girls. Such a difference is reasonable, given the greater pressure placed on boys to adopt the typical and approved gender role (Sandnabba & Ahlberg, 1999). Girls are allowed greater leeway in behaving in ways typical of boys than boys are allowed in acting like girls (Martin, 1995). That is, being a "tomboy" is more acceptable than being a "sissy." Indeed, younger women report being a tomboy more often than older women, and attitudes toward tomboys were quite positive (Morgan, 1998).

People hold different attitudes toward masculine girls and feminine boys, with masculine girls receiving more positive ratings. These differences appear in college men and women (Martin, 1995), in elementary school boys (Zucker, Wilson-Smith, Kurita, & Stern, 1995), and in parents of young children (Sandnabba & Ahlberg, 1999). Thus it is not surprising that, beginning around age 3, boys tend to show greater stability of gender-typed preferences than girls do (Powlishta, Serbin, & Moller, 1993).

Both gender schema and gender script theory predict that children attend to and master information about their own gender more rapidly than about the other gender (Levy & Fivush, 1993). Research has confirmed these predictions: Young children have better organized knowledge of events and behaviors stereotypically associated with their own rather than the other gender (Levy, 1999; Martin, Wood, & Little, 1990). In addition, children evaluate their own gender more positively than the other gender, with girls saying that "girls are better" and boys contending that "boys are better." In elementary school-aged children, these positive evaluations were not based on the value of the traits but rather on the children's association of positive characteristics with their own group (Powlishta, 1995).

Adolescence and Adulthood

The widespread belief that gender development is complete by the end of childhood has resulted in relatively little research conducted with adolescents and adults; however, some researchers have examined continuing changes in gender identity and attitudes. Much of this research has concentrated on the development of gender role flexibility, which seems limited during childhood but becomes more apparent during adolescence and adulthood.

Some evidence suggests that gender role development continues into adolescence and adulthood. A study of 7th graders, 12th graders, and adults (Urberg, 1979) considered changes in stereotyping at various ages. The 12th graders showed the most gender-related stereotyping, and the adults showed the least. This result indicates that stereotyping does

GENDERED VOICES

Yuck—I'm a Girl

The woman knew that her young son would not like the outfit that he was to wear for the wedding, so she decided to distract him as she dressed him. She was successful, but when he looked down at the finished product, he exclaimed, "Yuck—I'm a girl!" in a surprised and disgusted tone.

When we talked about gender development in class, she said that she now understood why he was so upset. She thought that he had meant that he looked like a girl, but instead, she now understood that he had not developed a concept of gender stability and he believed that, by dressing him in a frilly shirt and velvet suit, his mother had turned him from a boy into a girl.

not increase with gender knowledge in a linear fashion. Rather, the relationship between age and gender stereotyping showed a curvilinear relationship: low at early ages, before gender becomes an important factor for dealing with people; then higher, when dating and career choices become important; and finally, lower, when young adults accept greater flexibility for gender-related behavior.

Other studies have found a linear relationship between gender flexibility and age—that is, as age increases, so does gender flexibility (Katz & Ksansnak, 1994; Welch-Ross & Schmidt, 1996). When children acquire gender role knowledge, they tend to apply it inflexibly, but with increasing familiarity with stereotypes comes an increasing willingness to make exceptions, especially when applied to self.

The discrepancies among the studies of gender role flexibility may be due to the different research methods used and variations in the measurement of flexibility (Bigler, 1997; Signorella, Bigler, & Liben, 1993). For example, when forced to choose whether a behavior is performed by or is an occupation held by women or men, children are likely to show increasing evidence of gender stereotyping as they get older. On the other hand, if they are allowed the option to indicate that both perform the behavior or either can have that occupation, even middle-school children show signs of gender flexibility. This difference highlights the importance of the format and wording of questions, especially in research with children. Children and adolescents also tend to be more strict in applying inflexible standards for gender-related behavior to others than to themselves. Therefore, researchers who ask only about others or about cases that are typical may overlook the exceptions that children and adolescents are willing to make for themselves.

Nevertheless, children, adolescents, and even adults vary in their gender role flexibility, and several researchers have explored factors that relate to flexibility versus inflexibility. In one study (Katz & Ksansnak, 1994), a complex pattern of gender role flexibility appeared: both family and peer social environment influenced gender-related behavior but participants showed a general increase in tolerance for gender-atypical activities for self and others with increasing age. Another study (Welch-Ross & Schmidt, 1996) found that increases in gender role knowledge preceded increases in gender role flexibility, with flexibility beginning to develop during middle childhood. Figure 6.2 shows the course of development for gender knowledge and for application of gender-related rules over the life span: the knowledge component and application of gender-related rules increase throughout childhood, indicating decreases in flexibility. During adolescence, application of gender-related rules declines, signaling increased flexibility.

Gender role flexibility increases during adolescence, but young women and men apply different standards to their own gender than to the other. One study (Urberg, 1979) found that male and female participants described the other gender in more stereotypical terms than they described themselves. Male and female participants had similar self-perceptions for characteristics such as affiliation, personal effectiveness, control, and impulsivity, but they tended to perceive the other gender in more stereotypical ways.

Other than age, what factors relate to gender flexibility versus inflexibility? Gender is one factor, and girls endorse more flexibility than boys throughout adolescence (Jackson & Tein, 1998; Signorella et al., 1993). Girls show more flexibility in their activity preferences and tolerance for gender flexibility in others. In addition, family factors (Levy, 1989) and the combination of family and social environment (Katz & Ksansnak, 1994) have been the focus of research attention. Children who interacted more with their parents showed *less*

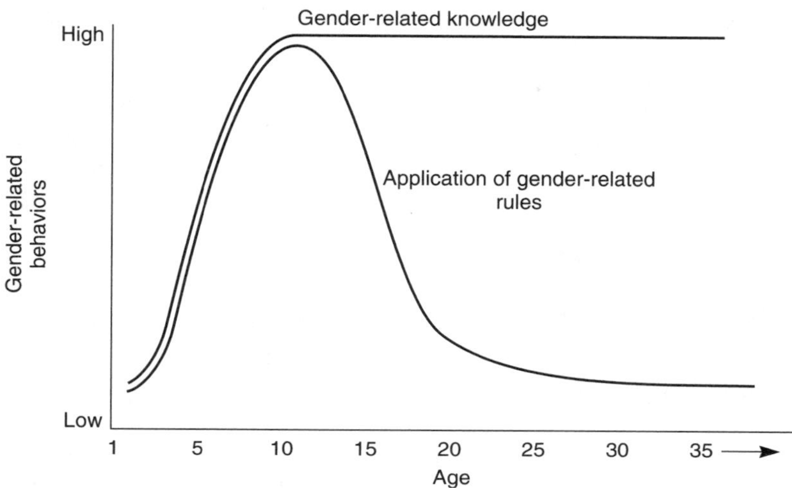

FIGURE 6.2 Course of Knowledge and Application of Gender-Related Rules for Behavior throughout the Life Span

gender role flexibility than children who spent less time with their parents, and children with fewer siblings showed *more* gender role flexibility than those with more brothers and sisters (Levy, 1989). Girls whose mothers worked outside the home and girls who expressed a preference for educational television showed more gender role flexibility than other girls. Siblings and peers are also important in developing gender flexibility; indeed, they may be more important than parents (Katz & Ksansnak, 1994). Same-sex siblings showed an especially important effect in the development of gender flexibility—either increasing or decreasing flexibility, depending on siblings' attitudes.

Some research has traced the correlates of both gender flexibility and inflexibility in men. Men who were stereotypically masculine tended to see women as stereotypically feminine; that is, men who show little gender flexibility in their own roles also show little toward women (Hudak, 1993). In adolescents, inflexibility increases as traditional young men approach high school graduation and begin to contemplate marriage and careers (Jackson & Tein, 1998).

Some men have very different attitudes, however, and tend to reject stereotypically masculine and feminine roles (Christian, 1994). Those who did were demographically diverse but showed several commonalities. Their early life experiences differed from those of more typical men in the study, with many of them having nurturing fathers and mothers in the workforce. In addition, most of these gender-flexible men had had at least one adult relationship with a feminist woman. These two themes echo the findings on the development of gender flexibility, which demonstrate that both parenting and social environment are related to gender flexibility.

It is apparent that gender identity continues to develop during adolescence and even into adulthood. When children have developed the cognitive and motivational components of gender identity, they tend to be inflexible in applying their understanding of these rules;

they are intolerant of gender-atypical behavior in themselves and even more so in others. Young children appear to be tolerant of gender flexibility, but this apparent tolerance is due to a lack of understanding of gender-typed behaviors. Children are "sexist piglets" who apply rigid rules of gender-related behavior to themselves and to others, but this inflexibility begins to dissipate as early as middle childhood. Adolescents and adults tend to be more flexible in their application of gender-related rules of behavior.

Which Theory Best Explains the Data?

Each of these theories of gender development presents an orderly pattern of development, but the research shows a complex pattern with many components that do not necessarily match the theories. That is, none of the theories is able to explain all the data from research on gender development.

Social learning theory predicts a process of learning gender roles that results in a gradual matching of gender-related behaviors to the culturally prescribed pattern through modeling and reinforcement of gender-appropriate behaviors. Although the research shows that children begin learning information consistent with gender stereotypes at an early age, gender knowledge consists of several different concepts that do not appear incrementally. The finding that children learn gender labeling before gender-typical toy and clothing preferences indicates a pattern of gender knowledge development that social learning theory does not predict.

Research has substantiated the influence of parents, siblings, and peers in directing gender-related behaviors. Social learning theory predicts that family, peers, teachers, and media images of men and women affect children in their learning and performance of gender-appropriate behaviors. Modeling can be a powerful force in prompting the performance of gender-related behaviors (Bussey & Bandura, 1984, 1992, 1999), and same-sex siblings, parents, peers, and teachers are all important influences in the child's development of gender flexibility (Katz & Ksansnak, 1994). These findings are consistent with the predictions of social learning theory.

Social learning theory allows that girls and boys might differ not only in their gender-related behaviors, but also in cross-gender behaviors. The male gender role carries more power, and power is one of the factors that affects children's modeling. During childhood, boys are discouraged from performing feminine behaviors, whereas girls may not be discouraged from performing behaviors typical of boys. These differences lead to the prediction that boys should be more strongly gender typed than girls, and research supports this difference. Cognitive developmental theory does not allow for a different pattern of development for boys and girls, whereas gender schema theory hypothesizes that parental attitudes and family patterns may produce variations in individual schemata. This theory does not specifically address differences in schemata between girls and boys.

Cognitive developmental theory hypothesizes that gender development comes about through cognitive changes that occur by way of general cognitive development. Research has indicated that gender development produces cognitive changes in accuracy and memory for gender-related information, but gender schema theory also predicts that cognitive changes come with the development of gender schema, making findings that support these cognitive changes applicable to either theory.

The prediction that gender constancy is the basis for developing all other gender knowledge has not been substantiated. Indeed, research has shown that gender constancy develops late, with many other components of gender knowledge appearing earlier. This failure is a serious problem for cognitive developmental theory. Another problem for this theory is that gender development continues during adolescence. According to cognitive developmental theory, children undergo no additional cognitive changes after early adolescence, but research has shown that late adolescence is a time during which individuals gain flexibility of gender beliefs.

Gender schema theory predicts that children develop a cognitive organization for gender, a schema, that forms the basis for their understanding of gender and directs their gender-related behaviors. The types of cognitive changes that this theory predicts have been found in modes of information processing, such as accuracy of judgments and memory effects. In preschool children, gender schematicity was a significant predictor of masculine and feminine gender-typed behaviors, but gender constancy was not related (Levy et al., 1998). In addition, women in traditional versus nontraditional jobs have different conceptualizations of gender-appropriate behavior (Lavallee & Pelletier, 1992), a finding consistent with gender schema theory.

Gender development seems to consist of several different cognitive abilities. One team of researchers (Hort, Leinbach, & Fagot, 1991) proposed that the cognitive components of gender development do not have a great deal of coherence; they postulated that such knowledge varies among individual children of the same age and stage of cognitive development. That is, gender knowledge may not fall into a pattern sufficiently coherent to be called a schema.

Gender script theory makes many of the same predictions as gender schema theory. Differentiating scripts from schemata allows for some additional predictions, and some research has confirmed children's abilities to learn and behave according to sequentially ordered patterns like scripts. Gender script theory has not been the subject of sufficient research to make firm conclusions, but it may offer advantages over gender schema theory.

It is evident from this discussion that all of the social theories of gender development make predictions that research has supported, and all make predictions that research has failed to confirm. The picture drawn from the research shows that gender development presents a more complex process than any of the theories can fully explain. Gender development consists of separate components—gender labeling, preferences for gender-typed activities, gender stereotyping, and gender constancy. These components appear to develop in a pattern, but the pattern does not exactly conform to any of those predicted by the theories. Thus, all of the social theories of personality development have been useful and have been partially confirmed, but none is without weaknesses.

Considering Diversity

Most children adopt the gender-related behaviors typical for their biological sex. Those who do not readily adopt typical gender-related behaviors experience increasing pressure to do so. For example, one study (Raag & Rackliff, 1998) showed that most 4- and 5-year-old boys believed that their fathers would think it was "good" if they played with boys' toys and "bad" if they played with girls' toys. None of the boys who imagined their fathers would disapprove played with girls' toys in an observed play situation. Thus, children feel pressure to adopt typical gender-related behaviors, and boys experience more pressure than girls.

Most children show behaviors that represent a combination of the typical masculine and the feminine, which does not indicate any type of gender confusion. For example, one 5-year-old boy wanted a pink bicycle because pink was his favorite color (Rosenfeld, 1998). His parents knew that the color would be a problem, but they accepted his choice; the salesman did not and tried to convince him that a "boy's" color would be much better. His peers, including the girls, also teased him for having a pink bicycle.

Although boys receive greater pressure to adopt the traditional gender role, more boys than girls exhibit **gender identity disorder.** This disorder occurs when a child rejects the gender role that corresponds to biological sex and adopts cross-gender behaviors and possibly an identity. A small number of children show evidence of gender identity disorder, and these children not only display cross-gender behaviors but also reject their own gender identity and behaviors associated with it and often wish to be magically transformed into the other gender.

Richard Green (1987) studied boys who showed signs of gender identity disorder in order to discover differences between these boys and others who had more typical gender role development. His study indicated that some of these "sissies" had received reinforcement for their cross-gender behaviors, whereas others were ignored by parents or other adults for such behavior. The majority of these boys continued to have gender identity disorders into adulthood, with some attempting to change their biological sex through transsexual surgery, and others developing sexual attraction to men or to both men and women.

Green chose not to include girls in his study because too few girls showed symptoms of gender identity disorder. In a clinic study of gender identity disorder, boys were more than six times more likely than girls to receive a referral (Zucker, Bradley, & Sanikhani, 1997). Girls showed more cross-gender behaviors than boys but were less prevalent in the clinic referrals, suggesting a greater social tolerance for such behavior from girls. Indeed, girls see advantages in being boys (Baumgartner, in Tavris & Wade, 1984). When asked what would happen if they changed sex, elementary school girls imagined advantages, whereas boys imagined disaster. Adults make similar judgments, believing that being male offers advantages and being female presents disadvantages (Cann & Vann, 1995). Nevertheless, more boys than girls reject their gender and receive a diagnosis of gender identity disorder.

The individuals who receive this diagnosis experience many negative consequences of their cross-gender behaviors. People tend to confuse gender dysphoria (feeling unhappy and dissatisfied with one's gender—feeling "trapped in the wrong body") with homosexuality (feelings of sexual attraction for people of one's own gender) and transvestism (dressing in clothing appropriate to the other gender). These phenomena may overlap, but they are separable. As Green (1987) found, many individuals with gender identity disorder do not grow up to be heterosexual, but the large majority of gay men and lesbians have no gender dysphoria. Only 17% of male transvestites reported feeling trapped in a man's body (Docter & Prince, 1997). Therefore, dissatisfaction with one's gender may be associated with other cross-gender behaviors, but most individuals who exhibit these behaviors do not do so as part of gender identity disorder. Indeed, one study (Cole, O'Boyle, Emory, & Meyer, 1997) indicated that these individuals do not exhibit a high degree of other psychopathology. Being unhappy with one's biological sex does not imply a broad range of mental problems.

Indeed, controversy exists over whether gender identity disorder should be classified as a disorder (Zucker & Bradley, 1995). As children, these individuals are subject to diagnosis and treatment, but as adults they are free to seek sexual reassignment surgery and become **transsexual,** individuals who receive hormonal and surgical treatment to be changed to the other sex. Although transsexuals may have some problems in being accepted by society, studies (Cohen-Kettenis & van Goozen, 1997; Rehman, Lazer, Benet, Schaefer, & Melman, 1999) indicate that their gender dysphoria disappears and their overall functioning improves.

Not all cultures see cross-gender behaviors as a problem. When Europeans arrived in North America, they found many Native American tribes in which gender roles were less fixed than in European societies (Wieringa, 1994). More than 130 Native American societies accepted *berdaches*—men or women who adopted the gender-related behaviors of the other gender. Male berdaches were more common than female berdaches, but both versions existed. For example, the Zuni saw gender roles as learned rather than fixed by biology. Each gender had a specific role, but individuals were not necessarily tied to that role by their biological sex. Boys who wanted to dress like women, perform work typical of women, and marry a man were well accepted rather than discouraged. Indeed, the category of berdache carried a special spiritual status (Roscoe, 1993), and berdaches were respected members of the community rather than the outcasts that transsexuals often are now in North America.

Summary

The social theories of gender development provide alternatives to psychoanalytic theory to explain how infants come to identify themselves as male or female, to understand gender, and to behave in ways that their culture deems gender-appropriate. The social learning approach, a variation on traditional learning theory, relies on the concepts of observational learning and modeling to explain how children learn and perform gender-related behaviors. Initially the family, and later the broader culture, provide models and reinforcements for adopting certain gender-related behaviors while discouraging others. Research has supported the power of children's family and social surroundings to influence the development of gender-related behaviors, but the orderly pattern of gender development that occurs is not consistent with this theory.

Cognitive developmental theory holds that gender identity is a cognitive concept that children learn as part of the process of learning about the physical world and their own bodies. Children younger than 2 years of age have no concept of gender and cannot consistently label themselves or others as male or female. When children learn to classify genders, they have developed gender constancy, the understanding that gender is a permanent personal characteristic that will not change with any other physical transformation. According to cognitive developmental theory, additional facets of gender development arise from gender constancy; however, research has indicated that gender constancy is among the last types of gender knowledge to be acquired. These findings present a problem for this theory.

Gender schema theory is an extension of cognitive developmental theory that explains gender identity in terms of schemata—cognitive structures that underlie complex concepts. When children acquire a gender schema, they change the way that they deal with information concerning gender and also change their behavior to conform to gender roles. This theory suggests that gender stereotyping is a natural extension of the process of developing gender schemata, and that children become stereotypical in their gender behavior and judgments. Parents who wish to raise nonsexist children can attempt to substitute alternative schemata that are less sexist than the ones predominant in their culture, although completely avoiding the formation of gender schemata is not possible for children.

Gender script theory is an extension of gender schema theory. Rather than holding that children develop gender schemata, this theory says that children learn about gender by acquiring scripts—ordered sequences of behavior with a gender stereotype component. These scripts allow children to organize their knowledge and facilitate social relationships. This theory shares many predictions with gender schema theory, but the body of research testing this theory is smaller than that for other theories. Thus, assessment of this theory is difficult at this point.

The process of gender development may begin during infancy, but between ages 2 and 3, most children learn to apply gender labels and to understand some behaviors and features as stereotypically associated with gender. Their understanding of gender is far from complete, however, and children may be 7 or 8 years old before they have a complete understanding of all the components of gender, including gender constancy, gender consistency, and gender stability.

When children develop an understanding of gender, they tend to be rigid and inflexible in their application of gender rules to themselves and others. Gender stereotyping is not as strong during adolescence and adulthood, indicating that additional gender development occurs after childhood. Evaluating the social theories of gender development leads to the conclusion that although each has supporting research, this research fails to confirm any one theory to the exclusion of the others.

The large majority of children develop gender identities that are consistent with their biological sex, but some do not. Those children who identify with and want to be the other gender may be diagnosed as having gender identity disorder. As adults, these individuals may seek sexual reassignment surgery and fulfill their wish to be the other gender. This choice is poorly accepted in modern North America, but over 100 Native American cultures included berdaches, who represented cross-gender roles and behaviors and were accepted, respected members of their societies.

Glossary

gender constancy the knowledge that gender is a permanent characteristic and will not change with superficial alterations.

gender identity individual identification of self as female or male.

gender identity disorder a disorder that occurs when a child rejects the gender role that corresponds to biological sex and adopts cross-gender behaviors and possibly a cross-gender identity.

gender labeling the ability to label self and others as male or female.

gender role a set of socially significant activities associated with being male or female.

operant conditioning a type of learning based on the administration of reinforcement or punishment. Receiving reinforcement links the reinforcement with the behavior that preceded it, making the behavior more likely to be repeated.

punishment any stimulus that decreases the probability that a behavior will be repeated.

reinforcement any stimulus that increases the probability that a behavior will be repeated.

schema (plural, **schemata** or **schemas**) an internal cognitive structure that organizes information and guides perception.

transsexual an individual who receives hormonal and surgical treatment to be changed to the other sex.

Suggested Readings

Beal, Carole R. (1994). *Boys and girls: The development of gender roles.* New York: McGraw-Hill. Chapters 3, 5 through 7, and 9 in Carole Beal's book concentrate on the social forces that pertain to gender role development. Her careful review and good examples make this book a good summary of the research in this area.

Bem, Sandra Lipsitz. (1985). Androgyny and gender schema theory: A conceptual and empirical integration. In Theo B. Sonderegger (Ed.), *Nebraska Symposium on Motivation, 1984: Psychology and gender* (pp. 179–226). Lincoln, NE: University of Nebraska Press. Bem evaluates the other theories of gender development and presents gender schema theory, the research supporting her theory, along with advice about raising nonsexist children.

Pollack, William. (1998). *Real boys.* New York: Holt. The first two chapters of Pollock's book about boys explores the rigid gender role socialization that boys undergo and the damage that this socialization can do to boys.

Ruble, Diane N.; & Martin, Carol Lynn. (1998). Gender development. In Nancy Eisenberg (Ed.), *Handbook of child psychology, Vol. 3: Social, emotional, and personality development* (5th ed., pp. 933–1016). New York: Wiley. Ruble and Martin's massive review of gender development, presented in Chapter 14 of the handbook, may be a bit overwhelming in length, but their discussion of the research is clear and well-organized. The article includes other material in addition to a review of social factors in gender development. The first half of Chapter 14 is more pertinent to this topic than the last.

Chapter 7

Gender Stereotypes

Masculinity and Femininity

HEADLINE

The Stereotype Trap

Newsweek, November 6, 2000

> *From 'white men can't jump' to 'girls can't do math,' negative images that are pervasive in the culture can make us choke during tests of ability.... The power of stereotypes, scientists had long figured, lay in their ability to change the behavior of the person holding the stereotype.... But five years ago, Stanford University psychologist Claude Steele showed something else: It is the* targets *of a stereotype whose behavior is most powerfully affected by it. A stereotype that pervades the culture the way "ditzy blondes" and "forgetful seniors" do makes people painfully aware of how society views them—so painfully aware, in fact, that knowledge of the stereotype can affect how well they do on intellectual and other tasks" (Begley, 2000, pp. 66–67).*

According to Sharon Begley (2000), stereotypes present a trap into which many people can fall. In 1995, Claude Steele and Joshua Aronson reported on a study that showed how the existence of negative stereotypes can affect those who are part of the stereotyped groups. They proposed that people feel threatened in situations in which they believe that their performance will identify them as examples of their group's negative stereotype. Steele and Aronson labeled this situation *stereotype threat* because the presence of these negative stereotypes threatens performance and self-concept. Even if the person does not believe the stereotype or accept that it applies, the threat of being identified with a negative stereotype can be an ever-present factor that puts a person in the spotlight and creates tension and anxiety about performance.

By setting up a situation that manipulated expectations of the implications of taking a test, Steele and Aronson showed that those expectations affected participants' performance.

For example, African Americans who believed that the test they were taking was a test of basic scholastic ability performed worse than African Americans who thought the test was just another test. Women who believed that the mathematics test would reveal their underlying ability performed more poorly than women who had different beliefs about the test's diagnostic ability (Steele, 1997). In addition, African Americans and women performed more poorly than White men, who are not threatened by negative stereotypes of their abilities. "Stereotypes seem to most affect the best and the brightest. Only if you're black and care about academics, or female and you care about math, will you also care if society thinks you're bad at those things" (Begley, 2000, p. 67).

Begley's article also described how other aspects of stereotypes can be powerful and how easily they can be summoned. Reminding people of their membership in a stereotyped group, such as asking them to mark a question about their gender just before starting the test, was enough of a cue to affect performance negatively. However, when reminded of their affiliation with a positively stereotyped group, Asian American women's math performance improved. Stereotypes thus have the capacity to be a positive influence, but much more evidence indicates that they can do damage. This powerful process affects both those who impose the stereotypes and those who are the targets of stereotyping.

From Gender Roles to Gender Stereotypes

As Chapter 6 explored, a gender role consists of activities that men and women engage in with different frequencies (see Williams & Best, 1990). For example, in the United States, repairing cars and repairing clothing are associated predominantly with men and women, respectively. These gender-related behaviors thus become part of a pattern accepted as masculine or feminine, not because of any innate reason for these differences, but because they are associated with women and men.

A **gender stereotype** consists of beliefs about the psychological traits and characteristics of, as well as the activities appropriate to, men or women. Gender roles are defined by behaviors, but gender stereotypes are beliefs and attitudes about masculinity and femininity. The concepts of gender role and gender stereotype tend to be related. When people associate a pattern of behavior with either women or men, they may overlook individual variations and exceptions and come to believe that the behavior is inevitably associated with one gender but not the other. Therefore, gender roles can become gender stereotypes.

Gender stereotypes are very influential; they affect conceptualizations of women and men and establish social categories for gender. These categories represent what people think, and even when beliefs vary from reality, the beliefs can be very powerful forces in judgments of self and others, as the headline story for this chapter showed. Therefore, the history, structure, and function of stereotypes are important topics in understanding the impact of gender on people's lives.

Stereotypes of Women and Men

The rigid formulation of what is acceptable for women and men is not unique to children or even to contemporary society. The current gender stereotypes, especially those about women, reflect beliefs that appeared during the 19th century, the Victorian era (Lewin,

1984c). Before the Industrial Revolution, most people lived and worked on farms where men and women worked together. The Industrial Revolution changed the lives of a majority of people in Europe and North America by moving men outside the home to earn money and leaving women at home to manage households and children. This separation was unprecedented in history, forcing men and women to adapt by creating new behavior patterns. As men coped with the harsh business and industrial world, women were left in the relatively unvarying and sheltered environments of their homes. These changes produced two beliefs: the Doctrine of Two Spheres and the Cult of True Womanhood.

The Doctrine of Two Spheres is the belief that women's and men's interests diverge—that women and men have their separate areas of influence (Lewin, 1984a). For women, the areas of influence are home and children, whereas men's sphere includes work and the outside world. These two spheres are different, with little overlap, forming opposite ends of one dimension. This conceptualization of opposition forms the basis not only for social views of gender, but also for psychology's formulation of the measurement of masculinity and femininity.

The Cult of True Womanhood

The Cult of True Womanhood arose between 1820 and 1860. "The attributes of True Womanhood, by which a woman judged herself and was judged by her husband, her neighbors, and society could be divided into four cardinal virtues—piety, purity, submissiveness, and domesticity" (Welter, 1978, p. 313). Women's magazines and religious literature of the 19th century furnished evidence of society's emphasis on these four areas. The Cult of True Womanhood held that the combination of these characteristics provided the promise of happiness and power to the Victorian woman, and without these no woman's life could have real meaning.

Religion formed the basis for the Cult of True Womanhood (Welter, 1978), and its first virtue was piety. During this time, society saw women as more naturally pious than men. This tendency toward religion was part of women's natural moral superiority, and the belief in the moral superiority of women was stronger in the United States than in Europe and England (Lewin, 1984c). Women's natural superiority also appeared in their refinement, delicacy, and tender sensibilities. Religious studies were seen as compatible with femininity and deemed appropriate for women, whereas other types of education were thought to detract from women's femininity. Included in these other types of education were not only any studying through formal means, but also reading romantic novels, either of which might lead women to ignore religion, become overly romantic, and lose their virtue, or purity (that is, their virginity).

Although women were seen as uninterested in sex, they were vulnerable to seduction. The loss of the second virtue, purity, was a "fate worse than death." Having lost her purity, a woman was without value or hope: "Purity was as essential as piety to a young woman, its absence as unnatural and unfeminine. Without it she was, in fact no woman at all, but a member of some lower order" (Welter, 1978, p. 315).

Men, on the other hand, were not naturally as religious and thus not naturally as virtuous as women. According to this view of True Womanhood, men were, at best, prone to sin and seduction, and at worst, brutes. True Women would withstand the advances of men, dazzling and shaming them with their virtue. Men were supposed to be both religious and pure, although not to the same extent as women, and through association with True Women, men could increase their own virtue. True Women could elevate men.

The third virtue of the Cult of True Womanhood was submissiveness, a characteristic not true of and not desirable in men (Welter, 1978). Women were expected to be weak, dependent, and timid, whereas men were supposed to be strong, wise, and forceful. Dependent women wanted strong men, not sensitive ones. These couples formed families in which the husband was unquestionably superior and the wife would not consider questioning his authority.

The last of the four virtues, domesticity, was connected to both submissiveness and to the Doctrine of the Two Spheres. True Women were wives whose concern was with domestic affairs—making a home and having children: "The true woman's place was unquestionably by her own fireside—as daughter, sister, but most of all as wife and mother" (Welter, 1978, p. 320). These domestic duties included cooking and nursing the sick, especially a sick husband or child. Table 7.1 summarizes the elements of the Cult of True Womanhood.

Women who personified these virtues passed the test of True Womanhood. Of course, the test was so demanding that few, if any, women met the criteria. However, beginning in the early 1800s, women's magazines as well as teachings from social and religious leaders held these virtues as attainable. They urged women to work toward these qualities, and women tried to match these ideals. Although the Cult of True Womanhood was dominant during the 19th century, remnants remain in our present-day culture and influence current views of femininity.

Masculinities

The 19th-century idealization of women also had implications for men, who were seen as the opposite of women in a number of ways. Women were passive, dependent, pure, refined, and delicate; men were active, independent, coarse, and strong. These divisions between male and female domains, the Doctrine of the Two Spheres, formed the basis for the polarization of male and female interests and activities. The Cult of True Womanhood reached its height in the late Victorian period, toward the end of the 19th century. The Victorian ideal of manhood was the basis for what Joseph Pleck (1981, 1995) referred to as the Male Sex Role Identity. Pleck discussed the Male Sex Role Identity as the dominant conceptualization of masculinity in our society and as a source of problems, both for society and for individual men.

TABLE 7.1 Elements of Stereotyping of Women and Men

The Cult of True Womanhood	Male Sex Role Identity
Piety: True Women were naturally religious.	*No Sissy Stuff:* A stigma is attached to feminine characteristics.
Purity: True Women were sexually uninterested.	*The Big Wheel:* Men need success and status.
Submissiveness: True Women were weak, dependent, and timid.	*The Sturdy Oak:* Men should have toughness, confidence, and self-reliance.
Domesticity: True Women's domain was in the home.	*Give 'Em Hell:* Men should have an aura of aggression, daring, and violence.

SOURCES: Based on "The male sex role: Our culture's blueprint of manhood and what it's done for us lately," (p. 12). In Deborah S. David & Robert Brannon (Eds.), *The forty-nine percent majority,* 1976. Reading, MA: Addison-Wesley; and "The cult of true womanhood: 1820–1860." In Michael Gordon (Ed.), *The American family in social-historical perspective* (2nd ed.). New York: St. Martin's Press.

R. W. Connell (1995) explored the historical origins of attitudes toward masculinity. Connell looked back into 16th-century Europe and the changing social and religious climate to trace the development of individualism. He contended that industrialization, world exploration, and civil wars became activities associated with men and formed the basis for modern masculinity. Pleck (1984) reviewed the social climate of the late 19th century, citing examples from the late 1800s of the increasing perception that men were not as manly as they once had been. Growing industrialization pressured men to seek employment in order to be good providers for their families, roles that became increasingly difficult for men to fulfill (Bernard, 1981), thus endangering their masculinity. In addition, education became a factor in employment, and men often held better jobs (and were thus better providers) when they were educated. Pleck discussed how the occupation of early-childhood educator became the province of women, and how these female elementary school teachers tried to make boys into well-behaved pupils—in other words, "sissies."

The prohibition against being a sissy and the rejection of the feminine are strong components of modern masculinity. According to Robert Brannon (1976), No Sissy Stuff is one of the four themes of the Male Sex Role. The other three themes include The Big Wheel, which describes men's quest for success and status as well as their need to be looked up to. The Sturdy Oak component describes men's air of toughness, confidence, and self-reliance, especially in a crisis. Finally, the Give 'Em Hell aspect of the Male Sex Role reflects the acceptability of violence, aggression, and daring in men's behavior. Table 7.1 summarizes these elements.

The more closely that a man conforms to these characteristics, the closer he is to being a "real man." As Brannon pointed out, the pressure is strong to live up to this idealization of masculinity, which is equally as ideal and unrealistic as the "true woman" of the Cult of True Womanhood. However, even men who are fairly successful in adopting the Male Sex Role Identity may be poorly adjusted, unhappy people—this role prohibits close personal relationships, even with wives or children, and requires persistent competition and striving for achievement. These difficulties lead men to make significant departures from the role's requirements.

Pleck (1981, 1995) proposed a new model, which he called Sex Role Strain (now Gender Role Strain), which departs in many ways from the Male Sex Role Identity. Pleck argued that during the 1960s and 1970s, both men and women started to make significant departures from their traditional roles as men began to behave in ways that violated the Male Gender Role. He also suggested that the features of the Male Gender Role Identity have retained a powerful influence over what both men and women believe men should be. Many men deviate from the role, and some even believe that the role is harmful to them personally and to society, making adherence to the role a strain. Even men who succeed feel the strain in doing so, and the toxic components of the role present problems even for the successful.

Connell (1987, 1992, 1995) argued that gender has been constructed as part of each society throughout history, a view that is consistent with the belief that gender is something that people do rather than part of what people are (West & Zimmerman, 1987). This construction of masculinity includes both sanctioned and less accepted behaviors. Thus, masculinity varies with both time and place, creating a multitude of masculinities. For each society, Connell contended that one version of masculinity is sanctioned as the one to which men should adhere, which he termed *hegemonic masculinity*. This version of masculinity

GENDERED VOICES

Raising a Sissy

"Being twins, my brother and I were closer than most brothers and sisters. We didn't look alike, but we were together a lot," a college student told me. "We had different interests. I was the one who went outside and helped my dad, while my brother stayed inside with my mother. Everybody always said I should have been the boy and he should have been the girl.

"He didn't want to play alone, so he played with me and my friends—dolls, or whatever we played. He never got to choose. And when we played dolls, he got the one that was left after me and my friend chose the ones we wanted. My mom said, 'Let him play with the Ken doll—you have two Ken dolls—don't make him play with a Barbie,' but we didn't. So he got the Barbie with one arm missing or something.

"I always liked the outdoor activities, and my brother didn't. I was so upset that I couldn't join the Cub Scouts. My dad was a troop leader, and I just couldn't understand why I couldn't join; I had always done outdoor things with my dad. Besides, the Brownies did wimpy things, and the Cub Scouts did neat stuff. I was so ticked off.

"When we were in about the 7th grade, I told my mother, 'Mom, you're raising a sissy,' and I told her that my brother should stop hanging around with her and start doing things more typical of boys. She was really angry with me for saying so.

"Did we change as we grew up? I don't consider myself very feminine—I don't take anything off anybody. My mom can't believe that her daughter acts like I do. I still like outdoor activities—camping, hiking, bicycling. I don't think I've changed as much as my brother has. I wouldn't consider him a sissy now. In high school he played football, and he started being more in line with what everyone would consider masculine. As an adult, he's not a sissy at all, but I'm still kind of an adult tomboy."

attempts to subordinate femininity as well as less accepted versions of masculinity, such as male homosexuality. Like Pleck, Connell recognized many disadvantages to this narrow, dominant form of masculinity and saw many problems for society and for individual men who adhere to it.

Development of Stereotypes

In examining the research on social theories of gender development, Chapter 6 reviewed the process of developing gender knowledge and identity, including some information about forming gender stereotypes. This body of research indicates that gender learning consists of several components, which children begin to acquire around 2 years of age and may not complete until they are 7 or 8 years old. The first of the components to be learned is the ability to label the sexes, and this initial gender information may be adequate to allow children to begin to develop gender stereotypes: "Once children can accurately label the sexes, they begin to form gender stereotypes and their behavior is influenced by these gender-associated expectations" (Martin & Little, 1990, p. 1438). Thus, children as young as 3 years old start to show signs of gender stereotyping.

A pattern of selective stereotyping occurs in the course of gender stereotype development. The study that demonstrated this effect (Martin, Wood, & Little, 1990) questioned children between 4 and 6 years old about toy interests for themselves and other children. The children demonstrated selective stereotyping; they made gender-stereotypical judgments about children whose toy interests were similar to their own, but failed to make stereotypical judgments for children whose interests were different from their own. This finding demonstrated not only the complexity of stereotypes, but also the tendency for children to develop an understanding of their own gender before they understand the other gender.

Even more gender stereotyping appeared in a second study with 6- to 10-year-olds (Martin et al., 1990). The 6-year-olds made the same stereotypical judgments as the children in the first study; that is, their judgments were stereotypical for children of their own gender but not for children of the other gender. The older children, however, made stereotypical judgments for both genders, demonstrating that stereotype development is not complete until middle childhood.

After considering their results and reviewing research by others, Martin et al. proposed a pattern of stereotype development. This pattern is presented in Table 7.2. Children in the first stage have learned characteristics and behaviors associated directly with each gender, such as the toy preferences of each. In this stage, they have not learned the many indirect associations with gender, associations that are essential for stereotypes to form. In the second stage, children have begun to develop the indirect associations for behaviors associated with their own gender, but not yet for the other gender. In the third stage, children have learned these indirect associations for the other gender as well as their own, giving them the capability of making stereotypical judgments of both women and men.

A specific cognitive process allows children (and adults) to maintain stereotypes once they have formed (Meehan & Janik, 1990). This process is called **illusory correlation:** "the erroneous perception of covariation between two events when no correlation exists, or the perception of a correlation as stronger than it actually is" (Meehan & Janik, 1990, p. 84). These researchers maintained that people perceive that relationships exist between gender and various behaviors when no relationship exists, or when the relationship is not as strong as their perception indicates.

Illusory correlation was demonstrated in a study in which children in 2nd and 4th grade saw pictures of women and men engaged in gender-stereotypical, gender-astereotypical, or gender-neutral activities and were asked to remember who did what activity (Meehan & Janik, 1990). Although there was actually no relationship between the activities and gender for the set of pictures, the children remembered more stereotypical than astereotypical or neutral activities. For example, the children were more likely to recall a male than a female carpenter and a female rather than a male librarian. The perception of correlations can be an important factor in maintaining stereotypes for both children and adults; when people

TABLE 7.2 Stages of Gender Stereotype Development

Stage	Gender Knowledge	Status of Gender Stereotypes
1	Behaviors and characteristics directly associated with gender	Undeveloped
2	Beginnings of indirect associations with gender for own sex but not other sex	Self-stereotype but none for other sex
3	Complex, indirect gender-related associations for same and other sex	Stereotypes for self and other sex

SOURCE: Based on "The development of gender stereotype components" (pp. 1891–1904) by C. L. Martin, C. H. Wood, & J. K. Little, 1990, *Child Development, 61.*

believe that activities are related to one or the other gender, then they feel comfortable in thinking in terms of these categorizations.

Gender knowledge increases during childhood, and this knowledge forms the basis for stereotyping. Thus, older children stereotype more than younger children. One study (Durkin & Nugent, 1998) showed that 5-year-olds stereotyped more strongly than 4-year-olds when asked to make predictions concerning what jobs women and men can do. The stereotyping was not equal; activities associated with men were stereotyped more than those associated with women. By the time they reach elementary school, children stereotype less than they did as preschoolers (Helwig, 1998), and the tendency to stereotype decreases during the elementary school years. Girls were less ruled by stereotypes than boys were when children expressed preferences for occupations, and that tendency has increased over the past several decades. This finding shows that changes have occurred in children's stereotyping, decreasing their power for girls but not for boys.

With increased gender stereotype knowledge comes not only the acceptance of stereotypes, but also the ability to make individual exceptions to those stereotypes. This latter ability allows for gender flexibility rather than the rigid acceptance of gender stereotypes. College students showed such flexibility when they deviated from gender stereotypes in evaluating men and women; they relied more on information about the individual than on gender-stereotypical information, showing that college students can be flexible in their evaluations (Locksley, Borgida, Brekke, & Hepburn, 1980).

Studying gender stereotyping in individuals ranging from kindergarten children to college students showed that the flexible application of gender stereotypes increases with age (Biernat, 1991). Younger children relied more on gender information than on information about individuals when making judgments about people, whereas older individuals took into account information about deviations from gender stereotypes. This pattern of development indicates that the acquisition of full information concerning gender stereotypes is accompanied by greater flexibility in the use of stereotypes. The tendency to rely on the stereotype is always present, and both children and adults showed a tendency to attribute gender-stereotypical traits to women, men, and children, including a reluctance to attribute feminine characteristics to males and a tendency to associate femininity with being childlike (Powlishta, 2000).

Therefore, the development of gender stereotypes begins early, with 3-year-olds knowing about gender-related differences in behavior. As children acquire information about gender, they become capable of forming and maintaining elaborate stereotypes for men and women, but they also become more willing to make exceptions to the gender rules they have learned. Older children and adults are more willing to allow for deviations from stereotypes when they consider people's characteristics and past behaviors. Nevertheless, gender stereotypes provide a system for classifying people that operates as a standard throughout people's lives; these influence their expectations for self and others, as well as the judgments they form about people based on their gender-related characteristics and behaviors.

Function of Stereotyping

The term *stereotyping* has negative connotations, but contrary to the headline story for this chapter, some theorists have contended that stereotypes have positive as well as negative effects. They proposed that inaccuracy is not one of the inevitable consequences of the process (Jussim, McCauley, & Lee, 1995). Consistent the with the negative view of stereotyping, other theorists have argued that stereotyping produces such a magnitude of distortions and incorrect generalizations that its disadvantages are overwhelming (Allen, 1995; Fiske, 1993).

One view (Martin & Halverson, 1981) contends that gender stereotyping is a normal cognitive process. In this view, gender stereotyping is an especially useful type of information processing that allows children to form categories based on gender and to understand this important attribute, if in a simplified and distorted way. The simplification and distortion inherent in stereotyping can have negative effects, but the positive benefits to children of forming gender stereotypes outweigh the negative effects of making some mistakes and thinking too narrowly about gender-related behaviors. Therefore, the function of gender stereotyping can be understood in developmental terms as a useful way to approach the complexities of gender.

A knowledge of gender stereotyping in children does not necessarily lead to an understanding of the factors that maintain stereotypical behavior in adults (Eagly, 1987b). The existence of gender stereotypes in children does not necessitate that adults maintain gender stereotypes. Research has indicated that older children, adolescents, and adults are willing to make exceptions to the dictates of their gender stereotypes, both for themselves and for others. The tendency to see gender stereotypes as inflexible prescriptions for behavior lessens with age. Then what is the point of keeping a rule with so many exceptions?

The "kernel of truth" position holds that stereotypes have some valid as well as some inaccurate points (Martin, 1987). Gender roles, the set of behaviors performed more often by men or women, form the basis for gender stereotypes. That is, the social roles that women and men fulfill allow people to perceive differences between men and women and to extend these differences to areas where none exists.

Several researchers have conducted studies to assess the accuracy of gender stereotypes, but no agreement has yet been reached. Part of the controversy is due to the difficulty in assessing gender-related behaviors (Allen, 1995). Should persons report on their own behavior, should some observer record behavior, or should researchers rely on standardized tests for their assessments? All three approaches are subject to errors that complicate assessing stereotypes accurately.

One side of the controversy proposes that gender stereotypes are accurate representations of actual differences between men's and women's reported characteristics. The inaccuracy comes from exaggeration, with stereotypes being much more inclusive than actual gender differences (Martin, 1987). A meta-analysis (Swim, 1994) of studies on the accuracy of gender stereotyping confirmed and extended this finding: Both overestimation and underestimation occur. Perceptions of gender differences may be accurate when measuring average group judgments, but individuals differ a great deal, and some individuals exhibit substantial inaccuracies (Hall & Carter, 1999).

The other side of the controversy contends that gender stereotypes contain a great deal of inaccuracy (Allen, 1995). People make errors in which they sometimes underestimate and often overestimate gender differences. Stereotypes may not be systematic exaggerations (McCauley, 1995), but inaccuracies are usually part of the process. Although the evidence concerning the accuracy of stereotypes is not completely clear, the findings lead to the conclusion that people are not very accurate in understanding the differences between the genders.

The process of rationalization may be an important factor in maintaining stereotypes. Observation cannot form the basis for stereotyping because many gender differences are too small to rely on personal observation as their basis (Hoffman & Hurst, 1990). Rather, people form stereotypes and perpetuate them by adjusting their attitudes. Confirmation for this view comes from two clever experiments that provided descriptions of people in two fictional categories, with the majority in each category differing from the minority in their preferred occupational activities. These descriptions did not specify a total division of labor; one study described one group as 80% "child raisers" and another group as 80% "city workers." The study investigated whether participants would explain the differing activities by rationalizing different personalities suited to the activity most common in each group.

The results showed strong evidence of this type of stereotyping, with participants imagining differences in personality traits that supported the division of labor. When a habitual activity was specified, people deduced an underlying personality trait that explained why this difference existed. Rather than believing that circumstances are important in activities, people tend to attribute differences in behavior to underlying personality traits. Thus, the unequal distribution of activities is sufficient to form the basis for gender stereotypes, including beliefs about intrinsic personal characteristics.

People feel better, for example, about women being child-care workers or homemakers if they believe that some element of women's personalities suits them to do such work. Additionally, this view holds that if women have the personal qualities that are necessary for such jobs, then men should not hold these jobs. Such rationalizations would also extend to racial or ethnic stereotyping as well as stereotypes based on gender roles. This view of stereotyping proposes that such cognitive processing offers rationalizations for existing situations that allow people to avoid thinking about the complexities of gender (see According to the Media/According to the Research).

Power rather than cognitive processing is an additional explanation for stereotyping (Fiske, 1993). Power encourages stereotyping through differential attention paid by the powerless and the powerful. The powerless attend carefully to the powerful to help understand their motives and predict their behaviors. This attention promotes the formation of complex perceptions of the powerful rather than stereotypes. The powerful, on the other hand, do not have the need to attend to the powerless, who do not exert control over the powerful. Their lack of close attention is conducive to stereotyping.

In addition, the powerful are often overloaded by many sources that vie for their attention, making superficial attention common for them. They may also have a high need for dominance, making them willing to control others. Furthermore, "stereotyping and power are mutually reinforcing because stereotyping itself exerts control, maintaining and justifying the status quo" (Fiske, 1993, p. 621).

Thus, several lines of research highlight the negative aspects of stereotyping and point out that stereotyping has more impact simply by being convenient for cognitive processing. The function of gender (or any other type of) stereotyping may be ease of cognitive processing: Stereotypes omit some individual details. This neglect of details allows people to think in simplified ways about a class of individuals rather than considering each person on an individual basis. For children, such simplification may be a necessary part of dealing with a complex world. In contrast, adolescents and adults are capable of considering information about individuals and allowing for nonstereotypical behaviors. However, adolescents and adults still have access to strong stereotypes, and these views influence their expectations

ACCORDING TO THE MEDIA...

The Voice of Authority Comes from a White Man

In television commercials during the 1990s, White men were the source of authority. According to a content analysis of these commercials, White male characters were more prominent than any other group (Coltrane & Messineo, 2000). Male prominence extended to those who appeared in voice only—male voices narrated commercials more than 10 times more often than female voices. The patterns of men in positions of authority and men as the voice of authority exist in the United Kingdom, Europe, Australia, and Asia as well as in the United States (Furnham & Mak, 1999). Women are also more likely than men to be shown as dependent, and around the world, women appear more often at home than in other settings.

In the United States, African Americans appeared in the background more often than as main characters in commercials and they were often subordinate to Whites (Coltrane & Messineo, 2000). In addition, their portrayals varied by gender. African American men tended to be shown as aggressive but were less likely to be shown in home settings or with women. African American women were less visible; they did not get the romantic and sexual attention that White women received, nor were they portrayed in home settings with the frequency that White women were.

The proportion of African Americans in television commercials was not substantially different from their proportion in the actual population—about 11% (Coltrane & Messineo, 2000). Eighty-six percent of characters in commercials were White, which is more than in the general population. This proportional representation of African Americans and overrepresentation of Whites means that Hispanic Americans and Asian Americans were practically invisible—only 1% and 2%, respectively. In addition, a disproportionate number of Hispanic and Asian Americans in commercials were children, an additional representation of their lower status and powerlessness. Indeed, ethnic minorities did not appear as often as Whites in situations that reflect the pursuit of happiness—in romantic situations, in prestigious careers, or in family settings.

Gender stereotyping in commercials extends to those advertisements aimed at children, and similar patterns of stereotyping appear (Browne, 1998). Boys are portrayed more frequently and as more dominant and instrumental than girls. These patterns occur more often in the United States than in Australia. In many countries, television commercial advertising presents stereotypical depictions of male and female characters and of ethnic groups.

about gender-related behavior. For adults, such simplification may be a convenient rationalization for relegating women and men to stereotypical activities or for explaining the consequence of power differentials that exist between men and women in many societies.

Perceptions of Women and Men

How have these stereotypes influenced people's perceptions of men and women? What are the components of stereotypes for women and men? Do people measure women by the standards of the Cult of True Womanhood? What problems will men experience if they deviate from the Male Gender Role Identity? Or have the changes in women's and men's behaviors produced changes in the stereotypes and broadened the boundaries of acceptable behaviors for men and women?

The content of gender stereotypes include four separate components that people use to differentiate male from female—traits, behaviors, physical characteristics, and occupations (Deaux & Lewis, 1984). All these components are relatively independent, but people associate one set of features from each of these with women and another set with men. On the

ACCORDING TO THE RESEARCH...

Biased Media Portrayals Perpetuate Stereotyping

When people see women and ethnic minorities portrayed in stereotypical ways, those presentations influence the way they think about and judge individuals from those groups (Murphy, 1998). That is, biased portrayals perpetuate stereotyping. This effect appeared in a study in which participants read a fake autobiography about an African American man who was aggressive, lazy, unintelligent, and criminal—the most prominent of the negative characteristics associated with this ethnic group. By presenting this stereotypical information, the participants were "primed" to believe negative things about African Americans, and this priming exerted an effect. In a later survey, the same participants judged that the events that happened to Rodney King (receiving a beating from police) and Magic Johnson (being infected with HIV) were situations that they had "brought on themselves." Participants who read neutral or counterstereotypical stories made significantly different judgments. Therefore, negative stereotypes in the media influence judgments in subtle ways.

Concerning gender stereotypes on television, there is bad news and good news. The bad news is that stereotypical portrayals of women and ethnic minorities abound on television, and these presentations have the power to do harm. Regardless of people's knowledge that "it's only on television," these messages are persuasive and powerful (Murphy, 1998). The good news is that the media can also work to counteract stereotyping. Commercials and programming that present counterstereotypical information can counteract stereotypes. These presentations can offer models who behave in ways contrary to stereotypes and open behavioral possibilities (Browne, 1998). Therefore, the media tend to perpetuate negative stereotypes, but changes in portrayals could have a very different, positive influence.

basis of knowledge of one dimension, people extend judgments to the other three. Figure 7.1 shows the components of this model; the arrows indicate the associations people make among components. Given a gender label for a target person, people will make inferences concerning the person's appearance, traits, gender role behaviors, and occupation. Information about one component can affect inferences made about the others, and people will attempt to maintain consistency among the components.

People viewed men and women as differing more in physical features than in psychological characteristics, and people relied more on physical information than on trait, behavioral, or occupational information in making gender-related judgments (Deaux & Lewis, 1984). As Figure 7.1 shows, physical appearance was the most influential of these components, affecting the other components more strongly than information about traits, behaviors, or occupations influenced judgments about appearance. Given information about behaviors, people make inferences about traits, and information about occupations can affect judgments about behaviors. In addition, specific personal information can outweigh gender as a factor in subsequent judgments about a person. For example, men who were described as managing the house or taking care of children were also judged as likely to be

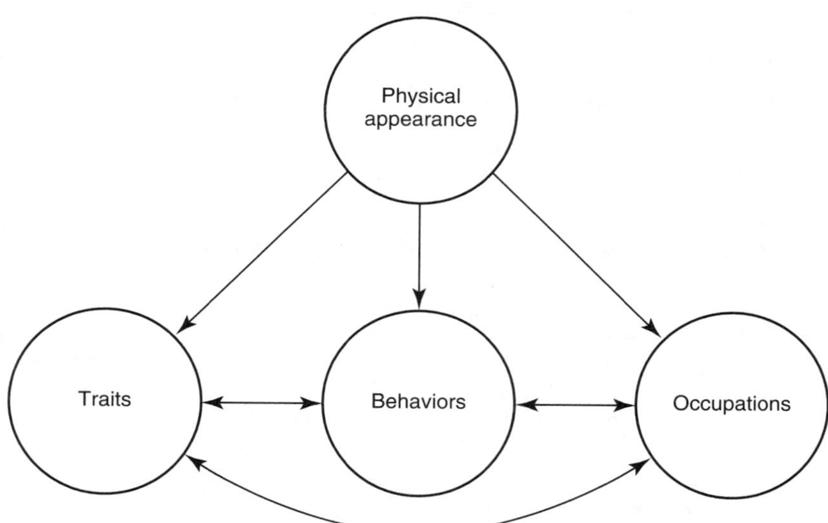

FIGURE 7.1 Components of Deaux and Lewis's Model of Gender Stereotyping

emotional and gentle. Such counterstereotypical information about men also increased the likelihood that such men would be judged as likely to be homosexual.

Although the participants in this stereotyping study saw differences in the traits, behaviors, physical characteristics, and occupations of women and men, their ratings of the two categories reflected the possibility that women may have some characteristics more typical of men, or men may have some characteristics more typical of women. That is, people do not view the stereotypes for women and men as separate and dichotomous, but as probabilistic and overlapping, categories. Participants judged the probability of a man and woman having certain characteristics on a scale of 0 (no chance) to 1.00 (certainty). The participants judged the probability that a man would be strong as .66, a high probability but not a certainty. However, they also judged the chances that a woman would be strong as .44. Although these judgments reflected stereotypical views of the relative strength of men and women, being male was not perfectly associated with strength, nor was being female associated with complete lack of strength.

Therefore, people use several dimensions to categorize men and women, drawing inferences on one dimension based on information from another. What is the content of these stereotypes? Studies in the 1960s and 1970s often found evidence for beliefs that matched elements of the Male Gender Role Identity or the Cult of True Womanhood, but some more recent research has shown changes in attitudes.

Beliefs held by college students in the 1960s showed strong acceptance of gender stereotypes by both college men and women (Rosenkrantz, Vogel, Bee, Broverman, & Broverman, 1968). Table 7.3 shows the items that differentiated women and men, which describe many of the characteristics of the Cult of True Womanhood and of Male Gender Role Identity. These college students applied these standards to themselves, evaluating themselves as

TABLE 7.3 Stereotypic Traits of Men and Women

Male-Valued Traits	
Aggressive	Knows the ways of the world
Independent	Feelings not easily hurt
Unemotional	Adventurous
Hides emotions	Makes decisions easily
Objective	Never cries
Easily influenced	Acts as a leader
Dominant	Self-confident
Likes math and science	Not uncomfortable about being aggressive
Not excitable in a minor crisis	Ambitious
Active	Able to separate feelings from ideas
Competitive	Not dependent
Logical	Not conceited about appearance
Worldly	Thinks men are superior to women
Skilled in business	Talks freely with men about sex
Direct	
Female-Valued Traits	
Does not use harsh language	Interested in own appearance
Talkative	Neat in habits
Tactful	Quiet
Gentle	Strong need for security
Aware of feelings of others	Expresses tender feelings
Religious	

SOURCE: From "Sex-role stereotypes and self-concepts in college students" (p. 291) by P. Rosenkrantz, S. Vogel, H. Bee, I. Broverman, and D. M. Broverman, 1968, *Journal of Consulting and Clinical Psychology, 32*.

masculine or feminine. In addition, both the women and the men in the study showed more positive ratings for masculine than feminine traits, and both the women and men showed some prejudice against stereotypically feminine traits, and preferred stereotypically masculine characteristics. A later study (Broverman, Vogel, Broverman, Clarkson, & Rosenkrantz, 1972) confirmed the bias in favor of characteristics associated with men.

The social roles of men and women began to change during the 1960s, which might have prompted changes in male and female stereotypes. One line of research indicating changes has come from Alice Eagly and her colleagues (Eagly, Mladinic, & Otto, 1991), who have found that women as a gender class receive more favorable evaluations than men. These researchers acknowledged that women may be poorly evaluated in some situations, but people have positive feelings about the characteristics stereotypically associated with women: People believe that these characteristics provide fine examples of human qualities. Results from a meta-analysis (Feingold, 1998) indicated that women received slightly more favorable ratings than men.

GENDERED VOICES

The Problem Disappeared

"Our car was having some problem, and my wife took it to be repaired," a man said. "She called me from the auto repair place, furious with the treatment she had received. The men there were stonewalling her—failing to listen to what she was telling them and treating her as though she couldn't possibly be capable of relating problems concerning an automobile. She was steamed.

"I went down there, and the problem disappeared. I was a man and apparently privy to the innermost secrets of automobiles. They treated me as though I would understand everything perfectly. Both my wife and I thought it was really absurd."

"One of my friends was upset that it cost $3.20 to get her shirt dry-cleaned," a woman told me. "She asked them why it was so much—the shirt was a tailored, plain shirt. They told her that women's blouses cost more than men's shirts, regardless of the style, because women's clothes don't fit on the standard machine for pressing and must be hand-pressed. She wondered if that was really true, and she gave the shirt to a male friend to take to the same dry cleaners. The problem apparently disappeared, because they charged him $1.25 for the very same garment. Isn't that beyond stereotyping?"

According to several studies, attitudes toward women have changed over time. Administering the Attitudes Toward Women Scale (AWS) to students at the same university over a 20-year period showed that students were least egalitarian during the 1970s and most egalitarian during the 1990s (Spence & Hahn, 1997). Using the same assessment over the same time period, a study with Canadian university students (Loo & Thorpe, 1998) revealed parallel changes. A meta-analysis of studies that used the AWS revealed a positive relationship between the extent of feminist attitudes and the year of administration (Twenge, 1997). For women, the relationship was strong, and for men, the relationship was still positive but not as strong. Therefore, these studies show that attitudes toward women have become more feminist/egalitarian over the past 25 years, which signals some changes in the traditional stereotypes of women, but questions remain concerning changes in attitudes toward men.

According to several studies, men may be the victims of more stringent stereotyping than women. College students who described their views of women and men applied more stereotypical terms to men than to women (Hort, Fagot, & Leinbach, 1990). For both physical and social characteristics, the masculine stereotype was more extreme than the feminine. In addition, men are the targets of some negative attitudes. Assessments of women's attitudes toward men have revealed that women hold ambivalent (Glick & Fiske, 1999) and negative (Stephan, Stephan, Demitrakis, Yamada, & Clason, 2000) attitudes toward men. The ambivalence includes feelings of hostility toward men and their gender role combined with admiration and attraction. The disapproving attitudes originate with women's negative contacts with men more than with the influence of negative stereotypes of men. Not only are men subject to more stringent stereotyping, but also men have become the target of negative attitudes.

Indeed, women negatively stereotype men (Edmonds & Cahoon, 1993). In several studies, women and men made judgments about the opinions of same- and other-gender individuals. These studies indicated that men made more accurate judgments about women's opinions than women made concerning men's opinions. In addition, women tended to believe that men held higher degrees of bias concerning women than the men expressed. That is, women showed negative stereotyping of men. One study (Hudak, 1993) found that men who scored high in stereotypical masculinity viewed women in more stereotypical terms than men who were not so strongly stereotypical.

Therefore, some of the positive attitudes about men and negative attitudes about women found in earlier studies seem to be changing. More recent studies have shown a shift toward greater acceptance of gender role flexibility for women and an increase in positive attitudes toward women. Some studies have indicated that men have now become the object of more severe stereotyping and some negative opinions from women.

Some evidence suggests that men and women may not apply stereotypes to themselves as strictly as they apply these stereotypes to others. U.S. college students hold stereotypical beliefs about gender, but they have also shown that they are willing to exempt themselves from these stereotypes (Williams & Best, 1990). That is, these students rated themselves as varying from the stereotype. Although people hold stereotypical views of men and women, they may make exceptions for themselves, allowing themselves a wider variety of behaviors than the stereotype would permit. By allowing such personal exceptions as routine, people decrease the power of stereotypes to control and restrict their lives.

Research has tended to confirm not only the existence of gender stereotypes, but also the characteristics these stereotypes share with the ideal woman from the Cult of True Womanhood and the model man from the Male Gender Role Identity. Over the past 30 years of research on gender stereotypes, earlier studies found prejudice in favor of the characteristics typical of men, but more recent studies have found more favorable ratings for the feminine traits. Research also has indicated that people may be willing to make exceptions for themselves in deviating from stereotypical gender-related behaviors, thus decreasing the power of these stereotypes to control behavior. The structure of gender stereotypes is complex; they include multiple components and inferences about these components based on information about others.

Masculinity, Femininity, and Androgyny

The concepts of *male* and *female* are relatively easy for people to understand because these words relate to biological differences understood by everyone except young children. But the concepts of masculine and feminine are much less closely related to biology and thus much more difficult to separate into two nonoverlapping categories: "One can be more or less feminine. One cannot be more or less female" (Maccoby, 1988, p. 762). Nonetheless, these dimensions seem important—perhaps essentially important—and psychologists have attempted to conceptualize and measure masculinity and femininity along with other important personality traits. After many years of difficulty with such measurements, the concept of **androgyny**—having both masculine and feminine characteristics—appeared as an addition to the conceptual framework. Several techniques now exist for measuring this attribute.

Psychologists' attempts to understand and measure masculinity and femininity have a long history but not a great deal of success (Constantinople, 1973; Lewin, 1984a, 1984b). The problems began with the first measures developed, and no measurement technique used since has escaped serious criticism.

Lewis Terman (who adapted the Binet intelligence test into the Stanford-Binet test) and Catherine Cox Miles constructed the Attitude Interest Analysis Survey, a 456-item test that appeared in 1936 (Lewin, 1984a). This test yielded masculinity–femininity (MF) scores that were increasingly positive in the masculine direction and increasingly negative in the feminine direction. Therefore, this early test conceptualized masculinity and femininity as a single dimension, with strong masculinity lying at one extreme and strong femininity at the other. The test was not valid in any way other than distinguishing men from women, and critics (Lewin, 1984a) thus argued that the test actually measured Victorian concepts of masculinity and femininity rather than the masculinity and femininity of individuals. This test is no longer used, but its existence influenced others to develop measurements of masculinity and femininity.

When the Mf scale of the Minnesota Multiphasic Personality Inventory (MMPI) appeared in 1940, it soon became the most common measure of masculinity and femininity, largely because of its inclusion in this personality test developed to measure psychological disorders (Lewin, 1984b). This scale was also unidimensional and bipolar, with masculinity and femininity at opposite ends of the scale. The psychologists who developed the MMPI were more interested that their Mf scale was able to measure homosexual tendencies in men than masculinity and femininity in heterosexual men and women. As a result of this interest, their **validation** procedure included a comparison of the Mf responses of 13 homosexual men to the responses of 54 heterosexual male soldiers. They used the responses of the 13 homosexual men as a standard for femininity, thus defining femininity as the responses of these men.

The test makers knew that the scale should not be used as a valid measure of femininity, and they were initially tentative in describing its use for a nonhomosexual population. But the test was soon extended to thousands of people, and the reservations disappeared. "It is rather staggering to realize that the *femininity dimension of this popular test was 'validated' on a criterion group of 13 male homosexuals!*" (Lewin, 1984b, p. 181; emphasis in original). The scale was not even very successful in diagnosing homosexuality in men, and this confusion of masculinity–femininity and sexual orientation posed a problem for understanding both concepts.

An alternative means of conceptualizing masculinity and femininity used the terms *instrumental* and *expressive,* with men's behaviors considered instrumental and women's behaviors as expressive (Lewin, 1984b). This distinction was based on an analysis of families around the world, with the conclusion that men occupy the role of autonomous- and achievement-oriented leaders, whereas women provide nurturance and support. This terminology has become important to those who have attempted to reconceptualize and measure psychological masculinity and femininity.

Despite the problems with a unidimensional measure of masculinity–femininity and the limited success with identifying homosexuals with these scales, this approach to the measure of masculinity and femininity was the most common until the 1970s. When theorists realized that the dimensions of masculinity and femininity were separate from sexual orientation, the measurements of both changed, helping to clarify both areas.

In 1974, Sandra Bem published a different approach to the measurement of masculinity and femininity by adding the concept of androgyny. She proposed that some people have characteristics associated with both masculinity and femininity; that is, some people are androgynous. The androgyny concept requires both masculinity and femininity in combination, so it is incompatible with a unidimensional view of masculinity–femininity. Instead, Bem constructed two scales to capture her concept of androgyny. Her test, the Bem Sex

GENDERED VOICE

Some Things Are Different There

"I think of femininity more in terms of what a woman wears than anything else," a young man told me. He had grown up on an island in the Mediterranean, lived in Paris for two years, and now lives in the United States. He sees some differences in what is considered feminine and masculine in the three cultures he has known. "Where I grew up, there was very little sexual activity among teenagers; it was a very conservative culture, and adolescent sexuality was strictly discouraged. The girls didn't dress in any way that was sexual, so they didn't seem very feminine to me. I guess I would consider some of them more feminine than others, probably in the same way that a person in the U.S. would: Small and dainty girls were more feminine. So I don't see any differences there.

"In Paris, nothing was hidden—things were openly sexual. The U.S. is a very sexualized culture, but there are differences. For example, kinds of clothing that people wore in Paris were different from in the U.S., and those differences related to femininity. Wearing jeans and tennis shoes would be considered very unfeminine rather than just another way to dress. I remember one girl in my student group who often wore tennis shoes, jeans, and a big sweater, and she was considered very unfeminine. Not that her way of dressing kept her from being pretty or attractive, but she didn't seem feminine. I guess I would say that Paris was less casual, and the women seemed more feminine than in the U.S. or in the Mediterranean.

"There were also some differences in what was considered masculine. At home, men tend to be small, so masculinity is not determined by size but more by behavior. Even men who are 5'4" or 5'6" can be macho, depending on what they do. Gangsters are very masculine, and so are those who are involved in politics, especially radical politics. The communists are considered the most masculine—lots of testosterone there. Men can demonstrate their masculinity by drinking—it has to be liquor and straight, without ice—and by smoking unfiltered cigarettes. Also, women who drink or smoke are considered masculine. So masculinity is a matter of what you do in the Mediterranean, not how you look—except the gangsters always have a three-day growth of beard.

"One of the differences in what is considered masculine involves bodybuilding and weight lifting. Men in the Mediterranean and in Paris just didn't do anything like that. They wouldn't consider bodybuilding masculine; it would be considered odd rather than a way to demonstrate masculinity. If they exercise, it's oriented more toward fitness than bodybuilding, so that seems very American to me.

"Political activism is masculine where I come from, whether men or women are involved. As I said, the communist radicals are considered very macho, and women who become involved in politics or become lawyers are considered masculine. As career opportunities increase for women, this may change, but now, women lose their femininity when they gain power through legal or political careers—even more than in the U.S.

"Also, on the island where I grew up, there was a status for women that I haven't seen anywhere else. Postmenopausal women lose their sexuality but they gain power and can become very influential in the community. They are considered almost neuter in terms of sexuality, so they are not feminine at all, but these women can have a lot of power, whereas younger women do not. As long as a woman is young and unmarried or married, she has almost no voice in the community, but these older women can make a transition to a position of respect and power.

"The only men who lose their sexuality in a similar way are artists, who are not considered feminine but almost neutral. Being an artist is well accepted and doesn't really carry any connotations of femininity, unlike homosexuality, which is strongly prohibited. It is a conservative culture, and homosexual activity is not tolerated at all—unlike Paris, where gay men and lesbians are very open about their sexuality. The U.S. seems to be the worst of both cultures in that respect; homosexuality is fairly open but poorly tolerated. That seems like a bad combination to me. As far as masculinity and femininity and homosexuality are concerned, I can't see any relationship. I know I can't tell who is homosexual by how masculine the men seem or how feminine the women seem. So sexual orientation does not seem to coincide with these characteristics to me."

Role Inventory (BSRI), included a scale to measure masculinity and another to assess femininity. Figure 7.2 shows the difference between the traditional unidimensional approach to personality measurement and Bem's two-dimensional approach.

People who take the BSRI respond to 60 characteristics by rating how well each of these characteristics applies to them on a 7-point scale. Of the 60 items, 20 represent cultural stereotypes of masculinity (ambitious, independent, competitive), 20 represent femininity (gentle, warm, understanding), and 20 are filler items. The 7-point scale ranges from *Always or almost always true* to *Never or almost never true.* Scores on the masculinity and femininity scales yield four different possibilities: masculine, feminine, androgynous, and undifferentiated. People who score high on the masculinity scale and low on the femininity scale would be considered *masculine,* whereas people who score high on the femininity scale and low on the masculinity scale would be considered *feminine.* These people not only accept cultural stereotypes of masculinity or femininity, but they also reject the other role. Thus, such individuals fit the stereotypical notions of masculinity or femininity, classifications similar to those obtained on other MF tests.

Bem labeled those people who score high on both scales *androgynous* and those who score low on both scales *undifferentiated,* classifications that do not appear in traditional tests of masculinity–femininity. Androgynous people evaluate themselves as having many of the characteristics that our culture associates with men and women, whereas those people who are undifferentiated report few traits of either gender.

The concept of androgyny experienced a rapid growth in popularity. Another test, the Personal Attribute Questionnaire (PAQ) (Spence, Helmreich, & Stapp, 1974), soon appeared to overcome problems with the BSRI (see Spence & Helmreich, 1978). The PAQ also identified people as masculine, feminine, androgynous, and undifferentiated, and both tests have continued in use. Although the MMPI Mf scale is still widely administered as part of that personality test, researchers interested in measuring masculinity or femininity usually choose some other assessment, such as the BSRI and the PAQ.

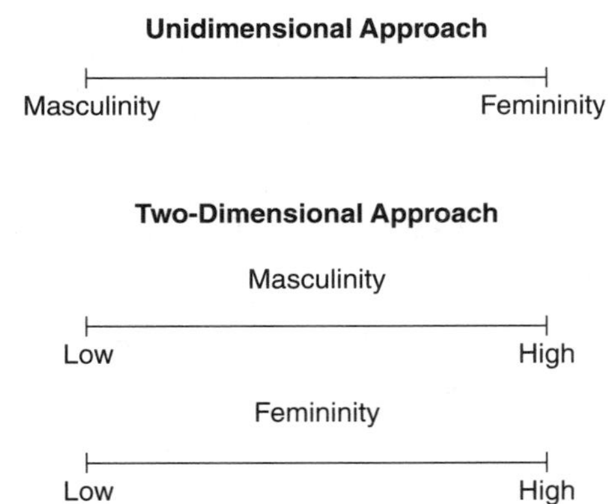

FIGURE 7.2 Two Approaches to the Measurement of Femininity and Masculinity

Not all researchers accept that the concept of androgyny offers improvements. Critics contend that tests that include measures of androgyny have provided no revolutionary reconceptualization of the measurement of masculinity and femininity (Lewin, 1984b). The masculinity scales of these tests measure instrumentality, and the femininity scales measure expressiveness; they do not necessarily measure actual masculinity and femininity. Indeed, many researchers now refer to scores on these two scales in terms of instrumentality and expressiveness, rather than masculinity and femininity. Janet Spence (1985; Spence & Buckner, 2000), one of the developers of the PAQ, has acknowledged the weaknesses of this conceptualization of masculinity and femininity and now uses the terms *instrumental* and *expressive* to describe the traits that such tests measure. She discussed the conceptual inadequacies of psychology's measurements of masculinity and femininity and proposed that gender identity is multifactorial and complex (Spence & Buckner, 2000). Thus, none of the existent tests provide adequate assessments of these constructs.

Some researchers have adopted David Bakan's (1966) terminology. He used the term *agentic* to refer to the assertive, controlling tendencies that are associated with men, and the term *communal* to refer to the concern with the welfare of others associated with women. Other research (Ricciardelli & Williams, 1995) has tested an alternative conceptualization that involves four dimensions: positive and negative masculinity plus positive and negative femininity. Table 7.4 gives examples of these four characteristics. The PAQ contains only positive aspects of masculinity and femininity, and the BSRI includes mostly positive aspects of both but has some examples of negative femininity. Although more research is necessary on this four-factor conceptualization, it seems to offers advantages over the two-factor approach.

Although the terms *masculinity* and *femininity* are meaningful to most people, psychologists have not yet managed to measure them in theoretically meaningful and valid ways. Problems exist both in the measurement of masculinity and femininity as well as in the concept of androgyny (Constantinople, 1973; Lewin, 1984b). In answering the question, "Are MF tests satisfactory? [The answer is] No. There is no evidence that the MF tests of the last sixty years provide a valid measure of the relative femininity of women or the relative masculinity of men" (Lewin, 1984b, p. 198). Instead, these tests measure our society's conceptualization of what women and men should be by using values that date from the Victorian era, although research indicates that society and self-concepts of masculinity

TABLE 7.4 Examples of Positive and Negative Femininity and Masculinity

Femininity		*Masculinity*	
Positive	Negative	Positive	Negative
Patient	Timid	Strong	Aggressive
Sensitive	Weak	Confident	Bossy
Devoted	Needs approval	Firm	Sarcastic
Responsible	Dependent	Forceful	Rude
Appreciative	Nervous	Carefree	Feels superior

SOURCE: Lina A. Ricciardelli & Robert J. Williams, 1995, "Desirable and undesirable gender traits in three behavioral domains," *Sex Roles, 33,* 637–655.

and femininity are changing. The MF tests purport to measure masculinity and femininity, but actually measure gender stereotypes rather than personality characteristics.

Considering Diversity

Gender stereotypes affect how women and men think of themselves and how they evaluate their own behaviors as well as the behaviors of others. Additional categories are equally important to stereotypes. "Although every individual belongs to at least one sexual, racial, and social class category simultaneously, such categories do not have an equal social meaning" (Unger, 1995, p. 427). How do these factors interact to form the basis for stereotypical categories? Do cultures around the world and ethnic groups in North America make similar distinctions between what is considered masculine and feminine? Do other cultures stereotype gender-related behaviors, and are these stereotypes similar to those in North America?

Within the United States, stereotypes exist for various ethnic groups and for men and women within those groups. The gender stereotypes for African Americans differ from those of European Americans, and history can explain these differences (Davenport & Yurich, 1991). Slavery and the manner in which Africans came to America have created long-standing effects of stereotypes perpetuated against slaves. Slavery disrupted the patriarchal family patterns that existed in Africa. It rendered the men powerless and imposed a type of equality between women and men based on their slave status. After slavery ended, racist attitudes toward ex-slaves restricted their earning power and kept African American men from attaining the type of power usually associated with the breadwinner role in patriarchal families. Instead, women not only worked at caring for their children, but they also worked outside their homes to support their families.

The employment of African American women has led to the view that African American families are matriarchies, but this stereotype is not completely accurate (Davenport & Yurich, 1991). African American families fit several different patterns, depending on economic level and geographical location. Middle-class African American families tend to be similar to middle-class families of most other ethnicities, with the family made up of a husband, a wife, and children. Poor families are more likely to consist of a single woman and her children.

Different stereotypes exist for African Americans at different economic levels. Poor African Americans are stereotyped as lazy and dangerous; the women are perceived as being sexually promiscuous and having many children; the men are perceived as being unemployed, and possibly involved in criminal activities. Media portrayals and news stories perpetuate these stereotypes despite their lack of validity for the majority of poor African Americans.

For middle-class African Americans, gender stereotypes vary from those of European Americans. Because of racism, African American men have trouble attaining the power associated with the White male stereotype, but African American women, with their greater likelihood of attaining a college education, can become successful, independent professionals. These lifestyle options can put such African American women in the position of not needing men to provide for them, and the self-reliance of these women has added both to the tension between the sexes and to the stereotype of African American women as strong, resourceful women who value both motherhood and employment.

Do African American women and men differ from European Americans in their beliefs about self and others? A comparison of African American and European American students in the United States showed no differences between the two ethnic groups, but did show differences in gender (Bailey, Silver, & Oliver, 1990). Both European American and African American women held more positive attitudes toward women than men did in either ethnic group. Thus, these researchers found a stronger effect for gender than for ethnic background for U.S. college students' views.

Hispanic American women have also been the topic of research on gender stereotypes related to their ethnic backgrounds. One component of the stereotype of Hispanic Americans is true—25% of Hispanic American families are poor, compared to less than 10% of White families. A contributor to this situation is the discrimination that Hispanic American women experience, which is more severe than the discrimination White women experience in employment and salary (Ginorio, Gutiérrez, Cauce, & Acosta, 1995). Stereotypes of Hispanic Americans include portraying the women as passive and compliant and the men as oppressive (Davenport & Yurich, 1991). Several researchers (Davenport & Yurich, 1991; Ginorio, et al., 1995; Vazquez-Nuttall, Romero-Garcia, & De Leon, 1987) have questioned the traditional concept that Hispanic culture values male dominance and female submissiveness and have conceded that the dynamics of the relationships are often more complex than the stereotypes would suggest. This complexity is especially true for Hispanic American women who have come into contact with European American culture by pursuing education and professional careers.

Some research (Vazquez-Nuttal et al., 1987) indicates that Hispanic American women hold a more feminine stereotype of the ideal woman than African American or European American women, but they see themselves as more masculine than this ideal. In other words, the stereotype of Hispanic American women may be feminine, but these women feel that they do not fit these stereotypes well. This discrepancy is similar to the gap between stereotype and personal perception that appeared in European American college students (Williams & Best, 1990); living up to stereotypes is a difficult task in all ethnic groups.

An attempt to understand the development of gender differences across many cultures led to a large cross-cultural study of the development of social behaviors (Whiting & Edwards, 1988). Children from 12 different communities in Kenya, Liberia, India, the Philippines, Okinawa, Mexico, and the United States were studied to better understand the development of gender in various regions of the world. Some differences appeared in the treatment and subsequent behavior of boys and girls, but many similarities also emerged in the types of interactions children experienced. The analysis showed that age was more important than gender in predicting the experiences of children in these various cultures. These differences were more apparent in the lives of older children, whose chores differed according to gender. For example, girls were more likely than boys to participate in the care of younger children, which related to greater nurturance among women. Beginning in middle childhood, especially in male-dominated cultures, boys were allowed more freedom to roam and be independent, which also related to the development of adult gender roles in men. In many of these cultures, girls experienced more pressure than boys to behave in socially acceptable ways.

Another cross-cultural investigation of gender stereotypes (Williams & Best, 1990) took place in 30 different countries in North America, South America, Europe, Asia, Africa, and Oceania. The study included children, but the emphasis was on gender stereotypes held by young adults. College students in these countries rated a list of 300 adjectives according to the extent to which each was more frequently associated with men or women. The goal was to study the associations that people in different cultures make about women and men and to look for female and male stereotypes.

The results revealed more similarities than differences in the gender stereotypes. Six adjectives were associated with males in all of the cultures—adventurous, dominant, forceful, independent, masculine, and strong—and three adjectives were identified with females in all cultures—sentimental, submissive, and superstitious. In addition, a wide list of adjectives appeared as male-associated or female-associated in a large majority of the cultures, and only a few adjectives were male-associated in one culture and female-associated in another. These findings furnish evidence for similarities in gender stereotypes across cultures, but the similarities were far short of being universal.

In the study of college students' stereotypes (Williams & Best, 1990), some cultures evaluated the male stereotype more favorably than the female stereotype, but this pattern did not appear consistently. For the entire group of countries, no tendency appeared to evaluate one stereotype more favorably than the other. In addition, the young adults in some of the cultures sharply differentiated the characteristics they attributed to male and female stereotypes, whereas others made relatively few such distinctions. For example, the male stereotype was much more positive than the female stereotype in Nigeria, with views that males are much more active and much stronger than females. In Italy, the differences were reversed or minimized: The female stereotype was the more positive, and beliefs about activity and strength were not given as great a weight.

Despite similarities in many aspects of gender stereotypes, not all cultures hold the same views of what traits, characteristics, and patterns of behavior men and women should exhibit. Despite the existence of gender role differences in all cultures, a cross-cultural review (Gibbons, Hamby, & Dennis, 1997) found that no one gender distinction applied to all cultures. In many cultures, women hold more liberal views of women and women's roles than men endorse, but even this difference is not universal. No differences in attitudes toward women appear in Malaysia or Pakistan, and men in Brazil hold more liberal views of women than women do. The distinction between traditional beliefs and beliefs concerning equal opportunity and equal power might apply to all cultures, but the specifics of what constitutes traditionality vary. Therefore, the only universal seems to be the division of activities and behaviors into male and female domains, without worldwide agreement about what those activities and characteristics are. Such divisions of activities, however, form the basis for gender roles and furnish the potential for gender stereotyping.

Summary

The term *gender role* refers to the activities or behaviors typically associated with women or men, whereas *gender stereotype* refers to the beliefs associated with the characteristics and personalities appropriate to men and women. Current stereotypes of women and men have been influenced by historical views of women and men. The Cult of True Womanhood that arose during Victorian times held that women should be pious, pure, submissive, and domestic. For men, several models of masculinity show gender role stereotypes. One of these is the Male Gender Role Identity, which holds that to be successful as men, males must identify with the elements of that role, including the need to avoid all feminine activities and interests, have an achievement orientation, suppress emotions, and be aggressive and assertive.

Gender stereotyping begins early in development and results in children holding rigid rules for gender-related behavior. Stereotyping is maintained by the illusion that more activities and characteristics are associated with gender than actually are. Children become flexible in applying gender rules as they approach adolescence, allowing themselves more exceptions for individual variation. Research indicates that children and adults accept elements of these stereotypes and use the stereotypes in making decisions and judgments, but adults apply the rules less strictly than children do because they have the ability to make many personal exceptions.

During childhood, stereotyping may serve to simplify cognitive processing and allow children to make easier decisions and judgments. During adulthood, such simplification is no longer needed, but the structure still exists. Several concepts have been proposed to explain the function of stereotypes: convenience of cognitive processing, rationalization of existing gender-related divisions, or maintenance of power differences between men and women.

Gender stereotypes have four different aspects—physical characteristics, traits, behaviors, and occupations. Each aspect may vary independently, but people make judgments about one based on information about another, to form an interdependent network of associations. People use this network of information in making deductions about gender-related characteristics.

The concepts of masculinity and femininity have a long history in the field of psychology as personality traits measured by various psychological tests. The first such test was the Attitude Interest Analysis Survey, which conceptualized masculinity and femininity as opposite poles of one continuum. The Minnesota Multiphasic Personality Inventory still uses this unidimensional approach. In addition, the MMPI also attempted to measure homosexual tendencies in men. This test even went so far as to define femininity in terms of the responses of a small group of homosexual men.

A more recent approach to the measurement of masculinity and femininity includes the concept of androgyny. Several tests have adopted this strategy, and such tests include separate scales for masculinity and femininity. People who score high on one but not on the other are considered masculine or feminine, but those who score high on both scales are considered to be androgynous. However, some critics have argued that none of the personality tests that purport to measure masculinity and femininity do so; rather, these tests measure characteristics that would be better labeled as instrumental–expressive or agentic–communal dimensions of personality. At present, the underlying concepts of masculinity and femininity remain elusive.

Cross-cultural research on gender roles and gender stereotyping indicates that all cultures delegate different roles to men and women. Gender stereotypes have more similarities than differences across cultures, with the male stereotype fitting the instrumental, or agentic, model and the female stereotype fitting the expressive, or communal, model. However, not all cultures make sharp divisions between the characteristics and behaviors of men and women.

Glossary

androgyny a blending of masculinity and femininity, in which the desirable characteristics associated with both men and women are combined within individuals.

gender stereotype the beliefs about the characteristics associated with, and the activities appropriate to, men or women.

illusory correlation the incorrect belief that two events vary together, or the perception that the relationship is strong when little or no actual relationship exists.

validation the process of demonstrating that a psychological test measures what it claims to measure; the procedure that demonstrates the accuracy of a test.

Suggested Readings

Deaux, Kay (1987). Psychological constructions of masculinity and femininity. In June Machover Reinisch, Leonard A. Rosenblum, & Stephanie A. Sanders (Eds.), *Masculinity/femininity: Basic perspectives* (pp. 289–303). New York: Oxford University Press. Deaux reviews not only the leading theories of gender role development, but also the efforts to measure masculinity and femininity.

Levant, Ronald F. (1996). The new psychology of men. *Professional Psychology, Research and Practice, 27,* 259–265. Levant summarizes the theory and research that has emerged in men' studies over the past 20 years, including the problems that men face in constructing a masculinity they can live with and that society can accept.

Lewin, Miriam (1984). "Rather worse than folly?" Psychology measures femininity and masculinity: 1. From Terman and Miles to the Guilfords (pp. 155–178); and Psychology measures femininity and masculinity: 2. From "13 gay men" to the instrumental–expressive distinction (pp. 179–204). In Miriam Lewin (Ed.), *In the shadow of the past: Psychology portrays the sexes.* New York: Columbia University Press. Lewin's two articles critically review attempts in the field of psychology to measure masculinity and femininity. She points out the difficulties and the mistakes, including conceptualizing femininity as the responses of 13 gay men.

Chapter 8

Emotion

HEADLINE

Big Fat Lies about Men

Mademoiselle, August, 1996

Andrew Postman (1996) listed several "big fat lies about men" and offered counterarguments for each. One of the lies was that "men don't show emotion" (p. 187). Postman argued that men and women both show emotion, but sometimes the situations that elicit the emotion differ. His girlfriend cried at a romantic movie, but he couldn't stay interested. He, on the other hand, cried at the Normandy memorial to the D-Day invasion, but his girlfriend was not as moved.

There are some situations in which men and women have similar emotional reactions. Both Postman and his girlfriend watched women's basketball, and his girlfriend noticed how emotional the women were during their playoff game. The losing team sat on the bench after the game, and most were crying. When they watched the men's final, she predicted a different emotional reaction from the men than they had seen from the women. Yet, "When the clock ran out, the camera focused on the losing bench. A bunch of 6'6" men, crying furiously" (p. 187), was not the emotional reaction that his girlfriend had expected from men.

Postman's "big fat lies about men" were stereotypes of men (and women) concerning emotionality. He pointed out how expectations concerning emotionality are incorrect for men and argued that women and men are similar in emotionality (and in many other ways). Although the situations that provoke emotion for women and men sometimes differ, the range of emotions are the same, and even the situational differences are not always present. Despite the appearance on national television of these 6-foot 6-inch crying male basketball players, the widespread perception is that women are more emotional, that they experience a wider variety of emotion and a higher level of emotional intensity than do men. On the other hand, men are restricted to a few emotions, especially anger. This chapter explores the experience and expression of emotion for women and men, and then examines two emotional reactions stereotypically associated with women and men: maternal instinct and aggression.

Physiological, Cognitive, and Behavioral Aspects of Emotion

Emotion has been a subject of interest in the field of psychology since its early years as a discipline. Even before psychologists began experimental investigations of behavior, emotion was a topic of interest to philosophers. From the start, western philosophers tended to conceptualize emotions as irrational and to place emotion opposite the rational thought processes (Averill, 1982). This attitude shaped the rational–emotive dichotomy that persists today.

Psychologists have devised several theories to explain the various components of emotion and their relative contribution to the experience. Early theories (McDougall, 1923) emphasized the physiology of emotional reactions and proposed their instinctual nature. Other theories attempted to integrate the contribution of cognition to explain the physiological reactions that accompany emotion (Cannon, 1927; James, 1890). All approaches held that both the physiology and the cognitive components were important to experiencing emotion.

An experiment by Stanley Schachter and Jerome Singer (1962) demonstrated that similar levels of physical arousal could result in different emotions, depending on the setting and the expectation of the participants. This study showed that both physiological arousal and cognitive labeling are important components in the individual's experience of emotion. Despite the results from Schachter and Singer's study, the relative contributions of physiology and cognition have been the source of continued controversy in psychology. Some theorists have asserted that the physiological component is more important (Zajonc, 1984), and others have argued that cognitions are more critical to the experience of emotion (Lazarus, 1984).

The primacy of either physiology or cognition has important implications for understanding emotion. If cognition were the primary factor in emotion, then an emotional experience should be dependent on the setting and expectation, and the physiology of the underlying emotion should be the same, regardless of the emotion evoked. If physiology were the primary factor, then the emotional experience should vary with bodily states, and each emotion would have a characteristic pattern of physical responses.

Both theories may be correct: one for men and the other for women (Pennebaker & Roberts, 1992). In this view, women rely more on cognitive information, whereas men use physical cues, to identify their experiences. Several types of evidence support this view. In laboratory studies, men are better than women at gauging their internal physical states such as heart rate, blood pressure, and blood glucose levels. These gender differences do not appear in studies done in more naturalistic settings, where women and men are equally adept in judging their internal physical responses. Outside the laboratory, women are better than men in gauging the emotions of others. They cannot know others' physiological responses, so this expertise must come from reading the situation. Women's reliance on situational and contextual cues in interpreting emotion may be the result of socialization that teaches them not to listen to their bodies. Women, therefore, may become skilled in interpreting cues from the environment, whereas men do not undergo this social pressure and continue to use internal bodily cues to understand their emotion. This intriguing hypothesis of a "his and hers theory of emotion" allows that two competing theories of emotion may both be true and that both describe some gender-related differences in perception of emotion.

Paul Ekman and his colleagues (Ekman, 1984; Ekman, Levenson, & Friesen, 1983) have concentrated on similarities between genders in emotional experience. They hold that some facets of emotional experience are universal, not only for women and men, but also for people around the world. These researchers studied the different facial movements that accompany the experience of emotion and found that certain facial expressions are characteristic of emotional states across societies. That is, people experience a standard set of emotions regardless of the culture of origin. Ekman argued that this consistency exists because emotions have evolved to help people deal with life tasks.

This evolutionary view can be traced to Charles Darwin (1872), who believed that both humans and animals innately experience emotions. Although Ekman's view of emotion does not exclude cognition as a factor in emotion, his evolutionary explanation emphasizes the role of physiology and the consistency of emotional experience for people in all cultures. Other investigations have tended to confirm Ekman's view, but not all investigators (Russell, 1994) accept the universal nature of emotions. When researchers use methods of investigation other than facial expressions, such as examining language for emotion-related words or investigating the social context of emotion, the results no longer support a universality of emotional experience.

Regardless of the consistency of emotional *experience,* people do not show similar consistency in emotional *expression.* That is, the behaviors associated with emotion show some cultural and individual variation. Some associations are known to exist between emotion and expression in terms of behavior, for example, between anger and aggression. However, the experience of emotion requires no behavioral manifestation: People do not have to *do* anything when they feel an emotion. The emotional experience is internal, and behavior is not an inevitable consequence of that experience.

The lack of correspondence between emotion and behavior results in the ability to disguise or conceal emotion. People can experience an emotion and yet manifest no overt behavior that signals their inner experience. Ekman (1984) defined the concept of **display rules** as "overlearned habits about who can show what emotion to whom and when they can show it" (p. 320). These display rules make it possible to experience one emotion and display another, or to display no emotional reaction at all despite the internal experience of strong emotion. In addition, the learning of display rules provides an explanation for the variability of emotion from person to person and from culture to culture.

How does learning provide an explanation for the gender differences in emotion? Do men and women learn different display rules and show different emotions, or do they experience differing types and intensities of emotions?

Gender and the Experience of Emotion

"From the 19th century onwards, rationality and emotionality have largely become associated with the supposedly different natures of men and women, the former fitted for productive labor and the latter for household and emotional labor" (Fischer, 1993, p. 303). This emotional double standard holds that women are more emotional than men, but only for a restricted range of emotions—happiness, sadness, disgust, fear, and surprise. Anger is notably absent from the list of emotions stereotypically associated with women. Men are also subject to a parallel stereotype—one of restricted emotionality for most emotions except anger (Heesacker et al., 1999).

The stereotypes of overemotional women and restrained men do not apply to all emotions or all situations. College students revealed similar gender stereotyping of emotions in two studies. In one study (Kelly & Hutson-Comeaux, 1999), college students rated how characteristic underreactions and overreactions were in relationship and achievement situations. The results showed a stereotypical view of emotionality according to context. For women in personal relationships—a domain associated with women—people rated women's overreactions as more characteristic than men's. For men in achievement situations—a domain associated with men—participants expected men to overreact. The exception to this general finding was anger, which was rated as characteristic of men regardless of the situation. The second study (Plant, Hyde, Keltner, & Devine, 2000) also showed a bias in associating anger with men and not women. Participants tended to interpret women's reactions as sadness rather than anger and had trouble seeing women as angry, even when women's expressions were clearly angry. Therefore, people have stereotypes for emotionality that are among the strongest gender stereotypes.

Another study showed that the association between anger and boys applies to infants as well as adults. Participants ratings of infants' emotional responses varied according to their belief that the infant was a boy or a girl (Condry & Condry, 1976). They tended to see the same reaction as anger from a "boy" and as fear from a "girl". Bias in evaluating emotion may also be a factor when people judge their own emotions. Evidence that women experience more intense emotions than men (Fujita, Diener, & Sandvik, 1991) comes from self-reports of emotional experience in which women reported having a greater emotional intensity than men. The process of recalling and reporting emotional experience may introduce gender bias. Indeed, when women and men gave immediate reports of their current emotions in everyday situations (Larson & Pleck, 1999), the results showed very few differences. Overall, men and women probably have very similar emotional experiences, just as Postman's (1996) headline story suggested.

Rather than detailing the gender differences and similarities in a list of emotions, this chapter concentrates on two types of emotional experience that have figured prominently in the stereotypes of emotion: the concept of maternal instinct (a "feminine" expression of emotion), and the concept of aggression (a "masculine" expression of emotion). In addition, the concept of instinct, connected with biological determinism, is often associated with both maternal behaviors in women and aggression in men. These two concepts provide a good contrast for considerations of gender and emotion. Psychologists have considered both as primary instincts basic to humans and animals (Hilgard, 1987). Those who consider these two instincts as primary believe that large gender differences exist, with nurturing and caregiving behaviors being the province of the female of many species, and anger and aggression being a male specialization.

The Myth of Maternal Instinct

The concept of maternal instinct holds that nurturing behaviors of mothers toward their children are determined by biological factors and are largely insensitive to environmental or situational conditions. Charles Darwin and the late-19th-century scientists who accepted maternal instinct have shaped subsequent research on the topic (Shields, 1984). Notions of instinctive nurturing can be traced to assumptions belonging to the 19th century, which accepted both women's intellectual inferiority and their emotional reactions to infants and children. Scientific thought of that time held that women could not be as intellectually developed as men because their energies were required to go toward reproduction and caregiving. Nature had suited them to focus on immediate situations rather than abstract ones (hence their intellectual inferiority) and to be more perceptive and emotional (hence their attraction to small and helpless beings).

Instinct as an explanation of behavior fell into disfavor among psychologists with the rise of behaviorism and its emphasis on learning and certain environmental factors known to shape behavior (Hilgard, 1987). Despite the decline of instinct as a general explanation for behavior, the concept of maternal instinct did not fade from psychological explanations of behavior. Fields as disparate as primate biology and social policy have shown the influence of assuming that biology determines motherhood and fatherhood (Silverstein, 1993). Scientists and social policy makers have accepted the views of early primatologists, who linked manhood with male aggression and sexuality, and feminine pursuits with female passivity and nurturance. Despite this acceptance, research evidence from studies of human parenting as well as cross-species work failed to support this view (Silverstein & Auerbach, 1999).

According to primatologist Sarah Blaffer Hrdy (1981), observations of various primate species have changed the view of mothers as primary caregivers and fathers as only marginally involved with offspring. These observations showed that male primates' involvement with infants varies from being the primary caretaker to showing benign disinterest, with researchers observing little dangerous aggression from adult males. Individual differences appeared in the amount of involvement with infants within their species; some males formed numerous relationships with infants and young primates, even those they had not fathered, whereas other males of the same species were less involved with the young (Silverstein, 1993). The evidence from studies of other primate species shows the behavioral flexibility of caregiving and does not support the concept of maternal instinct (and paternal disinterest). The behavior of primates offers no evidence for biological invariance of nurturing among females and lack of nurturing among males.

Despite the growing unpopularity of the concept of instinct during the 1940s and 1950s, many scientists selected the evidence they considered appropriate, and thus they continued to believe in the concept of maternal instinct. As Judith Lorber (1997, p. 13) quipped, "Believing is seeing." One of these scientists was psychologist Harry Harlow, whose research ironically provided evidence *against* the validity of the concept of maternal instinct.

Maternal Deprivation and Its Consequences for Nurturing

During the 1950s, Harry Harlow and his colleagues (including his wife, Margaret) conducted a series of experiments concerning affection and attachment. Harlow (1971) was concerned about the nature of attachment—of mothers for their babies, of babies for their mothers, of fathers for their babies, of children for each other, and so forth. One of Harlow's questions concerned the effects of maternal deprivation on children, but ethics prevented him from using human subjects. Therefore, he chose to experiment on monkeys.

Harlow's research on maternal deprivation originated from his desire to raise infant monkeys in a controlled environment, but he noticed that the infant monkeys raised in isolation behaved abnormally. They stared into space for hours, circled their cages or rocked repetitively for long periods of time, and repeatedly injured themselves, especially when humans approached (Harlow & Harlow, 1962). Not only did these young monkeys behave oddly when alone, but they also exhibited abnormal behavior when placed in a social group of other monkeys. They failed to fit into the social group; they fought more and interacted less than monkeys raised normally. They were also sexually abnormal; they appeared interested in sex but unable to mate. Thus, Harlow noticed that the experience of maternal deprivation seemed to have permanent effects on the social and sexual behavior of these monkeys.

Isolation also affected the monkeys' maternal behavior. When the isolated female monkeys became mothers themselves, they made spectacularly poor ones. These monkey mothers were negligent and abusive, refusing to allow their infants to nurse and sometimes beating them for trying to establish physical contact. Such negligent and abusive behavior did not support the concept of maternal instinct, but rather suggested that the experience of isolation from their mothers affected their nurturing behavior. That is, this research suggests that caregiving is dependent on experience and not on any inherent biological factors.

Harlow (1959) initially believed that being mothered was the critical experience that would allow a monkey to become an adequate mother, but subsequently, a series of studies revealed that other social experiences could substitute for being mothered. Harlow and his associates discovered that physical contact was an important factor in learning "mothering." They constructed two types of surrogate mothers, one a wire "mother" and the other a cloth-covered wire "mother." Neither type of surrogate was very much like a real monkey's mother; neither moved, held the infants, or responded to them in any way. In some of Harlow's studies, both types of surrogates offered milk for nursing, whereas in some conditions, only the wire surrogate offered milk. Although the surrogate mothers were unresponsive, the infants were not. The infants strongly preferred the cloth-covered surrogates to the wire surrogates, even if the wire surrogate was the sole source of food. Infants nursed from the wire "mother" but clung to the cloth-covered surrogate for hours and ran to it when frightened. Harlow concluded that the cloth-covered surrogates provided some comfort that the wire surrogates could not, and he called this factor *contact comfort,* the security provided by physical contact with a soft, caring, or comforting object. However, even these monkeys did not become socially, sexually, or maternally normal, indicating that the cloth surrogate had failed to provide the experiences that are necessary for normal monkey development.

Additional research showed that the experiences that promote normal nurturing and caregiving in monkeys involve contact with other monkeys. Despite the logic of modeling and imitation, such contact does not have to include the experience of being mothered. That is, being a good mother does not require being adequately mothered. Harlow and Harlow (1962) reported on studies that indicated that age mates can provide the social experiences necessary for normal development. The study involved separating infant monkeys from their mothers and raising them together as a group. Although these monkeys showed some abnormal behavior as infants—they clung together practically all the time they were together in their cage—these infants developed into normal adolescent monkeys. In addition, another study in which infants were raised with their mothers but without peer contact showed that mothering alone would not be adequate for normal development; some contact with peers appeared to be essential.

Therefore, the studies by Harlow and his colleagues demonstrated (at least in monkeys) that maternal behavior is not instinctual. As Table 8.1 shows, nurturing and caregiving are not behaviors that appear in all females. Instead, Harlow's research showed that specific social experiences are necessary for the development of adequate maternal (and other social) behavior. Without these experiences, adequate maternal behaviors fail to appear.

Attachment

Although research has demonstrated no innate, fixed pattern of caregiving, the contention that nurturing behavior has innate components has not disappeared from psychological the-

TABLE 8.1 Types of Deprivation and Effects on Nurturing in Monkeys

Type of Deprivation	Adequacy of Nurturing
No deprivation—contact with mother and peers	Normal
Complete isolation	Inadequate and abusive
Wire or cloth "mother"	Inadequate
Contact with mother only	Inadequate
Contact with peers, but not with mother	Normal

ory. Instead, that notion has been transformed into the concept of attachment, or **bonding,** an emotional attachment that develops between infant and caregiver within a few days after birth (Shields, 1984). Bonding, however, is not restricted to mother–infant attachment, but can also occur between fathers and infants, or with any others who happen to be present during the critical time period.

The concept of **critical periods** in development comes from ethnology, the study of animal behavior in natural settings, and the work of Konrad Lorenz, who discovered one type of attachment in geese (Eyer, 1992). Lorenz researched the factors that are important for baby geese as they developed an attachment to their mothers. He found a critical period in the lives of young geese, a time during which they learn to follow their mother. During this critical period, goslings learn to follow their mother after only one exposure to her walking past, showing that critical-period learning is not like typical learning, which requires repetition or practice.

In addition to the timing, the mother's behavior during the critical period is also important: She must walk past the goslings within two days after they hatch. If the timing and the mother's behavior coordinate, then the goslings *imprint* on their mother and follow her, which helps them to avoid danger and to learn behaviors important to their survival. If the critical period passes without the mother walking past, then the goslings do not imprint on her, leaving them without making an attachment to a caretaker and increasing their risk for the many dangers that may befall small fowl. Although the mother's behavior is important, the attachment may occur to animals other than geese, as Lorenz himself demonstrated. By timing his behavior to the critical period, groups of goslings were imprinted to follow Lorenz as though he were their mother.

The concept of imprinting could apply to the attachment that forms between babies and their caregivers, but it does not explain how the attachment develops between mothers and their infants. That is, Lorenz's work should not be used to resurrect the concept of maternal instinct because he studied *infant* attachment to a caregiver, not maternal (or paternal) behavior toward a child. Of course, geese and humans are very different, and one should be hesitant about applying Lorenz's findings to humans.

The popular concept of bonding is similar to imprinting, but bonding is a reciprocal process; it applies to mother–infant as well as infant–mother attachments. This concept is a variation on the idea of maternal instinct because bonding also depends on innate components that are known to occur in the early interaction between infant and caregiver. However, bonding is not restricted to mothers, so the concept definitely varies from that of maternal instinct.

The concept of bonding was popularized with published research (Klaus & Kennell, 1976) contending that in the first few hours after children's birth, their attachment to mothers is critically important. Not only do infants form a bond with their mothers, but mothers bond with their babies, forming attachments that are important for the duration of the relationship. Studies showed that mothers who were allowed to cuddle their babies felt a stronger attachment to the infants and showed more interaction with them during the children's infancy than mothers who were not allowed this physical contact. However, other researchers have failed to confirm these results and have criticized the concept of bonding (Chess & Thomas, 1982; Eyer, 1992). As a result, the concept of bonding remains more favored by the popular press than by developmental researchers. Indeed, the popularity of the concept may be connected with the desire to explain caregiving in biological terms—another version of maternal instinct (Eyer, 1992).

Gender and Caring for Children

Although research has failed to find a biological basis that explains women's nurturing, women remain the primary caregivers for children in the great majority of cultures, but fathers' involvement varies from high levels to no contact (Silverstein & Auerbach, 1999). The circumstances of childbearing and nursing place many women in continued contact with children. This association with caregiving is the basis for the classification of women as more nurturant than men. Two possible explanations for gender-related differences in nurturing behavior exist: responsiveness to children and pleasure in taking care of children (Shields, 1984). That is, perhaps girls and women respond more quickly and strongly to children or derive greater satisfaction from caring for children than men do, or both.

Gender differences in responsiveness to babies appear by age 3 years (Blakemore, 1998) and increase throughout childhood (Melson & Fogel, 1988a, 1988b). Many of the studies that have shown gender differences in responsiveness to babies used self-report measures that are subject to biases from expectation (Berman, 1980), but some studies have measured behavioral reactions. One study (Melson & Fogel, 1988a) found that preschoolers' interest in babies was similar before age 4, but with age, involvement with an infant in a play situation increased for girls and decreased for boys. The tendency for girls and boys to behave differently toward infants also appeared in a study in which preschool children posed for photos with either a baby or a peer (Reid, Tate, & Berman, 1989). The girls stood closer to the baby than the boys did, and when asked to play "mommy" or "daddy," girls stood closer than boys. In a naturalistic situation, girls showed more interest and nurturance toward babies than boys did, even at age 3 years (Blakemore, 1998). This pattern was stronger for boys whose parents held traditional gender roles compared to boys with more egalitarian parents. Therefore, parental and social encouragement are clearly factors in responsiveness to infants.

Girls' responsiveness to babies may not reflect a complete picture of nurturance. Boys tended to care for and nurture pets as they became less interested in babies (Melson & Fogel, 1988b). This behavior may represent the tendency for boys to become aware of the gender role they should follow. This awareness would prompt a decrease in their responsiveness to babies, but boys would still have the capacity to be nurturant caregivers, as expressed by their feelings for and behavior toward pets. Boys may be as nurturant as girls, although this nurturance may be expressed in different ways.

The studies that have used behavioral measurements of responsiveness to infants and children have revealed complex findings (Berman, 1980); many show no simple gender-

GENDERED VOICES

If Men Mothered

"I think that men could do as good as women at taking care of children," two college students told me. Both the young man and the young woman said that they believed that women have no instinctive advantage in nurturing children. Both of them said that the differences were due to experience rather than inherent biological factors. Indeed, both said that they believed there were few differences in ability to care for children.

"Well, men can't breast-feed," the young man said, "but I think that is about the only advantage women have except for experience. They have a lot more experience in caring for children. Girls babysit, and boys don't." He knew how difficult it was for men to get experience caring for young children because he had attempted to obtain such experience. He had volunteered to care for the young children in his church while their parents attended the service and had answered advertisements for babysitters. Neither of these efforts had met with enthusiasm from others; he had gotten the impression that wanting to care for children was considered odd for a man. He considered the possibility that people might think he was a pedophile, when all he really wanted was to learn to be more nurturant.

"I think if men were responsible for caring for children, there would be more changes in men than in children. If men had to learn to care for children, then they would. It wouldn't be automatic, because they don't have the experience, but they could learn. I don't believe in maternal instinct—that women have some innate advantage over men in caring. But women do have more experience, and men would have to learn the skills they lack.

"Men would learn to care for children if they had to, and they would become more nurturant in other aspects of their lives, maybe even in their careers. They might not care so much about competition and high-status careers.

The young woman had a slightly different view: "I think that the children would be different. This opinion is based on my own family and the differences between my mother and my father. My father was more willing to let us be on our own, but my mother was more involved. My mother took care of us, but my father let us make our own decisions. Maybe that wouldn't be good for young children, but I think I would have learned to be more self-reliant with my father's style of caretaking. But maybe if he had been the one who had to look out for us,

related differences, but rather interactions between gender and situational factors. For example, the gender of the experimenter and the gender of the participant might interact, producing different behaviors in male experimenter–male participant interactions than in male experimenter–female participant interactions or some other combination of testing situations. The lack of clear gender-related differences in behavioral and physiological measures of responsiveness confirms the view that social roles may be the most important factor in the gender-related differences in responsiveness to infants.

The differences in patterns of child care—namely, that women perform the vast majority of child care—complicate comparisons of the pleasure that women and men derive from these activities. Although some fathers are involved in all aspects of child care, the accepted role for fathers is helper, and the role for mothers is primary caregiver. "Mothers provide the 'continuous coverage' that babies require, [and] fathers are novel, unpredictable, physical, exciting, engaging, and preferred playmates for young children" (Thompson & Walker, 1989, p. 861). Any comparison of the pleasure of nurturing experienced by mothers and fathers is not based on a direct comparison of the satisfaction each derives from specific caregiving activities, but rather on a comparison of their roles as mothers or fathers and the types of caregiving each provides. Within the context of these differences, men rate their emotional experience within the family setting more positively than in work settings (Larson &

Pleck, 1999). That is, men experience more positive and less negative emotion at home than at work.

The time and effort mothers spend in child care lead to feelings of both satisfaction and dissatisfaction (Thompson & Walker, 1989). The experience of involvement in parenting, coupled with their feelings of the social value of nurturing children, produce satisfaction, but the loss of freedom and the irritation of attending to the demands of small children lead mothers to feel dissatisfaction. Indeed, many mothers feel disappointment over mothering because they had expected the experience to be both easier and more fulfilling.

Mothers tend to find more pleasure in taking care of their children than do fathers, unless the fathers are as involved with child care as are mothers. Fewer fathers have become the primary caregivers of young children, although several researchers have managed to investigate situations in which men are equally as involved as women in child care.

One such situation occurs in families in which the fathers are gay. The majority of gay fathers are men who have fathered children in heterosexual relationships. These men do not often get custody of their children, but an increasing number of gay couples are adopting or choosing surrogacy in order to become fathers (Patterson & Chan, 1997). These men are highly motivated to become fathers, and they place a high value on relationships with their children. Without gender roles to attach to themselves, gay fathers tend to divide child care more evenly than heterosexual couples and to be more satisfied with this division of labor.

Heterosexual fathers who participated in the care of their children experienced feelings and behavior toward their young children that were similar to those of women who provided similar levels of care (Risman, 1989). Those fathers who were very involved in child care expressed high feelings of satisfaction with their choice, even though they made career sacrifices to be involved fathers (Duindam & Spruijt, 1997). Therefore, the greater pleasure that women derive from caring for children seems to be a function of their greater involvement with their children, and men who have similar levels of involvement experience similar feelings.

If no instinctive force compels women toward and men away from nurturing, why, then, have men been involved so little in caring for children? Powerful forces operate to prevent fathers from becoming more intimately involved with their children, but those forces are social and not biological. In industrialized societies, fathers hold the role of breadwinner, which usually takes them outside the home and away from their children's lives. Social pressures toward achievement and monetary success have convinced men that they can best contribute to their families by devoting themselves to their jobs, and this devotion results in many hours at work.

The traditional pattern of the male breadwinner who is a distant, uninvolved father has undergone changes over the past 40 years (Pleck & Pleck, 1997), but the well-publicized image of the "new" father who is involved with children's upbringing may be an overstatement (Silverstein, 1996). Nevertheless, fathers are more involved with their children than in past decades, and an increasing number of fathers feel motivated to be more intimately involved in their children's lives (Duindam & Spruijt, 1997; Pleck, 1997). Few institutional supports exist for increased paternal nurturance (Silverstein, 1996). The fathers who have created such relationships diverge from traditional expectations, which can make them targets of disapproval when they decrease their income in efforts to make additional time to spend with their children (Riggs, 1997). The limited research on these fathers indicates that the children, mothers, and fathers all can benefit from positive involvement by fathers in their children's lives (Pleck, 1997).

The Prominence of Male Aggression

Aggression has also been the primary focus of gender role studies of instinct, again with explanations of men's evolutionary advantage (Cairns, 1986). The standard version says that during human prehistory, while the women were at home caring for the children, the men were out hunting and defending the group against various threats. In both the hunting and the defending, aggressive actions could be adaptive and even essential. Thus, women became passive homebodies and men became aggressive conquerors.

This view of human prehistory may be fictionalized and based more on the theorists' personal views than on prehistoric human behavior. There have been questions about both the idea of female passivity and whether men had an adaptive advantage from aggression (Benderly, 1987; Hrdy, 1981; Weisstein, 1982). Women in the hunter–gatherer societies of prehistory probably not only gathered plants for food, but also participated in small-game hunting, thus making them essential contributors to their groups' food supply and far from passive. As for aggression, it can offer advantages if directed at the proper targets outside the group, but it can also be disruptive and dangerous within a group. The men in these societies must have needed to become selectively rather than pervasively aggressive; therefore, natural selection would not favor those who were aggressive in all situations.

Despite the widespread acceptance of an instinct for aggression, a definition has been difficult to formulate. Although most people would agree that aggression is active and behavioral and that the result (or at least the intent) is harm to another, not all people would easily agree on which behaviors should be included and which consequences of these behaviors constitute harm. Actions such as hitting, kicking, and biting obviously fit into the definition of aggression, but aggression can cause not only physical but also psychological harm (Tavris, 1982). Relational and indirect aggression are additional categories that also fit into the definition. *Relational aggression* involves behaviors that harm others through damage to personal relationships, such as sulking or the "silent treatment" (Crick et al., 1999), and *indirect aggression* causes harm through indirect means, such as arranging for someone to be blamed for a serious mistake at work, or mocking someone's actions (Bjorkqvist, 1994). In addition, intent as well as action are both important considerations. Therefore, a definition of aggression presents problems for researchers.

Psychologist Leonard Eron (1987) discussed how he had solved the dilemma of defining aggression after 30 years of aggression research. He decided on a behavioral, objective definition of aggression, which he defined as "an act that injures or irritates another person" (p. 435). Eron contended that intentionality is very difficult to measure, especially in children; his definition avoided this problem by ignoring aggressive intent and sticking to harm or irritation as the outcome. He acknowledged that some accidents would be included in his definition, but he argued that assertive acts would largely—and in his opinion, correctly—be excluded. His approach avoided not only the issue of intent, but also the complex relationship between anger and aggression.

Anger and Aggression

Anger and aggression seem intimately related—anger is the internal emotion and aggression is its behavioral reaction (Plutchik, 1984). However, the two are not inevitably connected: A person can experience anger and take no action, aggressive or otherwise, but a person can also act aggressively without feeling anger, such as the violence shown by a hired killer.

Psychological and popular explanations of aggression have accepted that aggression is the outcome of some prior circumstance, either in the emotions or in the environment. Psychologist William McDougall and psychoanalyst Sigmund Freud believed that aggression was the result of instinctive expressions of frustrated wishes. This contention gave rise to the frustration–aggression hypothesis (Dollard, Doob, Miller, Mowrer, & Sears, 1939), which holds that aggression is the inevitable result of frustration, and frustration is the inevitable consequence of aggression. In this formulation, anger is not an important concept (Averill, 1982). The volume of research testing the frustration–aggression hypothesis has been conducted primarily in laboratory settings with a limited set of frustrating stimuli and measures of aggression. These experiments have yielded information about one facet of aggression but have failed to explore aggression prompted by everyday events in more natural settings.

Several investigations have surveyed people about their experience of anger and subsequent aggression. Although these surveys rely on self-reports and do not directly measure either anger or aggression, the survey method provides a way to investigate a wider range of topics than is possible through laboratory experiments. Among 4th- and 5th-grade rural, urban, and suburban students (Buntaine & Costenbader, 1997), no gender differences appeared in levels of reported anger, but boys said they expressed their anger as aggression more often than girls did. In a survey of university students in eight European countries, Klaus Scherer and his associates (Scherer, Wallbott, & Summerfield, 1986) found that anger occurred more often than other emotions, with about 75% of participants reporting anger within the four weeks prior to the survey.

What is the relationship among the three factors involved: the angry person's experience of emotion, the consequences of anger, and gender? By surveying community residents and college students in the United States about their experiences of anger and subsequent aggression, James Averill (1982) sought to answer these questions. He found that anger was very common—85% of those surveyed reported at least one experience of anger within the week. However, Averill also found that physical aggression was rare during anger, and that even the impulse to use physical aggression is not all that common. Although aggression may be a visible manifestation of anger, Averill concluded that anger could be expressed in a great variety of ways.

This survey yielded surprisingly few gender differences in the experience of anger. Gender differences appeared in the targets of anger, with men being somewhat more frequent targets of anger than women. However, the relationship between the two people was also an important factor. Among people who were not well-known to each other, men were more likely than women to be the targets of anger. Among loved ones, men and women were equal targets. Among friends, anger toward same-gender friends was the most common pattern. Averill also found that women reported more intense experiences of anger than did men, and women's responses were more varied, especially in their tendency to cry when they were angry.

The tendency for women to cry when they feel angry was a circumstance that June Crawford and her colleagues (Crawford, Kippax, Onxy, Gault, & Benton, 1992) discovered. Crawford and her research group conducted their study by exploring their own memories of emotional experiences, including those involving anger. They found a common experience of crying in response to anger. They explained this experience as an acceptable means for girls and women to express anger, whereas physical aggression is less acceptable. However, crying is often misinterpreted as sadness or grief, especially by men. If the situation is one in which anger is appropriate, then women would appear to behave differently from men by exhibiting an inappropriate response of sadness. This tendency may be a major reason for women to be labeled as overemotional.

Few gender differences appear in the experience of anger. For girls and boys as well as for women and men, the experience of anger is similar (Larson & Pleck, 1999). In addition, both men and women feel angry in response to the same types of provocations. These include actions that lead to violations of their plans or expectations, personal insults, and persons breaking social rules (Tavris, 1982). However, what counts as a personal insult may differ for women and men, which produces some apparent differences in the circumstances that prompt anger. In addition, the expression of anger has many negative social consequences and a limited effectiveness in bringing about change. Therefore, expressions of anger tend be construed as more destructive than constructive.

Gender role—not gender—has a consistent relationship to anger and the expression of anger (Kopper & Epperson, 1991; 1996). In one study (Kopper & Epperson, 1996), masculinity (rather than being male) was related to the expression of anger and aggression, and femininity (rather than being female) was related to the suppression of anger. These studies show that the stereotypical association of men and anger is incorrect, although men are more likely than women to respond to anger with physical aggression.

In summary, the relationship between anger and aggression is far from automatic, with feelings of anger occurring far more often than acts of aggression. Of the studies that have explored gender differences in the experience of anger, few have found differences between men and women. Instead, these studies have shown that men and women both experience anger from being similarly provoked. Other studies have indicated that gender role—not gender—shows a relationship between the expression of anger as physical aggression.

Developmental Gender Differences in Aggression

Observing gender differences in aggression during the early months and even early years of life is very difficult, because what counts as aggression in an infant is virtually impossible to define. Rather than attempting to assess aggression in young children, researchers have used other behaviors, beginning with children's activity level during infancy. Some studies have failed to find a gender difference in activity level, but Maccoby and Jacklin's (1974) review concluded that boys showed higher activity levels than girls.

The existence of gender differences in aggression among preschool children is controversial, but researchers have found elementary school boys to be more aggressive than girls. Using the definition of aggression as physical action, boys are more aggressive than girls. One meta-analysis (Hyde, 1984) evaluated the developmental nature of these differences and their magnitude. This analysis indicated that gender differences decrease with age; that is, boys and girls show greater differences in aggression during elementary school than during college. In addition, a decrease in the magnitude of aggression occurs over the course of development, with both boys and girls becoming less aggressive as they develop into adults.

Another way to approach the question of the stability of aggression over the course of development is through longitudinal research—in studies that test the same group of people over many years. Eron and his colleagues (Eron, 1987; Huesmann, Eron, Lefkowitz, & Walder, 1984; Lefkowitz, Eron, Walder, & Huesmann, 1977) conducted one such longitudinal study of aggression that tested 600 children, beginning when the children were in the 3rd grade (approximately 8 years old) and continuing for 22 years. The researchers assessed the children's opinions about who acts aggressively with questions such as "Who in the class pushes other children?" This measure provided an assessment of peer-defined aggression.

In the initial phase of the study, the researchers compared this aggression score to parenting styles and found that parents who were less nurturant and acceptant at home tended to have children who behaved more aggressively at school than the children brought up by more nurturant and acceptant parents. Ten years later, both the girls and boys rated as aggressive at age 8 received similar peer ratings. These children saw themselves as aggressive, rated others as such, and saw the world as an aggressive place, demonstrating the persistence of aggression.

This longitudinal study also investigated the influence of watching violent television programs; the researchers found that the violence on television acted as an effective model for aggressive children. Indeed, the preference for violent television programs at age 8 was a good predictor of how aggressive the male adolescents would be at age 19. Another longitudinal study (Eron, Huesmann, Brice, Fischer, & Mermelstein, 1983) found that violent television viewing was significantly related to aggression in both boys and girls. In addition, the relationship between viewing violence on television and aggression increased until children were 10 to 11 years of age, demonstrating both a cumulative effect for observing violence and a developmental period during which children are especially sensitive to the effects of televised violence.

In the third phase of this 22-year longitudinal study (Eron, 1987; Huesmann et al., 1984), participants were around age 30, and aggression during childhood predicted a number of aggressive behaviors during adulthood, including criminal behavior, traffic violations, convictions for driving while intoxicated, aggressiveness toward spouses, and severity of punishment of children. Table 8.2 shows the stability of aggression among the participants in these studies. The results of this longitudinal study demonstrated that adult

TABLE 8.2 Aggression over the Life Span

Children identified at 8 years of age by their peers as aggressive toward other children.

At Age 8	At Age 18	At Age 30
Had less nurturant and acceptant parents	Were still rated by peers as aggressive	Were more likely to have a criminal record
also	*also*	*also*
Preferred violent TV programs	Rated themselves as aggressive	Were more likely to abuse spouse
	also	*also*
	Rated others as aggressive	Were more likely to have DWI (DUI) conviction
	also	*also*
	Saw the world as a dangerous place	Were more likely to have traffic violations
		also
		Were more likely to use severe punishment with children

aggression can be predicted to some degree from childhood aggression, indicating that the two are related on a conceptual level. However, the specific behaviors that constitute adolescent and adult aggression will differ substantially from the behaviors measured in studies of children. Although children may fight and provoke trouble at home and at school, physical maturity and access to weapons makes adolescents and adults much more capable of doing serious harm.

Another longitudinal study (Cairns, Cairns, Neckerman, Ferguson, & Gariépy, 1989) explored the developmental differences in aggression between boys and girl from 4th through 10th grade. The researchers found that 4th-grade boys were much more likely to have confrontations that involved physical aggression with other boys than with girls, and this pattern became stronger over the 6-year time span. As adolescents, boys were much more likely to engage in physical confrontations but little cross-gender aggression. Expressions of aggression among girls in this age group tended to be indirect and relational, involving attempts to alienate or ostracize another girl from the social group or to defame her character. This type of social aggression increased for the girls but occurred rarely for the boys.

Social standards for the expression of anger in the form of physical aggression differ for men and women, but both boys and girls are discouraged from being physically aggressive by their parents and teachers. However, by middle childhood, both boys and girls have developed different expectations about expressing aggression. Boys expected less parental disapproval for their aggression, and both expected less parental disapproval for aggression against a boy than against a girl (Perry, Perry, & Weiss, 1989). Even with general parental disapproval for aggression, children learn about circumstances under which their aggression is more acceptable and more effective, and boys learn different rules for displaying aggression than girls learn.

Boys tend to enact the most serious types of aggression more often than girls do (Cairns et al., 1986). Some girls appear in the same range of violence as the most aggressive boys, but a study of girls in gangs (Campbell, 1993) showed that male and female violence served different purposes. Men use aggression to exert control over others, whereas women's aggression usually represents a loss of emotional self-control. The violence in male gangs is consistent with this interpretation: Boys in gangs use aggression and violence to gain social recognition and to get money. Girls in gangs also use violence to create recognition, but unlike boys, they do not seek money as much as they seek to avoid becoming victims by creating a reputation for being tough. These gang girls represent an extreme, but their use of violence to achieve their goals is similar to their male counterparts, even though their goals differ from those of boys.

Therefore, a developmental trend occurs toward a decrease in aggression from middle childhood to young adulthood, and gender-related differences appear in the use of aggression. Boys and girls use different strategies and behaviors in their displays of aggression, with boys using more confrontational, physical aggression. This aggression is much more dangerous than childhood aggression. With their size, strength, and greater likelihood of owning a weapon, adolescent boys become more likely to use aggression that causes serious damage and violations of the law than are adolescent girls.

Gender Differences in Aggression during Adulthood

If gender-related differences in aggression decrease during development as children age, then few differences should exist between adult men and women, although differences might exist in the styles of expression. Reviews of the experimental research on aggression have confirmed these predictions, finding that the differences between aggression in men and women are not large, but that significant differences exist in circumstances and styles.

Both literature reviews and meta-analyses have been used to explore gender differences in aggression. One such review (Frodi, Macaulay, & Thome, 1977) evaluated experimental studies in psychology, omitting surveys and crime statistics and concentrating on laboratory studies. These situations are artificial but controlled. Several meta-analyses have evaluated research on gender differences in aggression (Bettencourt & Miller, 1996; Eagly & Steffen, 1986).

The earlier analyses (Eagly & Steffen, 1986; Frodi et al, 1977) found that men were more aggressive than women under neutral and unprovoked situations. When women were provoked or felt justified, however, they became as aggressive as men. The later meta-analysis (Bettencourt & Miller, 1996) was directed toward understanding the factor of provocation, and this analysis showed that gender differences decreased or disappeared with some types of provocation. For example, women do not as readily respond aggressively to insults to their intelligence as men do, but both respond similarly to the frustration of someone blocking their path through an intersection. This analysis showed that some of the gender differences found in experimental research are due to the various provocations researchers have used. Table 8.3 summarizes some gender-related differences in tendencies to respond with anger and aggression for both children and adults.

Aggression can be a very effective way of exerting power and forcing others to behave according to one's wishes (Cairns, 1986; Campbell, 1993). When considering aggression as a method of exerting power, women may be reasonably concerned about the potential for reprisal; the size and strength differential between men and women makes women more vulnerable to the effects of aggression. Women's reluctance to use aggression is related to their fear of retaliation. Even when women and men hear the same description of a situation, women's fear of retaliation is greater than men's, and this factor decreases their likelihood of responding with physical aggression (Bettencourt & Miller, 1996).

When the action inflicts psychological or social harm, however, women are likely to become as aggressive as men. These situations are more common among adults than other situations involving physical aggression (Bjorkqvist, 1994). Although not without the danger of retaliation, relational and indirect aggression are less risky than physical confrontation, and women are more likely to use this strategy than men. This difference is the major reason that research has shown men as more aggressive than women: Laboratory studies offer a limited range of choices in carefully controlled (and contrived) situations that focus on physical aggression. With more comprehensive definitions of aggression and in more naturalistic situations, women are as aggressive as men.

For example, women are not generally aggressive in public, though they may be in private (Ben-David, 1993). Women have been shown to be as likely as men to initiate domestic-partner violence and more likely than men to hit and mistreat children (U.S. Department of Health and Human Services [USDHHS], 1997). Domestic violence is less likely than public violence to result in arrest, so women and men do not have similar levels of involvement with the criminal justice system.

Gender and Crime. Despite the small-to-nonexistent gender difference in aggression, the statistics on societal aggression reveal large gender differences. Men commit many more

TABLE 8.3 Gender Differences in Situations that Provoke Anger and Aggression

*For Children**	
Type of Provocation	Tendency toward Anger
Being hit accidentally	Boys report more anger
Not being invited to a party	Girls report more anger
*For Adults***	
Type of Provocation	Tendency toward Aggression
No provocation	Men respond with much more aggression in everyday contacts
Physical attack	Men respond with slightly more aggression Men consider attacks more serious
Insults:	
Insensitive behavior	Women consider insults more serious
Condescending behavior	Women respond with more aggression
Impolite treatment	
Rude comments	
Frustrations:	Men respond with more aggression
Not able to succeed	
Not able to finish task	
Recognize own inability	
Traffic congestion	
Negative feedback concerning intelligence	Men respond with much more aggression Women are much less angered by this type of provocation

SOURCES: *Roberta L. Buntaine & Virginia K. Costenbader. (1997). "Self-reported differences in the experience and expression of anger between girls and boys," *Sex Roles, 36,* 625–637. **B. Ann Bettencourt & Norman Miller. (1996). "Gender differences in aggression as a function of provocation: A meta-analysis," *Psychological Bulletin, 119,* 422–447.

criminal acts than do women, and their arrest and incarceration rates are much higher. According to the U.S. Department of Justice (1999a), men are about four times more likely than women to be arrested for various types of offenses, such as murder, robbery, vandalism, fraud, drunkenness, and so forth. Although not all of these violations involve violence, many do; as Table 8.4 shows, such offenses are more likely to be committed by men than by women.

Not all crimes result in arrest, and the possibility exists that the ratio of crimes committed by men and women is more equal than the arrest rates suggest. Surveys have indicated that although the reported rates of crime exceed the arrest rates, men still outnumber women in committing crimes (Osgood, O'Malley, Bachman, & Johnston, 1989).

Crime was so strongly associated with men before the 1970s that most criminologists and officials in the criminal justice system assumed that crime was an almost exclusively male problem (Warren, 1981). During the 1970s, research interests turned to female offenders, prompted by the increase of criminal activity among women. Although one hypothesis

TABLE 8.4 Percent of Male and Female Offenders Arrested for Various Offenses

Offense	Men	Women	Offense	Men	Women
All violent crimes	83.8%	16.2%	Forgery	61.4%	38.6%
All property crimes	72.2%	28.8%	Fraud	53.9%	46.1%
Murder	89.7%	10.3%	Embezzlement	52.9%	47.1%
Rape	98.7%	1.3%	Vandalism	85.1%	14.9%
Robbery	90.2%	9.8%	Prostitution	39.8%	60.2%
Aggravated Assault	81.2%	18.8%	Domestic violence	79.8%	20.2%
Burglary	88.1%	11.9%	Drunkenness	87.7%	12.3%
Larceny/theft	65.4%	34.6%	Disorderly conduct	77.9%	22.1%
Motor vehicle theft	85.0%	15.0%	Curfew violation/loitering	69.2%	30.8%
Arson	85.0%	15.0%	Runaway	41.8%	58.2%

SOURCE: Based on information from "Sourcebook of criminal justice statistics, 1998" (1999). U.S. Department of Justice, Washington, DC: U.S. Government Printing Office.

about this increase is that it resulted from the women's movement—equal opportunity applied to crime—research indicated that female offenders tended to be traditional rather than feminist in their beliefs. Even considering the increase in crime rates among female offenders, the rate of offenses remained lower, and the offenses committed by women were less serious than those committed by men (Tjaden & Tjaden, 1981). That is, the increase in crimes committed by women was due more to nonviolent rather than violent crimes. Therefore, the gender difference in violent crime persists, but the role of gender in criminal behavior remains poorly understood (Burton, Cullen, Evans, Alarid, & Dunaway, 1998).

Men are not only more likely to commit acts of violence, but they are also more likely than women to be the victims of crime (see "According to the Media/According to the Research"). This pattern of male-against-male violence substantiates research on aggression during childhood and adolescence (Cairns et al., 1989). Those findings showed that boys were much more likely than girls to use confrontation and aggression as a strategy for managing conflict, and that physical aggression between boys and girls decreased during adolescence. Despite decreases in physical violence among male adolescents, their size, strength, and likelihood of owning weapons made young men more likely than young women to become both perpetrators and victims of physical aggression.

Despite their lower rate of victimization, women are more likely than men to fear being the victims of crime. Women's perceived risk of crime victimization follows two principles: perceived severity of the crime and feelings of personal vulnerability (Warr, 1985). In general, the more severe the crime, the less likely it is to occur, and the less at risk women feel, with one exception—rape. Women of all ages reported a fear of rape, and among women aged 35 and younger, it was the most feared crime—more than assault, robbery, or murder.

Sexual Violence. Women's fears of sexual violence are not misplaced—rape is a common crime. In addition, rape often goes unreported, making the official estimates lower than actual occurrences (Koss, 1992). The U.S. Department of Justice (1999b) reported that rape—defined as some form of forced sexual intercourse (vaginal, oral, or anal) by the use of force or threats of force—occurs at a rate of 67 per 100,000 women. This estimate is restricted to women as the only victims and is based on the number of rape reports. Men's exclusion and women's reluctance to report rape has led to the belief that the actual rate may be several times larger.

A study of U.S. college students (Koss, Gidycz, & Wisniewski, 1987) clarified the rate of sexual violence. Asking both men and women about their sexual behaviors revealed that 15.4% of the women reported being raped since the age of 14 years, and another 12.1% reported experiences that met the legal criteria for attempted rape. Yet only 7.7% of the men reported behaviors that met the legal definition of rape or attempted rape. These rates yielded estimates for rape that were 10 to 15 times greater than the arrest rates for this crime, as well as perpetration rates that were 2 to 3 times higher than official estimates for the risk of rape. These results suggest that many rapes go unreported.

Not only does rape go unreported to legal authorities, many women are reluctant to tell anyone about being raped. Although this reluctance is common, women from some ethnic backgrounds are more reluctant than others. Despite a similarity in the numbers of attempted and completed rapes for African American and European American women, African American women are significantly less likely to tell anyone about being raped (Wyatt, 1992). Women from both ethnic groups had difficulty in identifying attacks by their acquaintances as "real" rape, and other research (Pino & Meier, 1999) confirmed the reluctance to discuss rapes. All rape victims share some commonality, yet African American women have a unique history of rape during slavery, and that history has had an impact on attitudes toward rape among women of this ethnic group.

Asian Americans hold more negative attitudes toward women as rape victims than European Americans (Mori, Selle, Zarate, & Bernat, 1994). Both Asian American men and women were more likely than European Americans to endorse rape myths, such as the myth that rape is the woman's fault or that women secretly enjoy rape. Asian American men had more negative attitudes about women than any other group, so Asian American women's acceptance of blame for rape may make them particularly unlikely to report this crime.

The stigma of rape involves the sexual nature of the crime and the tendency to blame the victim. Blaming and stigmatization are particularly common in rape cases, but the stigma is even more severe when men are the victims (Dreyfus, 1994). Male victims of rape or other types of sexual coercion have been accorded much less attention than female victims, partly because they are not victimized nearly as often, and partly because of the difficulty of accepting that men can be raped (Struckman-Johnson, 1988). Men are even less likely than women to report rape, and a major reason for their reluctance is that rape violates their masculine self-identity (Pino & Meier, 1999).

Despite these obstacles, a growing body of research indicates that men are sexually coerced and victimized by women as well as by men in ways similar to women's experience of coercion: through bribery, threats of withdrawal of affection, intoxication, physical intimidation, physical restraint, and physical harm (Struckman-Johnson & Struckman-Johnson, 1994). Both men and women are victims of sexual coercion, and both are censured for being victimized. The problem of female victimization is much more urgent because of its frequency and because women are more traumatized by coercive sexual experiences than men are (Struckman-Johnson & Struckman-Johnson, 1993). Therefore, a great deal of research has concentrated on understanding the characteristics of men who rape and coerce women into sex.

ACCORDING TO THE MEDIA...

Women Are Stalked by Crazed Killers

Since the 1970s, the "slasher" film has captured large audiences, especially among adolescents (Nolan & Ryan, 2000). *The Texas Chainsaw Massacre* was one of the early films of this genre and exemplified many of the common elements of slasher movies, including a maniac killer stalking young women with frightening weapons. These young women (often dressed very scantily) ran screaming with fear, only to be caught and killed. The slasher posed a threat to women, and the films sometimes showed the action of stalking through the eyes of the slasher, who was always a man. Thus in slasher movies, the victims are young women, and the killers are men.

As intended by the filmmakers, men and women react differently to slasher films (Nolan & Ryan, 2000; Oliver, Sargent, & Weaver, 1998). In general, men find these movies more exciting and enjoyable than do women, who find the films more frightening and disturbing. These reactions are not surprising, if viewers identify with the characters: Female victims are the targets of graphic violence, whereas men are the perpetrators who menace sexy young women.

Rape was once considered a rare form of deviation, but a recent book by Randy Thornhill and Craig Palmer (2000) portrayed rape as not only normal, but also adaptive, behavior. Their argument came from evolutionary psychology, a new field within psychology that studies the evolutionary benefits of various behaviors and tends to concentrate on sexual and reproductive behaviors. Part of the problem with this approach is that "unlike bones, behavior does not fossilize, and understanding its evolution often involves concocting stories that sound plausible but are hard to test" (Coyne, 2000, p. 27). Thornhill and Palmer's argument suffers from this weakness, but some of their contentions are testable. For example, they contended that rape allows men who would have no other chances to reproduce, to do so. A study of convicted rapists (Scully, 1990) provided evidence that failed to confirm this notion; most of these rapists had wives or girlfriends at the time they committed rape and presumably could have had sex with these women. This finding also refutes the notion that rape occurs as a result of sexual frustration.

Additional evidence also fails to support the contention that rape increases reproduction. If rape were a reproductive strategy, then victims would tend to be in the age range of fertility (Coyne, 2000). At least one-third of rape victims are younger than age 11 or older than menopause. For rapists to be reproductively successful, ejaculation must occur, but it does not in about half of rape cases. Of course, men who rape other men are not engaging in any reproductive strategy. Other explanations for rape seem more promising.

Diana Scully (1990) studied convicted rapists by conducting extensive interviews that revealed some of their motivations and attitudes. Her results revealed that the rapists had not experienced an unusually high level of treatment for psychopathology or an unusually high rate of childhood physical or sexual abuse. Their family histories were filled with instability and violence, but so were the backgrounds of other felons in Scully's study. The

ACCORDING TO THE RESEARCH...

Men Are More Often the Victims of Violent Crime, and Women Are Most Often Killed by Intimate Partners

Men are more likely than women to be the perpetrators of violent crimes such as assault and murder, but they are also more likely to be the victims of such crimes (U.S. Department of Justice, 1999a). Men are more involved in all types of crime than women are, but men are much more likely than women to be involved in violent crime.

Of course, the movie image of the maniac killer stalking beautiful young women is inaccurate in several ways. First, most people who commit murder kill people whom they know well, rather than people whom they do not know or know only slightly. Second, most people with psychological problems are not violent. Of those people who are violent and have psychological problems, most commit crimes that lead to their prompt arrest, giving them no opportunity to continue with a series of killings. Indeed, serial and mass murder are much more common in the media than in real life. Third, young women are not the most typical victims—young African American men are disproportionately the victims of violence in the United States (U.S. Bureau of the Census, 1999).

When women are the victims of violence, crazed killers are rarely the perpetrators. Instead, husbands and boyfriends are more likely to be the ones who harm women. Women are more likely to be assaulted or killed by men whom they love than by strangers (Heise, Ellsberg, & Gottemoeller, 1999). Therefore, the portrayal of deranged, menacing stalkers with female victims is not how most real-world violence occurs. For most female and male victims, violence has a familiar, male face.

---

rapists were able to form relationships with women, but their attitudes toward women showed a combination of beliefs: that women belong "on a pedestal," and that men have the right to treat women with violence. Many of these rapists told Scully that they planned their actions because they were angry with their wives or girlfriends and wanted to do violence to some woman. These men reported that the common characteristic of their victims was their vulnerability: They were in the right place at the wrong time—usually alone somewhere at night. Their physical appearance made no difference—many of the rapists had trouble describing their victims. This disregard for appearance highlights the violence of the act and argues against a sexual motive for this type of rape.

Scully's sample underrepresented rapists who were acquainted with their victims; acquaintance rape is less likely to result in complaint, prosecution, or conviction than stranger rape. Yet the violent attack by a stranger is the vision of rape that women fear, even though the most common experience of rape is an attack by an acquaintance, termed *date rape* or *acquaintance rape*. One survey (Koss et al., 1987) of rape and attempted rape included questions that allowed participants to estimate their involvement in various types of sexual coercion. A total of 54% of the women in the survey reported some type of forced or coerced sexual activity, but only 25% of the men in the survey admitted to some level of sexual aggression. The discrepancy in the rates for men and women is not due to a few sexually predatory men, but rather to some degree of denial or failure by many men to recognize their own sexual aggression. This failure to recognize sexual aggression also occurred among the convicted rapists in Scully's study and in a study with a representative sample of U.S. residents (Laumann, Gagnon, Michael, & Michaels, 1994). All of these researchers have found that men may have trouble recognizing their own behavior as sexually coercive.

One view of rape holds that coerced sex is the action of men behaving in ways that their culture allows and perhaps even encourages under some circumstances (Brownmiller, 1975; Herman, 1989). A relationship exists between acceptance of traditional social beliefs and sexual aggression in men (Walker, Rowe, & Quinsey, 1993). Acceptance of rape myths, acceptance of interpersonal violence, desire for dominance, and hostility toward women are all factors known to be related to the appeal of sexual aggression. Although all men who find sexual aggression appealing may not act, this factor is a predictor of sexually aggressive behavior.

Neil Malamuth and his colleagues (in Malamuth, 1996) have worked toward developing a model to predict sexual aggression. Drawing from the fields of evolutionary psychology and feminist scholarship, Malamuth proposed that the convergence of two factors relate to rape: (1) high levels of uncommitted, impersonal sex, and (2) hostile masculinity—hostility toward and desire to dominate women. When combined, these two factors relate to men's use of sexual coercion. Figure 8.1 presents this model and the paths leading toward

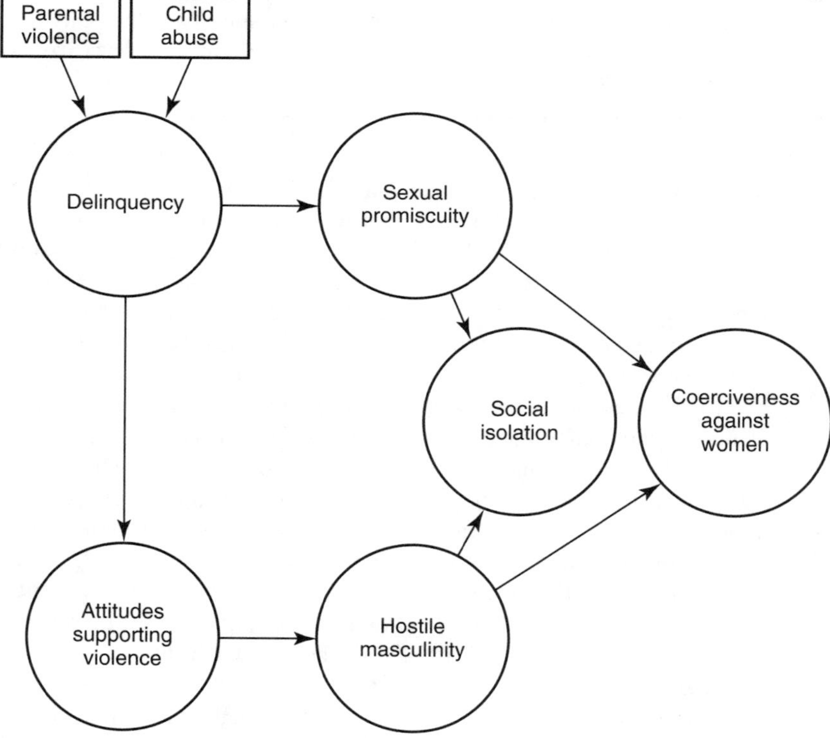

FIGURE 8.1 Model of Characteristics of Men Who Are Coercive against Women

SOURCE: Adapted from N. Malamuth, R. Sockloskie, M. P. Koss, & J. Tanaka, 1991, "The characteristics of aggression against women: Testing a model using a national sample of college students," *Journal of Consulting and Clinical Psychology, 52,* p. 676. Adapted by permission of Neil Malamuth and the American Psychological Association.

coercive sexuality. Malamuth's research team has conducted several studies that validate the model and its ability to predict coercive tactics to obtain sex.

In summary, male aggression is not a myth, but the notion that men are aggressive and women are passive is not true. Both genders experience similar levels of anger, but men are more likely to express their anger as physical aggression. This likelihood can be traced to different social expectations and reinforcements for aggression experienced by boys and girls. As adults, men are more likely to be violent in public, to use aggression to gain power over others, and to experience legal problems associated with their aggression. Women are more likely to be violent in private, to use indirect or social aggression, and to respond violently if they feel justified in doing so and protected from retaliation. These patterns of aggression show gender-related differences, but they do not suggest that aggression is a male instinct.

Expressivity and Emotion

The similarities in the feelings that men and women experience and the differences in their behavior suggest that the gender differences in emotion may occur in the way emotions are expressed. Indeed, women have been described as the expressive gender, whereas men are described as failing to express their emotions (Fischer, 1993). This interpretation is possible only by using a selective definition of what counts as emotion (Shields, 1994). Only by concentrating on the emotions of fear and sadness in women and by overlooking aggression in men could women be considered more expressive than men. Such evidence agrees with Postman's view from the headline for this chapter—it's a big, fat lie to believe that men are not emotional. As Postman proposed, both women and men feel similar emotions under similar circumstances, but women are more likely to express the emotions of sadness, anxiety, and fear than men are, and men are more likely than women to express their anger. This difference in expressivity can be explained by differences in display rules: Men and women are supposed to restrain displays of certain emotions, yet are free to show others.

In his discussion of compliance with the Male Sex Role Identity model, Robert Brannon (1976) listed four criteria, two of which relate to these gender differences in emotionality: (1) No Sissy Stuff, meaning men must avoid anything vaguely feminine, and (2) Give 'Em Hell, meaning men are proud to display anger and aggression. (See Chapter 7 for a discussion of all four components.) The stereotype holds that because women are emotional, anything feminine that is prohibited would include displays of most emotions. Anger is acceptable, however, because it is the essence of "giving 'em hell." These two components are essential elements of the display rules for men, which allows women to express more of what they feel, with the exception of anger.

The discrepancies among the three types of measures of emotionality (self-reports, observed behavior, and physical arousal) support these gender differences in display rules. When researchers have used participants' self-reports to measure emotion, they often find that women are more emotional than men. For example, one review of self-reports of emotionality (Maccoby & Jacklin, 1974) showed that girls and women were more likely than boys and men to admit to feelings of fear and anxiety. When researchers have used observations of participants' behavior in public, they have measured the enactment of display rules and the potential bias of observers, who may be influenced by the stereotypes governing emotion. Such studies tend to find gender differences (Eagly & Steffen, 1986), although the differences are not large, on the average. When researchers unobtrusively measure behavior

GENDERED VOICES

They Put a Lot of Effort into Showing Nothing

I talked to a psychologist who had been employed as a therapist in a prison, and he told me that the prisoners exhibited what he considered to be an inappropriate level of emotion—none. He said, "I thought they put a lot of effort into showing no emotion. Their goal seemed to be to show no sign of any emotion. For example, even if they were hurt, their faces didn't change expression. Every once in a while, I would see a slip, and a prisoner would show some sign of pain when he got hurt. I assume that they had feelings that were similar to anyone's, but their expression of emotion was very abnormal.

"Showing no emotion didn't mean that they let things go. They would retaliate against another prisoner who had hurt them, even if it was mostly an accident and he hadn't meant to hurt anyone. But they didn't show any emotion when they were hurt or when they hurt the other guy. It was part of the prison society to keep their faces like masks, showing nothing about what they felt, closing themselves off from the others."

in private, participants are more likely to display their emotions, and such studies often fail to find gender differences (Eisenberg & Lennon, 1983).

Measuring the physiological component of emotion provides a method of comparing the emotional responses of women and men, and some studies have used physiological measures of emotionality, often in combination with self-report or behavioral measures. One such study (Frodi & Lamb, 1978) measured behavioral and physiological responses of children who were interacting with babies. A behavioral difference appeared between girls and boys—the girls responded to and interacted with the babies more than their counterparts—but no difference appeared in the physiological measures.

Women learn a slightly different set of display rules for emotion than men do, and the behavior of both men and women tends to conform to the display rules they have learned. According to these display rules, women should be more nurturant than men, and in self-reports and in public behavior, they are. Boys and men should not be interested in babies or responsive to them, and under some circumstances, they are not. However, boys tend to nurture pets, and men who care for children are as nurturant and responsive as women who perform these tasks. According to these display rules, men should be more physically aggressive than women, and in self-reports and in public behavior (including criminal violence), they are. However, women experience anger as strongly as men do, and when they feel justified (and anonymous), women are as likely to show as much physical aggression as men. Women also use indirect aggression, which involves doing harm indirectly. Therefore, the gender differences in emotion are more a function of circumstances and social learning of display rules than biologically determined differences due to instinct.

Considering Diversity

Emotions show both consistency and diversity across cultures. One such cross-cultural study (Scherer, Walbott, & Summerfield, 1986) surveyed students in Belgium, France, Great Britain, Israel, Italy, Spain, Switzerland, and West Germany to investigate similarities and differences of emotion. More similarities than differences appeared, one being the tendency for everyday situations to be the main source of strong emotion. Of the emotions, anger was the most commonly reported, followed by joy. Close relationships were the main source of both positive and negative emotions. This survey revealed the expected stereotypical gender differences—women reported more expressions of emotion than men—but the study also found a small magnitude of gender difference.

This survey revealed some evidence against the emotional stereotypes associated with these countries: The English were very talkative rather than reticent; the Italians were very concerned with achievement rather than personal relationships; and the Swiss were very emotional rather than very reserved. Overall, this study showed fewer differences in emotion than the researchers had expected. Perhaps these similarities are not too surprising, considering how similar to each other European cultures are tending to become.

Other cross-cultural studies have included a wider geographical variety of cultures, and these have found more variation in the situations that prompt emotion as well as in the emotional responses. James Russell (1991) reviewed the cross-cultural work on the categorization of emotion by using emotion words and facial expressions. He concluded that "people of different cultures and speaking different languages categorize the emotions somewhat differently" (p. 444). However, Russell also concluded that more similarities than differences exist in the categories of emotion across different cultures and languages.

Another cross-cultural study (Mesquita & Frijda, 1992) analyzed the evidence on emotion by examining the components of emotion rather than only their categorization. By doing this type of analysis, similarities and differences appeared across cultures: "There exists some evidence that, by and large, certain kinds of events elicit emotions in widely different cultures and that they tend to elicit the same emotions in these different cultures" (Mesquita & Frijda, 1992, p. 181). These similar emotions included anger, disgust, joy, fear, sadness, and surprise. For example, loss of a loved one was associated with sadness in all cultures. Interaction with strangers was a source of anger in many cultures. Within these broad similarities in emotion, specific differences appeared. For example, interactions with strangers were a source of anger for 52% of Japanese, compared with 15% of Americans and 20% of Europeans—a substantial cultural difference.

The experience of shame is common to all cultures as a response to being observed doing bad things, but what constitutes "bad things" varies enormously among cultures. For example, among the Bedouins, a loss of honor is cause for shame, so their culture is very sensitive to the many causes of diminished honor. Signs of dependency or weakness cause a loss of honor, and the Bedouins believe that women are at constant peril because they are weak and dependent by nature. Women in Bedouin society must be very careful when they are in the presence of men lest they do something that will dishonor them and their families. On the other hand, the Japanese are shamed by displays of emotion because their code of modesty demands that true feelings remain hidden. Not all emotions bring shame to the Utku Eskimos, but anger does; it is considered dangerous, and its display is completely unacceptable for adults.

The Vanatinai also believe that anger and aggression are unacceptable (Lepowsky, 1994). The inhabitants of this small island society in the south Pacific near New Guinea value independence and assertiveness but find physical aggression shameful; adults who commit such acts are thought to be out of control and embarrassing to their families. Fighting is rare, even among children. This society is notable for its egalitarian values as well as for its lack of aggression, and women are somewhat more likely than men to be physically aggressive. This culture is not passive, nor are the gender roles reversed. The men are fierce warriors, and women are not allowed to participate in warfare or use spears. However, this society holds different display rules than Western societies.

At an abstract level of analysis, emotions show many similarities across cultures—the types, the antecedent situations, the labels used, and the physical reactions and facial responses people exhibit. However, cultural differences exist in the specifics of each component, especially in the processes regulating emotion (Mesquita & Frijda, 1992). Cultures vary both in restricting and in prescribing the display of emotion—who should express what emotion under what circumstances. That is, although many similarities exist across cultures, the rules that govern the display of emotion and the rules that govern what emotion should be experienced vary enormously among cultures: "Although there are universal patterns of expressive behavior, there also are culture-specific behavior modes, deriving from culture-specific models and from culturally based expectations regarding behavior that is appropriate under particular circumstances" (Mesquita & Frijda, 1992, p. 199). People may all feel the same emotions, but they do not express them in the same ways or under the same circumstances.

Summary

The stereotype of gender and emotion presents women as emotional and men as rational, but research on the different components of emotion has revealed that there may be few gender differences in the inner experience of emotion. Gender differences appear in how and when emotion is displayed. Included in the components of emotion are the physiological dimension and the cognitive dimension. Both expectation and social setting exert significant effects on the experience of emotion, and psychologists continue to debate the relative contributions of physiology and cognition to the experience of emotion.

The notion that some emotions are the result of instincts can be traced to Charles Darwin's theory of evolution. In psychology, the explanation that emotion is instinctive has faded, with the exception of beliefs about a maternal instinct and an instinct toward aggression. Belief in a maternal instinct has continued, although research by Harlow and his colleagues demonstrated that monkeys deprived of contact with other monkeys during the first 6 months of their lives failed to show adequate nurturing and caregiving. Another version of maternal instinct supports the concept of bonding—the attachment formed between adult and infant during the first hours of the infant's life—although this concept has not found as much research support.

Research on gender differences in responsiveness to babies has shown differences in self-reports, but not in physiological measures, of responses to babies. These findings indicate that girls and women show more responsiveness to babies because they believe they should, and that boys and men show less responsiveness for the same reason. Women still have a great deal more involvement in child care than men. Self-reports indicate that the greater pleasure of women in caring for children is coupled with their greater irritation in caring for them; however, men who are very involved in child care tend to report similar feelings. Although fathering has not included the type of intimate caregiving that mothering has, research indicates that fathers have increased their involvement with their children, demonstrating their interest and ability in nurturing. Therefore, the concept of maternal instinct has no support as a biologically based explanation for caregiving, and both men and women have similar emotions related to nurturing.

Aggression has also been nominated as an instinct, with the belief that men have more innate tendencies toward showing aggressive behavior than women. When considering the link between anger and aggression—that is, between emotion and behavior—few gender differences appear. Women and men experience anger similarly, but there are gender differences in emotional expression. Boys and men tend to be more likely to use direct, physical confrontation when they are angry, whereas girls and women are more likely to use more indirect and relational aggression. There is no difference in the use of verbal aggression; however, girls and women are more likely to cry when angry, an expression that men often misunderstand.

Developmental gender differences in aggression exist, with boys more likely than girls to use physical aggression at all ages. Longitudinal studies have revealed that aggression is moderately stable over time, and aggressive children are more likely than less aggressive children to become violent adults. However, both boys and girls tend to become less aggressive as they develop, and by adulthood, the gender difference in aggression has diminished.

Despite small gender differences in aggression in laboratory studies, very large gender differences exist in crime rates—men are about four times more likely than women to commit a violent crime. The victims of these violent crimes are more likely to be other men. However, women fear crime victimization more than men, especially sexual violence. Their fear has some basis: Official reports indicate that about 8% of women will be raped during their lifetime, and surveys indicate the rate of rape might be as high as 15%. Explanations of rape have changed historically from the view that a few pathological men commit sexual violence, to the current view that cultural factors support violence against women.

Although men have more experience with violence and less experience with nurturance than women, these differences may relate to how emotion is expressed rather than to women's or men's subjective experiences of emotion. The cultural display rules that govern the behaviors associated with emotion differ for men and women, and these allow women more expression and restrain men from expressing many emotions. Therefore, the gender differences in emotion may more accurately reflect differences in expressivity.

Emotions show both consistency and diversity across cultures. Research indicates that people across the world experience the same range of emotions, but the situations that evoke these emotions differ enormously across cultures.

Glossary

bonding an emotional attachment that develops between primary caregiver and infant within a few days after birth.

critical period a time early in development during which baby animals are capable of rapid learning when presented with the necessary stimulus. Once the critical period has passed, no amount of exposure will produce the learning.

display rules the learned social rules that govern who may display which emotion to whom, and in what situation each emotion may be displayed.

Suggested Readings

Eyer, Diane E. (1992). *Mother–infant bonding: A scientific fiction.* New Haven, CT: Yale University Press. Eyer critically reviews not only the concept of bonding, but also other versions of biological determinism in caregiving. Her book also offers a criticism of science in the media and how medical practice can be influenced more by popular beliefs than by valid research.

Larson, Reed; & Pleck, Joseph. (1999). Hidden feelings: Emotionality in boys and men. In Dan Bernstein (Ed.), *Nebraska Symposium on Motivation, 1999: Gender and motivation* (pp. 25–74). Lincoln, NE: University of Nebraska Press. Larson and Pleck review theories of emotion and present results from several studies that compare emotional responses of girls, boys, women, and men in a variety of situations. Their gender-as-process approach and innovative methodology provide an interesting presentation of gender and emotionality.

Silverstein, Louise B.; & Auerbach, Carl F. (1999). Deconstructing the essential father. *American Psychologist, 54,* 397–407. Silverstein and Auerbach analyze the changes in views of fathering, considering research and social policy.

Tavris, Carol. (1982). *Anger: The misunderstood emotion.* New York: Simon & Schuster. This popular book is not recent, but Tavris provides a readable review of research on the subject. She contends that the benefits of getting in touch with and expressing anger have been overrated, and she argues that the benefits of control outweigh the advantages of expression.

Chapter 9

Relationships

HEADLINE

The Science of a Good Marriage

Newsweek, April 19, 1999

The scientist behind "The Science of a Good Marriage," (Kantrowitz & Wingert, 1999) is psychologist John Gottman. This science includes a variety of techniques to measure reactions of partners in the "Love Lab," the Family Research Laboratory on the Seattle campus of the University of Washington. Most researchers who have studied marriage used surveys and self-reports, but Gottman (1998) chose to gather direct behavioral observations and to make physiological measurements of partners as they interacted. Gottman prefers to collect information of partners as they experience conflict, and his approach has shown some surprising findings.

One surprising finding was that anger is not the problem in bad marriages. Indeed, anger was common to both good and bad marriages. Thus, angry couples do not necessarily have relationships that are in trouble. The danger signs for a marriage come from what Gottman calls the Four Horsemen of the Apocalypse—criticism, contempt, defensiveness, and stonewalling. These reactions to conflict situations signal troubled relationships, and Gottman claims that he can predict divorce with 90% accuracy.

Several relationship patterns characterize couples whose relationships are in trouble, and those patterns differ from what many people assume. For example, Gottman's research also contradicts the Mars–Venus school of relationships, which holds that men and women come from two very different emotional worlds. According to his studies, "gender differences may contribute to marital problems, but they don't cause them" (Kantrowitz & Wingert, 1999, p. 54).

According to Gottman's research, one problem in marital relationships is an unequal balance of power. Husbands tend to have more power than wives, and when they do not share the power, the relationship suffers. Gender differences also occur in connection with other problems. For example, wives are more likely to engage in criticism, but husbands are more likely to stonewall, that is, to disengage during conflict. Both behaviors are typical of couples with unstable relationships. In addition, a clear signal of problems is a facial ex-

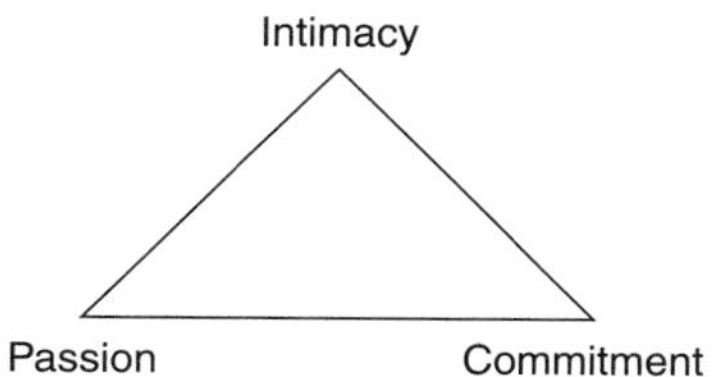

Liking = Intimacy without Passion or Commitment
Companionate love = Intimacy + Commitment without Passion
Romantic love = Intimacy + Passion without Commitment
Empty love = Commitment without Passion or Intimacy
Fatuous love = Passion + Commitment without Intimacy
Infatuated love = Passion without Commitment or Intimacy
Consummate love = Passion + Commitment + Intimacy

FIGURE 9.1 Sternberg's Triangular Theory of Love

SOURCE: Adapted from "A triangular theory of love," (pp. 123, 128) by R. J. Sternberg, 1986, *Psychological Review, 93.* Adapted by permission of Robert Sternberg and the American Psychological Association.

pression reflecting contempt. These behaviors all relate to a pattern of negative reaction with few attempts to reinstate any positive interaction. That is, couples headed toward splitting up tend to interact differently than couples who will stay together. Gottman's observation and physiological measurements allowed him to know which aspects of marital interaction were important in predicting divorce.

The gender differences in patterns of behavior in problem marriages may relate in part to women's and men's different styles in relationships, which have implications for friendships and love relationships, both with same-sex and other-sex individuals. Robert Sternberg (1986) proposed a model for understanding all relationships, including friendship and romantic love. He called this model the triangular theory of love because it hypothesizes love's three points: intimacy, passion, and commitment. His conception of intimacy encompasses feelings of closeness, passion includes romantic and sexual attraction, and commitment involves the decision that love exists and the relationship should continue. Figure 9.1 shows Sternberg's model and the different types of relationships that result from the combinations of these elements.

Sternberg argued that if none of these components exists, there is no relationship. His model distinguishes between two types of friendships—liking and companionate love. Liking occurs when people share intimacy, but not passion or commitment. Sternberg (1987) included both sharing feelings and sharing activities as intimacy. The combination of intimacy and commitment without passion results in **companionate love,** a definition that would come close to what most people regard as close but platonic friendship.

Friendships

Although Sternberg's triangular theory of love makes no distinction between intimacy developed through sharing feelings or through sharing activities, these two styles tend to be associated with women and men, respectively. These gender differences in relationship styles have made some men feel that their friendships are deficient because they do not share emotional intimacy the way that women do (Nordheimer, 1991). The view that men are deficient at friendship has not always existed, nor do all cultures discourage intimate, emotional friendships between men (Nardi, 1992a). The Greeks believed that true friendships could exist only between free and equal individuals, which restricted true friendship to a limited number and omitted all women, slaves, and men of lesser social standing.

During the 19th century, intimate friendships were common for both men and women (Nardi, 1992a). Courage and loyalty were seen as the basis for a special type of friendship that men could share, and men were considered capable of experiencing closeness and feelings for other men that women could not feel for other women, and that women and men could feel for each other. Those beliefs have changed, and currently, women are seen as more capable of intimate friendship, and women's style of friendship is viewed as more intimate than men's relationships.

Development of Styles

Children tend to segregate themselves according to gender starting at preschool age and continuing throughout elementary and middle school (Maccoby, 1988). This segregation is noticeable during preschool, and it becomes much more pronounced during the elementary school years, and may be imposed by parents or teachers. When the two are put into situations in which they must interact, they do, but the tendency to group into same-gender associations is a persistent pattern for children. Furthermore, the interaction patterns of boys and girls differ, beginning very early in development.

Children show gender differences in interactions as early as 33 months (Jacklin & Maccoby, 1978). Researchers studied pairs of children who interacted in all possible combinations—boys with boys, girls with girls, and boys with girls. The results showed that children interacted more with children of the same than with the other gender, for both positive and negative behaviors. Children in same-gender pairs were more likely to offer toys to their partners or try to take toys from their partners than the children in mixed-gender pairs. The girls in mixed-gender pairs tended to be passive and the boys unresponsive. Girls in such pairs tended to stand by and watch the boys play or to withdraw and seek their mothers. The boys in such pairs tended to ignore what the girls said to them. In contrast, girls and boys behaved similarly when they interacted with children of the same gender: The girls were active in their exchanges, and the boys were responsive to their partners' messages. Their reactions when partnered with an other-sex child, however, fell along stereotypical lines, which may relate to the gender segregation that is typical of children's play and friendships. Playing would not be that much fun if your partner failed to react and did not listen. These interactions may make each gender more eager to seek the company of others of the same gender.

Children as young as 2nd grade have a concept of friendship and expect friends to behave differently toward them than toward other children who are only acquaintances (Furman & Bierman, 1984). At this age, their notion of friendship centers mostly around what friends should do for each other, such as helping each other and sharing secrets. As they develop, children add to their notion of friendship so that personal characteristics such as loyalty become important. Children also begin to rely on friends for emotional and tangible support during the elementary and junior high school years, and they consider these types of support important to friendship (Berndt & Perry, 1986). During preadolescence, children become increasingly able to integrate the notion that conflict is an acceptable part of friendship, forming a more complex concept of friendship during the years of middle childhood and preadolescence.

During elementary school, children begin to rely on peers for companionship and intimacy rather than on siblings and parents (Buhrmester & Furman, 1987). These relationships reflect the closeness or intimacy component of Sternberg's triangular model of relationships. The research on elementary school children demonstrated that same-gender friends were important sources of companionship for the 2nd, 5th, and 8th graders. Gender differences in the development of intimate friendship also appeared, with girls both seeking and valuing intimacy at younger ages than boys. Like other investigations, the children showed a resistance to cross-gender friendships; only the eighth graders valued the company of the other gender.

One possible basis for the gender differences in friendships during middle childhood comes from the different activities that girls and boys enjoy during these years. For example, boys are more fond of rough-and-tumble play than girls are. Such play involves play-fighting and chasing and is very common among preschool children, especially boys (Humphreys & Smith, 1987). The persistence of rough-and-tumble play throughout middle childhood and into preadolescence might seem to escalate into aggression, but such play is actually done in a spirit of fun. Boys also tend to play in somewhat larger groups, to spend more time outside (Maccoby, 1990), and to be more fond of activities that involve **gross motor skills,** such as running, jumping, and throwing a ball.

Activity preferences may also be a reason for gender segregation during childhood (Bukowski, Gauze, Hoza, & Newcomb, 1993). Boys who preferred high levels of motor activity preferred the company of other boys, and girls who disliked such activities preferred the company of other girls. However, the conception of girls playing quietly with their dolls is stereotypical rather than typical: Girls engage in active and even athletic play, but their preferred partners are other girls rather than boys. The more active, assertive girls—the "tomboys"—tended to have the strongest preference for the companionship of other girls (Maccoby, 1988).

A large part of children's play time is occupied by gender-neutral activities, but the decision to play with children of the same gender persists (Maccoby, 1990). The play groupings of girls tended to be smaller than those of boys, and girls' group interactions differ from those of boys (Maccoby, 1988, 1990). For example, girls make more polite requests and use persuasion to get their way, whereas boys make more direct demands and attempt to get their way through dominance within their group. Girls try to involve other girls in the ongoing activities of the group, whereas boys tell other boys what to do. During middle childhood, the less direct style of persuasion typical of girls begins to be less effective with boys than with other girls, providing an additional basis for restricted association.

Gender is not the only basis for self-segregation during the early school years. Ethnic and racial background are also characteristics that children notice and use as a basis for forming groups, but ethnic background showed less of an effect than gender as a basis for groupings among junior high school students (Schofield, 1981). When put into a position to choose, children crossed ethnic lines before gender lines. Some interracial friendships formed in school (DuBois & Hirsch, 1990), but they tended to revolve around school rather than extending to the range of activities that most friendships did. Even with these restrictions, friendships between children of different ethnic groups were more common than cross-gender friendships, revealing that the most salient type of segregation for children is by gender.

Gender segregation is a strong force during elementary school, with few children voluntarily crossing the boundary (Thorne, 1993). Children imposed this division on themselves, but the organization of the schools and the teachers contributed to this gender segregation. For example, teachers often organized classroom competitions in which the girls formed one team and the boys the other, and school staff considered one section of the playground to be the girls' and another to be the boys' area. Thus, schools and adults may be perpetuating the tendency for girls and boys to form separate work and play groups.

The segregation is so strong, that the boundary crossings are of interest; animosity often accompanies such interactions. "It's like girls and boys are on different sides," an 11-year-old girl said (Thorne, 1993, p. 63). The animosity took the form of name-calling, invading another's space, pollution games and rituals ("cooties"), and occasional fights. Some of the hostile interactions contained the hint of heterosexual awareness and future romantic relationships, but sexuality was more commonly used as a way to taunt. Situations of comfortable interaction appear only rarely between girls and boys. These situations tended to be either very absorbing activities, such as group projects or interesting games, or activities organized by an adult so as to include both girls and boys, such as games involving assigned rather than chosen teams. Few children traveled easily between the social worlds of both girls and boys.

Preadolescents must avoid members of the other gender except under certain sanctioned circumstances, yet each gender must have sufficient contact to learn about the other. Maintaining the sanctioned balance of separation from and interaction with the other gender is important (Sroufe, Bennett, Englund, & Urban, 1993). Preadolescents who maintained gender segregation were both more popular with their peers and rated as more socially competent by adults than children who violated the boundaries between the genders. Same-gender friendships during childhood may serve the function of allowing individuals to learn how to form relationships without the pressure of sexual contact. Referring back to Sternberg's model of relationships, these relationships allow the development of intimacy and commitment without passion. Childhood friendships, then, might be regarded as a type of practice for adolescent and adult romantic relationships.

Despite their avoidance, preadolescent children are acutely aware of their future roles as romantic partners. At times, gender segregation during preadolescence seems forced (Maccoby, 1988), and children of both genders use threats of contact and proposed romantic feelings—threats to kiss, teasing about who "likes" whom, and avoidance of physical contact for fear of catching "cooties"—as ways to harass each other (Thorne, 1993). This active avoidance changes to active interest during adolescence; contact between girls and boys becomes more common, but friendships between girls and boys remain uncommon.

Friendships over the Lifespan

Friendships during adolescence are similar to those of preadolescence, but adolescents intensify the intimacy in their relationships with a greater degree of personal sharing and self-disclosure than those of younger children. The gender differences in the value and attainment of intimacy persist, with girls more likely to be interested in forming emotionally intimate friendships with a smaller set of girls, and boys more likely to form activity-based friendships with a more extensive set of boys. This pattern results in boys being alone less often than girls, but girls talking with each other more often than boys do (Smith, 1997).

Adolescent girls use talk as a way to develop intimacy, to reveal and learn intimate knowledge about each other (Berndt, 1982). A meta-analytic review (Collins & Miller, 1994) showed that self-disclosure is an important factor in friendship, increasing liking in those who hear disclosures. Self-disclosure is not as characteristic of boys' as of girls' friendships, and this difference may relate to different conceptualizations of friendship for boys and girls (Berndt, 1982). Alternatively, disclosure may be something that boys feel they cannot do. An interview study with poor, urban, adolescent boys (Way, 1997) revealed that the boys wanted intimacy but did not trust their peers sufficiently to disclose important thoughts to them. These boys expressed regret over that situation and longed for the closeness of a "best" friend to whom they could really talk.

This attitude of aloofness and withdrawal from intimacy is a set of behaviors that Richard Majors and his colleagues (Majors & Billson, 1992; Majors, Tyler, Peden, & Hall, 1994) labeled *cool pose.* Cool pose is a way that African American men present themselves, used as a compensation and coping strategy. The poses, postures, humor, readiness to use violence, and suppression of emotional displays are intended to create visibility for those who have been made invisible by a society that fails to grant African American men the status of European American men. The violence and suppression of emotion are elements of the masculine gender role, and cool pose uses an exaggeration of this role. This exaggeration allows African American men to feel a sense of masculinity. Cool pose magnifies some of the destructive elements of the masculine gender role, creating problems for those who take this pose. In addition to the violence associated with interpersonal conflicts, the emotional remoteness that is essential to the cool pose also inhibits the development of intimacy, both with women and with other men.

Fear of homosexuality is another factor that discourages boys from forming the same type of intimate friendships that girls experience (Berndt, 1982; Way, 1997). The current prohibitions against same-gender sexual activity make men hesitant about emotional closeness in friendships, and the activity-based relationships of adolescent boys and adult men illustrate one strategy for avoiding the emotional intimacy that could suggest homosexuality (Nardi, 1992a). Gay men do not have this obstacle, and their friendships with both gay and straight men show similarities and differences to heterosexual men's friendships (Fee, 2000). Gay men are often more willing than straight men to discuss personal relationships and problems; thus their friendships with both differ from the activity-based relationships typical of men. Their friendships with straight men are often tinged with caution over potential sexual attraction.

Studies of friendship among college students (Caldwell & Peplau, 1982; Roy, Benenson, & Lilly, 2000) confirmed the gender differences in the bases for friendships in men and women. These studies failed to find differences in the number or importance of friendships or in the time spent with friends. Men were more likely than women to choose an activity to do with a friend rather than "just talk" and to choose their friends on the basis of shared activities rather than shared attitudes. Women were more likely to talk about personal problems and celebrate personal accomplishments with female friends. These differences did not lead to differential evaluations of intimacy; women and men were equally likely to consider their friendships intimate.

Unmarried, childless college students may have the most time to devote to friends, making this often-studied group different from others. In addition, the demands of friendship for men and women may be most similar among college students (Caldwell & Peplau, 1982). As individuals become involved with romantic relationships, families, and careers, existing friendships often change, occupying less time and possibly becoming less intimate.

Marriage or other committed love relationships introduce a different pattern of friendship, when relationships with other couples are added to relationships with individual friends. Interviews with married couples were used to explore the factors that relate to the formation and maintenance of these people's social networks (Wellman, 1992). Traditionally, men have formed friendships as a result of their work and public lives, whereas women have formed networks of friends and family relationships centered around the home. The home became the base for friendships for both the male and female working-class participants in one study. Furthermore, the women were the monitors of social activity, arranging most social gatherings as well as get-togethers with other couples. These associations with other couples did not require both members of a couple to be equally close friends; the most typical pattern was for either the husbands or the wives to be friends with each other, and for their counterparts to be tolerant of these friends. This pattern of friendship tends to promote fairly superficial friendships, at least for one member of the couple.

The men in this interview study also had buddies whom they saw separately from couple-oriented activities. These buddies were likely to be companions for activities such as going to ball games, but these buddies also helped with small services (fixing a car) or large services (roofing a house). The men in this sample got less emotional support from their friends than their wives received from their friends, but then the men did not necessarily feel that their friends should provide emotional support; husbands tend to rely on their wives rather than their male friends for emotional support, and the husbands in this study behaved similarly.

During the early years of marriage, both spouses may relinquish other relationships to develop their marriage, seeking emotional intimacy and support from each other. In addition, when couples have children, the children take up time that might have been devoted to friends (or even to spouses.) Thus, young marrieds, especially those with children, tend to devote less time to other friendships than people who are unmarried or childless. The men in one study (T. Cohen, 1992) had restricted their friendships both when they were first married and again after the births of their first children. Some of those restrictions were due to time limitations and the obligation to fulfill the husband and father role, but some withdrawal from friendship was due to friends' perception of the married friends' roles. That is, unmarried men perceived that married men were not supposed to spend as much time with their friends, so they restricted their attempts to stay in contact when a friend married. Married men reported that they felt they should restrict their other relationships so as to maintain greater intimacy with their wives rather than with other male or female friends. This process may also apply to women. Thus, each member of a married couple may restrict their outside friendships.

When children become adults, their family members may become their friends. Due to the wide difference in power and authority between parents and children, this possibility is not likely during childhood or adolescence, but adult children and their parents can form relationships that have the emotional sharing and self-disclosure that characterize other friendships. These relationships also show gender differences consistent with other findings: Daughters and mothers are closer than other combinations of family members (Lye, 1996). Indeed, the closeness of families with adult children often depends on mothers' efforts to maintain contact. In addition to parent–adult child relationships, siblings are often close after they become adults, maintaining relationships that are as close as friends (Floyd, 1995).

Aging produces changes in friendships, with the elderly needing more practical support while their number of friends decreases due to death. Children often become the source of this caregiving and practical support, but the elderly attempt to maintain social networks (Akiyama, Elliott, & Antonucci, 1996). Women become more numerous in the social networks of the elderly because men die at younger ages, leaving more women. Thus, men's same-gender friendships tend to be replaced with relationships with women. Therefore, friendship becomes more female-based among the elderly.

Flexibility of Styles

Men may find emotional intimacy easier with women than with other men. As Francesca Cancian (1987) proposed, love has come to be "feminized," that is, to be defined in feminine terms, as the expression of feelings and as self-disclosure. These characteristics are commonly associated with women and are actually more common in women's than men's friendships. Some evidence exists that men can also use this style of relationship and tend to do so when they relate to women. That is, men may be able to use different styles of relating to different friends. This flexibility appeared in a study (Reid & Fine, 1992) that focused on self-disclosure in same-gender and cross-gender friendships. One of the important factors in self-disclosure was the type of relationship between the two people. For instance, lovers and spouses reported more intimate self-disclosure than close platonic friends.

Cross-gender friendships face more constraining rules than same-gender friendships. Cross-gender friendships are a recent development that did not exist 100 years ago when Western societies were strongly gender segregated, when women governed the home and men occupied the world of work, politics, and business (Swain, 1992). Although gender segregation still exists in many situations, school and work offer opportunities for cross-gender relationships, and women and men have formed such friendships. Such friendships may experience difficulties in a society that emphasizes same-gender friendships and cross-gender sexual relationships, but some research (Monsour, Harris, Kurzweil, & Beard, 1994) found that these problems affect only a small percentage of cross-gender friendships. For most cross-gender friends, these special challenges and problems were "much ado about nothing," (Monsour et al., 1994, p. 55).

The ability to adapt to the situation by using a more "feminine" or "masculine" style of interaction indicates that styles of friendship are indeed roles that men and women learn. Although not all men may learn the intimate sharing and self-disclosure that are typical of women's friendships, most do, and these men use this style when they form friendships with women. Men may feel uncomfortable in enacting this friendship style for several reasons. As several researchers have pointed out, **homophobia**—the unreasonable fear and hatred of homosexuality—restrains men from seeking emotional intimacy with other men. Even when men know the style, they may be reluctant to use it. When they use it, they may feel more comfortable in this type of relationship with women rather than with other men.

The constraints on women's behavior are not as strong; their typical style of emotional intimacy with other women carries no homosexual connotations. However, emotional intimacy between women and men often has an element of a sexual relationship, so women who seek friendships with men also must be vigilant in maintaining these as nonsexual friendships. Women who adopt an activity-based style of relationship with men, being "one of the boys," can participate in the same activities that men enjoy with each other—playing baseball, poker, or other recreational activities. This choice creates a style of relationship typical of men and not necessarily one infused with emotional intimacy. Some men and women have chosen to break the boundaries established during preschool and form friendships with members of the other gender. The research indicates that men and women know about both friendship styles, suggesting that any limitations in creating cross-gender friendships come from reluctance to apply these styles.

The restriction of one style of relationship to women and the other to men has forced each into a way of relating that fails to allow the development of full potential for either (Cancian, 1987). With women, the designated experts in relationships, many men feel incompetent at relationships because they may have problems with the emotional, intimate style of relating. These restrictions have affected love relationships even more strongly than friendships. Both styles have benefits, and the equation of emotional intimacy with romantic love has negative consequences. The history of love relationships suggests the possibility that the male and female roles restrict the development of both men and women.

Love Relationships

As the headline story on John Gottman (Kantrowitz & Wingert, 1999) described, maintaining love relationships proves difficult. Women's greater ease in emotional sharing can make men uneasy, and men's tendency to emotionally withdraw from a discussion is one of the warning signs that a marriage is in trouble. Currently in the United States, divorce is common, but problems in relationships are not new. The changes have come from what is expected of marriage and the ease of divorce, not with relationship problems. Elaine Hatfield and Richard Rapson (1996) contended that romantic, passionate love is universal, but this type of love has not been the basis for permanent relationships until recently in industrialized Western countries.

Historically, passionate, romantic love has posed a threat to the existing social structure and has rarely been the basis for permanent relationships (Hatfield & Rapson, 1996). Many cultures have literature or legends about lovers who have died tragically as the result of their passion and the unsuitability of any permanent relationship. The story of Romeo and Juliet is an example familiar to English-speaking cultures, but Hatfield and Rapson have described similar stories from ancient and modern societies around the world. Passionate love has been seen as madness rather than a good basis for marriage. The more common pattern for forming permanent relationships has been (and in many cultures remains) arranged marriages in which families choose mates for children. In such arranged marriages, financial considerations rather than love or passion have been the motivations for the match.

Several different patterns of love relationships have existed over the past several centuries in Western cultures (Cancian, 1987). Before the 1800s, agriculture was the basis for most people's livelihood, and both men and women worked together on family farms, making the family the center of both men's and women's lives. Although men were the heads of households, both men and women believed that marriage gave them the duty to love and help one another. Despite sharply divided gender roles in the home and community, love was not differentiated according to gender.

In Sternberg's (1986) triangular model of love, this Family Duty blueprint ensured an equal relationship between the partners. Such marriages were formed around commitment, and the sharing of home life made intimacy very likely, but the component of passion might have been missing from such duty-bound relationships. In arranged marriages, this component might never be part of the relationship of a married couple.

By the end of the 1700s, the Industrial Revolution had changed the pattern of many people's lives, including marriage and family. Work and family was separated, with men working in jobs in factories and offices rather than around the home. Women, too, might work in factories, but the ideal pattern of family relationship was for men to fulfill the Good Provider role (Bernard, 1981) and for women to be mothers and wives. This division led to the Doctrine of the Two Spheres (Welter, 1978), the division that resulted in women's preeminence in family life and men's dominance in the outside world.

Women became responsible for the maintenance of the home and family, a sanctuary from the hostility of the outside world of business and factory. This responsibility made women the experts in love: They were the ones who had the tender feelings and experienced the emotions; they were the ones who needed love and depended on men and children for it; they were the ones most capable of providing love to others.

Through this family arrangement, women became dependent on men for financial security, so maintaining the love of a husband was essential to women's financial security. During the 1920s, however, women started to invade the male world of work, taking paid jobs outside the home. With increasing economic power, women were less dependent on men for financial security, which changed the blueprint for marriage to the Companionship model (Cancian, 1987). Cancian credited the Companionship blueprint for love relationships with the feminization of love. This model focused on affection and support for each other, but women were still the experts on love and held the responsibility for the relationship: "Marriage was to be all of a woman's life but only part of a man's" (Cancian, 1987, p. 34).

The Companionship model for marriage emphasized the similarity of the partners, and personal characteristics in the selection of marriage partners became important as this model of marriage became better accepted. Spouses were supposed to love each other before they married and to choose their partners rather than relying on partners chosen by family. Using Sternberg's model to analyze these relationships, consummate love was the ideal, with an equal mixture of intimacy, passion, and commitment. However, romantic love was also a possibility, with its combination of passion and intimacy but lack of commitment. As evidence for the rising lack of commitment under the Companionship blueprint, the divorce rate increased (Cancian, 1987).

The emphasis on personal compatibility and romance in marriage prompted a different method of selecting marriage partners. Rather than relying on the family to choose their partners or making decisions on an economic basis, individuals started to choose their own mates. Dating arose as a way of finding suitable marriage partners for Companionship-style marriages.

Dating

Although dating began during the 1920s as a form of courtship, it has expanded to fulfill other functions—recreation, status and achievement, socialization, learning about intimacy, sexual exploration, companionship, and identity formation (Santrock, 1993). Since the

1940s, dating has become less formal and structured (Miller & Gordon, 1986). Rather than following the traditional pattern in which boys ask, plan, and pay for dates, current dating patterns include girls taking the initiative in asking, planning, and paying for dates in addition to a pattern of mixed-gender group dating.

Dating has become an important part of adolescent life, and most young people in the United States have their first date between the ages of 12 and 16 years, with girls dating slightly earlier than boys. By age 16 years, more than 90% of adolescents have had a date (Santrock, 1993). Dating becomes more frequent for older teenagers, with about 50% of adolescents in high school having at least one date per week.

Dating serves important functions throughout adolescence, but those functions change from the years of young adolescence to young adulthood. Younger adolescents (6th graders) said that they dated as a recreational activity or as a way to achieve status (Roscoe, Diana, & Brooks, 1987). Early adolescents wanted to have fun or to impress their peers with good-looking or well-dressed dating partners. Older teenagers showed more concern for personal characteristics, such as kindness and confidence. Boys and girls in this study showed some differences in the characteristics they valued in a date, with boys being more concerned with physical appearance and more interested in dating a sexually active partner than were girls. Adolescent boys who hold traditional attitudes toward masculinity reported more sexual partners, less intimacy with their sexual partners, and a greater belief that relationships with girls are adversarial than have adolescent boys who have less traditional views of masculinity (Pleck, Sonenstein, & Ku, 1993). For girls, confidence, kindness, dependability, parental approval, and abstinence from alcohol were more important characteristics in a date than they were for boys (Roscoe et al., 1987).

Traditional gender role behavior is evident in dating behavior. Young men's and women's behavior on dates follows a script, a model that people use to guide their behavior (Rose & Frieze, 1993). College students adhered to this script in describing an actual and a hypothetical first heterosexual date, with a great deal of agreement between the two scripts but a difference in the scripted roles for women and men. Following the script leads men to act and women to react. The man's active role includes initiating the date, controlling the activities, and initiating sexual activity. The woman's reactive role includes being concerned about her appearance, participating in the activities her partner planned, and reacting to his sexual advances. Both the hypothetical and actual dates reflected this script, which follows traditional gender stereotypes.

Although dating is the method through which most people now choose mates, only around 7% of the college students, and even fewer of the younger adolescents, said that mate selection was the reason for dating (Roscoe et al., 1987). However, the characteristics preferred by late adolescents in dating partners and the list of characteristics that young married adults find desirable in a mate were very similar (Buss & Barnes, 1986). People seek both dates and mates who are kind, intelligent, physically attractive, and socially exciting. In this study of mate selection as in the selection of dating partners, men valued physical attractiveness more than women did.

Evolutionary psychology is an area of psychology that examines how adaptation pressures have shaped contemporary behavior. "Evolutionary psychologists believe that females and males faced different pressures in primeval environments and that the sexes' differing reproductive status was the key feature of ancestral life that framed sex-typed adaptive problems" (Eagly & Wood, 1999, p. 408). According to this concept, remote pre-

GENDERED VOICES

I Was Terrible at Being a Girl

"I was fairly bad at being a girl when I was a child," a middle-aged woman told me. "I did tomboy-type things. But I was really terrible at it when I was a teenager and trying to date and attract boys. Dating seemed like a game, and the rules were so silly. And I was bad at the game. Flirting was a disaster—I felt so silly and incompetent.

"My mother practically despaired of my ever behaving in ways that would lead to dates. She would give me advice, such as 'Hide how smart you are, because boys don't like to date girls who are smarter than they are,' and 'Wait for him to open the door for you.' I thought both those things were pretty pointless. Why should I hide how smart I was? I had gone to school with most of the guys in my high school since we were all in elementary school, so they knew how smart I was. Besides, if I could have fooled one, I didn't think that I could have kept up the charade. I wasn't smart enough to play dumb for all that long. Also, why would I want to date a guy who wanted a dumb girl? Sounded like a poor prospect to me.

"I know that opening doors became an issue in the 1970s feminist movement, but my objections were about 10 years earlier. It just seemed silly to me that a perfectly capable person, me, should inconvenience a guy to open a door. I was more than capable of doing so, and I never saw why I shouldn't—still don't for that matter. I now see having doors opened as a courtesy, which is O.K. I open doors for both men and women. There's probably too much made of that particular issue, but when I was a teenager, it was something my mother warned me about on numerous occasions. I just had a hard time getting the rules of the game—I was terrible at the girl stuff. I am much better at being a woman than I was at being a girl."

human history left gender-related differences that appear today in peoples' selection of mates. This view hypothesizes that men's best strategy was to reproduce as often as possible, whereas women are limited in their reproductive abilities because they can bear a limited number of children. Thus they must select mates that will help them raise their children (Buss, 1994). Preference for physical attractiveness is one of the factors that evolutionary psychology sees as a gender difference, with men valuing attractive partners because attractiveness is a sign of health and reproductive fitness.

Men do emphasize the attractiveness of their partner more than women do, but the adaptive advantage of that preference is questionable; attractiveness is not closely related to health. Many women considered beautiful have fertility problems. A more reliable sign of reproductive capability is having borne children; however, the evolutionary psychologists do not hypothesize that women with young children are the most attractive potential mates, despite their demonstrated reproductive success.

Evolutionary psychology also predicts that attractiveness should be more important in heterosexual attraction than for gay or lesbian couples. A test of this hypothesis failed: Few differences in partner preference appeared in the descriptions of desirable partner characteristics in male–male, female–female, as well as male–female couples (Howard, Blumstein, & Schwartz, 1987). All said they wanted romantic partners who were kind, considerate, and physically attractive. The partners in same-gender couples expressed a preference for partners who were more athletic and expressive about their feelings than the mates described by partners in male–female couples, but these differences were small. Regardless of sexual orientation, people seek similar qualities in romantic partners.

Other characteristics that attract people to romantic partners include similarities of personal values. Mate selection is more a matter of "birds of a feather flock together" than "opposites attract" (Antill, 1983). That is, people are romantically attracted to others who are more like them than different from them. These similarities include not only personal values, but also social class, religion, and gender role acceptance. The notion that opposites attract may relate to the concepts of masculinity and femininity and the belief that the two lie on opposite ends of a continuum. (See Chapter 7 for a discussion of the inaccuracy of this conceptualization.) According to this view, masculine men should be attracted to their "opposite"—feminine women—and vice versa.

An alternative interpretation of compatibility and gender roles holds that men and women who have traditional beliefs about gender roles are not opposite, but similar to each other; both accept stereotypical gender roles. This match might make people more compatible because similarity is important in close relationships (Aubé & Koestner, 1995).

In studying gender roles and relationship stability, a longitudinal study (Peplau, Hill, & Rubin, 1993) followed dating couples beginning in the 1970s and continuing over 15 years. A great deal of variability in gender role attitudes existed during the 1970s; some couples held traditional attitudes, and some believed in egalitarian relationships. Both members of a couple tended to be similar in their beliefs, but the men were more conservative than the women. No relationship emerged between satisfaction and gender role attitudes, with both traditional and egalitarian couples forming equally satisfactory relationships. Gender role traditionalism was more strongly related to relationship stability for the women than for the men. College women with traditional gender role attitudes were more likely to marry their boyfriends and to be married to them 15 years later than were more liberal women.

Despite the opinion of adolescents that their dating is not oriented toward mate selection, dating is the process through which most men and women find partners. The patterns of relating to each other established during dating carry over into marriage, but marriage is a major life transition. When people marry, they assume the new roles of husband and wife.

Marriage and Committed Relationships

Marriage is not the only form of committed romantic relationship. Gay and lesbian couples cannot legally marry in most places, and heterosexual couples sometimes choose to live together without marrying. The number of cohabiting heterosexual couples has dramatically increased since the 1960s. In the United States in 1960, less than half a million heterosexual couples were cohabiting, but in 1998, over 4 million were, representing an increase of almost 1,000% (U.S. Bureau of the Census, 1999). This change is the most dramatic trend in committed relationships. For some couples, cohabitation has replaced marriage; for many more, cohabitation precedes marriage. Marriage and divorce have also changed over that time span. The number and rate of marriages has declined. Divorce dramatically increased, but now has begun to decrease. Figure 9.2 shows these trends.

Despite the increased prevalence of cohabitation, the majority of research on gender and committed relationships has focused on marriage. Several styles of marriage now exist, following the patterns Cancian (1987) called the Companionship, the Independence, and the Interdependence blueprints. The Companionship blueprint discussed earlier was the model for most marriages in the United States from the 1920s until the 1960s. Partners who follow this pattern tend to have well-defined and separate gender roles, and women are re-

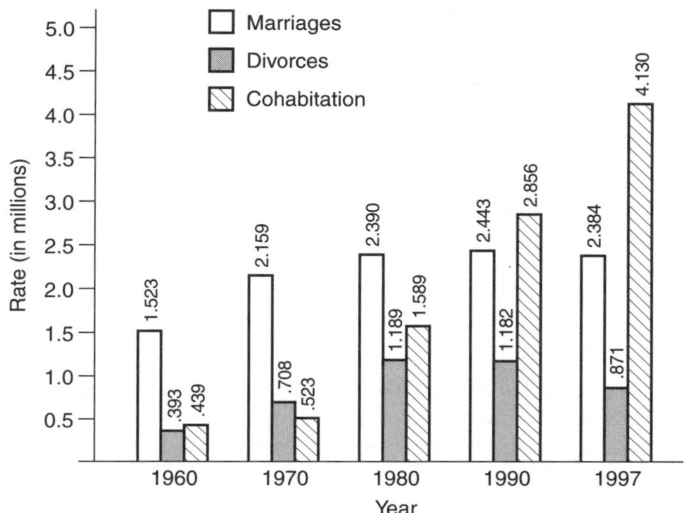

FIGURE 9.2 Trends in Marriage, Divorce, and Cohabitation from 1960 to 1997

Source: From *Statistical Abstracts of the United States, 1999* (119th ed.) (pp. 60, 75), U.S. Bureau of the Census, 1999. Washington, DC: U.S. Government Printing Office.

sponsible for maintaining the love relationship. This type of marriage is now considered traditional, because its adherents oppose self-development for women, a major tenet of the Independence blueprint.

The Independence blueprint arose during the 1960s, a period of personal freedom and change. Increases in paid employment for women and the women's movement led to an examination of the ground rules for relationships, and both men and women started to believe that marriage should be a partnership of equals. This model emphasizes self-development over commitment and obligations, holding that relationships are the meeting of two independent individuals. The emphasis on self-development resulted in less well-defined gender roles, and the concept of androgynous marriage arose. Cancian criticized this blueprint for encouraging empty relationships without sufficient commitment.

Interdependence is an alternative to the Independence blueprint. The Interdependence model also includes flexible gender roles, but calls for commitment based on mutual dependence. Cancian argued that self-development and interdependence were compatible goals for relationships, and that partners are always dependent on each other in marriage. Both the Companionship and Independence blueprints ignore this inevitable interdependence. Table 9.1 shows the three blueprints and the important characteristics of each.

Sternberg's (1986) triangular model of love explains these different blueprints for marriage as differing in the three components of intimacy, passion, and commitment. Companionship-style marriages would have all three components but not in equal proportion for men and women. Under this blueprint, women seek more intimacy than men, producing an unequal balance between such partners. As Cancian contended, the Independent

TABLE 9.1 Cancian's Blueprints for Love Relationships

	Companionship (devotion to each other)	Independence (self-development)	Interdependence (mutual dependence)
Are traditional gender roles maintained?	yes	no	no
Is the relationship stable?	yes	no	yes
Who is responsible for maintaining the relationship?	women	neither partner	both partners
Who develops personal interests?	men	both partners	both partners

blueprint lacks the component of commitment, but Interdependent marriages should fit what Sternberg called consummate love, the equal balance of all three components.

Marriages and other committed relationships may follow any of the blueprints, and contemporary couples may build any of these various types of relationships. However, a longitudinal study of expectations for marriage (Botkin, Weeks, & Morris, 2000) revealed that changes have occurred in women's conceptualizations of marriage. Between the 1960s and the 1970s, a large shift occurred toward beliefs in egalitarian marriages. After the 1970s, those beliefs have persisted, and the percentage of college women who believe in egalitarian marriage relationships is over 90%. This percentage has implications for several facets of committed relationships, including men's and women's concepts of romantic love and marriage, communication between partners, division of labor in households, power and conflict in marriage, and the stability of love relationships.

Concepts of Love and Marriage

Contrary to popular expectation (see "According to the Media/According to the Research"), men have more traditional concepts of love and marriage and are more romantic than women. Although men and women tend to choose partners who have similarly traditional or nontraditional beliefs about gender roles, the man of any given couple is likely to be more traditional than the woman and more likely than women to endorse statements such as "Women's activities should be confined to the home" (Peplau & Gordon, 1985). This tendency for men to be more traditional concerning gender roles appears in many cultures (Hatfield & Rapson, 1996), but some research (Mirowsky & Ross, 1987) has indicated that these discrepancies become smaller through the years of marriage. The continued association of marriage partners does not produce identical beliefs, however, and the majority of the differences remain. Thus, even after years of marriage, husbands are more likely than wives to hold traditional, conservative beliefs about gender roles.

Despite the stereotypical view that women are the romantics, a review of the research (Peplau & Gordon, 1985) has indicated that men are more romantic than women. Men report that they fall in love earlier in relationships than women. Also, women say that they would be more likely to marry someone they did not love, whereas a majority of men say they would not marry without love. Men are also more likely to have romantic beliefs such as "Love lasts forever" and "There is one perfect love in the world for everyone." Women, however, are more likely to report physical symptoms of being in love, such as feeling like they are "floating on a cloud." This willingness to report on physical symptoms of love is the only sign of romanticism in which women exceed men. In most ways, men are more romantic than women.

Romanticism does not necessarily make men feel more favorably toward marriage. Men are supposed to elude marriage, considering it a "trap," whereas women are perceived as planning and scheming to "land a husband." Jessie Bernard (1972) pointed out that this characterization is unfair; men tend to profit from marriage more than women do. Bernard contended that in any marriage there are actually two marriages—his and hers. She further argued that "his" marriage is more of an advantage to him than "hers" is to her. That is, marriage offers benefits to men that do not accrue to women. Married men are physically and mentally healthier than unmarried men, but married women are less healthy than their unmarried counterparts.

Married men report higher levels of life satisfaction and happiness than unmarried men, and studies have found few gender-related differences in marital satisfaction (Peplau & Gordon, 1985). Most of the studies of marital satisfaction have questioned only European American participants, however, and this choice has limited the conclusions about attitudes toward marriage (Ball & Robbins, 1986). Investigating marital satisfaction among African Americans showed that married African American women were more satisfied with their lives than single women were, but this difference disappeared when these researchers controlled for demographic factors such as age and health. Thus, the positive attitudes about marriage may be attributable to factors associated with marriage, such as having a stable life and financial security, rather than to positive feelings about marriage itself. The life satisfaction of African American men, on the other hand, was lower among married than single men, and these differences did not disappear when controlling for demographic factors. These results suggests that African American men may differ from African American women and European American couples in their feelings of satisfaction in marriage.

Communication between Partners

The issue of communication in marriage has also been a topic for gender researchers. Indeed, it has become an industry; John Gray's (1992) *Men Are from Mars, Women Are from Venus* topped the bestseller list for years, prompting sequels, and allowing Gray to hold seminars and to train other counselors. His concept of men and women from different planets originated from his advise to women to communicate with their husbands as if they were beings from another planet. Gray's characterization of men and women from different planets is an overstatement of gender differences in communication, but differences do exist.

The same gender differences that researchers have found in friendship styles also influence communication in marriage: Women create emotional intimacy through talk and self-disclosure, whereas men do so through activity. In marriage, sex is often the activity that men use to create intimacy. Cancian (1987) argued that in most contemporary couples, wives do not count sex as communication or as a method for establishing intimacy. This difference can produce a discrepancy in what each thinks is the level of communication in their relationship. Her survey of couples revealed that wives value talking about feelings more than husbands do, but husbands may feel threatened when their wives want to talk. "Talking about the relationship as she wants to do will feel to him like taking a test that she has made up and he will fail" (Cancian, 1987, p. 93).

Communication is a major task for couples, and the differences between men's and women's typical styles of communication provide one potential source of conflict in

ACCORDING TO THE MEDIA...

Bad Men Can Be Transformed by Women's Love

Movies are filled with images of selfish, roguish scoundrels transformed into heroes by women's love (Aronson & Kimmel, 1997). Self-absorbed scoundrel Rick Blaine (played by Humphrey Bogart) becomes a hero in the film *Casablanca* out of love for Elsa (Ingrid Bergman). Indeed, his love was so great that he gave up that love for the Allied cause—a true hero. Charlie Allnut (again, Humphrey Bogart) is transformed from a drunk into a hero by the love of Rose (Katharine Hepburn) in *The African Queen.* Humphrey Bogart was not the only actor who played this transformation repeatedly. Clark Gable also experienced a change for the better through the love of a woman in many movies.

Women have been affected by these portrayals, coming to believe that their love has the power to transform a bad man into a good one. *New York Times* columnist Anna Quindlen (reported in Aronson & Kimmel, 1997) asked female readers to choose a mate—either a kind, faithful, careful man or a roguish, self-interested scoundrel, and the vote was overwhelmingly for the nice guy. When she identified one as Ashley Wilkes and the other as Rhett Butler, however, some women felt differently. One woman said, "Well, that's different.... Rhett Butler's never been loved by me. When I love him, he'll change" (Aronson & Kimmel, 1997, p. 32). This quotation demonstrates the extent to which some women believe in the transformational power of their love, a romantic fantasy perpetrated by the media.

marriage. Deborah Tannen (1990) examined the barriers to communication for men and women, citing different strategies for men and women even when the goals are similar. Tannen argued that men and women see communication as "a continual balancing act, juggling the conflicting needs for intimacy and independence" (p. 27). She contended that women's communication is oriented toward intimacy, focusing on forming communal connections with others, whereas men's communication is oriented toward hierarchy, focusing on attaining and demonstrating status.

The differences in communication styles make it difficult for women and men to talk to each other. Both interpret the underlying messages as well as the words, and the differences in styles may lead men and women to understand messages that their partners did not intend to send. For example, Tannen cited an example of a husband who had failed to tell his wife about a pain he had been feeling in his arm. When his wife found out, she was very upset with him for withholding information that was important to her. She felt excluded from his life. He had not intended to exclude her from anything important, but instead had wanted to protect her from worrying about his health. Tannen contended that such miscommunication is common for women and men and constitutes a persistent problem for couples.

According to Tannen, learning the conversational style of the other is not the answer to all communication problems. She described sensitivity training as an attempt to teach the

ACCORDING TO THE RESEARCH...

Bad Men Are Dangerous to the Women Who Love Them

When women hope to change bad men through love, they put themselves in danger of being victimized by these men. Perhaps some scoundrels change through love, but many remain scoundrels who harm the women who love them. Violence directed toward women shows a different pattern than violence directed toward men (Heise, Ellsberg, & Gottemoeller, 1999). Women are more likely than men to be victimized by family members or intimate partners, putting women in danger of physical, psychological, and sexual abuse. Indeed, these types of abuse tend to co-occur, and women who experience one will likely be targets of the others as well. In addition, abuse typically occurs over a period of time, including repeated incidents. Women are abused in a variety of ways and at a high rate—over 25% of women reported some type of abuse by an intimate partner (Tjaden & Thoennes, 2000).

Women may be reluctant to leave an abusive partner, partly for the reasons that attracted them to the partner. In addition, the notion that "he will change," and "this time will be the last time he will hit/be unfaithful to/humiliate me," allows women to believe that their abusive partners will become the men they fantasized. Another factor that keeps women with abusive partners is the women's emotional commitment to these men combined with the men's lower commitment to their partners. The partner whose emotional commitment is higher has lower power in the relationship (Sprecher & Felmlee, 1997), putting women who love scoundrels at risk. Their love binds them to men who care less than their female partners do.

Women who do leave an abusive partner do not necessarily escape the danger they have experienced. Indeed, women who leave abusive partners are at increased risk for harm (Tjaden & Thoennes, 2000). Angry, resentful, or jealous former partners may stalk and do violence to the women who have left them. Indeed, women are more likely to be killed by an intimate partner during a separation than when living with these violent men. Staying with them is also dangerous—women experience over 1.3 million physical assaults from male partners each year. Therefore, the romantic notion that the love of a woman can transform a bad man into a good one appears more often in movies than in daily life.

conversational style of women to men, and assertiveness training as a method to teach the conversational style of men to women. Although flexibility of styles has benefits, Tannen expressed pessimism concerning changes in communication that would blend these divergent styles—both women and men like their ways of communicating.

In addition to differences in styles of communication, influenceability is another factor in communication in intimate relationships. Research has indicated that men and women differ in ability to be influenced and in styles of influence. Gender differences in influenceability can be understood in terms of power (Eagly & Wood, 1985). In laboratory experiments, few gender differences appear in influenceability, but outside the lab, women are more easily influenced than men. These differences may be a reflection of the subordinate role that women typically occupy in relationships with men. Subordinates are supposed to be easily influenced; it is part of the role. Their subordinate role is also a factor in patterns of communication in love relationships.

Thus, men and women tend to differ in style of intimate communication and in verbal styles. Women's reliance on self-disclosure and communal, empathic communication varies from men's reliance on sex and their competitive, hierarchical communication style. These differences can cause misunderstanding rather than foster communication, and women's subordinate role has an impact on many facets of the relationship.

Division of Household Labor

The division of household labor has become an area of interest to gender researchers, and their results have revealed another potential source of conflict for couples—an unequal division of this labor. Traditional gender roles include a division of labor in households, with men working outside the home for wages, and women working in the home providing housekeeping and child care. This division arose during the Industrial Revolution, when men started working for wages rather than working in agricultural or home-based trades, and domesticity became associated with women. Throughout the 20th century, however, an increasing number of women joined the paid workforce. Now, a majority of women, even those with young children, work for wages outside the home.

The changes in paid labor for women might have prompted a concomitant change in the division of housework, but instead, few changes have occurred in the division of household work. Sociologist Arlie Hochschild (1989) called this arrangement the Second Shift, an arrangement in which women work for wages outside the home plus perform the majority of housework and child care chores at home. This arrangement can result in a situation in which women work the equivalent number of hours of two full-time jobs. According to one extensive review (Thompson & Walker, 1989), wives do two to three times more housework and child care than husbands do. Looking at the division of labor in a different way, only 10% of husbands do as much work at home as their wives.

One factor that changes the balance of labor around the house is the status of wives' careers (Bernardo, Shehan, & Leslie, 1987). Wives who hold professional or managerial jobs spend less time on household chores than women in less prestigious careers or wives who do not hold paying jobs outside their homes. Husbands whose spouses also work spend proportionally more time on household chores than do other husbands, but they do not spend more hours than their wives doing housework. This situation may occur because the wives in dual-career families spend less time doing housework than other wives, making the husbands' contribution proportionally more, but not more in terms of number of hours. This finding suggests that wives who have professional or managerial careers do less housework. Because their husbands do not compensate by doing more chores, the housework either does not get done or is done by hired workers.

The types of household chores that men and women perform tend to be divided along gender-stereotypical lines: Women clean, cook, shop, care for children, do laundry, and straighten the home; men take out the trash, mow the lawn, garden, work in the yard, and make household repairs. This division is not only stereotypical, but also allots women repetitive, routine, time-locked tasks while allowing men chores with irregular hours that they can arrange to their convenience (Thompson & Walker, 1989). In addition, the timing of these chores differs during the day, with women's chores occurring both in the morning and during the early and late evening, whereas men often have leisure time during the evening. Men can often arrange their chores so that they can do them on the weekend, but women have daily housework as well as larger chores they do on weekends.

One measurement of the division of household labor confirmed the gender segregation of housework and the stereotypical nature of the division (Blair & Lichter, 1991). This analysis indicated that employment was not a significant factor in bringing about a more equitable division of household labor, but that earning power was. Employment and earnings alter the power structure within marriages and thus alter the balance of housework—as women's wages increase, they perform less housework and their husbands perform more.

Ironically, when wives earn more than their husbands, however, husbands perform less housework. Gender role stereotypes are important in perpetuating the division of labor in housework, but the power balance within a marriage is a big factor in who does the dishes. Table 9.2 summarizes some of the factors that relate to sharing of household work.

Gender role attitudes are also important in who does the dishes. Men are unlikely to do much household work unless both they and their wives hold egalitarian attitudes (Greenstein, 1996). That is, the interaction of husbands' and wives' attitudes determined whether husbands performed housework. When husbands or wives held traditional gender role attitudes, men did little work around the house. Even when men held egalitarian beliefs but their wives did not, men still avoided chores. Only the combination of both husbands and wives with egalitarian attitudes resulted in men performing a nearly equal share of household work—only 25% of the men studied performed as much as 40% of the household work. Equal sharing was rare. Egalitarian attitudes are increasing, which may predict an increasingly equitable sharing of chores.

Married couples allot tasks primarily on the basis of gender, but gay and lesbian couples cannot use this strategy and use different methods to determine who does what chores (Kurdek, 1993). Both gay and lesbian couples tended to share household work more equitably than heterosexual married couples, but the patterns of sharing differed. Gay couples were more likely to split tasks, with each partner performing a set of chores. Lesbian couples were more likely to alternate in sharing tasks, taking turns in performing the same chores.

The division of household chores may be a source of conflict in marriage (Stohs, 2000; Thompson & Walker, 1989). Between 25% and 33% of wives believe that their husbands are not doing a fair share of housework and want them to do more. These figures do not equal the discrepant contributions of husbands and wives, indicating that some wives are satisfied with the housework their husbands do even if the division is not equal. If wives do a disproportionate share of chores, husbands tend to be happier with the marriages. Perhaps some wives find the extra housework an acceptable price to pay for happier husbands.

On the other hand, some wives resent the disproportionate amount of housework they do. Wives who hold views of equal participation in housework for men and women and yet do more chores than their husbands might feel overburdened and perhaps have marriages at risk (McHale & Crouter, 1992). Husbands who hold traditional beliefs about segregation of household chores yet who are doing an equal share should also feel overburdened, and their relationships would also be at risk. Such wives and husbands rated their marriages less favorably than other spouses who felt less burdened, and for the wives, the feelings persisted

TABLE 9.2 Factors Related to Division of Household Work

Men Do More Household Work When…	Men Do Less Household Work When…
Wives' earnings approach their husbands' earnings	Wives are not employed outside the home
Chores are "masculine"	Wives earn less money than their husbands
Timing of task is flexible	Wives earn more money than their husbands
Wives' shiftwork schedule requires husbands' cooperation	Either husbands or wives hold traditional gender role beliefs
Both husbands and wives hold egalitarian beliefs	

over the time span of a year. The persistence of resentment may be a factor in the stability of marital relationships.

Division of chores can be a major source of marital conflict. In one study (Benin & Angostinelli, 1988), the greatest satisfaction occurred when the division of chores was almost equal (with wives doing more than husbands). Both husbands and wives were dissatisfied with inequitable divisions of household labor, but husbands wanted both an equitable division and a low number or hours spent doing housework. Wives wanted an equitable division plus their husbands' help. These shared goals of equitable sharing of chores may not be compatible with the secondary goals for husbands and wives. Therefore, even a mutual desire to share household work may not allow husbands and wives to negotiate this problem.

The division of household labor may fall into traditional "masculine" and "feminine" tasks, or the division may be one of necessity dictated by the time constraints of women's work schedules. For example, women who work the evening shift may have to go to work immediately after an early dinner, leaving their husbands and families with the night-time chores. Shift work is more common in working-class than middle-class or upper-middle-class families, making working-class couples somewhat more likely to share equally in housework than more affluent couples (Hochschild, 1997; Thompson & Walker, 1989). Although working-class men do not have more egalitarian attitudes than other men, their family situations may push them toward a greater sharing of household work. Therefore, social class is an important indicator in family patterns of housework.

Ethnicity is not an important factor in attitudes toward family work. In a study of couples from a variety of ethnic groups (Stohs, 2000), conflict over household work was common. The Hispanic American women worked fewer hours per week in their jobs outside the home than African American or Asian American women did, which might lead them to feel less burdened by doing more household chores. However, the feelings that husbands were not doing a fair share of household work was shared among all ethnic groups.

The differences in division of household labor by social class and gender role attitudes may relate to the differences of power in these couples. Working-class wives' economic contributions are more essential to their families' subsistence than middle-class wives' salaries. By making essential contributions, these women may gain power in their marriages, and their husbands may respond to the more equal balance of power by sharing housework. More equal contributions to family income related to shared household chores (Coltrane & Valdez, 1993). For middle-class Hispanic American couples, wives whose income made them coproviders were more likely to get their husbands' help than women who contributed less to family income. However, husbands' assistance was not easy to get; even the husbands who acknowledged the importance of their wives' income were often reluctant to do household chores and child care, using their own job demands as an excuse for not contributing to household work.

Wives who have high-status, highly paid employment (such as professional or managerial jobs), may also experience increased power in their marriages, and this increased power may give these wives the freedom to do less housework (Bernardo et al., 1987). When husbands and wives experience discrepancies in their attitudes about household labor, conflict may arise in the marriage. Therefore, the issue of household work may be related to both power and conflict within marriages.

Power and Conflict

Most dating couples believe that marriages should be an equal sharing of power and decision making, but the members of these couples acknowledged that their own relationships failed to show an equal balance of power (Felmlee, 1994; Peplau & Campbell, 1989; Sprecher & Felmlee, 1997). Although a large majority of both women and men said that they believed each partner should have an equal voice in the relationship, just less than half reported equal power in their relationships. This finding suggests that, even before couples marry, the balance of power is unequal. A longitudinal study (Sprecher & Felmlee, 1997) indicated that the power imbalances are fairly stable over time.

For those couples whose relationships are not equal in power, traditional gender roles dictate that the man will be the leader and head of the household. Current relationships reflect this tradition, and men are likely to have more power in marriages than women. According to an extensive survey of couples by Philip Blumstein and Pepper Schwartz (1983), almost 64% reported an equal balance of power. The remaining couples reported an unequal balance of power in their marriages—28% of husbands and 9% of wives said they had more power. Other studies have shown a higher percentage of male dominance in heterosexual couples (Peplau & Campbell, 1989; Sprecher & Felmlee, 1997). Table 9.3 shows the power structure in couples according to three studies.

One drawback of a majority of research is the educational and ethnic composition of the participants: Couples are often college-educated, and most are White. A consideration of other ethnic groups brings other factors relating to power. The concepts of **matriarchy** and **machismo** are associated with African American and Hispanic American families, respectively. A review of research on families, however, found that both patterns of unequal power were more myths than descriptions of the actual balance of power in these families (Peplau & Campbell, 1989). African American families are more likely to be headed by women than White families, but Black couples do not have significantly different power relationships in the family than White couples do. An equal sharing of power, the most common pattern in Blumstein and Schwartz's study, was also the most common pattern in African American couples. For couples with an unequal balance of power, male dominance was more common than female dominance. The same patterns appeared in Mexican American families, with the most common pattern being one of shared power. Despite the prominence of the concepts of matriarchy and machismo, a fairly equal balance of power seems to be the rule for most couples in the United States, regardless of ethnic group.

Saying that couples exhibit an equal balance of power does not mean that both partners have an equal say in all decisions, however. Decision-making power may be divided along traditional lines, with men making financial decisions and women making household decisions (see Peplau & Gordon, 1985). What couples report as an equal balance of power may

TABLE 9.3 Ideal and Actual Power Structure in Couples

	Peplau and Campbell Study (1989)		*Blumstein and Schwartz (1983)*	*Sprecher and Felmlee Study (1997)*	
	Men	Women	Couples	Men	Women
Believe in equal power	87%	95%			
Have equal power	42%	49%	64%	47%	48%
Husband has more power			28%	35%	29%
Wife has more power			9%	19%	24%

actually be a division of decision making into husbands' and wives' domains. This division may reflect wives' lack of real power; wives may be put into the position of making decisions that their husbands consider too trivial for their own attention. For example, wives may decide what to have for dinner and what brand of cleaning products to use, and husbands may decide which house to buy and where to live. One study (Sprecher & Felmlee, 1997) measured the discrepancy between power and decision making in dating couples and found that men's decision-making power was higher than their overall power. In addition, both male and female partners rated men's decision-making power as well as men's overall power as higher than women's decision-making and overall power.

Paid employment is a factor in the balance of power in marriage. Women who do not have paid employment tend to have less power in their marriages than women who earn money (Blumstein & Schwartz, 1983; Peplau & Campbell, 1989; Peplau & Gordon, 1985; Steil, 1989). The amount earned is also a factor: Husbands who earn more money have more power, but wives' earnings show a complex relationship to their power. In working-class couples, wives who earn more money have more power, but middle-class wives may not gain power by making money (Thompson & Walker, 1989). These differences may have to do with the necessity of wives' earning income in the two social classes. Working-class wives' salaries are more likely to provide essential incomes, whereas middle-class wives' salaries may not be as necessary to their families. When husbands know the importance of their wives' salaries, this knowledge may give wives more power. In the rare families in which wives earn more than their husbands, however, the balance of power does not tip in the wife's favor. These couples tend to be dominated by the husbands (Thompson & Walker, 1989), perhaps because wives abdicated the power that their incomes could give them. Therefore, wives' income has a curvilinear relationship to power in marriage; that is, wives who earn no income have low power, wives who earn money have increased power to the point of equal incomes, but wives who earn *more* than their husbands exercise *less* power than their spouses.

Consistent with the income and power interpretation, Blumstein and Schwartz (1983) found that money was an important factor in the power equation for unmarried couples, too. Blumstein and Schwartz studied not only married couples but also cohabiting couples—heterosexual as well as gay and lesbian. They found that money was an important factor in determining which partner had more power for all except the lesbian couples, who tried to maintain an equal monetary contribution in their relationship so as to avoid unequal power. The failure to do so was a source of problems for these women.

Some evidence suggests that men and women experience some differences in the sources of conflict and use different tactics to resolve conflict. Among recently married couples in one such study (Buss, 1991), the wives' most frequent complaint was that their husbands were inconsiderate, and the husbands' most frequent complaint was of their wives' moodiness. Not surprisingly, both husbands and wives who were low in emotional warmth, high in selfishness, low in security, and high in temper behaved in many ways that angered their spouses and caused conflict in the relationship.

Understanding and explaining conflict also shows gender differences in couples. The husbands in one study (Lavin, 1987) tended to take personal credit for both their own positive and negative behavior, attributing those behaviors to stable, internal traits, but husbands saw their wives' behavior as determined by unstable internal forces. Wives, on the other hand, did not attribute their husbands' behavior to different forces than they attributed

GENDERED VOICES

When I Got Sober

"The balance of power in my marriage didn't change when I went to work, but when I got sober," a woman in her 40s told me. She had been a homemaker for a number of years before she started a career, and she said that earning money didn't make much of a change in her marriage. By the time she began her job, she had already started drinking heavily, and she continued to do so.

"Everybody took care of me, so I could drink and take drugs and get away with it. So I did. My daughter took care of me for most of her childhood. My husband also let me get away with being drunk most of the time. I was dependent on them, but then I got sober, and things changed.

"When I got sober, I started being able to take care of myself, and my family wasn't used to it. The balance of power changed in my marriage, and we eventually split up. I was sober and involved in AA, and my husband was still drinking, but that wasn't the main problem. I started to become independent, and he couldn't adjust. I realize that it was quite an adjustment: I had never taken care of myself—never in my life—and then I started.

"I remember one incident in particular. I was trying to change the batteries in my small tape recorder, and my husband came over and took the recorder out of my hands and did it for me. I thought, 'I can do that for myself.' I started thinking that about a lot of things. As I started to become more independent, our marriage changed. In fact, our entire family changed, and most of those changes were good. The kids could come to me rather than go to their father for everything. I became a responsible person. With that responsibility came a growing desire to be independent, and now I am. The marriage became an emotional power struggle, with my growing self-reliance and my husband still trying to be in control."

their own behavior. In this light, husbands would be likely to resist their wives' requests to change because they believe their behavior reflects unchanging personality traits, whereas husbands expect their wives to change in response to their requests because they believe the wives' behavior is not only changeable but also under personal control. Thus, the husbands' beliefs about conflict management gave them more power in the relationship; they could rightfully demand changes, but could not reasonably be asked to change.

Wife battering illustrates both power and conflict in marriage. Historically, domestic violence has been considered appropriate, with women as targets of marital (and even premarital) violence in many societies and throughout many time periods (Bonvillain, 1998; Gelles & Cornell, 1990). Even though physical abuse is not the most common method of resolving conflicts in contemporary relationships, violence is not unusual between married or cohabiting partners. Both men and women use violence toward each other, but women are at a disadvantage in physical conflicts with men (Tjaden & Thoennes, 2000). The rate of violence may even be close to equal, but the rate of injury is not: Women are much more likely to sustain serious injury as a result of domestic violence.

Several national surveys of couples in the United States have revealed a decreasing amount of violence between partners. A survey in the 1980s (Straus & Gelles, 1986) showed 16% of homes reported some kind of violence between spouses within the previous year, which represented a 27% decrease from a similar survey in 1975. A more recent study (Tjaden & Thoennes, 2000) showed that 1.8% of the women and 1.1% of the men surveyed said that they had been the victims of domestic violence in the previous 12 months. The majority of these incidents were minor, but discounting the acts of minor violence in domestic conflict is not wise; even minor violence is predictive of more serious violence between spouses (Feld & Straus, 1989). Furthermore, women who fight back are likely to escalate rather than halt the violence directed toward them.

Unfortunately, many people find some level of violence between partners acceptable. About 25% of wives and over 30% of husbands found violence toward each other acceptable under some circumstances (Straus, Gelles, & Steinmetz, 1980). With these attitudes, the escalation of minor violence to abuse is not surprising, nor is it likely to change.

Marriages in which the partners have an equal balance of power are less likely to involve physical violence than marriages in which one partner is dominant (Thompson & Walker, 1989). Regardless of which partner has more power, both partners are more likely to be the targets of violence in couples with a dominant and a subordinate partner (Gelles & Cornell, 1990). Inequalities of power promote violent conflict in couples, putting both partners at increased risk.

Therefore, a connection exists between the issues of power and conflict in committed relationships. The majority of couples endorse equal power within their love relationships, but most also acknowledge that their relationships have not attained an equal balance of power. Men are more likely to be dominant than women, as they traditionally occupy the provider role and typically earn more money. Both gender roles and money affect the balance of power in relationships. Power also affects conflict and conflict management. When conflict results in violence, women are more likely than men to be injured in the confrontation. Many women and men find physical violence acceptable as a conflict resolution strategy under some circumstances, an attitude that perpetuates domestic violence.

Stability of Relationships

Relationships that involve physical violence are less stable than those with no violence, but some of these violent relationships endure. Many people find it difficult to imagine why a woman would stay with a man who repeatedly abuses her, but some women do. Abusive men often work to isolate their wives from family and friends, depriving them of social support and alternative residences (Gelles & Cornell, 1990; Heise et al., 1999). Abused women who are unemployed, with few marketable skills and young children in need of financial support may feel as though they have no options except to stay in the relationship, no matter how abusive. With the rise of shelters for women to escape abusive homes, abused women have an option, and thousands take this option each year.

Abusive relationships are an extreme case of conflict in love relationships, but all couples experience some level of conflict. These conflicts tend to decrease the stability of a relationship and increase the chances of the relationship ending. Blumstein and Schwartz (1983) found that couples who experienced conflicts over money, wives' employment, power, division of household labor, or sex were more likely to split up than couples who experienced fewer of these conflicts. They found that couples who were married were less likely to break up than cohabiting heterosexual, gay, or lesbian couples, but married couples also tended to have a lower level of conflict except in the early years of marriage. The institution of marriage often holds couples together when they might otherwise dissolve their relationships. Couples who do not have the support of the institution behind them are thus more likely to part.

Similarity is not only a factor in attraction, it is also a factor in the stability of relationships. Dating couples are more likely to stay together if their attitudes match rather than conflict (Felmlee, 1994; Hendrick, Hendrick, & Adler, 1988). Members of a couple are not the only ones whose opinions should match; parents of dating couples can also contribute to the stability and progress of a dating relationship (Leslie, Huston, & Johnson, 1986). Mothers' opinions are most important, and young adults try to influence their mothers to think well of their partners. The more serious the relationship, the more frequent the attempt to convince parents of the partner's merits.

As the headline story for this chapter related, conflict, even heated conflict, is not necessarily threatening to the stability of marriages. John Gottman (Gottman, 1991, 1998) and his colleagues (Levenson, Carstensen, & Gottman, 1994) have investigated the elements and styles of conflicts that strengthen relationships as well as those that signal problems in relationships over the long run. Surprisingly, their research indicated that marital satisfaction was not a strong predictor of separation, but that the level of physical arousal during conflict was. That is, couples whose heart rates, blood pressure, sweating, and physical movement during an argument were elevated were more likely to separate within the next 3 years than couples with lower levels of arousal. Couples whose physiological reactions were calmer tended to have marriages that improved over a 3-year span.

Behavioral factors also predicted divorce, including wives' tendency to be overly agreeable and compliant, and husbands' tendency to stonewall by withdrawing emotionally, avoiding eye contact, holding the neck rigid, and being unresponsive to their wives during an argument. In their conversations, both members of couples who were likely to separate were more defensive; additionally, the wives complained and criticized more and the husbands disagreed more than did couples who remained together. The couples who were headed toward separation also showed different facial expressions during their conversations, the most important of which was wives' expressions of disgust. Husbands' fear also related to later separation, as did a facial expression Gottman called the "miserable smile," a smile that affected only the mouth, as when people try to "put on a happy face." Gottman concluded that the couples who would later separate were in the process of dissolving their relationship emotionally, and their physiological reactions, conflict tactics, and facial expressions signaled their impending separation. Table 9.4 summarizes these factors.

TABLE 9.4 Factors Relating to Marital Separation

Factor	Prediction
Marital satisfaction	No strong relationship to separation
Physical arousal during conflict—heart rate, blood pressure, sweating, moving	Higher levels predict increased likelihood of separation; calmer reactions predict strengthening of relationship
Wives being overly agreeable	Increased likelihood of separation
Husbands participate in housework	Increased satisfaction for husbands and wives; increased health in husbands
Husbands stonewall	Increased likelihood of separation
Wives criticize and complain	Increased likelihood of separation
Husbands disagree with wives	Increased likelihood of separation
Couples are defensive	Increased likelihood of separation
Facial expressions during conflict—"miserable smile," wives' disgust, husbands' fear	Increased likelihood of separation

According to Sternberg's (1986, 1987) triangular theory of love, relationships that have only one of the components should lack stability. Two-component relationships will be less stable than those that have all three. Friendships will be less enduring if only intimacy is present, rather than intimacy plus commitment. Furthermore, love relationships that have two components will be more stable than those with only one. For example, romances that have only the passion component would not last as long as those with both passion and commitment. Indeed, passion alone is the classic "one-night stand," whereas passion plus commitment is a "whirlwind courtship." A combination of all three components in equal proportion would offer the most stability, but maintaining all three components is difficult.

The commitment component of Sternberg's model is the most important for relationship stability. Commitment "can be essential for getting through hard times and for returning to better ones. In ignoring it or separating it from love, one may be missing exactly that component of loving relationships that enables one to get through the hard times as well as the easy ones" (Sternberg, 1986, p. 123).

Dissolving Relationships

Relationships go through phases of attraction, development, and sometimes dissolution (Duck, 1991). All relationships are subject to these stages, but people expect the dissolution of casual relationships and believe that such breakups pose no problems for the people involved. Unfortunately, even relationships with commitment sometimes fail to endure. When close friendships or love relationships dissolve, the end of such relationships poses problems for both people involved as well as for their social network of friends and family, who must make adjustments in their relationships with the members of the separated couple.

Love relationships without institutional support, such as cohabitation, are more likely to break up than are marriages. Only about 10% of heterosexual cohabiting couples live together long-term without marrying (Brown & Booth, 1996). In their study of couples, Blumstein and Schwartz (1983) found that married couples were more likely to remain together than cohabiting couples. In follow-up interviews 18 months after the initial interviews, they found that lesbian couples were most likely to have broken up and that married couples were least likely to have done so. Figure 9.3 shows the separation rates for the four types of couples in Blumstein and Schwartz's survey.

The institutional support for marriage is no guarantee of stability for such relationships. Although marriages have never been permanent, divorce increased dramatically over the past 80 years (Hendrick & Hendrick, 1992), hit a high level in the 1980s, decreased slightly, and remains at a high level today (U.S. Bureau of the Census, 1999). The high divorce rate is not necessarily a condemnation of marriage as much as the failure of women and men to fulfill their vision of what they believe marriage should be. When partners' views of marriage run according to different narratives, their relationships are not stable (Sternberg, 1998).

In her extensive interviews with divorced men and women, Catherine Riessman (1990) found that both held an ideal of marriage as the fulfillment of three components: emotional intimacy, companionship and primacy (the belief that the relationship with the spouse constitutes the primary relationship in their lives), and sexuality. That is, these people's vision of marriage matches what Cancian called the Companionship blueprint for marriage. When they separated and divorced, women and men did not question the blueprint. Rather, they

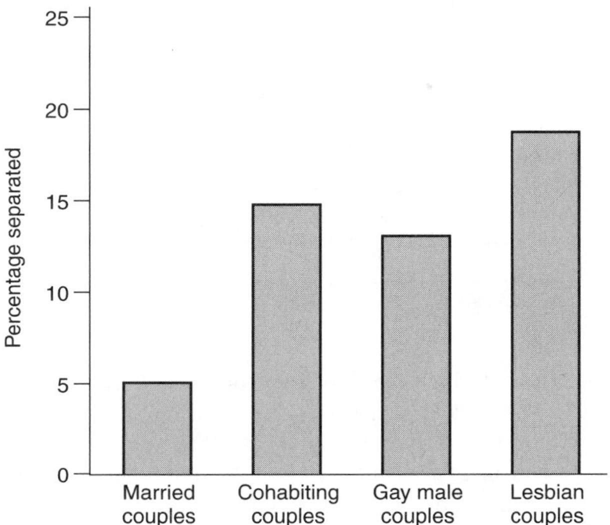

FIGURE 9.3 Separation Rates for Couples over an 18-Month Period

SOURCE: Based on *American couples* by Philip Blumstein & Pepper Schwartz, 1983, New York: Pocket Books.

found fault in their own marriages, blaming either their former spouses or themselves for failing to fulfill some component of their marital ideal. Riessman's interviews showed the ways in which men and women found fault in their marriages and how they coped with separation and divorce.

Although divorced men and women both described failures to live up to their ideals, their descriptions showed some variation according to gender and social class. Both women and men saw failures in achieving emotional intimacy, but each attributed the failures to

GENDERED VOICES

I Wasn't Any of His Business Anymore

A woman, talking with her friend about her ex-husband, said, "I saw Ed at a country western club last Friday night. He was there with some of his friends, drinking. I went there because I wanted to get out and have some fun. He didn't see me at first, and then he kept looking in my direction, trying to make sure he was seeing right.

"Finally, he came over to me and said, 'What are you doing in a place like this? You shouldn't be here.' I told him that what I did wasn't any of his business anymore. We were divorced, and I could do what I wanted. I didn't need his permission to go to a bar, and he didn't have any right to say anything to me. He said some pretty ugly things, calling me a bitch and a whore, and I just walked away from him. I had enough of his ordering me around when we were married."

GENDERED VOICES

My Ex-Wife Acts Like We're Still Married

"Although we were divorced three years ago, my ex-wife acts like we're still married," a man in his mid-30s said. "I understand why she calls me when something involves the kids, but she calls me when she needs things done to the house." He considered these requests inappropriate because he and his ex-wife had both remarried. "I can't help it if she married a wuss who can't fix the toilet. I don't think she should be calling me to do the chores. We're not married anymore, and taking care of her house is not part of my job now."

different reasons. Two-thirds of the women said that they did not get the emotional intimacy, which they defined as talking and sharing feelings, that they expected from their husbands. They claimed their husbands just didn't communicate with them.

Divorced men largely agreed with this assessment, blaming themselves for not communicating with their former wives and maintaining that they had difficulties in talking about their feelings and sharing the important elements of their work. One-third of the divorced men also believed that their wives had failed to give them emotional support, which they tended to define as physical affection. The working-class men repeatedly said that their wives were not waiting "with their arms open and a kiss" when the men came home from work. Such physical manifestations of intimacy were lacking, resulting in their feelings that their marriages lacked emotional intimacy. These gender-related differences reflected the talk-based versus action-based styles of showing support that are typical of women and men and highlighted the importance of these differences in the dissolution of relationships.

The divorced men and women also believed that their marriages had fallen short of the ideal in the second component of companionate marriage—companionship and primacy. Both the women and men in Riessman's study described differences in interests that prevented each from being primary companions for the other, and both reported that they felt slighted by this lack of shared interests. The discrepancy of leisure interests was a factor in this problem, especially for working-class women whose husbands' involvement with sports was a common complaint. The men reported that their wives' devotion to friends, family, and children was a problem; these other relationships made the husbands feel that they did not come first. The women did not resent such other relationships of their husbands, but some described their husbands' work as an intrusion, especially middle-class women whose husbands had prestigious, time-consuming careers.

Sex is the third component of the companionship model of marriage, and the divorced people in Riessman's study mentioned problems with sex in connection with their divorce. The men mentioned dissatisfaction with the frequency of sex and resentment over their wives' refusal to have sex as often as husbands wanted. Sexual affairs were a factor in 34% of the divorced people in this study, and both women and men believed that affairs had been the impetus for the dissolution of their marriage. The women took their own as well as their husbands' affairs as a sign of emotional betrayal, signaling that their marriage was over. The men did not necessarily share that attitude, but they also acknowledged that affairs had been a factor in their divorces. Wives found it difficult to forgive husbands' affairs, and wives who had affairs tended to leave their husbands for their lovers.

These feelings suggest that women might be the ones to initiate breakups; research (Duck, 1991) has confirmed this finding, stating that women initiate 80% of the breakups of heterosexual couples. This gender difference may be due to women's tendency to be more vigilant about monitoring their relationships so that they know when something is going wrong more quickly than men do. This finding highlights a substantial asymmetry in love relationships: Women fall out of love more quickly and fall in love more slowly than men do.

Women and men both experience different lives after the dissolution of a love relationship. For couples who have been married or have cohabited, the dissolution of the relationship is usually financially as well as emotionally difficult. Women's lower earning power coupled with their custody of children tends to create financial hardship, whereas men's financial position tends to improve after divorce. Divorced women experienced at least a 30% decline in income (Hoffman & Duncan, 1988) and possibly more (Weitzman, 1985), whereas men experienced a 42% increase in their standard of living a year after their divorce.

Both men and women find positive as well as negative consequences as a result of the divorce experience (Riessman, 1990). Both women and men said they enjoyed the freedom that came with divorce, but their feelings had different sources: Women liked being free from their husbands' dominance, whereas the men liked being free of their wives' expectations. The women in Riessman's study experienced more positive as well as more negative emotions in connection with their divorces than the men experienced. All of the women found something positive in the experience, whereas 15% of the men found nothing positive about their divorces. The women experienced more symptoms of depression, but they also discovered heightened self-esteem and feelings of competence through performing activities their husbands had done when they were married.

Dissolution of marriage often deprives men not only of companionship and emotional support from their wives, but also of their children and of their network of friends and family (a network typically maintained by women). Women tend to use these support networks after divorce, but men do not. The men in Riessman's study were surprised at the difficulties of being alone, but they also described feelings of satisfaction from their developing competencies in domestic chores.

Divorced men and women are likely to feel displeased with their ex-spouses rather than with marriage itself, and most showed their endorsement of marriage by remarrying. With the growing acceptability of cohabitation, some divorced people choose to live with a new partner rather than marry; cohabitation is also a form of trial marriage for some of these couples, who married after living together for 1 or 2 years (Blumstein & Schwartz, 1983). Some evidence exists that the second marriage is less traditional than the first, with a more equal balance of power and a more equal sharing of decision making and household chores (Furstenberg & Spanier, 1984). Second marriages are even more likely to end in divorce than first marriages, which Riessman interpreted as an increased unwillingness to endure an unhappy relationship combined with the knowledge that divorce offered positive as well as negative experiences.

Considering Diversity

The blueprints for marriage have changed over time in the United States (Cancian, 1987). In the 1800s, the Family Duty blueprint was the rule: Couples often entered arranged marriages for economic reasons, and their feelings revolved around a sense of duty to each other and their children. Looking further back into history and to other cultures, Nancy Bonvillain (1998) analyzed gender and marriage in a variety of settings, contrasting male-dominated and egalitarian societies. Her analysis pointed to economics as an important factor in the power that women have in their marriages and in the society in general.

In societies in which women contribute significantly to household subsistence, the women have power in their personal relationships. For example, the Ju/'hoansi are a society of foraging people who live in Botswana and Namibia. Ju/'hoansi society has differences in gender roles and behaviors, but women's foraging is essential to band survival, and this contribution is reflected in Ju/'hoansi women's full participation in social decisions. Parents typically arrange marriages between an older man who has gained some success as a hunter and a younger woman, which can tip the balance of power in favor of men. However, recently married couples live with the woman's family for the first years of marriage, and this arrangement protects women from male domination and violence.

The Inuit of Arctic North America are also a foraging band society, but they have a male-dominated culture (Bonvillain, 1998). Again, an economic analysis showed that the scarcity of foods to gather results in men's hunting as the main source of the food for these people. In Inuit society, women are forbidden to hunt. Consequently, women's contributions are perceived as less important, and their status is lower. In addition, the Inuit have a preference for couples' living in proximity to the husbands' family, leaving wives with no automatic allies. Wife beating is common and accepted, and husbands practice sexual exchange of wives for husbands' economic benefit.

For larger and more complex societies, the economic analysis still seems to reflect women's status and power within relationships. In tribal societies, both egalitarian and male-dominated societies have existed. When Europeans arrived in North America, the Iroquois allowed women access to economic resources, whereas the Yanomamo of Brazil and Venezuela were a tribal society that did not allow such access. These two societies showed the predicted patterns of egalitarianism and male dominance, respectively. In even larger and more complex groups such as state and industrialized societies, the restriction of economic production to men gives them power and puts women in the position of subordinates in many ways, including in marriages.

Bonvillain contended that when women's contributions are seen as minor, their status is lower, and they have little power in their relationships. Lack of power manifests itself in the inability to leave unhappy marriages or to avoid physical abuse. A cross-cultural analysis of violence against women (Heise, Ellsberg, & Gottemoeller, 1999) also related domestic violence to societies with strong male dominance. Consistent with Bonvillain's view, this analysis cited financial dependence and restriction of access to resources as contributors to domestic violence.

Examining domestic violence against women across cultures revealed a great deal of variation in the percentage of women who reported abuse (Heise et al., 1999). In cultures that endorse men's right to control women and to "discipline" wives, the rates of abuse were high—over 40% of women in studies conducted in Turkey, New Guinea, Ethiopia, Uganda, India, and Nicaragua reported physical abuse by their intimate partners. In societies that support abuse against women, men (and sometimes women too) find a variety of justifications for abuse, including failure to obey husbands' orders, asking for money, failure to take care of children, suspicion of adultery, or refusing sex. Other societies set stricter limits on domestic violence, and these societies have a lower rate of reported partner violence. Indeed, domestic abuse does not occur in all societies.

Social sanction is not the only factor that relates to domestic violence: Individual, family, and community factors also relate to it (Heise et al., 1999). These factors are similar around the world. Men who are victims of physical abuse or who observe domestic violence as children are more likely to be abusive as adults. Use of alcohol increases the chances of an individual becoming violent. Within the family context, an imbalance of power promotes violence among couples. At the community level, women's isolation and lack of support increases their chances of being victimized.

Therefore, the cross-cultural analyses of domestic violence have revealed many commonalities among societies and individuals who are abusive to intimate partners. Another commonality is the growing worldwide campaign against this type of abuse. Since 1993, when the United Nations General Assembly passed the Declaration on the Elimination of Violence Against Women, countries around the world have developed initiatives to curb domestic violence. China (Xinhua News Agency, 2000), Uganda (Africa News Service, 2000), Europe (Women's International Network, 2000), and countries throughout Latin America (Heise et al., 1999) have begun widespread efforts to decrease domestic violence through public health campaigns, government agencies, churches, women's advocacy groups, and legislative efforts. These many efforts aim to change societal attitudes, community standards, and individual behaviors to create a world that is safer for women in their intimate relationships.

Summary

Sternberg's triangular model of relationships provides a framework for understanding all relationships, including friendships and love relationships. Gender differences in friendship styles appear early in development; children voluntarily segregate themselves according to gender before age 5 years. Girls are fond of talking and sharing secrets, and boys tend to enjoy active games. Even the girls and boys who do not like their gender-typical activities are not welcome in cross-gender groups.

Adolescents are more concerned with developing emotional intimacy in their relationships, but girls emphasize this aspect of relationships more than boys. Although young men say that they value intimacy in relationships, they often find it difficult to develop such relationships, especially with other men. Some men develop emotionally intimate love relationships with women, and such relationships often decrease the amount of time and emotional energy men have to devote to male friends. Friendships tend to be tied to developmental stages of life, and marriage and the birth of children tend to restrict friendships.

Cancian has argued that love has become feminized. The current concept of love is emotional intimacy—a pattern closer to the typical relationship for women than for men. This definition slights the styles of intimacy men tend to adopt—the activities of providing help and doing things together. Some research has indicated that both men and women have a flexibility of friendship styles and that they use different styles to relate to male and female friends. Cross-gender nonsexual friendships are a recent phenomenon, and both men and women acknowledge that such relationships require special rules.

Love relationships currently form through dating, an activity that first arose during the 1920s as a response to changing patterns of mate selection. Dating has now become not only a method of courting, but also a forum for recreation, socialization, and sexual exploration. Adolescents tend to choose dates similar to future mates, preferring dates who are kind, considerate, socially exciting, intelligent, and physically attractive. People with either heterosexual or homosexual orientation describe their preferred partners in similar ways, but men emphasize the importance of physical attractiveness more than women do.

Currently, marriage and other committed relationships can follow several different blueprints:

Companionship, Independence, and Interdependence. The Companionship blueprint involves separate gender roles and emphasizes the woman's role in maintaining a love relationship. Both the Independence and Interdependence blueprints emphasize self-development for both men and women, but they differ in the importance of commitment.

Gender researchers have explored several issues in love relationships, including beliefs about love, communication, division of household labor, power and conflict, and relationship stability. Men are more romantic in their conceptualization of love than women are, and marriage tends to benefit them more, but they are not necessarily happier with their marriages. Men and women may have trouble communicating in love relationships, partly because their styles and goals of communication differ, with men trying to establish independence and dominance, and women trying to share feelings and make connections.

The division of household labor is usually unequal in marriages: Women perform far more of this work than men, even when women have paid employment outside the home. The ideal pattern of household work for both partners is closer to equal, but both women and men feel satisfied with women performing a disproportionate share. When women do most household work and hold outside jobs, their disproportionate work load may be a source of conflict. Although paid employment is a source of power, both partners do not usually have equal power in a marriage. Couples experience conflict from many sources, but some marital conflict results in violence. Over 25% of women and men find violence acceptable in their personal relationships under some circumstances, but women are more likely than men to be injured as a result of relationship violence.

Violence decreases the stability of relationships, but does not necessarily end them. Stable love relationships tend to occur in couples with similar attitudes and values, and the commitment factor in marriage produces greater stability than in other love relationships. But even marriages dissolve, and divorce has increased in the past several decades. People who have divorced tend to see the fault in their ex-spouses rather than in the institution of marriage. Although divorce brings financial and emotional problems, most women and men also find positive factors in divorce. Most remarry, and some evidence suggests that both women and men form more equitable second marriages.

Across time and cultures, many patterns of marriage have existed. Analyzing the economic contributions of women in a variety of societies leads to the conclusion that women experience more egalitarian relationships and roles in societies in which they make significant economic contributions. Male-dominated cultures restrict women's access to resources, tend to establish restrictive marriages, and tend to allow greater intimate-partner violence. A worldwide campaign against domestic violence has sensitized people in many countries to the problems that result from this type of abuse.

Glossary

companionate love a combination of commitment and intimacy without passion.

gross motor skills skills involving use of large muscles of the body, producing large movements, such as throwing, kicking, running, and jumping.

homophobia the unreasonable fear and hatred of homosexuality.

machismo a Spanish word meaning strong and assertive masculinity and implying complete male authority.

matriarchy a family pattern in which women are dominant or a pattern in which women are the head of the household due to the father's absence.

Suggested Readings

Blumstein, Philip; & Schwartz, Pepper. (1983). *American couples.* New York: Pocket Books. Although not recent, this book examines the relationships of all types of couples—married and cohabiting heterosexual partners as well as gay and lesbian couples. Through interviews with couples, Blumstein and Schwartz explore attitudes toward power, money, and sex, and their impact on individual happiness and relationship stability.

Gottman, John, (with Silver, Nan). (1994). *Why marriages succeed or fail.* New York: Simon and Schuster. Gottman's popular book summarizes his research on factors related to success and failure in marriage. In addition, he includes self-quizzes so that couples can assess their relationships.

Hatfield, Elaine; & Rapson, Richard L. (1996). *Love and sex: Cross-cultural perspectives.* Boston: Allyn and Bacon. Hatfield and Rapson's book examines love and sex across contemporary cultures as well as delving into history for additional examples. They consider attraction, the difficulties of forming relationships, and the problems involved in ending romantic relationships. Their cross-cultural and historical review adds a valuable (and fascinating) point of view to the understanding of passionate love.

Maccoby, Eleanor. (1990). Gender and relationships: A developmental account. *American Psychologist, 45,* 513–520. Maccoby summarizes and reviews the research on gender differences and similarities in social interactions and relationships. Her developmental approach includes children, adolescents, and adults, and this brief review is easy to read.

Chapter 10

Sexuality

HEADLINE

The Sex Drive

Men's Health, October, 1999

Gregg Gutfeld (1999, p. 118) described the experience of "cybersex," sexually explicit material and interactions on the Internet:

> *Sex online is the biggest thing since, well, sex. It's not real sex, but almost. In some ways it's much better than actual sex. And we'll never get rid of it.... It's here to stay because it gives men exactly what they want: Sex without commitment or cost. The harem has arrived, and it's waiting for you on your hard drive.*

Many people use their computers to bring sex into their homes and offices. "Sex is the number-one destination on the Internet. During a single month recently, 15 percent of the 57 million Americans using the World Wide Web accessed the 10 most popular adult Web sites" (Gutfeld, 1999, p. 118). Gutfeld contended that cybersex is so popular because it delivers the kind of sex that men want: a seemingly endless variety of great-looking women, easy availability, and no commitment or relationship issues. Sex on the Internet overcomes many of the barriers associated with sexual relationships; it is accessible, affordable, and anonymous.

For some people involved in online sex, their involvement becomes a problem for their real-life relationships. Gutfeld contended that real women cannot match the fantasy that the Internet offers and that online sex can become a dangerous addiction. A survey of people who use online sex services (Cooper, Scherer, Boies, & Gordon, 1999) indicated that a small percentage (8%) of individuals who engage in cybersex use the services extensively and experience problems related to their behavior. This low percentage means 92% of people who engage in cybersex spend only a few hours a week in this pursuit and report that it interferes little with their lives (Cooper et al.,1999). This optimistic assessment is based on the reports of those who use these services and not their partners, who may feel differently.

People who seek sex on the Internet are more likely to be men than women—85% of cybersex participants are men (Cooper et al., 1999). Some of these individuals become very involved in commercial sites that offer live action or video presentations of sexual activity, and with chat rooms that allow participants to interact with each other. Men tend to frequent the sites that offer pictures and videos, whereas the women who seek cybersex tend to use the chat rooms. Do these patterns reflect overall gender differences in sexuality? Are men interested in variety, adventure, and quantity of sexual encounters without relationship entanglements? Do women really concentrate on relationships and care less about the physical pleasures of sex? Researchers have attempted to answer these questions by conducting studies on sexual behavior.

The Study of Sexuality

Researchers who want to know about sexual behaviors and attitudes have several options in choosing a method of investigation. They may question people about their sexual behavior, as the survey on cybersex did (Cooper et al., 1999), or they may directly observe people's sexual behavior. Both of these approaches present scientific, practical, and ethical problems.

Those researchers who choose to question people about their sexual behaviors or attitudes are using the survey method. Chapter 2 described surveys, along with their advantages and disadvantages. One limitation is especially relevant to sexuality research: Some people feel that sex is a private, personal issue and do not want to share this information with researchers. These people refuse to participate in sex surveys, and they very likely differ from people who are willing to answer questions about their sexual attitudes and behavior. Potential participants who refuse to cooperate can bias results because their opinions are systematically excluded.

Another possibility for investigating sexual behavior is through direct observation of sexual activity. Most people are even less willing to participate in this type of research than in a survey, but nonhuman animals have (or at least have voiced) no such objections. The problems with generalizing results from these studies to humans are even more serious than with generalizing from one group of humans to another. Nevertheless, this strategy has been useful, adding breadth to the study of sexual behavior. A prominent example of this type of research appears in *Patterns of Sexual Behavior* (1951) by anthropologist Clellan Ford and psychologist Frank Beach. These two researchers presented not only a cross-cultural study of human sexual behavior, but cross-species comparisons as well.

Only a small percentage of people have been willing to have sex in a research laboratory. Such participants allowed William Masters and Virginia Johnson (1966) to study human sexual behavior in ways that no other researchers had managed. Not only were Masters and Johnson's participants willing to answer questions about sex, they were willing to have sex in the lab and to have their physical responses measured during the activity. Although the results of Masters and Johnson's research have become widely accepted, their participants were less typical of the general population than those of any of the major surveys, a situation that Masters and Johnson considered unimportant but that others have criticized.

Thus, although researchers who want to study sexual attitudes and behavior have several options, most researchers have surveyed people about their attitudes or behavior, or both, by asking questions and recording the responses. The problems with survey research include finding a **representative sample**—a group of people that reflects the characteristics of the population from which the sample was drawn—as well as securing truthful and accurate responses. Despite the problems connected with surveying people about sex, this approach has been the most common one. Sex surveys such as the one conducted online suffer from the problem of **self-selection of participants.** When participants rather than researchers choose who is to complete the survey, then the sample is not representative. Such surveys can still reveal interesting and important information, but self-selected participants prohibit researchers from generalizing the results to the general population. For example, over 9,000 people participated in the online sex survey (Cooper et al., 1999), but all were computer users who had participated in cybersex, making that sample far from representative of people in general.

Sex Surveys

Before Alfred Kinsey's groundbreaking survey of men's and women's sexual behavior in the 1930s and 1940s, several other investigators completed reports on sexuality (Brecher, 1969). Henry Havelock Ellis, a British physician, wrote a series of books between 1896 and 1928 in which he detailed the differences in sexual customs of various cultures and collected sexual case studies of women and men. These studies led him to the conclusion that the Victorian social norms of repression and denial of sexuality that he saw around him were not reflected in people's sexual behavior. Ellis came to a conclusion that is applicable today: "Everybody is not like you and your friends and neighbors," and even, "Your friends and neighbors may not be as much like you as you suppose" (in Brecher, 1969, p. 39). Ellis was one of several sex researchers in the 1800s who was important in making sex an acceptable topic for scientific research, and this research helped to end the sexual repression that was the standard of that time.

Clelia Duel Mosher was a physician who began questioning women in the United States about their sexual behavior and enjoyment in 1892 (Degler, 1974). Although Mosher's sample size was small—only 45 women—and far from representative—all were college students—the responses to her survey indicated that sexual repression might not have been as common as Victorian standards held. About half of the women reported that they had no knowledge of sex before their marriages, but 35 of the 45 women reported sexual desires, and 34 of the 45 said they experienced orgasm. This small, unrepresentative sample might not reveal the average woman's attitudes for that time, but the existence of women who enjoyed sex seems to contradict the prevalent view of the Victorian period. The marriage manuals of the day portrayed women as lacking in sexual feelings, but Mosher's data revealed that that view was not completely accurate.

Several other researchers completed small-scale sex surveys during the early 1900s. The most famous of the surveys on sexual behavior were those completed by Kinsey and his colleagues.

The Kinsey Surveys

In 1920, biologist Alfred Kinsey took a position as instructor at Indiana University. In 1937, he began to teach a newly created course in sex education, which at that time was a controversial topic. Kinsey found that little systematic research existed on sexuality, and this gap prompted him to begin such research. He started collecting data in 1938 with a preliminary interview that he later expanded to include extensive information about nine areas: social and economic background, marital history, sex education, physical characteristics and physiology, nocturnal sex dreams, masturbation, heterosexual history, history of same-gender sexual activity, and sexual contact with animals. Each of these areas included subdivisions, making the interview extensive and time consuming. Amazingly, Kinsey completed more than 7,000 such interviews himself. His associates, Wardell Pomeroy, Clyde Martin, and Paul Gebhard, conducted other interviews, for a total sample of 17,500 (Brecher, 1969).

Although the interviews were extensive and large numbers were conducted, Kinsey's sample was drawn primarily from the university and the surrounding community. He did not necessarily strive to obtain a representative sample, and the lack of a representative sample prevented generalization to the U.S. population. Kinsey questioned African Americans, but he excluded their data from his analysis because he knew that the individuals he had questioned were not a representative group. This choice further biased his results. His final groups of 5,300 men and 5,940 women were therefore White, well educated, mostly from Indiana, and largely Protestant.

Kinsey was skilled at getting a wide variety of people to talk with him candidly about their sexual histories (Brecher, 1969; St. Lawrence & McFarlane, 1999). His technique included asking questions that required participants to deny rather than admit a practice, such as, "At what age did you first experience full intercourse?" This approach assumed that everyone had done everything. Perhaps this strategy helped to make people more comfortable and encouraged them to tell the truth. Reinterviewing some participants 18 months after their first interview revealed mostly minor inconsistencies that came from memory lapses rather than intentional deception, indicating to Kinsey that they were telling the truth. Thus, Kinsey's surveys managed to overcome some problems associated with survey research.

The results from Kinsey's surveys appeared in two parts, *Sexual Behavior in the Human Male* (Kinsey, Pomeroy, & Martin, 1948) and *Sexual Behavior in the Human Female* (Kinsey, Pomeroy, Martin, & Gebhard, 1953). Kinsey's reports appeared during a time when sex was not a topic of polite conversation; when women were supposed to be reluctant to have sex; and when same-gender, premarital, and extramarital sexual activities were illegal in many areas. The results of the surveys surprised (and even shocked) many people, because the participants reported such a wide variety of sexual behaviors, including some that were socially unacceptable and even illegal.

Kinsey's results indicated that women enjoyed sex; that many men had participated in male–male sexual behavior; that children experienced sexual excitement and activity; and that masturbation, premarital sex, and extramarital sex were common for both women and men. Around 90% of the women in the study had experienced orgasm by age 35 years. Of the 10% who had not, another 8% reported experiencing sexual arousal, leaving only 2% of women who had failed to enjoy sexual activity, a figure much lower than most people imagined.

Some of Kinsey's most controversial findings concerned same-gender sex. People with sexual partners of their own gender have objected to the term *homosexual,* a term that Kinsey used to describe male–male and female–female sexual behavior. The term has become stigmatized because it highlights the sexual aspect of these individuals' lives. A relationship with a same-gender partner is much more than sexual (Blumstein & Schwartz, 1983), and other terms have replaced *homosexual.* The term ***gay*** is an alternative that many find preferable and that may apply to both men and women, but it is more often used to describe men, who have sexual relationships with men. The term ***lesbian*** refers to women who have sexual relationships with other women.

A total of 37% of the men in Kinsey's survey reported at least one sexual experience with another man; that is, an experience with another man that led to orgasm. This figure included men who had had sexual experiences with other men only as young adolescents, and men who had had only one such experience. Some of these men reported that they no longer felt sexual attraction toward other men or had no subsequent sexual experiences with other men. Both the percentage of men who had some type of sexual experience with other men (37%) and the percentage of men who primarily or exclusively had sex with other men (13%) were higher than previous estimates (Brecher, 1969). Kinsey's figures on female sexual activity with other women were similar to the figures for men, but the percentages were smaller. Twenty-eight percent of women had at least some sexual experience with other women, but only 7% reported primarily or exclusively lesbian sexuality. Table 10.1 shows these figures.

These figures for the frequency of same-gender sexual attraction and activity are at the center of a continuing controversy. Kinsey's figures for the number of men who primarily or exclusively have sex with other men are not only higher than previous estimates, but they are also higher than later estimates (Hunt, 1974). A biography of Kinsey (Jones, 1998) contended that Kinsey's figures were biased by his personal interest and participation in sexual activity with men and his desire to portray these sexual activities as common. He therefore chose to question a disproportionate number of gay men, inflating the figures for this type of sexual activity.

Many participants in the Kinsey survey reported that as children they had sexual feelings and sometimes acted on those feelings. The most common type of childhood sexuality was **masturbation,** manipulation of the genitals to produce sexual pleasure. Infants and young children masturbate, some to orgasm. A total of 14% of the women and 45% of the

TABLE 10.1 Percentage of Participants Reporting Sexual Activities in Three Sex Surveys

	Kinsey Surveys (1948, 1953)		Playboy Foundation Survey (Hunt, 1974)		National Opinion Research Council (Laumann et al., 1994)	
	Percentage Reporting Each Behavior					
Sexual Activity	Men	Women	Men	Women	Men	Women
Masturbation to orgasm	92.0%	58.0%	94.0%	63.0%	—	—
Masturbation before age 13	45.0	14.0	63.0	33.0	—	—
Masturbation during marriage	40.0	30.0	72.0	68.0	57.0	37.0
At least one homosexual experience	37.0	28.0	—	—	7.1	3.8
Primarily homosexual orientation	13.0	7.0	2.0	1.0	4.1	2.2
Premarital intercourse	71.0	33.0	97.0	67.0	93.0	79.0
Extramarital sex	50.0	26.0	41.0	18.0	<25.0	<10.0
Sexual abuse during childhood	10.0	25.0	—	—	12.0	17.0

men in Kinsey's survey said that they had masturbated before the age of 13 years. They also remembered other-gender and same-gender exploratory play with peers as well as sexual contact with adults. Men recalled preadolescent intercourse more frequently than women did. Almost one-fourth of the women recalled incidents during which adult men had shown their genitals, touched them, or attempted intercourse. Over half of the incidents reported by women involved acquaintances or family members. Adults' recollections of their childhood sexual activities are most likely not completely accurate, but Kinsey's results suggested that children experience sexual curiosity and exploration as well as sexual abuse by adults.

Kinsey's survey revealed that masturbation was a common sexual activity. A small percentage of people reported preadolescent masturbation, but the activity increased during adolescence. By the time they were adults, almost all of the men and about two-thirds of the women had reached orgasm by masturbating. Married women and men told Kinsey that they continued to masturbate, although they also had sex with their spouses. Around 30% of married women and 40% of married men reported that they masturbated. These figures contradicted the popular notion that masturbation was primarily a practice of adolescence and that people with a sexual partner no longer masturbated.

Kinsey surveyed people who lived in a society that accepted different sexual standards for men and women. Although both were supposed to be sexually inexperienced before marriage and to have sex only with their spouses, men were not held to this standard but women were. This **double standard for sexual behavior** has a history that stretches back at least a century, and Kinsey found evidence for it in the different rates for both premarital and extramarital sex. By 25 years of age, 83% of unmarried men but only 33% of unmarried women said that they had participated in intercourse. A similar discrepancy occurred in the reports of extramarital affairs—that is, about half the men but only 26% of the women admitted having extramarital affairs.

In summary, Kinsey and his associates interviewed thousands of men and women during the 1930s and 1940s to determine the sexual behavior of people in the United States. They questioned a variety of people, but not a representative sample, so the results have limitations. Kinsey's results suggested that people engage in a wide variety of sexual activities, beginning during childhood. He found that most women experience orgasm, and that masturbation and extramarital sex are common. In addition, Kinsey's results showed that more than one-third of men have had some type of sexual experience with another man, but that few were exclusively gay. The reports of female–female sexual activities were less common but with parallel findings: Few women were exclusively lesbian, but more had past or occasional sexual experiences with other women. After the Kinsey reports, many other sex researchers chose the survey method of investigation.

Hunt's Playboy Foundation Survey

In the 1970s, the Playboy Foundation commissioned a survey of sexual behavior in the United States, and in 1974, Morton Hunt reported the results in his book *Sexual Behavior in the 1970s.* The researchers involved in this survey wanted to update the Kinsey findings, and they attempted to obtain a more representative sample than Kinsey had managed.

The survey began with a sample of people randomly drawn from the telephone books of 24 U.S. cities, which is not a representative sample. In addition, 80% of those contacted declined to participate, which further biased the sample. Despite the problems with the sampling procedure, Hunt contended that the sample matched characteristics of the U.S.

population in terms of ethnic background, education, age, and marital status. The 2,026 participants filled out a lengthy questionnaire about their backgrounds, including sex education, attitudes toward sex, and sexual histories. A total of 200 also participated in an even more lengthy interview that was similar to the Kinsey interviews.

As Table 10.1 shows, this survey confirmed the prevalence of masturbation Kinsey had found, with an even higher rate of preadolescent masturbation and a similar rate of masturbation during adulthood. Hunt found a lower percentage and a different pattern of same-gender sexual activity than Kinsey had found. He concluded that most such activity occurs as a form of adolescent experimentation, with most of the women and men who had same-gender sexual experiences discontinuing this form of sexuality by age 16 years. Hunt estimated that 2% of men and 1% of women were exclusively gay or lesbian in their sexual orientation.

Hunt found some evidence for a sexual revolution in the form of increases in certain sexual activities. More unmarried people had engaged in intercourse than the Kinsey surveys reported. A total of 97% of the unmarried men and 67% of the unmarried women reported having intercourse by age 25 years, representing an increase in intercourse and a decrease in the double standard. According to Hunt, by the 1970s, extramarital sex was more common, especially among younger women.

The Playboy Foundation survey also found evidence that more people were engaging in a wider variety of sexual activities than Kinsey reported. For example, a higher percentage of respondents in the Playboy Foundation survey reported oral–genital sexuality than in Kinsey's surveys. **Fellatio** is oral stimulation of the male genitals, and **cunnilingus** is oral stimulation of the female genitals. Kinsey found a difference in popularity of oral–genital sexuality according to educational background: 60% of people with a college education, 20% of those with a high school education, and 10% of those with a grade school education had engaged in oral–genital sexual activity. Hunt reported that 90% of the young married couples in his survey said they had engaged in oral–genital stimulation, revealing a dramatic increase in prevalence and a leveling of social class differences.

In summary, Hunt's Playboy Foundation survey attempted to obtain a representative sample of U.S. residents and question them about their sexual attitudes and behavior. One of the goals was to complete an interview similar to Kinsey's technique so as to furnish updated comparisons. This survey showed that Kinsey was correct in concluding that people's sexual behavior is more varied than the social norms suggest, and it confirmed the prevalence of masturbation and childhood sexuality. Hunt's estimates for same-gender sexuality were much lower than Kinsey's figures, but Hunt found evidence for an increase in premarital, extramarital, and oral–genital sexual activity.

The National Opinion Research Center Survey

Two major U.S. sex surveys appeared during the 1990s, one conducted by Samuel and Cynthia Janus (1993), and the other by a team headed by Edward Laumann, John Gagnon, Robert Michael, and Stuart Michaels (1994) for the National Opinion Research Center (NORC). Although both groups claimed that theirs was the first survey to obtain a representative sample of adults in the United States, the NORC survey relied on a random sampling technique rather than on volunteers. After collecting their information, Laumann and his colleagues compared their sample to information known about U.S. adults, and they concluded their group was representative.

The NORC survey revealed a slightly different picture of sex in the United States than either the Kinsey or Hunt surveys had shown. One difference was a continuation of the trend toward more liberal sexual standards, with sex serving either as an important factor in love relationships (regardless of marital status) or as a recreational activity (without any necessity for a committed relationship). Only around 30% of respondents expressed the traditional, conservative view that sex outside marriage is always wrong and that procreation is the main reason for having sex.

The other difference expressed in the NORC survey indicated some degree of conservatism concerning sex. For example, a low percentage of participants reported attraction to and practice of a variety of sexual behaviors. Indeed, the NORC survey found that vaginal intercourse was not only the most frequent form of sexual activity with a partner, but also the most appealing to both men and women. Giving and receiving oral sex and watching a partner undress were at least somewhat appealing to a majority of participants, but group sex, anal intercourse, sex with strangers, and forcing or being forced to do something sexual were not appealing to the majority of participants.

This survey also found gender differences in sexuality, just as the other surveys had done. One large gender difference related to the experience of first intercourse: 28% of women but only 8% of men said that they did not want to have intercourse at the time, but either did so out of affection for their partners or were forced to do so. Men also reported more varied sexual interests and behavior, including more lifetime sex partners and a slightly higher interest in group sex, anal intercourse, watching others do sexual things, visiting sex clubs, viewing sexually explicit books or videos, and giving and receiving oral sex. Men were more likely to masturbate, but women were more likely to report feeling guilty about masturbating. Table 10.1 summarizes information from this survey.

"The general picture of sex with a partner in America shows that Americans do not have a secret life of abundant sex" (Michael, Gagnon, Laumann, & Kolata, 1994, p. 122). The most common category for frequency of intercourse was *a few times a month,* and only about 7% reported having sex four or more times a week. In addition, about two-thirds of both men and women said that they had only one sex partner within the past year, with reports showing only small variations across different ethnic groups, religious affiliations, or educational levels. The NORC survey reflected a less sexually varied United States than the media or people's imaginations often present, but it also showed an acceptance of sex for pleasure and outside the boundaries of marriage.

Gender Differences (and Similarities) in Sexual Attitudes and Behavior

The three major sex surveys have shown gender differences in several sexual behaviors and in some attitudes toward sexuality. Although the more recent surveys have indicated a smaller difference in sexuality of men and women, even the NORC report indicated that men are more sexually active at a younger age than women. A meta-analysis (Oliver & Hyde, 1993) revealed that gender differences exist in some aspects of sexuality but not in others.

Two large, gender-related differences emerged from this meta-analysis: incidence of masturbation and attitudes toward casual premarital sex. Studies of male adolescents and adults have indicated a higher rate of masturbation and a greater acceptance of casual premarital sex than for female adolescents and adults. These researchers pointed out that the magnitude of the differences for these comparisons surpasses other gender-related differences, such as those in mathematics or verbal abilities. (See Chapter 4 for a discussion of these cognitive differences.) The greater acceptance of casual premarital sex applies to men in a variety of cultures, including Canada, Africa, Hong Kong, Sweden, and all ethnic groups in the United States (Hatfield & Rapson, 1996). The term *casual* also seems to apply to online sex, and about 85% of those who engage in this type of sexual activity are men (Cooper et al., 1999).

Gender-related differences in other aspects of sexuality were smaller, and some of the meta-analysis (Oliver & Hyde, 1993) comparisons failed to show gender differences. Of the differences that appeared, men reported being, and actually were, more acceptant of those sexual behaviors than women were. Small differences also appeared in the acceptance of premarital and extramarital intercourse, sexual permissiveness, number of sexual partners, and frequency of intercourse. In addition, men reported feeling less sexual guilt or anxiety than women felt. Analysis of acceptance of the double standard for sexual behavior indicated, ironically, that women believed in the double standard more than men did. No gender differences appeared in attitudes toward same-gender sexuality, rights for gays or lesbians, attitudes toward masturbation, incidence of oral sex, or sexual satisfaction. Table 10.2 shows some of the behaviors and attitudes from this meta-analysis, along with the magnitude of gender-related differences.

Changes over time were also among the results of the meta-analysis (Oliver & Hyde, 1993): All gender differences showed signs of decreasing over time. Thus, this analysis confirms the trends that appeared in the comparison of the three major surveys, as shown in Table 10.1—that is, a decrease of differences between men's and women's sexual attitudes and behavior, along with a few persistent differences.

Masters and Johnson's Approach

As noted earlier, researchers who want to observe sexual behavior directly can conduct their studies on nonhuman animals, or they can enlist the cooperation of people who are willing to engage in sex in a research laboratory. Although such participants are far from average, they might furnish important information about the physiology of sex. Other researchers have taken this approach, but the most famous of these have been William Masters and Virginia Johnson.

Masters began his study of the physiology of the sexual response in the 1950s by interviewing prostitutes (Brecher, 1969). However, he was interested in taking measurements during sexual activity and considered prostitutes unsuitable participants. He sought volunteers from the medical community in St. Louis and found people who were willing to masturbate or have intercourse while being observed in the laboratory. During the time Masters was recruiting participants for the laboratory studies, he also recruited Virginia Johnson to assist him with the interviewing, and she became an essential part of the research.

Masters and Johnson chose a total of 694 people to serve as research participants, including 276 married couples as well as 106 single women and 36 single men. These participants not only had to be willing to have sex in the lab, but the researchers selected women who regularly experienced orgasm, a criterion that restricted the sample of participants. All participants received payment for their participation, resulting in an overrepresentation of medical school students who were interested in contributing to scientific research and who also needed the money. These criteria and procedures were reasonable, but resulted in a sample that was far from representative. Masters and Johnson were not as concerned with

TABLE 10.2 Sexual Attitudes and Behaviors Showing and Failing to Show Gender-Related Differences

Sexual Behaviors/Attitudes	Direction of Difference
Large Differences	
Incidence of masturbation	Higher for men
Acceptability of casual sex	Higher for men
Moderate to Small Differences	
Acceptability of sexual permissiveness	Higher for men
Incidence of sex in committed relationship	Higher for men
Incidence of intercourse by engaged couples	Higher for men
Acceptability of premarital sex	Higher for men
Age at first intercourse	Lower for men
Frequency of intercourse	Higher for men
Incidence of same-gender sexual experiences	Higher for men
Anxiety, fear, and guilt associated with sex	Higher for women
Acceptability of double standard of sexual behavior	Higher for women
Acceptability of extramarital sex	Higher for men
Number of sexual partners	Higher for men
No Differences	
Incidence of oral sex	
Incidence of kissing	
Incidence of petting	
Acceptability of masturbation	
Acceptability of same-gender sexuality	
Belief that gays and lesbians should be given civil rights	
Sexual satisfaction	

drawing a representative sample as other sex researchers were. They believed that the physiological sexual responses they were studying varied little from person to person; thus, any sample should include the characteristics of interest to them. Lenore Tiefer (1995) argued that Masters and Johnson's selection of participants biased their results. In addition, she contended that they knew what they wanted to find and interpreted their data according to their preconceived notions, forcing the sexual experience into stages that are not necessarily appropriate for everyone.

In these laboratory studies, the married couples had intercourse, masturbated each other, or engaged in oral–genital stimulation. The unmarried participants did not have sex with a partner; the men masturbated and the women either masturbated or were stimulated by an artificial penis designed to measure vaginal responses during sexual arousal and orgasm. In

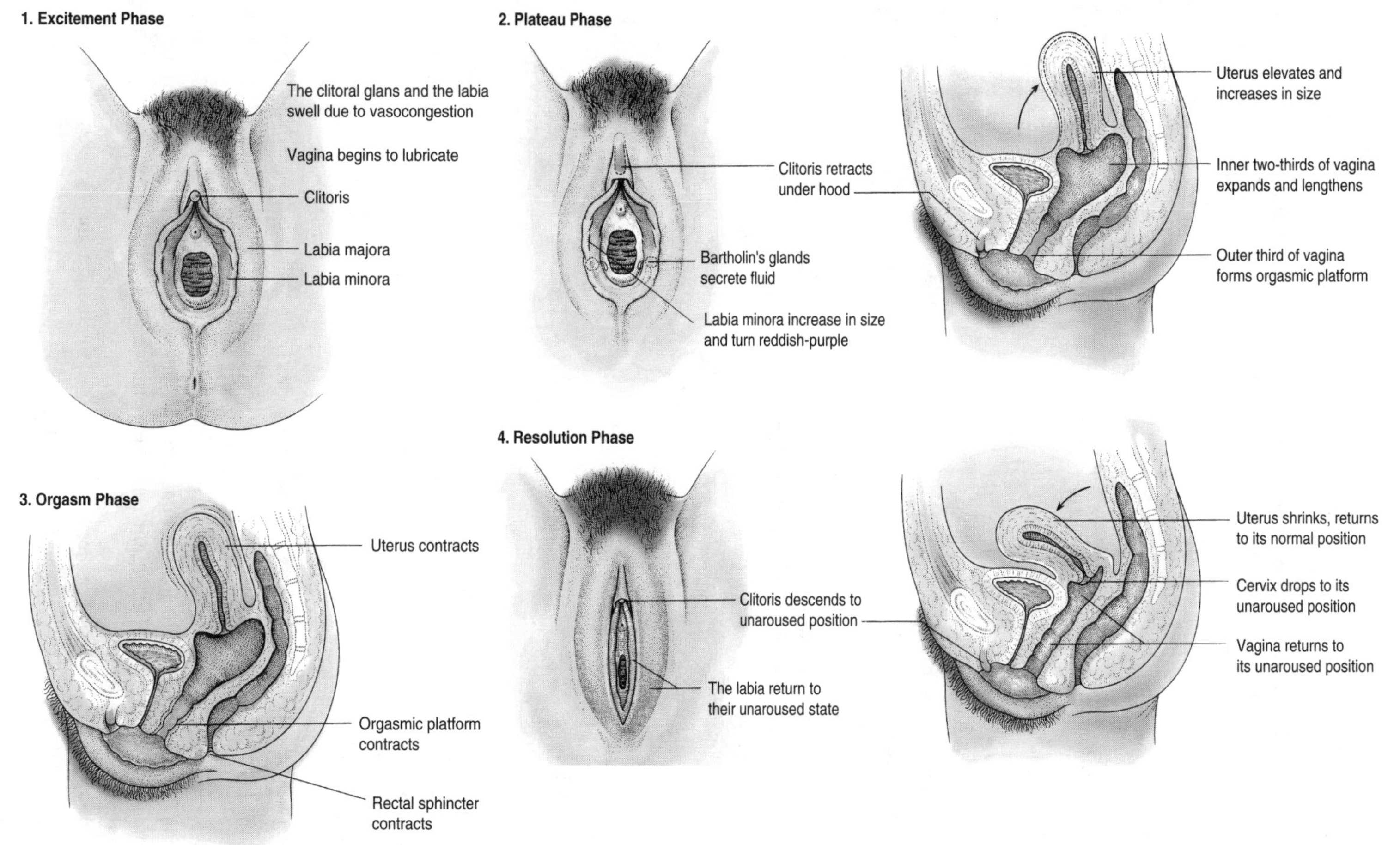
1. Excitement Phase
The clitoral glans and the labia swell due to vasocongestion
Vagina begins to lubricate
Clitoris
Labia majora
Labia minora
2. Plateau Phase
Clitoris retracts under hood
Bartholin's glands secrete fluid
Labia minora increase in size and turn reddish-purple
Uterus elevates and increases in size
Inner two-thirds of vagina expands and lengthens
Outer third of vagina forms orgasmic platform
3. Orgasm Phase
Uterus contracts
Orgasmic platform contracts
Rectal sphincter contracts
4. Resolution Phase
Clitoris descends to unaroused position
The labia return to their unaroused state
Uterus shrinks, returns to its normal position
Cervix drops to its unaroused position
Vagina returns to its unaroused position

FIGURE 10.1 Female Genitals during the Phases of the Sexual Response Cycle

addition to collecting information by measuring genital activity during sex, Masters and Johnson gathered physiological measurements such as heart rate, muscle contraction, and dilation of the blood vessels from both men and women.

Masters and Johnson measured physiological responses during more than 10,000 orgasms and presented their findings in *Human Sexual Response* (1966). Their findings suggested that four phases of sexual excitement exist—excitement, plateau, orgasm, and resolution. The two researchers contended that these four phases describe the sequence and experience of sexual arousal and orgasm for both women and men. Figures 10.1 and 10.2 show the four phases and the organs that are affected in both women and men.

The *excitement phase* refers to the initial physiological responses for sexual excitement—erection of the penis in men and the clitoris in women. The responses of both men and women are produced by vasocongestion, the swelling of tissues due to engorgement of the area with blood. The penis and clitoris are not the only areas affected; the testes, nipples, vaginal opening, and labia also swell, and the skin may become flushed. The vaginal walls secrete lubrication, and heart rate, blood pressure, and muscle tension increase.

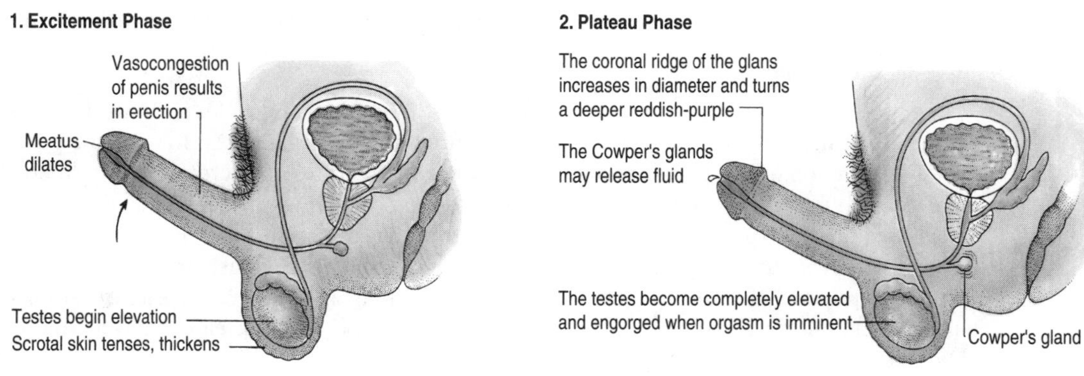
1. Excitement Phase
Vasocongestion of penis results in erection
Meatus dilates
Testes begin elevation
Scrotal skin tenses, thickens
2. Plateau Phase
The coronal ridge of the glans increases in diameter and turns a deeper reddish-purple
The Cowper's glands may release fluid
The testes become completely elevated and engorged when orgasm is imminent
Cowper's gland

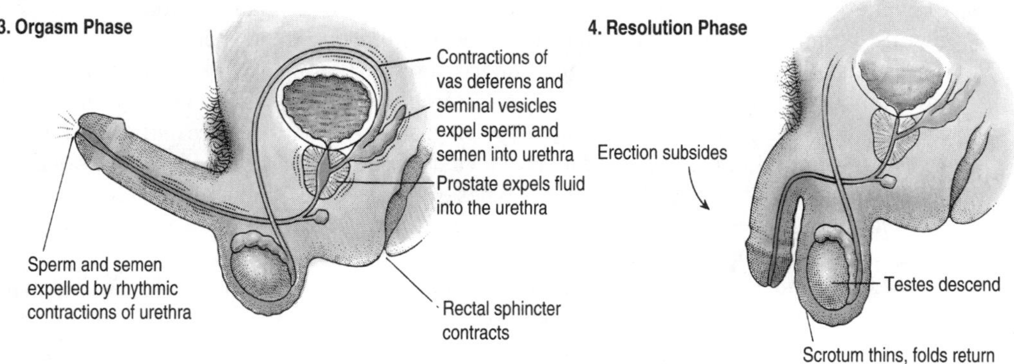
3. Orgasm Phase
Contractions of vas deferens and seminal vesicles expel sperm and semen into urethra
Prostate expels fluid into the urethra
Sperm and semen expelled by rhythmic contractions of urethra
Rectal sphincter contracts
4. Resolution Phase
Erection subsides
Testes descend
Scrotum thins, folds return

FIGURE 10.2 Male Genitals during the Phases of the Sexual Response Cycle

A leveling off of sexual arousal occurs during the *plateau phase,* with fewer dramatic changes than those experienced during the excitement phase. In women, the outer third of the vagina swells while the inner part expands. The clitoris withdraws beneath its hood, becoming shorter, and secretions from the Bartholin's glands appear. The labia minora deepen in color. In men, the penis may enlarge slightly more than in the excitement phase, and it turns a deep purple color. The testes elevate further, and the Cowper's glands secretes a small amount of fluid that appears at the tip of the penis. In both men and women, heart rate, blood pressure, and muscle tension increase slightly. Flushing of the skin is even more likely to occur in this phase than in the excitement phase.

The *orgasm phase* for both women and men consists of muscle contractions at 0.8-second intervals, releasing the tension that has built up during the first two phases. In women, between 3 and 15 contractions occur in the muscles that surround the vagina, and an additional 3 to 6 contractions may also occur, although these are weaker and slower. In men, orgasm occurs in two stages. In the first stage, seminal fluid collects in the urethral bulb due to muscle contractions of the vas deferens, seminal vesicles, and ejaculatory duct. In the second stage, semen is ejaculated from the body through the urethra due to a series of 3 or 4 muscle contractions at 0.8-second intervals, possibly followed by several additional, slower contractions. For both women and men, other spasmodic muscle movements occur for muscles in the abdominal region and throughout the body. Heart rate and blood pressure also peak in this phase.

In the *resolution phase,* the body returns to its normal prearousal level. In women, the clitoris, vagina, labia, nipples, and uterus all return to their normal sizes. In men, the penis loses its erection over a period of about a minute, and the testes and scrotum return to normal size. Both women's and men's skin returns to its normal, low level of flush. All of these responses are part of the decreased vasocongestion that occurs in this phase. The muscle tension has been dissipated during the orgasmic phase, and the decrease of vasocongestion returns to prearousal levels. This process may take as long as five minutes after experiencing orgasm, but for those who do not experience orgasm, return to prearousal functioning may take as long as an hour.

Not only did Masters and Johnson's research suggest that both women and men are similar in experiencing four stages of sexual response, but it also showed that women experience one type of orgasm. Freud hypothesized that women experience two types—clitoral and vaginal orgasm. He believed that girls experience clitoral orgasm during masturbation, beginning during early childhood, and that women are immature if they continue to require clitoral stimulation for orgasm. Freudian theory described women who experience orgasm through intercourse as healthier and more mature than women who have only clitoral orgasms. Masters and Johnson's results showed that women experience only one type of orgasm—a clitoral orgasm. Their data provided no evidence for different types of orgasms, thus refuting Freud's contention that two types of orgasm exist. Some women have clitoral orgasms during intercourse and some do not; intercourse may not provide sufficient clitoral stimulation to produce orgasm in some women.

Masters and Johnson's research has been both controversial and influential. As with other physiological processes, individual variations exist in whether stages are experienced, and Masters and Johnson ignored these variations (Tiefer, 1995). Their conceptualization has become so well-accepted that people who do not conform to these stages are open to being diagnosed with sexual dysfunctions. According to their findings, all people experience four phases of sexual response—excitement, plateau, orgasm, and resolution. Their research proclaimed similarities in sexual response for women and men, but it failed to address issues of individual differences. Their findings about the physiology of sexual response showed that women have one type of orgasm produced by clitoral stimulation, but they failed to test women who did not easily experience orgasm. The Masters and Johnson research has been valuable in measuring sexual physiology, but their research findings may not be as universal as they have contended.

Childhood Sexuality: Exploration and Abuse

As the Kinsey, Playboy Foundation, and NORC surveys have shown, sexuality begins before puberty. Even as infants, children take part in sexual exploration, and they are sometimes the victims of sexual abuse. Before birth, male fetuses have erections, infant boys have erections, and infant girls experience erections of the clitorises as well as vaginal lubrication (Masters, Johnson, & Kolodny, 1992). Infants touch their genitals as they explore their bodies, and this exploration teaches children that their bodies can produce pleasurable sensations. Preschool-aged children masturbate, sometimes several times a day.

Parents who notice their children's masturbation may accept it, or they may be surprised or shocked. Their attitude and their method of dealing with their children's masturbation can convey positive or negative messages about sexuality, and these messages can have a permanent impact (Masters et al., 1992). Parents who say, "That's not nice," or "Nice boys and girls don't do that," or who move their children's hands away from their genitals send negative messages about sexuality.

Another aspect of childhood sexuality that may make parents uncomfortable revolves around their children's questions about sexuality, pregnancy, and birth as well as their children's sexual exploration with other children. By age 4, most children have begun to form a concept of gender and the roles that women and men occupy. They know that women have babies and men do not, and pregnancy and birth are topics that stimulate curiosity and questions. Parents may feel embarrassed about giving straightforward descriptions and resort to analogies such as "Daddy plants a seed inside Mommy." Due to their concrete thought processes, children have the tendency to misinterpret these fanciful descriptions and analogies (Masters et al., 1992).

Children's tendency to invent and fill in the details of stories they do not fully understand means that concealing information will not keep children from knowing about sex. But what they "know" may be incorrect. Table 10.3 presents examples of children's descriptions of how babies come into being. As these explanations show, children have trouble understanding sex and birth, and even older children misunderstand some aspects of the process. Therefore, formulating appropriate answers to young children's questions about sex and birth requires a delicate balance of providing the correct amount of information without excessive details. Parents' discomfort with the topic of sex complicates these discussions.

"I would love for him to grow up to be a doctor, but I sure wish he'd wait another twenty years to specialize in gynecology," the mother of a 5-year-old said (Segal & Segal, 1993, p. 131). This mother humorously expressed her concern over her son and the neighbor's daughter, who were exploring each other's genitals. The Segals explained to the mother that her son's explorations were more curiosity than sexuality and that his behavior

TABLE 10.3 Examples of Children's Beliefs about Sex and Birth

How Do People Get Babies?

According to 3- to 5-year-olds:

"You go to the baby store and buy one."

"Mommy bought me in a shop."

"They grow inside. I don't know how it starts. It just grows."

"The babies are in the stomach. I already have a baby in my stomach.... It won't grow 'cause I'm little. When I'm big, then it can grow.... You have to be very careful because the baby may get loose in your stomach."

According to 4- to 6-year-olds:

"To get a baby to grow in your tummy, you just make it first. You put some eyes on it. Put the head on, and hair, some hair all curls. You make it with head stuff you find in the store that makes it for you."

"Maybe from people. They just put them in the envelope and fold them up and the mommy puts them in her 'gina and they just stay in there."

"From marrying people. They put seeds in their vaginas. The mommies open up their tummy, but sometimes they open up their vaginas. So the daddies, so they can put their eggs in them, and they can put the seeds in them."

According to 7- to 10-year-olds:

"Well, I first thought, when I was seven that all you have to do is get married. And then all you would have to do is read a book, and then you would have a baby."

"The sperm is like a baby frog. It swims into the penis and makes a little hole. It bites a hole in its little mouth and swims into the vagina."

"I don't know how they get the baby. Maybe some special germs."

"From the daddy. He has something that helps the mommy get the baby. Some sort of medicine. I don't know what it's called, but it's here. [She pointed to her crotch.] Well, it goes in to some sort of part, I think it's the vagina, and just fixes up and helps around there, and makes it have a baby."

"Well, I think, but I'm not sure, that the penis goes into the vagina and, well, I think it does something. I was thinking that it might touch something in a body, and then it starts growing a little sperm. Like it might touch some blood, or a blood vein or a bone, well doubtfully a bone, but something around the clitoris. Maybe the sperm comes out from that little thing, near the clitoris. It comes out and it starts. Then I think it might break off, come loose and break off and it stays in that one place, or goes up the stomach."

"I don't know much about it. Well, I know one thing. The man and the woman get together. And then they put a speck, then the man has his seed and the woman has an egg. They have to come together or else the baby, the egg won't really get hatched very well. The seed makes the egg grow. It's like plants. If you plant a seed, a flower will grow."

According to 11- and 12-year-olds:

"When the egg is fertilized it sort of comes to life. If you want to...the chemicals make it come to life. The sperm are injected to where the eggs are, and they just, I guess, coat them. There's some chemical in the sperms that activates another chemical in the egg, which starts the development of the baby."

"Sexual intercourse? Well, it should only be brought on by love, and it helps if you're married. And it's when the man and the woman come together, and the man sticks his penis into the lady's, near the womb, and then the egg that comes down through a little tube, down into the womb, is fertilized, and becomes a child."

SOURCE: From *The Flight of the Stork,* 1978, by Anne C. Bernstein, New York: Delacorte Press.

was normal. They advised this mother to set limits on her son's explorations and urged her not to be concerned about her son's curiosity about female genitals.

Punishing children for exploring their sexuality can convey the message that something is wrong with the genitals, giving negative messages about sexuality. Sexual explorations during preschool or elementary school are rarely harmful, but parental punishment can be, leaving a permanent impression that something is wrong with such activities (Masters et al., 1992). In addition, the double standard for sexual behavior starts during this age range; girls are warned about sexual exploration and sex play, and boys are allowed more freedom in their sexuality.

Parents may be unaware that sexual explorations during childhood include same-gender as well as other-gender sexual play (Masters et al., 1992). For example, parents are not aware of most sexual contact between siblings. The majority of such contact consists of examining the genitals and touching, and a low percentage of sibling sexual activity includes attempted or successful intercourse. Nonetheless, sexual activity between siblings qualifies as **incest**—sexual activity between family members. David Finkelhor (1980) reported that 15% of college women and 10% of college men recalled sexual experiences with their siblings. The majority of these college students did not believe that the experience had harmed them, but an important factor in this evaluation was the age difference between the two siblings; a large age difference was associated with a greater perception of harm.

Age has been a critical factor in defining sexual exploitation of children (Finkelhor, 1984). When sexual contact occurs between children who are close to the same age, this activity falls into the category of *exploration.* When a child has sexual contact with an adult or an adolescent at least 5 years older than the child, that activity falls into the category of *exploitation* or *sexual abuse.* Also included as abusive are sexual relationships between adolescents and adults whose age exceeds the adolescents' age by at least 10 years.

Incest is one form of sexually abusive relationships, but children can also be sexually abused by nonrelatives, including strangers and adults in positions of authority, such as neighbors, day-care workers, religious leaders, and teachers. The Kinsey et al. (1948, 1953) surveys included questions about childhood sexual experiences with adults, and his results revealed that 25% of girls and 10% of boys reported such contact. In over 50% of the cases, the activity consisted of an adult man exhibiting his genitals to the child. Kinsey also found that over half of the incidents involved adults whom the children did not know. Later research on the sexual abuse of children has confirmed the high percentage of abuse and the gender difference in rates of sexual abuse, but it has failed to confirm that most abusers are strangers.

Beginning in the 1970s, several groups of researchers attempted to determine the rate of sexual abuse of children. This research is even more difficult than other types of sex surveys. The honesty and memory problems that affect all surveys are more serious when adults are asked about sexual abuse during childhood; and honesty is a major problem when questioning adults about abuse they may have committed. Those who sexually abuse children are capable of convincing themselves that the relationships are "special" and have not harmed the child (Gilgun, 1995), which can lead them to distort their reports of the events.

Assessment of childhood sexual abuse has been conducted with a wide variety of people in different geographic locations using varying definitions of sexual abuse and several different research methods (Bagley & King, 1990). These variations resulted in differing percentages of people who reported being sexually abused as children, with percentages ranging from 11% to 40% for women and from 3% to 8.6% for men. Due to the sampling techniques in the various studies, these percentages might be underestimates; at least 15% of girls and 5% of boys are sexually abused during childhood or adolescence.

Despite the differences, the studies reviewed (Bagley & King, 1990) showed some commonalties: Girls were sexually abused more often than boys, and men were the instigators of abuse far more frequently than women. Both girls and boys are at risk during their entire childhoods and adolescence from family members, family friends, adult authority figures, and strangers, but the risk is not equal for all ages or from all adults. Table 10.4 shows the range of estimates and the characteristics of sexual abusers and victims.

Girls are not only more likely to be sexually abused, but they are also more likely to be abused at younger ages than boys. The preadolescence years are the riskiest age period for both, with girls between ages 10 and 11 years and boys between ages 11 and 12 years at the

TABLE 10.4 Summary of Offender and Victim Characteristics for Childhood Sexual Abuse

	Range of Estimated Occurrence	
Characteristic	Lowest	Highest
Girls abused while under age 16 (average age 10.2–10.7 years)	11%	40%
Girls who rated the experience negatively	66%	
Girls whose abuser was male	94%	100%
Boys abused while under age 16 (average age 11.2–12 years)	3%	8.6%
Boys who rated the experience negatively	38%	
Boys whose abuser was male	83%	84%
Children whose offender was a stranger	11%	51%
Children whose offender was a friend or an acquaintance	33%	49%
Children whose offender was a relative	14%	50%
Girls whose offender was a sibling	15%	
Boys whose offender was a sibling	10%	
Children whose offender was a biological parent	1%	6.8%
Girls whose offender was a stepfather	7.6%	17%
Children who had force or threats used against them	55%	
Children whose abuse consisted of exhibition	26%	28%
Children whose abuse consisted of being fondled	26%	40%
Children whose abuse consisted of forced fondling of offender	10%	14%
Children whose abuse consisted of intercourse	15%	18%

SOURCE: Based on *Child sexual abuse: The search for healing* by C. Bagley & K. King, 1990, London: Tavistock.

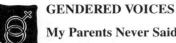

GENDERED VOICES

My Parents Never Said Anything Until…

"My parents never said anything to us about sexual abuse until my brother was molested," a teenager said. "Then our whole family talked sexual abuse. My brother had to tell us what happened, tell us what the person had done very explicitly. Maybe that wasn't a good thing for him to have to do, because he had to talk about it a lot, but we learned about what to be careful about. And they never said anything before he was molested.

"It was tough on the family, because the person who molested him was a cousin. He was about 4 or 5 years older than my brother, and our families don't speak to each other anymore. It was hard to know what to do, because the cousin had been molested when he was younger, so he was just repeating what happened to him. Should he be punished for doing what he had learned? My brother was still hurt, but it was difficult not to feel sorry for my teenage cousin.

"We went for counseling as a family, and I think it helped. I hear that it can be much worse to ignore it, because it won't go away if you don't talk about it. We talked about it afterward, but not before something happened."

highest risk. These ages represent the time during which the first victimization is most likely to occur. For many children, sexual abuse continues for years, often for as long as they remain in contact with their abusers.

Between 94% and 100% of those who abused girls were men, and around 84% of those who abused boys were men. Although abusers are sometimes strangers, more often these men are known to their victims as family members, family acquaintances, or as adult authority figures such as teachers, scout leaders, or religious leaders. Ethnic differences exist in sexual abuse for African American and European American women, and abusers tend to choose victims within their own ethnic group—in 81% of cases, ethnic backgrounds of victim and abuser matched (Wyatt, 1985).

Both female and male abusers exist, but the emphasis in research and therapy has been on boys and men as perpetrators and girls and women as victims. This emphasis is not entirely inappropriate, but not all abuse follows this pattern. Female–male abuse (female offender) occurs and differs from the male–female (male offender) pattern. Whereas male strangers represent approximately one-third of the cases of male abusers, almost all of female abusers are acquaintances of those whom they molest (Duncan & Williams, 1998). A common pattern among female perpetrators consists of babysitters molesting the children in their care (Johnson, 1989). In addition, female perpetrators are very likely to have themselves been the victims of abuse, most commonly by a family member.

The sparse research on female perpetrators and male victims has demonstrated that such abuse occurs, but some women victimize boys in the guise of initiating them into sexuality. These cases are rarely reported to authorities (Duncan & Williams, 1998; Sleek, 1994), making the proportion of male abusers seem higher than it actually is. The overwhelming focus on female victims and male perpetrators has left sexually abused men and sexually abusive women neglected in both research and treatment, but this situation is beginning to change.

Incest involving biological fathers and their daughters is not the most common type of sexual abuse; stepfathers are much more likely to force this type of relationship. Diana Russell (1986) found that 17% of stepdaughters were molested by their stepfathers, whereas only 2% of daughters were victims of sexual abuse by their biological fathers. Indeed, living with a stepfather is a major risk factor for sexual abuse. Other research (Finkelhor & Baron, 1986) came to similar conclusions. Living with a stepparent increased the risk for abuse, and this risk was proportionate for all ethnic and social class groupings. In addition, living apart from biological parents, or having a mother who was unavailable due to illness, handicap, or employment, increased the risk for abuse. Children whose parents had relationships filled with conflict and whose parents used harsh punishment as discipline were also at elevated risk for sexual abuse.

Cases of incest involving a father or father figure are the most serious and may have serious, long-term consequences, including difficulties in school and in personal relationships, sexual dysfunction, as well as alcohol and substance abuse (Heise et al., 1999). Some evidence exists for both the short-term and long-term effects of sexual abuse (Finkelhor, 1990; Heise et al., 1999). The short-term effects include fear, anxiety, depression, anger, and sexually inappropriate behavior. The long-term effects include anxiety, depression, poor self-concept, sexual adjustment problems, and substance abuse disorders. A review of sexually abused boys (Finkelhor, 1990) found that few gender differences exist between boys and girls who have been the victims of sexual abuse; both suffer similar negative effects from their victimization.

In one study (Herman, 1981), the fathers who committed incest tended to be traditional men who held unquestioned authority in their families and considered sexual activity with their daughters to be part of their right as the head of the family. Although this pattern of sexual abuse is not the most common, it suggests the underlying commonalty in child sexual abuse—power. Adults have social power and power in the family, and this power allows them to abuse children. The family structure usually grants more power to men than women, and this power differential may be an important reason why most perpetrators are male.

In summary, childhood sexuality is more active than most parents imagine; it begins during infancy when children explore and manipulate their own genitals and then progresses to curiosity about and exploration of others' genitals. Although parents may find these signals of sexuality distressing, they are normal. Sexual explorations during childhood are confined to activities with peers; when older adolescents or adults initiate sexual activity with children, abuse occurs. Various surveys have asked adults about their experiences of being molested as children, with the results indicating that at least 15% of women and 5% of men have been sexually abused as children. Girls are much more likely to be abused than boys, and men are much more likely than women to be abusers. There are few gender differences in short-term and long-term effects of childhood sexual abuse, which include anxiety, depression, and anger, as well as adult sexual and substance abuse problems.

Heterosexuality

Most people develop erotic or sexual interests that result in attraction to people of the other sex rather than people of the same sex. That is, most people develop a heterosexual, rather than a same-gender, **sexual orientation.** Signs of heterosexual erotic interest may begin during childhood, but sexual activity during childhood mainly takes the form of masturbation and exploratory play, which can be directed toward same- or other-gender children. Thus, children's sexuality often is not clearly heterosexual.

During late childhood and preadolescence, children seek the company of same-gender peers and avoid associating with other-gender peers (see Chapter 9). This gender segregation restricts the opportunities for heterosexual activity, but does not signal children's lack of interest in the other gender. Indeed, children often tease each other by announcing who "likes" whom and by threatening to kiss others who are unwilling (Thorne, 1993). Such games demonstrate an awareness of heterosexuality and an early knowledge of gender roles in heterosexual interactions.

During Adolescence

Although a distressing number of children are introduced to sexuality through force or coercion, adolescence is the period during which most people explore sexuality. These explorations consist of formal and far more informal education. The traditional view in the United States and many other societies has situated sexuality within marriage, which discourages adolescent sexual activity. These cultures also send many messages about sex and its pleasures, which pose problems for adolescents who see the promised joys of sex, but who are forbidden to participate.

These messages are not equal for girls and boys: Girls receive many more messages to beware of sex than do boys (Baldwin & Baldwin, 1997). Although a double standard of sexual behavior is sharply apparent in adolescent sexuality, neither boys nor girls experience adequate sexuality education (Fine, 1988; McCormick, 1994; Whatley, 1990). Publicity about teen pregnancy, date rape, and sexual exploitation conveys the impression that sexuality is dangerous, especially for young women, and this danger has been the focus of most sex education. Rather than emphasizing the pleasures of sex and how to develop successful sexual relationships, most sex education for teenagers focuses on abstinence as the best choice and pregnancy, sexually transmitted diseases, and vulnerability to rape as the alternatives.

This emphasis appears to be successful in conveying a sense of sexual vulnerability in young women; feelings of sexual vulnerability develop during adolescence (Burt & Estep, 1981). The men in this study expressed few feelings of sexual vulnerability compared to the women, but boys get negative images of male sexuality—that men are aggressive, uncaring lovers who focus on their partners' appearance and avoid commitment.

Although adolescents are exposed to sex education that does not help them develop healthy sexuality, they begin sexual exploration through several avenues, one of which is dating. A small percentage (2 to 17%) of adolescents in one study (Roscoe, Diana, & Brooks, 1987) listed sex as the motivation for dating. For the 6th graders, 11th graders, and college students, boys listed sex as a more important reason for dating than did girls, reflecting differential interests, or the double standard.

First intercourse has been a developmental milestone that traditionally has been associated with marriage. Kinsey's surveys during the 1930s and 1940s revealed that a majority of young men had intercourse before marriage. The substantially smaller percentage of young women who had intercourse before marriage reflected the double standard, but this discrepancy has decreased over the past 60 years (Brooks-Gunn & Furstenberg, 1989). In 1938, approximately 7% of European American girls had intercourse by age 16 years, but by the 1980s, the percentage had risen to 44%. Information does not exist to make comparisons for boys, but estimates suggest that boys were more sexually active than girls from the 1940s to the 1960s, with between one-third and two-thirds of boys having intercourse

GENDERED VOICES

Sex De-Education

"A shiver goes up my spine remembering my 'sex education' experience in the 6th grade. Now, I don't know if the teacher had some problems with sexuality in general, or if perhaps it was part of her job, but I'll never forget the fear of sex and sexual contact she put into about 95%, if not all, of the young girls in that class.

The majority of the information was in reference to reproduction and sexually transmitted diseases. My teacher brought in this old, old medical book and proceeded to show these pictures of people with severe stage STDs. These pictures showed people with ulcerated sores all over their bodies; parts of their flesh were falling and, and she said, 'This is what happens to people who have sex when they're not married.' It was disgusting, not to mention terrifying.

As if that wasn't bad enough, when she taught the section on the male genitalia, she brought another visual aid. She brought in a rubber replica of a male penis and testicles, and the thing was HUGE and she represented it as actual size. I've never heard so many young girls gasp in terror at the same time in my life. She was very quick to relay how painful sex with a man was. I never understood her motivation. She was married with three kids. Maybe her husband was that big, but it seems unlikely.

"To this day, I still wonder how many of these young girls were traumatized by their 'sex education' and how that affected their first sexual encounter with a man. I've also wondered what techniques were used to teach the boys in our school."

as teenagers. The difference diminished during the 1970s and 1980s. By age 18 years, 60% of young men have had intercourse, and by age 19 years, the percentage was similar for young women.

The average age of first intercourse now varies by gender only by a few months: 16.6 years for boys and 17.2 years for girls (Upchurch, Levy-Storms, Sucoff, & Aneshensel, 1998). Age of first intercourse shows more variation across ethnic backgrounds in the United States, however. A study of an ethnically diverse sample of adolescents from the Los Angeles area (Upchurch, et al., 1998) revealed a lower age of first sexual activity for African American adolescents (15.8 years), and a higher age for Asian American (18.1 years) than for White (16.6 years) or Hispanic American (17.0 years) adolescents. An analysis of the family indicated an influence: Adolescents living in two-parent families tended to have a higher age of first intercourse than those in other living arrangements.

The reasons for girls' and boys' decisions to have sex often differ. For boys, having sex is not only a means to pleasure, but also to social prestige (Baldwin & Baldwin, 1997). "For teenage boys, their first sexual experience may be the primary symbol of manhood—a rite of passage" (Stark, 1989, p. 12). Boys feel pressure from their peers to "score," and their sharing the stories are a way to gain admiration from their peers. The pressure boys experience may be conveyed to the girls they date by demands for sex. Boys may have sex to prove a point. Girls may refuse sex to prove a point, or they may give in to this pressure and have sex.

Sharon Thompson (1999) interviewed adolescent girls about their first sexual experiences, and found that girls' stories fell into two groups. Girls in the first group were unhappy with their first sexual experience and had sex because of pressure. They had not planned or wanted to have sex, and they tended to describe it as something that "just happened," depersonalizing the experience and absolving responsibility. Their stories were filled with pain and regret, but with little desire. Girls who told stories of wanting sex expressed different views. These girls grew up in homes with positive attitudes about sex, and the girls were knowledgeable and prepared. Having sex was a decision they clearly made, often with anticipation and desire.

Women who readily consent to sex are at risk for being considered promiscuous, and that potential consequence may influence the decision to say "No." Indeed, such refusals may be social rather than personal; women feel desire, but openly acknowledging that desire may lead to many unkind labels. Being labeled "easy" was one reason that women showed token resistance to sexual activity (Muehlenhard & Hollabaugh, 1988). That is, women sometimes said no when they were willing to have intercourse and had every intention of later saying yes. The double standard encourages women to deny their sexuality, and women's refusals provide them with a way to appear to resist and also a way to exert power in their relationships by withholding sex. The majority of women who say No mean what they say, but the double standard pressures women to be insincere about their desire. Communication about sex is not always honest.

Such dishonesty might relate to the high incidence of **date rape** or **acquaintance rape,** the forced sexual activity between people who are dating or otherwise acquainted. If No is not the final answer, what level of persuasion is permissible? Chapter 8 discussed rape as an aggressive crime disproportionately committed by men. Most people picture rape as an attack by a stranger, but the majority of rapes and other acts involving forced or coerced sex occur between acquaintances. Mary Koss and her colleagues (1987) surveyed college students about sexual activities and found that 54% of the young women in the survey claimed to have been the victims of some type of coerced or forced sexual activity at some time during their lives, and over 15% had been raped. Questioning a more representative group of women, the NORC survey (Laumann et al., 1994) found that 22% of women said that they had been forced to do something sexually by a man. Of these women, 46% said that they were in love with the man and another 22% said that they knew the man well who forced them. As this study shows, women are less likely to report sexual assaults if they know (and especially if they are in love with) the perpetrator, leading to an underrepresentation in crime statistics of the incidence of rape by acquaintances.

Miscommunication may be a factor in acquaintance rape. The dynamics of sexual negotiation are complex, but the acceptability of forced sex is an important factor in the prevalence of acquaintance rape. Some men consider forced sex acceptable, at least under some conditions (Muehlenhard, Friedman, & Thomas, 1985). Men with more traditional attitudes toward women rated date rape as acceptable under a wider variety of conditions than did men with nontraditional attitudes. If the woman asked the man out, the man paid the expenses of the date, and the woman agreed to go to his apartment, men found rape more justifiable than if the date followed another script. Women, however, may be unaware of these conditions and may not feel that they owe sex to their partners. Thus, dating partners follow complex, often unexpressed, and possibly unshared rules about sexual activities on dates. Their assumptions about the right to have sex may make men more likely to force women into the sex they believe they deserve—that is, to commit date rape. When women offer insincere refusals, they are contributing to men's reluctance to believe that the answer is really no.

Another issue for adolescent sexuality is concern over pregnancy. This anxiety affects girls more than boys. Although some pregnancy education is aimed at teenage boys, most is directed at girls and emphasizes the danger of sex. The concern is not without reason;

approximately 1 million teenage girls become pregnant each year in the United States (Centers for Disease Control and Prevention, 2000). Pregnancy during adolescence is associated with a number of negative factors, including a decrease in life satisfaction (McCabe & Cummins, 1998). Teenage boys are also involved in these pregnancies, but a substantial number of the fathers are at least 5 years older than their teenage partners (Lindberg, Sonenstein, Ku, & Martinez, 1997). The percentage of older partners was higher for younger girls (ages 11 to 12), and not surprisingly, these partnerships tended to produce more problems for these young girls (Leitenberg & Saltzman, 2000). Therefore, some teen pregnancies appear to involve sexual relationships that fit into the category of exploitation or abuse.

The recent emphasis on condom use as a method of contraception and also as a control for sexually transmitted diseases should signal a shift in the balance of responsibility for birth control from women to men. However, merely emphasizing condom use may not have prompted any change in responsibility. Gail Wyatt (1994) described a number of interventions for risky sexual behaviors in which women were the targets for change, but men's behaviors were the risk. These programs have often targeted African American and Hispanic American women to encourage them to avoid pregnancy or decrease their risk of sexually transmitted diseases. For example, some programs have encouraged women to be responsible for condom use to prevent HIV infection from male partners, and these programs tend to have disappointing success rates. Wyatt pointed out that Black women's resistance to these programs is reasonable: Why should they be the targets of these programs when men's behavior is the problem?

In summary, as adolescent sexuality becomes increasingly oriented toward heterosexual encounters, some gender differences appear. Girls receive messages of danger and vulnerability rather than pleasure, and boys receive messages about how pleasurable sex is, but also hear negative information about the damage their sexuality can produce. Sex education may not meet the needs of either girls or boys. Greater numbers of adolescent boys tend to have intercourse and have it at earlier ages than adolescent girls, but this gender difference has diminished over the past 50 years. Now the percentages of adolescent girls and boys having intercourse at each age are similar, as is the average age of first intercourse. Although these changes signal a decline of the double standard, sex may have a different meaning for boys and girls. Although peer pressure is a factor for both, boys use sex as proof of their masculinity, whereas validation of their femininity is not a common reason for girls to have sex.

During Adulthood

Traditionally, marriage has not only been a major transition, but also the primary context within which adult sexuality appears, often in the form of vaginal intercourse. The more recent studies of college students and surveys with more representative samples have indicated that the standards for sexual behavior have changed. Lower ages of first intercourse, increases in sexual activity among female adolescents, and increases in the acceptability of a variety of sexual activities suggest that more frequent and more varied sexual behaviors are now accepted for both women and men. Sexuality has become an important part of life for young adults, regardless of their marital status (McCabe & Cummins, 1998).

One specialized survey of Canadian college students (Netting, 1992) found evidence of three styles of sexuality among these young adults—celibacy, monogamy, and free experimentation. Although these styles can apply to same-gender sexuality, this survey concentrated on heterosexual college students. These styles represent very different choices, but "the only value shared almost universally was the right to choose" (p. 970).

Celibacy, refraining from sexual activity, was a fairly popular choice; about one-third of the students were in this category. This group included students who had never had intercourse plus those who had had no sexual partners for the previous year. A similar percentage of men and women were celibate, but for different reasons. For the women, celibacy was most often a choice; their most common reason for remaining celibate was that they were waiting for love. For the men, celibacy was often not a matter of choice—their most common reason was that they were waiting for an opportunity to have sex. A similar but smaller percentage of both men and women said that they remained celibate because of moral or religious reasons, but few students said that they were waiting for marriage to have sex.

Monogamy means having only one sexual partner in a committed love relationship. This style of relationship was the most popular alternative, being the choice for 61% of the women and 37% of the men. This choice represents the ideal for many, but is the actual lifestyle for fewer participants. Some endorsed monogamy but were celibate and waiting for a relationship; others practiced **serial monogamy,** in which a person has relationships with a series of partners, one at a time; and still others endorsed monogamy but "cheated" by having sex with other partners. Thus, many of these students subscribed to the ideal of monogamy without adhering to the practice of having one sexual partner for life. The percentage of men who had or wanted a monogamous relationship was lower than the percentage of women.

The students who chose the free experimentation style valued sexual freedom and wanted to participate in a variety of sexual relationships. Counting those who had more than one partner during their lives, about half the students were in this category. Some of these young adults were in a committed relationship with one partner at the time of the study, but believed in having different partners on the way to a monogamous relationship. More students believed in than practiced free sexual expression, but some in this group had many sexual partners and fit the description of experimenting freely with their sexuality. More men than women fit this pattern—28% of men but only 5% of women said that they were sexually active but not monogamous. Table 10.5 summarizes the styles of sexuality among the college students in this study.

All of the styles that appeared in this Canadian study are reflective of adult sexuality in Canada, the United States, and other western countries. Indeed, the western concepts of love and sex are spreading to other parts of the world (Hatfield & Rapson, 1996), making these patterns of sexual behavior more similar throughout the world than in the past. Some adults are celibate, some are monogamous, and others have many sexual partners and freely experiment with sexuality. In addition, the gender differences that appeared in the survey of Canadian students also are reflective of adult heterosexuality, though gender differences in attitudes and behavior can provide obstacles in forming and maintaining sexual relationships.

According to the NORC survey (Laumann et al., 1994), celibacy described the sexuality of about 9.8% of men and 13.6% of women in the year prior to the survey. Lifelong celibacy is, however, unusual—only 2.9% said they never had a sex partner. Those who are ill or whose partners have died are especially likely to be celibate, and both circumstances are associated with increasing age. Thus, celibacy increases sharply after age 60. Older women's longer life expectancy makes them far more likely to be celibate than men of the same age.

TABLE 10.5 Styles of Sexuality among College Students

Style Chosen	Percentage Women	Percentage Men	Reason for Choice
Celibacy	36%	32%	Women were waiting for love; men were waiting for an opportunity
Monogamy	61	37	Considered monogamy the ideal type of sexuality
	48	34	Were currently monogamous
	25	19	Had had only one partner during their lives
Free expression	14	33	Valued freedom of expression, including expression of sexuality
	5	28	Sexually active but not currently monogamous

Monogamy is most common for married couples. Indeed, 93.7% of married couples in the NORC survey were monogamous in the year prior to the study (Laumann et al., 1994). Unmarried cohabiting heterosexual partners (76.7%), those who had never been married and were not cohabiting (38%), and those who were divorced or separated (40.5%) were less likely to be monogamous.

The sexual attitudes and behaviors of women and men show few differences, but those few differences may have larger implications for heterosexuality, including the choices of monogamy or free experimentation. One way to understand these gender differences is through the framework of script theory (Simon & Gagnon, 1986). This view proposes that sexual behavior follows a sequentially organized set of steps, and that men and women learn and internalize somewhat different scripts. The sequence of events occurring during a couple's first intercourse are so tightly scripted that college students can arrange the sequence from a set of randomly organized statements (Geer & Broussard, 1990), demonstrating that young adults know the scripts very well.

The differences between male and female scripts can throw couples into conflict. One of the large gender differences in sexuality is in the acceptability of casual sex, with men being more acceptant than women (Oliver & Hyde, 1993). The script approach helps in understanding this gender difference and its implications. Women are encouraged to associate sex with love, and they come to believe that sex should occur in the context of a committed relationship, whereas the script for men is not so relationship centered (McCormick, 1994). Thus, sex may have different meanings for women and men.

The implications of this difference can be large, forming areas of conflict for couples. For women, the association between commitment and sex leads them to believe that commitment should exist before having sex, but men may not share these requirements or expectations. These differing beliefs lead to differences in expectations about the timing of intercourse in a relationship (Cohen & Shotland, 1996). As predicted, men expected sex after significantly fewer dates (9 to 11) than women did (15 to 18). These differing expectations could be a source of conflict if men begin to pressure women to have sex and the women do not feel ready, or if women refuse sex when men believe that their relationship warrants it.

The difference in acceptability of casual sex can also have an impact on sex outside the primary relationship. With less acceptant attitudes, women are more likely to be monogamous than men, and they are more likely to consider sex outside the relationship as violations of trust or as betrayals by their partners. People perceive "cheating" differently for women and men (Sprecher, Regan, & McKinney, 1998). When the man is the cheating partner, people predict that he will not necessarily leave his wife for his lover, but people see women's extramarital sex as more indicative of the end of the relationship. Thus, the gender difference in the acceptability of casual sex affects extramarital sex and people's beliefs about what affairs imply.

The other large gender difference in sexuality is the frequency of masturbation (Oliver & Hyde, 1993), with men masturbating more often than women. At first, any relationship between masturbation and partnered sex may not seem apparent, but Janet Hyde (1996) has explained a connection. She proposed that women's lower frequency and greater guilt concerning masturbation results in less familiarity with their bodies and less certain knowledge of how to reach orgasm. Women are less likely to experience orgasm during intercourse than are men, and this difference causes distress in many couples. Hyde pointed out that many sex therapists direct women who are having orgasmic difficulties to masturbate, thus demonstrating to them the importance of masturbation. She hypothesized that women's lower frequency of masturbation may lay the foundation for women to have difficulties in reaching orgasm during heterosexual sex.

Other gender differences may also have some relationship to the problems that heterosexual couples face. One issue is desire for and frequency of intercourse. The double standard proposes that women will be less interested in sex because they are less sexual creatures than men, and evolutionary psychology (Buss, 1994, 1996) holds that women must be more sexually selective than men in order to choose mates who will be able to provide for offspring. These two views agree that women are less sexual but disagree over the reason. Determining a social or biological explanation is very difficult because society influences everyone. And because many societies control women's sexuality, any interpretation of "natural" sexuality is impossible.

Sarah Blaffer Hrdy (1981, 1986) criticized the view that women are less sexual than men, which she called the Myth of the Coy Female, by reporting on females unaffected by cultural expectations and the double standard—nonhuman primates. She argued that male scientists who have seen female reluctance to engage in sex have been influenced by the double standard and have projected these human differences onto nonhuman primates.

According to Hrdy, the sexual behavior of nonhuman animals varies from species to species. The females of some species, such as baboons and chimpanzees, initiate multiple, brief sexual relationships and show no coy reluctance to engage in sex, whereas the females of other species, such as blue monkeys and redtail monkeys, are very selective about their mating habits. Their selectivity might appear coy. Hrdy argued that any tendency to see patterns similar to human sexual behavior in the behavior of other species tells more about the human observer than about the observed species.

Women's lower interest in sex may be related to accepting of the double standard for themselves, another difference revealed by meta-analysis (Oliver & Hyde, 1993). An alternative explanation comes from script theory, which suggests that women have internalized the cultural view that their sexuality is weaker. If women believe that they are or should be less sexual, they may behave accordingly and become less sexual. A meta-analysis of attitudes toward sexuality (Oliver & Hyde, 1993) showed that women accepted the double standard more strongly and felt more guilt over sex than men did, which is consistent with this interpretation. Masters and Johnson (1966) argued that women could be just as, or even more, sexual than men if women were free to express their sexuality and to participate in the activities that gave them sexual pleasure. Rather than loosening the constraints on female sexuality, however, Masters and Johnson's research may have added to these restrictions by prescribing that women should be as sexual as men and that the sexuality of the two genders should be similar (Tavris, 1992).

Is sexuality very different for women and men? Gender differences in sexual behavior have decreased over time since the older studies were done, suggesting that both female and male sexuality are subject to change and are influenced by social standards. During the Victorian era, women were presumed to be less sexual than men, and so they became. In our sexualized modern culture, women are portrayed as being more sexual than in the past but still less so than men, and so they have become. Sexuality is created by each culture and shows enormous differences in those cultures. Thus, women and men exhibit a wide variety of sexual behaviors depending on their physiologies, cultures, personal backgrounds, and personal expectations. Carol Tavris (1992, p. 245) summarized heterosexuality by saying, "The question is not whether women are more or less sexual than men. (The answer to that is yes, no, both, and sometimes.) The questions are: What are the conditions that allow women and men to enjoy sex in safety, with self-confidence, and in a spirit of delight? And how do we get there?"

Homosexuality

Some people develop erotic attraction toward people of the same gender and choose to engage in same-gender sexual activities. For years, psychologists failed to make a distinction between *gender role,* the social behaviors associated with one or the other gender, and *sexual orientation,* the erotic attraction to members of one or the other gender (or to both). Psychologists confused gender role and sexual orientation, when in fact the two are separate constructs (Constantinople, 1973; Lewin, 1984a, 1984b). This conceptualization of same-gender sexual orientation as an inversion of gender role was usually not productive, and a separation of gender role and sexual orientation has clarified the process of measuring masculinity and femininity and demonstrated that same-gender sexual orientation has a far from perfect relationship to these traits. That is, men who are erotically attracted to other men are not necessarily feminine in appearance or behavior, and women who find other women sexually attractive are not necessarily more masculine than other women.

The number of people with same-gender sexual interests, behavior patterns, and identities constitute a minority, but estimates vary on how small a minority. Most of the variation in estimates can be explained according to the definitions that the researchers have used. Is sexual attraction to those of the same gender sufficient? Are persons lesbian or gay if they have engaged in sexual activity with persons of the same gender at any time during their lives? Does having sex primarily or exclusively with members of one's own gender define homosexuality? Or must people identify themselves as gay or lesbian? These varying criteria produce different estimates.

Kinsey and his colleagues (1948) found that 37% of the men said that they had engaged in male–male sexual activity at some time during their lives. When asked the equivalent

GENDERED VOICES

Treated Like a Gender Traitor

"When I came out as gay, I got a lot of homophobia reactions" a college student in his 20s said. "Men were especially bad. Their reactions weren't exactly fear, although they were nervous. And it wasn't hatred. It was more like resentment. I wasn't a real man anymore and like I was some kind of traitor to the male gender."

question, 28% of women reported at least one female–female sexual experience during their lifetimes (Kinsey et al., 1953). Therefore, a substantial number of both men and women who participated in the Kinsey surveys reported sexual experiences with members of their own gender, but most did not engage in such relationships as the primary form of sexuality throughout their lives. About 13% of the men and about 7% of the women Kinsey's surveys identified themselves as primarily gay or lesbian, but this estimate has been controversial (Jones, 1998).

Other surveys have yielded lower estimates and have explored sexual orientation by asking different questions about attraction and behavior. Table 10.6 presents a comparison of the various measures of homosexuality for several studies, one of which questioned people in three countries. As this table reveals, the different measures (and cultures) show variations in the percentage of people who might be classified as gay or lesbian. Thus, same-gender sexual orientation is complex, and estimates depend on whether researchers ask about attraction or behaviors as well as the frequency of behavior and the age of respondents.

Attitudes toward same-gender sexuality vary from culture to culture, and some cultures have positive, acceptant attitudes. Among tribal societies in Africa, 64% accept same-gender sex, at least for some members of the tribe (Hatfield & Rapson, 1996). In ancient Greece, men (but not women) were free to engage in same-sex love affairs. European and North American societies came to disapprove of same-gender sexuality and to impose harsh social and legal penalties for such activities. During the 20th century, experts began to use the term *homosexuals,* which made sexuality the defining characteristic of the person.

The identification of persons exclusively with their sexuality allowed for a coalescing of negative attitudes:

> *According to many church leaders, homosexuals are sinners; according to the law, they are criminals. Mental health professionals until recently have viewed homosexuality as pathological.... Although these perspectives differ and are at points mutually exclusive, the underlying message is clear: Homosexuality is bad and shameful, to be feared and suppressed. (de Monteflores & Schultz, 1978, p. 59)*

This statement represents not only the current view in many (but not all) places in the world, but also attitudes from recent history. Homosexual activity has been condemned and suppressed, making the choice to express sexual feelings toward members of one's own sex difficult.

The social stigma associated with acquired immune deficiency syndrome (AIDS) has been an additional difficulty for gay men. During the early years of the epidemic, the vast

TABLE 10.6 Differing Estimates of Same-Gender Attraction and Behavior

	Percent	
Study	Men	Women
Kinsey et al. (1948, 1953)		
At least one same-gender sexual experience	37	28
Primarily or exclusively same-gender sex	13	7
Janus and Janus (1993)		
At least one same-gender sexual experience	22	17
Primarily same-gender sex	4	2
Laumann et al. (1994, NORC survey)		
Same-gender desires or experiences	10.1	8.6
Done anything sexual with same-gender partner	9.1	4.3
Same-gender sex partner since puberty	7.1	3.8
Same-gender sex partner in past year	2.7	1.3
Attracted to same-gender individuals	7.7	7.5
Self-identified as gay or lesbian	2.8	1.4
Sell, Wells, and Wypij (1995)		
United States		
Same-gender attraction but no activity	8.7	11.1
Same-gender sexual activity since age 15	6.2	3.6
United Kingdom		
Same-gender attraction but no activity	7.9	8.6
Same-gender sexual activity since age 15	4.5	2.1
France		
Same-gender attraction but no activity	8.5	11.7
Same-gender sexual activity since age 15	10.7	3.3

majority of those in North America infected with the human immunodeficiency virus (HIV), which causes AIDS, were gay men and intravenous drug users. A common perception developed that gay men carried AIDS, and that any type of association with them was dangerous (see "According to the Media/According to the Research"). This perception was and is, of course, incorrect. Most gay men are not infected with HIV, and most of the people in the world who are infected with HIV are heterosexual. Transmission of the HIV infection requires close contact with bodily fluids, such as blood or semen; casual contact will not transmit this infection.

Although many people already disliked and even feared gays, the association of gay men with the HIV infection fueled a growing homophobia, which has led to increased job and housing discrimination and even increased physical attacks. The widespread prejudice against gay men and lesbians has implications for many aspects of the lives of those who identify themselves as either. In addition, gays and lesbians must contend with identity issues concerning their sexual orientation. Many feel the pressure to be heterosexual, and many people consider sexual orientation a choice, putting gays and lesbians into the position to defend their stigmatized "choice." The changeability of sexual orientation has not been established. Indeed, the basis for the development of sexual orientation—either homosexual or heterosexual—remains elusive. This question is the center of a heated controversy: Is sexual orientation the result of biological or environmental factors, or some mixture of the two?

Early biological theories of sexual orientation focused on genetics and hormones, but research failed to confirm any simple relationship between sexual orientation and either genetic background or hormonal levels. Both genetics and hormone levels may exert an influence, but in complex ways that involve prenatal hormone levels and their influence on the developing brain (Breedlove, 1994; Money, 1987). The brains of women and men show some differences, including a difference in size of the third interstitial nuclei of the anterior hypothalamus. This structure is larger in men than in women, and in 1991, Simon LeVay proposed that this structure was smaller in gay men than in heterosexual men.

LeVay studied the brains of three groups: gay men (all of whom had died of AIDS), heterosexual men (fewer than half of whom had died of AIDS), and heterosexual women (only one of whom had died of AIDS). He found that the third interstitial nucleus of the anterior hypothalamus was on the average twice as large in the heterosexual men as in the gay men. LeVay claimed that he had found a biological basis for male–male sexual interest, but the differences in cause of death for the three groups may have biased the results. That is, the people in LeVay's three groups died of different causes, making them different in a way other than their sexual orientation. This bias weakens the study and casts doubt on his conclusions. In addition, these results have not yet been replicated (Bohan, 1996), raising additional doubts.

LeVay's evidence produced a great deal of controversy. The notion that sexual orientation might be traced to some biological difference fits into an essentialist view of sexual behavior, and essentialists hold that a biological basis places behavior beyond personal choice. Many people who want to restrict same-gender sexual activity want to believe that such behavior is a choice so that those who have made this choice can change their sexual behavior or be blamed for failing to do so. Members of the gay community have viewed LeVay's research with ambivalence (LeVay, 1996), with many agreeing that they feel as though their sexual orientation is innate, but disputing that their sexuality is a problem that should be changed. Rather, they see their sexuality as a difference to be accepted. Accepting that difference is a major issue for those adolescents who feel attracted to members of their own gender.

During Adolescence

Adolescence is a time of sexual exploration, and adolescent sexual activity has become more common and more accepted over the past 40 years—for heterosexual couples. Despite the increased opportunities for same-gender sex offered by the gender segregation during childhood and adolescence, the great majority of these contacts have no sexual connotations. These opportunities, however, may account for the larger number of people who have engaged in same-gender sexuality as adolescents but not as adults. Indeed, most of the people who have same-gender sexual experiences do so as part of adolescent experimentation and not as the beginning of a gay or lesbian sexual identity. However, some adolescents who are attracted to persons of the same gender do not act on these desires during adolescence (Savin-Williams, 1995). Therefore, sexual orientation and sexual activity during adolescence do not correspond completely to sexual identity or to sexual activity during adulthood.

ACCORDING TO THE MEDIA...

The People Who Die from AIDS Are Gay, White, and Male

On television, people who are HIV-positive are portrayed disproportionately as "the lonely gay White male dying of AIDS" (Hart, 1999, p. 201). In several episodes of the television series *Beverly Hills, 90210,* a character named Jimmy embodied all these stereotypical characteristics—a lonely gay White man who died of AIDS. This character became part of the show when Kelly Taylor, one of the show's major characters, began working in a hospice as part of her college work in psychology. The character of Jimmy was in his late 20s or early 30s, attractive, articulate, and sympathetic. Despite appearing healthy, Jimmy was in the final stages of AIDS and died after three episodes.

In the course of the developing friendship between Jimmy and Kelly, Jimmy is injured and Kelly gets his blood on her, setting off fears of HIV infection, prompting HIV testing and the trauma involved with this process, and causing Kelly to avoid Jimmy. As the physician in the episode correctly pointed out, intact skin is an effective barrier, and exposure to Jimmy's blood is not a big risk for HIV infection. Kelly's testing for HIV presented an opportunity to examine her risky behavior—a variety of sexual partners and a sexual relationship with someone involved with drugs. Despite her risky behavior, Kelly was not HIV positive, and despite his monogamous relationship with a longtime partner, Jimmy was dying of AIDS. In the last episode with Jimmy, he attended religious services and reconciled with his family. He was active and outgoing but died suddenly. These elements perpetuate stereotypical and inaccurate information about persons with AIDS (Hart, 1999).

Some gays and lesbians say they knew that they were different even before adolescence, but many of them have tried to develop heterosexual interests and fit into this accepted pattern of sexuality (Zera, 1992). Some may succeed, but it is more common for someone identified as heterosexual during adolescence and young adulthood to adopt a gay or lesbian identity than for a gay or lesbian adolescent to adopt a heterosexual orientation (LeVay, 1996). Rather than reflecting a change in sexual orientation, this trend probably occurs as part of developing a gay or lesbian identity.

The acceptance of same-gender attraction is a major challenge for gay adolescents. They often struggle with feelings that something is wrong with them, and self-esteem may be a problem. Self-acceptance is different (and often comes more easily) than revealing one's same-gender sexual orientation or behavior to family and friends. **Coming out** is the process of personally recognizing and publicly acknowledging one's gay or lesbian orientation to others (Bohan, 1996). The term originated with the phrase "coming out of the

ACCORDING TO THE RESEARCH...

An Increasing Number of AIDS Cases Are Ethnic Minorities and Women

Jimmy, the lonely gay White male dying of AIDS in *Beverly Hills, 90210,* is an accurate portrayal of a *decreasing* number of people who are HIV positive. As the lonely gay White male dying of AIDS, Jimmy represented the stereotypical person with AIDS, but each feature of that stereotypical portrayal is increasingly inaccurate.

The HIV epidemic among men who have sex with men represents the largest number of AIDS cases in the United States, but that number has sharply declined (U.S. Bureau of the Census, 1999). The spread of HIV infection among gay men has slowed the most dramatically of all the modes of transmission. The portrayal of Jimmy as involved in a long-term monogamous relationship would make his infection less likely, and this portrayal may be a case of heterosexism—the person who is afflicted with AIDS is the gay man rather than the heterosexual female character (despite her riskier sexual behavior). Indeed, the transmission of HIV through heterosexual sex is the mode of transmission that has increased most sharply in recent years.

Another biased feature of the presentation of Jimmy was the absence of his longtime partner as Jimmy was dying. Jimmy was in the hospice, alone until he is befriended by Kelly, who avoids him when she is faced with the thought that she may have been infected through her contact with him. Kelly avoids Jimmy, leaving him once more alone. This isolation of persons with AIDS is not accurate. Most are not abandoned by their partners or families.

The decision to portray the person with AIDS as White was also increasingly inaccurate (Hart, 1999). Minority ethnic groups are disproportionately represented among those who are HIV positive: 43% of AIDS cases are African Americans, 36% are European Americans, and 20% are Hispanic Americans (Brannon & Feist, 2000). The infection rate for ethnic minorities is increasing.

Another inaccuracy in the television depiction of AIDS was Jimmy's apparent health and vitality. People with advanced AIDS neither look nor feel healthy. Almost all experience severe weight loss, and the causes of death include a variety of infections that occur because of the loss of immune function. In the early stages of HIV infection, people appear healthy and may feel well. The improvements in drug therapy can prolong this period of healthy functioning, but these possibilities did not apply to Jimmy, who died in the third episode.

Therefore, persons with AIDS can be attractive, articulate, and sympathetic, but they are less likely to be alone, gay, White, and male than during the early years of the AIDS epidemic. As that epidemic progresses in the United States, people who are HIV positive are increasingly likely to be heterosexual, ethnic minority members, and female.

closet," referring to the hidden (closeted) nature of sexuality for many gays and lesbians. Thus, coming out is a positive affirmation of sexuality. This process may be part of adolescent development, or it may occur at any time during adulthood.

Coming out may include a public acknowledgment of sexual orientation, or the revelation may be limited to only friends and family. Parents may be acceptant and supportive, or they may be angry and have trouble accommodating the sexual orientation of this child (Bohan, 1996; Zera, 1992). In addition, friends may react negatively to coming out, and peer verbal or physical attacks are not unusual (Savin-Williams, 1995). Thus, gay and lesbian adolescents may be estranged from family and peers, and they are at increased risk for home- and school-related problems.

For adults, coming out often includes acceptance into the gay community. For adolescents, such acceptance is not as easy, because activities in the gay community are oriented toward adults. Charges of seducing adolescents or of promoting same-gender sexual activities present situations that make gay adults sensitive about including adolescents in the gay community.

Coming out can be a positive statement of sexuality for adolescents as well as for adults, but adolescents face many challenges in establishing a gay or lesbian identity: "Despite the pain and confusion in this process of development, it is important to bear in mind that most gay people do successfully resolve these issues and are able to be happy with themselves and participate in healthy relationships" (Zera, 1992, p. 854).

During Adulthood

Women and men who engage in same-gender sexual activities are often in danger of being arrested if they make their sexual activities public because such activities are often illegal. This lack of legal sanctions reflects the lack of social acceptability for gays and lesbians as well as for same-gender sexual activities (Kite & Whitley, 1996). Men have more negative attitudes than women do toward homosexuality, especially regarding gay men. This lack of acceptance is one reason for the formation of self-contained gay communities. In many large cities, such communities form the context for the lives of many gay people, who may rarely interact with the outside world of heterosexuals. This life is not typical of gays, however, and the vast majority must deal with disapproval and lack of acceptance from the larger society in which they live. This lack of societal approval means that the need to form friendships and social networks is an essential part of gays' and lesbians' social lives.

The development of friendships and sexual relationships differs in gay men and lesbian women (Nardi, 1992b). Gay men were much more likely than lesbians to have had sex with both casual and close friends. Indeed, among gay men, sexual activity can form the basis for later friendships, which may represent conformity to the traditional masculine gender role in which men use sexual activity as a means to establish intimacy.

Women's romantic friendships have a long history, but until recently these relationships have been presumed to be nonsexual (Faderman, 1989). Perhaps the passionate friendships that were common among women in the 18th and 19th centuries included no sexual activity, but in other respects, these love relationships were similar to today's lesbian relationships, having an emphasis on feelings of closeness and emotional expression (Peplau, Cochran, Rook, & Padesky, 1978).

Lesbians and gay men form love relationships that have the elements of intimacy, passion, and commitment in them, just as in heterosexual couples' relationships. Philip Blumstein and Pepper Schwartz (1983) surveyed gay male and lesbian couples as well as heterosexual couples, and their survey revealed similarities as well as differences among these various configurations of couples. The survey included questions about sexual activities and satisfaction with these activities.

Lesbian couples reported a lower level of sexual activity than any other type of couple and had some reluctance to perform cunnilingus. Blumstein and Schwartz speculated that lesbians' socialization as women might have had an influence on their sexuality, making both partners hesitant about initiating sex. The result was a lower frequency of sexual activity than in couples formed with men, who are socialized to initiate sex. Lesbians who had frequent oral sex were happier with their sex lives and with their relationships than those who had less oral sex. Nevertheless, only 39% of the lesbian couples in the survey reported having oral sex very frequently, and mutual masturbation was the most common sexual ac-

GENDERED VOICES

I Never Imagined the Pain

"Lesbians have been telling me about their problems in coming out," a female graduate student in counseling said. "For some reason, two women have confided in me about the problems with staying in the closet and coming out. They are women I knew and they came to trust me, but I'm not their counselor. I never imagined the pain and the problems. I guess I have led a sheltered life. I have known gays and lesbians, but I had never known or imagined the difficulties in essentially leading two lives—one for the public and the real, private one.

"One woman has been in a relationship for 17 years. During those years she and her lover have had to pretend to be 'just roommates' who share a house. She felt that she could never let the people at work know she was lesbian; she thought she would lose her job.

"She said that she felt pressured and tried to be heterosexual. She was even engaged to be married when she was in her early 20s, but her mother sensed something was wrong and told her that she didn't have to get married if she didn't want to. She broke the engagement and stopped trying to be something she wasn't, but she kept her sexual orientation secret for another 20 years.

"This woman has started to come out selectively to people she trusts. Her family still doesn't know—or at least she hasn't told them. She has found coming out a great relief and would like to be able to be completely out but does not feel comfortable enough to do so.

"The other woman has not yet come out. I guess you would say she is bisexual rather than lesbian; I'm not sure about these classifications. She is married and has a child, but she is attracted to women and has had a number of lesbian affairs, but they upset her. She says that she was 'good' when she went on a shopping trip to a large city and did not pursue a lesbian relationship, but 'bad' when she did. She is very unhappy and troubled over whether she should leave her husband and come out as a lesbian. I am really very concerned for her, because she is suicidal, and I am afraid that she might harm herself. This conflict is really a problem for her.

"In listening to these women, I was struck by their pain in essentially living a charade, pretending to be something they know they are not. That must be so difficult and so stressful. Coming out has been like removing a huge burden for the woman who has, but I see the problems in that choice, too. Talking to these two women has really been an education for me."

tivity among these couples. Lesbians also valued nongenital physical contact, such as hugging and cuddling, activities that promoted intimacy but not orgasm.

The validity of Blumstein and Schwartz's analysis has been questioned (Frye, 1997), with an accusation of a heterosexual bias that did not allow for an understanding of lesbian sex. "Having sex" was defined as genital contact and intercourse, and lesbian sex may not conform to these boundaries. What body parts must be touched for sex to occur? Did a couple "have sex" if neither experienced orgasm? "What violence did the lesbians do their experience by answering the same question the heterosexuals answered, as though it had the same meaning for them?" (Frye, 1997, p. 206). Therefore, simple comparisons of heterosexuality and homosexuality may not be valid.

Sex is a very important part of life for gay men, and their relationships typically include a lot of sexual activity, especially early in the relationship (Blumstein & Schwartz, 1983). Fellatio is an important activity for gay men, but their sex lives are varied, and mutual masturbation is also a common activity. Anal intercourse was never as common an activity as either oral sex or manual stimulation, and its dangers for spreading HIV infection have made it less common than before the appearance of AIDS. Gay men engage in a variety of sexual activities, and their frequency of sexual contact is higher than for any other configuration of couples during the early years of their relationships. The frequency of activity with their partners falls sharply after approximately the first 2 years of the relationship, but this decrease in frequency may only be a decrease in sex with their long-time partners, and not in total sexual activity.

Gay men are more acceptant of casual sex than lesbians are, and even gay men who are involved in long-term relationships often have sex with men other than their partners. Indeed, gay men often work out a relationship in which they may have sex with men other than their companions and yet keep their long-term relationships. Affairs can present a problem for any couple, but sex outside the relationship is not as likely to be a factor in the dissolution of gay men's relationships as it is for other couples. These relationships are more likely to break up than marriages are, since gay relationships lack the social acceptance that marriages have. In Blumstein and Schwartz's study (1983), gay men and lesbians were more likely to end their relationships than were married couples, and lesbians were even more likely to break up than gay men.

Many similarities appeared among all four configurations of couples that Blumstein and Schwartz studied. For example, sex was important to heterosexual, lesbian, and gay couples, and couples who had sex less than once a week were not as happy as couples who had sex more often. Sex formed a physical bond for all the types of couples and helped them maintain their relationships, but it was also a common source of problems. Those couples who fought about sex were less stable than those who were happy with their sexual relationships. For all of the couples, their sexual relationships reflected the problems that happened in other aspects of their relationships: Sex went well when the relationships went well, and unhappiness with the sexual activity in the relationships tended to be associated with unhappiness in the quality of affection in the relationships.

Bisexuality

In Kinsey's survey of sexual behavior, a relatively high percentage of men and women reported some same-gender experiences but did not have an exclusive same-gender sexual orientation. This situation suggested to Kinsey that sexuality should not be considered in terms of independent categories. He created a continuum for classifying people's sexual experience and attraction to members of their own and the other gender. This 7-point scale ranged from strongly heterosexual to strongly homosexual, with gradations in between representing people who have both types of sexual relationships in varying proportions. These gradations reflected people who are attracted to individuals of both genders, who are referred to as **bisexual.**

The status and even the existence of bisexuality remain controversial (Fox, 1996). In psychoanalytic theory, attraction to both sexes was part of sexual development, but it was abandoned in normal gender development. In this view, bisexuality is not an acceptable form of sexuality. Those who find homosexuality unacceptable will object to the same-gender sexual element of bisexuality. For gays and lesbians, bisexuality is seen as an unwillingness to acknowledge a gay or lesbian identity by clinging to heterosexuality. Therefore, bisexuality has been condemned by several discrepant groups.

Although one view of bisexuality holds that this sexual orientation represents conflict, another view sees it as flexible (Zinik, 1985). Both views may be correct. For some individuals, bisexuality represents a developmental step on the way to forming a gay or lesbian sexual orientation. These individuals experience conflict over their sexuality, and bisexuality is a way to postpone accepting their sexual identity. For others, bisexuality is a successful integration of same- and other-gender sexuality and represents flexibility.

The frequency of bisexuality is difficult to assess. With a behavioral criterion, the vast majority of gays and lesbians would be considered bisexual. That is, most gay men and lesbians have had heterosexual experiences at some time during their lives. In addition, some individuals whose primary sexual orientation is heterosexual have had same-gender sexual experiences. A behavioral criterion would count these groups of individuals as bisexual, making a substantial percentage.

Heterosexual activity may represent a type of adolescent sexual exploration among gay and lesbian adolescents (Herdt & Boxer, 1995). Just as many adolescents who go on to have a heterosexual sexual orientation experience some same-gender sex, many adolescents who develop a gay or lesbian sexual orientation experiment with heterosexuality. Indeed, they do so in greater proportions than heterosexual adolescents experiment with same-gender sex because heterosexuality is socially sanctioned, and many gay and lesbian adolescents want to "test" their unconventional sexual orientation.

Those who identify themselves as bisexual and who maintain romantic and sexual relationships with both women and men are found in much lower numbers than those who identify themselves as gay or lesbian. According to the NORC survey (Laumann et al., 1994), 0.8% of men and 0.5% of women identified themselves as bisexual. So few people are bisexual that no community exists to offer support, and most bisexuals are not integrated into the existing gay and lesbian communities, leaving many bisexuals isolated (Bohan, 1996). This situation is beginning to change, and many gay and lesbian community centers and agencies include services oriented to bisexuals. Despite this increased acceptance, bisexuality remains the least-researched and least-understood sexual orientation.

Considering Diversity

Cultures around the world have chosen a variety of sexual activities for acceptance as "normal" and have designated other choices as abnormal, sinful, or repulsive. Cultures shape sexuality by "choosing some sexual acts (by praise, encouragement, or reward) and rejecting others (by scorn, ridicule, or condemnation), as if selecting from a sexual buffet" (Vance, 1984, p. 8). This selection from the array of available choices has resulted in virtually no universally accepted and no universally rejected set of sexual behaviors. What some cultures have found disgusting, others have found essential.

Forced fellatio performed on adult men by adolescent boys would be the basis for criminal prosecution in many cultures, but the Sambia in New Guinea find this practice not only acceptable but also required (Herdt, 1981). According to their beliefs, a preadolescent boy must leave his mother and live with men in order to become a man himself. Part of the process involves swallowing semen, and the Sambia encourage boys to engage in fellatio with unmarried adolescent and adult men. The men must restrict their same-gender sexual activities to these boys, and fellatio with men their own age is strictly forbidden. When these adolescents and young men marry, they are supposed to make the transition to heterosexuality and to end all same-gender sexual activities.

Children in some societies are allowed and even expected to experiment with sex, whereas other societies restrict sexuality during childhood (Ford & Beach, 1951). For the societies that allow children to express their sexuality, genital touching and simulated intercourse are more likely to be allowed between peers than between a child and someone older. The Sambia, with their institutionalized adult–adolescent fellatio are an exception, and so are the Lepcha of India, who believe that girls will not mature unless they engage in early intercourse.

The variety of selected and rejected options are not equal across cultures. Some activities (kissing, heterosexual intercourse) are a common choice in many societies; other activities are less common but still appear in many societies (intercourse for unmarried adolescents, oral–genital stimulation); still other activities are very uncommon in the world but standard in one society, such as biting off one's partner's eyebrows during intercourse.

Societies that restrict childhood sexuality tend to do so not only through restricting intercourse, but also by limiting information about sex, prohibiting masturbation, and enforcing different standards of sexual behavior for men and women. That is, sexually restrictive societies tend to have a double standard and put more restrictions on the sexuality of girls and women than on that of boys and men.

Research in the United States has indicated that the double standard is diminishing, and attitudes toward sex are becoming more liberal. Other countries have experienced similar trends, often more dramatic than those in the United States. Jacqueline Scott (1998) studied British and American attitudes toward sexuality over time and compared these findings to attitudes in Ireland, Poland, Germany, and Sweden. Her results showed several cross-cultural differences as well as some similarities. For example, all of the countries has experienced an increase in acceptability of premarital sex. Indeed, this trend represented the biggest change in attitudes toward sex from the 1960s to the 1990s.

Changes have also occurred in attitudes toward same-gender sexuality, with all societies showing attitudes of greater acceptance. That acceptance was not as high in the United States as in the European countries in Scott's study. Indeed, the United States and Ireland were more conservative in sexual attitudes than the other countries in the study. Scott attributed much of the conservatism to the influence of religion and the prohibitions that Christianity places on sex for reasons other than procreation.

All countries were conservative in one attitude—extramarital sex. This sexual behavior was condemned in all countries, and women disapproved more than men. Scott's cross-cultural research measured attitudes, however, and attitudes and behavior are not the same. People's behavior is not always consistent with their attitudes. Therefore, disapproval of any specific sexual behavior does not mean that people do not engage in that behavior.

Summary

Gender differences in sexual attitudes and behavior have been the object of speculation and research. Most sex research has used the survey technique—questioning people about their sexual attitudes or behavior. Problems with this method include the possibility of inaccuracy with self-reports and the problem of obtaining a representative sample that allows generalization to the population. Although not the first sex surveys, Kinsey and his colleagues conducted the most famous sex surveys of male (1948) and female (1953) sexual behavior. The results showed the prevalence of many sexual activities, which differed from social norms, and the results shocked many people. Kinsey's results have been disputed, but the importance of his work has not. He made the study of sexuality a legitimate part of scientific research.

Many other sex surveys have been completed, including the Playboy Foundation survey during the 1970s and the National Opinion Research Council survey in the 1990s. Both of these surveys attempted to obtain a representative sample of U.S. residents and succeeded to a greater degree than Kinsey had. These surveys indicated some changes in sexuality over the intervening years—especially a decrease in the double standard of sexual behavior for men and women—but all of the surveys have shown that people engage in a wide variety of sexual behavior.

Masters and Johnson measured sexual responses directly during masturbation and intercourse in an attempt to understand the physiology of sexual response. Their 1966 book detailed four stages of the sexual response—excitation, plateau, orgasm, and resolution. Although the people who are willing to have sex for the sake of science are not representative of the general population, Masters and Johnson believed that sexual response is similar in all people.

Childhood sexuality includes both exploration and the potential for abuse. Exploration begins very early, with infants manipulating their genitals, young children masturbating to orgasm, and kindergarten children exploring each other's genitals. Parents may find these explorations disturbing, and condemning these behaviors may convey the impression that sexual feelings and activities are unacceptable.

The unequal power between children and adults can create situations for sexual abuse. Sex surveys have revealed that at least 15% of women and 5% of men were sexually abused as children. The large majority of the perpetrators of sexual abuse of children are men, often family members or those in positions of authority, but girls and women are also perpetrators of abuse. Abuse has both short-term and long-term negative effects for male and female victims.

Sex education tends to emphasize the dangers rather than the pleasures of sexuality, leaving boys with information about the damage that their male sexuality can do and leaving girls with a sense of vulnerability. Adolescence is a time of increasing heterosexual interest. Sexual activity is one of the reasons for dating, although boys emphasize sex as a reason for dating more often than girls do. Boys also tend to begin intercourse at a younger age than girls, and this difference appears in many ethnic groups. Gender differences in premarital intercourse as well as in other sexual activities have decreased over the past 50 years.

Marriage is no longer the only acceptable context for sexual activity; a majority of both young men and young women now have intercourse before age 25. Celibacy is a choice made by about one-third of college men and women, but more women than men choose monogamy as an ideal style of sexual relationship (61% versus 37%), whereas more men than women choose free sexual experimentation (28% versus 5%). This difference may relate to men's greater acceptance of casual sex, which is one of the largest gender differences in sexuality. Another large difference is frequency of masturbation, which may lead to women being less likely to experience orgasm during partnered sex.

Another difference that influences sexuality is the existence of a double standard for sexual behavior, which holds that girls and women are less sexual than boys and men. Comparisons of the data from the Kinsey surveys and more recent analyses show that acceptance of the double standard has declined, but its continuation is a factor influencing the sexuality of women and men and contributing to conflicts in couples.

Same-gender sexual activity is not uncommon among children and adolescents, but a minority of people experience erotic attraction to only members of the same gender. Estimates vary according to the definition, but a small percentage of men and an even smaller percentage of women have primarily or exclusively gay or lesbian sexual orientation. The underlying reasons for a gay or lesbian sexual orientation are not understood, but recent research has concentrated on biological factors that may relate to sexual orientation. The third interstitial nucleus of the hypothalamus seems to be larger in heterosexual men than in homosexual men and heterosexual women, but these conclusions are in question due to bias in the study that identified this difference.

Lesbian and gay sexuality is not well accepted, and adolescents who are attracted to members of their own gender may have trouble accepting themselves and their sexual orientation. The process of coming out, of revealing gay or lesbian interests and behavior, can be a process of positive self-acceptance, but can also create family conflict due to parents' difficulty in accepting a child's sexual orientation.

The sexuality of gay men and lesbian women differs, and these couples have both similarities with and differences from heterosexual couples. For instance, both gay men and lesbians value oral sex, but lesbians are more reluctant to perform cunnilingus than gay men are to perform fellatio. One survey indicated that lesbian couples have sex less often than other couples do, but the definition of what constitutes sex is typically intercourse, which does not fit within lesbian sexuality. Gay men value and have sex often, especially in the first several years of their relationships. For all types of heterosexual, gay, and lesbian couples, sex provides both a bond of pleasure and a potential for conflict in their relationships.

When individuals form romantic and sexual relationships with both men and women, they are bisexual. This sexual orientation is controversial and difficult to define because many individuals experiment with sexuality, having both male and female partners. Few, however, have a true bisexual sexual orientation, so this sexual orientation remains the least researched and most poorly understood of the sexual orientations.

Across the world, some cultures condemn the sexual behaviors that other cultures require, producing a wide variety of sexuality throughout the world. Some cultures are very restrictive, and those cultures tend to restrict women's sexuality more than men's. In western cultures, attitudes toward sex have become more liberal over the past 30 years, especially in the increased acceptability of premarital sex, but also in same-gender sexuality.

Glossary

bisexual a person who is sexually attracted to individuals of the same as well as the other gender.

celibacy refraining from sexual activity.

coming out the process of recognizing and publicly acknowledging one's gay or lesbian sexual orientation.

cunnilingus oral stimulation of the female genitals.

date rape or **acquaintance rape** forced sexual activity occurring between people who are acquainted with each other.

double standard for sexual behavior the social standard that allows men greater freedom of sexual expression than women.

fellatio oral stimulation of the male genitals.

gay an alternative for the term *homosexual,* emphasizing the entire lifestyle instead of only the sexual aspects of it; sometimes used to refer to both men and women, but more often to men, who feel sexual attraction for and choose sexual activity with people of the same gender.

incest sexual activity between family members.

lesbian a woman who feels sexual attraction for and chooses sexual activity with other women.

masturbation manipulation of the genitals to produce sexual pleasure.

monogamy having only one sexual partner.

representative sample a sample (subset) of the population that reflects the characteristics of the population from which the sample was drawn.

self-selection of participants when participants rather than researchers choose who will take part in the research. This problem biases the results and prevents generalization to a wider population.

serial monogamy the practice of having a series of monogamous sexual relationships.

sexual orientation the erotic attraction to members of the same or the other gender (or to both).

Suggested Readings

Blumstein, Philip; & Schwartz, Pepper. (1983). *American couples.* New York: Pocket Books. This book examines married, cohabiting, gay, and lesbian couples, interviewing them about money and work as well as sex. The chapter about sex is a fascinating examination of what couples do and enjoy as well as what role sex plays in conflict and maintenance of the relationship.

McCormick, Naomi B. (1994). *Sexual salvation: Affirming women's sexual rights and pleasures.* Westport, CT: Praeger. Although McCormick concentrates on women's sexuality, she addresses a range of topics for women's sexuality in an outspoken way. She believes that women can construct a sexuality that will give them salvation—freedom and pleasure.

Netting, Nancy S. (1992). Sexuality in youth culture: Identity and change. *Adolescence, 27,* 961–976. This study reports on sexual attitudes of college students in 1980 versus 1990 and analyzes the styles of sexuality in young heterosexual adults. The categories of celibacy, monogamy, and free experimentation correspond to choices for other adults.

Oliver, Mary Beth; & Hyde, Janet Shibley. (1993). Gender differences in sexuality: A meta-analysis. *Psychological Bulletin, 114,* 29–51. This meta-analysis concentrates on sexual attitudes and reports of sexual behaviors. The authors have determined the size of gender differences, finding large differences for a few aspects of sexuality, smaller differences for some attitudes, and no difference for others. Their interpretation is tied to the various theories of sexuality and makes an interesting summary of gender differences in sexuality.

Chapter 11

School

HEADLINE

Science for Girls Only

Newsweek, June 21, 1999

The heart of Silicon Valley hardly seems the setting to require a special school to promote science and technology, yet a number of people there saw a need for such a school. The result was the Girls' Middle School in Mountain View, California, devoted to developing girls' interest and abilities in science and technology. Patricia King's (1999) headline story reported that, even in Silicon Valley, girls "hit the wall of femininity" (p. 64), just like they do in other parts of the United States.

As the name implies, the students in the Girls' Middle School are all girls. This school is one of many founded during the 1990s on the basis of a report from the American Association of University Women (AAUW) (1992), that contended that schools shortchange girls by stereotyping and ignoring their educational needs. Those who are associated with these schools believe that, by isolating girls from boys, girls' educational needs can be better served. Girls' (and boys') schools have a long tradition, but coeducation has been the trend for the past 100 years. Do girls need to be isolated from boys to get a good education? Does the presence of the other gender hinder academic performance? Will single-sex classes help girls (and boys) achieve in school?

Proponents of single-gender education believe that "all-girl classes can be especially helpful in middle school, a transition period when conflicting messages about femininity and achievement, and the need to fit in, often erode girls' self-image," (King, 1999, p. 65). The girls who attend the Girls' Middle School get the attention from their teachers and the access to science facilities that they may miss in coeducational classrooms. Developing a positive attitude about science is important if girls are to continue in science. A study of women with high science anxiety (Brownlow, Jacobi, & Rogers, 2000) showed that these women took fewer college science classes than less science-anxious women and recalled less helpful and supportive science teachers. Therefore, educators are searching for ways to enhance girls' science experiences.

Gender segregation, however, is controversial. With gender, as with race, separate is usually not equal, and federal law permits few reasons for segregation by gender in public schools. Contact sports, singing groups, and human sexuality classes are among those exceptions, but science and literature are not, making gender-segregated classes legally questionable. A growing number of public schools have instituted such classes, usually for girls in science and math, but sometimes also for boys in language and literature. Private schools such as the Girls' Middle School in Mountain View increased 20% during the 1990s, reflecting the growing popularity of the view that this type of separation can be beneficial (King, 1999).

Others have questioned the long-term benefits of gender-segregated public school classes. After all, the world is coed, and girls and boys must learn to deal with each others' presence at some point. Single-gender schools can offer girls some advantages in terms of higher confidence (AAUW, 1992), but little research exists on advantages, especially in the long term, of single-gender classes in coed schools. Single-gender classes were not associated with decreases in gender stereotyping in one longitudinal study (Signorella, Frieze, & Hershey, 1996), which found the advantages of such classrooms questionable for most students. The feelings on the issue are strong, with both enthusiasts and skeptics looking for ways to remedy gender inequities in schooling. What are those inequities? When do they start? And what are the long-term consequences for women's and men's lives?

The School Experience

Even before children begin school, their parents and the society in which they live treat boys and girls differently. Chapter 7 included examples of the process of gender stereotyping: dolls for girls but trucks for boys, quiet games for girls but noisy games for boys, frilly dresses for girls but grubby jeans for boys, staying close to home for girls but venturing out for boys.

Not all girls or all boys conform to these stereotypes, but by age 4 or 5, children have developed a concept of gender and know what behaviors are expected and approved for each. (See Chapter 6 for a more complete discussion of the development of gender identity.) Thus, when children start kindergarten, they already hold beliefs about what clothes, games, and behaviors are appropriate for boys and girls, and they bring these beliefs to the school experience. Schools often reinforce these stereotypical beliefs, producing differences in attitudes and expectations about careers that result in differences in preparation to pursue careers.

Title IX of the Education Amendments of 1972 prohibits gender discrimination in school programs that receive federal funds. Although gender discrimination is now prohibited by law, a study by the AAUW (1992) presented a great deal of evidence illustrating a continuing lack of gender equity. Problems included unequal attention and access to education materials, promotion of stereotypical gender roles, unequal expectations concerning careers, and increased sexual harassment in school by classmates and teachers.

Attitudes of teachers and counselors allow the continuation of gender bias in schools, and several studies have indicated that educators exhibit both gender and ethnic biases. One study (Avery & Walker, 1993) measured future teachers' attitudes about students' potential for accomplishment, and the results indicated more bias related to ethnicity than to gender. Another study (Jones, 1989) asked if the recent emphasis on gender issues made a difference for recently trained teachers. The results from this study failed to show any effects of that recent emphasis; instead, it showed that both experienced and new teachers gave boys more attention, feedback, praise, and warnings than they gave girls. Regardless of teaching experience or gender of the teacher, interactions with female students were different and less helpful than were teacher interactions with male students.

Gender equity is not a large part of the curriculum for prospective teachers; neither is it a frequent topic of inservice training for teachers (AAUW, 1992; Sadker & Sadker, 1985). A 1980 examination of textbooks used for teacher training found that these texts devoted very little space to gender equity issues (Sadker & Sadker, 1980). This study concluded that teachers could not be trained to be gender fair when their training minimized these issues. In 1993, a similar study produced similar results (Titus, 1993). Thus, teachers may enter their profession with gender stereotypes that their training as teachers failed to address, leaving them with a tendency to treat their students in gender-stereotypical ways.

Early Schooling

The problem of teachers promoting stereotypical gender roles can begin very early in the school experience. Teachers channel children into gender-stereotypical activities, beginning during preschool; they encourage different play activities with boys than with girls and spend the majority of their time—60%—with boys (Jones, 1989). In addition, children have the experience of being taught by an overwhelming majority of female kindergarten and elementary school teachers. Several factors discourage men from teaching young children, including the poor salary, low prestige, and poor image of elementary school teachers (D. Cohen, 1992). The women who choose elementary teaching also differ from men who have made the same choice (Montecinos & Nielsen, 1997). Women reported that they decided to become elementary teachers when they were in elementary school more often than men did, and more women than men expected to teach in elementary school for the duration of their careers. Thus, the men and women who choose to teach young children had different expectations for their careers.

Male elementary school teachers are still rare, but their behavior is similar to female elementary school teachers: Both tend to reward children for being compliant (D. Cohen, 1992). Children benefit by having male elementary teachers by their decrease in students' gender stereotyping: Those with male teachers make significantly fewer stereotypical explanations for the behavior of men and women than do students who have had only female teachers during the elementary grades (Mancus, 1992). Both boys and girls benefit from seeing men perform the job of teacher during their early years of schooling, whereas there is no clear evidence that girls benefit and boys are damaged by the gender imbalance in elementary school teachers.

The preponderance of female elementary school teachers has led to the "myth that early-education environments meet the needs of girls better than boys" (AAUW, 1992, p. 18). The AAUW report argued that the opposite is true: Early schooling consists of activities in which girls have more proficiency than boys, giving boys more training in the skills they lack, such as reading, while ignoring skills that girls lack, such as science investigation. Girls need practice with gross-motor activities, investigatory activities, and experimental activities, but these activities tend to be considered part of "play" rather than part of their education, and thus they were excluded from the curriculum. Furthermore, these activities are more likely to result from boys' play than the play girls prefer. Thus, the activities of the early elementary classroom may strengthen the skills boys lack while failing to provide the same benefits for girls.

The early school situation also presents problems for boys (Connell, 1996). To benefit from the lessons that school presents, boys must be quiet, pay attention, and concentrate. To some boys, this behavior is out of line with the gender role they are developing; that is, school requires that they act like "sissies." Either due to rebellion or to difficulties in meeting the school requirements, boys are much more likely than girls to present behavior problems. Indeed, a great deal of the extra attention that boys get revolves around controlling boys' misbehavior.

Few gender differences exist in school achievement during the early years of school. Some standardized, national tests have shown that girls outscore boys on some types of verbal ability, but other similar tests have shown boys to have a small advantage (AAUW, 1992; Maccoby & Jacklin, 1974). Whatever the direction, the magnitude of the difference on standardized tests is small, but girls make better grades. Socioeconomic status is a much stronger predictor of elementary school achievement than is gender, with children from lower socioeconomic levels having consistently poorer school records than children from wealthier families. Even controlling for socioeconomic status, girls tend to make better grades in school, beginning during the elementary grades and persisting through college.

Several social factors combine to predict academic success and to explain gender differences during elementary school (Serbin, Zelkowitz, Doyle, Gold, & Wheaton, 1990). Girls' advantage relates to their tendency to respond to social cues and to comply with adults' requests. That is, the training that girls receive in complying with the female gender role is a factor in their early school success. Problems in school occur when students fail to comply with adults' rules and requests, and boys are more likely to behave in these ways, creating problems for themselves in school. Indeed, conformity to gender-typical behaviors relates to both girls' success and boys' problems.

Academic success is complex; both intellectual and social factors relate to success in school. Figure 11.1 shows a model of factors that one study (Serbin et al., 1990) related to academic success. As previous research had indicated, socioeconomic variables predicted

GENDERED VOICE

Treated Like a King

"I'm not sure why I wanted to work with kids," a young male elementary school teacher told me. "I started as a camp counselor, and that job was attractive because of the other counselors—lots of girls. They thought it was cool that I was a counselor and was good with kids. They seemed to think that getting along with children meant I was sensitive. I can get a line of my ex-girlfriends who will testify that I am not any more sensitive than most guys, but I do like working with kids, so I became a teacher.

"The principal and coach are both men, but there is only one other male teacher in my school, so I get a lot of attention from the students and from the female teachers. The kids love me; I'm treated like a king. When I walk down the hall, they want to be near me, and my attention is something special. Some of them live in single-parent families with their mothers, but even the ones who live with fathers seem starved for male attention. I believe that their fathers may not be too emotionally accessible, and I am, so they are drawn to me. I try to have good relationships with them, and it is work that I enjoy, but the administration keeps hinting that I should get a degree so that I can become an administrator. I don't want to; I'm satisfied doing what I'm doing."

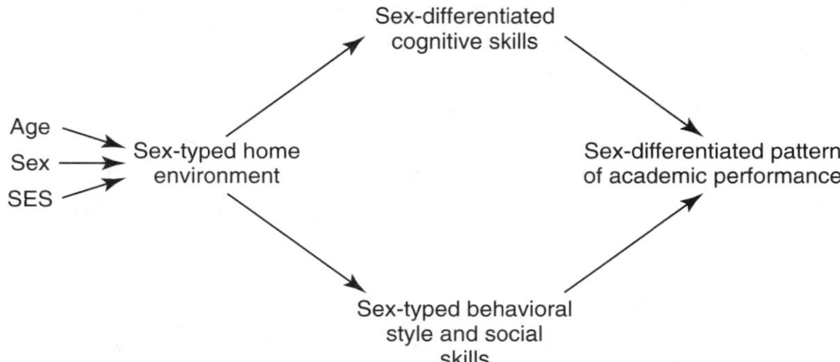

FIGURE 11.1 Model of Social and Cognitive Abilities Predicting Academic Performance

SOURCE: From L. A. Serbin, P. Zelkowitz, A. Doyle, D. Gold, & B. Wheaton, 1990, "The socialization of sex-differentiated skills and academic performance: A mediational model," *Sex Roles, 23,* p. 616. Reprinted by permission of Plenum Publishing and Lisa Serbin.

academic success, including mothers' occupational and fathers' educational levels. These variables also indirectly influenced the single cognitive factor most strongly related to academic success: visual–spatial ability. This study suggested that children's conformity to gender-typical behaviors plays a role in girls' academic success and in boys' poor performance. Thus, a complex picture emerges to describe academic success during elementary school, with socioeconomic factors, gender role socialization, and cognitive abilities all contributing.

Like the differences in academic success, the gender differences in self-perception are small during elementary school. These differences, however, reflect the beginnings of gender stereotypes (Eccles, Wigfield, Harold, & Blumenfeld, 1993). As early as first grade, children show differential beliefs in their abilities at various activities. Girls express more positive beliefs about their competence in reading and music, whereas boys are more positive about their mathematics and sports abilities. No gender differences exist for these skills at this age, so these differences reflect children's beliefs rather than their abilities. As children grow older, the gender associations of male and female begin to show greater differences.

Changes during Junior High

Gender differences in achievement start to appear during the junior high school years. Girls experience a decreased interest in math and science and a change in career orientation, with an increased interest in marriage and children and a narrowing of career interests to those careers most commonly occupied by women (Bush & Simmons, 1987). Adolescent girls believe that they will combine a family with paid employment, reflecting the current reality of contemporary family life, but their image of this combination may not correspond to the difficulty of balancing these different roles. Adolescent boys experience a widening of career interests and give less attention to their future family plans, assuming that they are preparing for a career that will be a primary focus of their lives.

During elementary school, girls and boys exhibit few differences in academic abilities, but girls make better grades. During junior high school, boys' achievement in math and science begins to exceed that of girls, although the differences are small and vary within different areas of math and science (AAUW, 1992). For example, the male advantage in math problem solving is minimal throughout junior high school. The gender difference in science achievement begins during these years, but does not affect all sciences equally. For example, girls do as well or better than boys in life sciences, and boys perform better in physical sciences (Lee & Burkam, 1996).

Achievement differences mirror girls' and boys' science experiences during junior high school (AAUW, 1992). There are no differences in *interest* in participating in science activities, but boys are more likely to participate in using equipment and performing science activities. Boys are more likely to use science equipment, such as microscopes and electricity meters, and these different experiences with science activities both in and outside of the classroom are a factor in girls' lower achievement and interest in science (Lee & Burkam, 1996). These inequalities are the target of schools such as the Girls' Middle School in Mountain View, California, described in the headline article for this chapter. By allowing girls access to science and technology, these schools strive to boost girls' interest and achievement in these areas.

Girls start to experience a decline in confidence in their academic abilities during junior high school, whereas boys start to feel more confident (Bush & Simmons, 1987). The AAUW report (1992) hypothesized that girls' diminished confidence might be a reason for their tendency to discontinue studying math and science, whereas boys who stop studying math and science might do so due to their difficulties in mastering the material. Girls tend to view their mastery problems in math as lack of ability, whereas boys explain their decisions to discontinue math courses as a lack of interest.

The decrease in academic confidence for girls and the increase for boys may be part of the developmental changes that accompany puberty, forming a complex interaction between school experience and social structures (Bush & Simmons, 1987). One possibility is that gender-related role expectations intensify during puberty for both boys and girls, with each becoming more stereotypical in their interests and achievement-related behavior (Hill & Lynch, 1983). A review of the research in this area (Eccles & Bryan, 1994) indicated that development of more stereotypical interests may be more typical of boys than of girls, with boys developing more gender stereotypical views about themselves and about girls. Girls, however, become more stereotypical in their view of academic subjects, developing the opinion that their math abilities are lower and their language abilities are higher than for boys, even when standardized tests reveal similar abilities.

The timing of puberty affects girls and boys differently (Tobin-Richards, Boxer, & Petersen, 1983). For girls, early puberty presents problems: They must deal with bodies that are more developed than those of their peers, and they must cope with people's reactions to their physical maturity. These reactions often include comments on or interest in their developing sexuality, which many girls find embarrassing. For boys, early onset of puberty is an advantage: As they increase in size and strength relative to their peers, they have advantages in social dominance and athletic performance, making for welcomed changes.

Athletic performance becomes more gender segregated during late childhood and early adolescence. "That's a game for girls" is an insult to boys, and few girls are competent at boys' sports. The preferred activities of girls and boys continue to differ along paths that appeared during early childhood: Boys more often engage in physical activities requiring gross motor skills that use the large muscles of the body. Games that include running, jumping, throwing, and kicking—namely baseball, football, soccer, and basketball—are preferred by boys more than by girls.

Girls are not necessarily more sedentary than boys, but their leisure activities are less likely to involve gross motor skills. Indeed, both boys and girls watch television and play video and computer games, resulting in a more sedentary lifestyle and decreased levels of physical fitness. The intensification of gender roles during junior high school pushes girls away from, and boys toward, athletics, producing gender differences in physical activity and in confidence in physical abilities.

Therefore, the junior high school years mark the beginning of differences in academic accomplishment for girls and boys. Girls continue to make better grades than boys, but girls become less assertive about classroom activities, such as science demonstrations and equipment use. Their decreased participation may be one reason for their decreased interest in science, but the continued lack of encouragement by their teachers and parents may also contribute to girls' declining interest in science and math during junior high school. Boys also experience a decline of interest in science during this time, but their interest remains higher than that of girls.

High School

The differences in academic achievement that begin during junior high school become more pronounced during the high school years, as do differences in confidence and attitudes toward various subjects. These changes in academic achievement, attitudes, and confidence relate to an even more important gender difference—in choices. During secondary schooling, students begin to have choices in their coursework, and girls and boys make different choices that can have life-long consequences. For example, girls' choice not to take advanced math and science courses can affect their access to certain college majors and careers; boys' choice to play sports can detract from study time and affect their grades, which can limit their career options.

Both girls and boys feel more confident in their abilities at age 9 than at age 17 (Freiberg, 1991). During elementary school, 60% of girls and 67% of boys have positive feelings about themselves and their abilities, whereas by high school, only 29% of the girls and 46% of the boys still hold these beliefs (see Figure 11.2). Although both experience a decrease, girls report less self-confidence than boys do. These feelings extend to physical appearance and abilities as well as academic subjects.

Physical appearance and athletic ability are important to high school students because both are ways to gain prestige in the school social structure (Suitor & Reavis, 1995; Suitor & Carter, 1999). Both female and male high school students have other ways to gain social status, but some changes have occurred. In comparing students from the late 1970s to those from the late 1980s, physical appearance remained a primary way for girls to attain social prominence in their schools, and athletics continued to be as important for boys (Suitor & Reavis, 1995). The 10-year comparison showed that sports had become more important, and cheerleading less important, ways for girls to gain prestige. For boys, having fast cars became less important, but having sex remained a way to gain prestige in the high school environment. For both girls and boys, getting good grades, being considered intelligent, sports participa-

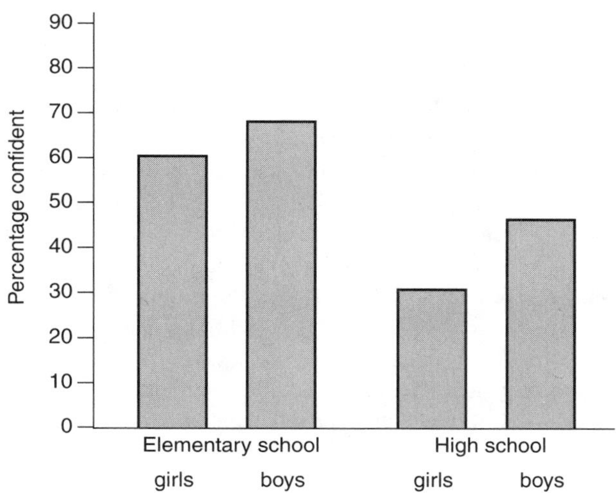

FIGURE 11.2 Self-Confidence of Girls and Boys during Elementary and High School

tion, and physical attractiveness conferred prestige. Sports dominated the avenue to prestige for boys, whereas all the factors contributed to girls' prestige (Suitor & Carter, 1999).

The increased emphasis on sports for young women has resulted in the current acceptance of sports as a way for young women to gain positive recognition. Their increased sports participation has been dramatic. In 1971, girls constituted only 7% of athletic participants in high schools, but in 1991, the percentage had grown to 36% (Mansnerus, 1992). Not only has the number of female athletes grown, but the variety of sports in which they participate has also increased. High schools have added women's teams in cross country, gymnastics, soccer, field hockey, softball, swimming, track, volleyball, and other sports. The success of U.S. women's teams in Olympic and world competition for soccer, basketball, and softball have provided exciting role models. Expanded opportunities for high school girls have allowed them to develop their physical abilities and talents in ways that previously were reserved for boys.

From junior high to high school, girls experience more of a decrease than boys in interest and confidence concerning math and science. A meta-analysis (Weinburgh, 1995) indicated that boys had more positive attitudes toward science than girls did, and that the relationship between attitudes and achievement were positive. Furthermore, the relationship was stronger for girls than for boys, indicating that their attitudes may have a stronger influence on their performance.

High levels of ability do not guarantee that students will have positive attitudes or high achievement. The lack of confidence in math and science extends to intellectually gifted young women, who have the ability to succeed at the highest levels, but fail to believe that they are academically gifted (Walker, Reis, & Leonard, 1992). Mathematically talented girls have lower aspirations than comparable boys, and girls do not use their abilities as much as boys do (Benbow, 1992). High-achieving girls, however, have positive attitudes toward science (Weinburgh, 1995), highlighting the importance of attitudes in achievement.

The lack of personal and academic confidence is a factor in the choice of coursework for both boys and girls during high school. The overall gender differences in mathematics course participation are small and decreasing, however (U.S. Department of Education [USDE], 1999). Until the 1990s, boys and girls completed an average of three math courses during high school, but boys were more likely to enroll in more advanced courses (AAUW, 1992). These differences have disappeared, and now girls and boys are equally likely to take advanced math classes (USDE, 1999). The differences in test scores on standardized tests have decreased over the past decade, but boys still score higher on tests such as the Scholastic Aptitude Test (Willingham & Cole, 1997).

Male and female high school students who pursue science are not equally represented in all types of science courses (AAUW, 1992). Female students are more likely to enroll in advanced biology and social sciences classes, whereas boys are more likely to take chemistry, physics, and physical sciences. In addition, students enrolled in the same course may have different views of how the course fits into their career plans. For example, young men who enroll in calculus and advanced science in high school are very likely to take these courses in preparation for careers in engineering, whereas very few young women enrolled in the same courses even consider engineering careers. Therefore, young women fail to develop the same level of interest in science careers, even when they have the ability and preparation to do so.

The differential enrollment of young men and women in advanced math and science courses has been considered a problem for women because they miss these educational experiences and the career preparation the courses offer. When education experts judge the enrollment of women as low, they are using men and their enrollment statistics as the standard (Noddings, 1991). The implication is that women's enrollment is deficient and something to be remedied. Nel Noddings suggested that educators have given too little consideration both to what women are doing and to the reasons behind their choices. She pointed out that stereotypical thinking has imposed limitations on both young women and young men, restricting both from a full range of choices in coursework and careers. Most of the criticisms and research have centered on girls and how they are diverted from math and science. Fewer considerations have been directed toward boys and how they might be steered toward math and science when those subjects and careers might not be the ones for which they have the highest interest or aptitude. That is, the current situation may reflect both an underrepresentation of women and an overrepresentation of men in math and science.

Counselors' stereotyping of gender-appropriate careers is a factor in the courses that boys and girls take in school as well as in the careers they choose. Gender bias in counseling may be either overt or covert (Hoffman, 1982). Overt bias includes sexist statements, such as telling girls that they are not expected to be good at math or discouraging boys from enrolling in cooking classes. Covert bias includes encouraging girls and boys to behave in stereotypical ways, such as providing information concerning traditional but not nontraditional careers, or failing to take nontraditional career interests seriously. Research on career education materials indicates that these materials are largely oriented toward boys, leaving girls unrepresented or portrayed in stereotypical ways (Hoffman, 1982). Only 3% of the materials contained clear references to both women and men, and 60% made reference to only one gender. These tests and materials used by counselors present barriers to career development, especially for girls.

Counselors tend to steer adolescents toward traditional careers (Hoffman, 1982). They may counsel girls about careers that require education and ability, but not careers that lead to high status and prestige. That is, counselors are more likely to recommend that girls be-

GENDERED VOICE

I Might Have Been an Engineer

"I probably would have been an engineer if I had been given the opportunity. Well, maybe *opportunity* isn't exactly the right word, because nothing really prevented me, but nobody encouraged me, either," a high school science teacher in her early 40s said. "I always liked science and did well in it, but none of my counselors mentioned engineering, or being a chemist, or any science career except teaching. I think they mentioned those careers to the boys who were good at science, but not to the girls. They steered us toward teaching. That's just the way it was, and I'm not sure how much it has changed.

"They just didn't expect girls to be good at science and math, and when we were, they didn't consider science careers, so they didn't tell us about being a scientist. Teaching science, yes, but not being a scientist. If a boy was interested in science, they wouldn't have mentioned teaching, even if that was what he would have been best at. I wonder how many women would have been better scientists and engineers than science teachers, and how many men would have been better science teachers."

come science teachers than chemists, and that boys become chemists rather than science teachers. Furthermore, girls are discriminated against at increasing levels as they get older and closer to a career choice.

Vocational education is another area in which girls and boys have received unequal attention: "Vocational education was originally designed to give work skills to high school boys who were not planning to attend college. But research indicates that it may not serve either males or females very well in the current environment" (AAUW, 1992, p. 42). This pessimistic assessment comes from the finding that men who complete vocational educational courses in high school earn less money than those who have not taken these courses. Vocational education also does young women a disservice, routing them into office and business occupations that are low-paying and often dead-end jobs. Only around 4% of the students enrolled in construction, mechanics, and machine repair are young women (Burge & Culver, 1990), and the choice to take nontraditional vocational courses places young women at risk for harassment from male classmates and sometimes from teachers.

Sexual harassment, unwanted sexual attention, from male students and teachers becomes a source of stress for young women at school. Although young men can also experience sexual harassment, few mention being troubled by unwanted sexual attention by their female peers or teachers (AAUW, 1992). This reticence may be part of the gender role young men are attempting to fulfill rather than because there is no sexual harassment.

Harassment involving gender may be sexually oriented or not; it consists of unwanted sexual remarks, statements about the unsuitability of women for various types of jobs, or derogatory remarks about women and their abilities. As the AAUW (1992) report pointed out, harassment is about power and authority, and the vast majority of incidents involve boys harassing girls. Although sexual and other harassment that affects the educational process is prohibited by Title IX of the Education Amendments of 1972, those who harass are often allowed to continue. The attitude is often "boys will be boys," with harassment not considered a serious offense. Thus, fear of harassment may make girls reluctant to enroll in courses with a majority of boys or to enroll in nontraditional vocational courses.

ACCORDING TO THE MEDIA...

Boys Are Not Sissies in Children's Books

During the 1970s, when gender became a legal issue in schools, the presentation of gender roles in children's books became a topic of interest. Children's readers tended to ignore women and girls, containing more boy-centered than girl-centered stories, more adult male than female characters, more biographies of men than women, and even more stories of male than female animals. Even the illustrations in children's books showed more boys and men and portrayed them in more active, powerful ways (Sadker, Sadker, & Steindam, 1989). An examination of the contents of the stories before the 1980s (Hoffman, 1982) showed that male characters were (1) more numerous than female characters and (2) more likely than female characters to show creativity, bravery, curiosity, and achievement. Female characters were often portrayed as passive, fearful, and incompetent. Adult characters fit the gender stereotypes of female domesticity and male achievement.

Publishing houses became sensitive to gender equity in children's books, and the presentations of male and female characters changed. The frequency of male and female characters became more evenly distributed (Evans & Davies, 2000; Turner-Bowker, 1996), but the portrayals did not change as much as the proportions. For example, even though male and female characters were central characters equally often, male characters appeared more often in titles and in illustrations for these books, making these male characters more prominent (Turner-Bowker, 1996). In addition, the characters still behaved in stereotypical ways. The male characters were aggressive, argumentative, and competitive significantly more often than female characters, who were more emotionally expressive, tender, and affectionate than male characters (Evans & Davies, 2000).

Despite the continuation of stereotyping, changes in children's books have occurred since the 1970s, affecting female more than male characters (Evans & Davies, 2000). Female characters are more likely to behave in ways that cross gender boundaries, but male characters do not. That is, boys do not act like "sissies" in books for children. Instead, they stick to stereotypical male gender role behaviors. These portrayals leave boys who read these stories without models for affection, nurturance, emotional expressiveness, and other positive characteristics open to girls.

A survey of 8th- to 11th-grade students in public schools in the United States (AAUW, 1993) revealed that sexual harassment was a common experience. Four out of five students said they had been the target of unwelcome sexual behavior while at school or a school function. Adult school employees were the perpetrators in 25% of incidents when girls were targets and in 10% of incidents when boys were targets, showing that the majority of harassment incidents are perpetrated by other students. Girls were more common targets than boys, but both girls and boys admitted perpetrating sexual harassment. The student perpetrators tended to consider harassment part of school life and "no big deal" (Bryant, 1995, p. 41). The targets felt differently. Harassment made school more difficult; victims were less interested and involved in school, made lower grades, and expressed more doubt about graduating (see "According to the Media/According to the Research"). Although sexual harassment may be part of high school life, it is a major problem with serious consequences.

In summary, both overt and subtle forces affect adolescents during high school, with both girls and boys making more traditional, stereotypical choices. Enrollment in math and science classes is now comparable for boys and girls, but attitudes about those subjects differ. Those girls who complete advanced math and science courses tend not to view these courses as part of their career preparation, forming the basis for a gender imbalance in math and science careers. High school counselors are a source of gender bias, steering more boys

ACCORDING TO THE RESEARCH...

Students Who Do Not Conform to Gender Stereotypes Face Harassment in School

The consequences of failing to conform to gender stereotypical behaviors can be very serious, opening children and adolescents to criticism, punishment, and harassment in school. Many people fail to conform to stereotypes of masculinity and femininity, but those who bear the brunt of the harassment are gays and lesbians. Those who disclose gay or lesbian sexual orientations as adolescents are at increased risk of harassment at school, especially from peers. Indeed, the majority of sexual harassment in school comes from other students. Accusations of homosexuality are frequent occurrences and may even be taunts aimed at students who are heterosexual but not conforming to someone's standards of masculine or feminine behaviors (AAUW, 1993). The harassment sometimes goes beyond name calling and into physical attacks, with young gay men in particular peril:

> *"Faggot" is the ultimate insult used by kids and teenagers all over the country to designate those who are different or simply disliked, whether they are gay or not. It was the epithet of choice the students at Columbine High School hurled at the Trench Coat Mafia, helping to drive two of its nail-painting, Hitler-worshipping techies into their murderous rage. It was the word young gay bashers carved into the flesh of the 17-year-old Marin County lad whom they beat senseless after he founded a Gay-Straight Alliance at the high school in his supposedly liberal and tolerant community. Most teachers and school administrators haven't a clue how to tackle the root causes of antigay verbal violence and the physical violence and psychological trauma it engenders. (Ireland, 1999, p. 8)*

These incidents of harassment and violence take their toll, making school unpleasant and dangerous not only for gay and lesbian students, but also for others who do not conform to gender stereotypes. Gay and lesbian students are more likely to drop out of school and attempt suicide than other students (Lock & Steiner, 1999). Some schools approach the problem by beginning counseling programs and by appointing personnel to coordinate services for gay, lesbian, and bisexual students (Livingston, 1994). Some schools do nothing, and those schools can be a major problem for gay and lesbian adolescents.

than girls toward prestigious careers. In vocational education, boys are more likely to be guided toward higher-paying skilled craft jobs, and girls into lower-paying business jobs. However, vocational education may not serve boys well, because those who have and have not completed this coursework earn comparable salaries. Girls who enroll in nontraditional courses face the possibility of sexual or other harassment, and, although illegal, this behavior is often not considered a serious infraction of the school's rules.

College and Professional School

The effects of stereotyping and gender bias influence young women and men before they enter college, creating differences in expectations and choices. Young men receive messages from society, the media, and specific people in their lives that they should prepare for careers that will support a family. Young women get a different message: Their careers will be less important than their husbands' employment, so their college majors need not lead to specific job-related skills.

These differing expectations are consistent with the history of women's roles, but not necessarily with contemporary employment patterns. College education for women developed gradually during the 19th century, but never approached equal education for men and women, either in numbers or in type of training (Fox, 1989). Instead, women went to college to find husbands and to prepare for careers that would last only until they married. Thus, higher education for women confined them to careers that would be flexible, but chances for advancement were unimportant. One of the early careers available to women was teaching, and beginning in the 1800s, women were in demand as teachers in the growing public school system. One of the reasons female teachers were in demand was their willingness to work for low salaries.

Throughout most of the 20th century, men attended college in greater numbers than women, but the number of female college students in the United States and Canada has grown to the point that women now receive more undergraduate degrees than men do (Jacobs, 1996). This pattern applies to few other countries. Especially in countries that are less industrialized, women do not participate in higher education nearly as often as men do. Table 11.1 presents the percentage of women in the entire college enrollment in various countries. This table shows the percentage of students who are women, but it does not reveal what percentage of students who are eligible to attend college actually do so. In the United States, a higher percentage of high school graduates enroll in college than in most other countries, even compared to other industrialized countries. That high percentage combined with the proportion of female U.S. college students results in U.S. women being better educated than their counterparts in most other countries (USDE, 1999).

Men have historically received the overwhelming majority of advanced and professional degrees (such as medical, dental, law, veterinary), but that pattern also has changed (Fox, 1989). In the 1960s, women earned only about 3% of professional degrees, but by the 1980s, the percentage had grown to 33%, and in 1996, women received 56% of all master's, 40% of all doctoral, and over 30% of professional (such as medicine, dentistry, law) degrees granted in the United States (U.S. Bureau of the Census, 1999). This growing number of women in professional fields has changed the composition of most professions, but past differences will take many years to equalize. Like undergraduate and professional degrees, doctoral degrees also show patterns of gender segregation: A greater proportion of doctoral

TABLE 11.1 Percentage of All Female College and University Students in Various Countries

Country	Percentage of Women	Country	Percentage of Women
Argentina	47%	Japan	29%
Australia	53	Kenya	28
Brazil	53	Mexico	45
Canada	55	Nigeria	27
China	20	Peru	34
France	55	Russian Federation	50
Germany	41	Saudi Arabia	42
India	32	South Africa	48
Iran	31	Switzerland	40
Israel	51	United States	53

SOURCE: Adapted from "United Nations International Conference on Population and Development," 1995, New York: United Nations.

degrees in physical sciences and engineering still go to men, whereas a greater proportion of doctoral degrees in education and psychology go to women.

Table 11.2 shows the percentage of degrees awarded to women in 1971 compared to 1996 for different majors. Most professions now have a larger proportion of women as a result of the changes in degrees awarded during the past 20 years. Some areas, however, have become even more strongly dominated by women, and other areas have experienced few changes. In addition, the concentration of doctoral recipients in some areas, such as in education and ethnic studies, is even more pronounced for African American and Hispanic women. Over half of the doctoral degrees earned by these women are in the field of education (Fox, 1989).

TABLE 11.2 Percentage of Degrees Awarded to Women in Various Fields, 1971 versus 1996

	Bachelor's Degree		*Master's Degree*		*Doctoral Degree*	
Field	1971	1996	1971	1996	1971	1996
Agriculture	4.2%	36.8%	5.9%	42.0%	2.9%	26.4%
Architecture	11.9	36.1	13.8	40.9	8.3	31.9
Ethnic studies	52.4	65.7	38.3	53.4	16.7	48.9
Biology	29.1	52.7	33.6	52.9	16.3	42.0
Business and management	9.1	48.6	3.9	37.6	2.8	28.8
Communications	35.3	58.8	34.6	61.3	13.1	44.9
Computer and information science	13.6	27.5	10.3	26.7	2.3	14.5
Education	74.5	75.1	56.2	76.3	21.0	62.2
Engineering	0.8	16.1	1.1	17.2	0.6	12.5
English/literature	65.6	66.0	60.6	64.3	28.8	61.6
Foreign language	74.0	69.8	64.2	67.4	34.6	55.8
Health science	77.1	81.6	55.3	79.0	16.5	56.6
Home economics	97.3	88.1	93.9	83.0	61.0	71.7
Law	5.0	72.9	4.8	36.4	—	36.2
Liberal studies	33.6	60.6	44.6	65.4	31.3	56.0
Library science	92.0	86.2	81.3	79.0	28.2	81.1
Math	37.9	45.7	27.1	38.8	7.6	20.4
Philosophy and religion	25.5	30.2	27.1	39.1	5.8	18.4
Physical Science	13.8	36.0	13.3	32.2	5.6	23.1
Protective services	9.2	38.4	10.3	36.5	—	42.1
Psychology	44.4	73.0	40.6	72.4	24.0	66.1
Public administration	68.4	78.8	50.0	71.4	24.1	55.9
Social sciences	36.8	47.9	28.5	46.1	13.9	37.8
Visual and performing arts	59.7	59.2	47.4	57.6	22.2	50.9

SOURCE: From *Statistical abstract of the United States, 1999* (119th ed.), pp. 204–205, U.S. Bureau of the Census, 1999, Washington, DC: U.S. Government Printing Office.

Gender disparities also exist on college athletic fields, and the attempts to remedy these inequities have become the center of continuing controversy. Title IX of the Educational Amendments of 1972 prohibited discrimination in educational programs that receive federal funding, including college athletic programs. Funding has been far from equal in athletics, as men's sports receive far more scholarships, equipment, facilities, staff, and publicity than women's sports do. Colleges have struggled (and sometimes mounted legal challenges) against increased funding for women's athletics (Tarkan, 1995).

Critics of Title IX argue that women and men do not show the same interest in sports participation, making equal funding unfair to men who want to participate. Supporters contend that female students' low level of interest in college athletics reflects the bias against women in sports that begins even before girls go to school (Tarkan, 1995). Increased opportunities for women to participate in competitive athletics have increased the number of women who compete. In the 1970s, only 7% of college women participated in organized athletics, but that percentage has grown to about 35%. The increase has not resulted in equal participation, equal funding, or equal acceptance for women in athletics. Enforcement of Title IX has not yet resulted in equal opportunities for training, use of locker rooms, medical services, or scholarships (Suggs, 1999).

Women compete in a growing variety of sports and athletic activities, which allows them to begin to break down some of the stereotypes about female athletes. The stereotype of masculine-looking, unattractive (and possibly lesbian) female athletes has begun to diminish (Theberge, 1991). Increased media coverage of a variety of athletics has allowed people to see a wider variety of female athletes, including many who meet most people's definition of female beauty.

The growing number of women who compete in college athletics receive support in the form of scholarships from their colleges and universities, but they have also received encouragement to develop their athletic abilities before they reach college. Mothers, older siblings, friends, and coaches in high school and junior high were all forms of social support to women who were college athletes (Weiss & Barber, 1995). Furthermore, these sources of support have improved over the past 15 years. Therefore, today's female athletes have benefited not only from the laws that mandate access to sports, but also from the changes in attitudes that have made athletic competition more acceptable and admired for women.

Athletic departments have struggled to provide funding for women's athletics in times of dwindling budgets. Indeed, much of the controversy over women's athletics concerns money rather than a desire to prohibit women from participating in sports (Sandomir, 1997). After a 1988 U.S. congressional affirmation that campuses cannot discriminate in funding for sports and athletics, and a 1997 U.S. Supreme Court ruling that leaves Title IX intact, college athletic departments must become reconciled to following this law. In many ways, college amplifies the gender inequities that occur in high school, making the college experience different for women and men in the classroom as well as in the locker room. Although both women and men report a generally positive campus climate (Fischer & Good, 1994), women experience more feelings of gender bias than men, and these feelings relate to the number of male instructors and classmates. Men also reported some negative feelings, including indifference and lack of recognition from their instructors. Both men and women agreed that women were not as well represented in the curricula as men are.

The choice of coursework results in some majors and classes that are dominated by one gender or the other. Although men are in the minority in many college classrooms, they

GENDERED VOICES

I Didn't Get to Play

"When I was a teenager, I was interested in sports, and I was good, especially at baseball," a woman in her 40s told me. "That was before Title IX, and there was no effort at all to allow women access to athletics, so I didn't get to play. It was partly social censure. Girls weren't supposed to be athletic, except for acceptable athletics. Dancing and cheerleading were acceptable for girls, but not baseball, which was the sport I liked.

"My mother didn't like my athletic inclinations and tried to urge me away from baseball and volleyball. I think I could have made the boys' baseball team, but of course, that was out of the question. No more. The changes are amazing. Girls play on boys' teams in baseball and even football in junior high and high school. Of course I regret not being able to play the sports I liked, but the changes in access to sports for women and even in attitudes toward athletic women are substantial.

"Rather than being discouraged from pursuing sports, my cousin got a volleyball scholarship that paid for her college education. I saw a news story about a girl who played linebacker on her junior high school football team. Those changes have not come easily, but I can remember when things were much different for athletic women. There has definitely been improvement."

may still dominate. For example, men interrupt more often in college classroom discussions and take leadership roles in mixed groups (Condravy, Skirboll, & Taylor, 1998). College instructors are more likely to be men, and this factor influences classroom interaction styles. Women and men have different preferences for classroom interactions with teachers and peers (Kramarae & Treichler, 1990). Women feel more comfortable in discussions in which teachers and students collaborate than in situations in which teachers try to impose their views on students. Men feel more comfortable in classrooms with a clear hierarchy and an emphasis on specified goals. That is, women and men carry their conversational preferences (see Chapter 9) into classroom interactions, and the preferences of each gender may make the other uncomfortable.

Women's uneasiness with the campus climate extends to professional and doctoral training, at which point women feel less encouraged and supported than their male colleagues (Fox, 1989). The majority of professors are men, and they tend to support, encourage, and assist their male students more than their female students (Schroeder & Mynatt, 1999). The lower percentage of female faculty causes female undergraduates to be less likely to attain advanced degrees (Rothstein, 1995). Role models and mentoring relationships can be very important to career advancement, not only in academia, but also in business (Wilbur, 1987), where young professionals benefit from the guidance and aid of older, more experienced professionals. Mentors tend to choose protégés who reflect themselves, so there is a tendency for men to choose men and women to choose women. With fewer women in high positions in academia and business, young women are thus at a disadvantage in finding mentors, and cross-gender mentoring does not offer the same benefits as same-gender mentoring, especially for women (Schroeder & Mynatt, 1999).

The close working relationships of mentoring provide situations that can lead to sexual attraction and action. With the imbalance of power between students and faculty, sexual relationships are almost inevitably exploitative. According to a 1980 court interpretation of Title IX of the Education Amendments of 1972, unwanted sexual remarks and advances constitute sexual harassment. The imbalance of power in the university is an arena in which instructors, professors, and administrators addicted to power may sexually harass students, staff, and instructors (Carr, 1991).

A review of sexual harassment in college (Paludi, 1997) noted the frequency of incidents, with both men and women as the targets. That frequency does not mean that students see themselves as sexually harassed; labeling sexual harassment is a problem for college students, but they report behaviors that meet the definition (Shepela & Levesque, 1998). The problems come from interpreting the behaviors as sexual harassment or even as inappropriate. Confirmation of problems with such incidents came from a study in which college students read scenarios of situations that met the legal definition of sexual harassment (Olson, 1994). When students evaluated whether they thought the scenarios constituted harassment, both women and men had difficulty. These college students tended to see these situations as free speech issues and hesitated to label even offensive remarks as harassment. In addition, these students tended to see women as responsible for letting men know that their remarks were offensive and to see men as blameless unless they had received a warning about the offensiveness of their behavior.

Therefore, asking students if they have been the targets of sexual harassment by teachers or peers will not yield accurate estimates of the frequency of campus harassment. Students do not recognize and label harassment. To understand the frequency of sexual harassment, researchers must ask about specific behaviors that meet the criteria of harassment. One study that focused on behaviors (Shepela & Levesque, 1998) found that harassment was very common. Between 50% and 78% of women and 29% to 74% of men had experienced incidents of peer sexual harassment in school. Behaviors such as sexual comments and pushing, shoving, and sexual intimidation were common. Between 20% to 55% of women and 15% to 44% of men had been the targets of faculty sexual harassment, such as sexist language and inappropriate sexual touching.

Students most often cope with harassment by trying to avoid the harassing faculty member and the situation—evading professors, changing majors, and altering examining committees (Hotelling, 1991). Although harassment produces stress for the one targeted, these incidents usually go unreported, because the reporting process causes additional stress. Whether reported or unreported, students' careers are affected by harassment from those in positions of power.

Therefore, like high school, college is another school situation in which women and men receive different treatment, which becomes a factor in making different choices, including their majors and careers. Women and men choose a similar range of majors and careers, but not in equal numbers. Women choose majors in education and social science more often than men do, who choose engineering and physical science majors more often than women do. Although women now receive more undergraduate degrees than men, they do not receive equal numbers of professional and doctoral degrees. The number of women in professional programs has increased in the past 25 years, and these women have had to contend with less attention and support than their male peers receive. Sexual harassment is not an uncommon experience on college campuses, despite legal prohibition, and women are more likely than men to be harassed by those in positions of authority as well as by their male peers. The problem is more common for female graduate students than for female undergraduates, providing an additional barrier to women in professional training.

Achievement

Achievement can have many meanings, including success in school. As the previous section showed, girls and women are successful in school, as measured by grades, but men are more successful when the criteria include prominence in prestigious careers and high salaries. How achievement is defined determines the extent to which women and men are high or low achievers.

Achievement Motivation

Traditionally, researchers have defined job success and recognition as achievement and have not considered personal or family relationships as comparable achievements. Therefore, neither women's nor men's roles in homemaking and family care have gained the same type of recognition as business, scientific, and political accomplishments. Indeed, women did not play a prominent part in psychology's early studies on achievement.

David McClelland and his colleagues (McClelland, Atkinson, Clark, & Lowell, 1953) studied the motivation to achieve, formulating the concept of *need for achievement.* These researchers looked at the expression of this need by asking people to interpret ambiguous drawings; that is, to tell a story about a picture that had many possible interpretations. The rationale behind this technique is that people reveal inner wishes and motivations in interpreting ambiguous situations by projecting their personal thoughts and feelings into unclear situations.

McClelland and his colleagues used this type of projective technique, reasoning that people would reveal their need for achievement by including achievement-related imagery in their stories about the pictures. Their results confirmed this prediction, revealing that people varied in the amount of achievement-related imagery in their stories. The need for achievement not only varied among people, but was stronger in people who had chosen achievement-oriented careers and in college students who had chosen careers with high risk and high responsibility.

This definition of achievement ignores forms of achievement other than business careers, which may be too restrictive (Mook, 1987). In addition, the need-for-achievement construct was formulated by examining only men, even though McClelland et al. found some overlap in the achievement needs of some men and women. However, another achievement-related concept has been applied specifically to women—fear of success.

Fear of Success

As David McClelland and his colleagues had done, Martina Horner (1969) also investigated the imagery associated with achievement and success. When she presented women and men with a description of a successful medical student, the women sometimes imagined negative consequences for the successful female medical student, but the men usually described the successful male medical student in positive terms.

Horner interpreted the women's descriptions of negative consequences accompanying success as a **fear of success,** or a motive to avoid success. She reasoned that women equate success with loss of femininity and feel anxious about success, especially when it involves competing with men. Her investigations showed that women often do better when working alone or when in competition with other women than when they must compete against men. Men, on the other hand, often perform better when they are in competition than when they work alone. Horner concluded that competition is a negative factor in women's achievement and that women see achievement situations differently than men do.

Although Horner used the terms *fear of success* and *motive to avoid success,* these labels are somewhat misleading, as they imply that women do not wish to succeed. What she called fear of success may have been women's acknowledgment that success in male-dominated professions is not socially well accepted for women, and that success will have negative as well as positive consequences for women. What Horner found was that competition may pose problems for women. She did not demonstrate that women try to avoid success, but that they anticipate and attempt to manage some of the negative consequences they believe will accompany success in male-dominated fields. Rather than finding that women fear success, Horner may have demonstrated that women understand the social consequences of competing with men in school and careers.

The social consequences of success in nontraditional careers may be negative for both men and women. An early study (Cherry & Deaux, 1978) found that men showed fear of success when describing a man in nursing school compared to a man in medical school, and women indicated awareness of negative consequences of success for a woman in medical school but not for a woman in nursing school. That is, perceptions of the negative aspects of success were related to the perceived gender appropriateness of the occupation rather than the gender of the person making the evaluation. Both women and men showed misgivings about violating gender stereotypes related to occupations.

A review during the 1980s (Paludi, 1984) showed that both men and women recognized the negative aspects of success at similar rates. In 64 studies on the topic, a median of 49% of women and 45% of men exhibited the "fear of success." These figures represent a considerable acknowledgment of the negative aspects of success, but show few gender differences.

More recent studies (Krishnan & Sweeney, 1998; Yoder & Schleicher, 1996) have indicated changes in these negative evaluations, possibly related to changes in the gender composition of occupations. When an occupation is no longer dominated by one gender, then it is not "gendered," and neither women nor men in the occupation should receive negative evaluations for pursuing that career. Such a change seems to have occurred in medicine; women no longer receive negative evaluations when they are described as being at the top of their medical school class, and no difference exists between women's and men's fear of success imagery and achievement motivation (Krishnan & Sweeney, 1998). Indeed, both men and women in nontraditional occupations received positive evaluations concerning their competence and success (Yoder & Schliecher, 1996). Women, however, were seen as less socially competent and less attractive when they were successful in nontraditional occupations. Therefore, women are no longer judged to fear success, but their success is seen as having personal costs.

Examining the dilemma of achievement from both a gender and an ethnic point of view (Gonzalez, 1988), achievement for Mexican American women can be a double-bind situation. This dilemma occurs as a result of the desire to form relationships with men from the same ethnic background plus the tendency of Mexican American men to feel threatened by women's achievements. The men in the survey reported that they were not threatened by women's accomplishments, but that the women believed otherwise. This situation creates stress in the women from what they see as conflicting demands for achievement and relationships. Wanting to preserve their ethnicity, these Mexican American women may be caught more severely in the dilemma of all women who strive for high achievement because they "experience conflict as their behavior is changing more rapidly than their sex role attitudes and the attitudes of their male counterparts" (Gonzalez, 1988, p. 378).

Self-Esteem and Self-Confidence

Self-esteem is conceptualized as a global evaluation of self that can range from positive to negative (Kling & Hyde, 1996). Although men and women have comparable concerns about success in nontraditional fields, their self-esteem and confidence in their own abilities show some differences. The AAUW (1992) contended that girls experience a sharp drop in self-esteem during junior high school, which negatively influences their education and careers. Two meta-analyses failed to find evidence of a dramatic decrease in self-esteem for girls during adolescence, however.

Both meta-analyses compared women's and men's self-esteem, but one (O'Brien et al., 1996) concentrated on adolescence, and the other (Kling & Hyde, 1996) included adolescence through later adulthood. Both studies found that boys and men have higher levels of self-esteem than girls and women have. These differences were small, however, even during adolescence. Within the United States, European Americans showed a small advantage for men, but for African Americans, no gender differences appeared in self-esteem (Kling & Hyde, 1996). Table 11.3 summarizes findings from several countries, showing that not all have the pattern that appears in the United States. Therefore, gender differences in self-esteem may be of little practical importance.

Self-esteem may be a factor in confidence, but other factors seem more important and more specific. Situational factors are important to one's confidence in achievement (Lenny, 1977). That is, no global concept of confidence applies to all situations. Similar to fear of success, confidence in one's ability to succeed varies with the gender typing of the activity.

TABLE 11.3 Differences in Self-Esteem for Males and Females

Age Group	Sample Population	Size of Effect	Higher In
Children	U.S. residents	Small	Males
Young adolescents	Norwegian	Small	Males
Adolescents	Chinese	Small	Females
Adolescents	Finnish	None	—
Young adults	Japanese	Small	Males
Young adults	Canadian	Small	Males
Adolescents to adults	U.S. European Americans	Small	Males
Adolescents to adults	U.S. African Americans	None	—
Adolescents and adults	Australian	Moderate	Males
Adults	U.S. residents	Small to moderate	Males
Elderly	U.S. residents	Moderate	Males

Men express more confidence in their abilities than women do when they perceive a task as "masculine," but this advantage disappears when the task is perceived as "feminine." Women showed lower expectancy of success on a masculine task than on a feminine or neutral task (Beyer, 1998), but this bias did not apply to men. Women's low predictions underestimated their performance, indicating that women have inaccurately low confidence in their performance on masculine tasks.

In addition, ability for specific tasks is an individual factor differentiating the self-confidence of men and women. When such information is available, the ability estimates of men and women are similar, but when this information is absent, men estimate their ability more highly than women estimate theirs. The same is true for situations in which people expect their performance to be compared to others; that is, women make lower estimates of their performance than men do, but they make similar estimates when they expect comparisons to be based on social rather than performance factors. Thus, situational factors are important in self-confidence, and women experience no overall deficit in self-confidence.

Other peoples' evaluations also influence men's and women's self-assessments of their performance in achievement situations, with women tending to be more responsive to others' evaluations than men are (Roberts, 1991). That is, women are more likely than men to revise estimates of their performance based on the evaluations they receive from others. This responsiveness might be due to women's greater social responsiveness or to lower confidence, but it may also be due to women's tendency to accept the feedback from others as more informative than men would.

A later study (Roberts & Nolen-Hoeksema, 1994) confirmed this finding while demonstrating that differences in self-confidence were not the source of women's more ready acceptance of evaluative feedback. Girls' and boys' experiences with evaluative feedback may lead to a difference; girls receive less feedback about their classroom performance, so they take what feedback they get quite seriously. Boys, on the other hand, tend to receive information not only about their performance, but also about their (mis)behavior. Indeed, a great deal of the attention that classroom teachers give to boys is oriented toward misbehavior. This situation could lead them to discount evaluative feedback, which sets up a gender difference. Women tend to consider the evaluations of others important, whereas men tend to reject these evaluations. Either strategy has advantages and disadvantages (Roberts, 1991; Roberts & Nolen-Hoeksema, 1994). Women may be overly responsive and rely too little on their own evaluations, but men may be overly resistant to advice from others and fail to change their behavior when changes would improve their performance.

Confidence and ability are not the same; one may be inappropriately confident or inappropriately unsure of one's abilities. Unduly low expectancies are more characteristic of girls and women than of boys and men. For example, women estimate their IQs as lower than men judge their IQs (Furnham & Gasson, 1998), and women predict lower college grade point averages than men do (Beyer, 1999). In some cases, the lower estimates may be underestimates, but these judgments are more accurate in some cases (Furnham, 1999). However, men's predictions are overestimates that represent a tendency toward positive self-presentation (Brown, Uebelacker, & Heatherington, 1998). Therefore, men have a tendency to see themselves as more intelligent and academically capable than women do. This tendency may lead them to be more confident in academic (and perhaps many other) situations, but it may also make them resistant to advice and feedback that would be helpful.

Attributions for Success and Failure

Research has also indicated that gender differences exist in explanations for success and failure. People can attribute success or failure to either internal factors, such as ability and effort, or external factors, such as luck and the difficulty of the task. Although both ability and effort are factors that come from within each person, ability is a stable factor, whereas effort can vary from situation to situation. Persons who believe that they succeeded because they worked hard have no assurance that they will succeed again without additional, similar effort. On the other hand, those who attribute their successes to intelligence should believe that similar success will continue—that is, they will still be intelligent next week and next year. Likewise, the external reasons for success and failure also differ in their stability. People who believe they failed because of bad luck would believe that their luck can change, leading to success on another attempt at the same task. People who attributes their failure to the difficulty of the task should believe that the task will always be difficult and that they will fail on each attempt. Therefore, people can explain their success or failure in terms of internal or external factors, and they can see each as either stable or unstable. Figure 11.3 shows the possibilities in combining these two dimensions. These explanations, or attributions, for success and failure can affect the amount of effort and time a person is willing to expend in order to succeed.

Some research (Karabenick, Sweeney, & Penrose, 1983; Rosenfield & Stephan, 1978) has revealed that the gender typing of the activity is a factor in preferences and attributions for success. One study (Karabenick et al., 1983) demonstrated that men preferred tasks with a high skill components when the tasks were "masculine," and women showed the same preference pattern on "feminine" tasks. Expectancy of success was influenced by the gender typing of the tasks. Another study (Rosenfield & Stephen, 1978) showed that the task need not actually be gender typed to show differences; describing the task as gender typed is sufficient. Men tended to explain success on a task described as "masculine" as due to internal factors and failure as due to external factors. That is, if they succeeded, they took personal credit, but if they failed, bad luck was to blame. The women showed a similar pattern for the task described as "feminine." Both men and women tended to use different attributions for their performance on the cross-gender task, explaining success or failure in

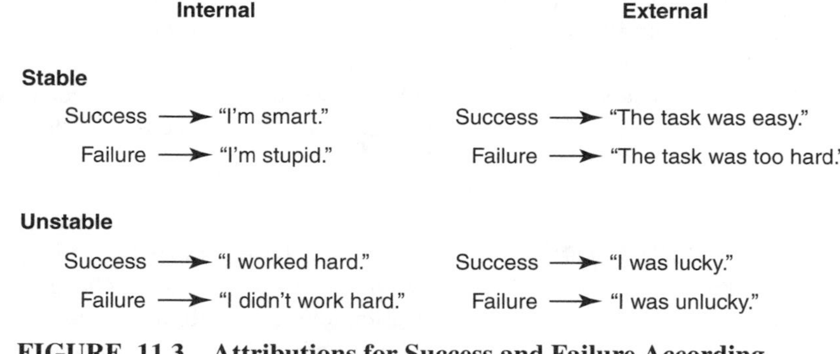

FIGURE 11.3 Attributions for Success and Failure According to Two Dimensions

less personal terms and attributing the outcome, either positive or negative, more to external factors, such as luck or task difficulty.

When asked to explain their grades in college classes, gender differences appeared (Campbell & Henry, 1999). Female college students were less likely to attribute their success to ability than were male college students. Although no difference appeared in attributional style (a pattern of explaining outcomes), and effort was the most common explanation for both, women chose this explanation significantly more often than men did. Effort can change, and this study suggests that women tend to believe that they need to continually put forth effort to succeed, but men feel more confident in their abilities. These gender differences may signal significant differences in women's and men's achievement efforts.

In summary, achievement may consist of a variety of attainments, but career success, rather than success in relationships or families, has been the standard definition. Under this definition, men have higher achievement motivation than women do. The fear of success, or the motivation to avoid success, became a popular explanation for women's lower levels of achievement, but further studies have indicated that negative evaluations of people and predictions about the future may be related to the gender appropriateness of the achievement situation. Men as well as women exhibit misgivings about achievements in gender-inappropriate occupations. The social consequences of achievement are a double bind for all women, but for women from minority ethnic groups, these problems are compounded by the desire to retain their ethnicity.

Studies have shown that women exhibit less confidence in their ability to achieve than do men, but these gender differences in confidence depend on the situation and the gender typing of the activity rather than on a general trait of men or women. The gender typing of the task also influences the attributions that women and men use to explain their performance, with both men and women attributing success to internal, personal sources on gender-typed tasks and resorting to external, situational explanations for failure. However, women tend to attribute success to effort rather than to ability, which may indicate significant gender differences in explanations for achievement.

Considering Diversity

Gender equity is a major diversity issue in education, but other diversity concerns are also important. The ethnic diversity and social class composition of the United States present problems to the educational system, and these two factors often combine to produce serious barriers to education. During the 1990s, between 35 and 40% of students in elementary and high schools were ethnic minorities, and around 5% of them had trouble speaking and understanding English (USDE, 2000).

Over the past 40 years, high school graduation rates have increased for all groups, but substantial differences exist among ethnic groups in the United States (U.S. Bureau of the Census, 1999). Asian Americans and Whites have comparable and high graduation rates (over 80%), but African Americans and Hispanic Americans finish high school at lower rates—76% and 55%, respectively. Employment opportunities have decreased for high school dropouts, but increased for those who attend college (*Business Week,* 1999); thus, those who fail to finish high school have decreasing job options. Gender differences are small in high school completion rates, with the biggest difference for African American women, who finish high school at slightly higher rates than African American men.

The percentage of ethnic minority students entering college increased between the 1970s and the late 1990s (USDE, 2000). These increases were not equal for all minorities, and most of the increases were due to greater numbers of Asian Americans and Hispanic Americans attending college. Despite their growing number, fewer ethnic minority than White students finish high school well-prepared to enter college (McCombs, 2000). Hispanic American, African American, and Native American students are not often among the highest achieving high school students, and they lack the academic records to be competitive at selective colleges. Indeed, these ethnic groups are more likely to enter 2-year than 4-year colleges (U.S. Bureau of the Census, 1999). The percentage of ethnic minority students decreases as the number of years required for college degrees increases, resulting in a very low percentage of doctoral and professional degrees granted to people from ethnic minorities.

Ethnic minorities are underrepresented in college for all types of higher and professional education. The exception is Asian Americans, who are more numerous in college than in the population, especially in prestigious research universities (USDE, 2000). Other ethnic minority students are more likely to attend public than private schools, and financing is one reason for their low college attendance and their choice of 2-year rather than 4-year programs. The cost of college has increased rapidly (U.S. Bureau of the Census, 1999), and minorities disproportionately live in poverty. Thus, even academically capable minority students may not be able to afford higher education. Ethnic minority students may be restricted to less expensive college options, even when their academic ability and preparation are adequate to make them competitive.

The gender differences in high school graduation rates are small, but larger differences appear in college (U.S. Bureau of the Census, 1999). Over the past 40 years, women have become more numerous on college campus (and at graduation ceremonies) than men. These differences are even more dramatic for ethnic minority women. Slightly more Asian American women than men attend college, substantially more Hispanic and Native American women do so, and the differences for African Americans is even larger.

The gender differences in advanced degrees produces differences in university faculties, in which ethnic minorities are also underrepresented (U.S. Bureau of the Census, 1999). Despite years of pressure to include diversity not only in curriculum but also in faculty, African Americans, Hispanic Americans, and Native Americans are underrepresented among the faculty in U.S. colleges and universities. Using medical school faculty as an example, one study (Fang, Moy, Colburn, & Hurley, 2000) showed that minority faculty experienced lower rates of promotion than White faculty. Therefore, ethnic minorities are not common on university faculties and advance at slower rates than their White colleagues.

The overall picture of education is one of increasing diversity but not always increased educational opportunities for those diverse groups in the United States. Ethnic minority students have not enjoyed the rapid progress that women have in gaining access to college and professional training. Indeed, African Americans received a lower percentage of doctoral degrees in 1998 than in 1981 (U.S. Bureau of the Census, 1999). Asian Americans are an exception, but Hispanic American, African American, and Native American students have to face many barriers to obtaining an education. Those barriers block the academic achievement of many, as reflected in the higher dropout rates and lower college attendance and graduation rates for these students.

Summary

Men and women have different experiences in education. Although Title IX of the Education Amendments of 1972 prohibits discrimination based on gender in schools, girls and boys do not receive the same treatment in schools. Beginning during the earliest school years and continuing throughout college and professional training, boys receive more attention and feedback about their performance in classroom work than girls do. Despite the different treatment, girls and boys have similar levels of achievement during elementary school. During junior high school, however, girls become less confident of their academic and physical abilities, and their achievement in math and science begins to lag.

During high school, girls and boys make different choices in coursework. Until recently, girls pursued advanced courses in math and science less often than boys did. The difference in number of math courses completed has disappeared, but girls are still less likely to take advanced physical science courses. Counselors convey higher career expectations to boys and fail to present the full range of career options to girls. Boys who enter vocational education programs are more likely to be steered toward lucrative skilled trades, whereas women in vocational education learn low-paying clerical skills. Athletics continues to be a way for boys to gain prestige, but the increase in sports participation among girls has led to greater acceptance of female athletes. Sexual harassment, especially from peers, becomes a problem for both girls and boys during high school. Gay and lesbian adolescents become targets of sexual harassment especially often, making school an unpleasant and even dangerous place for them.

Although women have not historically attended college in numbers comparable to men, that pattern has changed. Women now receive more undergraduate degrees than men do, but gender differences in choices of major persist, with a small percentage of science and engineering degrees and a large percentage of education and liberal arts degrees going to women. An increasing number of women are receiving advanced and professional degrees, however, and many majors are becoming less dominated by one gender.

The campus climate is less supportive of women's than men's achievement, both in the classroom and on the athletic field. Although Title IX of the Educational Amendments of 1972 also applies to athletics, women are less likely than men to be involved in college athletics, and equitable funding for women's athletics has become a source of controversy. Despite legal challenges, support for women's athletics is part of the law mandating equal opportunities in education, and this situation has resulted in a large increase in the number of women involved in sports.

Although achievement consists of a variety of attainments, studies of achievement have focused on career success rather than success in relationships or families. This emphasis has led to the portrayal of men as having a higher motivation for achievement than women. In considering women and achievement, the fear of success or the motivation to avoid success have become popular as a way to explain women's lower levels of achievement. Under this definition, women who exhibited fear of success acknowledged that negative as well as positive consequences will accompany success. Further studies have indicated that negative evaluations of people and predictions about the future may be related to the gender appropriateness of achievement situations. Men as well as women exhibit misgivings about achievements in gender-inappropriate occupations, but women continue to make pessimistic predictions about their personal characteristics and future lives when they succeed in nontraditional occupations. The social consequences of achievement are a double bind for all women, but for women from ethnic minority groups, these problems are compounded by the desire to retain their ethnicity.

Contrary to widely publicized reports, girls do not experience a sharp decrease in confidence during adolescence, but boys and men show slightly greater self-esteem than girls and women from adolescence through middle adulthood. Women also exhibit less confidence in their ability to achieve than do men, but these gender differences in confidence depend on the situation rather than on a general trait. Again, the gender typing of the situation plays a role in the confidence of both men and women, with each having more confidence in gender-appropriate compared to gender-inappropriate situations. The gender typing of the task also influences the attributions that women and men use to explain their performance, with both attributing success to internal, personal sources on gender-typed tasks and resorting to external, situational explanations for failure. Thus, gender role stereotypes are an important factor in achievement, with both men and women being influenced by their perceptions of the characteristics of the achievement situation.

Ethnic minorities in the United States face barriers to education. Over the past 40 years, high school graduation rates have increased for all groups, but African Americans, Hispanic Americans, and Native Americans graduate at lower rates than Asian Americans and Whites. This same disparity carries over into college, graduate, and professional training. Women from all ethnic groups attend college at higher rates than men from the same groups. Thus, at all levels, ethnic minorities experience educational disadvantages.

Glossary

fear of success negative consequences associated with success.

sexual harassment unwanted sexual attention.

Title IX of the Education Amendments of 1972 the federal act that prohibited educational institutions that receive federal funds from discriminating on the basis of gender.

Suggested Readings

Connell, R. W. (1996). Teaching the boys: New research on masculinity, the gender strategies for schools. *Teachers College Record, 98,* 206–235. The research and publicity on girls' treatment in schools has overlooked how schools can shortchange boys, too. Connell describes the problems that boys experience in school and how school can be an unfriendly place for them.

Jacobs, Jerry A. (1996). Gender inequality in higher education. *Annual Review of Sociology, 22,* 153–182. This review provides an evaluation of access to higher education, along with a historical and cross-national comparison. The experience of attending college is also critically reviewed, as well as the gender differential in majors and students' likelihood to be the target of sexual harassment.

Paludi, Michele. (1997). Sexual harassment in schools. In William O'Donohoue (Ed.), *Sexual harassment: Theory, research, and treatment* (pp. 225–240). Boston: Allyn and Bacon. Paludi presents information about the legal definition of sexual harassment along with a variety of examples and accounts of sexual harassment in various school environments.

Serbin, Lisa A.; Zelkowitz, Phyllis; Doyle, Anna-Beth; Gold, Dolores; & Wheaton, Blair. (1990). The socialization of sex-differentiated skills and academic performance: A mediational model. *Sex Roles, 23,* 613–628. This article is neither easy reading nor recent, but the presentation and integration of information concerning gender differences in academic achievement into a model are good.

Chapter 12

Careers and Work

HEADLINE

The Global Glass Ceiling

Fortune, October 12, 1998

Women who enter the world of corporate careers rarely become top-level executives; they tend to hit the glass ceiling and stay in middle-management or leave the company. The **glass ceiling** is the description for the invisible barrier that seems to prevent women and ethnic minorities from advancing to the highest levels of their professions. As Cora Daniels's (1998) article pointed out, this phenomenon occurs in other countries as well as in the United States. Indeed, the number of female managers is lower in Europe and Asia than in the United States—20% to 30% in Europe versus 40% in the United States (Daniels, 1998).

Even these figures represent changes: The number of women who have occupied top-level positions has grown during the 1980s and 1990s. For example, throughout the world, 45 women have become president or prime minister, and 25 of them have done so since 1990 (Daniels, 1998). The corporate world is restricted in the United States, but it is even less open in other countries. Women are more numerous and more prominent in the corporate world than they were, but the glass ceiling is still in place.

Throughout the world, some women have broken through the glass ceiling. According to Daniels (1998), several circumstances ease the trip to the top. Having a family business gives women many advantages in climbing the corporate ladder. Starting a business and entering businesses that are too new to have developed corporate climates unfriendly to women are other routes that make corporate success easier. In the established world of Fortune 500 companies, however, women fare poorly. In 1999, 49% of managerial positions were occupied by women, but only 5.1% of top executives and 3.3% of the top earners were women (Catalyst, 1999). These figures reflect how unfriendly corporate culture is for women and how strong the glass ceiling remains.

Careers

"Career, in its broadest sense, means 'life path' and thus includes all the roles a person plays throughout life," (Farmer & Sidney, 1985, p. 338). This definition places careers in a developmental framework and emphasizes the lifelong nature of career development and the many choices and roles that contribute to career development. Ideally, all people should choose a career on the basis of their interests, abilities, and potential contributions to society, but obstacles prevent the full development of both men's and women's potentials. Gender stereotyping is one of the obstacles.

Despite the encompassing social definition of career as the role people play throughout their lives, the study of career development has been limited to the choices and patterns that men have taken, with little study or attention given to women's career development. Barbara Gutek and Laurie Larwood (1989) wrote, "There was little reason to study the career development of women. It was easily summarized: There was none. Men had careers; women had temporary employment or jobs that took second place to family interest and obligations" (p. 8). This view led to research and theory on men's career development, the neglect of women's career development, and the assumption that the existing research and theories about men would extend to the women who pursued careers.

Women's careers, however, do not easily fit into the same framework as those of men, and men and women are likely to continue to have different career paths in the near future (Williams, 2000). One reason for this difference relates to the expectations about the types of careers each gender will occupy. Although both men and women are now violating these expectations by making gender-atypical choices at higher rates than in the past, most continue to choose gender-traditional occupations. Another expectation is that wives' careers will be secondary to those of their husbands. If someone must stay home with a sick child or if one person must relocate due to job demands, the husband's career nearly always takes precedence, and the wife must accommodate her schedule and employment. These expectations tend to result in interruptions in the careers of women, who may take years away from employment to care for children or to support a husband's career before rejoining the work force.

Women are more likely to hold part-time employment than men are—62% of part-time workers are women (U.S. Bureau of Labor Statistics, 2000). Part-time employment means not only lower salaries for women, but also problems for them in career advancement. Men's careers are more likely to follow a smooth line of development, meaning clear career choices during schooling, uninterrupted employment, and continuing career advancement throughout adulthood (Larwood & Gutek, 1989).

Indeed, homemaking is considered a legitimate career for women, but one that excludes them from the paid workforce. Homemaking is not directly comparable to paid work in a number of ways: It has no training requirements, no wages, no retirement benefits, no job security, and no opportunity for advancement (Betz, 1993). For most women, homemaking does not allow them to use and develop their abilities and talents: "This is not to discount the importance of childrearing, but only its insufficiency as a lifelong answer to the issue of self-realization" (Betz, 1993, p. 629).

Helen Astin (1984) formulated a model showing gender similarities and differences to explain career development for both women and men. Astin's model includes four components—motivation, expectations, gender role socialization, and opportunity. She assumed that motivation was the same for men and women but that their expectations differed due to differing gender role socialization patterns. Both the differences in gender role socialization and in opportunities create different outcomes in the workforce for men and women. Men have had the opportunity to participate in more highly paid, more prestigious work and in a wider variety of work than women have. Astin contended that changes have occurred, which give women greater freedom to choose careers dominated by men and which equalize the opportunities in those careers. Yet Lucia Gilbert (1984) questioned the adequacy of Astin's model, especially her optimism about women's greater freedom in career choices and success. Does research on motivation, expectations, gender role socialization, and opportunity support Astin's model? Do women have strong career motivations?

An exploration of college women's career orientations (Baber & Monaghan, 1988) indicated that some young women were innovators who planned nontraditional careers (as engineers, regional planners, or military officers), whereas others fit into the traditional category (teachers, day-care workers, social workers). All of the young women in this study were planning a working life that fit more closely into the category of career than job. Although this study did not compare women and men, it did demonstrate that young women have strong career motivations, substantiating this factor in Astin's model.

This strong motivation also applies to older women who have chosen and are pursuing careers. A survey of adults in New Jersey (Sigel, 1996) included women of varying ages and educational levels ranging from high school dropout to advanced professional degrees. The women in this study valued meaningful, rewarding work and showed ambition and dedication to their various careers.

Career Expectations and Gender Role Socialization

Young women still have family- and child-related expectations, but the career expectations of college women changed between the 1940s and the 1970s (Phillips & Imhoff, 1997; Komarovsky, 1982). In the 1940s, few college women planned to continue their careers after they married, but beginning in the 1970s, the opposite was true—very few planned to discontinue their careers after marriage. However, most women, regardless of their career plans, also anticipated marriage and children as part of their life goals. The requirements of combining family duties and paid work could account for women's lower career aspirations (Phillips & Imhoff, 1997).

College women have begun to anticipate combining marriage, motherhood, and careers (Baber & Monaghan, 1988). Young women have expanded their career choices to include some areas traditionally dominated by men, but the young women in this study still anticipated few difficulties in meshing career and family demands. The choices to remain single or to have no children were infrequent, with less than 2% of the young women planning to remain single and less than 3% anticipating lives without children

These expectations about marriage and motherhood demonstrate what Joan Williams (2000) described as force fields that pull women toward domesticity and away from careers. Similar forces affect men, drawing them toward careers and away from family. Despite college students' beliefs that few difficulties will arise in combining career and family, research presents a different picture. Arlie Hochschild (1997) found the situation of families squeezed by a lack of time as employed parents devoted hours to work and resented spouses and children for the time they demanded.

One factor that created Hochschild's (1997) "time bind" for families was the movement of women into nontraditional careers. Women who work as managers and engineers were as devoted to their careers as the men who held these jobs and almost as reluctant to go home to household work and child care as men were. That is, when women pursue high-prestige careers, they are more likely to behave in the same career-driven ways that men do. Indeed, acceptance of traditional gender role is related to the likelihood of women being in more traditional occupations (Schutte, Malouff, Curtis, Lowry, & Luis, 1996).

In addition, beliefs concerning egalitarianism contribute to nontraditional choices for both women and men. The belief that they and other women should be allowed the opportunity to develop their individual abilities makes women more likely to act on these beliefs by pursuing nontraditional careers (Phillips & Imhoff, 1997). Having employed mothers, supportive fathers, highly educated parents, and positive female models also contribute to women's likelihood of pursuing nontraditional careers. Family and personal beliefs also influence men (Christian, 1994). Those men with employed mothers, nontraditional fathers, and experience in personal relationships with nontraditional women are more likely to be egalitarian and to pursue nontraditional careers.

Ethnicity also plays a role in career expectations. Compared with European American women, African American women are more likely to expect that they will be employed throughout their adult lives (Betz, 1993). Those expectations are consistent with history: African American women have been more likely than European American women to be the heads and sole supporters of their households. The proportion of African American women who enter professional occupations is higher than for European American women, but African American women are even more concentrated in traditionally female occupations, which influences their incomes.

In comparing Mexican American and European American high school students, both gender and ethnic differences appeared (McWhirter, 1994). Female students perceived more barriers to careers than male students did, and Mexican American students saw more barriers and had less confidence in their abilities to overcome these barriers than European American students. For the young women, family-related problems were more common reasons for their lack of confidence than were their abilities, and the Mexican American students were more likely than the European American students to expect negative attitudes from their families should they attend college. The average ratings for the perception of barriers indicated uncertainty rather than pessimism, but ethnicity and gender both affected perception of barriers to careers.

Gender role expectations also influence the occupations men and women choose. Gender segregation of occupations is so prominent that choosing certain occupations often places persons within gender roles strongly identified with these occupations, whereas other careers do not have similar role demands. For example, caring about others and taking care of others is associated with the female gender role (Cancian & Oliker, 2000), and the "caring professions" of teaching, nursing, and child-care work are overwhelmingly female.

The percentage of women in the U.S. work force has risen to 46% (U.S. Census Bureau, 1999; see "According to the Media/According to the Research"), yet during the 1980s, over two-thirds of employed women were concentrated in occupations that were more than 70% female (Jacobs, 1989). Table 12.1 shows the percent of women in various occupation in 1983 and 1998. These occupations reflect a concentration of women in a narrow range of clerical, service, or professional positions, such as clerical workers, secretaries, child-care

TABLE 12.1 Percentage of Women in Various Occupations, 1983 versus 1998

Occupation	1983	1998	Occupation	1983	1998
Managerial	41%	49%	Administrative support	80%	79%
Accountants and auditors	38	58	Records processing	82	79
Public officials and administrators	39	49	Secretaries	98	98
Advertising, marketing, and public relations	22	39	Billing clerks	88	87
Professional	48	53	Sales	48	50
Architects	13	18	Mechanics	3	4
Engineers	6	11	Production and skilled crafts	21	23
Lawyers and judges	16	29	Construction	2	2
Mathematics and computer scientists	30	29	Labor	19	22
Natural scientists	21	31	Service occupations	60	60
Nurses	96	93	Household service	96	95
Physicians	16	27	Firefighters	1	3
Teachers, college	36	42	Police and detectives	9	16
Teachers, noncollege	71	75	Food preparation	63	57
Social workers	64	68	Hairdressers	89	91
Technical	48	54	Machine operation	42	37
Health technicians	84	82	Farm workers	25	17
Science technicians	29	43			

SOURCE: From *Statistical Abstracts of the United States, 1999,* U.S. Bureau of the Census, Washington, DC: U.S. Government Printing Office.

workers, teachers, and nurses. An examination of that table reveals some changes, with an increased percentage of women in occupations dominated by men, but fewer decreases in the percent of women in female-dominated fields. That is, women are moving into male-dominated occupations at a higher rate than men are moving into female-dominated jobs (Gutek, 1985). Even with these changes, a gender-segregated work force persists, with the majority of employed women and men working in jobs occupied by others of the same gender. This gender segregation promotes traditional gender role identification and hinders the career development of both women and men, especially those who have an interest in gender-atypical careers.

Career Opportunities

Women and men do not have equal career opportunities on several counts. Different education and training create unequal preparation for careers, which is the first point for gender inequity at work (see Chapter 11 for a review of these issues). The gender stereotyping that affects access to education and training also influences hiring decisions. Both gender differences in career choices and gender discrimination in hiring create differences in career opportunities (Gupta, 1993). Discrimination in hiring represents a second point at which women are disadvantaged in careers.

Discrimination in Hiring

Discrimination in hiring may be the primary factor in the gender gap in wages. Table 12.2 shows the gender gap in wages, and the differences are dramatic. For *every* occupational category, women earned less than men.

An examination of the wage differential between men and women who worked in a large private firm (Gerhart, 1990) showed that the women's salaries were 88% of the men's salaries, even after controlling for background, training, length of service with the company, and job title. This difference was attributable to inequitable initial salaries, and when this factor was taken into account, the salary advancements were comparable. The initial salary differences, however, prevented women's salaries from ever equaling the men's salaries.

Gender stereotypes are one source of discrimination in hiring, with both men and women subject to positive and negative discrimination on the basis of gender stereotypes (Martinko & Gardner, 1983). The gender role of the job positions is a major factor in discrimination: Men have the advantage in applying for "masculine" jobs, and women have a disadvantage. On the other hand, men can face negative discrimination when they apply for "feminine" jobs, whereas women can have the advantage. Specific, job-related information about applicants can overcome some gender stereotypes and can thus eliminate some discrimination, but the tendency toward gender stereotyping is a factor in hiring decisions.

TABLE 12.2 Weekly Earnings of Men and Women in Various Occupations, 1999

Occupation	Women's Earnings	Men's Earnings
Executive and managerial	$681	$952
Professional	707	939
Lawyers and judges	971	1,369
Technical	528	728
Engineering	625	673
Administrative support and clerical	427	539
Sales	399	666
Mechanics	592	622
Production and skilled crafts	352	582
Construction	423	571
Labor	301	357
Food service	286	311
Protective service (firefighters, police, guards)	492	613
Other service (food, healthcare, cleaning, and personal services)	302	336
Machine operation	340	487
Handlers, helpers, and laborers	314	377
Farming, forestry, and fishing	283	341

SOURCE: Labor force statistics from the current population survey, annual average tables from the January, 2000, issue of *Employment and Earnings,* Table 39, http://stats.bls.gov/cpsaatab.htm.

ACCORDING TO THE MEDIA...

Few Women Are Employed

Television programs frequently include characters' occupations as part of the plot, thus presenting a picture of occupations and the people who pursue those occupations. A content analysis of women on television in the 1990s (Elasmar, Hasegawa, & Brain, 1999) examined the portrayal of women and their employment. Regardless of employment, women appeared on television programs less often than men—only 39% of the speaking roles were female. In addition, women were more often minor rather than major characters. The figures are similar for music videos on MTV, where 63% were male characters versus 37% of female characters (Seidman, 1999). The figures for television programs and music videos, however, represent an increase over television portrayals of women in the 1970s and 1980s (Signorielli & Bacue, 1999) and music videos in the 1980s (Seidman, 1999).

About 10% of television women held professional, white-collar occupations, whereas almost 20% held blue-collar jobs (Elasmar et al., 1999). Those women with professional roles were more likely to be minor characters than major characters. About 15% held jobs in the entertainment industry, such as model, musician, or actress. About 16% had no job, 11% were portrayed as homemakers, and the occupation of about 30% of female television characters was unclear. Female major characters were more likely to have no job than to be employed. Although the percentage of women on television has increased since the 1970s, the percentage of employed women on television has not (Signorielli & Bacue, 1999).

In music videos, the portrayals of occupations are gender stereotypical (Seidman, 1999). More men than women appeared with a designated occupation, and women were underrepresented in both blue- and white-collar jobs. For example, 5% of police officers were female on MTV, compared to 13% in the population. Of the women portrayed in white-collar jobs, 8% were nuns, which is a substantial overrepresentation. Some occupations appeared more often in music videos than on television programming, but the gender stereotyping was similar.

Children are not a prominent part of women's lives on television (Elasmar et al., 1999). Only 13% of women on television shows had the primary responsibility of caring for children, yet the majority of women on television were in their 20s or 30s—the years when women are likely to have and care for children. Older women are not often employed on television (Signorielli & Bacue, 1999). Indeed, older women are practically invisible on television—less than 3% of characters are elderly. In addition, the definitions for elderly differ for men and women on television. Men over age 65 are more likely to have continuing employment than women over 65, which may be a factor in men's portrayals as middle-aged versus women's portrayals as elderly at the same age.

The world of work on television is not as gender-stereotypical as it was in television of the 1970s and 1980s (Signorielli & Bacue, 1999). Women are more likely to appear in occupations traditionally dominated by men than they were in decades past. If women are to appear on television, then they must hold such jobs because the jobs women actually hold do not appear—only 10 of the 68 job categories portrayed on television are jobs traditionally dominated by women. Employment on television is largely a man's world, even when women appear on the screen.

Additional evidence of gender discrimination in hiring came from a study of gender stereotypes in hiring decisions (Glick, Zion, & Nelson, 1988). Fabricated résumés went to business professionals for evaluation. Some résumés contained information giving the female or male applicants some characteristics more typical of the other gender, some résumés had information magnifying the stereotypical characteristics of the applicant's gender, and some résumés had neutral personal information. These researchers hypothesized that both men and women would be affected by gender discrimination based on stereotypes, but that specific, personal information in the résumés could overcome this bias.

ACCORDING TO THE RESEARCH...

Most Women Are Employed

The demographic picture of women and employment varies substantially from the television portrayal. On television, a minority of women are employed, whereas in the United States, about 60% of women are employed (U.S. Bureau of the Census, 1999). Indeed, television's presentation of female employment has been misleading throughout the history of television; women have always been employed at a higher rate in real life than in screen life.

In some respects, women's jobs are better in real life than on television. About 10% of female characters hold professional jobs on television, whereas the employment statistics reveal that about 50% of such jobs are held by women. In other respects, the television versions of professional women may be better than reality; television portrays the professional woman as a high-level executive. Ten percent would be too high a figure for this group—only about 5% of the highest level executives and managers are women. Despite the workforce changes of the past several decades and the portrayals of women in nontraditional jobs, the majority of women continue to work in occupations traditionally dominated by women.

Family situations are also different in real life than on television. About 60% of married women are employed (U.S. Bureau of the Census, 1999) versus about 30% on television (Metzger, 1992). About 70% of employed women have children, and the majority of child care is performed by women. Thus the 13% of women on television with primary child care responsibilities differs substantially from the situation of most women. Therefore, the portrayals of women and work on television present a picture that diverges from the demographics of work life for women in the United States.

The information in the résumés affected the business professionals' ratings of the applicants' personalities and suitability for the job, but not exactly in the ways the researchers had predicted. Their evaluations showed a bias toward masculinity for all occupations. Those applicants with "masculine" characteristics were more likely to be rated as worthy of interviews for employment, even when the job's characteristics were "feminine." When the personal information was neutral rather than gender stereotypical, the business professionals were more likely to choose the male rather than the female applicants for interviews. Thus, business professionals appeared to discriminate in favor of men.

A similar bias appeared in a study that concentrated on academic hiring and promotion (Steinpreis, Ritzke, & Anders, 1999). Academic psychologists who evaluated a résumé were more likely to endorse hiring when the résumé had a man's rather than a woman's name (although the résumés were identical in content). These evaluators also showed bias in commenting on qualifications for promotion, questioning the female but not the male professor's accomplishments. These biases appeared in the evaluations of both female and male academicians, indicating that discrimination in hiring and promotions continues to occur, even among academic psychologists.

Therefore, discrimination based on gender, and especially on the match between gender and gender stereotypes associated with the job, presents problems in making fair hiring decisions. Such discrimination is an important factor in the wage gap between men and women. Providing specific information that shows that applicants have some characteristics of the other gender can diminish stereotypical perceptions of these applicants and influence hiring. Unfortunately, gender stereotyping is resistant to change, and women experience more disadvantages than men because of such discrimination.

Barriers to Career Advancement

The barriers to career advancement can come from situational and organizational as well as individual sources. One of the organizational sources is the glass ceiling—the subject of this chapter's headline story. Only 5% of senior-level managers in major corporations are women, and these women tend to be concentrated in jobs traditionally associated with women, such as human relations or communications (Chartrand, 1996). Women in corporate jobs often believe that they have hit the glass ceiling.

A total of 52% of female executives blamed male stereotyping for their lack of advancement, whereas 82% of male chief executives said that women did not have sufficient experience to be promoted (Chartrand, 1996). Half of the women believed that they were excluded from informal networks at work—the "old boy's networks"—whereas only 15%

GENDERED VOICES

How Can I Do That to the Women?

Toni had been the auditor for the bank in the small town where she grew up, and she was the first woman to be promoted to vice-president of the bank. After three years as vice-president, she had a talk with the president of the bank.

She knew that she had made some big mistakes, and she was afraid that she might lose her job. He assured her that she was in no danger of losing her job, but he agreed that she had made some pretty serious mistakes and couldn't expect the bonuses she had gotten last year.

In their conversation, Toni told the president of the bank that she didn't really like being a vice-president as much as she had liked her auditing job, and he mentioned that it might be possible for her to have that job again, if she wanted. She said, "Oh no, I couldn't do that to the women." She felt that her promotion was so visible and her performance so crucial to other women in business in the town that she couldn't leave the job she disliked—it would be an admission of failure not only on a personal level but for all women. She couldn't consider the possibility.

of men believed that women were excluded. To succeed, female vice presidents reported the necessity of working harder and taking more risks than men in similar positions. Thus, women in corporate life see the glass ceiling as real and a barrier to their advancement, whereas male executives do not see the situation in the same way.

Although the concept of the glass ceiling was created to describe corporate careers, barriers also exist in other prestigious occupations. Science and engineering have been inhospitable to women and ethnic minorities (Long & Fox, 1995). The low participation rates can be attributed to a "filtering" of women and minorities out of science and engineering through choices to not pursue the required education (see Chapter 11 for a discussion of this process). Differential advancement in scientific careers is similar to business: Female and ethnic minority scientists and engineers are more likely to be employed in less prestigious academic settings and at lower rank than White men. Their academic situations and ranks limit their opportunities to participate in research, and these limitations affect their likelihood of receiving recognition. The specific factors that limit career success in the field of science differ from business, but the barriers are similar—a glass ceiling exists in science careers.

Ironically, women have no advantages in attaining higher positions in traditionally female-dominated fields. Indeed, men seem to have advantages in all types of jobs. The advantages that men have in female-dominated fields has been referred to as the *glass escalator* (Williams, 1992). This term conveys the image that some invisible force produces an easy ascent to higher positions, in contrast with the glass ceiling, which prevents women and minorities from reaching the highest levels of career achievement. Men who choose careers traditionally dominated by women face some discrimination from society in general, but these men have career advantages in terms of rapid promotion. These advantages may come as a result of the perception that men should not be in jobs that women usually perform, and thus men receive promotions to administrative or supervisory positions within that occupation.

For example, a male librarian described how happy and confident he had felt in his abilities as a children's librarian. Reading stories to children and helping them find books were part of his job, but many people mentioned to him that this was inappropriate for a man to do, and he was transferred to another library and given the position of research librarian. When asked why he did not consider a discrimination lawsuit, the man reported that his new job was really a promotion to a more prestigious position, so he felt benefited rather than being harmed from these clearly discriminatory actions. Gender role discrimination and occupational stereotypes provide the basis for both the glass ceiling and the glass escalator.

Gender stereotyping and discrimination in promotion contribute to the phenomena of the glass ceiling and the glass escalator, but the *sticky floor* is also a factor in women's lower wages and problems in career advancement. The concept of a sticky floor contrasts with the glass ceiling as a means to describe low-status occupations with little opportunity for advancement. That is, occupations in which employees get stuck at the lowest levels. Many of the occupations dominated by women fit this description, including clerks, secretaries, beauticians, garment workers, and household service workers. Greater numbers of ethnic minority women tend to be concentrated in these low-level jobs, with both African American and Hispanic American women more likely to occupy blue-collar jobs than White women (Green & Russo, 1993). Ethnic differences exist within blue-collar occupations; African American women are more likely to work in health service jobs, and Hispanic American women are more likely to be employed in manufacturing. All of these jobs have lower wages than jobs typically occupied by White women or by men.

GENDERED VOICES

I Never Felt Discriminated Against

A man who had gone to nursing school almost 30 years ago told me, "I decided to be a nurse when I was in the 10th grade, after I had surgery. The woman who lived across the street told me about the salaries of nurse-anesthetists, and the work interested me and the money sounded good. I don't remember my parents saying anything, my school counselor got information about nursing, and I didn't discuss it with my friends, so I don't recall any negative comments.

"During a career day at school, we had to choose the areas to attend, and I wrote down that I wanted to be a nurse. Much to my surprise, so did one of my friends, and neither of us knew that the other had thought about becoming nurses. One other guy wanted to be a surgeon, and we were the only three who had signed up for the health care option. The guy who wanted to be a surgeon was really mad at us, because he thought we were kidding about being nurses and were making fun of him.

"There were only two men in our nursing class. Now many men go into nursing, but then it was uncommon. There had been another guy about 10 years earlier and the two of us. That's it. I never felt discriminated against by either the teachers or the female students. Everybody was supportive and more than fair. My fraternity brothers were another story—they gave me a lot of static about majoring in nursing. The jokes were pretty good-natured, but there were a lot of jokes. I joke around a lot too, so it wasn't really a problem, but it was something that came up a lot.

"The women I have worked with were great. If anything, I think that being a man has been an advantage to me in my career. Rather than being discriminated against, I think that I was at some advantage. Maybe I got promotions and advancement faster than women, but those who chose me and recommended me were almost always women. I think I was competent and deserved the promotions, so I would have a hard time saying that I advanced in my career because I was a man, but I certainly never felt that it held me back."

I told him about the frequency of sexual harassment in jobs in which the gender ratio is far from equal and asked him if his female-dominated work situation had led to harassment. He replied, "Did I ever feel sexually harassed? That's hard to say. I never was put in the position of 'You do this or it's your job.' Never. But I've had my butt grabbed, and I've gotten a lot of offers. If that's harassment, then I guess I've been harassed, but I can't say that it really bothered me."

Factors other than gender stereotyping and discrimination contribute to the gender gap in wages—different career choices, career schedules, and workplace climate. Women occupy jobs and pursue careers that are less prestigious and not as well paid as those that men occupy. For example, only 29% of lawyers and judges are women compared to 89% of nursing aides, orderlies, and attendants; only 39% of managers in marketing, advertising, and public relations are women compared with 98% of secretaries and stenographers (U.S. Bureau of the Census, 1999). In addition, women in science, engineering, and management tend to choose public institutions rather than private industry. This choice may be due to the different climates that these work settings offer to men and women, but the consequences are lower salaries for women (Melamed, 1996).

The gender wage gap decreased during the 1980s, mostly due to an increase in women training for and entering fields that paid better (Loury, 1997). Therefore, the choices are not as different as they once were, and wages have changed as a result. For college-educated women and men, the situation is not as discrepant as for the workforce in general (Hecker, 1998). The gender wage gap narrows and even disappears when comparing women and men who had completed the same college majors. This narrowing was even more prominent as a trend for younger workers, demonstrating that the changes in workforce composition have made a difference in closing the wage gap.

The differences in women's and men's career development schedules also differentiate the genders in promotions and wages. Women are more likely than men to take time off from their careers to attend to family needs, such as staying home with young children. These employment gaps take women out of the work force, pull them off the track to advancement, and slow their progress. Employment gaps are even more damaging to men's career advancement plans (Schneer & Reitman, 1990), but women are more likely to interrupt their careers, so the overall impact of interrupted employment decreases women's wages and limits their opportunity for advancement more than it does for men.

What about those women who place a high priority on their careers? Does equal emphasis on work create equal rewards for women? Answers to those questions can come from women's satisfaction with their careers or from an assessment of their career progress. A group of successful male and female MBAs (people who have earned master's degrees in business administration) showed similar motivation, involvement, and enjoyment for work as well as similar tendencies to be "workaholics" (Burke, 1999). A study of the career progress of corporate men and women (Stroh, Brett, & Reilly, 1992) led to the conclusion that the same behavior did not result in the same success. "Although the women had done 'all the right stuff'—getting a similar education as the men, working in similar industries, not moving in and out of the workforce, not removing their names from consideration for a transfer more often—it was still not enough" (Stroh, 1992, p. 251). When women followed the traditionally male pattern of career advancement, they still did not advance at comparable rates. However, both women and men who did not do "all the right stuff" fared more poorly in terms of career progress than the women who did.

If deviating from the standard pattern does not work and following the pattern does not work, then women have no way to succeed to the extent that men do. As the headline article for this chapter discussed, being born into a business family or starting a business were the best routes to chief executive officer rather than climbing the corporate ladder.

Another factor in career advancement comes from the work climate and the informal social structure at work, which can help or hinder the advancement of new employees. Women perceive their work environments as more hostile in terms of the informal social structure, standards they must meet for advancement, sexist attitudes, and the possibility for solving problems that arise at work (Stokes, Riger, & Sullivan, 1995). For example, people working in business settings demonstrated their tendency to discriminate against women by choosing a man rather than a woman as the company representative for an important assignment, but choosing a woman for a less important assignment (Trentham & Larwood, 1998). Indeed, these business people believed that they were conforming to the social norms for business by favoring men, even when the individuals themselves believed in equal treatment. This tendency to comply with the norm of discrimination burdens women in their career advancement.

Achievement-oriented women who pursue careers in male-dominated fields are in the minority, and minority status can handicap career advancement through isolation from the informal power structures (Kanter, 1977). When a minority member (either a woman or a member of an ethnic minority) enters the corporate world, the person becomes a **token** of the minority group. The token stands out, becoming more visible than other employees, and feels pressure to succeed and to reflect well on the ability of everyone in his or her minority group.

As tokens try to fit into the existing corporate and social structure, the dominant group may work toward keeping them on the periphery. The process of excluding women and minorities may function either overtly or in a subtle manner (Benokraitis, 1997; Lorber, 1989). New workers either become part of the "inner circle" or not, and those who are not accepted never fit into the organization. As a result of this failure to fit in, these employees never gain the trust and confidence of coworkers. Such mistrust can isolate tokens and prevent them from joining interaction with the dominant work group.

Tokens are also handicapped in forming mentoring relationships, the relationships between younger and more experienced workers that offer younger workers valuable support in the form of friendship, advice, or even direct intervention in the organization. Mentor–protégé relationships tend to form within gender and ethnic lines. Neither women nor ethnic minorities are common in the upper echelons of organizations, and this situation places barriers on finding mentors (Leong, Snodgrass, & Gardner, 1992). Access to mentors can be an advantage for those who find them, and an impediment to advancement in the careers of those who do not (Wilbur, 1987).

For example, women and ethnic minority graduates from one MBA program were less likely to have mentors than White men who had completed the same program (Dreher & Cox, 1996). Establishing a mentor relationship with a White man was advantageous. Those MBAs who did form such relationships earned over $16,000 more per year compared with those without mentors and those whose mentors were women or ethnic minorities. Therefore, women and minority employees are at a disadvantage in finding mentors who can further their careers, whereas White men have advantages in this aspect of their careers.

The workplace environment and interactions in it affect performance and influence both colleagues' and supervisors' ratings of female workers. Management is a category that has been associated with men and has thus traditionally been considered male (Kanter, 1975). Despite a growing number of women entering management, the perception continues that management is a male position. Studies on perceptions of managers confirm the association of men and management. One study (Heilman, Black, Martell, & Simon, 1989) questioned male managers concerning characteristics of men and women as well as male and female managers. The results indicated an association between men and management and negative stereotypes of women as managers. A more recent study (Deal & Stevenson, 1998) questioned college students about their perceptions of male and female managers. The male students expressed negative opinions of women in management, but the female students indicated significantly more positive perceptions of female managers. A study of business managers (Rosenthal, 1996), however, showed no gender bias in managers' evaluations and explanations of their subordinates' performance.

This finding of no gender bias in a field study is particularly optimistic because research participants were managers rather than students, and research took place in organizations rather than in labs. Therefore, the existence of persistent stereotypes may be more of a factor for laboratory research than for ratings that appear as part of work settings with real people. Indeed, the opportunity to know persons allows managers to make ratings that are individual and specific rather than relying on stereotypes, as participants in laboratory research often must. This single finding does not overrule the possibility of gender bias operating in organizations, but it does suggest that knowing persons can allow some people to overcome the stereotype bias.

Some researchers have found that there are situations in which gender stereotypes produce more favorable views of women than of men. Alice Eagly and her colleagues (Eagly, Mladinic, & Otto, 1991) found that college students rated the social category of women more favorably than the social category of men, but Eagly (1994) contended that this positive evaluation depended on women adhering to the traditional gender role. When women diverge from this role, they no longer receive such positive evaluations.

Women can also receive more positive ratings by overcoming perceived discrimination (Abramson, Goldberg, Greenberg, & Abramson, 1977). When college students evaluated the competence of a male or female attorney or a male or female paralegal worker, they rated the female attorney as the most vocationally competent due to the barriers to achievement for women. Unusual success magnified the individual's achievement.

These studies demonstrate that women can be perceived as competent and capable of high levels of achievement, but the stereotype holds women as less competent. Therefore, to break through the gender stereotype, some evidence must exist to the contrary. That evidence can come from specific information about a person or from information about that person's competence. Without information that women are exceptions, men receive higher ratings of competence than do women.

Therefore, women and ethnic minorities encounter several barriers to their career advancement. Many of those barriers relate to negative stereotypes of women and minorities, involving questions of their abilities, competence, and dedication to work. Even with similar qualifications and performance, few women and ethnic minorities attain the highest levels of career advancement, which suggests that discrimination is a deciding factor in the difference.

Balancing Career and Family

Family demands influence careers paths for both men and women. Although most people marry and have children, the historic association of women with household work and child care has made family concerns more of an issue for women's than men's careers. The association between women and domesticity has created a "force field" that pulls women toward household work and child care, which often decrease the amount of time they spend on their careers (Williams, 2000). This pull toward domesticity prevents women from fulfilling the "ideal worker" role, a worker able and willing to devote full time and overtime to work. Men who want to be involved with their families also fail as ideal workers and also may suffer penalties in their career advancement. The assumption still operates in most workplaces that workers will devote themselves to their careers and someone will be at home to support these ideal workers by taking care of household and children.

A large majority of people marry and have children, placing them in the situation of balancing work and family demands. Figure 12.1 shows the increase in employment for married women, including women with young children. Society, employers, and many husbands assume that women will be the ones who perform most household chores and become the primary caregivers for children. Thus, women who choose to concentrate on their careers are perceived as neglecting their families (Hochschild, 1997).

On the other hand, assumptions about men place them under suspicion when they do *not* concentrate on their careers. Men's traditional role in families is breadwinner, which puts men into careers as a way of showing devotion to their families. Thus, traditional family

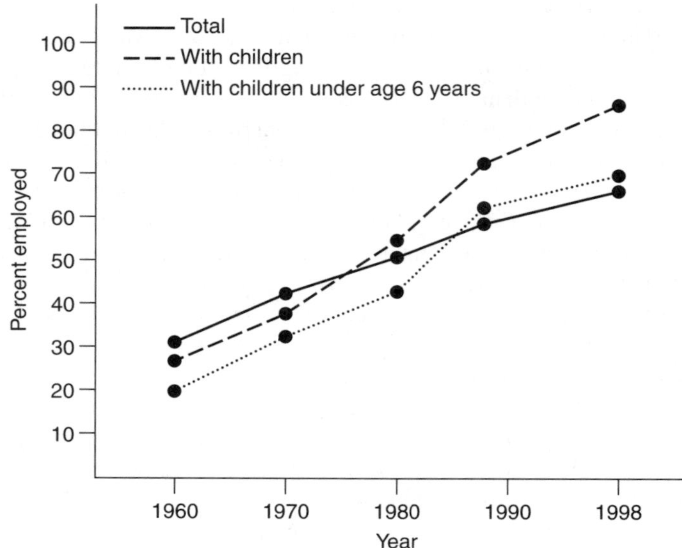

FIGURE 12.1 Employment Trends for Married Women, Including Women with Children, from 1960 to 1998

SOURCE: *Statistical Abstract of the United States: 1999* (119th ed.) (p. 417), U.S. Bureau of the Census, 1999, Washington, DC: U.S. Government Printing Office.

demands take men away from their families while they devote time to careers. Therefore, the choice to spend time away from family has been (and remains) more socially approved for men than for women (Steil, 1995). Changes have occurred and continue to occur as men want to participate more fully in their children's lives (Adler, 1996). These desires to become active fathers as well as good providers can conflict. The most lucrative careers tend to be the ones that take the most time. When men work 80 hours a week, they have little time to attend Little League games.

When men want to provide for their families but work hard at their jobs, they spend time away from their families and leave the wives (who often are also employed outside the home) to take up the slack in child care and household chores. This situation, therefore, decreases the time (and energy) that the wives have to devote to their careers and the time and energy that men have to devote to their families. These societal factors form barriers to women's career advancement and to men's involvement in family life.

What does it take to balance these demands? Several researchers have studied couples and companies to understand how some people manage this balancing act while others do not. Pepper Schwartz (1994) found that couples with children had a much more difficult time than those without children. The added demand of raising children coupled with the expectation that wives would be the primary caregivers prevented many couples from forming equitable relationships. Arlie Hochschild (1997) studied women and men in a large, multinational corporation and found that, even when the company had a variety of "family friendly" policies, the corporate climate pushed women toward domesticity and men toward career advancement.

The societal assumption that women will be family caregivers makes it difficult for women to develop their careers. One form of inequity often occurs: Women reduce the number of hours they work and allow their husbands to develop their careers. This strategy may seem reasonable because most husbands make more money than their wives, so wives' careers seem like the obvious ones to sacrifice. When this situation occurs, women undermine their careers and are likely to form unequal partnerships with their husbands. Schwartz found that couples who had formed equal partnerships often had chosen to sacrifice high-prestige careers. For many such couples, the decision was a deliberate acknowledgment that current corporate, scientific, and academic careers require more than full-time devotion to the job.

The social structure of work and family make it difficult for women to fulfill both career and family demands. "In our society, both families and professional careers are 'greedy' institutions. Until changes occur, women who want both can expect to face conflicting and overwhelming demands" (Kaufman, 1995, p. 302). With men wanting (and often expected to) be involved in family life, men as well as women feel the demands from career and family life to be "greedy."

Gender Issues at Work

The gender gap in wages reflects the barriers that women face when entering and advancing in careers. Although women have entered male-dominated professions in greater numbers in the past decades than at any previous time, women remain underrepresented in the highest levels of their professions. Even when factors such as education, age, position, job tenure, and type of job are equated, women earn less money than men (Landau & Arthur, 1992). About 25% of the wage gap between men and women is the result of gender segregation of occupations (Jacobs, 1989).

Gender Segregation on the Job

The gender-typical choices that most men and women make in careers have resulted in gender segregation in most jobs. That is, in most work situations the large majority of jobs are held by either men or women but not by an equal (or nearly equal) mix of both. These associations have created the perception that the jobs are gendered. That is, regardless of the job demands, some jobs have become so associated with either men or women as to be considered male occupations or female occupations.

According to Barbara Gutek (1985), women have a less diversified range of occupations than men. Consequently, women are concentrated in a few occupations, whereas men are employed in a wider variety of jobs. Over two-thirds of women have jobs in clerical or professional fields, but the professional fields are those traditionally dominated by women—nursing and teaching. Gutek pointed out that women are most underrepresented in skilled blue-collar jobs, such as electricians, mechanics, and plumbers. (Refer to Table 12.1 for the percentages in the "construction," "mechanics," and "production and skilled crafts" categories.)

In Gutek's study of employment in the Los Angeles area, over 60% of men worked in occupations that were dominated by men (defined as 80% representation by men for that job category). Women were also employed in gender-segregated occupations, but not to the same extent as men: About 40% of women worked in jobs that were female dominated. Furthermore, women have entered traditionally male-dominated fields, but men have not as often entered traditionally female-dominated occupations. Both the unequal gender distribution and the unequal movement into cross-gender jobs have resulted in more women in male-dominated occupations than men in female-dominated jobs. As of 1990, an end to gender segregation would have required a change in jobs for more than half of the men and women in the workforce (McCann & McGinn, 1992).

Gender integration at work poses strategic problems, especially during the early stages of the process. Men in mixed-gender work settings reported less satisfaction and more depression about their jobs than men in either male-dominated or female-dominated work settings (Wharton & Baron, 1987, 1991). Men were significantly less satisfied with gender-integrated compared to gender-segregated work situations. Not surprisingly, women were most dissatisfied in work situations in which women were in the majority and the few men received preferential treatment. Women in both male- and female-dominated workplaces reported more job-related demands than did men in the same jobs (Hochwarter, Perrewe, & Dawkins, 1995). Therefore, the process of gender integration presents problems for both men and women.

The dissatisfaction may be greatest at the beginning of the integration process (Allmendinger & Hackman, 1995), when either men or women dominate the workplace. When women held between 10% and 40% of positions within an organization, both genders were dissatisfied, and the organization did not function as effectively as it had previously. As the proportion of women increased toward 50%, many of the problems and conflicts diminished. When the workplace was integrated, no gender differences appeared in the perception of work-related demands (Hochwarter et al., 1995). Although the integration process may create problems, those problems diminish when gender integration progresses.

Gender segregation is often more extreme in specific work situations than in any occupation as a whole (Groshen, 1991). For example, both men and women wait on tables, but some restaurants hire only waiters, whereas others hire only waitresses. Even people who choose occupations that are not dominated by one gender may work in companies or offices in which that occupation is gender segregated and will spend their time with same-gender colleagues. Gender segregation tends to raise men's and lower women's salaries. At least 11% and as much as 26% of the gender wage gap is attributable to gender segregation, with the variation depending on the industry.

Gender segregation declined between 1970 and 1980, which may be related to a decreasing wage gap (Fields & Wolff, 1991). Not all occupations showed decreasing gender segregation, and occupations that experienced rapid growth during this time period showed the greatest decline in gender segregation. As the headline story for this chapter related, one of the routes for women to the top of a field occurs when the field has not yet had time to develop gender bias. New, rapidly growing fields are associated with lowered barriers for women entering the field as well as diminished practices of wage discrimination.

Although jobs are gender segregated for most workers, the workplace is likely to include both men and women, who, though they may hold different jobs, must work together in the same setting. For example, most secretaries are women, most managers are men, and most managers have secretaries. Thus, men and women often work together but not at the same job. Indeed, the work situations that allow for interaction between men and women often involve a power differential, with men having the more powerful positions and women the more subordinate.

Gender, Communication, and Power in the Workplace

Communication style is one possible explanation for the gender differences in career advancement. Robin Lakoff (1975) contended that "women's language" differs from "men's language," with women adopting a more tentative and deferential style of communication than men. She hypothesized that this style of speaking fails to convey the assertive, commanding qualities necessary for leadership, which makes women's speech style a handicap in their careers.

Would women be more successful at work if they talked like men? This question was tested by asking participants to evaluate applicants who presented one of two versions of a job interview (Wiley & Eskilson, 1985). The two versions varied only in speech style, with one version having many pauses, hedges, and questions and the other none of these characteristics. Each style was used by a female and male applicant, for a total of four conditions. The results indicated a complex pattern of relationships for speech style, gender of applicant, and gender of rater. Raters judged applicants with the hesitant style as less likely to be successful, but neither the applicant's nor rater's gender produced a significant effect. The complex patterns of interactions that occurred suggested that no simple relationship exists between speech style and ratings of ability. For instance, speech style made less difference to male raters than to female raters; in addition, male raters liked women who used the hesitant speech style and disliked women whose speech style was more assertive, but women rated women higher when they used assertive speech styles.

Elizabeth Aries's (1987; 1996) reviews on gender and communication confirmed these results: No distinctive patterns of communication are uniquely associated with success or even with women or men. That is, the hesitant speech style that Lakoff characterized as "women's language" and the assertive style that she identified as "men's language" are not specific to either. Although women and men may have different goals in speaking, the notion of a male versus a female way of talking is not supported by research. Even the tendency for men to interrupt more than women is small (Anderson & Leaper, 1998). Furthermore, the emphasis on group differences obscures more important individual differences. Gender-related differences in communication are complex, and both the setting and situation in which communication takes place are critical factors in men's and women's speech patterns.

Conversational style also reflects power, and power is one of the situational differences that affects speech. Speakers with more power speak differently than speakers with less power (Aries, 1987, 1996). Those in positions of power tend to use more assertive language. In the workplace, power and gender are related, and this power differential reflects the power differential in society. Thus, work roles mirror social roles just as social stereotypes of gender affect behavior and expectations in the workplace. Aspects of the female role carry over into the workplace to produce **sex role spillover** (Nieva & Gutek, 1981), gender role characteristics that spill over into the workplace, creating stereotyping and a sexualized atmosphere. Gutek (1985) expanded the concept, emphasizing that sex role spillover focuses on gender role behavior that is irrelevant (or even an impediment) to the work role. Sex role spillover can take several different forms, including the expectation that women will be more nurturant or loyal than men, that women will occupy subordinate positions, and that women will be sexual at work.

When men and women are together in the workplace, they may rely on their habitual patterns of interaction, including roles and stereotypes. As Gutek pointed out, most men have experience with women as mothers, girlfriends, wives, daughters, and secretaries, but possibly not as their professional colleagues. When a man is faced with a women in the same job, he may rely on one of the other role relationships to guide his interaction with her. Although treating the new female executive like his mother or his secretary may not be appropriate, these relationships are familiar and may be the chosen patterns. His stereotypes of women will thus inevitably affect his behavior, because he has no experience in forming an equal relationship with a female colleague.

The new female executive may also fall back on habitual patterns of interacting with men on the job, perpetuating inappropriate work behavior for everyone involved. On the other hand, her behavior may be shaped by the account executives she has known, most of whom were men, as well as her beliefs about how an executive should act. Thus she may act like a male executive, enacting a version of the role with which she is most familiar. Some evidence exists that women who occupy jobs most commonly filled by men adopt a male style of work-related behavior, and this behavior demonstrates how powerful situational demands can be. A review of the research on gender and leadership roles (Eagly & Johnson, 1990) showed that both women and men who have attained managerial status in organizations tend to be similar in leadership styles. Male leaders described themselves as somewhat more aggressive, instrumental, and risk-oriented than female leaders (Lewis & Fagenson-Eland, 1998), but their supervisors failed to see this difference. Job requirements and the selection of people for the job make managers more alike than different, regardless of gender.

When women adopt the same power styles as men, they may not be evaluated equally positively. Men are not more effective leaders than women (Eagly, Karau, & Makhijani, 1995), but their styles of leadership can be perceived as differing in effectiveness, depending on the extent to which the style matches the gender stereotype. Authoritative and even autocratic styles of management are common for men, but women are expected to be more "people oriented" and interpersonally sensitive. When managers exhibit different styles, the choice of autocratic versus democratic often corresponds to the male versus the female style (Eagly & Johnson, 1990). The choice of a democratic style is a wise one on the part of female leaders (Eagly et al., 1995; Eagly, Makhijani, & Klonsky, 1992), and women who use the directive male power style of leading are devalued by their associates, in contrast to the men who choose this style.

The story of Ann Hopkins provides a dramatic example of what can happen when women violate gender stereotypical expectations on the job (Fiske, Bersoff, Borgida, Deaux, & Heilman, 1991). Ann Hopkins was an employee of Price Waterhouse, and she was so successful that she was nominated for partner in that company, the only woman nominated that year. She was not chosen as a partner, and she became the object of criticism for being too aggressive and "macho" as well as for not being sufficiently feminine in her behavior and appearance. Hopkins sued the company for applying different criteria to its male and female employees, contending that gender stereotyping was a factor in their decision. Eventually, the U.S. Supreme Court agreed with these arguments and condemned the double bind that women face—they are penalized for using an aggressive, powerful style when only this style can lead to success.

If women are penalized for using the same methods to gain power that men use, how do women achieve power at work? Women have many obstacles that inhibit them from accumulating power in organizations (Ragins & Sundstrom, 1989). The social system and most organizational systems work to prevent women from gaining power. Different career expectations, entry-level jobs, assignments within the company, and promotion rates all favor the accumulation of power by men rather than women. One method open to women is the use of expert power—that is, using their specific expertise to accomplish tasks. Studies of successful female executives have shown that these women tended to accumulate power by being expert in performing their jobs and that such power was especially important early in their careers. After they had a power base, these women were more likely to turn their attention to gaining power through interpersonal skills and influence.

Expert power can be very effective in determining social dominance. One study (Dovidio, Ellyson, Keating, Heltman, & Brown, 1988) manipulated who had expert power and observed the effects on the nature of the social interaction. The results revealed an interaction between gender and expert power: When women had expert power, they behaved in dominant ways, and their male partners acknowledged this dominance by their reactions. When the women gained no power in the situation, the nature of the male–female interactions fell into more gender-stereotypical patterns: The men showed signs of social dominance and the women of social submission. Thus, expert power can change the power dynamics away from gender-stereotypical patterns, giving women ways to assert and accumulate power at work.

In summary, although research has failed to support the notion of different communication styles that are unique to women or men, it has shown that communication styles relate to the power of the speaker and the communication situation. The issues of gender, communication, and power also relate to adherence to stereotypical gender roles in the workplace, which give power to men and place obstacles in the way of women's career advancement. Using habitual patterns of interaction between men and women in the workplace produces a power differential, with men having the advantage. When women use the same behaviors as men to exert power, they are often perceived as behaving inappropriately and are penalized. Women have the option of relying on expert power to gain a power base and working from it to attain power at work, but the spillover of gender roles to work situations gives men an advantage in the accumulation and use of power.

The power difference between men's and women's positions offers not only the opportunity for men to be more successful at work, but also the opportunity for men to sexually exploit the women who work for them. Although sexuality at work can also be interpreted as a power issue, the term ***sexual harassment*** is now used as the label for sexual exploitation in the workplace.

Sexual Harassment at Work

According to Gutek (1985), "sex role spillover facilitates the expression of sexuality at work to the extent that the sex object aspect of the female sex role and the sexual aggressor aspect of the male sex role carry over into the work setting" (p. 18); sexual harassment is a function of sex role spillover. Men and women also choose to enter sexual relationships in the workplace, making it difficult to distinguish between this type of sexuality and sexual harassment.

In 1976, sexual harassment became illegal as a form of gender discrimination in the United States through a court interpretation of Title VII of the 1964 Civil Rights Acts (Fitzgerald, Swan, & Magley, 1997). The first form of sexual harassment to be recognized was **quid pro quo sexual harassment,** in which employers or supervisors demand sexual favors as a condition of employment or as a condition for promotion. This form of harassment involves a supervisor using threats or pressure toward a subordinate, making it a clear abuse of power. Men are more often supervisors and women more often subordinates, resulting in women as the common targets of this form of harassment.

In 1986, another form of sexual harassment was legally recognized in the United States—**hostile environment sexual harassment.** This concept of harassment is based on the notion that psychological harm or reduced effectiveness at work can result from unwanted sexual attention as well as from offensive or hostile behavior (Fitzgerald et al., 1997). A third classification of sexual harassment is **gender harassment,** which occurs when people are subjected to offensive or hostile behavior because of their gender. This type of harassment is distinctive because it does not involve sexuality; rather, it involves hostile or disparaging remarks directed toward a person because of that person's gender. Table 12.3 gives examples of each type of sexual harassment.

Over the past decade, sexual harassment accusations have increased dramatically (Simon, Scherer, & Rau, 1999), and the U.S. Supreme Court made a series of decisions that

TABLE 12.3 Examples of the Three Types of Sexual Harassment

Quid Pro Quo Type
Demands for sex in exchange for hiring
Demands for sex in exchange for promotion or favorable job evaluation
Demands for sex to keep a job
Demands for sex to avoid being placed in an undesirable job
Hostile Environment Type
Sexual touching
Sexual comments and jokes
Displays of sexual material, such as drawings or photographs
Nonverbal sexual posturing, including sexual gestures
Personal remarks about sexuality
Sexually oriented comments about appearance
Discussions about a person in sexual terms in the person's presence, including comments phrased as though the person were not present
Gender Harassment Type
Degrading comments about the ability of women (or men)
Hostile comments about women's (or men's) behavior as a group; not confined to sexual comments
Insults directed toward women or men because of their gender, rather than because of any action or characteristic of the individual

strengthened sexual harassment law, making lawsuits easier to win (Gould, 2000). During the 1990s, the number of cases filed with the Equal Employment Opportunity Commission more than doubled, and the monetary awards increased by more than fourfold. Protection against sexual harassment has been extended to men as well as women (although 90% of complaints are filed by women against men), and men have received monetary awards because of harassment by female supervisors. Sexual harassment is now an issue that has captured the interest of businesses and the general public, and most companies in the United States have policies and training to prevent harassment.

Many countries also have laws and regulations that have been used to prohibit sexual harassment, and some countries have laws that specifically apply to sexual harassment (Barak, 1997). The United Kingdom, Canada, Australia, Israel, Austria, Ireland, and New Zealand have laws that prohibit sex discrimination or sexual harassment, and the establishment of the European Community led to additional laws. The cities of Berlin and Tokyo enacted regulations of their own rather than wait for Germany and Japan to pass legislation. Yet sexual harassment is a common experience throughout the world. For countries where surveys have been done, the prevalence of the crimes fall between 30% and 50%.

The forms of sexual harassment are not equal in frequency or in perceived severity; the hostile environment form is more common, but the quid pro quo form is perceived as more serious (Riger, 1991). Despite the perceived lack of severity of hostile environment sexual harassment, Louise Fitzgerald (1994) found that workplaces that spawn this type of harassment

GENDERED VOICES

Hardly a Day Went By

In two stories I heard about sexual harassment, the behaviors of the two harassers were amazingly similar. Both harassers, a woman and a man, harassed a coworker. The behaviors of the targets were also very similar to each other.

A man told me, "I worked in a car dealership selling cars after I graduated, and one of the other salespeople was a woman—the only woman who was in sales. She sexually harassed the finance manager. It was blatant. She propositioned him in front of everybody, saying things like 'Let's go in the back room now,' and things much more vulgar.

"He seemed embarrassed and usually didn't reply; he tried to ignore her. He was married, and he never gave her any encouragement at all. She would go over and stand very close to him, never touching him, but standing close and making him uncomfortable. And she would proposition him; rarely a day went by when she didn't. The guy was clearly uncomfortable, but nobody ever did anything."

A young woman said, "I worked as a cashier in a discount store, and one of the department managers sexually harassed me. He would come over to the cash register where I was working, and he would proposition me. He made reasons to be close to me, and he kept saying what a good idea it would be for us to have sex. I didn't think it was such a good idea. I always said no, and I asked him to stop asking. His offers embarrassed me. Hardly a day went by without some sexual offer from him or some remark with sexual connotations. He never touched me or fondled me, but he made my job harder, and he embarrassed me.

"I complained to my supervisor, but she told me to just ignore him. He wasn't my boss, and he never made any threats or attacked me or anything. But I think that he shouldn't have been allowed to harass me the way he did. Nobody did one thing to stop him. I don't think that the store manager ever said a word."

tend to also have the quid pro quo type, and a 1998 U.S. Supreme Court decision agreed (Gould, 2000). Fitzgerald contended that all of the types of sexual harassment are interrelated, as Figure 12.2 shows. Fitzgerald emphasized environmental rather than personal factors in sexual harassment and reported that environments that allow insulting remarks and unwanted sexual attention also tend to be permissive of sexual coercion. Despite the separate legal definitions for the types of sexual harassment and the differences in frequency and their perceived severity, they often coexist.

Women are more frequently the targets of all sexual harassment, when defined in terms of *unwanted* sexual attention. In Gutek's (1985) study, men reported a comparable number of sexual overtures as women did and as many instances of sexual touching, but men were less likely than women to consider sexual attention unwanted and thus to label their experience as harassment. These different standards may contribute to miscommunication and exacerbate harassment.

Gender differences appear in what are perceived as sexual signals (Saal, Johnson, & Weber, 1989). When people observed social interactions between men and women, the male participants saw less friendliness and more sexiness in the women's behavior than the female observers saw. These findings suggested that men and women may not have the same interpretations of sexual intention, even when they observe the same behavior. These differences may lead to misunderstandings about sexual intentions, with men incorrectly believing that women are sending signals of interest when men perceive such signals.

Gender-related differences in perceptions of sexuality are also problematic when defining sexual harassment. Gutek (1985) found that the biggest gender difference concerning sexuality at work had to do with attitudes about sexual propositions. She found that two-thirds of the men in her study said that they felt flattered by such propositions, but only 17% of women felt the same way. Indeed, over 60% of the women said that they would feel insulted by a sexual proposition at work. The main problem, however, comes from the per-

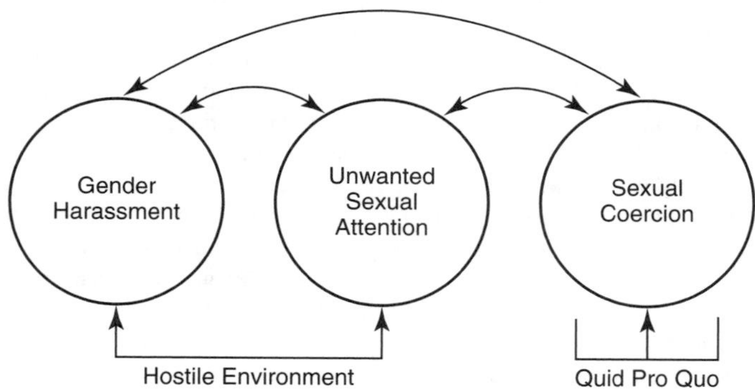

FIGURE 12.2 A Model of Sexually Harassing Behaviors

SOURCE: From Louise F. Fitzgerald, Suzanne Swan, & Vicki J. Magley, 1997, "But was it really sexual harassment? Legal, behavioral, and psychological definitions of the workplace victimization of women." In William O'Donohue (Ed.), *Sexual harassment: Theory, research, and treatment,* (p. 11). Copyright © 1997 by Allyn and Bacon. Reprinted by permission.

ceptions of both; neither the men nor the women in Gutek's study were aware of the perceptions of the other gender. The men believed that the women felt flattered by sexual attention when in actuality a majority of the women felt insulted or angered.

If the sexual attention that men receive at work is welcome, are men exempt from being the targets of sexual harassment? The legal definition did not specify the gender of the target, and a 1998 U.S. Supreme Court decision (Oncale vs. Sundowner Offshore Services, Inc.) specified that men could be victims of sexual harassment. The vast majority of the complaints are brought by women against men, but men are sometimes the targets of sexual harassment. Surveys of employed men and women (Berdahl, Magley, & Waldo, 1996) and of military personnel (DuBois, Knapp, Faley, & Kustis, 1998) revealed that sexual harassment with male targets was much less common than with female targets.

No men reported sexual coercion in the workplace study (Berdahl et al., 1996), but incidents of sexual hazing, including rape, occurred in the military study (DuBois et al., 1998). Gender harassment violations also occurred, with women using examples of such comments as "You men are all alike" and "Men have only one thing on their minds" (Berdahl et al., 1996, p. 540). In addition, several men mentioned a type of gender harassment that women did not. This type of harassment came from other men and involved comments about the target man not living up to standards of manliness by showing too much concern or sympathy with women. For example, a man who failed to share a joke that is derogatory toward women might be censured by other men who enjoyed the joke.

Although women often feel insulted and angered by sexual comments and propositions from supervisors and coworkers, they may have problems in labeling these behaviors as harassment (Gutek, 1985). Therefore, the estimates about rates for harassment may be low if the figures are based on personal reports. Gutek estimated that 21% of women in the United States had definitely been the targets of sexual harassment at some time during their work lives, and that up to 53% were probable victims. For men, at least 9% and up to 37% had experienced sexual harassment. Thus, sexuality at work is common, but women are more likely than men to label sexual experiences at work as harassment.

Men who sexually harass women do not differ from employed men in general (Gutek, 1985), but an analysis of the situational as well as personal factors has been more useful in understanding those who harass (Pryor & Whalen, 1997). Men who are likely to sexually harass tend to view sex and power as linked, making them more likely to use their power at work to sexually exploit women who are their subordinates. Women who are targets of harassment differ in some ways from typical women in the workforce; they are more likely to be unmarried, younger than the average employed woman, and attractive. Women who initiate sexual relationships at work are much less likely to be perceived as harassing men than vice versa, and, like the women who are the targets of harassment, they are younger and more likely to be unmarried than the average employed woman. In cases of men who reported that they were sexually harassed, their harassers were similar to both the women who initiated sex at work and to the women who were targets of harassment—young, unmarried, and attractive.

Another difference between male and female perpetrators of harassment is their status. Man who harass are likely to be in supervisory positions and thus have power over the women whom they harass, but women who initiate harassment are not, giving them no power to demand or coerce sexual favors from men with whom they work. Gutek hypothesized that the small percentage of men (as few as 9%) who describe incidents of being sexually harassed by women may feel harassed by the seductive behavior of their coworkers or subordinates, but the men's careers are not at risk from the sexual behavior of women at work. In contrast, men who are the targets of other men's sexual harassment tend to experience more serious consequences than women do (DuBois et al., 1998)

Careers are often endangered by sexual harassment. Over 30% of employed women had experienced some negative job consequences as a result of sexual harassment, compared to around 10% of men (Gutek, 1985). These problems included quitting their jobs, asking for transfers, or losing their jobs for refusing to have sex with employers or supervisors. In a survey of attorneys (Laband & Lentz, 1998), the experience of sexual harassment was associated with decreased job satisfaction and increased intentions to quit. Therefore, even among informed professionals, sexual harassment is a problem that can negatively affect women's careers.

Perhaps these differences in consequences of sexuality at work explain the differences in perceptions of harassment: Why should men feel harassed by sex at work when they are very unlikely to experience negative consequences? Why should women welcome sexual attention at work when their careers are so much more likely to be harmed? Given an equal interest in sexual relationships with people at work, the unequal consequences of sexual behavior on careers suggests that men and women should have different views of sexuality at work—and they do.

Considering Diversity

Diversity—or more specifically, a lack of diversity—is evident in most workplaces. Not only are most workplaces segregated by gender, but also by ethnicity, and ethnic minorities have disadvantages in hiring and career advancement. Like women, problems for ethnic minorities begin during school, when stereotyping pushes some people toward and others away from certain courses and majors and, thus, careers.

As a result, ethnic minorities are less common among the upper ranks of corporate management, science, law, and technology than are women in general. Table 12.4 shows the underrepresentation and overrepresentation in various occupations held by women, African Americans, and Hispanic Americans. The categories of African American and Hispanic American represent both men and women from these ethnic groups, not just women, so the percentages in the women category overlap with the other two categories.

The percentage of women in the general, working-age population is 52%, whereas 12% are African American, and 10% are Hispanic Americans. The negative percentages in Table 12.4 reflect underrepresentation, and positive numbers show overrepresentation, of these groups in various occupations. All three groups are underrepresented for most of the managerial and professional categories, meaning that women, African Americans, and Hispanic Americans do not occupy these prestigious, lucrative jobs as often as White men do. In contrast, all three categories are overrepresented in low-paying, low-prestige jobs such as clerical and personal service work. As Table 12.4 shows, Hispanic Americans are vastly overrepresented in the categories of farm worker and household service, and African Americans are overrepresented in the categories of clerks and household service. These jobs are premier examples of the "sticky floor," positions in which people get stuck at the bottom of the job hierarchy.

TABLE 12.4 Percentage of Variation from the Population of Working-Age Women, African Americans, and Hispanic Americans in Various Occupations

Occupation	Women	African Americans	Hispanic Americans
Managerial	–3%	–4%	–5%
Professional	+1	–4	–6
Architects	–34	–10	–6
Engineers	–41	–7	–7
Lawyers and judges	–23	–7	–6
Mathematicians and computer scientists	–23	–5	–6
Natural scientists	–21	–8	–6
Nurses	+41	–2	–7
Physicians	–25	–6	–5
Teachers, college	–10	–6	–6
Teachers, noncollege	+23	–2	–5
Social workers	+16	+12	–3
Technical	+2	–1	–4
Health technicians	+30	+2	–3
Science technicians	–9	–1	–3
Administrative support	+27	+2	–1
Records processing	+27	+5	+1
Secretaries	+46	–3	–2
Billing clerks	+35	+4	–1
Sales	–2	–3	–2
Mechanics	–48	–4	0
Production and skilled crafts	–29	–2	+3
Construction	–50	–5	+5
Labor	–30	+4	+7
Service occupations	+8	+6	+5
Household service	+43	+3	+19
Firefighters	–49	–1	–4
Police and detectives	–36	+3	–1
Food preparation	+5	0	+6
Hairdressers	+39	0	0
Machine operation	–15	+3	+9
Farm workers	–35	–11	+37

SOURCE: Labor force statistics from the current population survey, annual average tables from the January, 2000, issue of *Employment and Earnings,* Table 11, http://stats.bls.gov/cpsaatab.htm.

Some African Americans succeed in attaining the highest levels of career success. But the achievements of even these individuals are suspect, according to Stephen Carter (1991), who contended that African Americans have to work harder than Whites to achieve, and they receive less credit when they do. Part of the suspicion comes from the stereotyping of African Americans as less capable and less motivated than Whites. Additional suspicion comes from affirmative action, which gives ethnic minorities and women advantages in education and hiring to compensate for past (and, in many cases, continuing) discrimination. Many people believe that the only reason such individuals attend prestigious schools or get lucrative jobs is because of affirmative action. Affirmative action, Carter argued, allowed African Americans to enter elite schools and prestigious jobs; the criteria for entry were lower for ethnic minorities than for others. The chances for advancement, however, were slimmer: "Once hired, people who are not white face difficulties in finding mentors, powerful institutional figures to smooth their paths; then they will naturally advance more slowly" (Carter, 1991, p. 64).

Later research (Biernat & Kobrynowicz, 1997) confirmed Carter's beliefs: Stereotypes influence judgments and evaluations of ability and performance in much the same way that Carter himself had experienced. When judging African Americans and women, participants set lower competency standards. Thus, it may be easier for ethnic minorities and women than for White men to stand out in a job interview or application process. The standards for judging performance were higher for African Americans and women than for White men, putting them in the position that Carter described—having to work twice as hard to be considered half as good.

Asian Americans are also subject to stereotyping, but this process can help them in certain careers. The stereotype holds that Asian Americans are hard-working, intelligent, and oriented toward science and technology, which pushes them toward careers in these areas, but hinders the choice for other careers. Their success has ruled Asian Americans out of the category of "real" minorities, and workplace initiatives to diversify may thus exclude Asian Americans, leaving them at a disadvantage in terms of hiring and promotions (Ragaza, 1999).

Women and ethnic minorities are not the only groups at a disadvantage in the world of work. People with disabilities face prejudice and discrimination, and disabled women in the workforce encounter barriers on the basis of both their gender and their handicapping condition (McLain & Perkins, 1990). These biases result in these women's unemployment and underemployment. The unemployment rate among women with disabilities is 50% to 90%, and those who are employed earn 64 cents for each dollar able-bodied women earn. This high unemployment and underemployment results in poverty; these women's disabilities are more likely to bring their living standards below the poverty level. Women with disabilities have disadvantages compared not only to able-bodied women but also to men who are disabled. Such women have the lowest percentage of employment compared to both able-bodied women and men with and without disabilities (Altman, 1985); they are "at the bottom of the work heap" (McLain & Perkins, 1990, p. 54).

Many characteristics and circumstances can prevent a person from being an "ideal worker" (Williams, 2000). The model for the ideal worker is male, which presents problems for women who want to pursue careers. The ideal is also White and able-bodied; many people in the workforce fail to meet this ideal. Despite the enormous changes that have made the current U.S. workforce more diverse than it has ever been, the assumption of White, male breadwinners continues to influence the cultural perception of workers, to the disadvantage of all the groups that fail to meet this assumption.

Summary

Career development has been associated with men, because women's careers have traditionally revolved around their families rather than their employment. Although career motivation is similar for men and women, social forces still pull women toward domesticity rather than toward careers. Research indicates that college women expect to combine both career and family, but employment statistics indicate that women have fewer career opportunities than men have.

The limitations on women's careers come from their career choices, interruptions in their employment, and discrimination in hiring and promotion. Career choices and preparation lead men into a wider, more prestigious, and more lucrative group of occupations than are available to women. Interruptions in employment affect both men's and women's careers negatively, but women more often interrupt their careers to devote time to families. Discrimination in hiring is a major factor in the wage gap between men and women. Specific, personal information about job applicants can partially overcome the gender stereotyping that affects hiring decisions, but the bias in favor of men is a factor that still exists.

Women occupy a very small percentage of executive positions, often being blocked in their career progress by an invisible barrier called the glass ceiling, which limits women's careers throughout the world. Many factors have contributed to the formation of barriers to the advancement of women and ethnic minorities. The informal social structure in corporations excludes newcomers who differ from the majority. Thus, token women or minorities have difficulty being trusted and have trouble forming important mentoring relationships. Gender stereotypes influence perceptions of female managers' performance by making their competence difficult to acknowledge. Gender stereotypes can boost men in gender-typical careers, providing them with easier access to promotions. Even women who have comparable training, personal backgrounds, and performance do not advance in their careers as rapidly as men do, which shows evidence of discrimination in career advancement.

Gender-based interactions at work obstruct women from gaining power and from demonstrating their competence, as these characteristics are not part of the feminine stereotype. Women who fail to adhere to traditional standards of femininity can be penalized, but by following these "feminine" standards, women cannot succeed in the corporate world. Women can gain power through using their expertise, but they also have to overcome many barriers to gain power at work.

Balancing work and family is a task for both men and women, but the gender role for women holds that they, rather than men, should devote themselves to family concerns. These social expectations lead men toward and women away from career success by placing the burdens of household chores and child care on women. Ironically, taking care of their families by being the primary breadwinner takes men away from their families. Work and family both require time and effort, and, currently, prestigious careers require support at home, so these careers are unlikely for partners who have equitable relationships.

The workforce is gender segregated: Most men and women work with colleagues of the same gender, and few occupations have an equal proportion of men and women. Even in occupations that are not gender segregated, job situations may be. This segregation is more pronounced for men than for women, as women have moved into traditionally male-dominated fields more rapidly than men have moved into female-dominated jobs. Gender segregation on the job has resulted in certain jobs being associated with one gender, and this situation has resulted in spillover of male and female characteristics into the work environment. This gender role spillover tends to produce stereotypical patterns of interaction between men and women, rather than interaction between equal coworkers, bringing sexuality into the workplace.

Another consequence of sexuality at work is sexual harassment. Although illegal, both women and men are pressured for sexual favors from employees and supervisors and are subjected to unwanted sexual attention or hostile comments concerning characteristics and behaviors of their gender. Women are more likely than men to find sexual attention unwanted, possibly because they are more likely to be harmed by sexual relationships with coworkers. Men are likely to find sexual attention flattering that women find insulting. Although there is little difference in the amount of sexual attention men and women receive at work, women are more likely to label their experiences as sexual harassment than are men.

Ethnic minorities also experience barriers to career success, and African Americans and Hispanic Americans are affected by stereotyping, discrimination in hiring and promotions, and gender segregation. Asian Americans are advantaged by their stereotypes in some ways, but restricted in other ways, especially in terms of job hiring and promotions. All ethnic minorities and women suffer from their discrepancy from the ideal worker model, which also poses a disadvantage for disabled people.

Glossary

gender harassment a type of sexual harassment that occurs when people are subjected to offensive or hostile behavior because of their gender.

glass ceiling the invisible barrier that seems to prevent women and ethnic minorities from reaching the highest levels of their professions.

hostile environment sexual harassment the type of sexual harassment that occurs when employers allow offensive elements to exist in the work environment.

quid pro quo sexual harassment sexual harassment in the form of demands for sexual favors in exchange for employment or promotion.

sex role spillover the hypothesis that gender role characteristics spill over into the workplace, creating stereotyping and a sexualized atmosphere.

sexual harassment unwanted sexual attention.

token a symbol or example, in this case, of a minority group.

Suggested Readings

Fitzgerald, Louise F.; Swan, Suzanne; & Magley, Vicki J. (1997). But was it really sexual harassment? Legal, behavioral, and psychological definitions of the workplace victimization of women. In William O'Donohue (Ed.), *Sexual harassment: Theory, research, and treatment* (pp. 5–28), Boston: Allyn and Bacon. Fitzgerald is one of the leading researchers and theorists in the field of sexual harassment, and this article provides a review of both. In addition, the brief legal history and examination of the psychological definitions of harassment add clarity to a confusing issue.

Hochschild, Arlie Russell. (1997). *The time bind.* New York: Metropolitan Books. Hochschild's study of workers in a large, multinational company presents the problems of balancing work and family and how work seems to be winning the time battle. Her book tells stories of women and men who have made various choices in combining the two, and of the problems they face from family and work as a result of their choices.

Phillips, Susan D.; & Imhoff, Anne R. (1997). Women and career development: A decade of research. *Annual Review of Psychology, 48,* 31–59. This lengthy review covers only women's career development, but it provides a comprehensive examination of careers and topics related to career choices.

Williams, Joan. (2000). *Unbending gender: Why family and work conflict and what to do about it.* New York: Oxford University Press. Williams is an attorney who explores the social, psychological, and legal issues in balancing work and family concerns. Her analysis holds that forces push women and men toward traditional choices, and that individuals face overwhelming difficulties in departing from these traditions.

Chapter 13

Health and Fitness

HEADLINE

Is the Longer Life the Healthier One?

New York Times, June 22, 1997

The male–female mortality gap starts in the womb, holds into very old age and has widened in recent decades. It is now about seven years in the United States, compared with two to three years early in this century. As longevity improves for both men and women, it is uncertain whether the gap will grow. (Altman, 1997, p. 18)

Despite the advantage in years, women are not necessarily healthier. The phrase "Women are sicker; men die quicker" (in Altman, 1997, p. 18) expresses this apparent contradiction. As Altman's (1997) story discussed, the evidence for women's poorer health is not clear, and the reason for their longer lives is likewise unknown.

Women's poorer health is widely accepted, possibly because women make more doctor and hospital visits than men do. This situation leads to the acceptance of women's higher **morbidity,** that is, higher rate of illness. Altman interviewed an epidemiologist who contended that the health care system may be part of the reason why women are considered less healthy. Women receive more health care than men receive due to birth control and childbearing. During health care visits, providers may routinely ask about other problems, prompting patients to become vigilant concerning problems and to report problems that might otherwise be too minor to prompt doctor visits. Mentioning a problem leads to more health care. With more routine health care visits, women have more opportunities to experience such situations of expanding treatment.

The reasons for women's lower death rate, that is **mortality,** are also poorly understood. Women and men have different explanations for their varying life expectancies (Wallace, 1996). Men attributed their shorter life spans to their greater physical labor and more stressful lives, whereas women reported that they live longer because they take better care of themselves. These opinions came from college students and not health experts, but the notion that health habits may play a role in longevity has merit.

The combination of more sickness and longer life poses a distressing question: Do women's longer life spans offer only additional years of poorer health? The additional 7 years of life that women have beyond men in the United States are not filled with greater illness and disability than men's later years. Indeed, women and men experience comparable proportions of their later years with disability. Disability-free life expectancies beyond age 65 are about 8 years for men and 10 years for women, but overall life expectancies are 14 years and 19 years, respectively (Robine & Ritchie, 1991). Therefore, both women and men experience health problems that produce disabilities during their later years, but women live longer with such disabilities.

Mortality: No Equal Opportunity

As the headline story related, women's advantage in life expectancy is not a recent development; this discrepancy has existed for over 100 years and throughout the world. Figure 13.1 highlights the longer life expectancy for women in the United States over the past 90 years. Notice the increasing discrepancy between men and women in the first half of the 20th century and the recent narrowing of figures for women's survival. Also notice the difference between life expectancy for Whites and nonwhites, including the small discrepancies between men and women in the early 1900s, the advantage for Whites, and the increasing discrepancy in life expectancies for nonwhite women and men after 1910.

In addition, these gender differences are prominent in economically developed countries for the leading causes of death—cardiovascular disease, cancer, and accidents. These three causes of death account for about 70% of all deaths in the United States. For cardiovascular disease and cancer, men tend to die at younger ages than women, resulting in not only an excess of overall deaths of men, but death at younger ages.

Cardiovascular Disease

Cardiovascular disease (CVD) includes a group of diseases involving the heart and circulatory system, some of which are life threatening and some of which are not. For example, angina pectoris is one of the disorders in this category; this disease causes shortness of breath, difficulty in performing physical activities, and chest pain, but it poses no immediate threat to life. On the other hand, myocardial infarction (heart attack) and stroke can be immediately fatal. Cardiovascular disease is the leading cause of deaths accounting for 40.7% of deaths in the United States (U.S. Bureau of the Census, 1999). Deaths from cardiovascular disease have decreased over the past 25 years, with deaths from stroke decreasing more rapidly than deaths from heart disease.

As Table 13.1 shows, heart disease mortality for women and men does not differ greatly over the life span, and women have more fatal strokes than men do, but men die from CVD at younger ages than women do. The discrepancy in heart disease deaths for men and women between ages 35 and 74 is especially dramatic, showing how much men are affected by premature death from CVD.

Cardiovascular disease is one of the **chronic diseases**—those health problems that develop over a period of time, often without noticeable symptoms, and persist over time without a complete recovery. Such diseases differ from acute conditions such as infectious

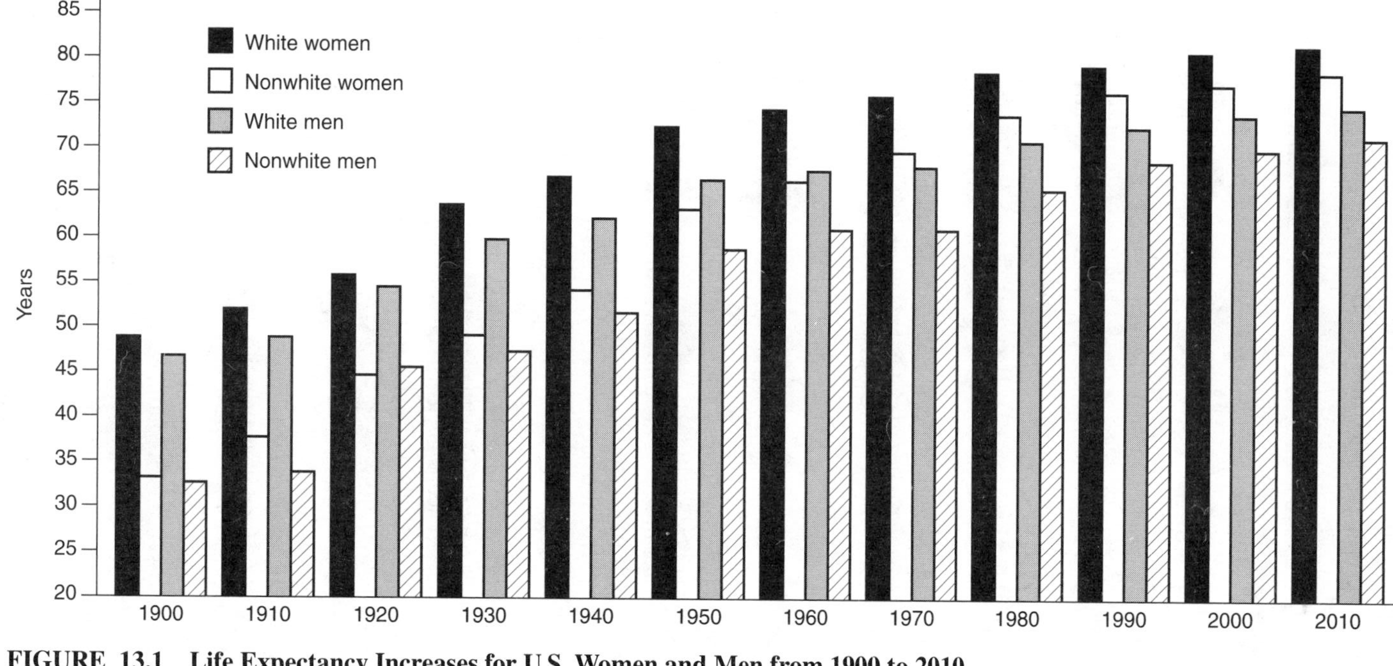

FIGURE 13.1 Life Expectancy Increases for U.S. Women and Men from 1900 to 2010

SOURCE: From *Historical statistics of the United States, Colonial times to 1970,* (p. 55), U.S. Bureau of the Census, 1975. Washington, DC: U.S. Government Printing Office; and *Statistical abstract of the United States, 1992* (112th ed.), (p. 76), U.S. Bureau of the Census, 1992, Washington, DC: U.S. Government Printing Office.

TABLE 13.1 U.S. Death Rates for Cardiovascular Disease in Men and Women, 1998 (rates per 100,000 population)

	Women		*Men*	
Age Range	Stroke	Heart Disease	Stroke	Heart Disease
15–24	0.4	2.1	0.6	3.5
25–34	1.8	5.8	1.7	10.8
35–44	5.7	17.3	6.2	44.0
45–54	14.6	52.8	18.5	152.2
55–64	36.3	173.9	49.5	411.1
65–74	117.2	522.6	145.7	997.3
75–84	442.6	1,579.5	474.7	2,377.2
85+	1,563.3	6,013.7	1,347.2	6,330.6
All ages	70.4	268.3	46.3	268.0

SOURCE: From *Health, United States, 2000* (pp. 185, 188) by National Center for Health Statistics, Hyattsville, MD: U.S. Government Printing Office.

diseases or accidents. Acute conditions have rapid onsets accompanied by specific symptoms, and people can recover completely. CVD develops over years but exhibits few symptoms until the condition is serious. For many people, heart attack is the first symptom of cardiovascular disease (Ellestad, 1986).

As with other chronic diseases, the causes of cardiovascular disease are not well understood. No infection or other specific agent appears to be responsible; instead, several physical conditions and behaviors are risk factors in the development of CVD. A **risk factor** refers to a condition associated with the increased probability that a disorder will develop. For example, high blood pressure is a risk factor for CVD; people with elevated blood pressure have an increased risk of heart attack and stroke.

Gender is a risk factor for CVD, with men at elevated risk to develop CVD before age 65. The source of this difference is unclear. The hormone estrogen plays some role in protecting premenopausal women from CVD, but this inherent difference is not the only factor producing the difference. If hormone levels were the only reason, then the gender differences in CVD would apply to all times and all societies. The current gender discrepancy is a fairly recent development; the gender gap was much smaller during the 1800s, began to widen during the 1920s, and has now begun to decrease (Nikiforov & Mamaev, 1998). These changes suggest factors other than biology are involved in this gender difference (Weidner, 2000).

Some authorities have suggested that behaviors associated with the male gender role may be dangerous (Harrison, 1978; Matthews, 1989; Messner, 1997). A study that investigated the components of masculinity and femininity as they related to risk of heart attack (Helgeson, 1990), negative masculinity (such as aggression and hostility) was related to heart attack severity for both men and women. Lifestyle factors such as smoking and eating a high-fat diet are risk factors for cardiovascular disease, and more men than women smoke and eat diets high in fat. However, lifestyle factors alone do not account for gender differences in CVD. In a study that statistically adjusted for lifestyle factors (Fried et al., 1998), men were still about twice as likely to experience CVD than women. Therefore, gender differences in CVD risk remain poorly understood.

Women who develop CVD have several disadvantages (Knox & Czajkowski, 1997), some of which relate to the disease itself, and some of which relate to women's treatment in the medical system. Since 1984, women have died of cardiovascular disease at higher rates than men. But women with CVD tend to be older and have more medical problems than men with CVD (Mark, 2000), and this situation may produce treatment differences. Women experience differences in treatment for CVD for additional reasons, however. Physicians refer men who report symptoms of CVD for further testing and treatment more often than they refer women with similar symptoms (Ayanian & Epstein, 1991; Steingart et al., 1991). Some of the difference in referrals for additional testing and treatment may be a correct assessment of women's risks and poorer condition, so similar treatment may not be a reasonable goal. In addition, a great deal of this difference in likelihood to refer is the hesitancy of physicians to refer African American women for additional testing (Mark, 2000). Thus, the bias may not be simply against women, and White women may receive treatment comparable to men.

In summary, cardiovascular disease, including heart disease and stroke, is the leading cause of death in the United States and other industrialized nations, accounting for about 40% of all deaths. Men die of heart disease at younger ages than women do, but overall, more women than men die of CVD. The death rates from both heart disease and stroke have fallen in the past 25 years, with strokes decreasing at a more rapid rate than heart disease. These gender differences in risk are not clearly understood, but both physiological and lifestyle differences between the two genders contribute to differences in risk.

Cancer

Cancer is the term applied to a variety of malignant neoplasms—tissues that have sustained uncontrolled growth that may form a tumor, as well as spread to other areas of the body. Most types of tissue can develop cancers. These growths are not restricted to human or even to animal tissues: Plants and all types of animals develop malignancies. Such uncontrolled tissue growth can become life threatening; cancer is the second leading cause of death in the United States, accounting for about 23% of all deaths (U.S. Bureau of the Census, 1999).

Men have higher overall death rates from cancer for most types of cancer and at most ages than women do. Table 13.2 presents the mortality rates for women and men for various types of cancer at various ages. As the table shows, some gender differences exist. For example, women are much more likely to develop breast cancer than are men (although men do get breast cancer), and women have earlier mortality rates for cancer of the genitals and reproductive organs than men do. Lung cancer is the leading type of fatal cancer for both men and women, but more men than women die of lung cancer.

Cigarette smoking is a major factor in lung cancer death rates. The gender rates for smoking also differ: Until recently, men smoked at a much higher rate than women. Smoking takes time to cause health problems, so smoking differences among men and women in the past continue to appear in recent health statistics (U.S. Department of Health and Human Services, 1989). However, the increase in women's and the decrease in men's rates of smoking have begun to alter this pattern: Women have begun to develop lung cancer at

TABLE 13.2 U.S. Death Rates for Cancer in Women and Men by Age, 1996 (rates per 100,000 population)

	Women					
Age Range	Lung	Breast	Digestive System	Genital	Leukemia	Urinary
35–44	5.3	14.2	5.5	6.5	1.7	0.6
45–54	29.0	38.8	20.2	16.4	3.5	2.8
55–64	102.2	67.4	63.6	37.1	8.5	8.7
65–74	209.0	99.1	147.1	65.9	20.0	20.0
75–84	251.1	139.8	280.5	95.0	40.8	39.9
85+	190.6	204.9	478.3	117.5	64.6	67.4
Average: 191.0 per 100,000*						

	Men					
Age Range	Lung	Breast	Digestive System	Genital	Leukemia	Urinary
35–44	6.5	—	8.7	0.6	2.1	1.4
45–54	48.5	0.3	36.6	2.9	5.1	6.9
55–64	190.7	0.7	117.1	22.2	14.0	22.1
65–74	424.6	1.1	255.0	107.8	37.1	52.7
75–84	566.9	2.4	418.7	321.7	71.4	101.0
85+	543.2	4.2	644.0	775.2	120.7	192.8
Average: 219.5 per 100,000*						

SOURCE: From *Statistical abstracts of the United States, 1999* (119th ed.) (p. 105), U.S. Bureau of the Census, 1999. Washington, DC: U.S. Government Printing Office.

*For all ages, including individuals under age 35 and cancers of other sites (1995 data).

increased rates, whereas men's rates have leveled off. In 1986, lung cancer surpassed breast cancer as the leading cause of cancer deaths among women.

Use of tobacco products accounts for about 30% of cancers, and diet for another 30% to 40% (Doll & Peto, 1981; Willett, 1999). In addition to foods that contain known or suspected carcinogens, dietary components have been implicated in the development of cancer, especially a high-fat diet. A substantial amount of evidence indicates that people who eat a high-fat diet are at increased risk for cancers of the digestive tract, including an elevated risk for breast cancer (Willett, 1999). On the average, women eat lower-fat diets than men, so this behavioral difference may explain part of the discrepancy in cancer death rates.

The "meat and potatoes" men may be at increased risk for cancer. The meat is much more of a risk than the potatoes; an increasing body of evidence indicates that high levels of animal-fat consumption increase the risk for several types of cancer (Willett, 1999). Some dietary components increase risk, and others lower risk. For example, lycopene, folic acid, selenium, and vitamin E are all nutrients that seem to lower the risk of various cancers.

GENDERED VOICES

I Have Breast Cancer

An announcement of breast cancer is shocking but not unusual—unless the person is a man. That unusual situation happened to Robert Riter (1997), who noticed a lump in his breast. Like many people, Riter thought it was a cyst and that it would go away. When he started bleeding from his nipple, he sought medical advise and treatment. His treatment included a biopsy, which revealed a malignancy. Although breast cancer is rare among men, the disease affects over 1,000 men per year in the United States.

Riter's experience was both similar to and different from women's experience of breast cancer. Like many women, he had a mastectomy and chemotherapy. Unlike many women, losing the breast was not as traumatic an event for him. His greatest distress came from examining the survival statistics, which are virtually identical for men and women. Riter learned that his chances of surviving for 5 years were about 80%, but his likelihood of living 10 years was only about 60%.

Riter was the first man to join his area's support group for breast cancer survivors. "I'm probably not the only male in this area with the disease, but... men find it hard to discuss their prostate cancer, let alone a 'female' disease," he said (Riter, 1997, p. 14). He also encountered some surprised reactions, like the lab technician who questioned the referral slip with the diagnosis of breast cancer. He felt odd going to a "women's imaging center" to get a mammogram and he said, "My follow-up letter from the center was addressed to Ms. Robert Riter. The radiology tech did note that I had the hairiest chest she's ever seen in a mammogram room" (p. 14).

Riter noted that his experience with breast cancer had taught him more about women's health issues that he would otherwise have known, but having a life-threatening "female disease" was a difficult way for him to gain knowledge and empathy.

People who eat diets high in these nutrients develop cancer at lower rates than people whose intake of these nutrients is lower. Therefore, food can raise or lower the risk for a variety of cancers, and women's diets tend to be healthier than men's diets.

Occupational exposure accounts for another 4% of cancer deaths (Doll & Peto, 1981). Men are at increased risk for cancer due to their exposure to workplace hazards (Waldron, 1991). Men are more likely than women to hold jobs that bring them into contact with carcinogens such as asbestos, benzene, and various petroleum products. Exposure to such substances may also be a factor in the difference in cancer deaths between women and men.

Sexual behavior and reproduction also contribute to the development of cancer, and about 7% of cancers are attributable to these factors (Doll & Peto, 1981). Women who have sexual intercourse at an early age and have many sexual partners are at elevated risk for cancers of the reproductive tract (Levy, 1985). These cancers constitute less of a risk than breast cancer. Furthermore, women who complete pregnancies before age 20 are at decreased risk for breast cancer compared to women with later pregnancies and to women who do not bear children. Thus, early intercourse presents a risk for cancer, but early pregnancy is a protection against cancer.

Men's sexual behavior can place them at risk for cancer, but their behavior can also be a risk for their female sex partners (Levy, 1985). In addition, men who are the receptive partner in unprotected anal intercourse are at increased risk for anal cancer as well as for infection with the human immunodeficiency virus (HIV), which is related to the development of acquired immune deficiency syndrome (AIDS). One of the diseases associated with

AIDS is a form of cancer called, Kaposi's sarcoma. Thus, receptive anal intercourse is a direct risk for anal cancer and an indirect risk for Kaposi's sarcoma. Men who have many sexual partners, especially those who have sex with prostitutes, endanger their female partners by elevating the women's risk for cervical cancer. In addition, poor genital hygiene in men is associated with increased risk of cervical cancer in their female sexual partners.

As Table 13.2 shows, women experience higher mortality rates from cancers of the genitals than men do until after age 65 years. Cancer of the genitals and reproductive tract plus breast cancer deaths account for the large proportion of women's cancer deaths during their early and middle-adult years. Indeed, before age 65, cancer is responsible for a greater proportion of women's deaths than is cardiovascular disease. The opposite pattern occurs for cardiovascular deaths among men, who are more vulnerable to premature death from CVD than from cancer.

Violent Deaths

Violent deaths (unintentional injuries, suicides, homicides), the fourth leading cause of death in the United States, account for about 6% of deaths in the United States (U.S. Bureau of the Census, 1999). This reflects a relatively high rate of violence compared to other industrialized, economically developed countries. Violent death rates are lower in Australia, Canada, Japan, most of the countries in Western Europe, Scandinavia, and other countries scattered throughout the world (Britannica Book of the Year, 1999). In the United States, violent death is the leading cause of death for adolescents and young adults. Men are about three times more likely than women to die from violent deaths. This discrepancy holds for all ages, from birth until old age, and the differences are most pronounced early in life.

Ethnicity plays a major role in risk of violence. As Table 13.3 shows, African Americans in the United States are much more likely than European Americans to die from accidents and homicides, but European Americans are more likely to die from motor vehicle accidents and suicide. African American men are disproportionately vulnerable to deaths from homicide, but gender differences are more prominent than ethnic differences.

The gender differences in risky behaviors account for the differences in violent deaths. Men tend to behave in ways that increase their risks, such as heavy alcohol use, low seat belt use, occupational risks, and illegal activities. Alcohol use increases the chances of ac-

TABLE 13.3 U.S. Death Rates from Accidents and Violence, 1996 (rates per 100,000 population)

	European American		*African American*	
Cause	Women	Men	Women	Men
Motor vehicle	10.7	22.4	9.5	24.3
Other accidents	14.4	25.0	13.3	30.1
Suicide	4.8	19.3	2.0	11.4
Homicide	2.5	12.5	10.2	51.5

SOURCE: From *Statistical Abstracts of the United States, 1999* (119th ed.) by U.S. Bureau of the Census, p. 101. Washington, DC: U.S. Government Printing Office.

cidents, suicide, and homicide (Eckhardt et al., 1981). By slowing responses and altering judgment, alcohol contributes to traffic crashes. People who have been drinking (even those who are not legally intoxicated) are more likely to be involved in fatal traffic accidents; about half of all traffic fatalities are related to alcohol. Seat belt use is an important factor in reducing traffic fatalities, and women are more likely than men to use seat belts (NHTSA, 2000). For the same reasons that alcohol use increases the chances of traffic accidents, alcohol use is also related to deaths from falls, fires, and drownings as well as from boating, airplane, and industrial accidents. Others' intoxication also increases the chances of becoming a pedestrian victim of an auto accident (USDHHS, 1990).

About 62% of adults in the United States drink alcohol, but only about 7% are heavy drinkers (USDHHS, 2000). Any amount of alcohol consumption can increase the risk of accidents, but heavy and binge drinking is especially risky. The gender differences in drinking are disappearing, but men are more than three times more likely to binge drink than women. In addition, drinking varies by age group, with younger adults being heavier drinkers. These gender and age differences in drinking patterns correspond to the differential risks of violent death. With the increases in women's drinking have come increases in problem drinking among women (Rodin & Ickovics, 1990). These changes have the potential to decrease the current female advantage in avoiding violent death.

Men are also more likely to hold risky jobs than women are (Waldron, 1991). In addition to exposure to hazardous materials, which increases the chances of cancer, men are more likely than women to have jobs that involve working around or operating dangerous machinery. Around 95% of the fatalities at work involve men, and gender differences in workplace accidents account for between 2% and 3% of the overall gender difference in mortality in the United States (Waldron, 1991). Therefore, occupational hazards and violence are substantial factors contributing to the gender difference in accidental deaths.

Men are more likely to commit suicide, but women are more likely to attempt suicide (USDHHS, 2000). This difference in suicide rates for men and women began to appear during the 1950s, increased during the 1960s, and began to decrease during the 1970s. The ratio of attempted to completed suicides is about 10 to 1 (Travis, 1988a). The main reason for the higher rates among men of completed suicides is that they tend to choose more lethal methods, such as guns and jumping from high places, whereas women more often attempt suicide by taking drugs. (No method is certain to be nonlethal, so any suicide attempt is serious.) The lethality of the methods chosen produces higher suicide rates among men, despite women's more frequent suicide attempts.

Chapter 7 described a gender difference in crime rate, explaining that men are more likely than women to commit crimes. This discrepancy is even greater for crimes involving violence, with men more likely to both perpetrate crimes and be victims of crime (U.S. Bureau of the Census, 1999). The increase in lawbreaking among women in the past decades has not changed these figures, because this increase reflects primarily nonviolent crimes. Thus, homicide affects men to a larger degree than women and has an especially disproportionate impact on young African American men.

In summary, men are more often the victims of unintentional and intentional violence than are women. Men's increased risk comes from several sources, including their heavier use of alcohol, heightened risk of workplace accidents, greater success at committing suicide, and their greater involvement in illegal activities. In addition, men are less likely to take protective measures, such as using seatbelts. All of these causes of violent deaths put men at a survival disadvantage and account for some of women's survival advantage. Women, however, do not experience the same advantage when seeking health care; women experience greater morbidity than men and have more difficulty receiving treatment for serious conditions than men do.

The Health Care System

As the headline story for this chapter discussed, women live longer than men, but they are sick more often. Defining what constitutes being sick is not simple, but doctor visits, hospital admissions, restriction of activities, or reports of distress are some of the indicators; women meet any of these definitions of illness more often than men do (Travis, 1988a). The combination of greater morbidity with lower mortality seems a contradiction, but gender roles as well as physiology contribute to the situation. The possibility mentioned in the headline story is that women's reproduction and its medicalized treatment account for increased use of medical services among women—pregnancy and childbirth are functions that now receive medical attention, require medical appointments, and are cared for by hospitalization. Another explanation involves the difference in gender roles related to seeking and receiving health care. A third possibility is that women are not as healthy as men, but that their health problems are less often life threatening, producing the combination of poorer health but longer lives.

Gender Roles and Health Care

People seek and receive health care from a variety of formal and informal sources, and gender roles contribute to receiving help from each source. Traditional male and female gender roles differ in the amounts of vulnerability each is allowed and the permissibility of seeking help. One facet of the masculine role, the Sturdy Oak, holds that men are strong and invulnerable; this aspect of the role causes men to restrain from showing signs of physical illness or seeking medical care (Brannon, 1976). The traditional female role, on the other hand, allows and even encourages weakness and vulnerability for emotional and physical problems (Lorber, 1975). Adherence to traditional gender roles may, therefore, hinder men from seeking help for their symptoms, but elements of the traditional feminine gender role relate to greater distress for women as well as to their increased readiness to seek medical care. After women and men enter the health care system, they also receive different care.

Gender and Seeking Health Care

The decision to seek medical care is influenced by many factors, including the perception of symptoms and beliefs about the consequences of seeking or failing to seek treatment. People who feel healthy may enter the medical care system to receive routine exams, but many skip such screening procedures, finding it easy to ignore their health as long as they feel well. Men are more likely to avoid regular health care than women are (Muller, 1990). Men are less likely than women to have regular physicians, sometimes avoiding checkups for years. Men explain these omissions in terms consistent with the masculine gender role, saying that they feel fine and thus do not need to consult physicians. This belief can be fatal; the first sign of heart disease can be a fatal heart attack, and many cancers do not produce symptoms in the early stages. Nonetheless, the belief that a lack of symptoms equals good health can lead men to avoid regular contacts with the health care system.

Women, on the other hand, find it more difficult to avoid the health care system, regardless of how well they may feel. Young women must seek medical advice to obtain many forms of contraception, especially birth control pills (Kane, 1991). These young women count in the statistics as having consulted physicians, although their medical visits involve no illness. As Altman's (1997) headline story suggested, such medical consultations often include physical examinations that may reveal health problems that require additional treatment. For example, blood tests may reveal anemia, and blood pressure readings may show hypertension. Each of these conditions merits further treatment, which leads these women into additional physician visits and medication. Young men receive no comparable medical attention during young adulthood that might reveal physical problems, and these differences in treatment for healthy young men and women contribute to the statistics concerning gender differences in seeking health care.

The personal perception of symptoms is an important factor in seeking medical care. People who sense that their bodies are not working correctly are more likely to seek medical advice than those who sense no problems. Perceiving symptoms, however, is not sufficient to lead people to make appointments with their physicians. Although some people readily seek professional medical advice and care, most people experience some reluctance to become part of the health care system.

This reluctance has many origins, including financial resources, convenience and accessibility of medical care, and personal considerations. Health care costs have risen faster than personal incomes, creating problems for many people in paying for health care. Scheduling of appointments and changing daily routines to keep these medical appointments are additional barriers. Anxiety about the diagnosis or treatment may keep people from seeking professional care; the diagnosis may be threatening, or the treatment may be painful or expensive, or both.

The factors that influence reluctance to seek medical care may not affect men and women equally. Women are more likely than men to be outside the paid workforce and to be employed on a part-time basis, whereas men are more likely to have the types of jobs that offer health insurance benefits. Employment situations can put women at a disadvantage in seeking health care, which leaves them with less money to pay for health care and to be without the health insurance that might cover their expenses (Muller, 1990).

Unemployed women can receive these benefits if they are married to men who have good insurance plans. For both men and women in these situations, continued health insurance depends on the continued employment of the spouse and the continuation of the marriage. Not only can women lose their health insurance through divorce, but children can also lose insurance coverage due to their parents' divorce. Mothers are most often granted custody, and the children may lose their coverage unless their mothers have employment that includes these benefits. Thus, women and children are less likely to have health insurance than men, making health care less accessible for them.

Men and women may have similar experiences of daily symptoms, but women are more likely to seek medical care for these symptoms. The reasons for this readiness may lie in two circumstances. Women are more sensitive to their body's signals than men are, making women more capable of reporting these physical symptoms (Pennebaker, 1982). In addition, their traditional gender role allows women to seek help more readily than men do.

Men and women also seek health care from different types of providers (Kane, 1991). Both women and men are more likely to consult pharmacists than any other category of health care professional, and women make more inquiries than men. Women may ask pharmacists for advice about over-the-counter remedies for their entire families, so the number of consultations may not reflect any gender difference in personal need. Men experience more injuries due to accidents and sports participation, so they are more likely to seek the services of physiotherapists than are women. Women, on the other hand, are more likely to seek the services of chiropractors or nutritionists. Women are also more likely to use alternative health care services, such as herbal medicine and acupuncture. None of these differences is large; thus, the types of health care professionals that men and women seek vary only to a small extent.

The different preferences in seeking medical care may be partly attributable to access to medical care, with women at a disadvantage due to their lower financial resources and poorer insurance coverage. Another difference may lie in women's greater sensitivity to symptoms, but a difference also exists in the willingness to report symptoms. These differences are consistent with the gender roles, with men denying and women accepting help.

Gender and Receiving Health Care

After a person has contacted a health care professional and becomes part of the health care system, gender becomes a factor in treatment. Again, gender roles influence the behavior of both patient and practitioner. Although some patients and practitioners are coming to view their relationship as a collaboration, the traditional conceptualization of the patient–practitioner relationship has included the subordinate patient and the controlling practitioner. The patient role is thus more compatible with the stereotypically female than the stereotypically male role, whereas the practitioner role is more consistent with traditional masculinity. The combination of gender roles and patient–provider roles puts women at a disadvantage both in giving and receiving medical care.

Men seem to have more trouble adopting the patient role than women do. Being a patient requires a person to relinquish control and follow the advice or orders of the practitioner. Gender is not a reliable predictor of patient compliance (Brannon & Feist, 2000), but the combination of the demographic factors of gender, age, ethnic background, cultural norms, religion, and educational level relates to patients' compliance with physicians' treatment advice. For example, people who are part of a culture that trusts physicians and accepts their advice as the best way to get well are more likely to follow physicians' advice than people from cultures that accept herbalists as the preferred health care professionals. Therefore, gender is only one factor from among a configuration of variables that relate to compliance with medical advice. Indeed, the interaction between patient and practitioner is more important to the patient's willingness to follow health advice than a patient's personal characteristics, and gender often plays a role in that interaction.

The medical profession has been criticized for its treatment of female patients, and this criticism has taken several forms. The most radical form of criticism holds that women were healers throughout history but have been replaced by technological, male-dominated forms of healing, examples of which are male physicians but female nurses (Ehrenreich & English, 1973). Other criticisms (Travis, 1988a) have claimed that negative stereotypes of female patients have led to poorer levels of medical care for them than for men. Yet other criticisms (Tavris, 1992) have been brought against the use of men as the medical standard to which women are compared, claiming that omitting women from medical training and research leaves physicians ill-prepared to treat women.

Physicians often have stereotypical views of women, and these views influence their treatment of female patients (Travis, 1988a). Medical school educational standards have promoted the view that women are emotional and incapable of providing accurate information about their bodies. An increasing percentage of physicians are women, but gender bias still exists in medical education, with few provisions to remedy these problems (Bickel, 1997). Physicians tend to rely on gender stereotypes in treatment decisions when they do not have a positive impression of the patients (Di Caccavo & Reid, 1998). When they felt positively about their patients, physicians in this study made similar treatment decisions about women and men, but when their feelings were neutral or negative, gender stereotypes took over, and women received more prescriptions for psychoactive drugs (to treat "emotional problems"), whereas men received more referrals for additional services.

The view of "emotional females" may lead physicians to discount the information provided by female patients and to believe that women cannot participate in decisions concerning their own health and treatment. Some research (Benrud & Reddy, 1998) supports the view that women's health problems receive different treatment than men's. The results of this research indicated that people explain women's and men's health problems in different ways. The researchers manipulated the information such that the problems were the same for both genders, so the differences in attributions were not due to the type of problems, but to the use of stereotypes of women and men in making judgments. People saw women's health problems as the result of relatively uncontrollable biological and emotional factors, but judged men's problems as the result of controllable behavioral and situational factors. These attributions have the potential to make big differences in health care: women's health problems may be viewed as "emotional problems," but men may receive blame for causing their own poor health through misbehavior.

Another criticism is aimed at a more subtle type of discrimination in medicine: the view that medical training represents men as the standard by which to measure all health concerns (Tavris, 1992). Physicians receive instruction in how to dissect and prescribe drugs for the standard patient, a 154-pound man. With men as the standard, women become the exception. Thus, any condition that men do not develop comes to be considered as deviant, including even the normal conditions associated with women's physiology—menstruation, pregnancy, and childbirth.

In addition to holding men as the standard in medicine, a great deal of medical research has omitted women entirely; that is, many studies have failed to include women as research subjects. The rationale for omitting women is that women bias the research because of their low rates of certain diseases and their hormonal variations. For example, middle-aged women develop CVD at a rate lower than middle-aged men, so longitudinal studies that follow healthy people until they show signs of CVD would have to include many more women than men to obtain a group of women with this disorder. Using only male participants results in studies that are easier to complete, but these studies reveal nothing about CVD in women. Assuming that women are similar to men in their development of CVD is unwarranted, because women are excluded from these studies precisely because of their physical differences.

Medical researchers have also excluded women from studies that test the safety and effectiveness of new drugs, as women would bias results because they experience cyclic variations in their hormonal levels. The researchers have feared that hormonal variations may interact with variations due to medication, making the task of assessing the effects of a test drug more difficult. Omitting women from such studies may be convenient for research, but is dangerous for women. If women have not participated in the testing, then the drug's safety and effectiveness have not been clearly established for them.

During the 1980s, the practice of excluding women from medical research received increasing criticism, and pressure mounted to give women's health additional emphasis. That pressure resulted in the creation of the Office of Research on Women's Health, a part of the National Institutes of Health (Kirschstein, 1991). This office's mission is to improve the prevention and treatment of diseases in women, and one of its first steps was to attempt to end the exclusion of women from medical research studies with the help of U.S. government sponsorship.

One of the research projects on women's health sponsored by this organization is the Women's Health Initiative (Blumenthal & Wood, 1997; Matthews et al., 1997). This study is designed to investigate factors involved with health problems experienced by older women, including CVD, cancer of the breast and digestive tract, and osteoporosis. The plan includes a 16-year longitudinal study with over 150,000 women, with both medication and psychosocial components of assessment and treatment. Additional areas of interest include improving the accessibility and quality of mammograms, and research on infertility and contraception. The initiative includes both prevention and clinical trials, and some results have begun to appear from these studies.

Although medicine remains male dominated, men are not the focus of comparable health initiatives. Indeed, men may not receive optimum or even adequate care. During childhood, parents are somewhat more likely to take their sons to the doctor than their daughters (Kane, 1991), but once men are responsible for seeking their own medical care, they tend to avoid regular medical care. Men seek care for their injuries, but not for regular exams and screening tests. In a survey on recent health status (in Kane, 1991), men were more likely than women to say that they had been ill within the past 2 weeks but had failed to seek medical care. This study showed that men are less likely to have regular physicians than women, so getting an appointment to see a physician is a greater inconvenience for a man in that he must first find a physician. Prostate cancer kills almost as many men as breast cancer kills women, yet many times more funds go toward breast cancer research than for prostate cancer (Stipp, 1996). Men have not mobilized to exert political pressure that spurs funding in the same way that women have, leaving men's health issues with fewer vocal advocates.

Some authorities (Schofield, Connell, Walker, Wood, & Butland, 2000) have argued that the division of health care into fields of women's health versus men's health will not best serve either. Indeed, the implication of labeling these specialty areas is that the differences between women and men are their main health concerns, when sexual and reproductive health are not the entirety of health care for either. These authorities recommended an integration so that the fields of women's and men's health can be seen in relation to each other and to the cultural and situational factors that influence both, such as family, work, poverty, and ethnicity.

In summary, the Sturdy Oak component of the male gender role may be a factor in men's avoiding health care; feelings of invulnerability and the belief that illness represents weakness lead men to ignore their health. Such avoidance can result in serious health problems that might be prevented or detected through routine physical exams. Men can avoid regular physical exams more easily than women can, because men typically do not have the same contacts with the health care system connected with reproduction or contraception that women of reproductive age have. Thus, men seldom use the health care system until they become ill, perhaps to the detriment of their health. Not only do reproduction and contraception concerns prompt women but not men to seek medical care during the reproductive years, but the differences in their reproductive systems also account for a large proportion of the gender difference in seeking and receiving health care.

Reproductive Health

Many of women's encounters with the health care system do not involve illness but occur as a result of contraception, pregnancy, childbirth, and menopause. Although these functions were completed throughout history with little medical assistance, they became increasingly "medicalized" during the 19th and 20th centuries (Ehrenreich & English, 1973). During this time, college education was largely restricted to men, who came to dominate the growing profession of medicine.

This expansion of medicine included attending women during childbirth, a role that had been performed by midwives. Childbirth was not the only function to gain medical attention; pregnancy came to be considered an appropriate area for regular medical care. The increasing number of contraceptive technologies during the 20th century depended almost exclusively on controlling women's rather than men's fertility, and physicians assumed control over access to contraception techniques such as birth control pills. During the middle of the 20th century, even menopause became a "disease" that could be "cured" by hormone replacement (Wilson, 1966). Thus, medical technologies came to be involved in all facets of women's reproductive health, from contraception during adolescence to hormone replacement after menopause.

Some critics have argued that access to the medical field has burdened women by forcing them to give birth in sterile, impersonal surroundings and subjecting them to increasingly large hospital bills for these services. According to this argument, birth is a natural process requiring no medical intervention. However, comparing statistics from undeveloped countries and from times in the United States before routine medical care during pregnancy and delivery, death could also be seen as a natural process. There is no question that technological medicine has dramatically cut both maternal and infant mortality (Kane, 1991). Nonetheless, women may receive too much treatment in some areas (as in too many hysterectomies or cesarean section deliveries) and too little in other respects (as in too little testing for heart disease or too little treatment for high cholesterol).

Women's more numerous consultations with health care professionals are due largely to their complex reproductive systems (Kane, 1991). Not only do women get pregnant and bear children, but their reproductive organs are subject to a greater variety of problems than are male organs. Figures 13.2 and 13.3 show the female and male reproductive systems. Except for children under age 15 years, girls and women receive more treatment for problems related to their reproductive systems than boys and men do.

Both systems can develop problems during prenatal development, producing congenital conditions that are more common in boys than in girls. During infancy and early childhood, boys have more problems with their genitourinary system than girls do, requiring more hospital stays and physician consultations for these problems (Kane, 1991). Beginning

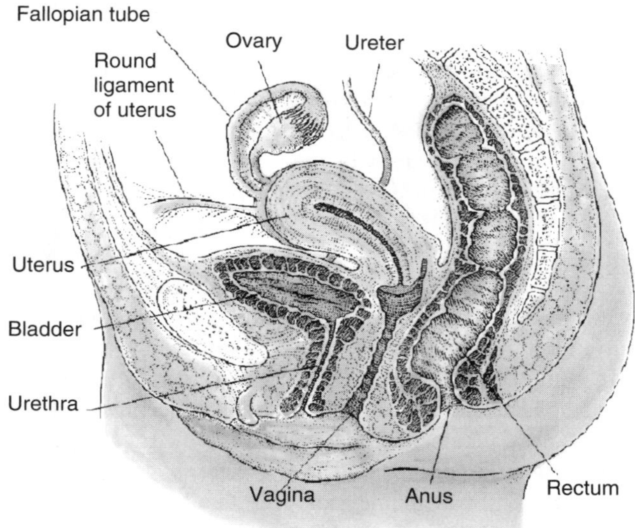

FIGURE 13.2 Female Reproductive System

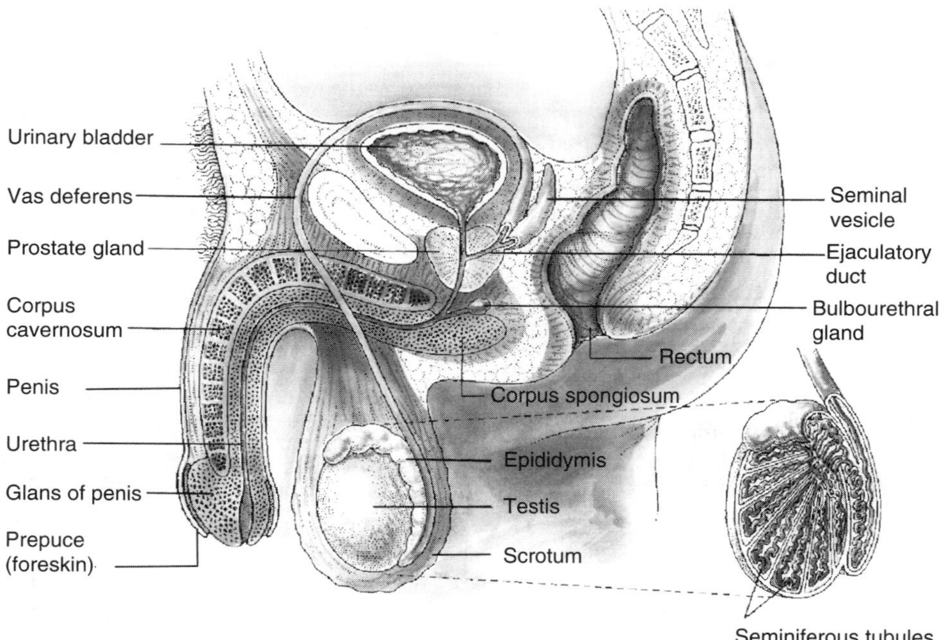

FIGURE 13.3 Male Reproductive System

at age 15 years, girls make more visits to health care professionals, and require more hospitalizations, regarding their reproductive systems.

The majority of the physician visits and hospitalizations for women during their reproductive years involve contraception, pregnancy, and childbirth; most of these contacts with the health care system are not due to illness or health problems but because women's reproductive functions have come under medical supervision. Although a large percentage of pregnancies and deliveries proceeds without any problem, most women in industrialized countries receive medical care during their pregnancies, and the majority of deliveries take place in hospitals. In addition, about one-fourth of the deliveries in the United States are by cesarean section (C-section) surgery (DiMatteo & Kahn, 1997). C-section deliveries can save mothers' and babies' lives, but the surgery carries morbidity and mortality risks. This system of medical treatment for childbirth has unquestionably decreased mortality for women during pregnancy and delivery, but these visits and hospitalizations count as statistics showing (and often put women into the situation of receiving) more health care.

Many of the methods of contraception for women—birth control pills, implants, intrauterine devices (IUDs), diaphragms, sterilization, abortion—not only require medical supervision, but also increase health risks. For example, birth control pills provide very effective contraception, but women over age 35 years who take contraceptive pills have significantly increased risks of stroke, and smoking multiplies this risk (Rodin & Ickovics, 1990). Therefore, contraception is not only more often a woman's responsibility, but also more of a health threat to women.

Both men and women are subject to **sexually transmitted diseases (STDs),** infectious diseases that are spread through sexual contact. The infectious agents can be bacterial, viral, fungal, or parasitic, and many can be transmitted by vaginal, oral, or anal sexual activity. These bacterial infections include gonorrhea, syphilis, and chlamydia, and do not always produce symptoms; women are especially likely to be symptom free until advanced stages of the diseases. Although bacterial infections can be cured by antibiotics, people without symptoms may not receive treatment until their diseases are serious. Furthermore, delays in treatment allow infected persons to transmit the disease to others.

Delays in treatment are also likely to escalate the growth of the fungal and parasitic STDs. *Candidiasis albicans,* a yeast-like fungus, produces itching and swelling of the genitals. It can be transmitted through sexual intercourse, but this infection is not always an STD; it is more common in women who take contraceptive pills or who are pregnant or diabetic. These conditions alter the chemistry of the vagina, allowing this fungus to grow at a rapid rate, producing annoying and painful symptoms. Chemical treatments exist to control this type of infection. Trichomonia is a one-celled parasite that can infect the vagina in women and the urethra in men. It is almost always sexually transmitted, and an effective drug treatment exists.

No drugs exist to cure viral diseases. Thus, the viral STDs pose an even more serious problem than other types of STDs. The human immunodeficiency virus (HIV) is the virus that produces acquired immune deficiency syndrome (AIDS), a virus that can be sexually transmitted. The virus damages the immune system, leaving the body open to a variety of opportunistic diseases that eventually lead to death. Years may pass between time of infection and the development of symptoms, allowing infected persons to be unaware of the presence of the condition and able to unknowingly transmit the infection to others.

Genital herpes, viral hepatitis, and genital warts are also viral STDs. Genital warts can sometimes be surgically removed, and several medications exist to manage the symptoms of herpes infections. Like other viral infections, these STDs are difficult to manage and are presently without a cure. Herpes infections are especially problematic, producing chronic problems with painful blisters on the genitals.

Not all medical problems of the reproductive organs are related to reproduction; that is, these organs can be the site of disease and cancer. Again, women are more likely than men to seek health care concerning problems with their reproductive organs. Although women are at greater risk for cancer of organs in the reproductive system than men are throughout young and middle adulthood, men are most likely to develop testicular cancer between ages 15 and 34 years (Parker, 1997). This form of cancer is quite rare, but rates are increasing; men are most likely to develop this form of cancer during the years when they tend to avoid regular physical checkups. A man may have no regular physician to tell about the lump he has detected on a testicle, and the tumor may go untreated for a dangerously long period. This form of cancer is rarely fatal if treated early, but fatality rates rise sharply with delays in treatment, going from a 90% survival rate to only a 25% survival rate. Thus, this rare form of cancer that affects men in their 20s and 30s may be fatal more often than it would be if men gave more attention to their health.

Prostate cancer is much more common than testicular cancer, and it tends to develop in older men. This form of cancer is not common until after age 75 years, when it increases sharply (U.S. Bureau of the Census, 1999). Even without malignancy, as the prostate enlarges, which begins during puberty, it can cause problems, such as difficulty during urination that can require surgery. Malignant tumors of the prostate typically are small and grow slowly, and many elderly men die *with* rather than *from* prostate cancer (Stipp, 1996). The development and use of a diagnostic test, the prostate specific antigen test, has allowed earlier diagnosis, and men are beginning to mobilize as advocates for improved treatment.

Endometrial cancer affects the uterine lining and is the most common form of cancer of the female genitals and reproductive tract (Paskette & Michielutte, 1997). Women can also develop cancer of the cervix, ovaries, vulva, vagina, and fallopian tubes. None of these sites is the most common site for cancer—the breast is. About one in nine women will develop breast cancer. (Even so, lung cancer is the leading cause of cancer death for both men and women due to its high fatality rate.) From ages 15 to 45, cancers of the reproductive system are a major cause of mortality for women but not for men.

During menopause, women lose their fertility; they cease ovulation and menstruation, and their production of estrogen and progesterone declines. Some women experience uncomfortable symptoms associated with menopause; the most common of these is the "hot flash," a sudden feeling of heat and skin flushing. These feelings may be uncomfortable and embarrassing but are not health threatening. Only 10% of menopausal women experience serious symptoms associated with menopause (Livingston, 1999). Estrogen replacement therapy can alleviate the symptoms, but this medical intervention remains controversial (Derry, Gallant, & Woods, 1997). Critics contend that hormone replacement is an example of overtreatment of women because menopause is not a disease. In addition, this treatment can increase the risk for breast cancer (Steinberg et al., 1991). Proponents cite the continued protection from heart disease and lowered risk of osteoporosis as benefits of hormone replacement therapy. Proponents and critics agree that hormone replacement therapy should be an individual decision made after considering both benefits and risks.

Men's hormone production also drops with aging, but they undergo no symptoms as visible as those of women during menopause. The decrease in hormone production in men results in the decline, but not the end, of their fertility. Men who lose the ability to get erections may receive hormone replacements, but many fewer men than women receive analogous hormone replacement therapy.

Thus, treatment for malignancies of the reproductive system accounts for only a small portion of the reproductive health care received by women, but for a larger portion of that received by men. Women not only get pregnant and bear children, but they also have the majority of responsibility for contraception. In addition, menstruation is often painful, and some women experience pain sufficiently serious to prompt them to consult health care professionals. The decline in hormone production associated with menopause also causes some women to seek medical treatment. Therefore, a great deal of the added health care received by women is due to their reproductive system needs, but this is only part of the reason for women's greater number of contacts with the health care system.

Gender, Lifestyle, And Health

Men have shorter average life spans than women in all developed and most undeveloped countries, now and in the past, yet women are more likely to use health care. Both men's shorter lives and women's poorer health may, as women believe (Wallace, 1996), be related to their lifestyles. That is, men may lose years from their life span by their behaviors, and factors in women's lives may increase their morbidity. Karen Matthews (1989) hypothesized that women's healthier lifestyles are a factor in their longer lives, and that men's lifestyle choices and occupational health risks place men in greater danger than women for life-threatening diseases and accidents. These risky behaviors are associated with the male gender role, which may be dangerous to men's health (Harrison, 1978; Messner, 1997).

The female gender role may likewise endanger health. Research findings (Gove & Hughes, 1979) have confirmed that the nurturant role that many women fulfill places them in the position of taking care of others better than themselves. The demands of providing social support and nurturant care can be emotionally and physically draining, but may not guarantee that women receive the same quality of care they give, leaving them without the support they offer to others. According to another study (Helson & Picano, 1990), those women who fulfilled the traditional female gender role when they were young were well-adjusted at the time, but were more poorly adjusted and less healthy than more nontraditional women were 20 years later, during middle age.

Therefore, both traditional gender roles carry health risks. Women's morbidity is a factor that significantly decreases the quality of their lives (Kaplan, Anderson, & Wingard, 1991), but their more frequent illnesses are usually not ones that threaten their lives. Men, on the other hand, tend to experience health problems that are more likely to be life threatening. In other words, "One sex is 'sicker' in the short run, and the other in the long run" (Verbrugge, 1985, p. 163). The causes of death, however, are similar, although men die earlier from these causes than women do.

Two behaviors that relate to health and longevity are eating and exercising, and these behaviors show gender-related differences.

Eating

Everyone eats, but people vary in their eating patterns and in the meaning they attach to eating (Belasco, 1989). Women's relationship with food is especially complex; women use food as comfort, but they also show more concern with eating to control weight and are more likely to diet than men. This concern with weight and their attempts to restrict food intake lead women to hold different attitudes toward eating than men do.

Gender differences in eating patterns start during early adolescence (Rolls, Fedoroff, & Guthrie, 1991) and become greater during the teen years. Figure 13.4 shows the changes in concerns about weight from fifth through ninth grades. Adolescent boys, on the average, eat enough food to obtain the required calories, but adolescent girls restrict their caloric intake to the point of risk for nutritional inadequacies. Adult women also eat less than adult men, but the discrepancy is not as great as during adolescence. Nonetheless, women may eat too little to receive adequate nutrition.

Not only do men eat more than women, but the eating patterns of each conform to the expectations of their respective gender roles. Observation of men and women (J. Green, 1987) showed that men ate more calories because they took bigger bites. Eating less and taking smaller bites may relate to efforts to appear feminine, and eating style can affect social perception, including impressions of femininity and personal concern about appearance (Chaiken & Pliner, 1987). In studies that paired female and male participants with same- and other-gender partners to snack and talk, women showed a tendency to eat less when paired with an attractive male partner but not with an unattractive male or with a female partner (Mori, Chaiken, & Pliner, 1987). Men, too, seem subject to the pressures to eat less to create a social impression (Pliner & Chaiken, 1990). Women's eating is motivated by the desire to appear feminine as well as the desire to give a good social impression.

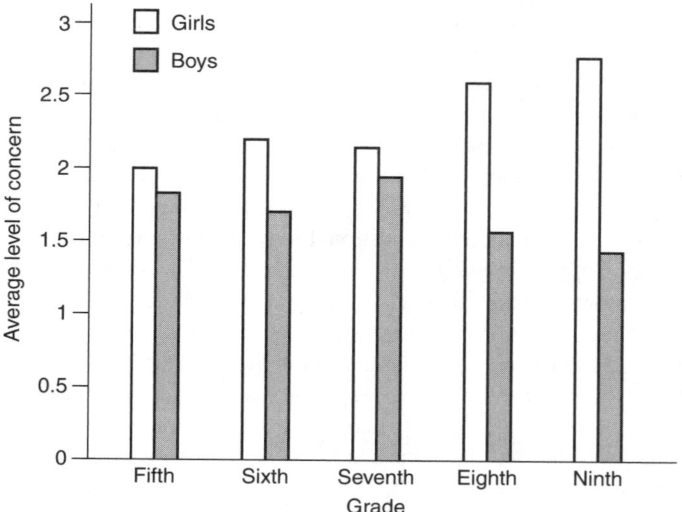

FIGURE 13.4 Gender Differences in Young Adolescents' Concerns about Weight and Eating, by Grade

SOURCE: Reprinted by permission of Elsevier Science from "Weight and eating concerns among pre- and young adolescent boys and girls," by M. H. Richards, R. C. Casper, and R. Larson, *Journal of Adolescent Health, 11,* pp. 203–209, Copyright © 1990 by The Society for Adolescent Medicine.

Thus, women have two constraints on their social eating, whereas men have only one. Therefore, women and men eat somewhat differently, partly due to men's greater caloric requirements and partly due to the impression that women may wish to convey through their eating style.

Difference in eating styles is more than a way to make an impression; the thinner ideal body image for women restricts most women's eating. Women have more body fat than men, but the ideal body image for women demands thinness. Thus, women may believe that they must diet to achieve the desired weight. Extreme concerns with weight and dieting can produce abnormal eating habits and serious eating disorders. A growing consensus holds that body image and eating disorders are linked; an unattainably thin body image can prompt these unhealthy eating patterns.

Body Image

The image of what constitutes an attractive female or male body currently emphasizes thinness for women and muscularity for men (see "According to the Media/According to the Research"). The contemporary ideal body image for women has developed over the past 100 years (Chernin, 1978; Wooley, 1994). In the past, plumpness was the ideal for women, signifying their health and wealth, but that ideal has faded. The thin image arose during the early part of the 20th century, signifying a departure from the plump image of traditional femininity. The thin ideal has a social-class basis (Polivy & Thomsen, 1988). When rich women began to have a preference for thinness, this preference began to spread throughout all social classes. This image now affects African American (Hsu, 1990), Hispanic American (Hsu, 1990), Asian American (Bradshaw, 1994), and Native American women (LaFromboise, Berman, & Sohi, 1994).

Overweight is a stigma for men as well as for women. Body image discontentment appears even in preadolescent children (Collins, 1991). As young as age 6 or 7, both girls and boys chose an ideal body thinner than their own, but girls made more extreme choices. This dissatisfaction continues into late adolescence and adulthood, and the gender differences persist.

Men who see themselves as overweight want to lose weight (Drewnowski & Yee, 1987), but being too heavy is not the problem most men experience. A different ideal body image exists for men—they are under pressure to conform to an ideal of muscularity (McCreary & Sasse, 2000). Adolescent boys (McCreary & Sasse, 2000) and college men (Drewnowski & Yee, 1987) expressed the desire to be more muscular rather than thinner. Among adolescents, this desire was related to low self-esteem and higher depression among boys but not girls. Boys and college men were more likely than girls and women to enact their attitudes about muscularity by working out with weights and to eat to increase bulk. The desire to increase muscularity may also be expressed by taking anabolic steroids, drugs that can help increase muscle mass. Unfortunately, these drugs have many negative side effects that can present physical and psychological risks.

Both women and men are somewhat mistaken in their estimates of what body type the other finds most attractive, but both are influenced by body shape. In addition, more recent studies have indicated more extreme body emphasis. Earlier research (Fallon & Rozin, 1985) indicated that women perceived the ideal female body as thinner than their own, and they believed that men found thinner female bodies attractive. Men expressed no such discrepancies for their own bodies, but they believed that women found heavier men more

ACCORDING TO THE MEDIA…

Attractive Women Are Thin; Attractive Men Are Muscular

Media portrayals of beauty influence the images of what women and men want to be. An examination of portrayals of many media images reflects the thin ideal for women and the muscular ideal for men. For example, an examination of magazines popular with young adults (Andersen & DiDomenico, 1992) found that women's magazines contained over 10 times as many advertisements and articles oriented toward weight loss compared to men's magazines. The magazines for men contained messages to change body shape rather than to lose weight. These messages promote the varying body ideals for women and men.

Several longitudinal analyses of magazines aimed toward women and men confirmed the difference in messages and suggested that the images have become more extreme over the past 40 years. The degree of change in the ideal body for women is reflected in *Playboy* centerfolds and in Miss America contestants (Garner, Garfinkel, Schwartz, & Thompson, 1980). Women in both categories became thinner over the 20-year period from 1959 until 1978. An extension of that research through 1988 (Wiseman, Gray, Mosimann, & Ahrens, 1992) showed that Miss America contestants became significantly thinner, and both images were significantly thinner than average women of comparable ages.

Playboy centerfolds did not continue their weight decline after 1979, but their weights stayed low (Spitzer, Henderson, and Zivian, 1999). Indeed, 99% of centerfolds and 100% of Miss American winners fell into the category indicating underweight, with an increasing number of weights for these women suggesting anorexia nervosa. As Brenda Spitzer and her colleagues (1999, p. 556) said, "Clearly the North American ideal for female beauty as portrayed in the media is at a weight deemed to be dangerous."

Playgirl centerfolds reflect the ideal for the male form, and an examination of those photos from 1986 to 1996 (Spitzer et al., 1999) showed an increase in weight. Those men were heavy, but the increase represented muscle, not fat. Again, the ideal in the media is extreme, and most men cannot meet this unreasonable ideal.

---

attractive than the women reported. These findings suggest that both women and men may strive for ideal bodies that are not perceived as ideal by the other gender.

More recent studies have confirmed that weight is not as critical as either women or men believe, but body shape is an important determinant of attractiveness. One study (Furnham, Dias, & McClelland, 1998) showed that ratings of attractiveness were not unique to any weight, but the body shape was. The important contributors were the ratio of waist size to hip size, breast size, and weight, and these factors combined in ways that were not surprising: Smaller waists and larger breasts contributed to higher attractiveness ratings. Women's ratings of men's body attractiveness showed a strong preference for a large upper body compared to waist and hip size (Maisey, Vale, Cornelissen, & Tovee, 1999).

Therefore, both women and men are subjected to pressures to have bodies that conform to the ideal, but the methods for achieving these changes differ. If these messages are effective, men and women would be likely to take different strategies to achieve their ideal bodies: Women would be more likely to experience eating disorders, whereas men would be more likely to encounter exercise-related problems.

Eating Disorders

Anorexia nervosa and bulimia are two eating disorders that have received a great deal of publicity, but dieting has reached such proportions and in some cases such severity that it may also

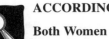

ACCORDING TO THE RESEARCH...

Both Women and Men Have Gotten Heavier

During the time that the media-promoted ideal body for women became thinner and the ideal for men became more muscular, research evidence suggests that both became heavier (Spitzer et al., 1999). The percentage of overweight U.S. residents increased from 24% during the 1970s to 34% during the 1990s (U.S. Bureau of the Census, 1999), and the number of overweight Canadians also increased during this time (Spitzer et al., 1999). As the ideals became thinner, the reality became heavier. "The ideal female weight, represented by actresses, models, and Miss Americas, has progressively decreased to that of the thinnest 5% to 10% of American women. Consequently, 90% to 95% of American women feel that they don't 'measure up'" (Seid, 1994, p. 8). The vast majority of women do not (and cannot) meet the standards presented as ideal, resulting in discontent with their weight as the norm.

On the one hand, women are discontent with their weights because almost half of the women who are not overweight believe that they are (U.S. Bureau of the Census, 1999). On the other hand, men are not as ready to believe or even to recognize that they are overweight. One-fourth of men who were not overweight believed that they were, and about 20% of those who were overweight failed to recognize it. Therefore, the percentage of overweight is very similar for men and women (between 33% and 35%), but the perception of being overweight varies. However, the title of one article summarizes the situation for both men and women concerning weight: "Nobody's satisfied" (Raudenbush & Zellner, 1997).

be considered an eating disorder (Polivy & Thomsen, 1988). Indeed, dieting is related to the development of the more serious eating disorders of anorexia and bulimia. **Anorexia nervosa** is a disorder caused by self-starvation in pursuit of thinness, and **bulimia** consists of binge eating followed by some method of purging (induced vomiting or excessive laxative use).

Dieting, anorexia, and bulimia are all more common among women than men. A survey of high school students and adult women and men (Serdula et al., 1993) showed, dieting was more common among women. About two-thirds of the girls and women were either trying to lose or trying not to gain weight, compared to about one-third of the boys in high school and one-half of the men. When considering lifetime dieting, 72% of the women and 44% of the men said they had dieted. The percentages are even more divergent for eating disorders, with around 90% of people who are treated for eating disorders being women (Rolls et al., 1991). Being female, therefore, is a predictor for dieting and for developing eating disorders.

Dieting itself produces physical and psychological effects, including fatigue, low blood pressure, anemia, headaches, cardiac problems, and other physical problems (Polivy & Thomsen, 1988). The psychological problems associated with dieting include irritability, anxiety, poor concentration, and depression. The relationship between dieting and depression is common in both women and men, but the relationship is stronger for men (Zimmer-Schur & Newcomb, 1994). Furthermore, the evidence is not entirely optimistic concerning the effectiveness of dieting as a way to control weight (Brownell & Rodin, 1994). Thus, dieting may not be the only answer to the problem of overweight. For some people, the risks of dieting outweigh the benefits.

Dieting is very common, but anorexia and bulimia are much less frequent. Anorexia is most common among young women, but only around 1% of adolescent girls have this disorder, and its appearance in the general population is even lower (Dolan, 1994). Bulimia is more common, occurring in about 2% of women. Again, young women are most likely to be bulimic; some estimates of the frequency of bulimia on college campuses run as high as 4%. Although these percentages are low, these disorders affect hundreds of thousands of people, so the problem is not a minor one.

Several factors relate to the development of eating disorders. As the rates of anorexia and bulimia suggest, both gender and age are factors, with women at a higher risk than men, and young women more subject to eating problems than older women (Hsu, 1990). Social class was once a major factor, but pressures for thinness now occur in all social classes and among all ethnic groups. Occupation is also a factor, with young women who are in modeling or dance school more likely to have eating disorders than comparable young women whose careers do not demand thinness (Garner & Garfinkel, 1980).

The underlying causes of eating disorders are not understood, but research has related eating disorders to problems and attitudes more common among women. Becky Thompson (1999) interviewed African American, Hispanic American, and White women with eating problems and found a history of sexual abuse and trauma among these women. Brett Silverstein and his colleagues (Perlick & Silverstein, 1994; Silverstein, Carpman, Perlick, & Perdue, 1990; Silverstein, Perdue, Wolk, & Pizzolo, 1988; Silverstein & Perlick, 1995) found that eating disorders were related to ambivalence over gender role, which arose from the conflict between rewards associated with achievement and the connection between achievement and masculinity. Other research (Lakkis, Ricciardelli, & Williams, 1999) has related disordered eating to gender role, specifically negative femininity, which consists of traits such as dependency, timidity, and weakness. Women who scored high in negative femininity were more likely to show signs of disordered eating. Thus, several lines of research have related eating disorders to traits and problems that are more common among women, which explains some of the gender-related difference in the rates of eating disorders.

About 10% of people with eating disorders are male (Rolls et al., 1991). Some of these men have occupations that require thinness, such as jockeys, dancers, or models. The demands of their careers make them subject to pressures for slimness in the same way as women who are dancers or models. Athletes also develop weight concerns so serious as to change their eating to a pathological pattern. Wrestlers and runners are at specific risk, and intensity of training is a factor. High-mileage runners have a greater chance of showing symptoms of eating disorders than those who run less (Kiernan, Rodin, Brownell, Wilmore, & Crandall, 1992).

Sexual orientation is also related to disordered eating in men. Gay men expressed higher body dissatisfaction than heterosexual men (Lakkis et al., 1999), and the preference for thinness is a risk for eating disorders. About a fourth of men who are anorexic are gay (Seligmann, 1994), but body dissatisfaction and traits of negative femininity in men are the factors predictive of eating disorders, just as they are in women. The majority of anorexic men are heterosexual, but among men, gay men are at an increased risk for eating disorders.

Both anorexia and bulimia are serious disorders, but anorexia is more likely to be life threatening. Between 5% and 15% of anorexics starve themselves to death (Hsu, 1990).

GENDERED VOICES

I'm Afraid Some of Them Are Not Going to Be Around

"I'm afraid some of them are not going to be around," a 14-year-old dancer told her mother concerning other dancers who showed symptoms of anorexia. The dancers in her classes were encouraged to be thin, and the girl believed that several were in danger; they were so thin that she had considered them in danger of dying. Her mother was angry because she believed that the instructor was encouraging unhealthy eating in students, by telling her normal-weight daughter that she needed to lose weight. The girl knew that she was heavier than many of the other dancers, but she believed that they had the problem, not her.

She had begun to hear criticisms about her weight when she was 12, and she started to become self-conscious about it, but she had resisted dieting, partly because she thought the other girls were too thin and partly because she didn't want to change her eating habits. She had also received conflicting messages about her weight, with her mother and others telling her that she wasn't too heavy, her dance teacher telling her that she needed to be thinner, and her classmates dieting to the point of anorexia.

Another girl's story confirmed the prevalence of weight consciousness among early adolescents. This 12-year-old came home from school one day and told her mother that when they had gone swimming for gym class, most of the girls had gone into the pool with their T-shirts over their bathing suits. She didn't understand why they had done so; a wet T-shirt made swimming more difficult. When she asked one why she had kept her shirt on, the other girl said, "Because I'm so fat. I don't want anyone to see me in a bathing suit." The 12-year-old told her mother, "But they're not fat." She considered her classmates' perceptions of their bodies very odd. Judging from the number of girls who had been reluctant to be seen in their bathing suits, her classmates' distorted perception was more common than her accurate assessment of what was normal and what constituted overweight.

Furthermore, treatment for anorexia is difficult. Anorexics do not cooperate with their treatment and persist in their desire to lose weight—even at the risk of their lives. Bulimia is more easily treated because bulimics typically feel guilty about their binge eating and purging and desire to change their behavior. Therapy can fail with both disorders, resulting in persistent eating problems that can lead to permanent damage to health.

Eating disorders, then, may be the result of concerns with body image and exaggerated attempts to attain thinness. Because their ideal body images are thin, women are more likely than men to develop eating disorders. Over the past several decades, both men and women have begun to feel increased pressure to attain and maintain attractive bodies, and women tend to try to achieve this goal through dieting and, to a lesser extent, through exercise; men on the other hand, use exercise as a primary means and dieting as a secondary means of shaping their bodies.

Exercise and Fitness

Exercise is a factor in the weight maintenance equation. To maintain a steady body weight, the energy (calories) from food consumed must equal body energy expenditures. Such expenditures come from the energy required to maintain basal metabolism and from the energy required for physical activity. Increases in physical activity require more calories, or weight loss occurs. Thus, increases in physical activity can produce weight loss.

As noted earlier, men are more likely to exercise and women are more likely to diet as their main strategies to lose weight. When dieters eat less, their basal metabolism slows, and their bodies require fewer calories, which protects against starvation but makes weight loss difficult (Polivy & Herman, 1983). To overcome this problem, the dieter must eat even less, increasing the chances of nutritional deficits and the difficulties in maintaining the diet. Thus, dieting is not only difficult, it also is not as effective for weight control as dieting plus exercise.

Increased concern with body image and the growing evidence that dieting may not be a good weight control strategy has led to an increased emphasis on exercise. Weight control, however, is a minor factor in considering the benefits of exercise; physical activity is a basic part of life. The amount of physical activity varies from person to person and from time to time, but people are physically active creatures.

The circumstances of contemporary life do not guarantee much physical activity. Most jobs in technological societies do not require a high level of physical effort. Some people enjoy exercise and participate in various types of leisure-time activities that require a great deal of physical effort, whereas others prefer television or other sedentary activities as a way to spend their leisure time. Differences in job and leisure-time activities show gender differences, with women being less likely to engage in physical activity than men (U.S. Bureau of the Census, 1999).

These gender differences begin during the preschool years, when boys are more active than girls. Throughout childhood, boys are more likely to engage in physical activities requiring gross motor skills that use the large muscles of the body. Boys' preferences for baseball, football, soccer, and basketball put them into more active situations than many girls' games require. Girls and boys do not play together often during childhood, decreasing the chances that girls will participate in many games and sports involving vigorous activity. Girls who do, however, are more likely to become college athletes than girls who engage in more traditional play activities (Giuliano, Popp, & Knight, 2000). (See Chapter 9 for a discussion of gender segregation and friendships during childhood and Chapter 11 for a consideration of athletics in schools.)

Watching television and playing computer games have become popular recreational activities for children. The computer game market has been dominated by games aimed at boys, with few oriented toward girls' interests. This situation is beginning to change, and some computer games with traditional feminine themes have appeared (Rothstein, 1997). Regardless of the content, computer games can take the place of more active games and decrease the physical activity of both boys and girls.

Although children with athletic talent are encouraged to participate in sports, the emphasis on sports may leave the majority of children without adequate encouragement to be active. Many children of both genders avoid physical activity. Not having the ability to excel, they shun exercise, resulting in poor fitness and an increased probability of obesity.

Gender differences in exercising increase during adolescence, with girls decreasing and boys increasing their participation in athletics. The traditional gender roles hold that women should look slender and dainty and should feel reluctant to compete. Men, on the other hand, should look muscular and strong and should feel eager to compete. Athletic participation, with its emphasis on size, strength, and competition, is more compatible with the male than the female gender role. Adolescents feel the pressures to adopt these gender roles; thus, boys are urged to "try out" for sports, whereas girls may not receive similar encouragement.

Title IX of the Education Amendments of 1972 prohibited sex discrimination in education, which included support for school athletics. The subsequent development of athletic programs for high school girls and college women has changed opportunities and attitudes toward women's athletics. More women now participate in athletics, establishing a pattern of physical activity that, like men's, can carry over into adulthood and provide long-term health benefits.

A growing body of research evidence indicates that exercise provides physical and psychological benefits to both men and women (King & Kiernan, 1997). A review of research on exercise and cardiovascular disease showed benefits, especially for men (Dubbert & Martin, 1988). Most of the studies on cardiovascular disease have excluded women, resulting in less conclusive evidence for the benefits of exercise for women. The role of exercise is better established in connection with **osteoporosis,** the process of bone demineralization. This disorder affects older individuals and is more common among women than men. Orthopedic problems such as fractures are common and can lead to decreased mobility, which is a major factor in decreased quality of life for the elderly (Robine & Ritchie, 1991). Exercise slows and may reverse this process.

In addition to the physical benefits, exercise promotes psychological benefits (President's Council on Physical Fitness and Sports, 1997). Exercise is related to improvements in mood and to feelings of psychological well-being and self-esteem. The efficacy of exercise to counter depression is particularly noteworthy. Thus, people who exercise show improvements in psychological and physical health, but relatively few people accrue these benefits; most children and adults in the United States lead sedentary lives (Dubbert, 1992).

Men's greater sports participation during adolescence makes them more likely than women to continue this athletic activity throughout their lives, but this background is no guarantee of an active lifestyle (Verbrugge, 1989). After they leave school, men become less likely to continue with physical activity, falling into the dominant pattern of desk jobs and sedentary hobbies.

Pressures on women to be thin have extended to fitness, with an increasing number of articles in women's magazines (Weisman, Gray, Mosimann, & Ahrens, 1992) and messages on magazine covers (Malkin, Wornian, & Chrisler, 1999) urging women to achieve thinness not only through diet but also through exercise. Although they may or may not have histories of participation in activities that promote physical fitness, women are subject to increasing pressures to exercise, mostly as a way to achieve weight goals rather than health goals.

An investigation of physically active men and women (McDonald & Thompson, 1992) looked at their exercise motivations, eating habits, and body satisfaction. Women were more likely than men to exercise to achieve good body tone and weight loss rather than fitness. In this study, both the women and men who exercised for reasons of health and fitness were less likely to show symptoms of eating disorders than those who exercised for weight control and to improve appearance.

Men's exercise motivations may also be symptomatic of body image problems. The drive to develop muscularity can lead boys and men to exercise excessively (McCreary & Sasse, 2000), which can lead to injury. Boys and men may be motivated to be muscular in a gender-stereotypical counterpart to girls and women, who are motivated to be thin. Exercise may allow both women and men to achieve fitness, but exercise may also provide a format for enacting body image dissatisfaction and unrealistic weight concerns. Therefore, despite the benefits of exercise, overcommitment to exercise is not always healthy.

In summary, exercise can be a healthy habit, that provides a number of physical and psychological benefits. Although men are more likely to have a background in sports, both women and men may pursue exercise for a variety of reasons. Men are more likely to use exercise as a way to shape their bodies, and women are more likely to use exercise as an adjunct to dieting to lose weight. Both of these goals may be the basis for pathological exercising, but moderate exercise is a factor in a healthy lifestyle, with men more likely to be physically active than women.

Considering Diversity

Health and mortality figures from around the world and within the United States reflect the influence of ethnicity and the economic conditions that are often related to ethnicity. One way to analyze world economies is the division into developed, or industrialized, countries; developing countries; and undeveloped countries. The economics of life in these countries also affects death in these countries. As Table 13.4 shows, life expectancy is longer in industrialized countries than in developing or undeveloped countries. In addition, the causes of death vary. In developed countries, leading causes of death are the chronic diseases (cardiovascular disease [CVD] and cancer) that are more common among older people. People in industrialized countries live long enough to develop these diseases. The death rates for CVD and cancer are much lower for the developing countries. In undeveloped countries, mortality is high from infectious and parasitic diseases, which are fatal for infants and young children more often than for other age groups. High mortality for infants and children lowers life expectancy and typically occurs in poor countries with inadequate nutrition and medical care.

As Table 13.4 illustrates, life expectancy and causes of death vary enormously throughout the world, but the gender gap in favor of women in life expectancy appears everywhere. That gap is larger in industrialized countries (7 to 10 years) and much smaller in undeveloped countries (a few months to 4 years). In some of the undeveloped countries, maternal mortality is high because of problems related to pregnancy and childbirth. Another practice that can decrease the survival advantage for girls and women is *son preference*—that is, the preference for sons over daughters (Kane, 1991). Son preference can lead to the murder of infant girls, but more often it is expressed through preferential treatment for sons, including better feeding and medical attention. In countries where girls and boys receive more equal treatment during infancy and childhood, girls have a survival advantage over boys, as women do when compared to men. Thus, the female survival advantage holds across many cultures. However, the life expectancy varies more than the magnitude of the gender gap, which indicates that social factors are important in life expectancy.

Worldwide, men are more vulnerable to disease and death in patterns similar to those in the United States: Men's rate of CVD death is higher than that of women of comparable age, they use tobacco at a higher rate, and they engage in risky behaviors that increase their vulnerability to violent death. In countries in which the death rate for CVD is high, the gender gap is larger than in countries with fewer deaths from this cause. The countries in eastern Europe, including those that were part of the Soviet Union, have a particularly high rate of CVD, and this rate has increased since the breakup of the Soviet Union (Weidner, 2000). The rise has affected those people most vulnerable to CVD—middle-aged men. The increase in Russia has been over 30%, the life expectancy in Russia has declined, and the gen-

TABLE 13.4 Average Life Expectancies, Infant Mortality, and Causes of Death for Developed, Developing, and Undeveloped Countries

	Life Expectancy			*Causes (per 100,000 population)*			
Country	Men	Women	Infant mortality (per 1,000)	Circulatory Diseases	Cancer	Accident/ Violence	Infectious/ Parasitic Diseases
			Developed Countries				
Australia	77	83	5.1	296.0	190.0	41.0	6.0
Canada	76	83	5.4	274.4	196.7	47.2	10.9
France	75	83	5.6	286.7	247.6	76.9	12.6
Germany	74	81	5.1	527.4	260.2	50.1	7.3
Japan	77	83	4.1	239.1	196.4	49.1	12.7
Sweden	77	82	3.9	544.5	229.9	32.6	7.5
United Kingdom	75	80	5.8	473.4	275.4	32.8	6.2
United States	73	80	6.3	353.9	202.4	54.4	25.1
			Developing Countries				
Brazil	59	69	35.4	238.0	94.0	104.0	41.0
Iran	68	71	29.7	304.0	61.0	108.0	34.0
Mexico	69	75	24.6	100.7	49.9	64.6	26.4
Thailand	65	73	29.5	250.0	162.0	104.0	(not available)
			Undeveloped Countries				
Angola	46	51	129.2	diarrheal diseases, 25.8%; malaria, 19%; cholera, 7%			
Bangladesh	61	61	69.7	typhoid, 19.8%; tetanus, 10%; tuberculosis, 8.7%			
Haiti	49	54	97.6	circulatory diseases, 11.9%; malnutrition, 8.5%; infectious/parasitic diseases, 46%			
Laos	53	56	89.3	includes bronchitis, influenza, malaria, diarrhea			
Mali	45	48	149.0	malaria, 62%; measles, 10%; STDs, 6%; influenza, 4.9%			

SOURCES: Adapted from causes of death from *Britannica book of the year, 1999* (pp. 778–782), 1999. Chicago: Encyclopedia Britannica; life expectancies from *The world factbook 2000,* Central Intelligence Agency, 2000, Washington, DC: U.S. Government Printing Office.

der gap in life expectancy has increased. The CVD death rate in Russia is about 500 per 100,000 population for men, but only 80 per 100,000 for women; the life expectancy is 59 and 72, respectively. The reasons for this dramatic increase in CVD are somewhat mysterious, but one hypothesis (Weidner, 2000) holds that psychosocial factors such as stress, economic uncertainty, inadequate social support, and depression are the basis of the problem.

The gender gap in life expectancy is not predicted to decline in the near future, nor are other causes of disease to which men are particularly vulnerable. An analysis of mortality statistics allowed researchers (Murray & Lopez, 1997) to predict death rates in the year 2020, and those predictions included no reversal of the epidemic CVD death rate among men in eastern Europe. In addition, those predictions included an increase in tobacco-related deaths and deaths due to violence, all of which affect men to a greater extent than women. Life expectancy will likely increase because infectious diseases are predicted to decline, but would benefit women more than men, which would increase the gender gap.

The United States is among the industrialized nations, but some ethnic groups in the United States have patterns of disease and death that look more like developing countries. The underlying reasons for these health disadvantages include poverty and discrimination, both of which affect living conditions and access to medical care. The provision of health insurance through employment or through private policies results in decreased access and often poor quality medical care for poor people. Ethnic minority groups are affected by these circumstances more than White people are (USDHHS, 1999a).

African Americans have higher infant mortality rates and shorter life expectancies than other ethnic groups in the United States. The infant mortality rate for African Americans is 13.7 deaths per 1,000 live births compared to a rate for Whites of 6 per 1,000 (U.S. Bureau of the Census, 1999). That is, African American babies die at a rate comparable to those in Kuwait, Costa Rica, and Bulgaria, whereas infant mortality for White babies is comparable to that of wealthy, developed countries. Other health indicators for African Americans show that they have a shorter life expectancy and a higher rate of several diseases, including cardiovascular disease, diabetes, and liver disease. African Americans also die from violence more often than Whites do—68.8 versus 45.8 per 100,000. Young men are especially likely to be the victims of unintentional and intentional injuries.

Hispanic Americans are disadvantaged by conditions similar to African Americans, but their mortality rates are more similar to non-Hispanic Whites than to African Americans. Young Hispanic American men are at elevated risk for injuries and death due to violence (Hummer, Rogers, Amir, Forbes, & Frisbie, 2000), but deaths due to cardiovascular diseases and cancer are lower than for non-Hispanic Whites. The overall death rate for Hispanics was comparable to that of non–Hispanic European Americans.

Native Americans experience a pattern of health problems that varies from other ethnic groups. Poverty and poor living conditions are major problems for the health of Native Americans, and their access to medical care is often through the Indian Health Service, which provides free medical care to Native Americans who live on reservations or in areas covered by the service (Weitz, 2001). This limitation restricts health care to many Native Americans. Infant mortality is higher for Native Americans than for Whites, but lower than that for African Americans (USDHHS, 2000). Youth violence is a bigger problem among Native Americans than any other ethnic group. Native Americans also have a genetic predisposition for developing diabetes, and their levels of alcohol abuse contribute to liver disease, violent deaths, and fetal alcohol syndrome.

As a group, Asian Americans experience health advantages rather than disadvantages when compared to European Americans (USDHHS, 1999a). Infant mortality rates for Chinese Americans, Japanese Americans, and Filipino Americans are among the best in the world (USDHHS, 2000). For Asian Americans as a group, CVD death rates and deaths from violence are about half of those for European Americans, and rate of cancer deaths is lower.

Therefore, some ethnic groups within the United States have health disadvantages whereas others have advantages. The health of non-Hispanic Whites and Asian Americans compares favorably with the industrialized nations throughout the world. For African Americans and Native Americans, health care and health indicators are comparable to those of developing nations.

Summary

Women live longer than men. This gender difference has existed in most countries and during most time periods. In economically developed countries such as the United States, Canada, Australia, and the countries of Scandinavia and western Europe, deaths from cardiovascular disease, cancer, and violence account for the majority of deaths. Women have lower rates of mortality than men from all these causes.

Cardiovascular disease (CVD) refers to diseases of the heart and circulatory system. Although not all CVD is life-threatening, heart attack and stroke account for almost half of the deaths in the United States. Men are more likely to die of CVD than women are before the age of 65 years, but the total mortality is similar for the two. Women with CVD may not have their reports taken as seriously as men with similar symptoms, which suggests a treatment bias on the part of physicians.

Cancer is the second most common cause of death, and men are more likely than women to die from this cause. Lung cancer, the deadliest form of cancer for both men and women, is strongly related to cigarette smoking. Until recently, men have smoked at a substantially higher rate than women. With the rise in women's smoking, their lung cancer rates have and will continue to increase. Both women and men develop cancer of the reproductive organs, but women are more likely to die of such cancers, especially before age 65 years.

The gender difference in violent deaths is large; men die of unintentional injuries, suicides, and homicides at higher rates than women. The male gender role, which holds that men are supposed to be reckless and aggressive, may play a part in the high death rates from these causes. Men's greater prevalence of heavy alcohol use increases their chances of dying of any of these violent causes. Violent deaths also vary from country to country, with the United States having one of the higher rates of violent deaths. Within the United States, different ethnic groups are not equally affected by violence—African Americans are especially vulnerable to violent death.

Although women live longer than men, women also seek health care more often. Gender and gender roles influence who seeks health care. The female gender role allows and even encourages vulnerability to illness, but the male gender role discourages the acceptance of any weakness, including illness. Women's sensitivity to physical symptoms tends to boost health care seeking, but their access to health care is diminished by lower rates of employment, lower salaries, and lower insurance coverage.

The interaction of gender roles of the patient and health care provider has an impact on the type of health care patients receive. Physicians have been the target of criticism concerning their treatment of female patients; three of these include being reluctant to believe female patients, using men as a standard against which all patients are judged, and omitting women from medical research. Concern over these problems has prompted the founding of the Office of Women's Health and the Women's Health Initiative.

Reproductive health is a major reason for the gender difference in receiving health care. Women not only become involved in the health care system due to pregnancy and childbirth, but contraception and menopause are also reasons for consulting physicians. Both women and men are affected by sexually transmitted diseases and disorders of the reproductive organs. Both develop cancer of the genitals, and among women, breast cancer is the most frequent cancer.

Lifestyle differences may account for some of the gender differences in morbidity and mortality. The thin body has become such a widespread ideal among women that dieting is now a way of life for millions of women. Because they cannot be as thin as the ideal, women develop body image problems and are more prone to eating disorders such as anorexia nervosa and bulimia. Men also experience body image dissatisfaction, but they tend to feel insufficiently muscular and are more likely to attempt to alter their bodies through exercise rather than through dieting.

Exercise can be a positive factor for fitness and weight control, and men are more likely to participate in sports and physical activity than women are. The passage of Title IX of the Education Amendments of 1972 removed some barriers that prevented women from participating in athletics, and increasingly positive publicity for female athletes encourages girls to become athletic. In an increasingly technological and sedentary society, most men and women must use their leisure time to pursue fitness. Athletic activities can build fitness and contribute to health, but excessive exercise can also be symptomatic of body image problems.

Life expectancy and health vary around the world, and economic factors contribute heavily to this variation. Wealthy, industrialized nations have longer life expectancies and the problems associated with long life—high rates of cardiovascular disease and cancer. Poor, undeveloped countries have shorter life expectancies and the problems associated with poverty—high infant mortality and death from infectious diseases. Within the United States, Asian Americans and European Americans have longer life expectancies and better health than African Americans and Native Americans.

Glossary

anorexia nervosa an eating disorder consisting of self-starvation in pursuit of thinness.

bulimia an eating disorder consisting of binge eating, followed by some method of purging, either by induced vomiting or excessive laxative use.

cardiovascular disease (CVD) a group of diseases involving the heart and circulatory system, some of which are life threatening; heart attack and stroke are the most common.

chronic diseases health problems that develop over a period of time, often without noticeable symptoms, and persist over time without a complete recovery.

morbidity illness.

mortality death.

osteoporosis the process of bone demineralization, resulting in greater likelihood of orthopedic problems and injuries.

risk factor any condition or factor that increases the probability that an illness will develop.

sexually transmitted diseases (STDs) infectious diseases that are spread through sexual contact, including bacterial infections, viral infections, fungal infections, and parasitic infections.

Suggested Readings

Brownell, Kelly D.; & Rodin, Judith. (1994). The dieting maelstrom: Is it possible and advisable to lose weight? *American Psychologist, 49,* 781–791. In this evaluation of the dieting controversy, Brownell and Rodin discuss healthy and unhealthy variations on dieting and seek to evaluate some of the myths and misinformation connected with dieting.

Brumberg, Joan Jacobs. (1997). *The body project.* New York: Random House. Brumberg explores the contemporary obsession with the body and how this emphasis affects girls and their relationship with their bodies.

Kane, Penny. (1991). *Women's health: From womb to tomb.* New York: St. Martin's Press. This book offers an interesting look at gender differences in health from a cross-cultural and developmental perspective. Kane draws on information from cultures throughout the world, offering not only information on these various cultures, but also an opportunity to see the differences among economically developed, developing, and undeveloped countries.

Weidner, Gerdi. (2000). Why do men get more heart disease than women? An international perspective. *Journal of American College Health, 48,* 291–294. This short, provocative article focuses on the gender gap in cardiovascular disease on an international level, and touches on many of the issues that differentiate men's and women's health.

Chapter 14

Stress, Coping, and Psychopathology

HEADLINE

Who Has the Most Stress?

Ladies Home Journal, March, 2000

Everyone encounters stress, but people have different experiences with stress and cope with their stresses with varying effectiveness. Kathryn Casey (2000) and *Ladies Home Journal* investigated the stress levels of five women throughout a typical day to determine how their stress varied and how they coped. The women included a married mother who had left her job as a physical therapist to stay home and care for her four young children, a married hairdresser who had one young daughter, an unmarried nurse with no children, a married teacher with an infant daughter, and a film executive with teenage children whose husband was her business partner. Casey reported on their perceptions of the stresses they encountered, but each also wore a heart rate monitor to give a physiological measurement of her reactions to the stresses of the day.

These women varied in marital status, number and age of children, employment status, and economic status of the family. The women in Casey's article were good examples of how these factors operate to produce stress and how people's perceptions of the stresses in their lives may not be an accurate assessment. For example, the homemaker had quit her job to stay home with her four children, and she imagined that giving up her job would decrease her stress level. She rated her stress level as low, but her heart rate monitor told another story. Caring for her children, especially when they squabbled, raised her heart rate into the high range, and she was not coping effectively.

The hairdresser combined her job with caring for her 6-year-old daughter, without much help from her husband. She expressed feelings that mirror those of many women: "At work, I worry that I don't spend enough time at home. At home, I'm stressed because I can't finish everything I want to" (in Casey, 2000, p. 153). She rated her stress level as moderate, but the heart rate monitor showed very high levels of stress, and an assessment of her daily routine showed poor coping skills. The woman whom many would rate as having the most stressful life was the nurse. She was unmarried, with no children, and worked 12-hour shifts in a busy trauma center emergency room. However, the most stressful event of her day was the commute to work and not the crowded, life-and-death work environment. Her job included many difficult situations, but her coping skills were very good, and she felt competent and in control.

Work was also not the most stressful time of the day for the teacher—instead, caring for her infant daughter was, especially getting up during the night to do so. Her husband was also a teacher and actively involved with child care. She rated her stress levels as moderately high, but her heart rates were lower than either of the other women who cared for children. The film executive rated her stress as high, and both her job and family life included several situations that most people consider stressful. Both she and her husband had teenaged children from prior marriages, and their blended family's rotating custody schedule and relationships with former spouses were sources of stress. In addition, the demands of running a business turn up the pressure. Despite her perception of high stress, her monitor ratings showed low to moderate levels, and the analysis of her reactions reflected good coping skills. Her highest heart rate occurred when she read an e-mail from her husband's former wife.

These women's experiences illustrate how job and family situations produce stress, how children can add to stress levels, and how employment is often not the main source of stress in women's lives. Are these women typical? Do the differences in men's work and family lives produce different patterns of stress for men? What types of problems develop for people who cannot cope?

Stress and Coping

The explanations for psychological problems have ranged from demonic possession to genetic vulnerability. The belief that madness results from possession has faded, but many authorities accept that some mental disorders, including depression and schizophrenia, have a genetic component. The gender differences in diagnoses, however, are too large to be accounted for by genetics (Cleary, 1987). Therefore, the search for risk factors for mental disorders has focused on life circumstances and stresses.

Stress is an inevitable part of life, so searching for the stresses that relate to the development of mental disorders becomes a complex task. Researchers cannot simply identify sources of stress but must, as did the headline article, investigate how people perceive various stressors and how they cope with the resulting stress in their lives.

Sources of Stress for Men and Women

The basic physiological reaction to stress is similar for men and women (Taylor et al., 2000), but sources of stress vary. As Chapters 9 and 12 explored, the many combinations of marriage, parenthood, and employment provide women and men with complex roles. Men have traditionally occupied the breadwinner role and have not been involved with providing much in the way of housekeeping or child care; that situation is beginning to change, and women are pressuring men to become more actively involved in household work. That pressure may be one source of stress for men. One research emphasis has been on multiple roles, including spouse, parent, and employee. As the women in the headline story showed, fulfilling these roles may be stressful and thus related to the development of problems.

Experiences with violence provide an additional reason for gender differences with stress. As Chapter 8 presented, men are more likely to be the perpetrators as well as the victims of violence. However, women are much more likely to be the targets of sexual abuse and violence in families, which places them at risk for the aftermath of such violence. Poverty, sexism, and gender discrimination are also potential sources of stress. How do these life experiences relate to the development of mental disorders—and are the gender differences in mental disorders related to these life experiences?

Family Roles

The gender differences in family roles revolve around marriage, parenthood, and employment. Marriage roles may be analyzed into "his" and "hers," and "his" tends to be more beneficial than "hers" (Bernard, 1972). Married men show better mental health than married women (Fowers, 1991; Hughes & Galinsky, 1994). Indeed, married people show the largest of the gender differences in mental health (Rosenfield, 1989). These differences may originate for reasons illustrated by the married women in our chapter headline: Women's roles include supplying care to other family members. Supplying care is often demanding, but it may not be reciprocated, leaving women with inadequate support for themselves.

Married women with children and single parents show higher rates of depression than married men and unmarried women (Aneshensel, Frerichs, & Clark, 1981; USDHHS, 1999b). That is, caring for children is one of the family roles that increases the risk for depression and anxiety. One explanation for this relationship involves the combination of low power and role overload (Rosenfield, 1989). The occupation of housewife is an example of a position with low power, and full-time employment plus caring for children constitute role overload. One of the women in the headline article for this chapter had left her job to care for her four children, and her life was more stressful than she thought. Another of the women combined full-time employment with caring for her young daughter. One study (Hughes & Galinsky, 1994) showed that women experienced higher levels of psychological distress than men did, which related to child care inequity and child care difficulties at home. Women who are mothers may benefit from that role, depending on their other roles and the assistance they receive in fulfilling their family and workplace obligations. Therefore, work and family can interfere with each other, and what causes stress for women is not the same for men.

Multiple roles do not inevitably lead to stress and stress-related problems, and the amount of strain from each role is important (Aneshensel & Pearlin, 1987). When employed mothers experience little strain in either role, they are at a low risk for depression, like the film executive and the teacher in the headline story. When married, employed mothers experience strain in each role; they are at a high risk for depression—a level of risk comparable to that of housewives. When family demands are equal for employed men and women, they have comparable rates of depression and anxiety disorders. When the burdens of family care fall disproportionately on women, these women's social circumstances pose risks for the development of depression.

Women have fewer mental health problems when they are employed, but their husbands may not. The shift in power that accompanies wives' employment may be a problem for their husbands (Rosenfield, 1992). If the wife's employment leads to a decrease in the husband's relative contribution to family income and an increase in his share of domestic duties, the husband's mental health suffers. Thus, men are also subject to role overload and the negative effects of loss of power and diminished personal control.

The research on stresses in men's lives has concentrated on job-related stress and its effects, but some investigators have explored men's multiple roles in the workplace and family. Family roles are important to men's psychological health (Barnett, Marshall, & Pleck, 1992; Larson & Richards, 1994). Work roles and family roles contribute equally to men's feelings of distress and well-being. Research has shown that the quality of men's marital relationships and the quality of their parental relationships are important factors in their lives. Men tend to feel more stressed at work and more relaxed at home (Larson & Richards, 1994). Satisfaction with family life can buffer men against the stresses of the workplace.

High commitment to the breadwinner role can be a source of strain for men, especially those who do not perceive their wives as supportive in their attempts to fulfill work and parenting roles (Greenberger & O'Neil, 1993). Women also experience strain when husbands spend many hours on their jobs and when they feel their husbands and neighbors are not supportive of their employment and parenting efforts. Thus, both husbands and wives can experience role strain when they believe that their efforts are not supported by their partners, but men tend to feel more strain and anxiety over their work roles than do women.

Parenthood is more likely to be a risk for distress in women than in men (USDHHS, 1999b). For men, pleasure in parenting can buffer against other stresses, but women who care for small children are more likely to experience psychological problems than women without child care responsibilities. This stress is ameliorated by sharing the responsibility for child care. Employment is related to positive mental health for both women and men, but women may experience stress and psychological problems from the overload of family and work responsibilities.

Violence

As discussed earlier, men are more likely than women to be both the perpetrators and the victims of violence. Women's victimization may be especially traumatic, because women are more likely to be the victims of violence by family and friends than by strangers (Russo, 1990; Walker, 1989). Furthermore, women are more likely to be injured in violent encounters by persons they know (Dutton, Haywood, & El-Bayoumi, 1997). A growing body of research has implicated violence as a risk to mental as well as physical health, and this research has concentrated on intimate violence in families—namely, childhood sexual abuse, rape, and marital violence. Although women are more often the victims of intimate abuse, men who are similarly victimized show comparable effects.

Mary Koss wrote, "Experiencing violence transforms people into victims and changes their lives forever. Once victimized one can never feel quite as invulnerable" (Koss, 1990, p. 374). A history of violence is related to the development of a wide variety of psychological problems, including posttraumatic stress disorder, depression, substance abuse, obsessive-compulsive disorders, eating disorders, and suicide attempts (Koss, 1993).

The American Psychological Association established a Task Force on Male Violence Against Women in 1991 (Goodman, Koss, Fitzgerald, Russo, & Keita, 1993). This task force estimated that between 21% and 34% of women in the United States are physically assaulted by men who have close relationships with them, and between 14% and 25% of adult women will be raped at some time during their lives. These figures suggest that male violence toward women puts a great many women at risk for mental disorders.

Despite the widespread publicity of male violence toward women, Clifton Flynn (1990) contended that the attention to domestic violence has been selective and that the rate of female violence toward men is nearly as high as male violence toward women. He examined evidence from many studies and concluded that the rates of violence toward intimate partners are similar for women and men, yet the patterns differ. Women are most likely to be violent in protecting themselves from and in retaliation for violent attacks by men, whereas men are more likely to initiate such attacks. Therefore, the rates of violence may be similar, but the repercussions are not. The aftermath of victimization has implications, especially for the mental health of women.

A body of research implicates violence as a risk in women's mental health. A meta-analysis of research on intimate partner violence (Golding, 1999) revealed that a history of such violence increases the risk for depression, suicide, posttraumatic stress syndrome, and substance abuse. Almost half of the women in the studies showed some type of mental health problem, demonstrating a greatly elevated risk.

Violence may be not only a significant contributor to the prevalence of depression among women, but also a main factor that accounts for the gender difference in this disorder (Cutler & Nolen-Hoeksema, 1991). Childhood sexual abuse is more common for girls than boys, and evidence links childhood sexual abuse with anxiety, depression, and low self-esteem. Support for this relationship has come from a study of women who were sexually abused as children (Yama, Tovey, & Fogas, 1993). A comparison of these women to those with no history of sexual abuse demonstrated that this type of childhood abuse has lasting effects for the development of anxiety and depression.

Other research has shown that sexual abuse at any age increases the risk for a variety of mental disorders in both men and women (Burnam et al., 1988; USDHHS, 1999b). This research revealed that being a victim of sexual abuse increases the chances of depression, substance abuse or dependence, phobic disorder, panic disorder, and obsessive-compulsive disorder, with the magnitude of increase reaching between two and four times that of men or women who have not been abused. The effects were especially dramatic for those whose abuse occurred during childhood. Women are much more likely to be the victims of sexual abuse than men, but this study found no gender difference in likelihood of developing psychological problems following abuse. The form of subsequent problems differed somewhat for men and women, with men more likely to experience drug and alcohol problems than women, but sexual victimization clearly increased the risk for a variety of problems for both genders.

Violence in the form of criminal victimization also relates to the development of psychological disorders, especially posttraumatic stress disorder (PTSD) (Resnick, Kilpatrick, Best, & Kramer, 1992). Those women who were victims of crimes involving violence or the threat of extreme violence were much more likely to develop symptoms of PTSD than women who were the victims of less violent crimes. However, all crime victims showed elevated risks of PTSD, demonstrating the psychological risks of criminal victimization. Direct involvement with violence is not necessary for the development of problems; exposure to violence is also a risk. Inner-city adolescents exposed to violence (an average of five incidents within the year of the study) also had elevated risks for PTSD (Mazza & Reynolds, 1999). Thus, exposure to violence is a risk to mental health.

The evidence concerning family roles and mental health problems are complex, with many different configurations and effects. Table 14.1 presents some of the influences of various roles on psychological health. The evidence for the relationship between violence

TABLE 14.1 Influences of Various Roles on Psychological Health

Role	Affects	Consequences
Caregiving	Women more than men	Stress; emotional and physical exhaustion
Marriage	Both genders	Positive
Parenthood	Both genders	Depends on other roles occupied and the support available
Child caregiving	Women more than men	At risk for mental and physical health problems
Employment	Both genders	Positive
Homemaker role	Women	At risk for depression
Breadwinner role	Men more than women	At risk for mental health problems
Employed wife	Men	At risk for mental health problems

and mental disorders is much more straightforward. Violence increases the risk for several mental disorders, and childhood victimization is especially harmful. Women are more likely to be the targets of childhood sexual abuse and rape, two types of violence that research has related to psychological disorders, but men who are victimized are also at elevated risk of such problems.

Poverty

Poverty also presents a risk for mental disorders for women, men, and children (Attar, Guerra, & Tolan, 1994; Neugebauer, Dohrenwend, & Dohrenwend, 1980). Those who live in poverty are at least two and a half times as likely to receive diagnoses of mental disorders compared to those who are not poor. Not only are poor people more likely to receive diagnoses of mental disorders, but a community study (Holzer et al., 1986) indicated that mental disorders are almost three times more common among those who are in the lowest as compared to those in the highest socioeconomic class.

Life circumstances associated with poverty are also associated with poor mental health (Belle, 1990). That is, not only is low income itself a problem, creating many stresses, but unemployment or underemployment, divorce, and single parenthood are all sources of stress that are associated with poverty. In addition, low income can lead to poor housing in high-crime neighborhoods, subjecting poor people to greater risks of violence and its psychological effects. Poverty may be an independent risk factor for mental disorders, but it is associated with other risks that increase the likelihood for problems.

Poverty affects women and ethnic minority families more than other groups (Belle, 1990). Single mothers are more likely to be poor than any other demographic group, affecting not only their mental and physical health, but also placing their children at risk for the stress associated with poverty. The National Institute of Mental Health has recognized the negative impact of poverty on women's mental health and has made the topic a priority for the Women's Research Agenda; however, poverty is also a risk to men's mental health.

Poverty has a negative impact on the ability to cope. Financial limitations deprive people of the ability to deal with other problems that can produce stress. Lack of money limits opportunities and choices, putting people in positions of dependency on government bureaucracy for housing, health care, food, and other essentials. The economically advantaged may be able to extricate themselves from problem situations and relationships that poor people cannot avoid. Both problem situations and the lack of any control over them can produce stress.

Discrimination

In addition to poverty and violence, a community study of mental health functioning (Hendryx & Ahern, 1997) identified racism as a factor related to lower levels of mental health functioning. Using the Schedule of Racist Events (Landrine & Klonoff, 1996), a sample of African Americans reported a high incidence of racist discrimination within the year before the study, and 100% reported having experienced racist discrimination during their lives. The study also examined the stressful effects of the experience of racist discrimination and found that a positive relationship existed between experiences of racist discrimination and psychiatric symptoms.

Sexist discrimination is also known to be a source of stress. The large traumas like childhood sexual abuse or criminal victimization can produce problems; however, so can being subject to frequent discrimination and harassment, such as being denied a job or promotion or having to listen to sexist jokes. A national survey of U.S. residents (Kessler, Mickelson, & Williams, 1999) revealed that the experience of discrimination was common—33.5% of the participants reported some incidence of major discrimination, and 60.9% said that they experienced less serious discrimination. This survey included all types of discrimination and focused on participants' perception of the extent and severity of discrimination. This study showed a substantial relationship between perceptions of discrimination and mental health problems.

The experience of sexist discrimination has also been related to mental health problems. In one study (Landrine, Klonoff, Gibbs, Manning, & Lund, 1995), the experience of sexist discrimination related to psychological distress in women and predicted some symptoms better than more general measures of stress. In a later study (Klonoff, Landrine, & Campbell, 2000), women who experienced a high amount of sexist discrimination exhibited more depression, anxiety, and physical complaints than women who experienced lower levels of sexist treatment. Indeed, the women whose experience with sexism was low showed symptom levels comparable to the men in the study. Thus, the experience of sexism may be a substantial factor in the greater number of psychiatric symptoms among women. Adding this factor to other sources of stress may help explain why women experience greater levels of distress than men do.

Coping Resources and Strategies

The number and intensity of stressors are important factors in any resulting problems, but resources and strategies for coping are even more important. Those who have resources to cope with the stresses in their lives may not perceive the situations as stressful. One theory of stress (Lazarus & Folkman, 1984) proposed that each person's appraisal of a potentially stressful situation varies according to his or her perception of the personal importance of the situation plus personal resources to deal with the situation. Those who do not have (or believe that they do not have) the resources to cope with events in their lives are vulnerable to stress, whereas others who experience the same events but have resources to cope do not experience stress from the events. Thus, stress varies according to perception, and that perception depends on the evaluation of resources for coping.

The resources for coping may differ for women and men; men often have more power and greater financial resources than women have. Power and money offer advantages for avoiding many of life's problems and for dealing with others. For example, the loss of a job may be more stressful for a single mother of two with only a high school education and skilled as a sales clerk than for a married male engineer with an employed wife and a sizable savings account. Neither of these jobless people will avoid stress; losing a job is stressful for almost everyone. However, the engineer has resources for dealing with his situation that the sales clerk lacks.

One of the most important differences between the male engineer and the female sales clerk is the social support the engineer has in the form of his family. The sales clerk may receive support from her children, but she must also offer them care and support. Women's roles generally carry obligations for providing support for others, whereas men's roles more often offer them the provision of emotional support (Gove, 1984). Providing care for others can be stressful, whereas receiving social support is more likely to relieve stress. On the other hand, the possibility exists that involvement in social relationships offers more advantages than costs in coping with stress.

Social Support

Social support is more than a matter of social relationships or social contacts; support implies providing emotional and material resources. Four different elements of social support are emotional concern, instrumental aid (such as money or other assistance), information and advice, and feedback (House, 1984). A person with few contacts with other people is more likely to be socially isolated than the person with many contacts, but social support requires more than contact or acquaintanceship. People who have a high amount of social support have a wide network of people on whom they can count for emotional and material support. Poor quality of support and small network size both relate to the development of anxiety and depression (Vandervoort, 1999).

As discussed in the "Friendships" section of Chapter 9, women are more likely than men to form friendships that include emotional intimacy, which may give them the advantage in creating networks that provide them with social support. Men's friendships tend to be activity oriented, which may offer them the material support but lack the emotional intimacy that is important for social support. Men's advantage in social support probably comes from their relationships with women, on whom men tend to rely for emotional support as well as for many aspects of physical care. Single and divorced men are at greater risk for mental health problems than married men, again suggesting the importance of social support. Those at greater risk typically have less social support, and those at lesser risk typically have more sources of social support.

The breadth and strength of social networks vary with ethnicity as well as with gender (Renzetti & Curran, 1992). Some ethnic groups maintain close family relationships, whereas in other ethnic groups, increased mobility and small families decrease the chances of having close friends. Also, these family patterns complicate family contact. The isolated nuclear family consisting of father, mother, and children has become the image of family life in the Western world, but many people live in extended families in close contact with other relatives.

Hispanic, African, and Asian American families often form extended family groupings, meaning grandparents, parents, children, and other relatives who live in close proximity. This pattern differs from the isolated nuclear family typical of many (but by no means all) European Americans, with resulting advantages and disadvantages. The advantages of an extended family include a wider range of people who offer their emotional and material support and advice. The disadvantages may include many demands for emotional and material support. If these other family members are poor (and members of ethnic minorities are more likely to be poor than members of the dominant ethnic group), then being part of a support network can lead to many demands and obligations to fulfill those demands. Thus, being part of an extended family network can provide social support, but it can also impose social costs, and these advantages and disadvantages operate among some ethnic groups more than others.

Coping Strategies

Coping is the process of changing thoughts and behaviors to manage situations that involve potential stressors (Lazarus & Folkman, 1984). How people deal with the events in their lives makes a critical difference in the amount of stress they experience, so having coping strategies is an essential factor in relieving part of the stress. These management strategies vary among people and situations, and these differences may distinguish among people who feel more or less stress. Table 14.2 lists coping strategies and gives examples of each.

The role of gender in coping with stress is not clear. Several models hold that gender-related differences exist, but research has not furnished results that fully clarify these varying views. One view (Taylor et al., 2000) holds that women react to stress in ways that differ from men's reactions. That is, the "fight or flight" reaction is more typical of men, and women's reactions to stressful situations can be described as "tend and befriend." This view ties together women's role as caregivers with neurohormonal reactions and evolutionary history, predicting that women's primary coping strategy will be seeking social support. Two alternative views of gender-related differences in coping include the socialization

TABLE 14.2 Examples of Coping Strategies

Coping Strategy	Behaviors That Exemplify This Strategy
Seeking social support	Talk to someone who could help Talk to someone who has experienced similar problems Talk to friends or family who will sympathize
Problem-focused	Analyze the situation Plan a strategy to solve the problem Take action to get rid of the problem Concentrate on the problem
Emotion-focused	Become upset Express negative feelings
Denial	Refuse to accept the reality of the problem Try to ignore the problem
Turn to religion	Seek God's help Pray
Disengagement	Work on other activities Sleep more than usual Engage in distracting activities Consume alcohol or other drugs

view, which holds that women and men are socialized to react to stress differently (women with emotional coping and men with active, problem-solving strategies) and the structural view, which holds that gender-related differences in coping come from the different stressful situations women and men encounter (Ptacek, Smith, & Zanas, 1992).

More evidence exists for gender differences in the experience of stress than for differences in coping strategies (Folkman & Lazarus, 1980). Consistent with the tend-and-befriend view, women are more likely than men to seek social support when they experience stress (Taylor et al., 2000). Consistent with the socialization view, men in one study (Folkman & Lazarus, 1980) were more likely to report experiencing stressful situations at work and using problem-focused coping strategies for those situations. However, the men in this study were more likely to be employed than the women, and no difference appeared for the frequency of emotion-focused coping. These results do not rule out the situational view. Indeed, both men and women tended to use both types of strategies to manage the various stresses. The gender difference in this study might not reflect a difference in strategies but a difference in situations; the women and men in this study did not have comparable lives.

Studies have attempted to assess coping strategies for men and women in comparable situations, including college students (Hamilton & Fagot, 1988) and industrial workers (Fontenot & Brannon, 1991). For the college students, both women and men reported the same types of events as stressful or not stressful and used the same strategies for dealing with each. This study showed few gender differences but did demonstrate that both men and women use similar coping strategies in similar situations. For the industrial workers, few gender differences emerged, but significant situational differences appeared. Both women and men said that personal conflict situations were more likely to prompt emotion-focused coping and that task-related stress situations were more likely to elicit problem-focused coping strategies. These findings suggest that specific situations were more likely than gender to be the source of differences in coping efforts.

Are situational factors the explanation for gender differences in coping? If so, gender differences in coping may be fairly large because men's and women's lives show many situational differences. Among these are the differences in gender roles that place women in more tend-and-befriend situations. Therefore, the capacity and tendency to use similar coping situations furnishes important information about gender-related capabilities, but the stresses related to women's and men's lives vary, as will their coping efforts. The magnitude of these gender differences do not account for the preponderance of women in treatment for behavior problems. Possibilities for the source of these differences lie in the criteria and in the processes used to diagnose mental and behavioral disorders.

Diagnoses of Mental Disorders

Before a sick person can receive appropriate treatment, the person must receive a **diagnosis,** a statement of the classification of a physical or psychological problem. Without a diagnosis, treatment would be haphazard and not connected with the problem. Thus, classification of both physical and mental problems is an essential step in receiving proper care. A good clinical classification system has several characteristics (Sarason & Sarason, 1993). Specifically, such a system should provide information about the cause of the condition, enable clinicians to make predictions about the course of the disorder, and suggest a course of treatment as well as methods of prevention. In addition, a system of classification should provide a set of common terminology for professionals to communicate among themselves. No system of diagnosis meets these goals perfectly, but the goals are common to the diagnosis of physical and mental problems.

Diagnosis is not a simple task; it consists of matching information about what constitutes a disorder against a description of symptoms. Because any person's symptoms will not match the textbook description of a disorder, clinicians use personal judgment in the diagnostic process. This judgment provides for the possibility that personal bias and subjective attitudes can enter the diagnostic process.

Diagnosis is a necessary part of treatment, offering patients disadvantages as well as advantages (Sarason & Sarason, 1993). The advantages include providing an accepted standard that allows reliable diagnosis of the same problem by different clinicians. One of the problems involves labeling—the need to apply a label to the diagnosis. With mental disorders, many labels carry a stigma, and people who have been labeled with diagnoses of mental disorders may be the targets of discrimination. Furthermore, labeling also puts people into categories, and grouping people tends to magnify the similarities and obscure the individual differences of those within a category.

The diagnosis of mental disorders dates back to the time of Hippocrates, who used a simple four-category classification—mania, epilepsy, melancholia, and paranoia (Lerman, 1996). During the late 19th century, interest in mental disorders increased, and in 1917 the National Committee for Mental Hygiene in the United States published a manual to aid in diagnosis. Currently, two systems exist for the classification of mental disorders—the International Classification of Diseases (ICD) of the World Health Organization and the *Diagnostic and Statistical Manual of Mental Disorders (DSM)* of the American Psychiatric Association. With the publication of the fourth edition of the *DSM,* the two systems became more compatible, but the *DSM* remains oriented to psychiatric diagnosis.

The DSM *Classification System*

The *Diagnostic and Statistical Manual of Mental Disorders (DSM)* of the American Psychiatric Association has become the standard for professionals who provide mental health care, especially in North America. The first version of the manual appeared in 1952, with a second edition in 1968 (Sarason & Sarason, 1993). These two editions were relatively brief, both were strongly influenced by psychoanalytic theory, and both were heavily weighted with psychoanalytic terminology. To make a diagnosis using the system of classification described in the *DSM-I* or *DSM-II,* the clinician needed to understand the patients' internal, unobservable psychological processes. Understandably, these schemes of classification led to a great deal of variation in diagnoses.

The third edition of the *DSM* appeared in 1980 and represented a substantial revision. The goal was to create a description-based system of classification for mental disorders—a set of unambiguous descriptions of mental disorders that would lead clinicians to make reliable judgments. A relatively minor revision of the *DSM-III* appeared in 1987. The *DSM-IV,* which appeared in 1994, contained no major changes but allowed for greater compatibility with the ICD.

The system of the *DSM* consists of five dimensions, or *axes,* which allow for comprehensive physical, psychological, and social diagnoses. The first three axes provide the diagnosis, and the two other axes provide an evaluation of stressors and overall functioning. The manual contains over 240 different diagnoses along with descriptions of the symptoms that characterize the disorders. Information also appears concerning typical age of onset, course of the disorder, and the gender ratio of the disorder; that is, how common the problem appears in men compared to women. In addition, the manual also contains information concerning the similarities among each diagnosis and other similar disorders so that clinicians can distinguish among disorders that have similar symptoms.

Axis I describes the major clinical disorders, such as schizophrenia, depression, and anxiety disorders, among others. Axis II includes mental retardation and personality disorders, such as antisocial personality, histrionic personality, and dependent personality disorders. Axis III contains a classification of physical disorders and is compatible with the ICD diagnosis system. Axis IV allows for reporting of psychosocial and environmental problems related to the diagnosis of psychopathology, including events such as death of a loved one, problems in school, homelessness, or loss of a job. Axis V allows for an overall rating of functioning on the Global Assessment of Functioning Scale, which takes psychological, social, and occupational functioning into account. Diagnosis includes a rating on each of the five axes.

For example, a diagnosis on Axis I might be **posttraumatic stress disorder (PTSD),** a subclassification within the category of anxiety disorders. The *DSM-IV* describes the diagnosis for this disorder as composed of several criteria. To be diagnosed with posttraumatic stress disorder, the person must meet five criteria: (a) "the person experienced, witnessed, or was confronted with an event or events that involved actual or threatened death or serious injury, or a threat to the physical integrity of self or others... [and] the person's response involved intense fear, helplessness, or horror" (American Psychiatric Association, 1994, pp. 427–428), (b) reexperience of the event in some form, (c) avoidance of stimuli associated with the traumatic event or numbing of responsiveness, (d) increased arousal, such as irritability, difficulty concentrating, or hypervigilance, and (e) duration of at least 1 month.

The combination of these criteria must be present and must produce "clinically significant distress or impairment in social, occupational, or other important areas of functioning" (American Psychiatric Association, 1994, p. 429) before a diagnosis of PTSD can be made. The *DSM-IV* offers guidelines to the clinician for the different forms of reexperiencing the event, the types of avoidance and numbing that might occur, and the symptoms of increased arousal that accompany PTSD.

In addition, the manual includes examples of the types of unusual events that might precipitate PTSD, examples of the behaviors of affected individuals, and descriptions of disorders that often accompany PTSD. Depression and substance-related disorders often coincide with PTSD, sometimes preceding and sometimes developing after the traumatic stress. If evidence of these disorders exists, the clinician should diagnose all of the conditions. Although the *DSM* provides the gender ratio for many diagnoses, no such information appears for PTSD.

For a person with a diagnosis of PTSD on Axis I, the Axis II diagnosis might or might not indicate pathology. That is, an Axis I diagnosis of a certain clinical disorder does not necessarily coincide with a problem in the developmental and personality disorders described on Axis II. Nor does one prohibit the other. The clinical disorders on Axis I and the personality disorders on Axis II can be related, but the diagnoses are made according to separate criteria. Thus, many people who receive a diagnosis of PTSD have no other conditions that predispose them to the disorder and might receive diagnoses of "no problem" on Axis II (Sarason & Sarason, 1993). Alternatively, people with PTSD might have other separate developmental or personality disorders, and these problems might relate to the PTSD. Some personality disorders, such as paranoid personality disorder, would tend to worsen PTSD.

If the person with a diagnosis of PTSD has developed the disorder as a result of a combat experience or rape, then the person may also have physical injuries that stem from the same situation. Indeed, some evidence exists to indicate a much greater likelihood of PTSD in soldiers (Helzer, Robins, & McEvoy, 1987) and in crime victims (Resnick et al., 1992) who have been injured. The Axis III diagnosis would note these or other physical conditions that could affect the person's psychological functioning.

Axis IV gives the clinician an opportunity to note any social and environmental problems that might affect the development, recurrence, or exacerbation of mental disorders. The *DSM-IV* instructs clinicians to note as many of these problems as are relevant and that have occurred within the prior year. PTSD is an exception, however; these events may have occurred more than a year before diagnosis and still be relevant to the problem.

Axis V allows the clinician to rate the global functioning of the person on the Global Assessment of Functioning Scale, based on overall psychological, social, and occupational functioning (excluding physical and environmental limitations). This scale ranges from 1 to 100, with low numbers indicating a low level of functioning and high numbers indicating fewer impairments. For example, a person with PTSD resulting from combat experiences might also show alcohol abuse, sleep problems, sensitivity to loud noises, and outbursts of violence with little provocation. Such a person would probably receive a global assessment rating between 50 and 60, indicating moderate difficulty in social and occupational functioning. But PTSD can produce symptoms that result in more or fewer problems in functioning.

The *DSM-III, DSM-III-R,* and *DSM-IV* represent improvements over the earlier versions of the *DSM.* The extensive descriptions of problem behavior allow clinicians to match patients' symptoms to the descriptions without relying on unobservable, internal psychological processes. The descriptive nature of the *DSM* makes diagnosis more reliable, but the system has sparked controversy. Criticisms include a lack of research support and adding diagnoses that may not be abnormal. The lists of behaviors that serve as criteria for each diagnostic category gives the impression of objectivity, but little research supports these criteria (Lerman, 1996). Therefore, the impression of objectivity is an illusion.

Criticism has also arisen concerning the *DSM*'s inclusiveness; some of the diagnostic categories describe behaviors that are arguably within the normal range. For example, nicotine dependence and nicotine withdrawal are diagnoses applied to smokers and smokers who have quit, respectively. Applying diagnoses in such cases implies that these behaviors represent diagnosable mental disorders. Many people, including mental health care professionals, disagree with the extension of diagnostic classifications to behaviors that fall within the range of normal for many people.

Gender Inequity in the Diagnosis of Mental Disorders

Criticisms of the multiaxial system of the *DSM* appeared immediately following its release in 1980. Some of these criticisms concerned gender bias in this diagnostic system. A number of critics (Kaplan, 1983a, 1983b; Lerman, 1996; Tavris, 1992) have asserted that the *DSM* system includes descriptions of disorders that make women likely to be diagnosed with problem behavior, even when the behavior is not due to any pathology. Indeed, the assumption that men provide a standard makes it likely that any behavior found more commonly in women will be viewed as pathological. The process of diagnosis is influenced by social values, and generally "professionals have used male-based norms to define healthy versus pathological behavior" (Cook, Warnke, & Dupuy, 1993, pp. 312–313). This bias has resulted in behaviors such as independence and assertiveness considered to be important for healthy mental functioning, whereas emotional expressiveness may be considered the sign of a problem.

The *DSM* system has also received criticism for its failure to consider the life circumstances of those receiving diagnoses (Cook et al., 1993; Lerman, 1996). The *DSM* system focuses on personal behavior, assuming that disorders are personal problems and not attributable to the circumstances or situational contexts of behaviors. A *DSM* diagnosis implies that the disorder is centered on the person, and that the person's circumstances, although possibly relevant, are not the source of the problem. Thus, if a battered woman experiences distress or depression, she will still be diagnosed by her symptoms as having depression or one of the anxiety disorders. The violence of her home life may be taken into account; however, even though the symptoms warrant a diagnosis of mental disorder, that diagnosis is given to her, not to her batterer or her home circumstances. Thus, people may receive diagnoses and then treatment for depression or substance abuse disorder without addressing the social context of the problem and without the clinician considering it appropriate to do so. A survey of clinical psychology interns (Middaugh, 1994) showed that 19% of male (but only 5% of female) interns believed that female clients must learn to adjust to their circumstances. Although these percentages indicate that a minority of clinicians hold such attitudes, this minority holds women responsible for the behavior of others. One example is an abused woman who could receive a psychiatric diagnosis and treatment when it is her abusive husband who has problems (Stephenson & Walker, 1979).

As noted in Chapter 13, the normal female functions of reproduction and childbearing have become "medicalized," as have other problems that should fall within the range of normal. This criticism applies to **premenstrual dysphoric disorder (PMDD),** the diagnosis applied to symptoms that are very similar to premenstrual syndrome (PMS). A diagnostic category limited only to women is destined to provoke controversy; such controversy has continued with the publication of the *DSM-IV* and its inclusion of PMDD.

The Axis II personality disorders have also been the target of criticism and a source of controversy. The diagnostic categories on this axis have much poorer research support than are necessary for their acceptance into the *DSM,* so the categories allow for effects of possible gender, ethnic, and social class biases on the part of clinicians. However, "The claims to a scientific basis for these diagnoses hang upon an extremely slender thread" (Brown, 1992, p. 215). The *DSM-IV* warns clinicians that they "must be cautious not to overdiagnose or underdiagnose certain Personality Disorders in females or in males because of social stereotypes about typical gender roles and behaviors" (American Psychiatric Association, 1994, p. 632), but research has suggested that such bias does occur and affects diagnoses.

Gender biases are not limited to stereotypes of the feminine role; some categories seem to be exaggerations of the traditional male gender role (Williams & Spitzer, 1983). For example, **schizoid personality disorder** is characterized by "detachment from social relationships and a restricted range of expression of emotions in interpersonal settings" (American Psychiatric Association, 1994, p. 638). **Antisocial personality disorder** appears as a "pervasive pattern of disregard for, and violation of, the rights of others" (p. 645),

GENDERED VOICE

I Think I Have It

Male psychologist: "Have you read the new description of PMS that will appear in the fourth edition of the *DSM?* I'm really very concerned."

Female psychologist: "Yes, I have. Premenstrual dysphoric disorder will replace **late luteal phase dysphoric disorder.** I'm concerned, too. It's supposed to appear in the main body of the classification under mood disorders, and I understand that the treatment will be antidepressant drugs. It's been very controversial, and I think that this move will keep it that way. What bothers you?"

Male psychologist: "According to my reading of the diagnostic criteria, I think I have it."

including lying, fighting, stealing, and physical cruelty. Both these personality disorders include exaggerations of the traditional male gender role (Brannon, 1976). Indifference to social relationships resembles the Sturdy Oak facet of the role, with its emphasis on self-reliance and lack of emotion. Elements of antisocial personality disorder resemble the Give 'em Hell facet, with its emphasis on dominance and aggression. Not surprisingly, men receive these two diagnoses more often than women do (American Psychiatric Association, 1994; Kass, Spitzer, & Williams, 1983). Table 14.3 shows some of the personality disorders, along with their prevalence and the gender-related differences in their diagnosis.

If some *DSM* diagnostic categories are biased against men, then why is there no protest from men against this categorization? The charges of gender bias in the *DSM* have come mostly from women who have contended that the system is unfair to them. Although some diagnostic categories are exaggerations of the male gender role and men receive these diagnoses more often than women, no analogous criticisms have come from men about gender bias in the *DSM.* Perhaps this silence is related to the overall lower rate of psychiatric diagnosis for men. The protests of gender bias coming from women apply not only to the *DSM,*

TABLE 14.3 Prevalence of and Gender-Related Differences in Personality Disorders

Disorder	Estimated Rate in General Population	Gender Difference
Paranoid	0.5–2.5%	More common among men in clinical populations
Antisocial	3% men, 1% women	More common among men in both general and clinical populations
Borderline	2%	More common in women—75% of those diagnosed are women
Histrionic	2–3%	More commonly diagnosed in women
Narcissistic	< 1%	More common among men
Dependent	Most common personality disorder	More commonly diagnosed in women
Schizoid	Uncommon	More common among men

SOURCE: Based on *Diagnostic and statistical manual of mental disorders* (4th ed.), American Psychiatric Association, 1994, Washington, DC: Author.

but also to diagnoses of mental disorder according to any system. That is, some critics have expressed concern that women will be considered less psychologically healthy than men because in any system, men constitute the standard for what is mentally healthy (Bem, 1993b).

An early study that laid the foundation for the concerns over gender bias in the clinical diagnosis of mental disorders was the influential work by Inge Broverman and her colleagues (Broverman, Broverman, Clarkson, Rosenkrantz, & Vogel, 1970). These researchers investigated what constitutes a well-adjusted, healthy adult and found that the description differed significantly from what constitutes a well-adjusted, healthy woman. The gender role for socially desirable behavior in women was not consistent with the psychological standards for a well-adjusted adult. For example, such stereotypically feminine traits as dependence and emotionality are not part of the concept for adult mental health. These researchers contended that the discrepancy between the ideal of mental health for a woman and that for an adult reflected a double standard.

Clinically trained psychologists, psychiatrists, and social workers exhibited a double standard for mental health in rating a normal adult, a normal adult man, and a normal adult woman (Broverman et al., 1970). These professionals' ratings showed that their concept of a healthy adult and a healthy man were similar, whereas their views of a healthy adult and a healthy woman differed. These results pointed out that the standard for mental health is male, whereas feminine traits were viewed as detracting from health.

This study has been influential and widely cited, but the choice of questions may have biased the results (Widiger & Settle, 1987). Alternatively, mental health professionals may have changed their views over time, showing less bias now than when Broverman et al. performed their study over 30 years ago. A later study with a comparable method (Phillips & Gilroy, 1985) showed no significant gender-related differences for standards of mental health. Unfortunately, these nonsexist attitudes concerning standards for mental health may not be translated into the practice of diagnosis.

Some research has suggested that gender bias does exist in the diagnosis of behavior problems. In one study (Adler, Drake, & Teague, 1990), clinicians received descriptions of patients that met the criteria for several different personality disorders. Two versions of these descriptions differed only in the gender of the patients; findings indicated that the patients' gender affected the clinicians' views in stereotypical directions.

In 1972, Phyllis Chesler proposed that diagnosis of mental disorders is fundamentally gender biased. Chesler contended that women who overconform or underconform to the traditional feminine gender role are subject to diagnosis; if they are either too aggressive or too submissive, they are deviant. Although Chesler's argument centered on the diagnosis of women's problems, the rationale can also extend to men. Those men who fail to conform to the male gender role may be at increased risk for diagnosis. This early critique of the diagnosis of psychological disorders created interest in gender bias, and subsequent research has confirmed Chesler's contention that adherence to and deviation from traditional gender roles are factors in the diagnosis of mental disorders.

Clinicians exhibit some bias in diagnosing personality disorders. Personality disorders are diagnosed on Axis II, which has less research support and is more controversial than diagnoses on Axis I. One study (Hamilton, Rothbart, & Dawes, 1986) included descriptions of histrionic personality disorder and antisocial personality disorder. Histrionic personality disorder is characterized by excessive emotionality and attention-seeking in a variety of situations, whereas antisocial personality disorder is characterized by a persistent disregard for and violations of the rights of others. The former is more often diagnosed in women, and the latter is more often diagnosed in men. When the case studies were equated for severity of pathology, case descriptions of women were found to receive more extreme ratings for histrionic personality disorder than case descriptions portraying men, even when the symptoms were identical. No comparable bias appeared for antisocial personality disorder, demonstrating a tendency to maximize female, but not male, pathology.

The differential diagnosis for mental disorders can be conceptualized by viewing personality disorders as extensions of gender role stereotypes (Landrine, 1987; 1989). Many of the characteristics of personality disorders are very close to stereotypes of male and female gender roles. Even without prejudice on the part of clinicians, differential rates of diagnoses seem likely. Indeed, not only clinical psychologists and psychiatrists (Landrine, 1987), but also college students (Landrine, 1989) were able to match descriptions of stereotypical cases to the various personality disorders. For example, participants assigned to the description of a lower-class man a diagnosis of antisocial personality disorder, the single middle-class woman was identified as histrionic, and the married middle-class woman received a diagnosis of dependent personality disorder. Only the married upper-class man was without pathology. Given descriptions of the personality disorders, college students supplied demographic information that was similarly stereotypical. Thus, both professionals and university students perceive consistent gender and social class patterns associated with the personality disorders, which correspond to the frequency of such diagnoses.

Gender differences also appear in several diagnoses for Axis I, such as anxiety disorders, depression, and substance abuse disorders. Gender role stereotyping relates to these categories of psychiatric diagnosis (Rosenfield, 1982). Women and men who showed signs of psychopathology that were more typical of the other gender were more likely to be judged as candidates for hospitalization than were those who showed gender-typical disorders. Men with depression or anxiety disorders, and women with personality disorders or substance abuse problems—patients displaying "deviant" deviance—were judged more likely to be candidates for hospitalization than were men who showed substance abuse disorders or women who showed depression—the more "normal" disorders for those genders.

These research studies have confirmed and extended Chesler's conceptualization of the relationship between deviance and gender role behaviors by showing not only that gender differences exist in diagnoses, but also that gender roles and stereotyping play a part in the clinician's process of arriving at diagnoses of mental disorders.

The process of diagnosis can include two types of judgment errors—overdiagnosis and underdiagnosis (López, 1989). The most commonly studied form of diagnostic bias has been *overdiagnosis,* identifying people as having disorders when they do not. *Underdiagnosis* is the mistake of failing to identify problems by overlooking symptoms. Research on under- and overdiagnosis has confirmed their existence but has also found a pattern of gender bias (Redman, Webb, Hennrikus, Gordon, & Sanson-Fisher, 1991). Overdiagnosis was more common for female patients, and underdiagnosis was more common for male patients. These gender differences appeared when contrasting the diagnoses on a questionnaire measuring psychological disturbance with physicians' ratings of the degree of disturbance. The questionnaire assessed a similar number of men and women as psychologically disturbed, but the physicians did not. Instead, physicians showed a tendency to underrate the psychological disturbances of men and to overrate those of women. Furthermore, no differences appeared between interns and practicing physicians, indicating that no recent changes in medical training have altered the gender stereotyping in physicians' diagnoses of psychological problems.

Underdiagnosis and overdiagnosis present problems for patients both by identifying problems in people who have no pathology and by failing to diagnose problems in others who have mental disorders. With the evidence that overdiagnosis is more common in female patients and underdiagnosis is more common in male patients, the picture is one of systematic gender bias.

Gender Comparisons in Psychopathology

Chapter 13 presented information about gender differences in seeking health care, showing that women are more likely than men to seek health care. This tendency also applies to psychological problems. Data from four large-scale surveys of mental health problems showed that women have a greater tendency than men to interpret nonspecific problems and distress as related to their mental health and thus to seek mental health care (Kessler, Brown, & Broman, 1981). All gender differences in mental health treatment are not due to women's greater tendency to seek help, but between 10% and 28% of the difference in treatment of women for mental health problems is due to their greater tendency to seek such care.

The circumstances that bring women and men to treatment vary. Women are more likely than men to consult general physicians about mental health problems, which opens the possibility for additional mental health consultations (Travis, 1988b). Men do not make as many physician visits as women (see Chapter 13), so a comparable number of opportunities do not arise for them. No gender difference appears in the use of mental health specialty services (Leaf & Bruce, 1987), suggesting that men who seek mental health consultations are likely to seek that service directly, whereas women are more likely to receive such care in the context of regular health visits. The overall rate of hospitalization for mental disorders is somewhat higher for women (Kane, 1991), but the difference is limited to the elderly. For men and women in other age groups, men have higher hospitalization rates than women.

Not all disorders show gender differences, but several do. Anxiety disorders, depression, and substance abuse disorders are among those problems that show marked gender differences, whereas other diagnoses are evenly distributed between women and men.

Depression

Use of the term *depression* has varied from the popular conception of minor, temporary, low mood to the extreme of severe, debilitating disorder that requires treatment (Miller, Norman, & Dow, 1988). Although depression is a common experience, the disabling problems of severe depression lie outside the range of normal experience. In the *DSM* system, depression is classified as a type of mood disorder and appears as a diagnosis on Axis I. Two subclassifications of depressive disorders exist—**major depression** and **dysthymia.**

Symptoms of major depression include dissatisfaction and anxiety, loss of interest and loss of pleasure, feelings of helplessness and hopelessness, changes in sleep or eating habits, and difficulty in concentrating. These symptoms must persist for at least 2 weeks to warrant a diagnosis of major depression. Dysthymia is milder than major depression and tends to be a chronic condition that may last for years. This diagnosis applies to people who chronically experience depressed mood, loss of interest, or other symptoms of depression, much as they would a personality trait. Major depression and dysthymia can co-occur or can exist separately.

Table 14.4 shows the prevalence and gender-related differences for mood disorders. The ratio of major depression in women compared with that in men is about 2 to 1, considering either the figures obtained from treatment or those from community surveys (American Psychiatric Association, 1994; Culbertson, 1997). These numbers apply to many (but not all) societies around the world, and the explanations for these figures have included biological as well as social and cognitive theories. The biological theories rely on the differences in reproductive hormones to account for gender differences in depression, but simple versions of hormonal theories have very little clear support (Nolen-Hoeksema, 1987).

Reproductive hormones may play some role in depression for both women and men (see "According to the Media/According to the Research"). Jill Cyranowski and her colleagues (Cyranowski, Frank, Young, & Shear, 2000) hypothesized that hormones associated with the onset of puberty, girls' needs for affiliation, and negative life events combine to make girls and women more vulnerable to depression. Alan Booth and his colleagues (Booth, Johnson, & Granger, 1999) researched the connection between testosterone to depression in men and found a complex relationship. For men with low testosterone levels, the lower their hormone level, the higher their rate of depression. For men with high testosterone levels, the relationship between the two factors was positive: the higher the hormone level, the higher the rate of depression. Booth et al. hypothesized that the relationship of negative life events and high testosterone is the basis of this association; men with high testosterone are more likely to exhibit antisocial, employment, and marriage problems, which are all risk factors for mental health problems. Therefore, hormones may be a factor in depression, but their role is not clearly established and is quite complex.

Although most societies show a ratio of female to male depression similar to that of the United States, several rural, nonmodern cultures have similar rates of depression in women and men. Among these cultures are the old-order Amish, a rural farming society in the United States. In addition, university students, the elderly, and the bereaved show no gender differences in rates of depression. These exceptions suggest a strong situational component for the gender differences in depression, and a number of researchers have pinpointed social and family roles as the source of this difference. (See the "Family Roles" section earlier in this chapter for a review of the gender differences in stress.)

TABLE 14.4 Prevalence of and Gender-Related Differences in Mood Disorders

Disorder	Estimated Rate in General Population	Gender Difference
Major depression	2–9%	More common in women, with a ratio of 2:1
Dysthymia	3%	More common in women, with a ratio of 2:1 to 3:1
Bipolar disorder	0.4–1.6%	No difference

SOURCE: Based on *Diagnostic and statistical manual of mental disorders* (4th ed.), American Psychiatric Association, 1994, Washington, DC: Author.

ACCORDING TO THE MEDIA...

Boys Are Depressed

When Julie Stephens (1999) began taking her 6-year-old son to movies, she noticed that several of the films aimed at young children featured boys who exhibited symptoms of depression. In *Barney's Greatest Adventure,* a movie for preschool children, a young boy has the opportunity to spend a holiday on a farm. He is not interested in this possibility, considering all the animals and barns boring. Two girls show him how much fun a farm can be. Indeed, these girls (along with a large pink dinosaur) help him to unlock his imagination.

The popular film *A Bug's Life* includes a main character who responds to failure or rejection by saying "I am hopeless," or "I can't do anything right." These statements are consistent with the things that depressed people say—expressions of incompetence and feelings of hopelessness. This character's body language also showed the characteristics of depression, with his head hung and shoulders slumped. The female characters in these films are the confident, competent ones (Stephens, 1999). The girls offer encouragement and practical suggestions about how to manage the challenges and dangers of the situations.

Although these movies offer positive portrayals of girls, the girls are still subordinate, which is consistent with the traditional female gender role. These female characters help the depressed male characters, offering nurture, encouragement, and practical suggestions. They help the boys' confidence and support their actions, but the girls are not main characters, even with their outstanding characteristics.

Alternative explanations for gender differences in depression come from differences in the use of cognitive strategies for dealing with distressing events. Susan Nolen-Hoeksema and her colleagues (Nolen-Hoeksema, 1987; Nolen-Hoeksema, Larson, & Grayson, 1999) proposed that the gender differences in depression come from a combination of differences in negative experiences, feelings of mastery, and strategies for dealing with negative feelings. Women have more negative experiences, lower feelings of mastery, and tend to ruminate on their feelings. Dwelling on problems and negative feelings tends to amplify the feelings, which can lead to depression. Men tend to take action, which may not solve problems but does provide distraction. Figure 14.1 shows the complex relationship among these factors. This pattern of interrelationships appeared in a large community study and suggested that women may become involved in a cycle of stress from negative events, low mastery, rumination, and depression.

Another cognitive explanation for women's higher rates of depression is that their genuine emotions, goals, and desires are suppressed (Jack, 1991; 1999). According to this view, women are more prone to depression because society devalues women and the feminine, placing women in a position in which they must deny who they really are to get along in the world and to maintain their relationships; when women lose their sense of self, they become depressed. Research support for this view is mixed. Several studies have confirmed that scores on Silencing the Self Scale relate to depression (Carr, Gilroy, & Sherman, 1996; Gratch, Bassett, & Attra, 1995; Page, Stevens, & Galvin, 1996), but not for everyone. This relationship was true for European American women, but not for African American women (Carr et al., 1996). In studies that included men (Duarte & Thompson, 1999; Gratch et al., 1995; Page et al., 1996), the relationship between self-silencing and depression was significant, but men showed higher self-silencing scores than women did. Finding that men's

ACCORDING TO THE RESEARCH…

Boys and Girls Are Equally Likely to Be Depressed

The ratio of depressed women to depressed men is about 2:1 and exists in many (but not all) cultures. This difference does not exist during childhood, and boys and girls are about equally likely to exhibit symptoms of depression (Cyranowski et al., 1999). Not only do boys and girls have similar rates for symptoms of depression, but they also have a low rate of such symptoms (Marcotte, Allain, & Gosselin, 1999). This situation changes during puberty. As they enter puberty, boys' depression decreases, but girls' depression increases.

For depressed adolescents, both girls and boys share attitudes and coping strategies (Marcotte et al., 1999). Depressed adolescents tend to have problems in seeing themselves as competent and have problems in the appropriate use of social problem-solving skills. Regardless of their gender, adolescents with such doubts and difficulties are more vulnerable to symptoms of depression.

scores are higher than women's complicates this conceptualization of depression and does nothing to explain women's higher rate of depression.

Although gender differences exist in the diagnosis of depression, perhaps no differences occur in the frequency of negative mood (Nolen-Hoeksema, 1987; Tavris, 1992). That is, women and men experience the negative feelings that underlie depression at similar rates, but they express their feelings differently. Women tend to turn their negative feelings inward, whereas men tend to take action. In women, the feelings produce symptoms consistent with the female gender role and hence with the *DSM* diagnostic criteria for depression. In men, the feelings produce symptoms such as substance abuse, risk taking, and violence.

Support for this conception comes from a study that examined symptoms among high school seniors (Casper, Belanoff, & Offer, 1996). The young men reported anger as their most common problem, whereas the young women listed sadness. Therefore, the symptoms of depression may be seen as an expression of gender role socialization for women, but men exhibit different symptoms that receive other diagnoses.

In summary, two types of depression appear in the *DSM* classification—major depression and dysthymia. Women from many cultures are more likely than men to report symptoms of and receive treatment for depressive disorders at a ratio of approximately 2 to 1. Several explanations exist for this gender difference, including factors that make women vulnerable to depression, such as family role differences, personal control differences, and cognitive differences in coping with negative events. Another view holds that the gender differences in depression are a product of the ways in which women and men deal with distress. Women become passive, expressing symptoms of depression, and men become active, expressing symptoms of risk taking, violence, drug use, or some combination of these three behaviors.

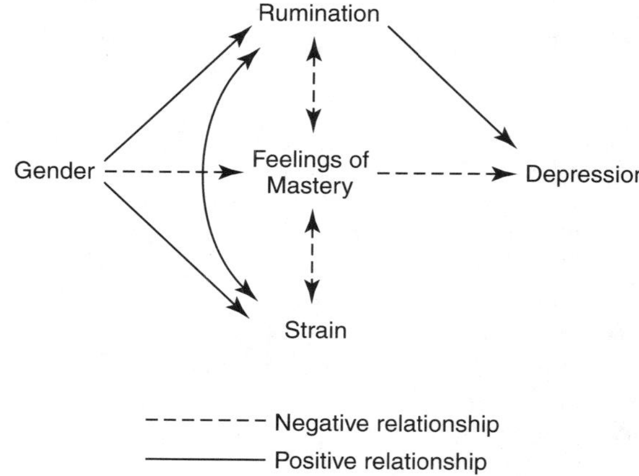

FIGURE 14.1 Effects of Gender, Rumination, Strain, and Feelings of Mastery on Depression

SOURCE: Adapted from "Explaining the gender difference in depressive symptoms," by S. Nolen-Hoeksema, J. Larson, and C. Grayson, 1999, *Journal of Personality and Social Psychology, 77,* p. 1067. Copyright 1999 by the American Psychological Association. Adapted by permission of Susan Nolen-Hoeksema.

Substance-Related Disorders

Substance-related disorders involve the use of **psychoactive substances,** drugs that affect thoughts, emotions, and behavior. Examples include alcohol, amphetamines, marijuana (cannabis), cocaine, hallucinogens, opiates, sedatives, and hypnotics. In order to be diagnosed as having one of the types of substance-related disorders, the person must not only use the drug, but also must exhibit a strong desire to use the substance and experience problems in social or occupational functioning due to drug use.

Alcohol is the most frequently used and abused substance, and men drink more than women in all categories of drinking (USDHHS, 2000). That is, more men than women fall into the categories of light, moderate, and heavy drinking. Drinking and drunkenness are associated with the male, and not the female, gender role (Capraro, 2000). People expect men to drink beer and to get drunk, but the same expectation does not apply to women. Indeed, women (and especially feminine women) are not expected to drink beer (but are expected to drink wine) and should *not* get drunk (Landrine, Bardwell, & Dean, 1988).

Alcohol is not equally intoxicating for men and women. Women tend to weigh less than men, and body weight affects intoxication, meaning that each drink has a greater effect the smaller the person is. In addition, some research has indicated that women's metabolism of alcohol produces a higher alcohol concentration in their blood compared to that in men's blood, even with the body-weight factor taken into account (Frezza et al., 1990). Both these factors result in greater risks to women who drink heavily than to men who do so. Because fewer women than men are heavy drinkers, however, men are more likely than women to experience the problems associated with heavy drinking, including the health risks and social problems associated with alcohol abuse.

A variety of evidence suggests that drinking is related to depression, both in men and in women. Alcohol consumption shows a relationship to depression and mood (Berger & Adesso, 1991). Among depressed and nondepressed men and women who were not problem drinkers, men expected more positive effects from drinking, and drank more, than women did. The depressed men consumed more alcohol than any other group, and drinking decreased these men's perception of depression. This study demonstrated the relationship between negative mood and drinking, especially for men. Perhaps these men are at risk for developing problem drinking, but their strategy of drinking to manage depression showed some signs of being effective.

Research has confirmed the relationship between depression and problem drinking. Among men and women in treatment for their drinking problems, those problem drinkers with a history of depression reported that they drank to relieve their depressive symptoms (Hesselbrock, Hesselbrock, & Workman-Daniels, 1986). Another study tested the relationship between depression and problem alcohol use over a 3-year time span (Horowitz & White, 1991). A significant relationship existed between depression at age 21 years and alcohol problems at age 24 for men, but no such relationship appeared for women. Thus, men who use the strategy of drinking to manage negative emotions are at increased risk for problem drinking.

Illegal drug use is also higher among men than women, with men more likely than women to use and abuse drugs such as heroin, amphetamines, cocaine, and marijuana—a pattern that parallels their alcohol use (USDHHS, 2000). On the other hand, women are more likely to use prescription tranquilizers and sedatives. That is, women are more likely to describe symptoms to physicians that lead to their diagnoses of having mental disorders treatable by drugs. The higher rate of prescription drug use by women and the greater use of illegal drugs by men result in similar rates but different patterns of substance use. Table 14.5 summarizes the prevalence and gender-related differences in substance use.

TABLE 14.5 Prevalence of and Gender-Related Differences in Substance-Related Disorders

Disorder	Estimated Rate in General Population	Gender Difference
Alcohol	5–8%	More common in men, with a ratio as high as 5:1, varying with age and cultural background
Amphetamine	Possibly as high as 2%	More common in men, with a 3:1 ratio
Cannabis	4%	More common in men
Cocaine	0.2%	No difference
Hallucinogen	0.3%	More common in men, with a 3:1 ratio
Opiates	0.7%	More common in men, with a ratio of 3:1 to 4:1
Sedatives, hypnotics or anxiolytics	1.1%	Women are at higher risk

SOURCE: Based on *Diagnostic and statistical manual of mental disorders* (4th ed.), American Psychiatric Association, 1994, Washington, DC: Author.

Men's drug use is more apt to be illegal, making them more likely to receive diagnoses because of their drug use. This diagnosis difference may not reflect much of a differential tendency in substance use. Perhaps women too might resort to illegal drug use if physicians were less willing to prescribe drugs for them: "The sex differences in the use of alcohol and prescription psychotropics are not inconsistent with the hypothesis that men and women are equally likely to resort to substance use for coping, and that the sex difference is merely in the choice of substances" (Biener, 1987, p. 336).

In summary, the research indicates that a relationship exists between depression and drinking; depressed people drink more than the nondepressed and even attribute their drinking to depression. The tendency to drink more heavily when depressed is stronger among men but not exclusive to them. Perhaps men choose this strategy for dealing with negative feelings more often than women do, so this difference in dealing with negative feelings may account for some of the gender differences in depression and substance-abuse disorders. The overall pattern of drug use for men and women probably differs little, but women tend to use legal prescription drugs, whereas men's drug use is more likely to come in the form of alcohol and illegal drugs.

Anxiety Disorders

The group of disorders labeled anxiety disorders includes panic attack, phobias, obsessive-compulsive disorder, and posttraumatic stress disorder, all involving features of anxiety and avoidance of problem situations. A survey of over 18,000 people indicated that anxiety disorders affect more than 7% of adults in the United States (Regier, Narrow, & Rae, 1990). No gender differences exist for some types of anxiety disorders, but other types appear much more often in women than in men.

Panic attack is characterized by periods of intense fear that occur without any fear-provoking situation. These attacks are typically accompanied by physical symptoms of distress, such as sweating, dizziness, and shortness of breath. This disorder is about equally common in women and men, but panic disorder with **agoraphobia** is about twice as common in women. "The essential feature of agoraphobia is anxiety about being in places or situations from which escape might be difficult (or embarrassing) or in which help may not be available in the event of having a panic attack...or panic-like symptoms" (American Psychiatric Association, 1994, p. 396). These feelings of anxiety lead people to avoid the situations that might provoke such feelings.

Agoraphobia can also occur without panic disorder, and women are also more likely to have this disorder (American Psychiatric Association, 1994; Cameron & Hill, 1989). Other **phobias,** unreasonable fears concerning some object or situation, constitute a second category of anxiety disorder. *Social phobias* appear as persistent fears of certain social situations, such as speaking in public, in which the person is judged by others or in which the person may do something embarrassing. The American Psychiatric Association (1994) stated that women in the general population are more likely to have social phobias, but in clinical populations, the gender ratio is either closer to equal, or men predominate. *Specific phobias,* fears of some object or situation other than anticipating a panic attack or being in a certain some social situation, are more common among women.

Obsessive-compulsive disorder is the combination of obsession, which refers to recurrent, intrusive thoughts about something the person would prefer to ignore, and compulsion, which refers to repetitive behaviors intended to prevent anxiety. To receive this diagnosis, a person must be distressed by the obsessive thoughts and must spend over an hour per day on the compulsive behaviors. According to the *DSM-IV* (American Psychiatric Association, 1994) and other research (Cameron & Hill, 1989), this pattern of behavior is equally common in women and men, but other research (Cleary, 1987) has found it more common among women.

Posttraumatic stress disorder (PTSD) (defined and discussed earlier in this chapter) was originally applied to men who suffered lasting effects from their war experiences. As research accumulated on PTSD, its wider application became evident. Now the diagnosis is given to people experiencing the prolonged aftereffects of many different types of trauma, including natural disasters, accidents, and violent crime as well as military combat. A random sample of women revealed that over 12% met the criteria for PTSD, a much higher percentage than previous estimates (Resnick, Kilpatrick, Dansky, Saunders, & Best, 1993). Both a community survey (Stein, Walker & Forde, 2000) and a study of 16- to 22-year-olds (Cuffe et al., 1998) showed that women were more vulnerable than men to PTSD.

Table 14.6 summarizes the prevalence figures presented in *DSM-IV* and the differences associated with gender for these disorders. Research has shown a consistent pattern of the higher prevalence for agoraphobia (with and without panic disorder) and for specific phobias among women. The findings are not so clear for social phobia and obsessive-compulsive disorder. Overall, more women than men receive the diagnosis of some type of anxiety disorder, indicating that agoraphobia and specific phobias are sufficiently common to cause women to dominate this diagnosis.

Women with anxiety disorders experience more severe symptoms than men with anxiety disorders do, and in one study (Scheibe & Albus, 1992) stress within marriage was the most frequent event that preceded the development of the disorder. Anxiety and fear are more characteristic of the feminine stereotype than of the stereotypical male role. The match

TABLE 14.6 Prevalence of and Gender-Related Differences in Anxiety Disorders

Disorder	Estimated Rate in General Population	Gender Difference
Agoraphobia with and without panic attack	1.5–3.5%	More common in women, with a ratio of 2:1 to 3:1
Agoraphobia (without panic attack)	More common (without panic attack) than agoraphobia with panic attack	Much more common in women
Specific phobias	9–11.3%	Women have 55% to 95% of specific phobias
Social phobias	2–13%	More common in women in general population; more common in men in clinical settings
Obsessive-compulsive disorder	1.5–2.1%	No difference
Posttraumatic stress disorder	1–14%	Not specified in *DSM-IV*

SOURCE: Based on *Diagnostic and statistical manual of mental disorders* (4th ed.), American Psychiatric Association, 1994, Washington, DC: Author.

between gender role traits and mental disorders that appears in personality disorders (Landrine, 1987, 1989) may also apply to anxiety disorders and may constitute an explanation for the higher overall rate of anxiety disorders among women. The gender differences among the different anxiety disorders suggest varying gender-related ways of expressing anxiety.

Other Disorders

Several important classifications of mental disorders show few or no gender differences in prevalence, but men and women with these disorders may not exhibit identical symptoms or the same time course of the disorder. For example, **schizophrenia**—a serious and complex disorder involving thought disturbances, problems in personal relationships, and possibly hallucinations—has been diagnosed equally in women and men.

This equal prevalence does not require that men and women have identical experiences with the disorder, and they do not. One study (Chu, Abi-Dargham, Ackerman, Cetingök, & Klein, 1989) found that male schizophrenics were younger than female schizophrenics at the time of their diagnosis, and that the men were less likely to be married than the women. In terms of symptoms, female schizophrenics tended to be talkative, agitated, irrelevant, and silly, whereas male schizophrenics were less active than normal, grandiose, withdrawn, and more likely to have auditory hallucinations.

Other research (Lewis, 1992) showed similar patterns, but male schizophrenics tended to have poorer functioning before the onset of their disorders and were more likely than female schizophrenics to be involved in substance abuse. In addition, women were more likely to respond favorably to treatment. Despite these differences, male and female schizophrenics exhibited more similarities than differences.

Bipolar disorder is one of the mood disorders, along with major depression and dysthymia (see Table 14.4). Bipolar disorder is characterized by periods of mania, high activity, and elevated mood alternating with periods of depression. These drastically different mood states change in a cyclic fashion such that the affected person experiences both mania and depression over a period of weeks or months, interspersed with periods of normal moods. Unlike the other two mood disorders, bipolar disorder shows no gender differences in prevalence (American Psychiatric Association, 1987; Cleary, 1987).

An examination of individuals with bipolar disorder in the United Kingdom (Sibisi, 1990) revealed that the time course of the disorder was somewhat different for men and women. No overall gender differences in prevalence appeared, but women were more likely than men to receive a diagnosis during their middle years. As with schizophrenia, men are more likely than women to be diagnosed at younger ages with bipolar disorder.

The **somatoform disorders** show some gender differences. This classification of disorders includes problems with physical symptoms of disease, but no physical basis for those symptoms. As a group, women are more likely to receive the diagnosis of somatoform disorder, but some of the disorders within this classification show no gender differences. *Conversion disorder,* the loss of physical function without any physical basis for the disability, was originally called *hysteria.* In the late 1800s, this disorder was so strongly associated with women that the extension of the label to men was controversial. The *DSM-IV* (American Psychiatric Association, 1994) stated that this disorder occurs rarely in men, and another study (Tomasson, Kent, & Coryell, 1991) found that the diagnosis of conversion disorder was three times more common in women than in men.

Another of the somatoform disorders is *somatization disorder,* the recurrence of physical complaints and the seeking of medical attention without receiving any diagnosis of a physical problem. These complaints are often dramatic or exaggerated, and the affected person seeks care from many medical professionals. Women account for 95% of somatization disorder patients (Tomasson et al., 1991). The diagnosis is so rare for men that some have questioned its existence in men. However, one investigation (Golding, Smith, & Kashner, 1991) found that this disorder does occur in men. In addition, the symptoms and the course of the disorder are similar for men and women.

The *DSM-IV* cautions that physical disorders that involve many variable symptoms can erroneously lead to the diagnosis of somatization disorder. Given physicians' tendency to dismiss the physical complaints of women and attribute those complaints to emotional problems (see Chapter 13), this diagnosis may be erroneously applied to women who have physical rather than mental problems. Indeed, physical and psychiatric disorders share many symptoms, and diagnostic bias can cause women to receive psychiatric diagnoses when they actually have physical disorders (Klonoff & Landrine, 1997).

Sexual disorders consist of two groups of disorders, paraphilias and sexual dysfunctions. **Paraphilias** are characterized by intense sexual feelings in response to objects or situations, such as nonhuman objects, children, nonconsenting persons, or even the suffering of self or others. The nonhuman objects include animals or items of clothing, and the situations include exposing one's genitals to strangers, fondling strangers in public places, observing sexual activities, or dressing in gender-inappropriate clothing. Sexual masochism—experiencing pleasure from receiving pain or humiliation—and sexual sadism—experiencing pleasure from inflicting pain or humiliation on one's sexual partner—are also among the paraphilias. About

GENDERED VOICES

The Doctor Wouldn't Listen

The case of a young women who was in one of my classes is a good example of a woman whose physician failed to take her complaints seriously. This young woman felt unwell, experiencing a variety of symptoms including chest pain, abdominal pain, and lack of energy. She consulted her physician, who had been her family's doctor since she was a child. He asked her about her symptoms and about her life. She described how she felt and where it hurt, along with the stresses and problems she had recently experienced: Her parents were getting divorced, and she felt so tired that school was difficult to manage. The physician said that she was experiencing stress and told her to relax, assuring her that she would feel better.

She tried but felt no better. After several visits, the woman was convinced that she had a problem that the physician was missing, and he was equally convinced that she had a mental problem that she failed to acknowledge. She consulted another physician, who might have behaved much as the first did, but instead, the physician did a series of tests that revealed a kidney tumor, which required immediate surgery. Her many symptoms and the stresses in her life were consistent with a number of diagnoses, but her family physician failed to take her physical complaints seriously, insisting that she was experiencing psychological distress rather than organically based physical problems.

This woman's experience is by no means unique. Men may also be erroneously diagnosed in a medical examination, but the overwhelming majority of horror stories of physical problems diagnosed as psychological disorders come from women who have experienced biased diagnosis and treatment. Therefore, biased diagnosis may be the source of some of the gender differences in somatization disorder.

20% of sexual masochists are women, and this disorder is the most common paraphilia among women, which indicates that women are rarely diagnosed as having any of the paraphilias.

Sexual dysfunctions, the other subcategory of sexual disorders, consist of abnormally low (or high) levels of sexual desire, or difficulty achieving arousal or orgasm. Women are more likely to receive diagnoses indicating abnormally low levels of sexual desire or inhibited orgasm, but men also experience these sexual problems. A summary of the prevalence and gender-related differences in schizophrenia, somatoform, and sexual disorders appears in Table 14.7.

When people receive diagnoses of abnormally low (or high) sexual interest or activity, these diagnoses require a standard of comparison, which may be their previous behavior as compared with their currently decreased (or increased) interest. The standard can also be the clinician's judgment about what is normal, and this standard may be biased or arbitrary. Despite warnings in the *DSM* concerning other physical or behavioral problems that can produce sexual dysfunctions, the possibility exists that patients may be held to some arbitrary standard of what constitutes normal levels of sexual activity, and they may be diagnosed on the basis of behavior that is deviant merely by definition.

In summary, several mental disorders show patterns of gender differences, and some disorders that have no overall discrepancy in prevalence do show gender differences in onset or experience. The most dramatic gender differences occur for anxiety and somatoform disorders, diagnoses overwhelmingly given to women, and sexual paraphilias, diagnoses overwhelmingly given to men. Schizophrenia and bipolar disorder show no gender difference in prevalence, but male schizophrenics show some behavioral differences compared to female schizophrenics. The gender differences in bipolar disorder relate to age of onset, with women receiving more diagnoses in middle age than men, who tend to be diagnosed at younger ages.

Although psychopathology constitutes more than exaggerated gender role behavior, all gender differences in mental disorders lend themselves to interpretations relating to gender

TABLE 14.7 Prevalence of and Gender-Related Differences in Rate of Selected Axis-I Disorders

Disorder	Estimated Rate in General Population	Gender Difference
Schizophrenia	0.2–2%	No difference in prevalence
Somatoform disorders		
Conversion disorder	11–300 cases per 100,000	More common in women, with a ratio of 2:1 to 10:1
Somatization disorder	0.2–2% in women; less than 0.2% in men	Rarely diagnosed in men
Sexual disorders		
Paraphilias	No estimate	Rarely diagnosed in women, with the ratio of men to women at 20:1
Sexual dysfunctions	No estimate	More common in women

SOURCE: Based on *Diagnostic and statistical manual of mental disorders* (4th ed.), American Psychiatric Association, 1994, Washington, DC: Author.

roles. People tend to exhibit pathology related to their gender roles; that is, women show signs of weakness and physical complaints, whereas men show violence and unusual sexuality. Male schizophrenics are more violent and socially withdrawn, whereas female schizophrenics are more talkative and silly; both behaviors are consistent with traditional gender roles.

The patterns in rates of mental disorders for men and women reflect the power of male and female gender roles. The most common patterns of disorder for both men and women show consistencies with what are considered to be appropriate gender-related behaviors. When violations of gender roles occur, clinicians are likely to perceive that these patients have more severe problems than patients who exhibit psychopathology consistent with their gender roles.

Considering Diversity

Gender stereotypes are not the only possibility for biased diagnosis with the *DSM* system; ethnic stereotypes can also influence the labeling of mental disorders. The *DSM* system represents the summary of the American Psychiatric Association's evaluation of mental disorders, and the psychiatrists who compose this organization are mostly male and mostly White. As previous sections of this chapter have proposed, the descriptions of categories within the *DSM* system may themselves include gender and ethnically biased components. The *DSM* system has been criticized for containing a western bias, which may be a problem for people from different cultures who live in a western country (Solomon, 1992). People may be judged by standards that they do not understand or accept. Alternatively, the application of the system may be biased by practitioners' ethnic stereotypes (Abreu, 1999; Landrine, 1987). Or both biases may occur in the process of psychiatric diagnosis.

In a study of clinician bias, psychiatrists received case descriptions for diagnosis with the gender and ethnic backgrounds of the cases varied to determine the effect on diagnosis (Loring & Powell, 1988). Even with clear-cut diagnostic criteria, the psychiatrists were influenced in the stereotypical direction by gender and ethnic information.

In one mental health agency, fewer ethnic differences in psychiatric diagnoses and treatment appeared than were expected for African American, Mexican American, Vietnamese American, Philippino American, and European American clients (Flaskerud, 1986). In this study of over 26,000 clients of a county mental health system, the relationship between ethnic background and psychiatric diagnosis showed differences for ethnic background in certain categories of diagnosis (Flaskerud & Hu, 1992). A greater proportion of African American and Asian American clients received diagnoses of serious mental disorders compared with European American clients, who, in turn, received more of these diagnoses than Latino clients did. Asian American clients were less likely than any other ethnic group to receive diagnoses involving substance abuse. Surprisingly, these researchers failed to find any differences in diagnoses relating to social class.

Other researchers have found that both ethnicity and social class relate to psychiatric disorders. An inverse relationship exists between socioeconomic status (SES) and psychiatric disorders; that is, as SES decreases, psychiatric disorders increase (Holzer et al., 1986). Diagnosis and social class have an inverse relationship for both African Americans and European Americans (Williams, Takeuchi, & Adair, 1992). The strongest relationship was for alcohol abuse, but other disorders showed similar relationships. For European

Americans, depression increased as SES decreased; for African Americans, no relationship appeared. White men with lower SES had a higher rate of mental disorders than their African American counterparts. Gender differences also appeared, forming complex interaction patterns of gender, ethnicity, and SES.

These findings suggest that to eliminate diagnostic bias, the criteria and the clinicians using them should be sensitive to the cultural background of the individual who is being diagnosed, and that diagnosis should relate to the individual rather than be an expression of the dominant culture. Behaviors that may seem dysfunctional to members of the dominant culture may not be so in minority cultures (Solomon, 1992). The fourth edition of the *DSM* addressed these problems by including information about various ethnic and cultural groups in each diagnosis to allow clinicians to take this information into account. Perhaps the professionals who use the *DSM* will be able to include this information to attain the cultural sensitivity that has been lacking in their diagnoses, but the listing of symptoms as shown in the multiaxial *DSM* system does not easily lend itself to the type of flexibility that will be necessary for culturally sensitive diagnoses.

Looking beyond the United States, similarities appear in psychopathology and in the factors related to its development around the world. However, different countries show different rates of problems (WHO International Consortium in Psychiatric Epidemiology, 2000). For example, a much higher percentage of people in the United States and the Netherlands (over 40%) reported some type of serious psychological problem during their lifetime than did people in Mexico (20%) or Turkey (12%).

The factors that relate to the development of mental disorders in the United States also operate throughout the world, including the disproportionate hazard to women (Desjarlais, Eisenberg, Good, & Kleinman, 1995). Inequitable treatment in family relationships, poverty and economic discrimination, and violence exert a negative impact on women, putting them at risk. Both women and men who live in war-torn areas are at increased risk for PTSD as a result of the violence in their countries, and women's lack of education, limited access to good jobs, and dependence on men for survival place women at risk for depression and anxiety disorders, which are more common diagnoses for women than for men throughout much of the world. Like men in the United States, men throughout the world receive more diagnoses of drug and alcohol abuse, suggesting that the gender role's pressures that prompt U.S. men to cope with negative feelings by alcohol and drug use operate in many cultures. As in the United States, psychopathology tends to follow gender role patterns.

Summary

Women experience more stress than men, and women's roles are the most probable sources of these differences. Women's roles often obligate them to provide physical and emotional care for their families, but they may not receive as much social support as they give. An increasing body of evidence has implicated violence as a factor contributing to a variety of mental disorders. Although men are the more common targets of violent crime, women are more commonly the victims of intimate violence, including childhood sexual abuse, rape, and spouse battering. Poverty is also a source of stress that disproportionately affects women and ethnic minorities, both of whom have higher rates of mental disorders than White men. Discrimination is a pervasive experience that increases stress in the lives of both ethnic minorities and women.

Comparisons of women's and men's coping strategies have been complicated by the need to examine differences in stressful situations in their lives. Studies that fail to control for these factors tend to support the stereotypical view that women use emotion-focused techniques more often and men use problem-focused coping. Not only do situational factors affect coping, but women and men seem ready to report the use of gender-stereotypical coping strategies, which suggests that self-report studies are biased.

Gender differences in patterns of psychopathology have been the source of accusations of gender bias in the way these mental disorders are diagnosed. These criticisms have centered around the *Diagnostic and Statistical Manual of Mental Disorders* (*DSM*) of the American Psychiatric Association. This publication contains a descriptive, multiaxial system for assigning diagnoses to people's behavioral problems. Using the *DSM* system, clinicians match each patient's symptoms against a description and make diagnoses on each of five axes. Axis I contains descriptions of the major clinical disorders, Axis II describes mental retardation and personality disorders, and Axis III provides a diagnosis of physical conditions. Axis IV contains a listing for the stressors in the patient's life, and Axis V allows for an overall rating of level of functioning.

Women's higher rate of treatment and the gender differences in some categories of disorders have led some researchers to argue that there is gender bias in the *DSM,* especially in the personality disorder diagnoses that appear on Axis II. The descriptions of these disorders appear to exaggerate traits of the female and male gender roles, and the expected gender differences appear.

The clinicians who apply the criteria may also be biased, holding men as the standard for both women's and men's mental health. Early research indicated that clinicians value masculine traits above feminine ones. These biases may be weakening, but physicians are more likely to overdiagnose women's and underdiagnose men's mental disorders. Although clinicians may not be personally prejudiced, their limited attention to gender and ethnic information can lead them to use this information in biased ways in their diagnoses, creating differences in the numbers of women and men who are given various diagnoses.

In addition to the personality disorders that show gender differences, the statistics concerning some Axis I diagnoses reflect different rates for women and men. Many categories of mental disorders show few gender differences, but major depression and substance-related disorders show marked gender differences, with women being more often diagnosed with depression and men more often diagnosed with substance abuse problems. Various explanations for these differences exist, including biological, social role, and cognitive theories. An alternative explanation holds that the gender differences in these two behavior problems reflect differences in expressing similar underlying, negative feelings: Women express their negative feelings in the form of depression, whereas men express their negative feelings in the form of alcohol and drug abuse.

Other mental disorders show some differences in women and men. Some anxiety disorders, such as phobias, are more common among women, but others, such as obsessive-compulsive disorders, show little gender difference in prevalence. Likewise, bipolar disorder and schizophrenia are about equally common in men and women, but the paraphilias are very rare in women. Somatoform disorders, on the other hand, are more common in women than in men. Therefore, the pattern of mental disorders seems to reflect the gender roles appropriate to men and women; that is, the patterns of abnormal behavior reflect aspects of the gender role of each.

Not only gender bias, but also ethnic bias may affect diagnosis of mental disorders, and several ethnic groups in the United States receive diagnoses at higher rates than Whites do. People in these ethnic groups tend to be more burdened with risks such as poverty, violence, and discrimination. Patterns of gender difference exist throughout the world, but so do the factors that relate to the development of mental disorders, including stresses in family life, poverty, violence, and discrimination.

Glossary

agoraphobia a phobic disorder characterized by anxiety about being in places or situations in which escape might be difficult or embarrassing.

antisocial personality disorder a personality disorder that is characterized by irresponsible and antisocial behavior such as lying, fighting, stealing, and physical cruelty.

bipolar disorder one of the mood disorders, characterized by periods of mania, high activity and elevated mood, alternating with depression.

diagnosis classification of a physical or psychological problem.

dysthymia diagnosis within the category of mood disorders that is applied to milder but chronic symptoms of depression, including depressed mood, loss of interest and pleasure, or other symptoms over an extended period, often for months or years.

late luteal phase dysphoric disorder a diagnosis with symptoms that resemble premenstrual syndrome. This controversial category appeared in the appendix rather than the body of *DSM-III-R,* along with other personality disorders that require more study.

major depression diagnosis within the category of mood disorders that is applied to severe symptoms of depression, such as dissatisfaction and anxiety, loss of interest and pleasure, feelings of helplessness and hopelessness, changes in eating and sleep habits, and difficulty concentrating.

obsessive-compulsive disorder the combination of obsession (recurrent, intrusive thoughts about something the person would prefer to ignore) and compulsion (repetitive behaviors intended to prevent anxiety).

panic attack one of the anxiety disorders, characterized by periods of intense fear that occur without any fear-provoking situation and accompanied by physical signals of distress.

paraphilias a type of sexual disorder characterized by intense sexual feelings in response to objects or situations that are unusual.

phobias unreasonable fears concerning some object or situation.

posttraumatic stress disorder (PTSD) one type of anxiety disorder that involves the experience of some distressing event outside the range of normal human experience, the reexperience of the event, avoidance of stimuli associated with the event, and increased sensitivity to associated experiences. These symptoms must persist for at least one month.

premenstrual dysphoric disorder (PMDD) a controversial diagnostic category that appears in an appendix of *DSM-IV.* Its symptoms are those of premenstrual syndrome, and the broad description of these symptoms presents the possibility that vast numbers of women could be diagnosed as mentally ill.

psychoactive substances drugs that affect thoughts, emotions, and behavior.

schizoid personality disorder a personality disorder that is characterized by lack of concern about personal and social relationships as well as a restricted range of emotional experience and expression.

schizophrenia a serious and complex disorder involving thought disturbances, problems in personal relationships, and possibly hallucinations.

sexual dysfunctions a subcategory of the sexual disorders that includes problems with low or high level of sexual desire, or difficulty achieving arousal or orgasm.

social support receipt of emotional and material resources from friends and family members.

somatoform disorders a classification of disorders that includes problems with physical symptoms of disease but with no physical basis for these symptoms.

Suggested Readings

Culbertson, Frances M. (1997). Depression and gender: An international review. *American Psychologist, 52,* 25–31. Culbertson's review provides a concise summary of the evidence on gender differences from a cross-cultural perspective. In addition, she considers explanations for depression with the goal of understanding how to approach its treatment.

Landrine, Hope. (1989). The politics of personality disorder. *Psychology of Women Quarterly, 13,* 325–339. Landrine demonstrated the congruence between social stereotypes and various descriptions of personality disorders. She argues that by incorporating these ethnic and gender stereotypes, the diagnosis of personality disorders becomes politicized.

Lerman, Hannah. (1996). *Pigeonholing women's misery: A history and critical analysis of the psychodiagnosis of women in the twentieth century.* New York: BasicBooks. Lerman's provocative book includes a historical review of the diagnostic process and many varieties of criticism of the ways that women's distress has been categorized.

Vandervoort, Debra. (1999). Quality of social support in mental and physical health. *Current Psychology, 18,* 205–222. Vandervoort thoroughly reviews the research on social support and its relationship to both mental and physical health.

Chapter 15

Treatment for Mental Disorders

HEADLINE

When Planets Collide

Psychology Today, May/June, 1997

John Gray, author of the best-selling self-help book, *Men Are from Mars, Women Are from Venus* (1992), began to franchise Mars & Venus counseling centers in 1997. These centers were another step in Gray's enterprise of counseling couples. Gray said that, despite the enormous success of his book, initially he had trouble finding a publisher: "New York publishers wanted nothing to do with it. They thought it was sexist" (in Marano, 1997, p. 29). These publishers are not alone—Gray's interplanetary version of gender difference has been the target of criticism that his approach is a repackaging of gender stereotypes and that his therapy perpetuates traditional roles for women and men (Marano, 1997). Indeed, by accentuating gender differences, Gray's approach may contribute to problems in relationships.

Gray holds to his beliefs about the opposing natures of women and men in his therapy for couples: "Whatever the therapy is about, it will take into consideration that a woman's from Venus, she has certain Venutian needs" (quoted in Marano, 1997, p. 30). Gray accepts that gender differences are biologically fixed and tied to hormones but acknowledges that "If a woman has to take the role of provider, she becomes more Martian" (p. 68). However, he stated that women's doing men's work along with household work is the reason for high divorce rates.

Gray has made his Mars & Venus approach into an industry, including several books, a series of counseling centers, a Broadway show, and a television talk show. Both men and women read his books as a way to help deal with relationship problems, and some seek counseling from Mars & Venus therapists. John Gray has become a voice for popular psychology in the public consciousness. Some critics have accused him of exaggerating gender differences and promoting traditional stereotypes rather than providing advice and therapy that helps couples form relationships with growth opportunities for both partners. Is the self-help approach a good way to deal with problems, or is more traditional therapy more effective? Is the accusation of perpetuating gender stereotypes unique to Gray, or do other approaches to therapy also share this problem?

Approaches to Therapy

Formal psychological treatment for mental disorders or behavior problems has a relatively short history, and throughout that history, the approach to treatment has been related to the conceptualization of the source of problems. Until the middle of the 19th century, the dominant belief was that abnormal and socially unacceptable behavior was a moral or spiritual problem, and few treatment procedures existed for people with mental disorders (Russell, 1995). The reconceptualization of mental disorders from possession by demons or moral deficiencies to problems in mental functioning came about during the 19th and early 20th centuries, and medicine became the model for understanding these problems. With the growing acceptance of mental illness as analogous to physical illness, medical researchers began to seek methods of treatment for abnormal behavior.

Therapies for the treatment of mental disorders arose and became part of psychiatry and psychology. The earliest modern therapy was **psychoanalysis,** Freud's version of talk-based treatment for psychological problems, although other therapists who were dissatisfied with psychoanalysis as the preferred method of treatment devised new talk-based therapies. In addition, psychological research on operant conditioning was applied to changing undesirable behavior, resulting in the therapy called **behavior modification.** Also, psychiatrists use psychoactive drugs in the treatment of behavior problems—sometimes instead of, and sometimes in addition to, psychotherapy. Therefore, these professionals now provide a variety of treatments for people with mental disorders.

Psychoanalysis

Sigmund Freud was among the early researchers who investigated causes of and sought cures for mental disorders. He developed a system of therapy that has influenced treatment as well as contemporary thinking about mental disorders. Freud's system of therapy is psychoanalysis, a talk-based approach geared toward understanding and alleviating psychological problems. Psychoanalysis was part of Freud's comprehensive theory of personality development and functioning. (Chapter 5 presented the Freudian approach to personality development.) Freud believed that psychological problems develop when people are incapable of dealing with problems and use **repression** to push problematic material into the region of the unconscious. The unconscious does not function rationally, so repressed material has the potential to remain in the unconscious throughout childhood and adulthood and can produce problems at any time.

Problems typically result from conflict during childhood, when the ego is not sufficiently well developed to deal with the many difficulties of early childhood. Adult problems often reflect childhood traumas that have been repressed and that leave the troubled person with mental conflict, distress, or problems in functioning. Psychoanalysts attempt to help patients resolve their problems by bringing unconscious material to consciousness so that patients may deal with these problems rationally. Once patients gain insight into the source of their conflicts, Freud believed that their conscious minds could deal with the problems, thus alleviating the source of conflict. Therefore, bringing repressed material to consciousness was a goal of psychoanalysis. Table 15.1 summarizes the elements of psychoanalytic therapy.

Although Freud and his colleagues were physicians, psychoanalysis developed as a psychological treatment for mental disorders. That is, the source of mental disorders was psychological, and the treatment was accomplished through talking about the source of the problem. This approach influenced popular thought and prompted the development of other talk-based treatments. Although medically based treatments for mental disorders also developed, talked-based psychotherapy remains a prominent approach to the treatment of problem behavior.

Some talk-based therapies arose in direct opposition to the Freudian system. Karen Horney (1939) was one of the psychoanalysts who protested the Freudian view of women and offered alternative approaches to dealing with psychological problems. Her theory and therapeutic interventions are the basis for contemporary talk-based therapy (Westkott, 1997). (See Chapter 5 for more about Freud's theory and Horney's alternatives to Freudian theory.) Other alternative therapies originated with Carl Rogers (1951), who developed a humanistic approach to therapy called client-centered therapy, and Albert Ellis (1962), who developed a cognitive therapy called rational-emotive therapy. These therapists objected to the emphasis on the unconscious in psychoanalysis and offered therapies that emphasized coping with current life problems rather than exploring developmental trauma from childhood.

Humanistic Therapies

The psychoanalytic view of human nature is rather pessimistic, holding that psychological development is filled with potentially debilitating problems and that few people develop into healthy adults. Psychoanalysis can help people resolve the problems that result from unconscious conflict and trauma, but helping them to maintain a healthy, functioning personality is always a delicate balancing act. The humanistic theories of personality, in contrast to psychoanalysis, hold the more optimistic view that people are innately drawn toward fulfilling their human potential. If they fail, the reasons lie in their circumstances and in their environments, which somehow prevent the complete development of their full potentials. This context-sensitive, optimistic view of humanity is reflected in humanistic

TABLE 15.1 Elements of Psychoanalytic Therapy

Category	Description
Underlying source of problems	Childhood trauma plus insufficient ego to deal with trauma
Cause of problems	Repression of unconscious conflict
Immediate source of problems	Repressed material escapes from unconscious
Goal of therapy	To bring repressed material to consciousness
Techniques	Talking, free association, dream analysis
Practitioners	Psychoanalysts (who are usually psychiatrists)

psychotherapy, as, for example, in Carl Rogers's client-centered therapy and Frederick (Fritz) Perls's Gestalt therapy.

Rogers (1951, 1961, 1980) proposed that human development follows a natural course toward health unless some event impedes this development. Rogers believed that problems originate from distortions in self-concept, and these distortions arise from a lack of acceptance of true feelings. When children get messages that the feelings they experience are unacceptable, they begin to deny these feelings. Lack of acceptance of feelings leads to inaccuracies in self-concept and interferes with many facets of development.

Client-centered therapy seeks to help people develop their full potential by providing a safe therapeutic environment (Kaplan & Yasinski, 1980). To form a relationship with an empathic, acceptant, and genuine counselor is of primary importance. Thus, client-centered counselors offer three conditions—unconditional acceptance, empathy, and congruence to their clients. The most important of these is congruence: "To be congruent means to be real or genuine, to be whole or integrated, to be what one truly is" (Feist & Feist, 2002, p. 474). These three conditions are essential for clients to experience growth, and all three arise from clients' relationship with the counselor. Given these three conditions, the process of therapy occurs.

A major goal of client-centered therapy is to eliminate discrepancies between clients' actual feelings and the feelings they recognize. By coming to recognize their true feelings—including negative feelings—clients can accept themselves. That is, clients develop congruence during the course of successful client-centered therapy. In addition, they become open to change and new experiences, develop a freshness of attitude, and come to trust in themselves.

The counselor does not work directly on changing clients, who must do that for themselves. The counselor's job is to provide clients with therapeutic relationships so that clients can reclaim their abilities to move toward personal growth and development. This approach focuses on allowing clients to think in undistorted ways, assuming that behavior changes in them will follow.

Gestalt therapy, another humanistic therapy, has similarities to client-centered therapy. The word *gestalt* means whole in German, and Perls (1969), the originator of this therapy, believed that the basis of psychological problems comes from feelings of not being whole. The failure to acknowledge their emotions leads people to this feeling of not being whole; they have a sense that parts of themselves have been psychologically disowned. Gestalt therapy seeks to help clients become whole again by allowing them to recognize and express their emotions, and Gestalt therapists use a variety of techniques oriented around understanding and integrating emotions to further this goal.

The humanistic therapies all share the view that fulfillment is a natural goal that people can reach, but barriers exist that block psychological growth. Humanistic therapists attempt to provide an atmosphere that permits clients to move in the natural direction of self-enhancement. Table 15.2 summarizes the elements of humanistic therapy.

Cognitive Therapy

Clients' thoughts are important in humanistic therapy, but these thought processes are the major focus in cognitive therapy. Cognitive therapists believe that thought processes are the basis of feelings and behavior; they create psychological problems and also provide the potential for alleviating those problems. Behavior and emotions follow from cognition, so changes in cognition provide the foundation for changes in behavior.

TABLE 15.2 Elements of Humanistic Therapy

Category	Description
Underlying source of problems	Discrepancy between genuine feelings and acknowledged emotions; feelings of not being whole
Cause of problems	Blockage of development toward full potential
Immediate source of problems	The problem that prompts a client to seek therapy
Goal of therapy	To provide an atmosphere that allows clients to move toward personal growth
Techniques	Empathic listening, providing unconditional positive regard, showing congruence
Practitioners	Psychologists, social workers, counselors

Ellis (1962) developed rational-emotive therapy, one of the earliest cognitive therapies, in response to what he saw as the failure of psychoanalysis to solve people's problems. Ellis objected to both the length and nondirective nature of psychoanalysis, insisting instead that therapists should set goals and that therapy should be brief and problem oriented.

Rational-emotive therapy views psychological problems as a result of people's irrational beliefs. Such beliefs lead people to unrealistic views of themselves and the world, and when these expectations go unmet, people make themselves miserable. Rational-emotive therapy attempts to change these irrational thoughts and assumes that a change in cognitions will produce changes in emotions and behavior. Correcting these irrational beliefs is the basic goal of rational-emotive therapy.

Aaron Beck (1985) developed a cognitive therapy specifically for depression, which concentrates on the distorted, self-defeating thoughts that accompany depression. Beck contended that depressed people overgeneralize personal failures into the belief that they are worthless, and that they explain positive occurrences as exceptions to the general rule of failure. Depressed people also magnify the enormity of negative events, seeing these events as catastrophic and unchangeable. Selective perception is another cognition that adds to depression, causing depressed people to notice the negative elements of their surroundings and ignore the positive ones. These distortions of thinking magnify and maintain negative cognitions and thus perpetuate depression.

Beck's cognitive therapy attempts to help clients change their negative thinking patterns by testing the beliefs to evaluate their validity. Rational-emotive therapy attempts to confront irrational beliefs with logic, but Beck's cognitive therapy is less directive and more experiential. Rather than arguing against such cognitions, Beck might formulate ways for clients to evaluate their thought processes and test their accuracy. Lack of pleasure is often a prominent component of depression, and Beck's cognitive therapy urges depressed people to introduce pleasurable experiences into their lives.

The headline story for this chapter presented John Gray's Mars & Venus approach to couples therapy. That technique is not one of the cognitive therapies, but it probably fits into this category better than in any other. The reason for the poor fit is that Gray's approach is not a formal therapy: It has no research or basis in psychological theory. Gray contended that he devised his planetary approach to couples counseling through his experience rather than through any research-based conceptualization.

Table 15.3 summarizes cognitive therapies. These therapies, such as Beck's cognitive therapy, assume that cognitions underlie psychological problems and that changing cognitions will change behavior. Rather than concentrating on behavior itself, these therapies concentrate on thoughts. Another therapeutic orientation takes an alternative approach—behavior modification emphasizes behavior rather than cognitions.

Behavior Modification

Behavior modification arose from laboratory research in psychology on the process of learning (Kantrowitz & Ballou, 1992). In exploring learning principles, researchers discovered that the principles of operant conditioning—reinforcement and punishment—are powerful forces in determining behavior. Not only do these principles apply to the nonhuman animals commonly used in laboratories, but they also apply to humans and their complex behaviors. As applied to behavior problems, behavior modification theory holds that such behaviors are learned and maintained by reinforcement and punishment, and application of these two principles can change unacceptable behavior.

Behavior modification strives to replace inappropriate or deviant behaviors with other, healthier behavior patterns through operant conditioning. Although both have been used in behavior modification programs, reinforcement for desirable behavior is more common than punishment for undesirable behavior.

Behavior modification is more specific and task-oriented than talk-based psychotherapies. For example, behavior modification is often used for various skills training, such as developing assertiveness, dealing with phobias, or changing eating patterns. In such programs, a client "learns a repertoire of behavior likely to produce desirable consequences in specific situations" (Blechman, 1980, p. 225). Women are the most common clients for behavior modification; they most often seek treatment for assertiveness problems, eating disorders, depression, and phobias.

Cognitive behavior therapy is a variation of behavior modification that incorporates the concept that cognition is an important factor in behavior, and the application of principles of reinforcement is used to bring about behavioral changes (Fodor, 1988). As with behavior modification, this therapeutic approach assumes that problems are the result of learned patterns of maladaptive behavior.

TABLE 15.3 Elements of Cognitive Therapy

Category	Description
Underlying source of problems	Irrational beliefs
Cause of problems	Application of irrational beliefs to personal circumstances
Immediate source of problems	The problem that brings a person to therapy
Goal of therapy	To change irrational beliefs to more rational beliefs
Techniques	Confronting and disputing irrational beliefs; testing the validity of negative cognitions
Practitioners	Psychologists, social workers, counselors

The process of cognitive behavior therapy typically differs from behavior modification in several ways, however. Rather than concentrating on behavior and ignoring internal cognitive processes, cognitive behavior therapy attempts to change thought patterns and thereby change behavior. This therapy tends to be more collaborative than behavior modification, with the client playing an active role. Client and therapist cooperate to establish goals, and the client, rather than the therapist, may monitor and reward the desired behavior. Table 15.4 summarizes behavior modification and cognitive behavior therapy.

Behavior modification and cognitive behavior therapy have been used as alternatives to more traditional therapies and differ from the psychoanalytic and humanistic approaches. The behavior modification approach emphasizes specific problems and the need to analyze the behavior that contributes to the problem. This behavior-oriented emphasis is also important in knowing when and how to apply reinforcement to change maladaptive to more adaptive behaviors. Therefore, behavior modification and cognitive behavior therapy represent different approaches to understanding and treating problem behavior.

Some therapists use behavior modification and cognitive behavior therapy with all clients and for all problems. Many therapists, however, take a more eclectic approach, using a variety of techniques rather than adhering to a single therapy orientation. These therapists argue that an eclectic approach offers them the opportunity to choose from a variety of approaches, fitting the problem and the client to the approach.

Medical Therapies

Talk-based psychotherapies and behavior modification are practiced by psychologists, social workers, counselors, and psychiatrists, but psychiatrists and other physicians can also use medical therapies for behavior problems. Psychoactive drugs are the most common of the medical therapies, but **electroconvulsive therapy** is also a medical approach to behavior problems. These medical therapies take the approach of altering brain functioning in order to change thoughts and behavior, but the exact mechanisms of the therapeutic benefits for both psychoactive drugs and electroconvulsive therapy are not completely understood. Nonetheless, physicians may use these therapies in conjunction with psychotherapy or alone.

Since the 1950s, both the use of and the number of psychoactive drugs has increased. Psychiatrists now use psychoactive drugs to treat schizophrenia, depression, and anxiety disorders.

TABLE 15.4 Elements of Behavior Modification and Cognitive Behavior Therapy

Category	Description
Underlying source of problems	None
Cause of problems	Behavior that is not adaptive or successful in specific situations
Immediate source of problems	The problem that brings a person to therapy
Goal of therapy	To change behavior (or cognitions that underlie behavior) to more acceptable alternative behaviors
Techniques	Reinforcement for acceptable behaviors, desensitization for phobias, assertiveness training
Practitioners	Psychologists, social workers, counselors

Women receive more drug prescriptions than men, and this difference is higher for both psychoactive as well as other types of drugs. Over 30 years ago, a review of the patterns of prescription psychoactive drug use in Canada, the United States, and the United Kingdom showed a consistently higher rate of use for women (Cooperstock, 1970). In addition, this review revealed evidence for both differences and similarities in patterns of drug use for men and women. The similarities included a higher rate of use for both women and men not in the workforce. The differences included a greater use of tranquilizers by women during early adulthood and middle age, compared to men's use of tranquilizers, which peaked at older ages.

Since that review, the prescription of psychoactive drugs has increased for both men and women, but the pattern remains similar (Ashton, 1991; Simoni-Wastila, 2000). The trend in psychiatry is toward a greater use of drug therapy and a decline in talk-based therapy. New drugs continue to appear for the treatment of schizophrenia, anxiety disorders, and depression, and women in North America and Europe have been prescribed psychoactive drugs 1.5 to 2 times more often than men.

Advertising of pharmaceuticals is one possible reason for overprescription of drugs. Drug company representatives and advertisements are major sources of information for physicians about drugs (Russell, 1995). An analysis of drug advertising (Nikelly, 1994) showed that the advertisements for drugs for depression tended to depict women far more often than men, to show women in stereotypical ways, to present depression as a medical problem, and to ignore the social contexts of depression. For example, one advertisement showed a color photograph of a well-ordered kitchen superimposed over a black-and-white photograph of a disorderly kitchen, with the message that the drug allowed patients to get back to their normal kitchen activities. Such drug advertisements convey not only the impression that female patients should receive such drugs, but also that these drugs are the best approach to treating depression, despite the evidence that occupational, marital, economic, and social factors contribute to the problem (see Chapter 14).

The use of electrical shock to alter behavior became common during the 1940s and remains in use today. This therapy involves delivering electric shocks to the brain, and the resulting convulsions have a therapeutic effect. Although the reasons for the beneficial effects remain unclear and serious side effects can occur, electroconvulsive therapy is now used almost exclusively for depression in patients who have failed to respond to antidepressant drugs (USDHHS, 1999b). Because a majority of the cases of depression occur in women, they are the most frequent recipients of this therapy.

Table 15.5 summarizes medical therapies. Despite the growth of medically based treatments for behavior problems, this approach is controversial. Drugs and electroconvulsive

TABLE 15.5 Elements of Medical Therapies

Category	Description
Underlying source of problems	Biological or biochemical abnormalities
Cause of problems	Chemical or biological malfunction in brain
Immediate source of problems	The problem that brings a person to therapy
Goal of therapy	To change biological functioning
Techniques	Psychoactive drugs, surgery, electroconvulsive therapy
Practitioners	Psychiatrists and other physicians

shock alter behavior and sometimes bring about substantial improvements, but both carry risks for serious side effects. In addition, these therapies do not cure mental disorders, but rather decrease or diminish the severity of symptoms. These effects can be beneficial, but not permanent; the symptoms tend to reappear when patients stop taking the drugs, and the therapeutic effects of electroconvulsive therapy rarely last for more than a few months (USDHHS, 1999b). Psychoactive drugs, like other drugs, can cause serious side effects, and electroconvulsive therapy typically produces some memory loss. The benefits of medical treatments can outweigh the risks for some people, but the risks exist.

Accusations of Gender Bias in Therapy

Psychoanalytic therapy and the Freudian theory and on which it is based have come under heavy criticism for their sexism (as Chapter 5 presented). Traditional therapy was designed primarily by men to treat women (Levant, 1990). The cultural views of gender roles during the late 1800s came to be incorporated into psychoanalysis, so the cases treated by Freud and his colleagues reflect men's views of women and their problems during that era. Freud's behavior in treating Dora, one of his most famous case studies, exemplified his mistreatment of female patients and the sexism of his system (Hare-Mustin, 1983); he refused to listen to or believe her and treated her as a child. Critics have long argued that psychotherapy in general and psychoanalysis in particular have failed to meet the needs of female patients.

The American Psychological Association's Task Force on Sex Bias and Sex-Role Stereotyping in Psychotherapeutic Practice (Brodsky & Holroyd, 1975) listed the sexist use of psychoanalytic concepts as one of the four main causes of gender bias in therapy. The gender bias in psychoanalysis comes from the notion that female development is a variation of male development, and that girls' perceptions of their gender inadequacy is a critical element in personality development. Freud and his followers accepted men as the standard and women as deviating from normal psychological development—a deviation that could never meet the male standard. Thus, critics have argued that psychoanalysis is inherently gender biased. This bias extends not only to psychoanalytic therapy, but also to all of the other therapies that have accepted Freudian concepts, which includes some (but not all) of the other talk-based psychotherapies.

Neither humanistic nor cognitive therapy is inherently gender biased in the way that psychoanalysis is, but both emphasize personal rather than social and environmental factors in functioning (Lerman, 1992). Such neglect makes client-centered counseling inadequate for women due to its emphasis on the individual and its failure to take the social and political aspects of personal problems into account (Waterhouse, 1993). By stressing the individual and orienting counseling toward the "here and now," women can be made to accept responsibility for the problem behavior of others, thus intensifying, rather than diminishing, their problems.

The practices of humanistic and cognitive therapy can become gender-biased if therapists apply their own personal values to therapy situations. Although not part of the therapy process, therapists might impose their personal values when they encourage their clients to adhere to traditional gender roles as a way to handle their problems. Such therapists may encourage clients to adopt more traditional gender roles, and such prescriptions are sexist.

Behavior modification is value free and has no theoretical component related to gender. Any behavior can be the target for modification, however, and the choice of which behaviors to encourage or discourage can reflect traditional or nontraditional values. Although behavior modification is not inherently gender biased, its practice can also be sexist (Blechman, 1980). Critics (Kantrowitz & Ballou, 1992) fear that behavior modification can and has been used to enforce women's conformity rather than their personal development.

Medical therapies have also been the target of criticisms of sexist bias. As Chapter 13 detailed, women and men receive different levels of treatment in the health care system. Physicians tend to take men's symptom reports more seriously than similar reports from women, and they tend to attribute women's complaints to psychological rather than physical causes. This tendency toward overdiagnosis of women and underdiagnosis of men results in inappropriate psychological treatment for women and a lack of appropriate psychological treatment for men.

Women are more likely to receive prescriptions for psychoactive drugs than men are, a pattern that has persisted since the 1960s (Ashton, 1991; Cooperstock, 1970). Some of these prescriptions are unnecessary, and both women and men may be overmedicated with psychoactive drugs (Ashton, 1991). Table 15.6 summarizes the potential sources of bias in the various types of therapy.

In an early and vehement indictment of gender bias in diagnosis and therapy, Phyllis Chesler (1972) argued that diagnosis has been used to identify women who deviate from their traditional gender roles and that therapy has been used to restore women to those roles. Chesler contended that women experience problems when they either conform too little or too much to traditional gender roles, and that therapy is a process used to reimpose the traditional feminine role. Women may behave in many deviant ways, but when they fail to be subservient and domestic, they are sometimes labeled as needing therapy.

This therapy may be of any variety, but according to Chesler, all therapies seek to restore women to the traditional female gender role. One of the respondents to a survey by the American Psychological Association (APA Task Force on Sex Bias and Sex-Role Stereotyping in Psychotherapeutic Practice, 1978) confirmed Chesler's view by saying, "I have had women report to me that they could not continue in therapy because the objective seemed to be for them to learn to adjust better to their roles as wives, mothers, daughters (underlings of one kind or another), and they needed to become free persons" (p. 1,122).

By surveying female psychologists, the APA Task Force (Brodsky & Holroyd, 1975) determined that sexist bias exists in four main areas of the practice of psychotherapy. As mentioned previously, sexist use of psychoanalytic concepts was one of the four. The other

TABLE 15.6 Sources of Gender Bias in Therapies for Behavior Problems

Type of Therapy	Source of Potential Gender Bias
Psychoanalysis	Psychoanalytic theory assumes that women are inferior.
Humanistic	Therapists may apply personal standards that are sexist; therapy focuses on the individual and ignores the social context of personal problems.
Cognitive	Therapists may apply personal standards that are sexist; therapy fails to address the social context of personal problems.
Behavior modification	Therapists may choose to reinforce traditional gender-related behaviors.
Medical	Women and men are diagnosed and treated according to stereotypical and traditional values.

areas included fostering traditional sex roles, having biased expectations concerning women, devaluing women's potential, and responding to women as sex objects, including therapists' sexual exploitation of clients. As the headline story detailed, Gray's Mars & Venus approach to couples therapy is guilty of fostering traditional gender roles and having biased expectations concerning women, making it unacceptable according to standards for nonsexist therapy.

Men are also subject to gender bias in therapy when practitioners urge the adoption of gender-typical behaviors. When a male patient in one study described a lifestyle that included providing housework and child care, therapists tended to concentrate on these atypical behaviors, emphasizing the gender role as a potential source of problems (Robertson & Fitzgerald, 1990). A second male patient who described his role as more typical of a breadwinner received no comments on his gender role behaviors as a potential source of problems. A more recent study (Guanipa & Woolley, 2000) confirmed the existence of gender biases in marriage and family therapy.

Counselors are likely to view both men and women stereotypically in terms of emotionality: women as overly emotional and men as lacking in emotion (Heesacker et al., 1999). These views influence the process of counseling when therapists blame husbands rather than wives for marital problems and when therapists set goals consistent with their stereotypes. Such a bias appeared in a study (Fowers, Applegate, Tredinnick, & Slusher, 1996) in which therapists did not encourage men to develop their expressiveness as much as they encouraged women to do so. In both work-related and relationship situations, therapists took an instrumental view concerning men's problems, but their orientation to women's problems was a more situation-specific mixture of instrumental and expressive views. Therefore, evidence exists that the practice of therapy is not value-free, and that therapy tends to work toward preserving traditional values, especially for men.

Gender Issues in Therapy

Besides therapist bias, treatment presents several other gender issues. One issue is the suitability of various types of therapy for women or men. Although women more often seek counseling and psychotherapy and tend to be better at the therapy tasks involved, their needs may not be met by the process itself. The gender bias in psychoanalytic approaches and the potential for gender bias in other therapies have presented important issues for therapy, and several alternative approaches have endeavored to correct these biases.

Recognizing the potential for bias in therapy has led to the notion that good therapy should be nonsexist (APA Task Force on Sex Bias, 1978), and professionals have worked toward the principles underlying nonsexist therapy. Feminist alternatives to therapy arose from the belief that ignoring gender issues does not make therapy gender fair. The contention that nonsexist therapy is not an adequate answer to the gender bias in therapy prompted the development of therapies that are specifically feminist, and oriented toward women's problems as well as practiced exclusively by women. "The sexism in so-called nonsexist brands of psychotherapy may be less blatant, but any approach to psychotherapy that conceptualizes women's social problems as personal pathology and promotes 'cures' for women's distress primarily through individual personal change strengthens the patriarchal status quo" (Rawlings, 1993, p. 90).

Feminist Therapy

A review of the history of feminist therapy (Enns, 1993, 1997) traced it to the early 1970s and the women's rights movement. Women, both inside and outside the mental health care professions, began to criticize therapy for its traditional goals and for its power in maintaining the status quo for women. Some women in professions that provide mental health care then responded by attempting to combine feminist goals with therapy; their results diverge from traditional therapy in several ways.

Two important principles underlie the practice of feminist therapy (Gilbert, 1980). The first principle is one borrowed from the feminist movement and states that "the personal is political." That is, personal experience is embedded within the social and political structure of the society, making the problems of any individual woman a reflection of the wider society.

Feminist therapy strives to enact this principle in several ways. Clients explore the influence of social roles on their individual behaviors, examining the difference between what they have been taught about appropriate behavior and what is actually appropriate. During feminist therapy, women have a forum for validating their experiences as women, including the situations and problems that are unique to women, and "Feminist therapists help clients see that their problems have social as well as personal causes" (Cammaert & Larsen, 1988, p. 15).

Feminist therapy is political, striving to bring about change in society. The early feminist therapists were politically active in the women's movement, and, indeed, such activity was a requirement for declaring oneself a feminist therapist. These therapists sought to bring about changes in the status of women and advocated political activism for their clients. Their position was that significant change was not possible in women's lives through personal changes in psychological adjustment; only change in society and in women's roles would lead to beneficial changes for women. Contemporary feminist psychotherapists may not emphasize the political as strongly as the founders did (Morrow & Hawxhurst, 1998), but feminist therapists have tried to maintain the emphasis on politics by continuing to discuss power issues as part of their therapy sessions (Marecek & Kravetz, 1998).

The second principle of feminist therapy states that therapists and clients should form an egalitarian relationship rather than the traditional therapeutic relationship in which therapists are powerful and dominant and clients are subordinate. This principle ensures that clients understand the types of therapy that they will receive and that they know about the options for other sources of assistance (Hare-Mustin, Marecek, Kaplan, & Liss-Levinson, 1979). This level of informed consent represents a consumer orientation to therapy, and feminist therapy tries to promote such an orientation.

The equal relationship between client and therapist also aims to "demystify" the therapist as a person who has special knowledge and power (Gilbert, 1980). The rationale for this position lies in the attempt to counter the typical subordinate position that women occupy and to promote the belief that feminist therapy is an appropriate place for women to begin to feel a sense of personal power. Research (Simi & Mahalik, 1997) has indicated that feminist therapists endorse more openness and self-disclosure with their patients than psychodynamic and other therapists.

Feminist therapists participate in therapy by modeling appropriate behaviors for their female clients and by sharing personal experiences with their clients. This degree of personal openness and the advocacy of political activity on the part of the therapist differentiates the role of feminist therapists from therapists in most traditional therapies. Feminist therapists consider these differences essential to their approach.

Theoretical Orientations of Feminist Therapy

Feminist therapists hold a variety of theoretical orientations. Indeed, feminist therapists have followed theories as diverse as psychoanalysis and behavior modification and all varieties of humanistic and cognitive therapies. The goals of feminist therapy differ somewhat, depending on the orientation of the therapist, and a common element of all feminist therapists is their striving to modify therapy techniques to make them more compatible with feminist goals (Hill & Ballou, 1998). These efforts have produced similarities in the goals of all feminist therapy: "The emphasis becomes growth rather than adjustment or remediation, development rather than blame or illness" (Cammaert & Larsen, 1988, p. 23).

With the amount of criticism of psychoanalysis for its sexism, it is ironic that psychoanalytic therapy is the orientation adopted by many feminist therapists. Yet revisions to traditional psychoanalytic theory now make it an appropriate basis for feminist therapy (Daugherty & Lees, 1988). These revisions retain the emphasis on early childhood development and the importance of unconscious forces in personality development and functioning but include the revised view from feminist psychoanalytic theorists (Chodorow, 1978; Dinnerstein, 1976).

The feminist psychoanalytic approach rejects the notion that a woman's personality is a variation on the male pattern; instead it attempts to explain both. These theorists have rejected the notion that women are developmentally inferior to men, specifically the beliefs that anatomy is destiny, that women unconsciously desire a penis, that female sexuality is oriented toward bearing sons, and that normal women are masochistic, dependent, narcissistic, and passive.

Feminist psychoanalytic therapy uses many of the techniques of traditional psychoanalysis, including "uncovering and exploring the traumatic memories and painful affects associated with childhood that develop into symptoms and psychological conflicts" (Daugherty & Lees, 1988, p. 78). Both versions of psychoanalysis have as their goal the process of uncovering unconscious conflicts and bringing this material to consciousness so that clients can make more reasonable decisions about their behaviors. Feminist psychoanalytic therapists share the principles of feminist therapy, conveying their feminist values to their clients and attempting to build egalitarian counseling relationships.

Feminist adaptations of cognitive, behavioral, and cognitive behavior therapy are easier than feminist adaptations of psychoanalysis. This family of therapies includes the behavioral treatment of phobias (Fodor, 1988), which was one of the earliest forms of behavior therapy. Women are the most common clients for such treatment. Cognitive behavior therapy is the integration of behavioral and cognitive therapy with research from cognitive and social psychology. During the 1970s, when feminist therapy arose, cognitive behavior therapy also gained prominence, and the goals of feminist theory were integrated into this therapy. The cognitive component of this therapy was especially compatible with feminist therapy; the goals of analyzing the social system and restructuring thought processes are consistent with an understanding of the personal as political.

For example, a woman who is stressed by her work situation might be urged to consider her supervisor's sexism rather than blaming herself for her difficulty in obtaining promotions.

Cognitive behavior therapy has social learning theory as its basis, with its view that the environment shapes behavior. This position is compatible with feminist therapy's view that the social context of behavior is essential to understanding the behavior.

Although behavior and cognitive behavior therapies are often selected for assertiveness and other skills training, these therapies are not the most ideal for feminist therapy. Both approaches to therapy view change as the responsibility of clients, so therapists must be vigilant to maintain a cooperative rather than dominant relationship with clients. Furthermore, these therapies originated and are used most successfully with White, middle-class clients.

Clients of Feminist Therapy

During the early years of feminist therapy, the majority of clients were White, middle-class women—a demographic description that matches many of the clients who seek therapy. Questions arose over the suitability of feminist therapy for all women: After all, some women who seek therapy do not endorse feminist goals, and many are not White or middle-class. Is feminist therapy appropriate for all women? And is it ever appropriate for men?

A study of women in feminist and traditional therapy evaluated the relative effectiveness of each (Marecek, Kravetz, & Finn, 1979). The results indicated that women who identified themselves as members of the women's movement evaluated feminist therapy as more helpful than traditional therapy, but women who did not identify themselves as part of the women's movement found the two types of therapy to be equally helpful. These results suggest that feminist therapy has the possibility for wider appeal than traditional therapy does.

Some women express a preference for feminist counselors, particularly college women seeking help for career counseling or sexual assault concerns (Enns & Hackett, 1990; Hackett, Enns, & Zetzer, 1992). In several studies, women showed some reluctance to see radical feminist therapists, and clients tended to prefer more moderate feminist therapists over traditional or nonsexist therapists, even those women with traditional gender role values.

Although men may seem to be unlikely clients for feminist therapy, this approach holds potential benefits for men (Ganley, 1988). Traditional therapy adheres to a gendered model of mental health that casts women as deficient for their femininity and that attempts to reconcile men with their role as breadwinners and competitors. Many feminist therapists adhere to an androgynous model that holds both masculine and feminine characteristics as beneficial to mental health.

Research has shown that a mixture of instrumental and expressive characteristics is related to positive mental health. In a study of masculine and feminine characteristics, the addition of expressiveness to instrumentality for men significantly added to the prediction of mental health (Sharpe, Heppner, & Dixon, 1995). That is, men who showed the expressiveness traditionally associated with femininity exhibited greater well-being than men who showed only the instrumentality traditionally associated with masculinity. This combination is also related to mental health in women (Hunt, 1993). Extremes of instrumentality or expressiveness are negatively related to psychological well-being (Helgeson, 1994; Saragovi, Koestner, Di Dio, & Aubé, 1997). Therefore, the combination of characteristics and behaviors that feminist therapists encourage in women and men is related to psychological well-being and mental health.

By taking this approach with male clients, feminist therapists attempt to develop relationship skills, appropriate emotionality, empathy, and communication skills—skills that men often lack due to their masculine socialization. Feminist therapy with men also works toward altering views of gender roles and seeks to change men's attitudes concerning what is appropriate for both women and men. By examining and questioning traditional gender roles, feminist therapy with men upholds the principle that the personal is political, one of the basic principles of feminist therapy. Most feminist therapists, however, believe that the practice of feminist therapy is restricted to women. Male therapists who adopt the principles of feminist therapy are labeled "profeminist." With either male or female therapists, male clients in feminist therapy can find both appropriate modeling and support through participation in group therapy.

Therefore, feminist therapy is appropriate for a wide range of people. From its beginnings as a radical therapy for women who were discontent with traditional therapy (both as therapists and as clients), feminist therapy has broadened its scope and clientele. Studies have shown that women with both traditional and feminist beliefs can profit from feminist therapy and that feminists are likely to have problems with traditional therapy. Its emphasis on the political and social aspects of mental health makes feminist therapy well suited for a variety of clients. In addition, men can benefit from feminist therapy by learning to develop communication and nurturing skills not associated with the masculine gender role. By adopting more androgynous behavior, both men and women can overcome gender role stereotyping and can gain greater flexibility in their lives.

Therapy with Men

Feminist therapy may be appropriate for men, but men rarely seek this type of therapy. Indeed, men are reluctant to seek even traditional types of psychotherapy. In seeking therapy, women outnumber men by a margin of two to one (Good, Dell, & Mintz, 1989). Although therapy tends to uphold traditional gender roles, the format of therapy emphasizes behaviors associated with the feminine rather than the masculine role, and both clients and counselors experience difficulties in the counseling process due to male clients' stereotypically masculine behavior (Brooks, 1998).

Male gender role expectations put men in situations of conflict and strain because those expectations hold that men should strive for power, control, and achievement (O'Neil, 1981; Pleck, 1981). Men can become obsessed with competition and success, which requires dedication to these goals. In addition, these strivings require that men reject all aspects of femininity, resulting in restricted emotionality as well as distrust and fear of women. These attitudes create problems for men in forming intimate relationships and in fulfilling their full potential as humans and, in addition, they present special problems for therapists in counseling men.

Investigations into the relationship between masculine gender role and attitudes toward seeking psychological counseling have revealed that stereotypical masculine beliefs negatively relate to willingness to seek help (Good, Dell, & Mintz, 1989). Furthermore, the emphasis on striving for success and restriction of emotional expression relate to depression, putting these men in greater need of help but with more reluctance to seek help (Good & Wood, 1995). Masculine socialization can keep men away from therapy (Brooks, 1998; Robertson & Fitzgerald, 1992). Men who show emotion, express their vulnerability, and seek help from others fail to fit the masculine gender role, and all of these elements are necessary for psychotherapy. John Robertson and Louise Fitzgerald wrote, "Many approaches to personal counseling require that clients bring a sense of self-awareness to the counseling room; yet men appear to be socialized away from self-awareness and encouraged to control (or hide) their feelings" (1992, p. 240). The masculine gender role demands that men hide their vulnerabilities, whereas counseling calls for disclosing them. Counseling urges clients to share their problems with other persons, and men have been socialized to hide their problems and approach problem solving in an intellectual rather than an emotional way.

Thus, counseling is a process that men might avoid. Studies have shown a negative relationship between traditional masculine attitudes and the willingness to seek psychological counseling (Good et al., 1989; Robertson & Fitzgerald, 1992). Men who rigidly held to stereotypical masculinity were less willing to seek counseling that involved emotional expression than less traditional men (Wisch, Mahalik, Hayes, & Nutt, 1995). In addition, men who adhere to stereotypical masculinity also found counseling more appealing when the process was presented in cognitive, problem-solving terms rather than as avenues of emotional expression.

One critic (Kipnis, 1991) maintained that some of men's reluctance to seek therapy comes from bias against men by mental health care professionals. This criticism contends that psychology has responded to women's needs by addressing women's problems, but no such changes have taken place for men. Examples of this bias included men who, along with their wives, had sought therapy and who had felt that the therapists had aligned themselves with the wives but had failed to see the men's points of view. These comments are consistent with the contention that a female communication style has become the language of psychotherapy, and this situation may alienate some men (Tavris, 1992). Table 15.7 presents some of the barriers that can deter men from seeking and succeeding in counseling.

Psychological services can be made more approachable for men through changing the description of those services (Robertson & Fitzgerald, 1992). When traditionally oriented men in this study read a brochure describing psychological service offerings in terms of classes, workshops, seminars, and videotapes, they rated these services as more attractive than when the services were presented as belonging to a college counseling center. This study demonstrated that masculine values may be barriers to seeking counseling and that traditional men may be more willing to seek counseling services that are presented in a way that is compatible with their masculine values.

Counseling offers advantages for men: "Men need counseling because many of them are unhappy, dissatisfied with their lives, and damaged by their roles" (Scher, 1981, p. 199).

TABLE 15.7 Barriers to Counseling Men

Help-seeking is discouraged by elements of the masculine gender role:

- Men should not require help.
- Men should deny and suppress their emotions.
- Men should not express their vulnerability.

Therapy often takes a talk-based rather than an action-based or intellectual approach to problem solving.

Emotional sharing is difficult for many men.

Men may believe that counselors are biased against men's needs.

Psychology has responded by addressing women's needs better than it does men's needs.

Presentation of psychological services may be in a format that does not appeal to men.

Men need help in relinquishing some of the negative elements of the masculine role so that they can learn to understand the value of being in touch with their emotions, ask for assistance when they need it, and encourage freedom from constraining gender roles in themselves and in others.

Gender Aware Therapy

Can therapy meet the needs of both women and men while not discriminating against either? Gender aware therapy (GAT) aims to integrate concepts of male and female gender development with the revised attitudes toward psychotherapy proposed by feminist therapists (Good, Gilbert, & Scher, 1990). This therapy approach has both similarities to and differences from nonsexist and feminist therapies. This approach acknowledges that society's conception of mental health is changing to a more androgynous standard, in which conforming to traditional standards is no longer a desirable goal for either gender.

The originators of GAT (Good et al., 1990) claimed that five principles should be part of all types of therapy. Gender aware therapy has its foundation in feminist therapy, and its five principles distinguish it from feminist therapy by extending and enlarging that approach. The first principle urges therapists to consider gender an integral aspect of counseling and mental health. Gender aware therapy "incorporates an understanding of gender effects and sexism in its therapeutic strategies and goals" (Good et al., 1990, p. 377). Nonsexist therapy strives for equal treatment of men and women by ignoring gender. However, the differences in women's and men's lives make ignoring gender unrealistic, and many issues raised in therapy relate to gender and gender roles.

The second principle of gender aware therapy echoes "the personal is political" basis of feminist therapy—it holds that consideration of the societal context of problems is essential. The third principle also incorporates the political activism of feminist therapy by urging therapists to question traditional gender roles, both for themselves and for their clients. The fourth principle urges gender aware therapists to form collaborative relationships with their clients, and the fifth principle directs therapists to respect their clients' freedom to choose. Table 15.8 presents these five points.

This freedom to choose includes the choice to adopt or reject traditional gender roles. Both traditional and nontraditional gender roles can be rigid and confining, and GAT urges therapists to allow their clients to find a combination that will enhance clients' full development. Gender aware therapy "eschews notions of political correctness" (Good et al., 1990, p. 377), urging clients to explore, find, and choose what is right for them. "In summary,

TABLE 15.8 Five Principles of Gender Aware Therapy

1. Regard the conception of gender as an integral aspect of counseling and mental health.
2. Consider problems within their societal context.
3. Actively seek to change gender injustice experienced by women and men.
4. Emphasize development of collaborative therapeutic relationships.
5. Respect clients' freedom to choose.

SOURCE: Based on "Gender aware therapy: A synthesis of feminist therapy and knowledge about gender," 1990, by G. E. Good, L. A. Gilbert, & M. Scher, *Journal of Counseling & Development, 68,* p. 377.

GAT supports the notion that particular behaviors, preferences, and attributes need not be categorized as falling into the domain of traditional or nontraditional, male or female, gender roles. Rather, what GAT advocates is simply choice, despite gender conceptions or political correctness" (p. 377).

Research with counselors in training (Brems & Schlottmann, 1988) indicated that the aims of gender aware therapy may be feasible. By studying graduate students in counseling and clinical psychology (who would soon be therapists), these researchers found that gender-bound definitions of mental health have decreased; gender role stereotyping was almost entirely absent in the counselors in training. These findings present an optimistic picture that therapists are now being trained who are less bound by gender stereotypes, for both themselves and their clients. Such therapists are necessary for gender aware therapy.

Therefore, gender aware therapy is an extension of feminist therapy, which attempts to incorporate the awareness of gender and its far-reaching implications for people's lives and yet emphasize individual needs. Many therapists have acknowledged that gender-fair counseling and therapy are imperative, and this approach may fulfill those needs.

Sexual Exploitation in Therapy

The preponderance of female clients and male therapists poses a situation in which gender is nearly always either an overt or covert issue in the therapy process (see "According to the Media/According to the Research"). The APA Task Force on Sex Bias and Sex-Role Stereotyping in Psychotherapeutic Practice (Brodsky & Holroyd, 1975) identified the treatment of clients as sex objects as a gender-related problem in psychotherapy. Erotic or sexual behavior with clients is included in this category. Sex between therapist and client is not unusual. Beginning with the founding fathers of psychoanalytic therapy and continuing today, clients are sexually exploited by the therapists to whom they come for help.

During the 1970s, a survey of licensed psychologists in clinical practice (Holroyd & Brodsky, 1977) disclosed attitudes toward sexual and nonsexual physical contact with clients. Nonsexual physical contact was acceptable under some circumstances to 27% of the therapists, but a large majority of the therapists reported that erotic contact between clients and therapists would *not* be beneficial to clients. Significantly more female than male therapists (88% versus 70%) believed that such contact would not be a beneficial component of therapy. Factors that contribute to therapists' willingness to enter into sexual relationships with their clients are their lack of preparation for sexual attraction to clients and their denial of the harm that such relationships can exert (Pope, 1988; 2000).

The possibility of sexual attraction on the part of clients toward therapists and for therapists toward clients is an important concept in psychoanalytical treatment, but the knowledge of this possibility did not deter several prominent early psychotherapists from forming sexual relationships with their patients. Other theoretical bases for therapies do not include the likelihood of mutual attraction between therapist and client; thus therapists adhering to other approaches were not prepared to deal with the possibility that they may develop sexual feelings for their clients (Pope, 1988). Most professionals considered such relationships unacceptable and unprofessional. This attitude led to a denial of the existence of therapist–client sex. Initially, journals were reluctant to publish articles, and conventions were unwilling to feature presentations on the topic (Pope, 1988).

During the 1990s, sexual relationships between therapists and clients became a widely publicized issue, and the helping professions began to address this problem. Therapists receive training concerning ethics and the unacceptability of sexual contact with their clients, but the emphasis is usually on the unacceptability of such behavior, rather than on how to deal with sexual feelings that therapists may experience. A survey of psychology internship programs (Samuel & Gorton, 1998) showed that 99% of programs provided some training on this topic. However, only about half of the graduates of counseling psychology programs remembered how their programs addressed this issue, and only 60% of that half thought that their program's training was adequate (Blanchard & Lichtenberg, 1998).

Although some therapists believe that personal and sexual relationships with clients are therapeutic for clients, research indicates otherwise. A variety of negative effects befall clients who have participated in sexual relationships with their therapists (Luepker, 1999; Pope, 1988). Clients may not exhibit any immediate negative effects of sexual intimacy with their therapists, but evidence indicates that at least 90% will eventually experience negative effects. These effects include posttraumatic stress disorder, depression, suicide, substance abuse, disputed personal relationships, and career problems. The effects are stronger when the relationship occurs concurrently with therapy, but clients who begin relationships with their therapists after the termination of therapy are still at risk.

GENDERED VOICES

Of Course I've Felt Attracted to My Clients

Both a counseling intern and a counselor with 30 years of experience told me, "Of course I've felt attracted to some of my clients. I think it's almost inevitable." Both reported that the attraction made them very aware of the nature of the counseling relationship and how inappropriate these feelings were. Both also became very conscious about behaving so as to conceal signs of their attraction, because it was considered professionally unacceptable.

"Part of our training includes the ethical unacceptability of any type of personal relationship with clients, especially any sexual relationship. It's completely unacceptable," the counseling intern said. "So feeling attracted to a client raised flags and made me aware that I needed to be very careful about what I did. I didn't want to convey my feelings to my client, and I didn't want to let my feelings affect my counseling. It's a difficult situation and an inevitable conflict, I think."

The veteran counselor agreed. "It's practically inevitable, although I have been sexually attracted to very few of my clients. When I felt attracted, those feelings made counseling more difficult. I tried to conceal how I felt, which is dishonest, while remaining honest in all other respects. And I tried very hard to do a good job in counseling the client. It made the counseling relationship more difficult."

"Nothing in our training taught me how to deal with these feelings," the intern said. "A great deal was oriented toward the ethics of counseling, but not how to handle my feelings or situations in which clients express some attraction for me. It was all 'Don't do that,' but nothing about what to do. I wouldn't feel comfortable talking to my supervisor about my feelings because of the ethical prohibition. I know it's unreasonable to imagine that counselors won't feel attracted to clients, but it's so forbidden that I feel I shouldn't have or admit to the attraction. I know that I will think about how to avoid letting any client know about my attraction, but teaching me how to deal with such feelings and what to do—no, that was lacking in my training."

The experienced counselor said that his training included how to deal with clients' attraction to him but not his toward clients. "The whole issue of sexual exploitation of clients hadn't been publicized or addressed in counselor training, so those issues were not part of my training."

ACCORDING TO THE MEDIA…

Male Therapists Are Crazy or Evil, and Female Therapists Have Sex with Their Patients

The image of psychotherapists in movies is often vague and usually not flattering. The profession of therapists is often left unclear—whether they are psychiatrists, psychologists, psychoanalysts, psychiatric social workers, or some other profession (Greenberg, 1992). In addition, how therapists are portrayed is not at all flattering. Therapists in the movies usually fall into one of three categories: Dr. Dippy, Dr. Evil, or Dr. Wonderful (Schneider, 1987). Dr. Dippy first appeared in a short film in 1906 as the therapist who was crazier than the patients, and about 35% of movie therapists fit into this category. Dr. Evil also appeared early in film history in a 1908 movie, *The Criminal Hypnotist,* and about 15% of movie therapists (excluding those in horror movies) have harmful motives. Dr. Wonderful is the ideal therapist—effective, caring, and available. These Dr. Wonderfuls devote large amounts of time to their on-screen patients doing talk-based therapy and rarely asking for payment. The psychiatrist in *Ordinary People* (1980) and the counselor in *Good Will Hunting* (1998) are good examples of Dr. Wonderful. About 22% of movie therapists fall into this category.

Female therapists are more likely to be Dr. Wonderful than Dr. Evil or Dr. Dippy, but their screen portrayals differ from male therapists. Female therapists are likely to be single or unhappy in their marriages, and in the movies, female therapists often "help" their male patients by becoming their lovers (Gabbard, 2000). In *Spellbound* (1945), Ingrid Bergman portrayed a competent but sexually repressed psychiatrist who fell in love with Gregory Peck's amnesiac character. More recently, movies such as *The Prince of Tides* (1991), *Basic Instinct* (1992), and *Twelve Monkeys* (1995) depicted female therapists who formed sexual relationships with their clients.

In the movies, female therapists who have sex with their patients do not seem to violate any rules or suffer any negative consequences. The patients sustain no harm, and the therapists experience benefits by "finding their femininity" (Gabbard, 2000) and often by abandoning their professional careers (Greenberg, 1992). When male therapists have sex with their patients, the relationship is usually more problematic, but again, the extent to which such behavior violates codes or professional conduct and the harm that comes to patients remains off screen.

The therapist–client relationship is one of trust and intimacy, but when sexual intimacy becomes part of the relationship, a betrayal of the client's trust has occurred. Thus, impaired ability to trust is a potential lifelong problem (Pope, 1988). This situation often leaves clients feeling ambivalent; they experience rage and a longing to escape combined with a fear of separation from the therapist. Sexually exploited clients may also feel guilt, isolation, emptiness, and sexual confusion. In addition, they have trouble finding help, contacting an average of 2.36 professionals before finding assistance they consider satisfactory (Luepker, 1999). Therefore, clients often experience a variety of serious problems after sexual involvement with their therapists and seek subsequent help for problems.

The growing awareness of the sexual exploitation of clients by therapists has produced changes in the codes of ethics for all of the professions that provide mental health care (Vasquez & Kitchener, 1988). The ethical codes that govern psychiatrists, psychologists, social workers, and marriage and family therapists all specifically prohibit sexual activity between therapists and clients. Sexual exploitation of clients has been the most common of reported ethical violations by therapists, accounting for half of the complaints to state licensing boards (Marecek & Hare-Mustin, 1991).

ACCORDING TO THE RESEARCH…

Male Therapists Are More Likely Than Female Therapists to Form Sexual Relationships with Patients

Movie portrayals of therapists are inaccurate in a number of ways. Therapists are not as dramatic as movie portrayals, failing to meet the standards for Dr. Dippy, Dr. Evil, or even Dr. Wonderful. Effective, concerned therapists exist, but currently, few psychiatrists are involved in the talk-based treatment that Dr. Wonderful dispenses (Gabbard, 2000). Drug treatments have replaced psychotherapy for most psychiatrists, and all types of therapists charge for their services.

Research also indicates that sexual relationships with patients are substantially different than the movies depict. In an early study (Holroyd & Brodsky, 1977), a significant gender difference appeared in the percentage of therapists who reported any type of sexual contact with clients—10.9% of male therapists and 1.9% of female therapists had some kind of sexual contact. When considering only those therapists who admitted having intercourse with past or present clients, the survey showed that 8.1% of the male therapists and 1% of the female therapists acknowledged this behavior. Of those therapists who admitted at least one sexual relationship with a patient, 80% acknowledged more than one such relationship. This figure suggests that some therapists have formed a pattern of habitual sexual exploitation of their patients. In the movies, sexual relationships are usually the result of two people falling in love rather than a powerful therapist exploiting a vulnerable patient.

Research indicates that another pattern of sexual relationship occurs as a series of steps of violations of the boundary between client and therapist (Simon, 1999). That is, therapists begin to behave in ways that are more intimate and personal, which eventually leads to sex. This situation is more likely to occur in gradual steps, with clients who are victims of childhood sexual abuse, and with therapists who are in a sole private practice, rather than to occur in other configurations of clients and therapists (Somer & Saadon, 1999). This picture of sexually exploitative therapists contrasts sharply with the movie portrayal: Therapists who form sexual relationships with their clients are more often male than female, tend to engage in a series of exploitative relationships, often prey on vulnerable clients, and understand that their behavior is a violation of their code of professional conduct.

The Self-Help Movement

A growing lack of confidence in psychotherapy, mounting awareness of sexual exploitation of clients, and increased cost have led to reluctance to seek therapy on the part of thousands of people with personal problems. "Across the country, in hospitals, churches, empty offices, and even shopping malls, small groups of individuals assemble to cope collectively with their unique challenges" (Davison, Pennebaker, & Dickerson, 2000, p. 205). People in self-help groups meet to share similar problems, and in the process, they receive emotional support as well as information that can assist in helping them cope.

Self-help groups began to proliferate during the 1980s. The 1987 Surgeon General's Workshop on Self-Help and Public Health brought the benefits of self-help groups to the attention of an increased number of health care providers (Hedrick, 1995). In 1992, the number of self-help groups had grown to more than 500,000, and over 7 million people were involved. By the end of the 1990s, the number of people in the United States who would be involved in some type of self-help group at some time during their lives was estimated at 25 million, a number that exceeded those in other types of therapy programs (Davison et al., 2000). The

United States is not unique in this proliferation; self-help groups exist in growing numbers in all industrialized countries and in most other countries in the world (Katz, 1993).

The prototype for the self-help movement is Alcoholics Anonymous (AA). Founded in 1935 by two alcoholics who had stopped drinking, AA proclaimed that people with drinking problems could stay sober through the social support of others with similar problems (Robinson, 1979). The format is a meeting in which people acknowledge their alcoholism and seek the support of others to continue in the struggle to abstain from drinking, one day at a time. This approach to dealing with problem drinking has been enormously influential, both in the treatment of problem drinking and in the formation of other self-help support groups. For example, addictions and other compulsive disorders were the concerns of early support groups such as Narcotics Anonymous, Gamblers Anonymous, and Overeaters Anonymous, but support groups now exist for a wider variety of problems. "There are groups for almost every serious medical problem and almost every presenting problem that clinicians confront, plus groups for dozens of conditions virtually unserved by therapists" (Jacobs & Goodman, 1989, p. 537). The variety of problems around which self-help groups form is vast, and Table 15.9 presents examples of these problems.

The philosophy of the self-help approach is that people with similar problems can offer each other social support and information, which can be helpful and beneficial. Rather than consisting of therapists who direct the therapy and clients who take direction, self-help and support groups may not involve professional therapists and may have no designated leaders (Jacobs & Goodman, 1989). Other groups have professionals who consult or even participate in meetings (Davison et al., 2000). Groups vary in size from a few members who have formed their own group to large, nationally affiliated groups, and they vary in organization from no specified format to tightly scripted (Jacobs & Goodman, 1989). Although the concerns of people in these groups vary, the underlying philosophies are similar.

The success of self-help groups is due in part to the comfort that people feel from being with others whose experience is similar (Jacobs & Goodman, 1989). Because individuals in these groups are similar, empathy is facilitated. The similarities among participants may be an important factor that draws people to support groups, especially for people with certain problems. For example, people with AIDS are 250 times more likely to join a support group than people with hypertension, and breast cancer has about 40 times more support groups than heart disease (Davison et al., 2000). For disorders that have a social stigma or visible effects, support groups of similar others may be especially helpful.

The financial advantages of self-help groups are another factor in the growth of this approach. These groups may charge participants a minimal fee, although many of them charge nothing. With the growing emphasis on cost containment, health care professionals have begun to promote cooperation between medicine and self-help groups as one way to contain treatment costs (Wituk, Shepherd, Slavich, Warren, & Meissen, 2000).

Free therapy is certainly cost-effective, but is it effective? Very little research has compared the effectiveness of self-help to traditional therapy (Christensen & Jacobson, 1994). Difficulties arise from researcher bias against self-help treatment and participants who are involved in multiple types of therapy, which makes assessment of the self-help group difficult. Some evidence exists for the effectiveness for self-help groups (USDHHS, 1999b), and the cost difference makes self-help attractive to a wide range of participants. The ease of access to support groups is another attractive feature, and the growing accessibility of the Internet has created an even more accessible form of self-help: online support groups.

TABLE 15.9 Examples of Self-Help Groups and Problems Served

Problem	Group	Problem	Group
Alcoholism	Alcoholics Anonymous	Alcoholic parent	Ala-Teen
Breast cancer survivors	Bosom Buddies	Overeating	Overeaters Anonymous
Gambling	Gamblers Anonymous	Divorced parents	Parents without Partners
Substance abuse	Narcotics Anonymous	Heart attack survivors	Mended Hearts
Parental bereavement	Compassionate Friends	Down syndrome	Parents of Children with Down Syndrome
Love addiction	Women Who Love Too Much		

Other Problems Served by Groups	
Cancer survivors	Incest survivors
Persons with AIDS	Adult children of alcoholics
Partners of persons with AIDS	Rape victims
Former dieters	Parents of children with cancer
Parents of children with diabetes	Parents of children with attention deficit hyperactivity disorder
Heart transplant patients	Persons with multiple sclerosis
Anorexics	Persons with arthritis
Parents and families of anorexics	Medical and psychological problems associated with being homosexual
People with disfigurements, including specific types such as victims of burns and neurofibromatosis	Impotence
Chronic money management problems	Parents of children with schizophrenia
Psychological problems associated with retirement	Sexual addiction
Alopecia (radical hair loss)	Narcolepsy (sleep disorder)
Couples with fertility problems	Codependency
Agoraphobia	
Caretakers of Alzheimer's patients	

Online Support Groups

Internet sites are available for a number of problems, allowing people without easy access to groups in their hometowns to meet in cyberspace. Preliminary evidence (Weinberg, Uken, Schmale, & Adamek, 1995) indicated that participants in online self-help groups receive some of the same benefits that other participants obtain. Later research has examined the participants and types of problems in online groups, the patterns of support that develop on line, and the differences from and similarities to face-to-face support groups.

The formation of online groups differs from face-to-face groups. Support groups may consist of only a few people, or as many as a few dozen, but online groups may have thousands of members (Galegher, Sproull, & Kiesler, 1998). No meetings take place, but participants can enter discussions 24 hours a day, 7 days a week. People can actively participate by posting comments and asking questions, or they may "lurk," reading the posted interactions but not offering comments themselves. Participants often use created names, which makes online interaction anonymous. Thus, the format for online support groups shows clear differences from other support groups.

The types of problems that prompt people to seek support on the Internet are somewhat different from those that bring people to face-to-face support groups (Davison et al., 2000). Rare and debilitating conditions are frequent topics on the Internet. Conditions such as chronic fatigue syndrome and multiple sclerosis seem well-suited to online support—people with these conditions have problems that impair them from going to meetings. People who have problems with oral speech can use a computer to communicate in a medium they can master and at their own pace (Finn, 1999).

The problems of participants in online support groups tend to center on physical health, but behavioral problems such as depression and attention deficit disorder are also common topics. Alcohol and substance abuse treatment form a large segment of the face-to-face support groups, but these problems are not as prominent in online support groups (Davison et al., 2000). However, cancer, diabetes, and AIDS bring people together on line as well as in person to share information and emotional support.

The same support processes that occur in face-to-face groups also take place on line (Finn, 1999). That is, online support groups also share information, work toward mutual problem solving, allow expressions of emotion, and show support and empathy. An analysis of the processes in online support groups (Finn, 1999) showed that the majority of messages (55%) could be classified as emotional or social exchanges, and 21% of messages showed empathy. Although participants exchanged a great deal of practical information, the main function of these groups was emotional support. Thus, online support groups show similarities to face-to-face groups in providing a format for the exchange of emotional support and practical advice from similar others.

Gender Issues in Self-Help

Just as women are more likely to seek therapy, women are also more likely than men to participate in self-help groups. More than two-thirds of those who attend support groups are women (Galegher et al., 1998). However, men are more likely than women to use the Internet, and men use online support groups more than women do. Although depression is more common among women and online support groups for depression are plentiful, only 40% of those who posted comments in such groups were women. This finding suggests that the Internet may furnish a forum in which men feel more comfortable in seeking help than they do in formal therapy or in face-to-face support groups.

Gender issues are often prominent in self-help groups because many such groups are formed around women's or men's issues. Consciousness-raising groups originated as a way for women to share their unique experiences, explore the similarities of their lives, and increase interaction with other women (Morgan, 1970). These groups began to form in the mid 1960s as part of the women's movement; thus, the aims of these groups were political as well as personal. The early emphasis on political ideology shifted to personal development (Kravetz, 1978). Instead of political activism, the most important goals became a sharing of thoughts and feelings about being women, learning about other women's experiences, increasing self-awareness, receiving emotional support, and examining the traditional gender role for women. Participants rated the groups as very successful in helping them to attain these goals, and the majority of participants encouraged other women to join groups. The personal changes experienced by women during consciousness-raising groups were likely to have been therapeutic, leading to these groups' becoming substitutes for or adjuncts to therapy (Enns, 1992).

The men's movement has also devised group meetings for men to share their concerns. In the 1970s, men's groups were similar to early women's consciousness-raising groups, with the purpose of making members more sensitive to the politics and the disadvantages of their gender role. Both concentrated on the social inequities women had experienced and how rigid gender roles had harmed men as well as women. Men sought to understand how they had participated in and had been harmed by society's mandates for their behavior.

In the 1980s, the goals of the men's movement began to diverge from those of the women's movement (Faludi, 1991). Men's oppression became the theme of many men's groups during that decade, and men sought to redefine masculinity (Bly, 1990; Kipnis, 1991). The format for this discovery is often in groups in which men discuss and explore their own experiences and problems with society's definition of masculinity. Men's groups have a greater diversity than women's consciousness-raising groups, but fewer men's groups exist. Women's groups tend to be oriented toward sensitizing women to the political goals of feminism, but men's groups have a variety of possible goals. Some men's groups have political goals, such as groups organized around gay rights, divorce, or custody rights; others supplement therapy for substance abuse; still others explore social conceptions of masculinity and ways to bring about positive personal and social changes. Unlike traditional psychotherapy, both women's and men's groups share the goals of reexamining gender roles and seeking possible avenues of change.

Considering Diversity

Based on an examination of mental illness and treatment throughout the world, Robert Desjarlais and his colleagues (1995, p. 51) concluded

> *how illness is understood and responded to actually shapes the illness itself, organizing symptoms, interpretations, and care-seeking activities in behavioral pathways that differ across societies and ethnic groups.... Every local system of medical knowledge and healing must cope with prolonged sadness and withdrawal, with violence and irrational anger, and with seizures, emotional distress, and acute and chronic forms of madness. (1995, p. 51)*

The views of different cultures often vary from those in the United States and western Europe by failing to make the distinction between physical and mental illness, which produce differences in treatments as well as in diagnoses.

Many people in Asia, Africa, and Latin America have views of treatment that are not compatible with psychiatric treatments involving drugs and psychotherapy. In these cultures, healing processes include folk healers, ritual dramas, herbal medicine, and possession rituals (Desjarlais et al., 1995). In some cultures, professionals using drugs and psychotherapy have little success in treating people because the individuals receiving treatment do not share the same views about their problems that the therapist holds, and they have no confidence in these therapies. For example, the Yolmo Sherpa of Nepal experience a disorder symptomized by a loss of energy; a loss of interest in eating, working, and socializing; sleep problems; and feelings of "dullness." In the United States, these symptoms would probably result in a diagnosis of depression, but the Yolmo believe that these symptoms occur because one of their spirits has left the body and wanders around the countryside. The treatment involves a lengthy and elaborate ritual performed by a shaman, who tracks the lost spirit and helps it return to the afflicted person. For the Yolmo, this course of treatment is a better choice and probably more effective than antidepressant drugs.

Every society has ways of treating behavioral problems, but conflicts arise when a society consists of various groups with differing views of the sources and appropriate treatments for problems. On a worldwide basis, this conflict has occurred when western treatment has been imposed on cultures that hold different views. Creating a mental health care system seems to be a worthy goal, but that system may not serve the people who receive the services. In most countries in Asia, Africa, and Latin America, providers must make adaptations to the culture for treatment to be effective (Desjarlais et al., 1995).

In the United States and Canada, people from many different ethnic groups receive treatment from mental health care professionals, yet this treatment may be as incompatible with their cultural beliefs as the same treatments would be in Asia, Africa, and Latin America. Effective treatment requires adaptations to the clients' culture and beliefs. The mixture of ethnic groups in the United States and Canada creates a challenge for those who provide mental health care.

The history of mental health care does not reflect the type of sensitivity required for effective care for ethnic minorities, and especially for women of color (Comas-Díaz & Greene, 1994b). Issues of inaccessibility of services, mistrust of health care professionals, and stigma associated with treatment create problems for ethnic minorities in the United States. Perhaps in response to these barriers, ethnic minorities have been less willing than Whites to seek mental health care, including self-help groups (USDHHS, 1999b). However, African Americans and Native Americans are represented more frequently in psychiatric hospitals than in the population (USDHHS, 1999b), which suggests that these groups are more likely to be subjected to involuntary treatment.

Feminist therapy may provide a model for therapy that is sensitive to the concerns of ethnic-minority clients (Mays & Comas-Díaz, 1988; Raja, 1998). Indeed, the desire to include diverse clients has been a goal for many feminist therapists (Comas-Díaz & Greene, 1994a). The sensitivity to environmental factors and the recognition of the impact of social reality on psychological functioning make feminist therapy better suited to ethnic-minority clients than therapies that conceptualize problems as personal and internal. Feminist therapy offers African American (Greene, 1994), Native American (LaFromboise, Berman, & Sohi, 1994), Asian American (Bradshaw, 1994), and Hispanic American (Vasquez, 1994) women a method to help them feel empowered, to give them skills to solve their problems, and to furnish opportunities to change society. By allowing these clients to center on family and community, feminist therapy can be useful to clients who are ethnic minorities.

Sexual orientation is another diversity issue, and the mental health care system has not offered appropriate treatment to lesbians and gay men. The emphasis on the social environment as a factor in psychological problems makes feminist therapy "one of few models of behavior change that intentionally perceives the variability of sexual orientations in human beings as a simple fact, rather than a matter for concern and intervention" (Brown, 1988, p. 206). Thus, feminist therapy is an obvious choice for helping lesbians and gay men in accepting their sexual orientation as well as in adjusting to problems that are unique to lesbians and gay men.

Summary

Psychoanalysis was an early form of treatment for mental disorders. Based on Freud's conceptualization of personality development and functioning, this therapy uses talk to help people bring unconscious material to consciousness. Alternative talk-based therapies were developed, including the humanistic approach to therapy, which attempts to help people fulfill their potential by accepting their emotions and feelings. Cognitive therapy focuses on thoughts and holds that changing irrational and self-defeating thoughts will produce a change in behavior. Behavior modification centers on applying the principles of operant conditioning to alter undesirable behaviors. Cognitive behavior therapy is a blending of cognitive therapy and behavior modification that attempts to alter cognitions and establish different behaviors.

Medical therapies are also used to treat behavior problems, including psychoactive drugs and electroconvulsive therapy. Psychoactive drugs for depression, anxiety disorders, and schizophrenia have become more popular, and women receive more prescriptions for psychoactive drugs than men do. Once used for many mental disorders, electroconvulsive therapy is now used largely for depression that has not responded to antidepressant drugs.

Charges of gender bias extend to all therapies. Psychoanalysis holds men as the standard for psychological development, a standard that women can never attain. Humanistic, cognitive, behavior modification, and cognitive behavior modification therapies are not inherently gender biased, but each offers a format in which therapists can impose their values. In addition, all concentrate on the individual and ignore the social and political aspects of problems. Research indicates that therapists focus on departures from traditional gender roles in their recommendations for treatment, and that therapy can be used to enforce traditional gender roles.

Nonsexist therapy was created in an attempt to remove the gender bias in therapy, but many female therapists believed that therapy should go further and even propose and promote feminist goals. Feminist therapists hold that personal problems are reflections of wider social problems, and they strive to maintain equality in the relationship between client and therapist. From its initial position of political activism, feminist therapy has expanded to a wide variety of clients, including men.

In general, men are less often therapy clients than women are. Men's reluctance to seek therapy relates to the masculine gender role, and men with more traditional values are less willing to seek help than men with less traditional values. Men might be unwilling to discuss emotions or acknowledge their vulnerability, but they might also feel discriminated against in therapy. Research indicates that therapy tends to encourage men to adopt the traditional breadwinner role.

Gender aware therapy is an attempt to extend feminist therapy to a form that applies to the full range of clients. By integrating an awareness of the impact of gender with encouragements to men and women to find what is right for them, gender aware therapy concentrates on individual needs rather than political correctness.

A growing number of complaints of gender bias in therapy has led the American Psychological Association to survey female psychologists about their experiences. The results of this survey revealed four areas of concern: (1) using sexist psychoanalytic concepts, (2) fostering traditional gender roles, (3) diminished expectations for female clients, and (4) treating women as sex objects, including having sex with clients.

Surveys of therapists have revealed that the sexual exploitation of clients by therapists occurs with between 9% and 12% of male therapists and between 2% and 3% of female therapists. The prevalence of this problem has led professional associations to include prohibitions against sexual relationships with clients, but this section nevertheless remains the most commonly violated of any of the ethical codes. A growing body of evidence indicates that intimate relationships with therapists do long-lasting harm to clients.

Rather than seeking therapy from professionals, a growing number of people join self-help groups. These groups mushroomed during the 1980s, and over 25 million people in the United States will participate in a self-help group at some time in their lives. Originating with the model of Alcoholics Anonymous, these groups offer emotional support and access to information from others who share the same type of problem. The low cost of self-help groups is attractive, and some research indicates that professional leaders may not be necessary for therapeutic effects to occur.

The increase in access to the Internet has led to the development of online support groups. These groups share many similarities with other support groups, but they are available to a wider group of participants. Men are more likely to participate in the online format for self-help than in face-to-face groups. Gender issues are often prominent in self-help groups: Many groups are organized around gender-related issues, are composed of all women or all men, and are devoted to examining gender roles.

People in Asia, Africa, and Latin America may not have the same views of psychopathology and thus will not accept psychotherapy or medical treatments for behavior problems. Treatment must be compatible with a culture to be accepted and successful, and providing culturally appropriate treatment presents challenges on a worldwide basis as well as in ethnically diverse societies such as the United States. With its emphasis on social context, feminist therapy is appropriate for people from a variety of cultures as well as for gays and lesbians.

Glossary

behavior modification the application of principles of operant conditioning to behavior, with the goal of changing undesirable behavior to more acceptable alternatives.

electroconvulsive therapy the application to the brain of electric current sufficient to induce a convulsion, which for unknown reasons produces therapeutic effects.

psychoanalysis Freud's talk-based treatment for psychological problems that consists of attempts to bring unconscious material to consciousness.

repression a defense mechanism used to push troubling material from the conscious into the unconscious.

Suggested Readings

Brooks, Gary R. (1998). *A new psychotherapy for traditional men.* San Francisco: Jossey-Bass. Brooks discusses the barriers that men face in therapy, men's needs for therapy, and how he came to change his approach as a therapist so that he could provide effective therapy to traditional men.

Enns, Carolyn Zerbe. (1997). *Feminist theories and feminist psychotherapies: Origins, themes, and variations.* New York: Harrington Park Press. For those who are interested in the history and variations on feminist therapy, this book details the history and development of liberal, radical, and cultural feminism and the therapies that have developed these social movements.

Marecek, Jeanne; & Hare-Mustin, Rachel T. (1991). A short history of the future: Feminism and clinical psychology. *Psychology of Women Quarterly, 15,* 521–536. For those who think that Enns's book is too long, this brief history of feminist criticism in clinical psychology will be easier to read. Marecek and Hare-Mustin review the history of clinical psychology and discuss the actual and potential contributions of feminist thought.

Pope, Kenneth S. (2000). Therapists' sexual feelings and behaviors: Research, trends, and quandaries. In Lenore T. Szuchman, Frank Muscarella (Eds.), *Psychological perspectives on human sexuality* (pp. 603–658). New York: Wiley. Pope reviews the research on prevalence of sexual contact among therapists and clients, details the evidence concerning the damage done to clients, and suggests ways to recognize therapists who are at risk and how to manage this problem.

Chapter 16

How Different?

HEADLINE

A Peace Plan for the Gender Wars

Psychology Today, March/April, 1996

> *Gender relations in contemporary society present a seemingly paradoxical picture. On one hand, we are told that women and men are rapidly becoming equal partners at home and in the workplace. With women and men moving into each other's traditional spheres, it would seem logical that we would finally be able to understand each other's experiences. Women have now had to compete day in and day out to financially support their family. They have set their sights on many of the same goals as their male counterparts.... Surely women can now understand the societal pressures to succeed that have always burdened their husbands. As wives have moved in even greater numbers into the workforce, husbands have had to take on more of women's traditional responsibilities for child care and homemaking. It would seem they can now understand the magnitude of these responsibilities, the never-ending routine of care and crisis.*
>
> *What has not changed, apparently, over the past 40 years is the desire of men and women to figure out what is appropriate for their own and the other gender—and to find ways to live together. What has changed is that we are now less sure about what is the right way to be a man or a woman. (White & Tyson-Rawson, 1996, p. 51)*

Despite women moving into men's sphere of work and men moving into women's sphere of household work and child care, the transitions have not been smooth. Mark White and Kirsten Tyson-Rawson (1996) examined the problems that women and men encounter in fulfilling these multiple roles. As an example, they presented Alex and Susan, who were trying to advance their careers and share household work and the care of their 5-year-old daughter. Their attempts to share equally ran into difficulty, and part of the problem was their reliance on traditional gender roles. Although they had deliberately tried to escape those traditional roles, they had not succeeded well enough to be comfortable.

Multiple Roles Have Become the Rule

The traditional assumptions hold that women will choose jobs to support themselves until they marry, but will make marriage their primary careers, and men will devote themselves to careers while remaining marginally involved in family life. These stereotypical assumptions no longer hold for many women and men. Like Susan and Alex in the headline story, a growing number of women pursue careers on a full-time, uninterrupted basis. As a result, many men are like Alex and no longer provide the sole support for their families. Also like this couple, many men and women are struggling with developing a way for both to have careers and be involved in family life.

Couples like Susan and Alex face problems stemming from social expectations. Despite joining the workforce of paid employment, women still are expected (and expect themselves) to occupy the role of wife and mother, including performing a majority of the household and family work. Men have experienced few changes in their roles (Tittle, 1986). The increasing number of employed women has led to increased acceptance of women in the workforce in addition to their role in the family, but men's roles have not undergone comparable changes and remain centered on the role of breadwinner. This expectation leaves men who want to be involved in household work and child care without social support for their choice.

Both men and women may be dissatisfied with the inequity in household work but have not managed to find a strategy for a more equitable division. Gender stereotypes push men away from household and child care work. Even when couples expect to share equally in household chores and child care, they often do not (Deutsch, Lussier, & Servis, 1993). Both husbands and wives expected husbands to participate in the care of their first child, but husbands actually participated very little—to the disappointment of both husbands and wives. Wives' work load from outside employment was a significant factor in the amount of child care their husbands performed, as were husbands' gender role attitudes. Not surprisingly, men with nontraditional gender role attitudes were more likely to participate in child care than men with more traditional attitudes. These results show that gender roles are a powerful force in determining who performs which tasks. Even when partners plan an equitable sharing of household work, they have difficulty implementing these plans.

Some jobs are especially problematic. High-level managerial and professional careers require long hours and extraordinary dedication. The corporate, male-dominated careers that women began entering in somewhat larger numbers during the 1970s have not changed to accommodate women's family duties (Hochschild, 1997). Men provided the model for these careers—men who had wives to provide a support system for their husbands' careers. These wives offered not only emotional support at home, but also social support in the public functions of the organization (Williams, 2000). That is, the "corporate wife" joins auxiliaries, organizes social functions, and boosts her husband's career. Women too need "wives" to provide this support, but few husbands are willing to be the homemakers who offer support to successful female breadwinners. Job demands in two-career families have been the precipitating source of conflict leading either to divorce or to women dropping off the track to success in high-prestige careers (Campbell, 1986).

GENDERED VOICES

I've Had This Conversation Before

Melinda was a single mother with a 2-year-old son who told me about her experiences with the woman she had hired to care for her son. She considered herself and her son extremely fortunate; the nanny was a retired pediatric nurse, ideally qualified to be a nanny, and a wonderful person. Like many mothers with careers, Melinda felt less than enthusiastic at the thought of leaving her son in the care of someone else, and she felt fortunate not only to be able to afford a full-time, live-in nanny, but also to have found a great person. Indeed, they had become like a family.

Melinda's business career was demanding but fulfilling. She had worked as a secretary during the time that she was married, but she had divorced and pursued a sales and management career and had become successful. Like other women with demanding and fulfilling careers, she worked long and sometimes irregular hours. Her son's nanny took care of him and the house, cooking dinner for herself and the child. She said that she could easily cook for Melinda as well; she would be glad to do so, but Melinda needed to be home to eat with them.

Melinda explained that she didn't always know when she would need to work late, and she couldn't be sure about being home in time for dinner every night. "But that doesn't matter. If I'm late, just leave my dinner. It's no big deal." The nanny said that it was a big deal; she didn't want to cook dinner and have her be late and have cold food. It just wasn't right. Melinda thought, "I've had this conversation before—when I was married. Only this time I'm being the 'husband,' and last time I was the wife. My husband said all the things I'm saying and gave all the excuses I'm giving, and I said the words I'm hearing from my nanny." Melinda was now the "husband."

Pepper Schwartz (1994) studied couples who had managed to construct marriages in which each shared equitably in family life, and she contrasted these couples with more traditional marriages. One factor that distinguished these two types of couples was level of employment: Few fast-track careers appeared among the marriages in which the partners shared equally. Schwartz found that these couples "maintain their relationship goals by folding work into the relationship rather than vice versa" (1994, p. 181). For both men and women, the relationship was more important than career. By making their relationship and home life primary, these couples have expanded the role for men, making them into full participants in their wives' and children's lives.

What are the consequences of role expansion for men and women? Three models hypothesize different consequences of multiple roles (Rodin, 1991). The *job stress model* holds that multiple roles lead to role conflict because people who try to fulfill many roles experience conflict when the multiple roles produce stress in their lives. This model proposes that role restriction would be healthier. An alternative model, the *health benefits model,* holds that employment offers direct benefits to women, such as feelings of control and self-esteem, social support from colleagues in the workplace, and financial gain. This model proposes that multiple roles are beneficial. The *role expansion model* emphasizes the indirect benefits of employment for women, proposing that the satisfaction of fulfilling several roles and the protection of occupying several different roles will be beneficial. Table 16.1 shows these three models and the position of each on the effects of multiple roles.

Research tends to support the advantages of multiple roles, especially the benefits that come from employment. Furthermore, a meta-analysis of job-related stress revealed no gender differences in experienced or perceived stress on the job (Martocchio & O'Leary, 1989). Employment may cause stress, but its impact is similar for men and women and does

TABLE 16.1 Three Models of Multiple Roles

Model	Results of Multiple Roles	Benefits
Job stress model	Role conflict	None
Health benefits model	Feelings of control and increased self-esteem; social support from coworkers; financial benefit	Direct
Role expansion model	Feelings of success at occupying several roles and of protection offered by these roles	Indirect

not harm women more than men. Indeed, multiple roles *decreased* psychological distress in business women, suggesting that the benefits of paid employment outweigh the stresses of fulfilling multiple roles (Abrams & Jones, 1994). Considering the economic and power benefits, women gain many advantages from paid employment. Put another way, "Being at work protects women from the full impact of marriage" (Archer & Lloyd, 1982, p. 194).

Men tend to receive greater benefits from marriage than women do (Barnett & Baruch, 1987), partially because their roles are less stressful than women's balance of career, household work, and child care. For men, participation in child care and family chores increased fathers' feelings of competence as parents, and men tended to feel less stressed at home than at work (Larson & Richards, 1994). For men, their jobs are their core role, and family enriches that role but should not interfere with it (Barnett & Baruch, 1987). Social expectations support this view, exempting men from family involvement to concentrate on their careers.

Although multiple roles have become the rule and evidence exists of the benefits of multiple roles, these changes may not be what women and men want. In the headline story, Susan was annoyed with Alex for being emotionally remote, but she was also irritated when he was "needy." Alex wanted Susan to take responsibility for tasks that men traditionally perform, yet he was angry when the salesman in a car dealership dealt with Susan rather than him, because buying a car is an activity that Alex considered to be part of the man's job. What do women and men want from each other, and will getting those things help to formulate a peace plan for the "gender wars"?

What Do Women Want? What Do Men Want?

Questioning what women want became popular after Sigmund Freud asked the question of Marie Bonaparte in the 1930s (Jones, 1955). His version of the question, as many others have been, was an exasperated plea prompted by a genuine lack of understanding of women's motivations (Feist & Feist, 2002). Other men have contended that women's goals are unreasonable rather than mysterious. Are women's motives so troublesome and difficult to understand? How different are the things that women and men want?

Men's motives have not been subject to the same degree of scrutiny, but the changes in women's roles have forced men to examine their own lives to consider what they want. Much of this examination has centered on what men want from women and the difficulties that changes in women's lives have created for men. Do men want traditional women, "new" women, or some combination?

Have Women Become More Like Men?

"Why can't a woman be more like a man?" was the title of a song in the musical play *My Fair Lady* (Lerner & Loewe, 1956). Henry Higgins sang about how unreasonable women were in comparison to men, and as he longed for women and men to be more similar, he was voicing the stereotypical belief that women and men differ in many ways. Although this view was common at the time the musical appeared (and for some people, is accepted even now), the differences between genders may have been exaggerations. Gender differences may not have been as large as people believed, but these beliefs have been perpetrated by focusing on the differences and maintaining the dichotomy by conceptualizing an "opposite" sex.

Women have begun to take the opportunity to pursue some of the goals that were reserved for men. If large differences once existed between men and women, perhaps the intervening years have allowed Higgins's wish to come true. Have women become more like men? And if this wish has come true, what do men think of these changes?

Higgins's wishes centered around emotionality; he listed negative emotions for women and positive ones for men. Of course, Higgins himself deviated from this ideal quite a bit, but his beliefs about differing emotionality in men and women may be partially correct. Women report more emotional intensity than men do; they experience more strongly positive as well as more strongly negative moods (Fujita, Diener, & Sandvik, 1991). This evidence offers some confirmation for the stereotype of emotional women, but other evidence suggests a more complex picture, in which social rules for displaying emotion shape the gender differences in emotionality.

Rather than women becoming more like men, the opposite trend has appeared in relationships; the typical feminine style of intimacy has become the standard for both men and women (Cancian, 1986). Although men often feel uncomfortable in sharing emotions with others, especially with other men, a growing number of men are seeking this style of relationship. Pressure for men to become more emotionally intimate has occurred in friendships, marriages, and other committed love relationships. Thus, women have not become more like men in this respect, but instead, men are in the process of becoming more like women.

Sexual behavior continues to show some gender differences. Some of those differences have decreased, but those that remain may be important. When Alfred Kinsey and his colleagues (Kinsey et al., 1948; Kinsey et al., 1953) conducted their surveys in the 1930s and 1940s, women reported more sexual activity and enjoyment than the popular image of women portrayed, but the double standard for sexual behavior constrained women from expressing their sexuality. Women were less likely to masturbate and to have intercourse outside marriage than men were. Later surveys (Janus & Janus, 1993; Laumann et al., 1994) have shown a decrease in the differences.

Differences in sexuality may have a significant impact on heterosexual relationships (Hyde, 1996). Women now endorse a greater variety of sexual behaviors and are likely to have their first sexual intercourse at younger ages than in previous decades, but men masturbate more and favor casual sex more than women do. The implications of these differences may be larger than the differences themselves (Hyde, 1996).

For example, women's lower rate of masturbation may relate to their difficulties in having orgasms during sex with their partners, a problem that prompts many couples to seek therapy and many others to experience conflict in their sexual relationships (Hyde, 1996). (The advice of sex therapists often includes masturbation to learn how to have orgasms.)

The difference in attitudes toward casual sex has a large influence on many relationships. When men and women bring different attitudes about commitment to sexual relationships, their varying standards can result in jealousy and conflict.

Changes in sexual attitudes have allowed women to explore their sexuality (Ehrenreich, Hess, & Jacobs, 1986). Women made substantial changes in their sexual attitudes and behavior between the 1930s and the 1970s. The conservatism of the 1980s and the growing fear of AIDS produced some decrease in the willingness for sexual exploration in both men and women, but women's exploration of their sexuality has taken them in directions that were not necessarily compatible with men's sexual preferences. Indeed, increased acceptance of sexuality other than intercourse led women to be less sexually dependent on men. This decreased dependence has become a source of men's discontent. Women have become more sexual, but not like men, and not necessarily to men's liking.

Women have become more like men in terms of their achievements; educational differences between men and women have decreased, with women and men receiving comparable numbers of college degrees. Differences still persist in several areas of training and in the advanced and professional degrees awarded, with men receiving more training for prestigious careers such as law, business, and medicine. Women's gains may overcome men's current advantage, and more women than men may be qualified for high-status jobs in the future (Tiger, 2000).

Interviews with women about their achievements in one study revealed a picture of women who are proud of their progress in careers and who believe that they have fought and succeeded in gaining recognition (Sigel, 1996). Not only professional women, but also working-class women expressed pride in women's accomplishments. Talking to men provided a different view: Men saw the changes in terms of letting women have more opportunities. This difference in view is very revealing, with each gender taking credit for the changes and seeing their own gender as responsible for those changes.

Employment gives women more economic advantages, but also produces greater demands. Some women have sought employment out of a desire for personal fulfillment, whereas economic necessity is the reason for most women's employment. The degree to which women are satisfied with their employment varies according to the support they receive from their families. Women whose husbands provide little assistance and emotional support for their employment are less satisfied than women with more supportive families.

In needing and providing support, women and men are now similar, but these similarities represent changes in their traditional roles. Female homemakers were the traditional caregivers, but employed women need to *receive* support from, as well as *provide* support to, their families. In the past, male breadwinners could expect the support of their wives, but they are now expected to provide their wives with emotional support and also help with household work. Through these changes, women and men have become more alike, but an increase in household chores was probably not what men like Henry Higgins had in mind.

Both women and men need the support of the other to be able to fulfill their dependency needs (Eichenbaum & Orbach, 1983). Men and women have similar needs, but the chances of fulfillment are usually not the same. Despite the helplessness and passivity some women display, they do not have someone on whom they can rely for emotional support, leaving dependency needs unmet. The lack of compatibility between meeting their own dependency needs and adopting the male gender role can make men feel ashamed of their dependency needs. In the past, men have been able to rely on women for emotional support, and women's increasing requests for emotional support from men can be an unwelcome change for many men.

These decreases in gender differences support the evidence that women and men have become more similar in education, employment, sexual attitudes and behavior, smoking rates, and athletic competition. The changes have occurred mostly in women, however. Whereas women have become more like men, men generally have not begun to adopt the positive aspects of women's behavior. This one-way change is not surprising when considering the situations that have produced the changes. Women have moved into the educational and employment worlds formerly occupied by men, but for the most part, men have not made corresponding moves into women's worlds. Thus, men encounter few, and women encounter many, situations that encourage the adoption of a more flexible style.

Despite superficial endorsement of the virtues of the traditional feminine role of homemaker and mother, society has accorded little value to nurturing skills or other traditional feminine behaviors (Cancian & Oliker, 2000). Men's traditional masculine style of assertive, independent, agentic behavior has set the mold for behavior in a variety of situations. Women who enter these situations tend to adopt the style of the situation, which is usually agentic rather than communal. Society's value of masculine over feminine traits results in women receiving rewards for adopting such active, instrumental behaviors and men receiving little encouragement for becoming more expressive or communal in their behavior. Thus, women have more freedom to become androgynous by combining the positive aspects of masculinity with the expressive, communal behaviors of femininity, but men have little encouragement to become more androgynous.

If they do, the outcome may not be entirely positive. Men who at age 12 expressed interests and traits more commonly associated with women showed poorer personal adjustment at ages 31 and 41 than men who had more traditionally masculine interests as children (Aubé & Koestner, 1992). Women who had endorsed nontraditional masculine interests and traits experienced no similar negative outcomes. Indeed, masculine instrumental traits were positively related to adjustment during adulthood for both women and men. That is, an androgynous combination of interests was a negative factor for men's, but not for women's, adjustment. Another study (Orlofsky & O'Heron, 1987) indicated that both women and men show better adjustment when they endorsed masculine instrumental traits than when they endorsed feminine expressive traits. Both of these studies demonstrated society's emphasis on masculine values and suggested that women have found it easier to become more like men because they receive social rewards for these behaviors.

How do women feel about these changes? According to Susan Faludi (1991), a great deal of media attention has focused on the negative effects of the changes in women's lives. Faludi contended that the negative publicity about women's increased economic and sexual independence represents a reaction against these changes, and that the stories misrepresent women's actual feelings; women would like more opportunities rather than a return to traditional gender roles. These media reports tend to focus on interviews with selected discontented women rather than presenting studies with more representative samples. Women in a survey and interview study (Sigel, 1996) confirmed this view. These women expressed pride in their workplace accomplishments and continued annoyance with discrimination, failures to be taken seriously, and lack of support and assistance from their husbands at home.

Men do not feel so positively about the changes in gender roles. Faludi (1999) also examined contemporary men and masculinity, and found many problems. The traditional models of masculinity no longer seem either valid or available. Men's role as breadwinner is compromised by the decreasing availability of good jobs and the increasing number of employed women who can provide for themselves. A culture that seemed to revolve around boys and men stopped doing so, and women's concerns became preeminent. Many men to whom Faludi spoke voiced feelings of lack of control and isolation from family, work, and society. Faludi concluded that men have been led to expect privileges that they no longer have, leaving them feeling (as the title of one of her books indicates) "stiffed."

Henry Higgins's wish may have come true. Women have, indeed, become more like men, but the changes are not everything that he (and men like him) had hoped for. Most people find change difficult and anxiety provoking, and changes in expectations for men and women have come about very rapidly. Indeed, the changes have occurred faster than social institutions have been able to change to accommodate them. People have few models to emulate in adopting new gender roles, and they live in a society that pressures them to be more traditional. When gender roles were narrowly defined, everyone knew what to do. Although the rules were unquestionably restrictive, which prevented people from performing gender-inappropriate activities, the roles were at least clear. Greater flexibility has produced uncertainty as well as options.

The power and privilege of men's traditional gender role put men in a position of having have more to lose through change than women do, and men are less content than women with the changes that have occurred. Although some men have welcomed the opportunities to form more intimate relationships with friends and partners and to be involved in their children's lives, many others have resisted making changes or have found themselves not knowing how to enact the changes they want to make. Few men want some of the new options, such as careers as elementary school teachers or secretaries. Employed wives bring home incomes that may be very attractive, but few men welcome the prospect of having more household chores. Therefore, many men have not gotten what they wanted as women have become more like men.

Women too may not be entirely satisfied with the changes in their lives. As the many polls indicate, the majority of women favor more equal treatment in politics and jobs, but they too may resist making other changes in the roles and underlying assumptions about their relationships with men, their sexuality, and their children. Women become less interested in change when "it requires profound individual change as well, posing an unsettling challenge that well-adjusted people instinctively avoid. Why question norms of sex and character to which you've more or less successfully adapted?" (Kaminer, 1993, p. 51). Women do not want to lose their femininity in gaining equal rights, and they do not want to give up relationships with men (Sigel, 1996).

Some women long for a return to traditionalism, but that longing is stronger in men, who believe that changes in gender roles have caused them to lose more and gain less than women have. Women tend to complain, not about what they have lost, but about what they have gained—the equivalent of two full-time jobs. Men tend to complain about what they have lost—services and subservience (Gallagher, 1987). These "new" women are more independent and more difficult for men to control (Skovholt, 1978).

Why Can't a Man Be More Like a Woman?

The status of styles of masculinity can be analyzed into three categories that describe men and their reactions to the changes in women's roles (Skovholt, 1978). *Traditional men* regret the changes that have occurred, seeing no advantages for themselves in women's greater freedom. Indeed, these men feel the competition for grades and jobs, and they resent the presence of women in the workplace. Traditional men have stereotypical attitudes toward their own gender role and prefer women to adhere to traditional femininity. These men do not feel the appeal of expanding their gender role to include behaviors traditionally reserved for women, so they see nothing but disadvantages connected with changing gender roles.

Men in transition are able to accomplish the task of interacting with women as people as well as with women as romantic partners. These men are not necessarily sympathetic with the goals of the feminist movement, but they are attempting to integrate the changes in women's roles by changing their own attitudes and behavior. Alex from this chapter's headline story fits into this category. He is able to interact with women as individuals as well as with Susan as his romantic partner, and he is struggling to become more sensitive and responsive.

Alex, however, fails to recognize as problems many of the issues that Susan finds troubling. The men in one survey and interview study (Sigel, 1996) were much like Alex in failing to see the problem of gender discrimination. Some of these men were traditional men who longed for the "good old days" when men ruled the workplace and home, but most endorsed gender equality and sympathy with women's quest for fair treatment. However, this issue did not capture their interest and commitment. These men in transition were grappling with the changes in gender roles, but they were not actively helping women to work toward equality.

The *male liberationists* embrace the feminist movement and extend the notion that gender roles are oppressive to men, highlighting the stresses of the male gender role and calling for changes for everyone. Table 16.2 summarizes these three categories of contemporary male attitudes toward changing gender roles.

Women have become more like men, but men more often have declined than accepted opportunities to become more like women. That is, women have developed a more instrumental orientation, but many men have failed to develop their expressive skills. The asymmetry of these changes may have created a situation in which women want men to change. Women are asking Henry Higgins's question from their own point of view: "Why can't a man be more like a woman?"

This question exists in two versions, one social and one personal. The first version applies to the question as a social one, challenging the wisdom of continuing to use men and masculine values as the preferred style. For example, what makes the hierarchical, directive (sometimes autocratic) style of leadership that men typically use preferable to the cooperative, democratic style women typically use? If differences in moral reasoning exist, why should the style dominant among women be considered inferior? Why can't men accept the

TABLE 16.2 Three Categories of Contemporary Men's Attitudes toward Changing Gender Roles

Approach	Characteristics	See Women As
Traditional	Wish to return to traditional gender roles for men and women	Subordinate
Men in transition	Attempt to adapt to the changes in gender roles	People as well as romantic partners
Male liberationists	See dangers of male gender role; embrace feminism	Equals

value of the feminine style? Why are men considered the standard and women the exception (Bem, 1993b)? The second version of the question is more personal, challenging men to include more expressiveness in personal relationships and to participate more fully in "women's work," that is, household work and child care. Women contend that both society at large, as well as their individual lives, would profit from men accepting the value of expressive behaviors.

Some evidence exists to indicate that people have no problems accepting the value of the communal qualities associated with women. Alice Eagly and her colleagues (Eagly, 1994; Eagly, Mladinic, & Otto, 1991) investigated evaluations of men and women, finding that women received more positive personal evaluations than men did. People think of women as a social category in very positive terms, a finding Eagly (1994) called the "Women are Wonderful" effect. These positive evaluations may signal a change in the social evaluation of women, allowing for a greater acceptance of feminine values.

However, these positive evaluations seem to contradict the disadvantages that women experience in so many realms. These positive evaluations were applied only to women in traditional roles, and they failed to carry over to women who diverged from those traditional roles; that is, people saw women as wonderful mothers, but not as wonderful business executives (Eagly, 1994). As Eagly et al. (1991) put it, "Although people evidently think that these qualities are wonderful human attributes, they may value them more in close relationships than in highly paid sectors of the workforce" (p. 213). Thus, the evidence concerning positive attitudes about women does not ensure the social acceptance of their style in roles other than traditional ones.

Some men have recognized the value of developing greater emotional expressiveness and have attempted to make changes in their behavior. Although these men believe that women and men should have equal power in relationships and equal access to education and careers, they may find these principles difficult to incorporate into their lives. Society offers few models of couples who develop equal relationships, but many examples of traditional couples.

Marriages between feminist men and women do not always work as the partners envisioned (Campbell, 1986). The lack of social support for equitable marriages pushes men and women toward traditional gender roles. Even men who have agreed to share in household work and child care find these promises difficult to keep, and women's success can leave men feeling neglected and jealous of the time their wives spend on work. While pursuing demanding careers, the wives do not have time to do household work and child care without their husbands' help. When their husbands refuse to help, their marriages experience trouble. Marriages that begin with the men being liberationists sometimes end with both partners realizing that the men were more traditional than either had believed.

The motivation to make personal changes in ways of dealing with partners and children has been a focus in many of the men's movement groups; here, men attempt to feel comfortable with emotional sharing and intimate disclosure. A growing number of men have accepted that the male gender role constrains their emotional expressiveness in ways that have harmed their relationships and possibly their well-being. This attitude has encouraged men to change.

What are the prospects for men becoming more like women? And how would women feel if they did? Currently, the rewards for men who adopt more expressive behaviors are not as great as for women who become more instrumental, which leads to the prediction that men may not change as much as women have. If the men who are involved in the men's movement provide any omen of changes to come, then men have little interest in adopting very many feminine qualities. Leaders in the men's movement, such as Sam Keen (1991) and Robert Bly (1990, 1994), have urged men to explore their masculinity and make changes in their attitudes and behavior, but their recommendations do not include listening to women to know what changes to make. The men's movement concept of authentic masculinity includes increased expressiveness and responsibility, making this view of what men should become correspond to the changes that many women want.

Will these views of masculinity influence men's attitudes and behavior? Although the vast majority of men are not involved in the men's movement, social changes become personal and affect people's lives (Sigel, 1996). The women's movement produced changes in society—for women's lives and for men's lives. The men's movement may have a parallel effect, and the discomfort may be similar, with women disliking some of the choices for change that men make in their lives.

Men and women may both want too much from each other, including things that appear to be contradictory. Each may want to be both independent and dependent, aggressive and passive, businesslike and romantic. These behaviors are not necessarily contradictory, but the rules that allow the display of both are more complex than the rules that allowed each gender only one pattern. Flexibility and acceptance of individual choices are goals for both the women's and men's movement, but both men and women are struggling with these new, more complicated rules.

Where Are the Differences?

One of the places where differences exist between the genders is in the theories used to explain psychological factors related to gender. The traditional dichotomy for theories of gender is the biological view versus the environmental view—attributing differences to either nature or nurture. Although these opposing points of view have influenced research in gender, another approach now encompasses the nature–nurture debate in gender—the maximalist versus the minimalist positions.

The maximalist view holds that men and women have large differences, whereas the minimalist view holds that the differences between men and women are small compared to their similarities. The older versions of maximalist theory are biologically based, emphasizing gender differences, and offering genetic or hormonal explanations for behavior as well as for anatomy. These theorists tend to accept biological explanations as evidence of unchanging, fixed patterns of behavior. Thus, offering the biological explanation means accepting inevitable differences. These theorists tend to rationalize the disadvantaged social position of women (and often of ethnic minorities) by citing biological programming as the source of differences. Naomi Weisstein (1982, p. 41) summarized this position by saying, "Men are biologically suited to their life of power, pleasure, and privilege, and women must accept subordination, sacrifice, and submission. It's in the genes. Go fight city hall."

Not surprisingly, feminist scholars have disputed the biological basis of behavioral differences between men and women, proposing that social experiences produce differences in learning and thus in behavior. According to this view, social learning, not biology, forms the basis for psychological gender differences. This approach holds that behavior varies according to circumstances and surroundings, and these theorists attribute gender differences to the different situations that women and men typically encounter. Those who hold this view tend to be minimalists, accepting few essential differences between men and women.

Newer versions of the maximalist position also rely on social learning to explain gender differences. Although these theorists see the differences between women's and men's behavior as learned, they believe that the differences are large and persistent. Many of these maximalist theorists are also feminists, advocating the superiority of women's style and characteristics. Rather than accepting the differences as deficiencies, they promote the female version as the better alternative.

These theorists (including Gilligan, Chodorow, and Tannen) are appealing to some women because "they offer a flattering account of traits for which they have historically been castigated" (Pollitt, 1992, p. 802). This view is a modernized version of the Doctrine of the Two Spheres, the Victorian view that women were moral, pure, spiritual, emotional, and intellectually inferior. It is no longer possible to separate the more positive from the very negative characteristics of this view. Unfortunately, the virtues that these maximalists idealize help rationalize the continued subordination of women. What's more, the popularity of this view is ironic, given that the roles of women and men are more similar than they have been at any time during the history of the West (Pollitt, 1992).

Both maximalists and minimalists look at the same research and find evidence to support their positions. The ability to maintain different interpretations of the same information highlights the constructed nature of theories; that is, those who support one view or the other have constructed their position in accordance with their beliefs about gender. Building and maintaining a theoretical position requires examining the research evidence, but theory goes beyond evidence. Therefore, it is possible for theorists to maintain discrepant positions with regard to gender differences, with some theorists holding maximalist and others minimalist positions.

Theories are not the only place that gender differences exist; gender-related differences also exist in behavior. The extent of gender-related differences, however, depends on the type of study considered. In considering studies on ability, few gender differences have appeared. In considering the choices that men and women have made about what to do in their lives, the gender differences are larger.

Differences in Ability

Considering the many comparisons of abilities of women and men, the gender differences are largest for physical strength. This difference relates to size and muscle mass, with men being significantly larger and stronger than women. The differences among individuals are also large; some women are stronger than other women, and some men stronger than other men. However, gender differences are larger than individual differences, making gender a good predictor of strength.

In the past, physical strength made a great deal of difference for a variety of activities, especially in the world of paid employment. Currently, few positions of prestige and power require strength, but the legacy of this position persists. In a survey and interview study of gender issues (Sigel, 1996), several men expressed the opinion that men should be paid more than women because men's jobs require more strength. Despite the high levels of skills that secretaries might need, they should receive less money, according to this view, because their jobs do not require heavy labor. The requirements for physical labor were also mentioned as a reason why men should not be expected to share household work or child care—they had already done physical labor and should not be expected to do more at home.

Gender is a very poor predictor of mental abilities. In both verbal abilities and mathematical abilities, only small gender differences exist. Despite the widespread belief that men have superior mathematical abilities and women have superior verbal abilities, the technique of meta-analysis has revealed that the gender differences are small (Hyde, 1996; Hyde, Fennema, & Lamon, 1990; Hyde & Linn, 1988). The largest difference in cognitive abilities is on one type of spatial task, the mental rotation task. Men have a large advantage in this type of task, but other spatial tasks show a complex relationship with gender.

Research conducted in laboratory settings often shows few if any gender differences. When men and women are put into situations without gender-related cues, their behavior tends to be quite similar. For example, a literature review (Frodi, Macaulay, & Thome, 1977) and a meta-analysis (Eagly & Steffen, 1986) of aggression have shown that women and men are similar in their willingness to behave aggressively in laboratory situations, but outside the laboratory, gender differences appear.

Perhaps the laboratory setting minimizes behavioral differences, which makes this approach unsuited to demonstrating gender-related differences. Because laboratory settings have a tendency to demonstrate gender similarities, researchers may have to look at behavior in social settings to find a difference. When examining the behavioral choices that men and women make, gender differences are larger than when considering abilities.

Differences in Choices

Women and men make different choices about important facets of their lives, and these choices reflect the behaviors that are encouraged for each gender. Saying that women make different choices than men implies that these choices are voluntary and freely made, but such is not the case. As Joan Williams (2000) described the situation, women and men are propelled by force fields that push them toward certain options and away from others, making the traditional choices the only available options for many individuals. Many barriers that prevented women and men from attempting some activities seem to have fallen away, but constraints remain in the form of expectations and encouragement. These choices are more important than abilities in determining what happens in people's lives. The gender differences that exist in education, employment, family life, relationships, sexuality, emotionality, health-related behaviors, body image, and behavior problems reflect these different choices and the expectations that foster them.

Although men and women have similar mathematical ability, young men are more likely than women to pursue careers that rely on math. Even women who complete the courses required for a good math background do not choose science and engineering careers as often as men do (AAUW, 1992). These discrepancies are larger than the differences in abilities would suggest: Fewer women enter mathematics and engineering than women who have the ability to do so (Hyde, 1996).

The expectation that men will pursue careers consistent with the breadwinner role and that women will seek careers compatible with family duties eliminates many options for each. Men are limited in their family involvement by careers that require dedication and long hours. Men do not receive encouragement when they make different choices, such as allotting time to family life by choosing part-time employment or by choosing to be homemakers. Indeed, this choice is considered deviant, and men who have made such decisions are encouraged to reconsider (Robertson & Fitzgerald, 1990).

The movement of women into the paid workforce has increased their options in some ways but not in others. Rather than giving women added choices concerning employment or homemaking, women now expect to be employed in addition to having a husband and children (Baber & Monaghan, 1988; Granrose & Kaplan, 1996). Women who have chosen to have a career and family experience the strains of juggling roles as they work to develop their careers, find adequate child care, and make time for children and husbands. Women who have chosen to be homemakers feel that their choice is not as well accepted or respected as the choice of pursuing paid employment, but they feel that the job they are doing is essential for their children's well-being. Women who have paid employment but would rather be homemakers, and those who had expected to pursue careers but are instead homemakers, face conflict between their expectations and their actual lives (Granrose & Kaplan, 1996). The change in patterns of employment for women has resulted in additional role responsibilities as well as an additional option.

Men and women tend to choose different styles of friendships, and this difference is clearly a choice. That is, most women and men are capable of adopting the style of friendship more common in the other gender. A woman can be "one of the boys," and a man can adopt the emotionally intimate friendship pattern more common among women, but each tends to choose a gender-typical style of relating to others. This choice gives women more intimate friendships with other women than with men, and it prevents men from forming intimate friendships with other men (and possibly with women). Friendships are one source of social support that brings advantages for physical and mental health. Women's style of friendship tends to provide more emotional support, whereas men's style of friendship tends to offer more material support. The advantages of social support come from both types of support and extend to both women and men.

Women's choice of achieving intimacy through emotional sharing and talk has become the accepted style for love relationships (Cancian, 1986), and men may feel deficient if they are not adept at this type of relating. Men's attempts to establish intimacy through sexual activity are not entirely compatible with women's choice to create intimacy through talk and sharing feelings. Thus, sexuality may have different meanings for women and men. Even with comparable levels of desire, men and women make different choices concerning expression of their sexuality.

Different choices also appear to be related to the varying life expectancies of men and women, with women choosing healthier and safer lifestyles in terms of their use of health care services, diet, alcohol intake, and seat belt use. On the other hand, men tend to make better choices by exercising and avoiding unhealthy dieting. Both patterns match the interpretation that men's and women's health-related behaviors are oriented toward maintaining their gender roles. Women behave in healthy ways not because of their health concerns, but due to their concern over thinness. Likewise, men exercise and choose risky health-related behaviors in an effort to maintain a muscular appearance, which matches the Give 'Em Hell component of the masculine gender role.

Men's and women's strategies for handling negative feelings can lead to different methods of dealing with emotions. These differences appear both in statistics on violence and in rates of various types of psychopathology. The display rules for emotion allow (and perhaps even encourage) men to openly express anger, leading to more acts of violence and crime committed by men. Women are encouraged to restrict their displays of anger, leading not to a decrease in the experience of anger, but to differences in the expression of anger. One difference is that women often cry when they are angry, whereas men typically do not.

Different choices for dealing with negative feelings may be reflected in the statistics on psychiatric diagnosis. Women are more likely to receive the diagnosis of depression than men are, but men are more likely to drink alcohol and use other illicit psychoactive substances than women are. Some evidence exists that men use alcohol to cope with negative feelings (Berger & Adesso, 1991), whereas women ruminate over negative events and become depressed (Nolen-Hoeksema, 1987; Nolen-Hoeksema et al., 1999). These different choices produce apparent differences in psychopathology, but may not indicate a difference in the experience of negative emotions.

The expression of psychopathology tends to fall along gender-stereotypical lines (Chesler, 1972; Rosenfield, 1982). The categories of psychopathology most common among women fall into the feminine gender role, but are exaggerated versions of the role: being dependent (dependent personality disorder), passive (major depression), self-sacrificing (self-defeating personality disorder), fearful (agoraphobia), and emotional (histrionic personality disorder). Likewise, men experience psychopathology that seems to have formed around elements of the masculine gender role, but exaggerates these traits: being irresponsible, untruthful, and violent (antisocial personality disorder), recklessness (psychoactive substance abuse disorder), and inappropriately sexual (paraphilias). Although these patterns may not represent intentional choices, they exist as reflections of gender-typical differences.

The choices that men and women make tend to fall along the lines sanctioned by tradition. Women's choices and men's choices tend to keep men and women each in their own category, which creates two domains—male and female—with limited "visitation privileges" from one to the other. Yet these two domains are not different planets, as the best-selling book *Men Are from Mars, Women Are from Venus* suggested. Rather, "the truth is, there is only one culture, and it shapes each sex in distinct but mutually dependent ways in order to reproduce itself" (Pollitt, 1992, p. 806).

The freedom to make cross-gender choices is still limited. An argument has been made that there are benefits derived from perpetuating gender categories. Although such categorization may be convenient to each gender, it limits options to only two well-defined choices. These choices ignore the inherent complexity of individual differences and fail to allow for the need for a wide range of individual choices. The abilities of men and women demand an equally wide range of choices—wider than the choices that are available in the bipolar classification of traditional gender roles.

Is a peace plan possible for the gender war? Have the forays into each others' worlds increased understanding and empathy? The current level of hostility would suggest not. Women's experiences in the world of work have had many positive attributes, but have also shown to women that they still are not treated equitably or taken seriously (Sigel, 1996). This continuing discrimination has escalated the hostility women feel toward their male counterparts, rather than encouraging women and men to initiate a peace plan.

Recent controversies have "put the traditional male sense of entitlements under the microscope. On the simple level, men don't know where the line is. But on a deeper level, there is anxiety" (Levant quoted in Gates, 1993, p. 50). Men's hostility has also increased, and women and ethnic minorities are sometimes the targets of their vehemence. Some men long for "the good old days" when men were privileged in the workplace and at home, and women "knew their place." Relinquishing power and privilege is not easy, and men are not eager to do so. When they lose their favored status, men become angry and resentful. "There are many more men who are taking care of the children than there are men on the freeway going berserk" (Pleck quoted in Gates, 1993, p. 53). But the resentment is there, which makes a peace plan difficult to formulate.

For society, peace in the gender war does not seem easily attainable. Several future scenarios are possible (Jones, 1996). Will the trend toward women as heads of households escalate into separatism in which women have exiled men? Will a male backlash prompt a superpatriarchy in which women are enslaved? Will technology create opportunities for people to do the work for which they are best suited regardless of gender? Or will things continue as they have for the past 30 years, with women gaining rights, roles, and extra work while men struggle with the changes in their own as well as in women's roles? None of these future options promises a truce.

For individuals, a peace plan is possible (White & Tyson-Rawson, 1996). Indeed, many couples have worked out equitable plans for living together and have built satisfying personal relationships (Schwartz, 1994). Building such relationships often requires analyzing the underlying assumptions connected with gender roles and finding ways to overcome the roles that society dictates for women and men. Alex and Susan in this chapter's headline story underwent such an analysis, and it helped them understand their gender scripts and how to rewrite the parts that were not working. Not all relationships can be mended so easily, but failing to understand the importance of gender will almost certainly allow the wars to continue.

Summary

The roles that men and women occupy have undergone changes in the past three decades, allowing women to move into careers that had formerly been the province of men. As women began to acquire careers and salaries comparable with men's, some men began to imagine that women would become more like them, which would make relating to each other easier. Some of these men have been disappointed, because women have made the changes in their lives, but not always the changes that many men had in mind.

The changes in women's employment have been additive rather than substitutive; that is, most women who are employed outside their homes also have family work to do when at home. Thus, most women are now employees, wives, and mothers. These multiple roles present stress in women's lives, but also offer rewards. Research indicates that the rewards outweigh the stresses for most women. Men also occupy multiple roles as employees, husbands, and fathers, but men do less family work at home than women do, which perpetuates the breadwinner role in the family structure. Research indicates that men find multiple roles rewarding, but they are less eager than women to allow family work to intrude on their employment obligations.

Men have long wondered what women want and have expressed the desire for women to behave in ways more similar to men. Gender differences may never have been as large as many people imagined, but men have gotten their wish in several respects: Women's behavior has changed to become more like men's behavior. These changes, however, have not resulted in the transformations that some men imagined. Men did not envision competition from women at work as a desirable outcome of gender similarity, but as women have moved into the world of paid employment, they have assumed roles and behaviors required by these situations. Men and women have become more alike in terms of education, employment, sexual attitudes and behavior, athletic competition, and rates of smoking. Few gender differences exist in experiencing emotion, but differences remain in how emotions are displayed. Men have become more like women, however, in their style of forming close personal relationships, and are beginning to explore the rewards of opening up to emotional sharing and talk.

Although the changes in women's lives have prompted men to change, these alterations have not been equal to the ones that women have experienced. A combination of the devaluation of traditionally feminine behaviors and the value placed on the activities that men perform has pushed women toward change. Some men dislike these changes and long once again for traditional roles for both; some men are trying to make the transition; and some men have welcomed the increasing similarities. Women, however, are more pleased with the changes in their lives than men are.

Women also wish for changes in men; they want men to accept and adopt some of the characteristics typical of women. Women would like for men to accept the validity of the feminine approach and to feel comfortable in adopting positive behaviors traditionally associated with women. One of these desired changes has occurred to some extent—the change in ways to communicate in intimate relationships. Women would like for men to be more emotionally expressive and to communicate intimate thoughts and feelings to their partners. Women would also like for men to become more active with their families, sharing household work and child care. These changes may be difficult to accomplish. The devaluation of women's characteristics and work means that men have few incentives for behaving more like women.

If women have become more like men in a number of ways, and if men have become more like women in some ways, how many gender differences remain? Differences continue in theories, with maximalist theories advocating that differences exist between the genders, and minimalist theories arguing for more similarities than differences.

Research on gender and ability has revealed relatively few differences. The largest of these differences in ability lies in men's greater physical strength, but few differences exist when measuring other abilities in laboratory situations. When examining the choices that men and women make concerning how to live their lives, larger gender differences appear. Indeed, the difference in choices may promote the idea that greater differences exist than research has confirmed.

The choices that women and men make tend to preserve well-defined gender roles rather than allow people to make freer choices and develop the most satisfying lives. Strict enforcement of gender-related behaviors may simplify rules of conduct, but preserving this dichotomy extracts a high price for individual women and men. On a societal level, the gender wars show no signs of diminishing in intensity, with many women wanting more changes and many men wanting a return to more traditional roles. On an individual level, peace between women and men is possible, and many couples have built relationships that allow them to participate fully in the workforce, household work, child care, and each other's lives.

Suggested Readings

Faludi, Susan. (1999). *Stiffed: The betrayal of the American man.* New York: Morrow. Faludi's book about men takes a sympathetic look at the dilemmas that men face in fulfilling the demands of their several roles. By examining many men in various situations, Faludi hears men's concerns and problems.

Kaminer, Wendy. (1993, October). Feminism's identity crisis. *Atlantic Monthly,* pp. 51–53, 56, 58–59, 62, 64, 66–68. Kaminer discusses the failure of most women to embrace feminism, despite their agreement with many of its goals, and she examines the implications of the maximalist and minimalist positions.

Schwartz, Pepper. (1994). *Peer marriage: How love between equals really works.* New York: Free Press. Schwartz examines couples' relationships, focusing on couples who have managed to construct marriage relationships in which both members are peers. Her report reveals the problems and advantages of working toward such relationships.

Sigel, Roberta S. (1996). *Ambition and accommodation: How women view gender relations.* Chicago: University of Chicago Press. Sigel interviewed men and women to determine their attitudes and experiences related to gender. Her book is an interesting mixture of quantitative results and personal experiences that reflect how the changes in gender roles have changed people's lives and how women and men are coping with the difficulties of living in a time of transition.

References

Abrams, Leslie R.; & Jones, Russell W. (1994, August). *The contribution of social roles to psychological distress in businesswomen.* Paper presented at the 102nd annual convention of the American Psychological Association, Los Angeles, CA.

Abramson, Paul R.; Goldberg, Philip A.; Greenberg, Judith H.; & Abramson, Linda M. (1977). The talking platypus phenomenon: Competency ratings as a function of sex and professional status. *Psychology of Women Quarterly, 2,* 114–124.

Abreu, Jose M. (1999). Conscious and nonconscious African American stereotypes: Impact on first impression and diagnostic ratings by therapists. *Journal of Consulting and Clinical Psychology, 67,* 387–393.

Adler, David A.; Drake, Robert E.; & Teague, Gregory B. (1990). Clinicians' practices in personality assessment: Does gender influence the use of DSM-III axis II? *Comprehensive Psychiatry, 31,* 125–133.

Adler, Jerry. (1996, June 17). Building a better dad. *Newsweek, 127*(25), pp. 58–64.

Africa News Service. (2000, February 4). Women want domestic violence law this year. Author, p. 1008032u6899.

Akiyama, Hiroko; Elliott, Kathryn; & Antonucci, Toni C. (1996). Same-sex and cross-sex relationships. *Journals of Gerontology, Series B., 51,* 374–382.

Allen, Bem P. (1995). Gender stereotypes are not accurate: A replication of Martin (1987) using diagnostic vs. self-report and behavioral criteria. (C. L. Martin's article, *Journal of Personality and Social Psychology,* vol. 52, p. 489, 1987) *Sex Roles, 32,* 583–600.

Allmendinger, Jutta; & Hackman, J. Richard. (1995). The more, the better? A four-nation study of the inclusion of women in symphony orchestras. *Social Forces, 74,* 423–460.

Altman, Barbara Mandell. (1985). Disabled women in the social structure. In Susan E. Browne, Debra Connors, & Nanci Stern (Eds.), *With the power of each breath: A disabled women's anthology* (pp. 69–76). San Francisco: Cleis Press.

Altman, Lawrence K. (1997, June 22). Is the longer life the healthier one? *New York Times,* section 14 (Women's Health), p. 18.

American Association of University Women (AAUW). (1992). *The AAUW report: How schools shortchange girls.* Washington, DC: American Association of University Women Education Foundation and National Educational Association.

American Association of University Women (AAUW). (1993). *Hostile hallways: The AAUW survey on sexual harassment in America's schools.* Washington, DC: American Association of University Women Educational Foundation.

American Psychiatric Association. (1987). *Diagnostic and statistical manual of mental disorders* (Rev. ed.). Washington, DC: Author.

American Psychiatric Association. (1994). *Diagnostic and statistical manual of mental disorders* (4th ed.). Washington, DC: Author.

American Psychological Association (APA) Task Force on Sex Bias and Sex-Role Stereotyping in Psychotherapeutic Practice. (1978). Guidelines for therapy with women. *American Psychologist, 33,* 1122–1123.

Andersen, Arnold E.; & DiDomenico, Lisa. (1992). Diet vs. shape content of popular male and female magazines: A dose-response relationship to the incidence of eating disorders? *International Journal of Eating Disorders, 11,* 283–287.

Anderson, Kristin J; & Leaper, Campbell. (1998). Meta-analyses of gender effects on conversational interruption: Who, what, when, where, and how. *Sex Roles, 39,* 225–252.

Aneshensel, Carol S.; Frerichs, Ralph R.; & Clark, Virginia A. (1981). Family roles and sex differences in depression. *Journal of Health and Social Behavior, 22,* 379–393.

Aneshensel, Carol S.; & Pearlin, Leonard I. (1987). Structural contexts of sex differences in stress. In Rosalind C. Barnett, Lois Biener, & Grace K. Baruch (Eds.), *Gender and stress* (pp. 75–95). New York: Free Press.

Angier, Natalie. (1999). *Woman: An intimate geography.* Boston: Houghton Mifflin.

Antill, John K. (1983). Sex role complementarity versus similarity in married couples. *Journal of Personality and Social Psychology, 45,* 145–155.

Apgar, Barbara. (2000). Premenstrual syndrome and the placebo response. *American Family Physician, 61,* 850.

Archer, John; & Lloyd, Barbara. (1982). *Sex and gender.* Cambridge, England: Cambridge University Press.

Aries, Elizabeth. (1987). Gender and communication. In Phillip Shaver & Clyde Hendrick (Eds.), *Sex and gender* (pp. 149–176). Newbury Park, CA: Sage.

Aries, Elizabeth. (1996). *Men and women in interaction.* New York: Oxford University Press.

Aronson, Amy; & Kimmel, Michael. (1997). The children's hour. *Tikkun, 12,* 32–33.

Ashton, Heather. (1991). Psychotropic-drug prescribing for women. *British Journal of Psychiatry, 158*(Suppl. 10), 30–35.

Astin, Helen S. (1984). The meaning of work in women's lives: A sociopsychological model of career choice and work behavior. *Counseling Psychologist, 12,* 117–126.

Astrachan, Anthony. (1986). *How men feel: Their response to women's demands for equality and power.* Garden City, NY: Anchor Press.

Attar, Beth K.; Guerra, Nancy G.; & Tolan, Patrick H. (1994). Neighborhood disadvantage, stressful life events, nd adjustment in urban elementary-school children. *Journal of Clinical Child Psychology, 23,* 391–400.

Aubé, Jennifer; & Koestner, Richard. (1992). Gender characteristics and adjustment: A longitudinal study. *Journal of Personality and Social Psychology, 63,* 485–493.

Aubé, Jennifer; & Koestner, Richard. (1995). Gender characteristics and relationship adjustment: Another look at similarity-complementarity hypotheses. *Journal of Personality, 63,* 879–904.

Averill, James R. (1982). *Anger and aggression: An essay on emotion.* New York: Springer-Verlag.

Avery, Patricia G.; & Walker, Constance. (1993). Prospective teachers' perceptions of ethnic and gender differences in academic achievement. *Journal of Teacher Education, 44,* 27–37.

Ayanian, John Z.; & Epstein, Arnold M. (1991). Differences in the use of procedures between women and men hospitalized for coronary heart disease. *New England Journal of Medicine, 325,* 221–225.

Baber, Kristine M.; & Monaghan, Patricia. (1988). College women's career and motherhood expectations: New options, old dilemmas. *Sex Roles, 19,* 189–203.

Baenninger, Maryann; & Newcombe, Nora. (1989). A role of experience in spatial test performance: A meta-analysis. *Sex Roles, 20,* 327–343.

Bagley, Christopher; & King, Kathleen. (1990). *Child sexual abuse: The search for healing.* London: Tavistock/Routledge.

Bailey, William T.; Silver, N. Clayton; & Oliver, Kathleen A. (1990). Women's rights and roles: Attitudes among Black and White students. *Psychological Reports, 66,* 1143–1146.

Bakan, David. (1966). *The duality of human existence.* Chicago: Rand McNally.

Baldwin, John D.; & Baldwin, Janice I. (1997). Gender differences in sexual interest. *Archives of Sexual Behavior, 26,* 181–210.

Ball, Richard E.; & Robbins, Lynn. (1986). Marital status and life satisfaction among Black Americans. *Journal of Marriage and the Family, 48,* 389–394.

Balmary, Marie. (1982). *Psychoanalyzing psychoanalysis: Freud and the hidden fault of the father* (Ned Lukacher, Trans.). Baltimore: Johns Hopkins University Press. (Original work published 1979)

Bandura, Albert. (1986). *Social foundations of thought and action: A social cognitive theory.* Englewood Cliffs, NJ: Prentice-Hall.

Banks, Terry; & Dabbs, James M., Jr. (1996). Salivary testosterone and cortisol in delinquent and violent urban subcultures. *Journal of Social Psychology, 136,* 49–56.

Barak, Azy. (1997). Cross-cultural perspectives on sexual harassment. In William O'Donohue (Ed.), *Sexual harassment: Theory, research, and treatment* (pp. 263–300), Boston: Allyn and Bacon.

Barnett, Rosalind C.; & Baruch, Grace K. (1987). Social roles, gender, and psychological distress. In Rosalind C. Barnett, Lois Biener, & Grace K. Baruch (Eds.), *Gender and stress* (pp. 122–143). New York: Free Press.

Barnett, Rosalind C.; Marshall, Nancy L.; & Pleck, Joseph H. (1992). Men's multiple roles and their relationship to men's psychological distress. *Journal of Marriage and the Family, 54,* 358–367.

Baumeister, Roy F. (1988). Should we stop studying sex differences altogether? *American Psychologist, 43,* 1092–1095.

Baxter, Susan. (1994, March/April). The last word on gender differences. *Psychology Today, 27,* 50–53, 85–86.

Bazzini, Doris G.; McIntosh, William D.; Smith, Stephen M.; Cook, Sabrina; & Harris, Caleigh. (1997). The aging woman in popular film: Underrepresented, unattractive, unfriendly, and unintelligent. *Sex Roles, 36,* 531–543.

Beal, Carole R. (1994). *Boys and girls: The development of gender roles.* New York: McGraw-Hill.

Beal, Carole R.; & Lockhart, Maria E. (1989). The effect of proper name and appearance changes on children's reasoning about gender constancy. *International Journal of Behavioral Development, 12,* 195–205.

Beck, Aaron T. (1985). *Anxiety disorders and phobias: A cognitive perspective.* New York: Basic Books.

Begley, Sharon. (1997, April 21). The science wars. *Newsweek, 129*(16), 54–57.

Begley, Sharon. (2000, November 6). The stereotype trap. *Newsweek, 136*(19), 66–68.

Belasco, Warren J. (1989, December). The two taste cultures. *Psychology Today,* pp. 29–36.

Belenky, Mary Field; Clinchy, Blythe McVicker; Goldberger, Nancy Rule; & Tarule, Jill Mattuck. (1986). *Women's ways of knowing: The development of self, voice, and mind.* New York: Basic Books.

Belle, Deborah. (1990). Poverty and women's mental health. *American Psychologist, 45,* 385–389.

Bem, Sandra Lipsitz. (1974). The measurement of psychological androgyny. *Journal of Consulting and Clinical Psychology, 42,* 155–162.

Bem, Sandra Lipsitz. (1981). Gender schema theory: A cognitive account of sex-typing. *Psychological Review, 88,* 354–364.

Bem, Sandra Lipsitz. (1985). Androgyny and gender schema theory: A conceptual and empirical integration. In Theo B. Sonderegger (Ed.), *Nebraska Symposium on Motivation, 1984: Psychology and gender* (pp. 179–226). Lincoln, NE: University of Nebraska Press.

Bem, Sandra Lipsitz. (1987). Gender schema theory and its implications for child development: Raising gender-aschematic children in a gender-schematic society. In Mary Roth Walsh (Ed.), *The psychology of women: Ongoing debates* (pp. 226–245). New Haven, CT: Yale University Press.

Bem, Sandra Lipsitz. (1989). Genital knowledge and gender constancy in preschool children. *Child Development, 60,* 649–662.

Bem, Sandra Lipsitz. (1993a). Is there a place in psychology for a feminist analysis of the social context? *Feminism & Psychology, 3,* 230–234.

Bem, Sandra Lipsitz. (1993b). *The lenses of gender.* New Haven, CT: Yale University Press.

Benbow, Camilla Persson. (1992). Academic achievement in mathematics and science of students between ages 13 and 23: Are there differences among students in the top one percent of mathematical ability. *Journal of Educational Psychology, 84,* 51–61.

Benbow, Camilla Persson; & Stanley, Julian C. (1980). Sex differences in mathematical ability: Fact or artifact? *Science, 210,* 1262–1264.

Benbow, Camilla Persson; & Stanley, Julian C. (1983). Sex differences in mathematical reasoning ability: More facts. *Science, 222,* 1029–1031.

Ben-David, Sarah. (1993). The two facets of female violence: The public and the domestic domains. *Journal of Family Violence, 8,* 345–359.

Benderly, Beryl Lieff. (1987). *The myth of two minds.* New York: Doubleday.

Benderly, Beryl Lieff. (1989, November). Don't believe everything you read.... *Psychology Today,* pp. 67–69.

Benenson, Joyce F.; Morash, Deanna; & Petrakos, Harriet. (1998). Gender differences in emotional closeness between preschool children and their mothers. *Sex Roles, 38,* 975–986.

Benin, Mary Holland; & Angostinelli, Joan. (1988). Husbands' and wives' satisfaction with the division of labor. *Journal of Marriage and the Family, 50,* 349–361.

Benokraitis, Nijole V. (1997). Sex discrimination in the 21st century. In Nijole V. Benokraitis (Ed.), *Subtle sexism* (pp. 5–33). Thousand Oaks, CA: Sage.

Benrud, Lisa M.; & Reddy, Diane M. (1998). Differential explanations of illness in women and men. *Sex Roles, 38,* 375–386.

Berdahl, Jennifer L.; Magley, Vicki J.; & Waldo, Craig R. (1996). The sexual harassment of men? Exploring the concept with theory and data. *Psychology of Women Quarterly, 20,* 527–547.

Berenbaum, Sheri A.; & Snyder, Elizabeth. (1995). Early hormonal influences on childhood sex-typed activity and playmate preferences: Implications for the development of sexual orientation. *Developmental Psychology, 31,* 31–42.

Berger, Bertrand D.; & Adesso, Vincent J. (1991). Gender differences in using alcohol to cope with depression. *Addictive Behaviors, 16,* 315–327.

Berman, Phyllis W. (1980). Are women more responsive than men to the young? A review of developmental and situational variables. *Psychological Bulletin, 88,* 668–695.

Bernard, Jessie. (1972). *The future of marriage.* New York: World Publishing.

Bernard, Jessie. (1981). The good-provider role: Its rise and fall. *American Psychologist, 36,* 1–12.

Bernardo, Donna Hodgkins; Shehan, Constance L.; & Leslie, Gerald R. (1987). A residue of tradition: Jobs, careers, and spouses' time in housework. *Journal of Marriage and the Family, 49,* 381–390.

Berndt, Thomas J. (1982). The features and effects of friendship in early adolescence. *Child Development, 53,* 1447–1460.

Berndt, Thomas J.; & Perry, T. Bridgett. (1986). Children's perceptions of friendships as supportive relationships. *Developmental Psychology, 22,* 640–648.

Bernstein, Dan. (1999). Introduction. In Dan Bernstein (Ed.), *Nebraska Symposium on Motivation, 1999: Gender and motivation* (pp. vii–xxiii). Lincoln, NE: University of Nebraska Press.

Bettencourt, B. Ann; & Miller, Norman. (1996). Gender differences in aggression as a function of provocation: A meta-analysis. *Psychological Bulletin, 119,* 422–447.

Betz, Nancy. (1993). Women's career development. In Florence L. Denmark & Michele A. Paludi (Eds.), *Psychology of women: A handbook of issues and theories* (pp. 627–684). Westport, CT: Greenwood Press.

Beyer, Sylvia. (1998). Gender differences in self-perception and negative recall biases. *Sex Roles, 38,* 103–133.

Beyer, Sylvia. (1999). The accuracy of academic gender stereotypes. *Sex Roles, 41,* 297–306.

Bickel, Janet. (1997). Gender stereotypes and misconceptions: Unresolved issues in physicians' professional development. *Journal of the American Medical Association, 277,* 1405–1406.

Biener, Lois. (1987). Gender differences in the use of substances for coping. In Rosalind C. Barnett, Lois Biener, & Grace K. Baruch (Eds.), *Gender and stress* (pp. 330–349). New York: Free Press.

Biernat, Monica. (1991). Gender stereotypes and the relationship between masculinity and femininity: A developmental analysis. *Journal of Personality and Social Psychology, 61,* 351–365.

Biernat, Monica; & Kobrynowicz, Diane. (1997). Gender- and race-based standards of competence: Lower minimum standards but higher ability standards for devalued groups. *Journal of Personality and Social Psychology, 72,* 544–557.

Bigler, Rebecca S. (1997). Conceptual and methodological issues in the measurement of children's sex typing. *Psychology of Women Quarterly, 21,* 53–69.

Bjorkqvist, Kaj. (1994). Sex differences in physical, verbal, and indirect aggression: A review of recent research, *Sex Roles, 30,* 177–188.

Blair, Sampson Lee; & Lichter, Daniel T. (1991). Measuring the division of household labor: Gender segregation of housework among American couples. *Journal of Family Issues, 12,* 91–113.

Blakemore, Judith E. Owen. (1998). The influence of gender and parental attitudes on preschool children's interest in babies: Observations in natural settings. *Sex Roles, 38,* 73–94.

Blanchard, Christy A.; & Lichtenberg, James W. (1998). Counseling psychologists' training to deal with their sexual feelings in therapy. *Counseling Psychologist, 26,* 624–639.

Blechman, Elaine A. (1980). Behavior therapies. In Annette M. Brodsky & Rachel Hare-Mustin (Eds.), *Women and psychotherapy* (pp. 217–244). New York: Guilford Press.

Blechman, Elaine A.; Clay, Connie J.; Kipke, Michele D.; & Bickel, Warren K. (1988). The premenstrual experience. In Elaine A. Blechman & Kelly D. Brownell (Eds.), *Handbook of behavioral medicine for women* (pp. 80–91). New York: Pergamon Press.

Blumenthal, Susan J.; & Wood, Susan F. (1997). Women's health care: Federal initiatives, policies, and directions. In Sheryle J. Gallant, Gwendolyn Puryear Keita, & Reneé Royak-Schaler (Eds.), *Health care for women: Psychological, social, and behavioral influences* (pp. 3–10). Washington, DC: American Psychological Association.

Blumstein, Philip; & Schwartz, Pepper. (1983). *American couples.* New York: Pocket Books.

Blustain, Sarah. (2000, November/December). The new gender wars. *Psychology Today, 33,* 42–45, 48–49.

Bly, Robert. (1990). *Iron John.* Reading, MA: Addison-Wesley.

Bly, Robert. (1994, August). *Where are men now?* Paper presented at the 102nd annual convention of the American Psychological Association, Los Angeles, CA.

Bohan, Janis S. (1996). *Psychology and sexual orientation: Coming to terms.* New York: Routledge.

Bonvillain, Nancy. (1998). *Women and men: Cultural constructs of gender* (2nd ed.). Upper Saddle River, NJ: Prentice Hall.

Booth, Alan; Johnson, David R.; & Granger, Douglas A. (1999). Testosterone and men's depression: The role of social behavior. *Journal of Health and Social Behavior, 40,* 130–140.

Booth, Alan; Shelley, Greg; Mazur, Allan; Tharp, Gerry; & Kittok, Roger. (1989). Testosterone, and winning and losing in human competition. *Hormones and Behavior, 23,* 556–571.

Boston, Martha B.; & Levy, Gary D. (1991). Changes in differences in preschoolers' understanding of gender scripts. *Cognitive Development, 6,* 417–432.

Botkin, Darla R.; Weeks, M. O'Neal; & Morris, Jeanette E. (2000). Changing marriage role expectations: 1961–1996. *Sex Roles, 42,* 933–942.

Bradshaw, Carla K. (1994). Asian and Asian American women: Historical and political considerations in psychotherapy. In Lillian Comas-Díaz & Beverly Greene (Eds.), *Women of color: Integrating ethnic and gender identities in psychotherapy* (pp. 72–113). New York: Guilford Press.

Brannon, Linda; & Feist, Jess. (2000). *Health psychology: An introduction to behavior and health* (4th ed.). Belmont, CA: Wadsworth.

Brannon, Robert. (1976). The male sex role: Our culture's blueprint of manhood and what it's done for us lately. In Deborah S. David & Robert Brannon (Eds.), *The forty-nine percent majority* (pp. 1–45). Reading, MA: Addison-Wesley.

Brecher, Edward M. (1969). *The sex researchers.* Boston: Little, Brown.

Breedlove, S. Marc. (1994). Sexual differentiation of the human nervous system. *Annual Review of Psychology, 45,* 389–418.

Brems, Christiane; & Schlottmann, Robert S. (1988). Gender-bound definitions of mental health. *Journal of Psychology, 122,* 5–14.

Bridge, M. Junior. (1995). What's news? In Cynthia M. Lont (Ed.), *Women and media: Content, careers, and criticism* (pp. 15–28). Belmont, CA: Wadsworth.

Britannica Book of the Year, 1999. (1999). Chicago: Encyclopedia Britannica.

Brodsky, Annette; & Holroyd, Jean. (1975). Report of the Task Force on Sex Bias and Sex-Role Stereotyping in Psychotherapeutic Practice. *American Psychologist, 30, 1169–1175.*

Brooks, Gary R. (1998). *A new psychotherapy for traditional men.* San Francisco: Jossey-Bass.

Brooks-Gunn, Jeanne; & Furstenberg, Frank F., Jr. (1989). Adolescent sexual behavior. *American Psychologist, 44,* 249–257.

Broverman, Inge K.; Broverman, Donald M.; Clarkson, Frank E.; Rosenkrantz, Paul S.; & Vogel, Susan R. (1970). Sex-role stereotypes and clinical judgments of mental health. *Journal of Consulting and Clinical Psychology, 34,* 1–7.

Broverman, Inge K.; Vogel, Susan Raymond; Broverman, Donald M.; Clarkson, Frank E.; & Rosenkrantz, Paul S. (1972). Sex-role stereotypes: A current appraisal. *Journal of Social Issues, 28*(2), 59–78.

Brown, Laura B.; Uebelacker, Lisa; & Heatherington, Laurie. (1998). Men, women, and the self-presentation of achievement. *Sex Roles, 38,* 253–268.

Brown, Laura S. (1988). Feminist therapy with lesbians and gay men. In Mary Ann Dutton Douglas & Lenore E. A. Walker (Eds.), *Feminist psychotherapies: Integration of therapeutic and feminist systems* (pp. 206–227). Norwod, NJ: Ablex.

Brown, Laura S. (1992). A feminist critique of personality disorders. In Laura S. Brown & Mary Ballou (Eds.), *Personality and psychopathology: Feminist reappraisals* (pp. 206–228). New York: Guilford Press.

Brown, Lyn Mikel; & Gilligan, Carol. (1992). *Meeting at the crossroads: Women's psychology and girls' development.* Cambridge, MA: Harvard University Press.

Brown, Lyn Mikel; & Gilligan, Carol. (1993). Meeting at the crossroads: Women's psychology and girls' development. *Feminism & Psychology,* 3, 11–35.

Brown, Susan L.; & Booth, Alan. (1996). Cohabitation versus marriage: A comparison of relationship quality. *Journal of Marriage and the Family, 58,* 668–678.

Browne, Beverly A. (1998). Gender stereotypes in advertising on children's television in the 1990s: A cross-national analysis. *Journal of Advertising, 27,* 83–96.

Brownell, Kelly D.; & Rodin, Judith. (1994). The dieting maelstrom: Is it possible and advisable to lose weight? *American Psychologist, 49,* 781–791.

Brownlow, Sheila; Jacobi, Tara; & Rogers, Molly. (2000). Science anxiety as a function of gender and experience. *Sex Roles, 42,* 119–132.

Brownmiller, Susan. (1975). *Against our will: Men, women and rape.* New York: Simon & Schuster.

Brumberg, Joan Jacobs. (1997). *The body project.* New York: Random House.

Bryant, Anne. (1995, March). Sexual harassment in school takes it toll. *USA Today Magazine, 123,* 40–41.

Buhle, Mari Jo. (1999, February 5). Feminism, Freud, and popular culture. *Chronicle of Higher Education,* p. B4.

Buhrmester, Duane; & Furman, Wyndol. (1987). The development of companionship and intimacy. *Child Development, 58,* 1101–1113.

Bukowski, William M.; Gauze, Cyma; Hoza, Betsy; & Newcomb, Andrew F. (1993). Differences and consistency between same-sex and other-sex peer relationships during early adolescence. *Developmental Psychology, 29,* 255–263.

Buntaine, Roberta L.; & Costenbader, Virginia K. (1997). Self-reported differences in the experience and expression of anger between girls and boys. *Sex Roles, 36,* 625–637.

Burge, Penny L.; & Culver, Steven M. (1990). Sexism, legislative power, and vocational education. In Susan L. Gabriel & Isaiah Smithson (Eds.), *Gender in the classroom: Power and pedagogy* (pp. 160–175). Urbana, IL: University of Illinois Press.

Burke, Ronald J. (1999). Workaholism in organizations: Gender differences. *Sex Roles, 41,* 333–346.

Burnam, M. Audrey; Stein, Judith A.; Golding, Jacqueline M.; Siegel, Judith M.; Sorenson, Susan B.; Forsythe, Alan B.; & Telles, Cynthia A. (1988). Sexual assault and mental disorders in a community population. *Journal of Consulting and Clinical Psychology, 56,* 843–850.

Burt, Martha R.; & Estep, Rhoda E. (1981). Apprehension and fear: Learning a sense of sexual vulnerability. *Sex Roles, 7,* 511–522.

Burton, Velmer S., Jr.; Cullen, Francis T.; Evans, T. David; Alarid, Leanne Fiftal; & Dunaway, R. Gregory. (1998). Gender, self-control, and crime. *Journal of Research in Crime and Delinquency, 35,* 123–147.

Bush, Diane M.; & Simmons, R. G. (1987). Gender and coping with the entry into early adolescence. In Rosalind C. Barnett, Lois Biener, & Grace K. Baruch (Eds.), *Gender and stress* (pp. 185–217). New York: Free Press.

Business Week. (1999, September 27). Ethnic gaps on campus. *Business Week,* 3648, 34.

Buss, David M. (1991). Conflict in married couples: Personality predictors of anger and upset. *Journal of Personality, 59,* 663–688.

Buss, David M. (1994). *The evolution of desire.* New York: Basic Books.

Buss, David M. (1996). Sexual conflict: Evolutionary insights into feminism and the "battle of the sexes." In David M. Buss & Neil M. Malamuth (Eds.), *Sex, power, conflict: Evolutionary and feminist perspectives* (pp. 296–318). New York: Oxford University Press.

Buss, David M.; & Barnes, Michael. (1986). Preferences in human mate selection. *Journal of Personality and Social Psychology, 50,* 559–570.

Bussey, Kay; & Bandura, Albert. (1984). Influence of gender constancy and social power on sex-linked modeling. *Journal of Personality and Social Psychology, 47,* 1292–1302.

Bussey, Kay; & Bandura, Albert. (1992). Self-regulatory mechanisms governing gender development. *Child Development, 63,* 1236–1250.

Bussey, Kay; & Bandura, Albert. (1999). Social cognitive theory of gender development and differentiation. *Psychological Review, 106,* 676–713.

Cairns, Robert B. (1986). An evolutionary and developmental perspective on aggressive patterns. In Carolyn Zahn-Waxler, E. Mark Cummings, & Ronald Iannotti (Eds.), *Altruism and aggression: Biological and social origins* (pp. 58–87). Cambridge, England: Cambridge University Press.

Cairns, Robert B.; Cairns, Beverley D.; Neckerman, Holly J.; Ferguson, Lynda L.; & Gariépy, Jean-Louis. (1989). Growth and aggression: 1. Childhood to early adolescence. *Developmental Psychology, 25,* 320–330.

Caldwell, Mayta A.; & Peplau, Letitia Anne. (1982). Sex differences in same-sex friendship. *Sex Roles, 8,* 721–732.

Cameron, Oliver G.; & Hill, Elizabeth M. (1989). Women and anxiety. *Psychiatric Clinics of North America, 12,* 175–186.

Cammaert, Lorna P.; & Larsen, Carolyn C. (1988). Feminist frameworks of psychotherapy. In Mary Ann Dutton Douglas & Lenore E. A. Walker (Eds.), *Feminist psychotherapies: Integration of therapeutic and feminist systems* (pp. 12–36). Norwood, NJ: Ablex.

Campbell, Anne. (1993). *Men, women, and aggression.* New York: Basic Books.

Campbell, Bebe Moore. (1986). *Successful women, angry men: Backlash in the two-career marriage.* New York: Random House.

Campbell, Constance R.; & Henry, John W. (1999). Gender differences in self-attributions: Relationships of gender to attributional consistency, style, and expectations for performance in a college course. *Sex Roles, 41,* 95–104.

Campenni, C. Estelle. (1999). Gender stereotyping of children's toys: A comparison of parents and nonparents. *Sex Roles, 40,* 121–138.

Cancian, Francesca M. (1986). The feminization of love. *Signs, 11,* 692–709.

Cancian, Francesca M. (1987). *Love in America: Gender and self-development.* Cambridge, England: Cambridge University Press.

Cancian, Francesca M.; & Oliker, Stacey J. (2000). *Caring and gender.* Thousand Oaks, CA: Pine Forge Press.

Cann, Arnie; & Vann, Elizabeth D. (1995). Implications of sex and gender differences for self: Perceived advantages and disadvantages of being the other gender. *Sex Roles, 33,* 531–541.

Cannon, Walter B. (1927). The James-Lange theory of emotions: A critical examination and an alternative theory. *American Journal of Psychology, 39,* 106–124.

Caplan, Paula J.; & Caplan, Jeremy B. (1994). *Thinking critically about research on sex and gender.* New York: HarperCollins.

Caplan, Paula J.; MacPherson, Gael M.; & Tobin, Patricia. (1985). Do sex-related differences in spatial abilities exist? A multilevel critique with new data. *American Psychologist, 40,* 786–799.

Capraro, Rocco L. (2000). Why college men drink: Alcohol, adventure, and the paradox of masculinity. *Journal of American College Health, 48,* 307–315.

Carr, Judith G.; Gilroy, Faith D.; & Sherman, Martin F. (1996). Silencing the self and depression among women: The moderating role of race. *Psychology of Women Quarterly, 20,* 375–392.

Carr, Rey A. (1991). Addicted to power: Sexual harassment and the unethical behavior of university faculty. *Canadian Journal of Counselling, 25,* 447–461.

Carrier, Joseph. (1997). Miguel: Sexual life history of a gay Mexican American. In Maxine Baca Zinn, Pierrette Hondagneu-Sotelo, & Michael A. Messner (Eds.), *Through the prism of difference: Readings on sex and gender* (pp. 210–220). Boston: Allyn and Bacon.

Carter, Stephen L. (1991). *Reflections of an affirmative action baby.* New York: Basic Books.

Casey, Kathryn. (2000, March). Who has the most stress? *Ladies Home Journal, 117,* 152–154.

Casper, Regina C.; Belanoff, Joseph; & Offer, Daniel. (1996). Gender differences, but no racial group differences, in self-reported psychiatric symptoms in adolescents. *Journal of the American Academy of Child and Adolescent Psychiatry, 35,* 500–508.

Catalyst. (1999). *Catalyst census of women corporate officers and top earners.* http://www.catalystwomen.org/press

CBS News Transcripts. (2000, August 15). *The Early Show.* New York: Central Broadcasting System.

Centers for Disease Control and Prevention. (2000). Teen pregnancy. Retrieved October 31, 2000, from the World Wide Web: http://www.cdc.gov/nccdphp/teen.htm.

Central Intelligence Agency. (2000). *World factbook.* Washington, DC: Government Printing Office.

Chaiken, Shelly; & Pliner, Patricia. (1987). Women, but not men, are what they eat: The effect of meal size and gender on perceived femininity and masculinity. *Personality and Social Psychology Bulletin, 13,* 166–176.

Chartrand, Sabra. (1996, June 2). Gender gap splits views of glass ceiling. *New York Times Job Market.* Retrieved July, 1996 from the World Wide Web: http://www.nytimes.com/search/daily.

Chehrazi, Shahla. (1986). Female psychology: A review. *Journal of the American Psychoanalytic Association, 34,* 111–162. Also in Mary Roth Walsh (Ed.). (1987). *The psychology of women: Ongoing debates* (pp. 22–38). New Haven: Yale University Press.

Chernin, Kim. (1978). *The obsession: Reflections on the tyranny of slenderness.* New York: Harper & Row.

Cherry, Frances; & Deaux, Kay. (1978). Fear of success versus fear of gender-inappropriate behavior. *Sex Roles, 4,* 97–101.

Chesler, Phyllis. (1972). *Women and madness.* New York: Avon.

Chess, Stella; & Thomas, Alexander. (1982). Infant bonding: Mystique and reality. *American Journal of Orthopsychiatry, 52,* 213–222.

Chodorow, Nancy. (1978). *The reproduction of mothering: Psychoanalysis and the sociology of gender.* Berkeley, CA: University of California Press.

Chodorow, Nancy. (1979). Feminism and difference: Gender, relation, and difference in psychoanalytic perspective. *Socialist Review, 46,* 42–64. Also in Mary Roth Walsh (Ed.) (1987). *The psychology of women: Ongoing debates* (pp. 249–264). New Haven: Yale University Press.

Chodorow, Nancy J. (1994). *Femininities, masculinities, sexualities: Freud and beyond.* Lexington, KY: The University Press of Kentucky.

Christensen, Andrew; & Jacobson, Neil S. (1994). Who (or what) can do psychotherapy: The status and challenge of nonprofessional therapies. *Psychological Science, 5,* 8–14.

Christensen, Larry B. (1997). *Experimental methodology* (7th ed.). Boston: Allyn and Bacon.

Christian, Harry. (1994). *The making of anti-sexist men.* London: Routledge.

Chu, Chung-Chou; Abi-Dargham, Annissé; Ackerman, Bette; Cetingök, Maummer; & Klein, Helen E. (1989). Sex differences in schizophrenia. *International Journal of Social Psychiatry, 35,* 237–244.

Cleary, Paul D. (1987). Gender differences in stress-related disorders. In Rosalind C. Barnett, Lois Biener, & Grace K. Baruch (Eds.), *Gender and stress* (pp. 39–72). New York: Free Press.

Cohen, Deborah. (1992). Why there are so few male teachers in early grades. *Education Digest, 57*(6), 11–13.

Cohen, Jacob. (1969). *Statistical power analysis for the behavioral sciences.* New York: Academic Press.

Cohen, Laurie L.; & Shotland, R. Lance. (1996). Timing of first sexual intercourse in a relationship: Expectations, experiences, and perceptions of others. *Journal of Sex Research, 33,* 291–299.

Cohen, Theodore F. (1992). Men's families, men's friends: A structural analysis of constraints on men's social ties. In Peter M. Nardi (Ed.), *Men's friendships* (pp. 115–131). Newbury Park, CA: Sage.

Cohen-Kettenis, Peggy T.; & van Goozen, Stephanie H. M. (1997). Sex reassignment of adolescent transsexuals: A follow-up study. Journal of the *American Academy of Child and Adolescent Psychiatry, 36,* 263–271.

Colby, Anne; & Damon, William. (1983). Listening to a different voice: A review of Gilligan's *A Different Voice. Merrill-Palmer Quarterly, 29,* 473–481. Also in Mary Roth Walsh (Ed.) (1987), *The psychology of women: Ongoing debates* (pp. 321–329). New Haven: Yale University Press.

Cole, Collier M.; O'Boyle, Michael; Emory, Lee E.; Meyer, Walter J., Jr. (1997). Comorbidity of gender dysphoria and other major psychiatric diagnoses. *Archives of Sexual Behavior, 26,* 13–26.

Collins, M. Elizabeth. (1991). Body figure perceptions and preferences among preadolescent children. *International Journal of Eating Disorders, 10,* 199–208.

Collins, Nancy L.; & Miller, Lynn Carol. (1994). Self-disclosure and liking: A meta-analytic review. *Psychological Bulletin, 116,* 457–475.

Coltrane, Scott; & Messineo, Melinda. (2000). The perpetuation of subtle prejudice: Race and gender imagery in 1990s television advertising. *Sex Roles, 42,* 363–389.

Coltrane, Scott; & Valdez, Elsa O. (1993). Reluctant compliance: Work-family role allocation in dual-earner Chicano families. In Jane C. Hood (Ed.), *Men, work, and family* (pp. 151–175). Newbury Park, CA: Sage.

Comas-Díaz, Lillian; & Greene, Beverly. (1994a). Overview: An ethnocultural mosaic. In Lillian Comas-Díaz & Beverly Greene (Eds.), *Women of color: Integrating ethnic and gender identities in psychotherapy* (pp. 3–9). New York: Guilford Press.

Comas-Díaz, Lillian; & Greene, Beverly. (1994b). Overview: Gender and ethnicity in the healing process.

In Lillian Comas-Díaz & Beverly Greene (Eds.), *Women of color: Integrating ethnic and gender identities in psychotherapy* (pp. 185–193). New York: Guilford Press.

Condravy, Jace; Skirboll, Esther; & Taylor, Rhoda. (1998). Faculty perceptions of classroom gender dynamics. *Women and Language, 21,* 18–27.

Condry, John; & Condry, Sandra. (1976). Sex differences: A study in the eye of the beholder. *Child Development, 47,* 812–818.

Connell, R. W. (1987). *Gender and power: Society, the person and sexual politics.* Cambridge: Polity Press.

Connell, R. W. (1992). Masculinity, violence, and war. In Michael S. Kimmel & Michael A. Messner (Eds.), *Men's lives* (2nd ed.; pp. 176–183). New York: Macmillan.

Connell, R. W. (1995). *Masculinities.* Berkeley, CA: University of California Press.

Connell, R. W. (1996). Teaching the boys: New research on masculinity, the gender strategies for schools. *Teachers College Record, 98,* 206–235.

Constantino, John N.; Grosz, Daniel; Saenger, Paul; Chandler, Donald W.; Nandi, Reena; & Earls, Felton J. (1993). Testosterone and aggression in children. *Journal of the American Academy of Child and Adolescent Psychiatry, 32,* 1217–1222.

Constantinople, Anne. (1973). Masculinity-femininity: An exception to a famous dictum. *Psychological Bulletin, 80,* 389–407.

Cook, Ellen Piel; Warnke, Melanie; & Dupuy, Paula. (1993). Gender bias and the DSM-III-R. *Counselor Education and Supervision, 32,* 311–322.

Cooper, Alvin; Scherer, Coralie R.; Boies, Sylvain C.; & Gordon, Barry L. (1999). Sexuality on the Internet: From sexual exploration to pathological expression. *Professional Psychology: Research and Practice, 30,* 154–164.

Cooperstock, Ruth. (1970). A review of women's psychotropic drug use. *Canadian Journal of Psychiatry, 24,* 29–34.

Cowley, Geoffrey. (1996, September 16). Attention: Aging men. *Newsweek, 128*(12), pp. 68–75.

Coyne, Jerry A. (2000, April 3). Of vice and men—The fairy tales of evolutionary psychology. *New Republic, 222,* 27–34.

Crandall, Christian S.; Tsang, Jo-Ann; Goldman, Susan; & Pennington, John T. (1999). Newsworthy moral dilemmas: Justice, caring, and gender. *Sex Roles, 40,* 187–210.

Crawford, June; Kippax, Susan; Onxy, Jenny; Gault, Una; & Benton, Pam. (1992). *Emotion and gender: Constructing meaning from memory.* London: Sage.

Crawford, Mary. (1989). Agreeing to differ: Feminist epistemologies and women's ways of knowing. In Mary Crawford & Margaret Gentry (Eds.), *Gender and thought: Psychological perspectives* (pp. 128–145). New York: Springer-Verlag.

Crawford, Mary; & Kimmel, Ellen. (1999). Promoting methodological diversity in feminist research. *Psychology of Women Quarterly, 23,* 1–6.

Crawford, Mary; & Marecek, Jeanne. (1989). Psychology reconstructs the female: 1968–1988. *Psychology of Women Quarterly, 13,* 147–165.

Crichton, Michael. (1999). Ritual abuse, hot air, and missed opportunities. *Science, 283,* 1461–1463.

Crick, Nicki R.; Werner, Nicole E.; Casas, Juan F.; O'Brien, Kathryn M.; Nelson, David A.; Grotpeter, Jennifer K.; & Markon, Kristian. (1999). Childhood aggression and gender: A new look at an old problem. In Dan Bernstein (Ed.), *Nebraska Symposium on Motivation, 1999: Gender and motivation* (pp. 75–141). Lincoln, NE: University of Nebraska Press.

Crook, Thomas H.; Youngjohn, James R.; & Larrabee, Glenn J. (1993). The influence of age, gender, and cues on computer-simulated topographic memory. *Developmental Neuropsychology, 9,* 41–53.

Cuffe, Steven P.; Addy, Cheryl L.; Garrison, Carol Z.; Waller, Jennifer L.; Jackson, Kirby L.; McKeown, Robert E.; & Chilappagari, Shailaja. (1998). Prevalence of PTSD in a community sample of older adolescents. *Journal of the American Academy of Child and Adolescent Psychiatry, 37,* 147–154.

Culbertson, Frances M. (1997). Depression and gender: An international review. *American Psychologist, 52,* 25–31.

Cutler, Susan E.; & Nolen-Hoeksema, Susan. (1991). Accounting for sex differences in depression through female victimization: Childhood sexual abuse. *Sex Roles, 24,* 425–438.

Cyranowski, Jill M.; Frank, Ellen; Young, Elizabeth; & Shear, M. Katherine. (2000). Adolescent onset of the gender difference in lifetime rates of major depression. *Archives of General Psychiatry, 57,* 21–56.

Dabbs, James M., Jr. (1992). Testosterone and occupational achievement. *Social Forces, 70,* 813–824.

Dabbs, James M., Jr.; Carr, Timothy S.; Frady, Robert L.; & Riad, Jasmin K. (1995). Testosterone, crime, and misbehavior among 692 male prison inmates. *Personality and Individual Differences, 18,* 627–633.

Dabbs, James M., Jr.; de la Rue, Denise; & Williams, Paula M. (1990). Testosterone and occupational choice: Actors, ministers, and other men. *Journal of Personality and Social Psychology, 59,* 1261–1265.

Dabbs, James M., Jr.; Hargrove, Marian F.; & Heusel, Colleen. (1996). Testosterone differences among college fraternities: Well-behaved vs. rambunctious. *Personality and Individual Differences, 20,* 157–161.

Dabbs, James M., Jr.; Hopper, Charles H.; & Jurkovic, Gregory J. (1990). Testosterone and personality among college students and military veterans. *Personality and Individual Differences, 11,* 1263–1269.

Dabbs, James M., Jr.; & Morris, Robin. (1990). Testosterone, social class, and antisocial behavior in a sample of 4,462 men. *Psychological Science, 1,* 209–211.

Dabbs, James M., Jr.; Ruback, R. Barry; Frady, Robert L.; Hopper, Charles H.; & Sgoutas, Demetrios S. (1988). Saliva testosterone and criminal violence among women. *Personality and Individual Differences, 9,* 269–275.

Daniels, Cora. (1998, October 12). The global glass ceiling. *Fortune, 138,* 102–103.

Darwin, Charles. (1872). *The expression of emotions in man and animals.* New York: Philosophical Library.

Daugherty, Cynthia; & Lees, Marty. (1988). Feminist psychodynamic therapies. In Mary Ann Dutton Douglas & Lenore E. A. Walker (Eds.), *Feminist psychotherapies: Integration of therapeutic and feminist systems* (pp. 68–90). Norwod, NJ: Ablex.

Davenport, Donna S.; & Yurich, John M. (1991). Multicultural gender issues. *Journal of Counseling and Development, 70,* 64–71.

Davis, Kathy. (1994). What's in a voice? Methods and metaphors. *Feminism & Psychology, 4,* 353–361.

Davison, Kathryn P.; Pennebaker, James W.; & Dickerson, Sally S. (2000). Who talks? The social psychology of illness support groups. *American Psychologist, 55,* 205–217.

Deal, Jennifer J.; & Stevenson, Maura A. (1998). Perceptions of female and male managers in the 1990s: Plu ca change.... *Sex Roles, 38,* 287–300.

Deaux, Kay. (1984). From individual differences to social categories: Analysis of a decade's research on gender. *American Psychologist, 39,* 105–116.

Deaux, Kay. (1987). Psychological constructions of masculinity and femininity. In June Machover Reinisch, Leonard A. Rosenblum, & Stephanie A. Sanders (Eds.), *Masculinity/Femininity: Basic perspectives* (pp. 289–303). New York: Oxford University Press.

Deaux, Kay. (1993). Commentary: Sorry, wrong number: A reply to Gentile's call. *Psychological Science, 4,* 125–126.

Deaux, Kay; & Lewis, Laurie. (1984). The structure of gender stereotypes: Interrelationships among components and gender label. *Journal of Personality and Social Psychology, 46,* 991–1004.

Degler, Carl N. (1974). What ought to be and what was: Women's sexuality in the nineteenth century. *American Historical Review, 79,* 1467–1490.

de Monteflores, Carmen; & Schultz, Stephen J. (1978). Coming out: Similarities and differences for lesbians and gay men. *Journal of Social Issues, 34*(3), 59–72.

Derry, Paula S.; Gallant, Sheryle J.; & Woods, Nancy F. (1997). Premenstrual syndrome and menopause. In Sheryle J. Gallant, Gwendolyn Puryear Keita, & Reneé Royak-Schaler (Eds.), *Health care for women: Psychological, social, and behavioral influences* (pp. 203–220). Washington, DC: American Psychological Association.

Desjarlais, Robert; Eisenberg, Leon; Good, Byron; & Kleinman, Arthur. (1995). *World mental health: Problems and priorities in low-income countries.* New York: Oxford University Press.

Deuster, Patricia A.; Adera, Tilahun; & South-Paul, Jeannette. (1999). Biological, social, and behavioral factors associated with premenstrual syndrome. *Archives of Family Medicine, 8,* 122–128.

Deutsch, Francine M.; Lussier, Julianne B.; & Servis, Laura J. (1993). Husbands at home: Predictors of paternal participation in childcare and housework. *Journal of Personality and Social Psychology, 65,* 1154–1166.

Di Caccavo, Antonietta; & Reid, Fraser. (1998). The influence of attitudes toward male and female patients on treatment decisions in general practice. *Sex Roles, 38,* 613–629.

Dietz, Tracy L. (1998). An examination of violence and gender role portrayals in video games: Implications for gender socialization and aggressive behavior. *Sex Roles, 38,* 425–442.

Dijkstra, Bram. (1996). *Evil sisters: The threat of female sexuality and the cult of manhood.* New York: Knopf.

DiMatteo, M. Robin; & Kahn, Katherine L. (1997). Psychosocial aspects of childbirth. In Sheryle J. Gallant, Gwendolyn Puryear Keita, & Reneé Royak-Schaler (Eds.), *Health care for women: Psychological, social, and behavioral influences* (pp. 175–186). Washington, DC: American Psychological Association.

Dinnerstein, Dorothy. (1976). *The mermaid and the minotaur: Sexual arrangements and the human malaise.* New York: Harper & Row.

Docter, Richard F.; & Prince, Virginia. (1997). Transvestism: A survey of 1032 cross-dressers. *Archives of Sexual Behavior, 26,* 589–605.

Dolan, Bridget. (1994). Why women? Gender issues and eating disorders: An introduction. In Bridget Dolan & Inez Gitzinger (Eds.), *Why women? Gender issues and eating disorders* (pp. 1–11). London: Athlone Press.

Doll, Richard; & Peto, Richard. (1981). *The causes of cancer.* New York: Oxford University Press.

Dollard, John; Doob, Leonard; Miller, Neal; Mowrer, O. Hobart; & Sears, Robert. (1939). *Frustration and aggression.* New Haven, CT: Yale University Press.

Dovidio, John F.; Ellyson, Steve L.; Keating, Caroline F.; Heltman, Karen; & Brown, Clifford E. (1988). The relationship of social power to visual displays of dominance between men and women. *Journal of Personality and Social Psychology, 54,* 233–242.

Dreher, George F.; & Cox, Taylor H., Jr. (1996). Race, gender, and opportunity: A study of compensation attainment and the establishment of mentoring relationships. *Journal of Applied Psychology, 81,* 297–308.

Drewnowski, Adam; & Yee, Doris K. (1987). Men and body image: Are males satisfied with their body weight? *Psychosomatic Medicine, 49,* 626–634.

Dreyfus, Colleen K. (1994, August). *Stigmatizing attitudes toward male victims.* Paper presented at the 102nd annual convention of the American Psychological Association, Los Angeles, CA.

Duarte, Linda M.; & Thompson, Janice M. (1999). Sex differences in self-silencing. *Psychological Reports, 85,* 145–161.

Dubbert, Patricia M. (1992). Exercise in behavioral medicine. *Journal of Consulting and Clinical Psychology, 60,* 613–618.

Dubbert, Patricia M.; & Martin, John E. (1988). Exercise. In Elaine A. Blechman; & Kelly D. Brownell (Eds.), *Handbook of behavioral medicine for women* (pp. 291–304). New York: Pergamon Press.

DuBois, Cathy L. Z.; Knapp, Deborah E.; Faley, Robert H.; & Kustis, Gary A. (1998). An empirical examination of same- and other-gender sexual harassment in the workplace. *Sex Roles, 39,* 731–750.

DuBois, David L.; & Hirsch, Barton J. (1990). School and neighborhood friendship patterns of Blacks and Whites in early adolescence. *Child Development, 61,* 524–536.

Duck, Steve. (1991). *Understanding relationships.* New York: Guilford Press.

Duindam, Vincent; & Spruijt, Ed. (1997). Caring fathers in the Netherlands. *Sex Roles, 36,* 149–160.

Duncan, Lauren E.; & Williams, Linda M. (1998). Gender role socialization and male-on-male vs. female-on-male child sexual abuse. *Sex Roles, 39,* 765–786.

Durkin, Kevin; & Nugent, Bradley. (1998). Kindergarten children's gender-role expectations for television actors. *Sex Roles, 38,* 387–402.

Dutton, Mary Ann; Haywood, Yolanda; & El-Bayoumi, Gigi. (1997). Impact of violence on women's health. In Sheryle J. Gallant, Gwendolyn Puryear Keita, & Reneé Royak-Schaler (Eds.), *Health care for women: Psychological, social, and behavioral influences* (pp. 41–56). Washington, DC: American Psychological Association.

Eagly, Alice H. (1987a). Reporting sex differences. *American Psychologist, 42,* 756–757.

Eagly, Alice H. (1987b). *Sex differences in social behavior: A social-role interpretation.* Hillsdale, NJ: Erlbaum.

Eagly, Alice H. (1994, August). *Are people prejudiced against women?* Paper presented at the 102nd annual convention of the American Psychological Association, Los Angeles, CA.

Eagly, Alice H. (1995). The science and politics of comparing women and men. *American Psychologist, 50,* 145–158.

Eagly, Alice H. (1997). Comparing women and men: Methods, findings, and politics. In Mary Roth Walsh (Ed.), *Women, men, and gender: Ongoing debates* (pp. 24–31). New Haven, CT: Yale University Press.

Eagly, Alice H.; & Johnson, Blair T. (1990). Gender and leadership style: A meta-analysis. *Psychological Bulletin, 108,* 233–256.

Eagly, Alice H.; Karau, Steven J.; & Makhijani, Mona G. (1995). Gender and the effectiveness of leaders: A meta-analysis. *Psychological Bulletin, 117,* 125–145.

Eagly, Alice H.; Makhijani, Mona G.; & Klonsky, Bruce G. (1992). Gender and the evaluation of leaders: A meta-analysis. *Psychological Bulletin, 111,* 3–22.

Eagly, Alice H.; Mladinic, Antonio; & Otto, Stacey. (1991). Are women evaluated more favorably than men? An analysis of attitudes, beliefs, and emotions. *Psychology of Women Quarterly, 15,* 203–216.

Eagly, Alice H.; & Steffen, Valerie J. (1986). Gender and aggressive behavior: A meta-analytic review of the social psychological literature. *Psychological Bulletin, 100,* 309–330.

Eagly, Alice H.; & Wood, Wendy. (1985). Gender and influenceability: Stereotype versus behavior. In Virginia E. O'Leary, Rhoda Kesler Unger, & Barbara Strudler Wallston (Eds.), *Women, gender, and social psychology* (pp. 225–256). Hillsdale, NJ: Erlbaum.

Eagly, Alice H.; & Wood, Wendy. (1999). The origins of sex differences in human behavior. *American Psychologist, 54,* 408–423.

Eccles, Jacquelynne S. (1987). Gender roles and achievement patterns: An expectancy value perspective. In June Machover Reinisch, Leonard A. Rosenblum, & Stephanie A. Sanders (Eds.), *Masculinity/Femininity: Basic perspectives* (pp. 240–280). New York: Oxford University Press.

Eccles, Jacquelynne S. (1989). Bringing young women to math and science. In Mary Crawford & Margaret Gentry (Eds.), *Gender and thought: Psychological perspectives* (pp. 36–58). New York: Springer-Verlag.

Eccles, Jacquelynne; & Bryan, James. (1994). Adolescence: Critical crossroad in the path of gender-role development. In Michael R. Stevenson (Ed.), *Gender roles through the life span: A multidisciplinary perspective* (pp. 111–147). Muncie, IN: Ball State University.

Eccles, Jacquelynne S.; Wigfield, Allan; Harold, Rena D.; & Blumenfeld, Phyllis. (1993). Age and gender differences in children's self- and task-perceptions during elementary school. *Child Development, 64,* 830–845.

Eckhardt, Michael J.; Harford, Thomas C.; Kaelber, Charles T.; Parker, Elizabeth S.; Rosenthal, Laura S.; Ryback, Ralph S.; Salmoiraghi, Gian C.; Vanderveen, Ernestine; & Warren, Kenneth R. (1981). Health hazards associated with alcohol consumption. *Journal of the American Medical Association, 246,* 648–666.

The Economist. (1994, September 24). The new Eve is no angel. Author, *332,* 91–92.

Edmonds, Ed M.; & Cahoon, Delwin D. (1993). The "new" sexism: Females' negativism toward males. *Journal of Social Behavior and Personality, 8,* 481–487.

Ehrenreich, Barbara; & English, Deirdre. (1973). *Witches, midwives, and nurses: A history of women healers.* New York: Feminist Press.

Ehrenreich, Barbara; Hess, Elizabeth; & Jacobs, Gloria. (1986). *Re-making love: The feminization of sex.* Garden City, NY: Anchor Press.

Ehrhardt, Anke A.; & Meyer-Bahlburg, Heino F. L. (1981). Effects of prenatal sex hormones on gender-related behavior. *Science, 211,* 1312–1317.

Eichenbaum, Luise; & Orbach, Susie. (1983). *What do women want: Exploding the myth of dependency.* New York: Coward-McCann.

Eisenberg, Nancy; & Lennon, Randy. (1983). Sex differences in empathy and related capacities. *Psychological Bulletin, 94,* 100–131.

Ekman, Paul. (1984). Expression and the nature of emotion. In Klaus R. Scherer & Paul Ekman (Eds.), *Approaches to emotion* (pp. 319–343). Hillsdale, NJ: Erlbaum.

Ekman, Paul; Levenson, Robert W.; & Friesen, Wallace V. (1983). Autonomic nervous activity distinguishes among emotions. *Science, 221,* 1208–1210.

Elasmar, Michael; Hasegawa, Kazumi; & Brain, Mary. (1999). The portrayal of women in U.S. prime time television. *Journal of Broadcasting & Electronic Media, 43,* 20–42.

Ellenberger, Henri F. (1970). *The discovery of the unconscious.* New York: Basic Books.

Ellestad, Myrvin H. (1986). *Stress testing* (3rd ed.). Philadelphia: Davis.

Ellis, Albert. (1962). *Reason and emotion in psychotherapy.* New York: Stuart.

Enns, Carolyn Zerbe. (1992). Self-esteem groups: A synthesis of consciousness-raising and assertiveness training. *Journal of Counseling and Development, 71,* 7–13.

Enns, Carolyn Zerbe. (1993). Twenty years of feminist counseling and therapy: From naming biases to implementing multifaceted practice. *Counseling Psychologist, 21,* 3–87.

Enns, Carolyn Zerbe. (1997). *Feminist theories and feminist psychotherapies: Origins, themes, and variations.* New York: Harrington Park Press.

Enns, Carolyn Z.; & Hackett, Gail. (1990). Comparison of feminist and nonfeminist women's reactions to variants of nonsexist and feminist counseling. *Journal of Counseling Psychology, 37,* 33–40.

Epstein, Cynthia Fuchs. (1988). *Deceptive distinctions: Sex, gender and the social order.* New Haven, CT: Yale University Press.

Eron, Leonard D. (1987). The development of aggressive behavior from the perspective of a developing behaviorism. *American Psychologist, 42,* 435–442.

Eron, Leonard D.; Huesmann, L. Rowell; Brice, Patrick; Fischer, Paulette; & Mermelstein, Rebecca. (1983). Age trends in the development of aggression, sex typing, and related television habits. *Developmental Psychology, 19,* 71–77.

Evans, Lorraine; & Davies, Kimberly. (2000). No sissy boys here: A content analysis of the representation of masculinity in elementary school reading textbooks. *Sex Roles, 42,* 255–270.

Eyer, Diane E. (1992). *Mother-infant bonding: A scientific fiction.* New Haven, CT: Yale University Press.

Faderman, Lillian. (1989). A history of romantic friendship and lesbian love. In Barbara J. Risman & Pepper Schwartz (Eds.), *Gender in intimate relationships* (pp. 26–31). Belmont, CA: Wadsworth.

Fagot, Beverly I.; & Hagan, Richard. (1991). Observations of parent reactions to sex-stereotyped behaviors: Age and sex effects. *Child Development, 62,* 617–628.

Fagot, Beverly I.; & Leinbach, Mary D. (1989). The young child's gender schema: Environmental input, internal organization. *Child Development, 60,* 663–672.

Fagot, Beverly I.; & Leinbach, Mary D. (1993). Gender-role development in young children: From discrimination to labeling. *Developmental Review, 13,* 205–224.

Fagot, Beverly I.; & Leinbach, Mary D. (1994). Gender-role development in young children. In Michael R. Stevenson (Ed.), *Gender roles through the life span: A multidisciplinary perspective* (pp. 3–24). Muncie, IN: Ball State University.

Fagot, Beverly I.; & Leinbach, Mary D. (1995). Gender knowledge in egalitarian and traditional families. *Sex Roles, 32,* 513–526.

Fagot, Beverly I.; Leinbach, Mary D.; & O'Boyle, Cherie. (1992). Gender labeling, gender stereotyping, and parenting behaviors. *Developmental Psychology, 28,* 225–230.

Fallon, April E.; & Rozin, Paul. (1985). Sex differences in perceptions of desirable body shape. *Journal of Abnormal Psychology, 94,* 102–105.

Faludi, Susan. (1991). *Backlash: The undeclared war against American women.* New York: Crown.

Faludi, Susan. (1999). *Stiffed: The betrayal of the American man.* New York: Morrow.

Fang, Di; Moy, Ernest; Colburn, Lois; & Hurley, Jeanne. (2000). Racial and ethnic disparities in faculty promotion in academic medicine. *Journal of the American Medical Association, 284,* 1085–1092.

Farmer, Helen S.; & Sidney, Joan Seliger. (1985). Sex equity in career and vocational education. In Susan S. Klein (Ed.), *Handbook for achieving sex equity through education* (pp. 338–359). Baltimore: Johns Hopkins University Press.

Fausto-Sterling, Anne. (1992). *Myths of gender: Biological theories about women and men* (2nd ed.). New York: Basic Books.

Fee, Dwight. (2000). "One of the guys": Instrumentality and intimacy in gay men's friendships with straight men. In Peter Nardi (Ed.), *Gay masculinities* (pp. 44–65). Thousand Oaks, CA: Sage.

Fee, Elizabeth. (1986). Critiques of modern science: The relationship of feminism to other radical epistemologies. In Ruth Bleier (Ed.), *Feminist approaches to science* (pp. 42–56). New York: Pergamon Press.

Feingold, Alan. (1988). Cognitive gender differences are disappearing. *American Psychologist, 43,* 95–103.

Feingold, Alan. (1994). Gender differences in variability in intellectual abilities; A cross-cultural perspective. *Sex Roles, 30,* 81–92.

Feingold, Alan. (1998). Gender stereotyping for sociability, dominance, character, and mental health: A meta-analysis of findings from the bogus stranger paradigm. *Genetic, Social, and General Psychology Monographs, 124,* 253–270.

Feist, Jess; & Feist, Gregory J. (2002). *Theories of personality* (5th ed.). Boston: McGraw-Hill.

Feld, Scott L.; & Straus, Murray A. (1989). Escalation and desistance of wife assault in marriage. *Criminology, 27,* 141–161.

Felmlee, Diane H. (1994). Who's on top? Power in romantic relationships. *Sex Roles, 31,* 275–295.

Fennema, Elizabeth. (1980). Sex-related differences in mathematics achievement: Where and why. In Lynn H. Fox, Linda Brody, & Dianne Tobin (Eds.), *Women and the mathematical mystique* (pp. 76–93). Baltimore: Johns Hopkins University Press.

Ferree, Myra Marx; & Hess, Beth B. (1985). *Controversy and coalition: The new feminist movement.* Boston: Twayne.

Fields, Judith; & Wolff, Edward N. (1991). The decline of sex segregation and the wage gap, 1970–80. *Journal of Human Resources, 26,* 608–622.

Fine, Michelle. (1988). Sexuality, schooling, and adolescent females: The missing discourse of desire. *Harvard Educational Review, 58,* 29–53.

Finkelhor, David. (1980). Sex among siblings: A survey on prevalence, variety, and effects. *Archives of Sexual Behavior, 9,* 171–193.

Finkelhor, David. (1984). *Child sexual abuse: New theory and research.* New York: Free Press.

Finkelhor, David. (1990). Early and long-term effects of child sexual abuse: An update. *Professional Psychology Research and Practice, 21,* 325–330.

Finkelhor, David; & Baron, Larry. (1986). Risk factors for child sexual abuse. *Journal of Interpersonal Violence, 1,* 43–71.

Finn, Jerry. (1999). An exploration of helping processes in an online self-help group focusing on issues of disability. *Health and Social Work, 24,* 220–227.

Fischer, Agneta H. (1993). Sex differences in emotionality: Fact or stereotype? *Feminism & Psychology, 3,* 303–318.

Fischer, Ann R.; Good, Glenn E. (1994). Gender, self, and others: Perceptions of the campus environment. *Journal of Counseling Psychology, 41,* 343–355.

Fiske, Susan T. (1993). Controlling other people: The impact of power on stereotyping. *American Psychologist, 48,* 621–628.

Fiske, Susan T.; Bersoff, Donald N.; Borgida, Eugene; Deaux, Kay; & Heilman, Madeline E. (1991). Social science research on trial: Use of sex stereotyping research in *Price Waterhouse v. Hopkins. American Psychologist, 46,* 1049–1060.

Fitzgerald, Louise F. (1994, August). *Sexual harassment—A feminist perspective on the prevention of violence against women in the workplace.* Paper presented at the 102nd annual convention of the American Psychological Association, Los Angeles, CA.

Fitzgerald, Louise F.; Swan, Suzanne; & Magley, Vicki J. (1997), But was it really sexual harassment? Legal, behavioral, and psychological definitions of the workplace victimization of women. In William O'Donohue (Ed.), *Sexual harassment: Theory, research, and treatment* (pp. 5–28), Boston: Allyn and Bacon.

Flaskerud, Jacquelyn H. (1986). Diagnostic and treatment differences among five ethnic groups. *Psychological Reports, 58,* 219–235.

Flaskerud, Jacquelyn H.; & Hu, Li-tze. (1992). Relationship of ethnicity to psychiatric diagnosis. *Journal of Nervous and Mental Disease, 180,* 296–303.

Floyd, Kory. (1995). Gender and closeness among friends and siblings. *Journal of Psychology, 129,* 193–202.

Flynn, Clifton P. (1990). Relationship violence by women: Issues and implications. *Family Relations, 39,* 194–198.

Fodor, Iris Goldstein. (1988). Cognitive behavior therapy: Evaluation of theory and practice for addressing women's issues. In Mary Ann Dutton Douglas & Lenore E. A. Walker (Eds.), *Feminist psychotherapies: Integration of therapeutic and feminist systems* (pp. 91–117). Norwood, NJ: Ablex.

Folkman, Susan; & Lazarus, Richard S. (1980). An analysis of coping in middle-aged community sample. *Journal of Health and Social Behavior, 21,* 219–239.

Fontenot, Kathleen; & Brannon, Linda. (1991, August). *Gender differences in coping with workplace stress.* Paper presented at the 99th annual convention of the American Psychological Association, San Francisco, CA.

Ford, Clellan S.; & Beach, Frank A. (1951). *Patterns of sexual behavior.* New York: Harper.

Fowers, Blaine J. (1991). His and her marriage: A multivariate study of gender and marital satisfaction. *Sex Roles, 24,* 209–221.

Fowers, Blaine J.; Applegate, Brooks; Tredinnick, Michael; & Slusher, Jason. (1996). His and her individualisms? Sex bias and individualism in psychologists' responses to case vignettes. *The Journal of Psychology, 130,* 159–174.

Fox, Mary Frank. (1989). Women and higher education: Gender differences in the status of students and scholars. In Jo Freeman (Ed.), *Women: A feminist perspective* (4th ed.) (pp. 217–235). Mountain View, CA: Mayfield.

Fox, Ronald C. (1996). Bisexuality in perspective: A review of theory and research. In Beth A. Firestein (Ed.), *Bisexuality: The psychology and politics of an invisible minority* (pp. 3–50). Thousand Oaks, CA: Sage.

Freeman, Ellen W.; Rickels, Karl; Sondheimer, Steven J.; & Polansky, Marcia. (1999). Differential response to antidepressants in women with Premenstrual Syndrome/Premenstrual Dysphoric Disorder: A randomized controlled trial. *Archives of General Psychiatry, 56,* 932–939.

Freiberg, Peter. (1991). Self-esteem gender gap widens in adolescence. *APA Monitor, 22*(4), 29.

Freud, Sigmund. (1959). An autobiographical study. In James Strachey (Ed. and Trans.), *The standard edition of the complete psychological works of Sigmund Freud* (Vol. 20). London: Hogarth Press. (Original work published in 1925)

Freud, Sigmund. (1989). Some psychical consequences of the anatomical distinction between the sexes. In Peter Gay (Ed.), *The Freud reader* (pp. 670–678). New York: Norton. (Original work published in 1925)

Freud, Sigmund. (1964). Femininity. In James Strachey (Ed. and Trans.), *New introductory lectures on psychoanalysis* (p. 112–135). New York: Norton. (Original work published 1933)

Frezza, Mario; di Padova, Carlo; Pozzato, Gabriele; Terpin, Maddalena; Baraona, Enrique; & Lieber, Charles S. (1990). High blood alcohol levels in women: The role of decreased gastric alcohol dehydrogenase activity and first-pass metabolism. *New England Journal of Medicine, 322,* 95–99.

Fried, Linda P.; Kronmal, Richard A.; Newman, Anne B.; Bild, Diane E.; Mittelmark, Maurice B.; Polak, Joseph F.; Robbins, John A.; & Gardin, Julius M. (1998). Risk factors for 5-year mortality in older adults: The Cardiovascular Health Study. *Journal of the American Medical Association, 279,* 585–592.

Frodi, Ann M.; & Lamb, Michael E. (1978). Sex differences in responsiveness to infants: A developmental study of psychophysiological and behavioral responses. *Child Development, 49,* 1182–1188.

Frodi, Ann M.; Macaulay, Jacqueline; & Thome, Pauline R. (1977). Are women always less aggressive than men? A review of the experimental literature. *Psychological Bulletin, 84,* 634–660.

Frye, Marilyn. (1997). Lesbian "sex." In Maxine Baca Zinn, Pierrette Hondagneu-Sotelo, & Michael A. Messner (Eds.), *Through the prism of difference: Readings on sex and gender* (pp. 205–209). Boston: Allyn and Bacon.

Fujita, Frank; Diener, Ed; & Sandvik, Ed. (1991). Gender differences in negative affect and well-being: The case for emotional intensity. *Journal of Personality and Social Psychology, 61,* 427–434.

Furman, Wyndol; & Bierman, Karen Linn. (1984). Children's conceptions of friendship: A multimethod study of developmental changes. *Developmental Psychology, 20,* 925–931.

Furnham, Adrian. (1999). Sex differences in self-stimates of lay dimensions of intelligence. *Psychological Reports, 85,* 349–350.

Furnham, Adrian; Dias, Melanie; & McClelland, Alastair. (1998). The role of body weight, waist-to-hip ratio, and breast size in judgments of female attractiveness. *Sex Roles, 39,* 311–326.

Furnham, Adrian; & Gasson, Lucinda. (1998). Sex differences in parental estimates of their children's intelligence. *Sex Roles, 38,* 151–162.

Furnham, Adrian; & Mak, Twiggy. (1999). Sex-role stereotyping in television commercials: A review and comparison of fourteen studies done on five continents over 25 years. *Sex Roles, 41,* 413–438.

Furnham, Adrian; & Rawles, Richard. (1999). Correlations between self-estimated and psychometrically measured IQ. *Journal of Social Psychology, 139,* 405–410.

Furstenberg, Frank F.; & Spanier, Graham B. (1984). *Recycling the family: Remarriage after divorce.* Beverly Hills, CA: Sage.

Gabbard, Krin. (2000, February 11). Therapy's 'talking cure' still works—in Hollywood, *Chronicle of Higher Education,* B9.

Galea, Liisa A.; & Kimura, Doreen. (1993). Sex differences in route-learning. *Personality and Individual Differences, 14,* 53–65.

Galegher, Jolene; Sproull, Lee; & Kiesler, Sara. (1998). Legitimacy, authority, and community in electronic support groups. *Written Communications, 15,* p. 493.

Gallagher, Maggie. (1987, May 22). What men really want. *National Review,* pp. 39–40.

Ganley, Anne L. (1988). Feminist therapy with male clients. In Mary Ann Dutton Douglas & Lenore E. A. Walker (Eds.), *Feminist psychotherapies: Integration of therapeutic and feminist systems* (pp. 186–205). Norwood, NJ: Ablex.

Garner, David M.; & Garfinkel, Paul E. (1980). Sociocultural factors in the development of anorexia nervosa. *Psychological Medicine, 10,* 647–656.

Garner, David M.; Garfinkel, Paul E.; Schwartz, Donald M.; & Thompson, Michael G. (1980). Cultural expectations of thinness in women. *Psychological Reports, 47,* 483–491.

Gates, David. (1993, March 29). White male paranoia. *Newsweek, 121,* 48–53.

Gay, Peter. (1988). *Freud: A life for our time.* New York: Norton.

Geer, James H.; & Broussard, Deborah Bice. (1990). Scaling heterosexual behavior and arousal: Consistency and sex differences. *Journal of Personality and Social Psychology, 58,* 664–671.

Gelles, Richard J.; & Cornell, Claire Pedrick. (1990). *Intimate violence in families* (2nd ed.). Newbury Park, CA: Sage.

Gentile, Douglas A. (1993). Just what are sex and gender, anyway? A call for a new terminological standard. *Psychological Science, 4,* 120–122.

Gentry, Margaret. (1998). The sexual double standard: The influence of number of relationships and level of sexual activity on judgments of women and men. *Psychology of Women Quarterly, 22,* 505–511.

Gergen, Kenneth J. (1985). The social constructionist movement in modern psychology. *American Psychologist, 40,* 266–275.

Gerhart, Barry. (1990). Gender differences in current and starting salaries: The role of performance, college major, and job title. *Industrial and Labor Relations Review, 43,* 418–433.

Geschwind, Norman; & Galaburda, Albert S. (1987). *Cerebral lateralization.* Cambridge, MA: MIT Press.

Gibbons, Judith L.; Hamby, Beverly A.; & Dennis, Wanda D. (1997). Researching gender-role ideologies internationally and cross-culturally. *Psychology of Women Quarterly, 21,* 151–170.

Gilbert, Lucia A. (1980). Feminist therapy. In Annette M. Brodsky & Rachel Hare-Mustin (Eds.), *Women and psychotherapy* (pp. 245–265). New York: Guilford Press.

Gilbert, Lucia A. (1984). Comments on the meaning of work in women's lives. *Counseling Psychology, 12,* 129–130.

Gilgun, Jane F. (1995). We shared something special: The moral discourse of incest perpetrators. *Journal of Marriage and the Family, 57,* 265–281.

Gilligan, Carol. (1982). *In a different voice: Psychological theory and women's development.* Cambridge, MA: Harvard University Press.

Gilligan, Carol; & Attanucci, Jane. (1988). Two moral orientations. In Carol Gilligan, Janie Victoria Ward, & Jill McLean Taylor. (with Bardige, Betty). (Eds.), *Mapping the moral domain: A contribution of women's thinking to psychological theory and education* (pp. 73–86). Cambridge, MA: Harvard University Press.

Ginorio, Angela B.; Gutiérrez, Lorraine; Cauce, Ana Mari; & Acosta, Mimi. (1995). Psychological issues for Latinas. In Hope Landrine (Ed.), *Bringing cultural diversity to feminist psychology: Theory, research, and practice* (pp. 241–263). Washington, DC: American Psychological Association.

Ginsburg, Herbert; & Opper, Sylvia. (1969). *Piaget's theory of intellectual development: An introduction.* Englewood Cliffs, NJ: Prentice-Hall.

Giuliano, Traci A.; Popp, Kathryn E.; Knight, Jennifer L. (2000). Footballs versus Barbies: Childhood play activities as predictors of sport participation by women. *Sex Roles, 42,* 159–182.

Glick, Peter; & Fiske, Susan T. (1999). The Ambivalence toward Men Inventory: Differentiating hostile and benevolent beliefs about men. *Psychology of Women Quarterly, 23,* 519–536.

Glick, Peter; Zion, Cari; & Nelson, Cynthia. (1988). What mediates sex discrimination in hiring decisions? *Journal of Personality and Social Psychology, 55,* 178–186.

Golding, Jacqueline M. (1999). Intimate partner violence as a risk factor for mental disorders: A meta-analysis. *Journal of Family Violence, 14,* 99–101.

Golding, Jacqueline M.; Smith, G. Richard; & Kashner, T. Michael. (1991). Does somatization disorder occur in men? Clinical characteristics of women and men with multiple unexplained somatic symptoms. *Archives of General Psychiatry, 48,* 231–235.

Goldsmith, Ronald E.; & Matherly, Timothy A. (1988). Creativity and self-esteem: A multiple operationalization validity study. *Journal of Psychology, 122,* 47–56.

Gonzalez, Judith Teresa. (1988). Dilemmas of the high-achieving Chicana: The double-bind factor in male/female relationships. *Sex Roles, 18,* 367–380.

Good, Glenn E.; Dell, Don M.; & Mintz, Laurie B. (1989). Male role and gender role conflict: Relations to help seeking in men. *Journal of Counseling Psychology, 36,* 295–300.

Good, Glenn E.; Gilbert, Lucia A.; & Scher, Murray. (1990). Gender Aware Therapy: A synthesis of feminist therapy and knowledge about gender. *Journal of Counseling & Development, 68,* 376–380.

Good, Glenn E.; & Wood, Phillip K. (1995). Male gender role conflict, depression, and help seeking: Do college men face double jeopardy? *Journal of Counseling and Development, 74,* 70–75.

Goodale, Gloria. (1999, September 24). His & hers TV: TV channels, video games, and Internet sites zero in on girls and boys. *Christian Science Monitor,* 13.

Goodman, Lisa A.; Koss, Mary P.; Fitzgerald, Louise F.; Russo, Nancy Felipe; & Keita, Gwendolyn Puryear. (1993). Male violence against women: Current research and future directions. *American Psychologist, 48,* 1054–1058.

Gorski, Roger A. (1987). Sex differences in the rodent brain: Their nature and origin. In June M. Reinisch, Leonard A. Rosenblum, & Stephanie A. Sanders (Eds.), *Masculinity/Femininity: Basic perspectives* (pp. 37–67). New York: Oxford University Press.

Gottman, John M. (1991). Predicting the longitudinal course of marriages. *Journal of Marriage and Family Therapy, 17,* 3–7.

Gottman, John M. (1998). Psychology and the study of marital processes. *Annual Review of Psychology, 49,* 169–187.

Gottman, John, (with Silver, Nan). (1994). *Why marriages succeed or fail.* New York: Simon & Schuster.

Gould, Ketayun H. (2000). Beyond Jones v. Clinton: Sexual harassment law and social work. *Social Work, 45,* 237–250.

Gould, Stephen Jay. (1996). *The mismeasure of man* (Rev. ed). New York: Norton.

Gove, Walter R. (1984). Gender differences in mental and physical illness: The effects of fixed roles and nurturant roles. *Social Science and Medicine, 19*(2), 77–84.

Gove, Walter R.; & Hughes, Michael. (1979). Possible causes of the apparent sex differences in physical health: An empirical investigation. *American Sociological Review, 44,* 126–146.

Granrose, Cherlyn Skromme; & Kaplan, Eileen E. (1996). *Work-family role choices for women in their 20s and 30s.* Westport, CT: Praeger.

Gratch, Linda Vanden; Bassett, Margaret E.; & Attra, Sharon L. (1995). The relationship of gender and ethnicity to self-silencing and depression among college students. *Psychology of Women Quarterly, 19,* 509–515.

Gray, John. (1992). *Men are from Mars, women are from Venus.* New York: HarperCollins.

Green, Beth L.; & Russo, Nancy Felipe. (1993). Work and family roles: Selected issues. In Florence L. Denmark & Michele A. Paludi (Eds.), *Psychology of women: A handbook of issues and theories* (pp. 685–719). Westport, CT: Greenwood Press.

Green, Judith. (1987). Patterns of eating in normal men and women. *Psychology—A Quarterly Journal of Human Behavior, 24*(4), 1–14.

Green, Richard. (1987). *The "sissy boy syndrome" and the development of homosexuality.* New Haven, CT: Yale University Press.

Greenberg, Harvey Roy. (1992). Psychotherapy at the simplex: Le plus ca shrink. *Journal of Popular Film and Television, 20,* 9–15.

Greenberger, Ellen; & O'Neil, Robin. (1993). Spouse, parent, worker: Role commitments and role-related experiences in the construction of adults' well-being. *Developmental Psychology, 29,* 181–197.

Greene, Beverly. (1994). African American women. In Lillian Comas-Díaz & Beverly Greene (Eds.), *Women of color: Integrating ethnic and gender identities in psychotherapy* (pp. 10–29). New York: Guilford Press.

Greenstein, Theodore N. (1996). Husbands' participation in domestic labor: Interactive effect of wives' and husbands' gender ideologies. *Journal of Marriage and the Family, 58,* 585–595.

Greenwald, Anthony G. (1975). Consequences of prejudice against the null hypothesis. *Psychological Bulletin, 82,* 1–20.

Gregory, Robert J. (1987). *Adult intellectual assessment.* Boston: Allyn and Bacon.

Groshen, Erica L. (1991). The structure of the female/male wage differential: Is it who you are, what you do, or where you work? *Journal of Human Resources, 26,* 457–472.

Guanipa, Carmen; & Woolley, Scott R. (2000). Gender biases and therapists' conceptualization of couple difficulties. *American Journal of Family Therapy, 28,* 181–192.

Gupta, Nabanita Datta. (1993). Probabilities of job choice and employer selection and male-female occupational differences. *American Economic Review, 83*(2), 57–62.

Gur, Ruben C.; Mozley, Lyn Harper; Mozley, P. David; Resnick, Susan M.; Kapr, Joel S.; Alavi, Abass; Arnold, Steven E.; & Gur, Raquel E. (1995). Sex differences in regional glucose metabolism during a resting state. *Science, 267,* 528–531.

Gutek, Barbara A. (1985). *Sex and the workplace.* San Francisco: Jossey-Bass.

Gutek, Barbara A.; & Larwood, Laurie. (1989). Introduction: Women's careers are important and different. In Barbara A. Gutek & Laurie Larwood (Eds.), *Women's career development* (pp. 7–14). Newbury Park, CA: Sage.

Gutfeld, Greg. (1999, October). The sex drive, *Men's Health, 14*(8), 116–120, 154–155.

Hackett, Gail; Enns, Carolyn Z.; & Zetzer, Heidi A. (1992). Reactions of women to nonsexist and feminist counseling: Effects of counselor orientation and mode of information delivery. *Journal of Counseling Psychology, 39,* 321–330.

Hall, Judith A.; & Carter, Jason D. (1999). Gender-stereotype accuracy as an individual difference. *Journal of Personality and Social Psychology, 77,* 350–359.

Halpern, Diane F. (1985). The influence of sex-role stereotypes on prose recall. *Sex Roles, 12,* 363–375.

Halpern, Diane F. (1992). *Sex differences in cognitive abilities* (2nd ed.). Hillsdale, NJ: Erlbaum.

Halpern, Diane F. (1994). Stereotypes, science, censorship, and the study of sex differences. *Feminism & Psychology, 4,* 523–530.

Halpern, Diane F. (1995). Cognitive gender differences: Why diversity is a critical research issue. In Hope Landrine (Ed.), *Bringing cultural diversity to feminist psychology: Theory, research, and practice* (pp. 77–92). Washington, DC: American Psychological Association.

Halpern, Diane F. (1997). Sex differences in intelligence: Implications for education. *American Psychologist, 52,* 1091–1102.

Hamilton, Sandra; & Fagot, Beverly I. (1988). Chronic stress and coping styles: A comparison of male and female undergraduates. *Journal of Personality and Social Psychology, 55,* 819–823.

Hamilton, Sandra; Rothbart, Myron; & Dawes, Robyn M. (1986). Sex bias, diagnosis, and DSM-III. *Sex Roles, 15,* 269–274.

Hantover, Jeffrey P. (1992). The Boy Scouts and the validation of masculinity. In Michael S. Kimmel & Michael A. Messner (Eds.), *Men's lives* (2nd ed.; pp. 123–131). New York: Macmillan.

Hardie, Elizabeth A. (1997). Prevalence and predictors of cyclic and noncyclic affective change. *Psychology of Women Quarterly, 21,* 299–314.

Harding, Sandra. (1986). *The science question in feminism.* Ithaca: Cornell University Press.

Hare-Mustin, Rachel T. (1983). An appraisal of the relationship between women and psychotherapy: 80 years after the case of Dora. *American Psychologist, 38,* 593–601.

Hare-Mustin, Rachel T.; & Marecek, Jeanne. (1988). The meaning of difference: Gender theory, postmodernism, and psychology. *American Psychologist, 43,* 455–464.

Hare-Mustin, Rachel T.; Marecek, Jeanne.; Kaplan, Alexandra G.; & Liss-Levinson, Nechama. (1979). Rights of clients, responsibilities of therapists. *American Psychologist, 34,* 3–16.

Harlow, Harry F. (1959). Love in infant monkeys. *Scientific American, 200*(6), 68–74.

Harlow, Harry F. (1971). *Learning to love.* San Francisco: Albion.

Harlow, Harry F.; & Harlow, Margaret Kuenne. (1962). Social deprivation in monkeys. *Scientific American,* 207, 136–146.

Harrison, James. (1978). Warning: The male sex role may be dangerous to your health. *Journal of Social Issues, 34*(1), 65–86.

Hart, Kylo-Patrick R. (1999). Retrograde representation: The lonely gay white male dying of AIDS on *Beverly Hills, 90210. Journal of Men's Studies, 7,* 201–214.

Hassler, Marianne; Nieschlag, Eberhard; & de la Motte, Diether. (1990). Creative musical talent, cognitive functioning, and gender: Psychobiological aspects. *Music Perception, 8,* 35–48.

Hatfield, Elaine; & Rapson, Richard L. (1996). *Love and sex: Cross-cultural perspectives.* Boston: Allyn and Bacon.

Hecker, Daniel E. (1998). Earnings of college graduates: Women compared with men. *Monthly Labor Review, 121*(3), 62–71.

Hedrick, Hannah L. (1995). The self-help sourcebook: Finding and forming mutual aid self-help groups (5th ed.) (Book review). *Journal of the American Medical Association, 274,* 847–849.

Heesacker, Martin; Wester, Stephen R.; Vogel, David L.; Wentzel, Jeffrey T.; Mejia-Millan, Cristina M.; & Goodholm, Carl Robert, Jr. (1999). Gender-based emotional stereotyping. *Journal of Counseling Psychology, 46,* 483–495.

Heilman, Madeline E.; Black, Caryn J.; Martell, Richard F.; & Simon, Michael C. (1989). Has anything changed? Current characterizations of men, women, and managers. *Journal of Applied Psychology, 74,* 935–942.

Heise, Lori; Ellsberg, Mary; & Gottemoeller, Megan. (1999). Ending violence against women. *Population Reports,* Series L, No. 11. Baltimore, MD: Johns Hopkins University School of Public Health, Population Information Program.

Helgeson, Vicki S. (1990). The role of masculinity in a prognostic predictor of heart attack severity. *Sex Roles, 22,* 755–776.

Helgeson, Vicki S. (1994). Relation of agency and communion to well-being: Evidence and potential explanations. *Psychological Bulletin, 116,* 412–428.

Helson, Ravenna; & Picano, James. (1990). Is the traditional role bad for women? *Journal of Personality and Social Psychology, 59,* 311–320.

Helwig, Andrew A. (1998). Gender-role stereotyping: Testing theory with a longitudinal sample. *Sex Roles, 38,* 403–423.

Helzer, John E.; Robins, Lee N.; & McEvoy, Larry. (1987). Post-traumatic stress disorder in the general population: Findings of the Epidemiologic Catchment Area survey. *New England Journal of Medicine, 317,* 1630–1634.

Hendrick, Susan S.; Hendrick, Clyde. (1992). *Liking, loving, and relating* (2nd ed.). Pacific Grove, CA: Brooks/Cole.

Hendrick, Susan S.; Hendrick, Clyde; & Adler, Nancy L. (1988). Romantic relationships: Love, satisfaction, and staying together. *Journal of Personality and Social Psychology, 54,* 980–988.

Hendryx, Michael S.; & Ahern, Melissa M. (1997). Mental health functioning and community problems. *Journal of Community Psychology, 25,* 147–157.

Herdt, Gilbert H. (1981). *Guardians of the flutes: Idioms of masculinity.* New York: McGraw-Hill.

Herdt, Gilbert H. (1990). Mistaken gender: 5-alpha reductase hermaphroditism and biological reductionism in sexual identity reconsidered. *American Anthropologist, 92,* 433–446.

Herdt, Gilbert; & Boxer, Andrew. (1995). Bisexuality: Toward a comparative theory of identities and culture. In Richard G. Parker & John H. Gagnon (Eds.), *Concerning sexuality: Approaches to sex research in a postmodern world* (pp. 69–83). New York: Routledge.

Herman, Dianne F. (1989). The rape culture. In Jo Freeman (Ed.), *Women: A feminist perspective* (pp. 20–44). Mountain View, CA: Mayfield.

Herman, Judith Lewis. (1981). *Father-daughter incest.* Cambridge, MA: Harvard University Press.

Herrmann, Douglas J.; Crawford, Mary; & Holdsworth, Michelle. (1992). Gender-linked differences in everyday memory performance. *British Journal of Psychology, 83,* 221–231.

Hesselbrock, Victor M.; Hesselbrock, Michie N.; & Workman-Daniels, Kathryn L. (1986). Effect of major depression and antisocial personality on alcoholism: Course and motivational patterns. *Journal of Studies on Alcohol, 47,* 207–212.

Heusel, Colleen; & Dabbs, James M., Jr. (1996, August). *Testosterone predicts engineer employment status in an oilfield service company.* Paper presented at the 104th annual convention of the American Psychological Association, Toronto, Canada.

Hilgard, Ernest R. (1987). *Psychology in America: A historical survey.* San Diego: Harcourt Brace Jovanovich.

Hill, John P.; & Lynch, Mary Ellen. (1983). The intensification of gender-related role expectations during early adolescence. In Jeanne Brooks-Gunn & Anne C. Petersen (Eds.), *Girls at puberty: Biological and psychosocial perspectives.* New York: Plenum Press.

Hill, Marcia; & Ballou, Mary. (1998). Making therapy feminist: A practice survey. *Women & Therapy, 21,* 1–16.

Hiscock, Merrill; Inch, Roxanne; Jacek, Carolyn; Hiscock-Kalil, Cheryl, & Kalil, Kathleen M. (1994). Is there a sex difference in human laterality? I. An exhaustive survey of auditory laterality studies from six neuropsychology journals. *Journal of Clinical and Experimental Neuropsychology, 16,* 423–435.

Hiscock, Merrill; Israelian, Marlyne; Inch, Roxanne; Jacek, Carolyn; & Hiscock-Kalil, Cheryl. (1995). Is there a sex difference in human laterality? II. An exhaustive survey of visual laterality studies from six neuropsychology journals. *Journal of Clinical and Experimental Neuropsychology, 17,* 590–610.

Hochschild, Arlie. (1997). *The time bind.* New York: Metropolitan Books.

Hochschild, Arlie. (with Machung, Anne). (1989). *The second shift: Working parents and the revolution at home.* New York: Viking.

Hochwarter, Wayne A.; Perrewe, Pamela L.; & Dawkins, Mark C. (1995). Gender differences in perceptions of stress-related variables: Do the people make the place or does the place make the people? *Journal of Managerial Issues, 7,* 62–74.

Hoffman, Curt; & Hurst, Nancy. (1990). Gender stereotypes: Perception or rationalization? *Journal of Personality and Social Psychology, 58,* 197–208.

Hoffman, Lorrie. (1982). Empirical findings concerning sexism in our schools. *Corrective and Social Psy-*

chiatry and Journal of Behavior Technology, Methods and Therapy, 28, 100–108.

Hoffman, Saul D.; & Duncan, Greg J. (1988). What *are* the economic consequences of divorce? *Demography, 25,* 641–645.

Hoffner, Cynthia. (1996). Children's wishful identification and parasocial interaction with favorite television characters. *Journal-of-Broadcasting-and-Electronic-Media, 40,* 389–402.

Holroyd, Jean Corey; & Brodsky, Annette M. (1977). Psychologists' attitudes and practices regarding erotic and nonerotic physical contact with patients. *American Psychologist, 32,* 843–849.

Holzer, Charles E.; Shea, Brent M.; Swanson, Jeffrey W.; Leaf, Philip J.; Myers, J.; George, L.; Weissman, M.; & Bednarski, P. (1986). The increased risk for specific psychiatric disorders among persons of low socioeconomic status. *American Journal of Social Psychiatry, 6,* 259–271.

Horner, Martina. (1969, November). Fail: Bright women. *Psychology Today,* pp. 36–38, 62.

Horney, Karen. (1967). The dread of women: Observations on a specific difference in the dread felt by men and by women respectively for the opposite sex. In Harold Kelman (Ed.), *Feminine psychology* (pp. 133–146). New York: Norton. (Original work published 1932)

Horney, Karen. (1939). *New ways in psychoanalysis.* New York: Norton.

Horowitz, Allan V.; & White, Helene R. (1991). Becoming married, depression, and alcohol problems among young adults. *Journal of Health and Social Behavior, 32,* 221–237.

Hort, Barbara E.; Fagot, Beverly, I.; & Leinbach, Mary D. (1990). Are people's notions of maleness more stereotypically framed than their notions of femaleness? *Sex Roles, 23,* 197–212.

Hort, Barbara E.; Leinbach, Mary D.; & Fagot, Beverly I. (1991). Is there coherence among the cognitive components of gender acquisition? *Sex Roles, 24,* 195–207.

Hotelling, Kathy. (1991). Sexual harassment: A problem shielded by silence. *Journal of Counseling & Development, 69,* 497–501.

House, James S. (1984). Barriers to work stress: I. Social support. In W. Doyle Gentry, Herbert Benson, & Charles deWolff (Eds.), *Behavioral medicine: Work, stress, and health.* The Hague, Netherlands: Nijhoff.

Howard, Judith A.; Blumstein, Philip; & Schwartz, Pepper. (1987). Social or evolutionary theories? Some observations on preferences in human mate selection. *Journal of Personality and Social Psychology, 53,* 194–200.

Hrdy, Sarah Blaffer. (1981). *The woman that never evolved.* Cambridge, MA: Harvard University Press.

Hrdy, Sarah Blaffer. (1986). Empathy, polyandry, and the myth of the coy female. In Ruth Bleier (Ed.), *Feminist approaches to science* (pp. 119–146). New York: Pergamon Press.

Hsu, L. K. George. (1990). *Eating disorders.* New York: Guilford Press.

Hubbard, Ruth. (1990). *The politics of women's biology.* New Brunswick: Rutgers University Press.

Hubbard, Ruth; & Wald, Elijah. (1993). *Exploding the gene myth.* Boston: Beacon Press.

Hudak, Mary A. (1993). Gender schema theory revisited: Men's stereotypes of American women. *Sex Roles, 28,* 279–293.

Huesmann, L. Rowell; Eron, Leonard D.; Lefkowitz, Monroe M.; & Walder, Leopold O. (1984). Stability of aggression over time and generations. *Developmental Psychology, 20,* 1120–1134.

Hughes, Diane L.; & Galinsky, Ellen. (1994). Gender, job and family conditions, and psychological symptoms. *Psychology of Women Quarterly, 18,* 251–270.

Hull, Gloria; Bell-Scott, Patricia; & Smith, Barbara. (Eds.). (1982). *All the women were White, all the Blacks were men, but some of us are brave: Black women's studies.* Old Westbury, NY: Feminist Press.

Hummer, Robert A.; Rogers, Richard G.; Amir, Sarit H.; Forbes, Douglas; & Frisbie, W. Parker. (2000). Adult mortality differentials among Hispanic subgroups and non-Hispanic Whites. *Social Science Quarterly, 81,* 459–476.

Humphreys, Ann P.; & Smith, Peter K. (1987). Rough and tumble friendship and dominancy in school children: Evidence for continuity and change with age in middle childhood. *Child Development, 58,* 201–212.

Hunt, Melissa G. (1993). Expressiveness does predict well-being. *Sex Roles, 29,* 147–169.

Hunt, Morton. (1974). *Sexual Behavior in the 1970s.* Chicago: Playboy Press.

Hyde, Janet Shibley. (1981). How large are cognitive gender differences? A meta-analysis using ω^2 and *d. American Psychologist, 36,* 892–901.

Hyde, Janet Shibley. (1984). How large are gender differences in aggression? A developmental meta-analysis. *Developmental Psychology, 20,* 722–736.

Hyde, Janet Shibley. (1986). Introduction: Meta-analysis and the psychology of gender. In Janet Shibley Hyde & Marcia C. Linn (Eds.), *The psychology of gender: Advances through meta-analysis* (pp. 1–13). Baltimore: Johns Hopkins University Press.

Hyde, Janet Shibley. (1994). Can meta-analysis make feminist transformations in psychology? *Psychology of Women Quarterly, 18,* 451–462.

Hyde, Janet Shibley. (1996). Where are the gender differences? Where are the gender similarities? In David M. Buss & Neil M. Malamuth (Eds.), *Sex, power, conflict: Evolutionary and feminist perspectives* (pp. 107–118). New York: Oxford University Press.

Hyde, Janet Shibley; Fennema, Elizabeth; & Lamon, Susan J. (1990). Gender differences in mathematics performance: A meta-analysis. *Psychological Bulletin, 107,* 139–155.

Hyde, Janet Shibley; Fennema, Elizabeth; Ryan, Marilyn; Frost, Laurie A.; & Hopp, Carolyn. (1990). Gender comparisons of mathematics attitudes and affect: A meta-analysis. *Psychology of Women Quarterly, 14,* 299–324.

Hyde, Janet Shibley; & Linn, Marcia C. (1988). Gender differences in verbal ability: A meta-analysis. *Psychological Bulletin, 104,* 53–69.

Idle, Tracey; Wood, Eileen; & Desmarais, Serge. (1993). Gender role socialization in toy play situations: Mothers and fathers with their sons and daughters. *Sex Roles, 28,* 679–691.

Imperato-McGinley, Julianne; Guerrero, Luis; Gautier, Teofilo; & Peterson, Ralph E. (1974). Steroid 5-α-reductase deficiency in man: An inherited form of male pseudohermaphroditism. *Science, 186,* 1213–1215.

Ireland, Doug. (1999, June 14). Gay ed for kids. *The Nation, 268*(22), 8.

Jack, Dana Crowley. (1991). *Silencing the self: Women and depression.* Cambridge, MA: Harvard University Press.

Jack, Dana Crowley. (1999). Silencing the self: Inner dialogues and outer realities. In Thomas Joiner and James C. Coyne (Eds.), *The interactional nature of depression: Advances in interpersonal approaches* (pp. 221–246). Washington, DC: American Psychological Association.

Jacklin, Carol Nagy; & Maccoby, Eleanor E. (1978). Social behavior at thirty-three months in same-sex and mixed-sex dyads. *Child Development, 49,* 557–569.

Jackson, Dorothy W.; & Tein, Jenn-Yunn. (1998). Adolescents' conceptualization of adult roles: Relationships with age, gender, work goal, and maternal employment. *Sex Roles, 38,* 987–1008.

Jacobs, Jerry A. (1989). Long-term trends in occupational segregation by sex. *American Journal of Sociology, 95,* 160–173.

Jacobs, Jerry A. (1996). Gender inequality in higher education. *Annual Review of Sociology, 22,* 153–182.

Jacobs, Marion K.; & Goodman, Gerald. (1989). Psychology and self-help groups: Predictions on a partnership. *American Psychologist, 44,* 536–545.

Jacobs, Michael. (1992). *Sigmund Freud.* London: Sage.

James, William. (1890). *Principles of psychology* (Vols 1–2). New York: Holt.

Janoff-Bulman, Ronnie; & Frieze, Irene H. (1987). The role of gender in reactions to criminal victimization. In Rosalind C. Barnett, Lois Biener, & Grace K. Baruch (Eds.), *Gender and stress* (pp. 159–184). New York: Free Press.

Janus, Samuel S.; & Janus, Cynthia L. (1993). *The Janus report on sexual behavior.* New York: Wiley.

Jermain, Donna M. (1999). Luteal phase sertraline treatment for Premenstrual Dysphoric Disorder: Results of a double-blind, placebo-controlled, crossover study. *Journal of the American Medical Association, 282,* 1705.

Jet. (1997, September 22). Walt Whitman Community School, nation's first private school for gays opens in Dallas. Author, 92(18), 12–13.

Johnson, D. Kay. (1988). Adolescents' solutions to dilemmas in fables: Two moral orientations—Two problem solving strategies. In Carol Gilligan, Janie Victoria Ward, & Jill McLean Taylor. (with Bardiger, Betty). (Eds.), *Mapping the moral domain: A contribution of women's thinking to psychological theory and education* (pp. 49–71). Cambridge, MA: Harvard University Press.

Johnson, Michael P. (1995). Patriarchal terrorism and common couple violence: Two forms of violence against women. *Journal of Marriage and the Family, 57,* 283–294.

Johnson, Toni C. (1989). Female child perpetrators: Children who molest other children. *Child Abuse and Neglect, 13,* 571–585.

Jones, Christopher B. (1996). Women of the future: Alternative scenarios. *The Futurist, 30,* 34–38.

Jones, Ernest. (1955). *The life and work of Sigmund Freud* (Vol. 2). New York: Basic Books.

Jones, James H. (1998). *Alfred C. Kinsey: A public/private life.* New York: Norton.

Jones, M. Gail. (1989). Gender issues in teacher education. *Journal of Teacher Education, 40,* 33–38.

Jussim, Lee J.; McCauley, Clark R.; & Lee, Yueh-Ting. (1995). Why study stereotype accuracy and inaccuracy? In Yueh-Ting Lee, Lee J. Jussim, & Clark R. McCauley (Eds.), *Stereotype accuracy: Toward appreciating group differences* (pp. 3–27). Washington, DC: American Psychological Association.

Kaminer, Wendy. (1993, October). Feminism's identity crisis. *Atlantic Monthly,* pp. 51–53, 56, 58–59, 62, 64, 66–68.

Kane, Penny. (1991). *Women's health: From womb to tomb.* New York: St. Martin's Press.

Kang, Mee-Eun. (1997). The portrayal of women's images in magazine advertisements: Goffman's gender analysis revisited. *Sex Roles, 37,* 979–996.

Kanter, Rosabeth Moss. (1975). Women and the structure of organizations: Explorations in theory and behavior. In Marcia Millman & Rosabeth M. Kanter (Eds.), *Another voice* (pp. 34–74). Garden City, NY: Anchor/Doubleday.

Kanter, Rosabeth Moss. (1977). *Men and women of the corporation.* New York: Basic Books.

Kantrowitz, Barbara; & Wingert, Pat. (1999, April 19). The science of a good marriage. *Newsweek, 133*(16), 52–57.

Kantrowitz, Ricki E.; & Ballou, Mary. (1992). A feminist critique of cognitive-behavioral therapy. In Laura S. Brown & Mary Ballou (Eds.), *Personality and psychopathology: Feminist reappraisals* (pp. 70–87). New York: Guilford Press.

Kaplan, Alexandra G. (1980). Human sex-hormone abnormalities viewed from an androgynous perspective: A reconsideration of the work of John Money. In Jacquelynne E. Parsons (Ed.), *The psychobiology of sex differences and sex roles* (pp. 81–91). Washington, DC: Hemisphere.

Kaplan, Alexandra G.; & Yasinski, Lorraine. (1980). Psychodynamic perspectives. In Annette M. Brodsky & Rachel Hare-Mustin (Eds.), *Women and psychotherapy* (pp. 191–216). New York: Guilford Press.

Kaplan, Marcie. (1983a). The issue of sex bias in DSM-III: Comments on the articles by Spitzer, Williams, and Kass. *American Psychologist, 38,* 802–803.

Kaplan, Marcie. (1983b). A woman's view of the DSM-III. *American Psychologist, 38,* 786–792.

Kaplan, Robert M.; Anderson, John P.; & Wingard, Deborah L. (1991). Gender differences in health-related quality of life. *Health Psychology, 10,* 86–93.

Karabenick, Stuart A.; Sweeney, Catherine; & Penrose, Gary. (1983). Preferences for skill versus change-determined activities: The influence of gender and task sex-typing. *Journal of Research in Personality, 17,* 125–142.

Kaschak, Ellyn. (1992). *Engendered lives.* New York: Basic Books.

Kass, Frederic; Spitzer, Robert L.; & Williams, Janet B. W. (1983). An empirical study of the issue of sex bias in the diagnostic criteria of DSM-III axis II personality disorders. *American Psychologist, 38,* 799–801.

Katz, Alfred H. (1993). *Self-help in America: A social movement perspective.* New York: Twayne.

Katz, Phyllis A.; & Ksansnak, Keith R. (1994). Developmental aspects of gender role flexibility and traditionality in middle childhood and adolescence. *Developmental Psychology, 30,* 272–282.

Kaufman, Debra Renee. (1995). Professional women: How real are the recent gains? In Jo Freeman (Ed.), *Women: A feminist perspective* (5th ed.; pp. 287–305). Mountain View, CA: Mayfield.

Keen, Sam. (1991). *A fire in the belly: On being a man.* New York: Bantam.

Keller, Evelyn Fox. (1985). *Reflections on gender and science.* New Haven: Yale University Press.

Keller, Teresa. (1999). Lessons in equality: What television teaches us about women. In Carie Forden, Anne E. Hunter, and Beverly Birns (Eds.), *Readings in the psychology of women: Dimensions of the female experience* (pp. 27–35). Boston: Allyn and Bacon.

Kelly, Janice R.; & Hutson-Comeaux, Sarah L. (1999). Gender-emotion stereotypes are context specific. *Sex Roles, 40,* 107–120.

Kessler, Ronald C.; Brown, Roger L.; & Broman, Clifford L. (1981). Sex differences in psychiatric help-seeking: Evidence from four large-scale surveys. *Journal of Health and Social Behavior, 22,* 49–64.

Kessler, Ronald C.; Mickelson, Kristin D.; & Williams, David R. (1999). The prevalence, distribution, and mental health correlates of perceived discrimination in the United States. *Journal of Health and Social Behavior, 40,* 208–230.

Kidder, Louise. (1994, August). *All pores open.* Paper presented at the 102nd Annual Convention of the American Psychological Association, Los Angeles, CA.

Kiernan, Michaela; Rodin, Judith; Brownell, Kelly D.; Wilmore, Jack H.; & Crandall, Christian. (1992). Relation of level of exercise, age, and weight-cycling history to weight and eating concerns in male and female runners. *Health Psychology, 11,* 418–421.

Kimball, Meredith M. (1995). *Feminist visions of gender similarities and differences.* New York: Haworth Press.

Kimmel, Michael S.; & Messner, Michael A. (1992). Introduction. In Michael S. Kimmel & Michael A. Messner (Eds.), *Men's lives* (2nd ed.; pp. 1–11). New York: Macmillan.

Kimura, Doreen. (1992, September). Sex differences in the brain. *Scientific American,* pp. 119–125.

King, Abby C.; & Kiernan, Michaela. (1997). Physical activity and women's health: Issues and future directions. In Sheryle J. Gallant, Gwendolyn Puryear Keita, & Reneé Royak-Schaler (Eds.), *Health care for women: Psychological, social, and behavioral influences* (pp. 133–146). Washington, DC: American Psychological Association.

King, Patricia A. (1999, June 21). Science for girls only. *Newsweek, 133,* 64–65.

Kinsey, Alfred C.; Pomeroy, Wardell B.; & Martin, Clyde E. (1948). *Sexual behavior in the human male.* Philadelphia: Saunders.

Kinsey, Alfred C.; Pomeroy, Wardell B.; Martin, Clyde E.; & Gebhard, Paul H. (1953). *Sexual behavior in the human female.* Philadelphia: Saunders.

Kipnis, Aaron R. (1991). *Knights without armor: A practical guide for men in quest of masculine soul.* Los Angeles: Jeremy P. Tarcher.

Kirschstein, Ruth L. (1991). Research on women's health. *American Journal of Public Health, 81,* 291–293.

Kite, Mary E.; & Whitley, Bernard E., Jr. (1996). Sex differences in attitudes toward homosexual persons, behaviors, and civil rights: A meta-analysis. *Personality and Social Psychology Bulletin, 22,* 336–353.

Klaus, Marshall H.; & Kennell, John H. (1976). *Maternal infant bonding.* St. Louis: Mosby.

Kling, Kristen C.; & Hyde, Janet Shibley. (1996, August). *Gender differences in self-esteem: A meta-analysis.* Paper presented at the 104th annual convention of the American Psychological Association, Toronto, Canada.

Klonoff, Elizabeth A.; & Landrine, Hope. (1997). *Preventing misdiagnosis of women.* Thousand Oaks, CA: Sage.

Klonoff, Elizabeth A.; Landrine, Hope; & Campbell, Robin. (2000). Sexist discrimination may account for well-known gender differences in psychiatric symptoms. *Psychology of Women Quarterly, 24,* 93–99.

Knox, Sarah S.; & Czajkowski, Susan. (1997). The influence of behavioral and psychosocial factors on cardiovascular health in women. In Sheryle J. Gallant, Gwendolyn Puryear Keita, & Reneé Royak-Schaler (Eds.), *Health care for women: Psychological, social, and behavioral influences* (pp. 257–272). Washington, DC: American Psychological Association.

Koehler, Mary Schatz. (1990). Classrooms, teachers, and gender differences in mathematics. In Elizabeth Fennema & Gilah C. Leder (Eds.), *Mathematics and gender* (pp. 128–148). New York: Teachers College Press.

Koeske, Randi K.; & Koeske, Gary F. (1975). An attributional approach to moods and the menstrual cycle. *Journal of Personality and Social Psychology, 31,* 473–478.

Kohlberg, Lawrence. (1966). A cognitive-developmental analysis of children's sex-role concepts and attitudes. In Eleanor E. Maccoby (Ed.), *The development of sex differences* (pp. 52–173). Stanford, CA: Stanford University Press.

Kohlberg, Lawrence. (1981). *The philosophy of moral development.* San Francisco: Harper & Row.

Komarovsky, Mirra. (1982). Female freshmen view their future: Career salience and its correlates. *Sex Roles, 8,* 299–313.

Kopper, Beverly A.; & Epperson, Douglas L. (1991). Women and anger: Sex and sex-role comparisons in the expression of anger. *Psychology of Women Quarterly, 15,* 7–14.

Kopper, Beverly A.; & Epperson, Douglas L. (1996). The experience and expression of anger: Relationships with gender, gender role socialization, depression, and mental health functioning. *Journal of Counseling Psychology, 43,* 158–165.

Koss, Mary P. (1990). The women's mental health research agenda: Violence against women. *American Psychologist, 45,* 374–380.

Koss, Mary P. (1992). The underdetection of rape: Methodological choices influence incidence estimates. *Journal of Social Issues, 48*(1), 61–75.

Koss, Mary P. (1993). Rape: Scope, impact, interventions, and public policy responses. *American Psychologist, 48,* 1062–1069.

Koss, Mary P.; Gidycz, Christine A.; & Wisniewski, Nadine. (1987). The scope of rape: Incidence and prevalence of sexual aggression and victimization in a national sample of higher education students. *Journal of Consulting and Clinical Psychology, 55,* 162–170.

Kramarae, Cheris; & Treichler, Paula A. (1990). Power relationships in the classroom. In Susan L. Gabriel & Isaiah Smithson (Eds.), *Gender in the classroom: Power and pedagogy* (pp. 41–59). Urbana: University of Illinois Press.

Kravetz, Diane. (1978). Consciousness-raising groups of the 1970s. *Psychology of Women Quarterly, 3,* 168–186.

Krishnan, Ahalya; & Sweeney, Christopher J. (1998). Gender differences in fear of success imagery and other achievement-related background variables among medical students. *Sex Roles, 39,* 299–310.

Kuhn, Deanna; Nash, Sharon C.; & Brucken, Laura. (1978). Sex role concepts of two- and three-year olds. *Child Development, 49,* 445–451.

Kurdek, Lawrence A. (1993). The allocation of household labor in gay, lesbian, and heterosexual married couples. *Journal of Social Issues, 49*(3), 127–139.

Kurzweil, Edith. (1995). *Freudians and feminists.* Boulder, CO: Westview Press.

Laband, David N.; & Lentz, Bernard F. (1998). The effects of sexual harassment on job satisfaction, earnings, and turnover among female lawyers. *Industrial and Labor Relations Review, 51,* 594–607.

LaFromboise, Teresa D.; Berman, Joan Saks; & Sohi, Balvindar K. (1994). American Indian women. In Lillian Comas-Díaz & Beverly Greene (Eds.), *Women of color: Integrating ethnic and gender identities in psychotherapy* (pp. 30–71). New York: Guilford Press.

Lakkis, Jacqueline; Ricciardelli, Lina A.; & Williams, Robert J. (1999). Role of sexual orientation and gender-related traits in disordered eating. *Sex Roles, 41,* 1–16.

Lakoff, Robin. (1975). *Language and woman's place.* New York: Harper & Row.

Landau, Jacqueline; & Arthur, Michael B. (1992). The relationship of marital status, spouse's career status, and gender to salary level. *Sex Roles, 27,* 665–681.

Landrine, Hope. (1987). On the politics of madness: A preliminary analysis of the relationship between social roles and psychopathology. *Psychology Monographs, 113,* 341–406.

Landrine, Hope. (1989). The politics of personality disorder. *Psychology of Women Quarterly, 13,* 325–339.

Landrine, Hope; Bardwell, Stephen; & Dean, Tina. (1988). Gender expectations for alcohol use: A study of the significance of the masculine role. *Sex Roles, 19,* 703–712.

Landrine, Hope; & Klonoff, Elizabeth A. (1996). The Schedule of Racist Events: A measure of racial discrimination and a study of its negative physical and mental health consequences. *Journal of Black Psychology, 22,* 144–168.

Landrine, Hope; Klonoff, Elizabeth A.; & Brown-Collins, Alice. (1992). Cultural diversity and methodology in feminist psychology: Critique, proposal, empirical example. *Psychology of Women Quarterly, 16,* 145–163.

Landrine, Hope; Klonoff, Elizabeth A.; Gibbs, Jeannine; Manning, Vickie; & Lund, Marlene. (1995). Physical and psychiatric correlates of gender discrimination: An application of the Schedule of Sexist Events. *Psychology of Women Quarterly, 19,* 473–492.

Larson, Reed; & Pleck, Joseph. (1999). Hidden feelings: Emotionality in boys and men. In Dan Bernstein (Ed.), *Nebraska Symposium on Motivation, 1999: Gender and motivation* (pp. 25–74). Lincoln, NE: University of Nebraska Press.

Larson, Reed; & Richards, Maryse H. (1994). *Divergent realities: The emotional lives of mothers, fathers, and adolescents.* New York: BasicBooks.

Larwood, Laurie; & Gutek, Barbara A. (1989). Working toward a theory of women's career development. In Barbara A. Gutek & Laurie Larwood (Eds.), *Women's career development* (pp. 170–183). Newbury Park, CA: Sage.

Laumann, Edward O.; Gagnon, John H.; Michael, Robert T.; & Michaels, Stuart. (1994). *The social organization of sexuality.* Chicago: University of Chicago Press.

Lavallee, Marguerite; & Pelletier, Rene. (1992). Ecological value of Bem's gender schema theory explored through females' traditional and nontraditional occupational contexts. *Psychological Reports, 70,* 79–82.

Lavin, Thomas J., III. (1987). Divergence and convergence in the causal attributions of married couples. *Journal of Marriage and the Family, 49,* 71–80.

Law, David J.; Pellegrino, James W.; & Hunt, Earl B. (1993). Comparing the tortoise and the hare: Gender differences and experience in dynamic spatial reasoning tasks. *Psychological Science, 4,* 35–40.

Lawton, Carol A. (1994). Gender differences in wayfinding strategies: Relationship to spatial ability and spatial anxiety. *Sex Roles, 30,* 765–779.

Lazarus, Richard S. (1984). On the primacy of cognition. *American Psychologist, 39,* 124–129.

Lazarus, Richard S.; & Folkman, Susan. (1984). *Stress, appraisal, and coping.* New York: Springer.

Leaf, Philip J.; & Bruce, Martha L. (1987). Gender differences in the use of mental health-related services: A re-examination. *Journal of Health and Social Behavior, 28,* 171–183.

Leder, Gilah C. (1990). Gender differences in mathematics: An overview. In Elizabeth Fennema & Gilah C. Leder (Eds.), *Mathematics and gender* (pp. 10–26). New York: Teachers College Press.

Lee, Valerie E.; & Burkam, David T. (1996). Gender differences in middle grade science achievement: Subject domain, ability level, and course emphasis. *Science Education, 80,* 613–650.

Lefkowitz, Monroe M.; Eron, Leonard D.; Walder, Leopold O.; & Huesmann, L. Rowell. (1977). *Growing up to be violent: A longitudinal study of the development of aggression.* New York: Pergamon.

Leinbach, Mary D.; & Fagot, Beverly I. (1993). Categorical habituation to male and female faces: Gender schematic processing in infancy. *Infant Behavior and Development, 16,* 317–332.

Leitenberg, Harold; & Saltzman, Heidi. (2000). A statewide survey of age at first intercourse for adolescent females and age of their male partners: Relation to other risk behavior and statutory rape implications. *Archives of Sexual Behavior, 29,* 203–216.

Lenny, Ellen. (1977). Women's self-confidence in achievement settings. *Psychological Bulletin, 84,* 1–13.

Leong, Frederick T. L.; Snodgrass, Coral R.; & Gardner, William L., III. (1992). Management education: Creating a gender-positive environment. In Uma Sekaran & Leong Frederick T. L. (Eds.), *Womanpower: Managing in times of demographic turbulence* (pp. 192–220). Newbury Park, CA: Sage.

Lepowsky, Maria. (1994). Women, men, and aggression in an egalitarian society. *Sex Roles, 30,* 199–211.

Lerman, Hannah. (1992). The limits of phenomenology: A feminist critique of the humanistic personality theories. In Laura S. Brown & Mary Ballou (Eds.), *Personality and psychopathology: Feminist reappraisals* (pp. 8–19). New York: Guilford Press.

Lerman, Hannah. (1996). *Pigeonholing women's misery: A history and critical analysis of the psychodiagnosis of women in the twentieth century.* New York: Basic Books.

Lerner, Alan Jay; & Loewe, Frederick. (1956). *My fair lady: A musical play in two acts.* Based on *Pygmalion* by Bernard Shaw. New York: Coward-McCann.

Leslie, Leigh A.; Huston, Ted L.; & Johnson, Michael P. (1986). Parental reactions to dating relationships: Do they make a difference? *Journal of Marriage and the Family, 48,* 57–66.

Levant, Ronald F. (1990). Psychological services designed for men: A psychoeducational approach. *Psychotherapy, 27,* 309–315.

Levant, Ronald F. (1996). The new psychology of men. *Professional Psychology, Research and Practice, 27,* 259–265.

LeVay, Simon. (1991). A difference in hypothalamic structure between heterosexual and homosexual men. *Science, 253,* 1034–1037.

LeVay, Simon. (1996). *Queer science: The use and abuse of research into homosexuality.* Cambridge, MA: MIT Press.

Levenson, Robert W.; Carstensen, Laura L.; & Gottman, John M. (1994). The influence of age and gender on affect, physiology, and their interrelations: A study of long-term marriages. *Journal of Personality and Social Psychology, 67,* 56–68.

Levy, Gary D. (1989). Relations among aspects of children's social environments, gender schematization, gender role knowledge, and flexibility. *Sex Roles, 21,* 803–823.

Levy, Gary D. (1999). Gender-typed and non-gender-typed category awareness in toddlers. *Sex Roles, 41,* 851–874.

Levy, Gary D.; Barth, Joan M.; & Zimmerman, Barbara J. (1998). Associations among cognitive and behavioral aspects of preschoolers' gender role development. *Journal of Genetic Psychology, 159,* 121–126.

Levy, Gary D.; & Boston, Martha B. (1994). Preschoolers' recall of own-sex and other-sex gender scripts. *Journal of Genetic Psychology, 155,* 369–371.

Levy, Gary D.; & Fivush, Robyn. (1993). Scripts and gender: A new approach for examining gender-role development. *Developmental Review, 13,* 126–146.

Levy, Jerre. (1969). Possible basis for the evolution of lateral specialization of the human brain. *Nature, 224,* 614–625.

Levy, Sandra M. (1985). *Behavior and cancer: Life-style and psychosocial factors in the initiation and progression of cancer.* San Francisco: Jossey-Bass.

Lewin, Miriam. (1984a). "Rather worse than folly?" Psychology measures femininity and masculinity: 1. From Terman and Miles to the Guilfords. In Miriam Lewin (Ed.), *In the shadow of the past: Psychology portrays the sexes* (pp. 155–178). New York: Columbia University Press.

Lewin, Miriam. (1984b). Psychology measures femininity and masculinity: 2. From "13 gay men" to the instrumental-expressive distinction. In Miriam Lewin (Ed.), *In the shadow of the past: Psychology portrays the sexes* (pp. 179–204). New York: Columbia University Press.

Lewin, Miriam. (1984c). The Victorians, the psychologists, and psychic birth control. In Miriam Lewin (Ed.), *In the shadow of the past: Psychology portrays the sexes* (pp. 39–76). New York: Columbia University Press.

Lewis, Andrea E.; & Fagenson-Eland, Ellen A. (1998). The influence of gender and organization level on perceptions of leadership behaviors: A self and supervisor comparison. *Sex Roles, 39,* 479–502.

Lewis, Carol D.; & Houtz, John C. (1986). Sex-role stereotyping and young children's divergent thinking. *Psychological Reports, 59,* 1027–1033.

Lewis, Shon. (1992). Sex and schizophrenia: Vive la difference. *British Journal of Psychiatry, 161,* 445–450.

Liben, Lynn S.; & Golbeck, Susan L. (1984). Performance on Piagetian horizontality and verticality tasks: Sex-related differences in knowledge of relevant physical phenomena. *Developmental Psychology, 20,* 595–606.

Lindberg, Laura Duberstein; Sonenstein, Freya L.; Ku, Leighton; & Martinez, Gladys. (1997). Age differences between minors who give birth and their adult partners. *Family Planning Perspectives, 29,* 61–66.

Linn, Marcia C.; & Petersen, Anne C. (1986). A meta-analysis of gender differences in spatial ability: Implications for mathematics and science achievement. In Janet Shibley Hyde & Marcia C. Linn (Eds.), *The psychology of gender: Advances through meta-analysis* (pp. 67–101). Baltimore: Johns Hopkins University Press.

Lips, Hilary M. (1989). Gender-role socialization: Lessons in femininity. In Jo Freeman (Ed.), *Women: A feminist perspective* (pp. 197–216). Mountain View, CA: Mayfield.

Livingston, Nancy. (1994, March 11). St. Paul, Minn., schools plan full-time coordinator for gay and lesbian students. *Knight-Ridder/Tribune News Service,* p. 0311 K2183.

Livingston, Martha. (1999). How to think about women's health. In Carie Forden, Anne E. Hunter, & Beverly Birns (Eds.), *Readings in the psychol-*

ogy of women: Dimensions of the female experience (pp. 244–253). Boston: Allyn and Bacon.

Lloyd, Barbara; Duveen, Gerard; & Smith, Caroline. (1988). Social representation of gender and young children's play: A replication. *British Journal of Developmental Psychology, 6,* 83–88.

Lock, James; & Steiner, Hans. (1999). Gay, lesbian, and bisexual youth risks for emotional, physical, and social problems: Results from a community-based survey. *Journal of the American Academy of Child and Adolescent Psychiatry, 38,* 297–304.

Locksley, Anne; Borgida, Eugene; Brekke, Nancy; & Hepburn, Christine. (1980). Sex stereotypes and social judgments. *Journal of Personality and Social Psychology, 39,* 821–831.

Long, J. Scott; & Fox, Mary Frank. (1995). Scientific careers: Universalism and particularism. *Annual Review of Sociology, 21,* 45–71.

Lont, Cynthia M. (Ed.). (1995). *Women and media: Content, careers, and criticism.* Belmont, CA: Wadsworth.

Loo, Robert; & Thorpe, Karran. (1998). Attitudes toward women's roles in society: A replication after 20 years. *Sex Roles, 39,* 903–912.

López, Steven Regeser. (1989). Patient variable biases in clinical judgment: Conceptual overview and methodological considerations. *Psychological Bulletin, 106,* 184–203.

Lorber, Judith. (1975). Women and medical sociology: Invisible professionals and ubiquitous patients. In Marcia Millman & Rosabeth M. Kanter (Eds.), *Another voice* (pp. 75–105). Garden City, NY: Anchor/Doubleday.

Lorber, Judith. (1989). Trust, loyalty, and the place for women in the informal organization of work. In J. Freeman (Ed.), *Women: A feminist perspective* (pp. 347–355). Mountain View, CA: Mayfield.

Lorber, Judith. (1997). Believing is seeing: Biology as ideology. In Maxine Baca Zinn, Pierrette Hondagneu-Sotelo, & Michael A. Messner (Eds.), *Through the prism of difference: Readings on sex and gender* (pp. 13–22). Boston: Allyn and Bacon.

Loring, Marti; & Powell, Brian. (1998). Gender, race, and DSM-III: A study of the objectivity of psychiatric diagnostic behavior. *Journal of Health and Social Behavior, 29,* 1–22.

Lott, Bernice. (1997). Cataloging gender differences: Science or politics? In Mary Roth Walsh (Ed.), *Women, men, and gender: Ongoing debates* (pp. 19–23). New Haven, CT: Yale University Press.

Loury, Glenn C. (1996, January-February). Joy and doubt on the mall: The Million Man March and me. *Utne Reader, 73,* 70–73.

Loury, Linda Datcher. (1997). The gender earnings gap among college-educated workers. *Industrial and Labor Relations Review, 50,* 580–593.

Luepker, Ellen T. (1999). Effects of practitioners' sexual misconduct: A follow-up study. *Journal of the American Academy of Psychiatry and the Law, 27,* 51–63.

Lye, Diane N. (1996). Adult child-parent relationships. *Annual Review of Sociology, 22,* 79–102.

Lyons, Nona Plessner. (1988). Two perspectives: On self, relationships, and morality. In Carol Gilligan, Janie Victoria Ward, & Jill McLean Taylor (with Bardige, Betty). (Eds.), *Mapping the moral domain: A contribution of women's thinking to psychological theory and education* (pp. 21–48). Cambridge, MA: Harvard University Press.

Maccoby, Eleanor E. (1988). Gender as a social category. *Developmental Psychology, 24,* 755–765.

Maccoby, Eleanor E. (1990). Gender and relationships. *American Psychologist, 45,* 513–520.

Maccoby, Eleanor Emmons; & Jacklin, Carol Nagy. (1974). *The psychology of sex differences.* Stanford, CA: Stanford University Press.

MacCoun, Robert J. (1998). Biases in the interpretation and use of research results. *Annual Review of Psychology, 49,* 259–287.

Maisey, D. S.; Vale, E. L. E.; Cornelissen, P. L.; & Tovee, M. J. (1999). Characteristics of male attractiveness for women. *Lancet, 353,* 1500.

Majors, Richard G.; & Billson, J. M. (1992). *Cool pose: The dilemmas of black manhood in America.* New York: Lexington.

Majors, Richard G.; Tyler, Richard; Peden, Blaine; & Hall, Ron. (1994). Cool pose: A symbolic mechanism for masculine role enactment and coping by black males. In Richard G. Majors & Jacob U. Gordon (Eds.), *The American black male: His present status and his future* (pp. 245–259). Chicago: Nelson-Hall.

Malamuth, Neil M. (1996). The confluence model of sexual aggression: Feminist and evolutionary perspectives. In David M. Buss & Neil M. Malamuth (Eds.), *Sex, power, conflict: Evolutionary and feminist perspectives* (pp. 269–295). New York: Oxford University Press.

Malkin, Amy R.; Wornian, Kimberlie; & Chrisler, Joan C. (1999). Women and weight: gendered messages on magazine covers. *Sex Roles, 40,* 647–656.

Mancus, Dianne Sirna. (1992). Influence of male teachers on elementary school children's stereotyping of teacher competence. *Sex Roles, 26,* 109–128.

Manger, Terje; & Eikeland, Ole-Johan. (1998). The effects of spatial visualization and students' sex on mathematical achievement. *British Journal of Psychology, 89,* 17–25.

Mansnerus, Laura. (1992, January 5). Women take to the field. *New York Times,* Sec. A4, pp. 40–41.

Marano, Hara Estroff. (1997). When planets collide. *Psychology Today, 30*(3), 28–30, 68, 70.

Marcotte, Diane; Allain, Michel; & Gosselin, Marie-Josee. (1999). Gender differences in adolescent depression: Gender-typed characteristics or problem-solving skills deficiency? *Sex Roles, 41,* 31–48.

Marecek, Jeanne; & Hare-Mustin, Rachel. (1991). A short history of the future: Feminism and clinical psychology, *Psychology of Women Quarterly, 15,* 521–536.

Marecek, Jeanne; & Kravetz, Diane. (1998). Putting politics into practice: Feminist therapy as feminist praxis. *Women & Therapy, 21,* 17–36.

Marecek, Jeanne; Kravetz, Diane; & Finn, Stephen. (1979). Comparison of women who enter feminist therapy and women who enter traditional therapy. *Journal of Consulting and Clinical Psychology, 47,* 734–742.

Mark, Daniel B. (2000). Sex bias in cardiovascular care: Should women be treated more like men? *Journal of the American Medical Association, 283,* 659–665.

Martell, Richard F.; Lane, David, M.; & Emrich, Cynthia. (1996). Male-female differences: A computer simulation. *American Psychologist, 51,* 157–158.

Martin, Carol Lynn. (1987). A ratio measure of sex stereotyping. *Journal of Personality and Social Psychology, 52,* 489–499.

Martin, Carol Lynn. (1995). Stereotypes about children with traditional and nontraditional gender roles. *Sex Roles, 33,* 727–751.

Martin, Carol Lynn; & Halverson, Charles F., Jr. (1981). A schematic processing model of sex-typing and stereotyping in children. *Child Development, 52,* 1119–1134.

Martin, Carol Lynn; & Little, Jane K. (1990). The relation of gender understanding to children's sex-typed preferences and gender stereotypes. *Child Development, 61,* 1427–1439.

Martin, Carol Lynn; Wood, Carolyn H.; & Little, Jane K. (1990). The development of gender stereotype components. *Child Development, 61,* 1891–1904.

Martinko, Mark L.; & Gardner, William L. (1983). A methodological review of sex-related access discrimination problems. *Sex Roles, 9,* 825–839.

Martocchio, Joseph J.; & O'Leary, Anne M. (1989). Sex differences in occupational stress: A meta-analytic review. *Journal of Applied Psychology, 74,* 495–501.

Masson, Jeffrey Moussaieff. (1984). *The assault on truth: Freud's suppression of the seduction theory.* New York: Farrar, Straus and Giroux.

Masters, William H.; & Johnson, Virginia E. (1966). *Human sexual response.* Boston: Little, Brown.

Masters, William H.; Johnson, Virginia E.; & Kolodny, Robert C. (1992). *Human sexuality* (4th ed.). New York: HarperCollins.

Matthews, Karen A. (1989). Are sociodemographic variables markers for psychological determinants of health? *Health Psychology, 8,* 641–648.

Matthews, Karen A.; Shumaker, Sally A.; Bowen, Deborah J.; Langer, Robert D.; Hunt, Julie R.; Kaplan, Robert M.; Klesges, Robert C.; & Ritenbaugh, Cheryl. (1997). Women's health initiative: Why now? What is it? What's new? *American Psychologist, 52,* 101–116.

Mays, Vickie M.; & Comas-Diaz, Lillian. (1988). Feminist therapy with ethnic minority populations: A closer look at Blacks and Hispanics. In Mary Ann Dutton Douglas & Lenore E. A. Walker (Eds.), *Feminist psychotherapies: Integration of therapeutic and feminist systems* (pp. 228–251). Norwood, NJ: Ablex.

Mazur, Allan. (1985). A biosocial model of status in face-to-face primate groups. *Social Forces, 64,* 377–402.

Mazur, Allan; & Booth, Alan. (1998). Testosterone and dominance in men. *Behavioral and Brain Sciences, 21,* 353–363.

Mazza, James J.; & Reynolds, William M. (1999). Exposure to violence in young inner-city adolescents: Relationships with suicidal ideation, depression, and PTSD symptomatology. *Journal of Abnormal Child Psychology, 27,* 203–214.

McCabe, Marita P.; & Cummins, Robert A. (1998). Sexuality and quality of life among young people. *Adolescence, 33,* 761–774.

McCann, Nancy Dodd; & McGinn, Thomas A. (1992). *Harassed: 100 women define inappropriate behavior in the workplace.* Homewood, IL: Business One Irwin.

McCauley, Clark R. (1995). Are stereotypes exaggerated? A sampling of racial, gender, academic, occupational, and political stereotypes. In Yueh-Ting Lee, Lee J. Jussim, & Clark R. McCauley (Eds.), *Stereotype accuracy: Toward appreciating group differences* (pp. 215–243). Washington, DC: American Psychological Association.

McClelland, David C.; Atkinson, J. W.; Clark, R. W.; & Lowell, E. L. (1953). *The achievement motive.* New York: Appleton.

McCombs, Barbara L. (2000, July). Reducing the achievement gap. *Society, 37,* 29–35.

McCormick, Naomi B. (1994). *Sexual salvation: Affirming women's sexual rights and pleasures.* Westport, CT: Praeger.

McCreary, Donald R.; & Sasse, Doris K. (2000). An exploration of the drive for muscularity in adolescent boys and girls. *Journal of American College Health, 48,* 297–304.

McDonald, Karen; & Thompson, J. Kevin. (1992). Eating disturbance, body image dissatisfaction, and reasons for exercising: Gender differences and correlational findings. *International Journal of Eating Disorders, 11,* 289–292.

McDougall, William. (1923). *Outline of psychology.* New York: Scribners.

McFarlane, Jessica; Martin, Carol Lynn; & Williams, Tannis MacBeth. (1988). Mood fluctuations: Women versus men and menstrual versus other cycles. *Psychology of Women Quarterly, 12,* 201–223.

McFarlane, Jessica Motherwell; & Williams, Tannis MacBeth. (1994). Placing premenstrual syndrome in perspective. *Psychology of Women Quarterly, 18,* 339–373.

McGuiness, Diane; Olson, Amy; & Chapman, Julia. (1990). Sex differences in incidental recall of words and pictures. *Learning and Individual Differences, 2,* 263–285.

McHale, Susan M.; & Crouter, Ann C. (1992). You can't always get what you want: Incongruence between sex-role attitudes and family work roles and its implications for marriage. *Journal of Marriage and the Family, 54,* 537–547.

McHugh, Maureen C.; Koeske, Randi D.; & Frieze, Irene H. (1986). Issues to consider in conducting nonsexist psychological research: A guide for researchers. *American Psychologist, 41,* 879–890.

McKeever, Walter F. (1995). Hormone and hemisphericity hypotheses regarding cognitive sex differences: Possible future explanatory power, but current empirical chaos. *Learning and Individual Differences, 7,* 323–340.

McLain, Susan June; & Perkins, Carol O. (1990). Disabled women: At the bottom of the work heap. *Vocational Educational Journal, 65*(2), 54–53.

McManus, I. C.; & Bryden, M. P. (1991). Geschwind's theory of cerebral lateralization: Developing a formal, causal model. *Psychological Bulletin, 110,* 237–253.

McWhirter, Ellen Hawley. (1994, August). *Perceived barriers to education and career: Ethnic and gender differences.* Paper presented at the 102nd annual convention of the American Psychological Association, Los Angeles, CA.

Meehan, Anita M.; & Janik, Leann M. (1990). Illusory correlation and the maintenance of sex role stereotypes in children. *Sex Roles, 22,* 83–95.

Melamed, Tuvia. (1996). Career success: An assessment of a gender-specific model. *Journal of Occupational and Organizational Psychology, 69,* 217–242.

Melson, Gail F.; & Fogel, Alan. (1988a). The development of nurturance in young children. *Young Children, 43,* 57–65.

Melson, Gail F.; & Fogel, Alan. (1988b, January). Learning to care: Boys are as nurturant as girls, but in different ways. *Psychology Today,* pp. 39–45.

Mesquita, Batja; & Frijda, Nico H. (1992). Cultural variations in emotions: A review. *Psychological Bulletin, 112,* 179–204.

Messner, Michael A. (1997). *Politics of masculinities: Men in movements.* Thousand Oaks, CA: Sage.

Metzger, Gretchen. (1992). TV is a blonde, blonde world. *American Demographics, 14,* 51.

Meyer-Bahlburg, Heino F. L. (1980). Sexuality in early adolescence. In Benjamin B. Wolman & John Money (Eds.), *Handbook of human sexuality* (pp. 61–82). Englewood Cliffs, NJ: Prentice-Hall.

Michael, Robert T.; Gagnon, John H.; Laumann, Edward O.; & Kolata, Gina. (1994). *Sex in America.* Boston: Little, Brown.

Middaugh, Anne. (1994, August). *Clinical psychology interns' attitudes and information about women.* Paper presented at the 102nd annual convention of the American Psychological Association, Los Angeles, CA.

Mifflin, Margot. (1999, December 13). Singing the pink blues. *Mothers Who Think.* Retrieved May, 2000, from the World Wide Web: http://www. salon.com/mwt/feature/1999/12/13/toys.

Miller, Randi L.; & Gordon, Michael. (1986). The decline in formal dating: A study in six Connecticut high schools. *Marriage and Family Review, 10,* 139–156.

Miller, Ivan W.; Norman, William H.; & Dow, Michael G. (1988). Depression. In Elaine A. Blechman & Kelly D. Brownell (Eds.), *Handbook of behavioral medicine for women* (pp. 399–418). New York: Pergamon Press.

Mirowsky, John; & Ross, Catherine E. (1987). Belief in innate sex roles: Sex stratification versus interpersonal influence in marriage. *Journal of Marriage and the Family, 49,* 527–540.

Mischel, Walter. (1966). A social-learning view of sex differences in behavior. In Eleanor E. Maccoby (Ed.), *The development of sex differences* (pp. 56–81). Stanford, CA: Stanford University Press.

Mischel, Walter. (1993). *Introduction to personality* (5th ed.). Fort Worth: Harcourt Brace Jovanovich.

Mittwoch, Ursula. (1973). *Genetics of sex differentiation.* New York: Academic Press.

Money, John. (1986). *Venuses penuses: Sexology, sexosophy, and exigency theory.* Buffalo, NY: Prometheus Books.

Money, John. (1987). Sin, sickness, or status? Homosexual gender identity and psychoneuroendocrinology. *American Psychologist, 42,* 384–399.

Monroe, Judy. (1995, December). The great debate: Gender differences. *Current Health 2, 22,* 22–25.

Monsour, Michael; Harris, Bridgid; Kurzweil, Nancy; & Beard, Chris. (1994). Challenges confronting cross-sex friendships: "Much ado about nothing?" *Sex Roles, 31,* 55–77.

Montecinos, Carmen; & Nielsen, Lynn E. (1997). Gender and cohort differences in university students' decisions to become elementary teacher education majors. *Journal of Teacher Education, 48,* 47–54.

Montello, Daniel R.; Lovelace, Kristin L.; Golledge, Reginald G.; & Self, Carole M. (1999). Sex-related differences and similarities in geographic and environmental spatial abilities. *Annals of the Association of American Geographers, 89,* 515–534.

Mook, Douglas G. (1987). *Motivation: The organization of action.* New York: Norton.

Morgan, Betsy Levonian. (1998). A three generational study of tomboy behavior. *Sex Roles, 39,* 787–800.

Morgan, Robin. (1970). Introduction: The women's revolution. In Robin Morgan (Ed.), *Sisterhood is powerful: An anthology of writings from the women's liberation movement* (pp. xv–xvii). New York: Vintage Books.

Mori, DeAnna; Chaiken, Shelly; & Pliner, Patricia. (1987). "Eating lightly" and the self-presentation of femininity. *Journal of Personality and Social Psychology, 53,* 693–702.

Mori, Lisa; Selle, Lynn L.; Zarate, Mylene G.; & Bernat, Jeffrey. (1994). *Asian American and Caucasian college students' attitudes towards rape.* Paper presented at the 102nd annual convention of the American Psychological Association, Los Angeles, CA.

Morrow, Susan L.; & Hawxhurst, Donna M. (1998). Feminist therapy: Integrating political analysis in counseling and psychotherapy. *Women & Therapy, 21,* 37–50.

Muehlenhard, Charlene L.; Friedman, Debra E.; & Thomas, Celeste M. (1985). Is date rape justifiable? The effects of dating activity, who initiated, who paid, and men's attitudes toward women. *Psychology of Women Quarterly, 9,* 297–309.

Muehlenhard, Charlene L.; & Hollabaugh, Lisa C. (1988). Do women sometimes say no when they mean yes: The prevalence and correlates of women's token resistance to sex. *Journal of Personality and Social Psychology, 54,* 872–879.

Muller, Charlotte F. (1990). *Health care and gender.* New York: Russell Sage Foundation.

Murray, Christopher J. L.; & Lopez, Alan D. (1997). Alternative projections of mortality and disability by cause 1990–2020: Global Burden of Disease Study (part 4). *Lancet, 349,* 1498–1504.

Murray, Kathleen. (1995, April). PMS: Is it for real? *Cosmopolitan, 218,* 208–211.

Murphy, Sheila T. (1998). The impact of factual versus fictional media portrayals on cultural stereotypes. *The Annals of the American Academy of Political and Social Science, 560,* 165–178.

Nardi, Peter M. (1992a). "Seamless souls": An introduction to men's friendships. In Peter M. Nardi (Ed.), *Men's friendships* (pp. 1–14). Newbury Park, CA: Sage.

Nardi, Peter M. (1992b). Sex, friendship, and gender roles among gay men. In Peter M. Nardi (Ed.), *Men's friendships* (pp. 173–185). Newbury Park, CA: Sage.

National Center for Health Statistics. (1995, May 22). *National Economic, Social, and Environmental Data Bank* (electronic database). Hyattsville, MD: Author.

National Highway Traffic Safety Administration (NHTSA). (2000). *1998 motor vehicle occupant safety survey, volume 2.* Retrieved Sept., 2000, from the World Wide Web http://www.nhtsa.dot.gov/ people/injury/research/SafetySurvey/TechDoc.hmt

Nelson, Katherine. (1981). Social cognition in a script framework. In John H. Flavell & Lee Ross (Eds.), *Social cognitive development: Frontiers and possible futures* (pp. 97–118). Cambridge: Cambridge University Press.

Netting, Nancy S. (1992). Sexuality in youth culture: Identity and change. *Adolescence, 27,* 961–976.

Neugebauer, D. D.; Dohrenwend, Bruce P.; & Dohrenwend, Barbara S. (1980). The formulation of hypotheses about the true prevalence of functional psychiatric disorders among adults in the United States. In Bruce P. Dohrenwend, Barbara S. Dohrenwend, M. S. Gould, B. Link, R. Neugebauer, & R. Wunsch-Hitzig (Eds.), *Mental illness in the United States* (pp. 45–94). New York: Praeger.

Newman, Leonard S.; Cooper, Joel; & Ruble, Diane N. (1995). The interactive effects of knowledge and constancy on gender-stereotyped attitudes. (Gender and Computers, part 2). *Sex Roles, 33,* 325–351.

Nieva, Veronica F.; & Gutek, Barbara A. (1981). *Women and work: A psychological perspective.* New York: Praeger.

Nikelly, Arthur G. (1994, August). *Drug advertisements and the medicalization of unipolar depression in women.* Paper presented at the 102nd annual convention of the American Psychological Association, Los Angeles, CA.

Nikiforov, Sergey V.; & Mamaev, Valery B. (1998). The development of sex differences in cardiovascular disease mortality: A historical perspective. *American Journal of Public Health, 88,* 1345–1353.

Noddings, Nel. (1991/1992, December/January). The gender issue. *Educational Leadership, 49*(4), 65–70.

Nolan, Justin M.; & Ryan, Gery W. (2000). Fear and loathing at the cineplex: Gender differences in descriptions and perceptions of slasher films. *Sex Roles, 42,* 39–56.

Nolen-Hoeksema, Susan. (1987). Sex differences in unipolar depression: Evidence and theory. *Psychological Bulletin, 101,* 259–282.

Nolen-Hoeksema, Susan; Larson, Judith; & Grayson, Carla. (1999). Explaining the gender difference in depressive symptoms. *Journal of Personality and Social Psychology, 77,* 1061–1072.

Nordheimer, Jon. (1991, August 14). When a fellow needs a friend, not just a buddy. *New York Times,* pp. C1, C8.

Norris, Jeanette; Nurius, Paula S.; & Dimeff, Linda A. (1996). Through her eyes: Factors affecting women's perception of and resistance to acquaintance sexual aggression threat. *Psychology of Women Quarterly, 20,* 123–145.

O'Brien, Edward J.; Jeffreys, Dorothy; Leitzel, Jeff; O'Brien, Jean P.; Mensky, Larissa; & Marchese, Marc. (1996, August). *Gender differences in the self-esteem of adolescents: A meta-analysis.* Paper presented at the 104th annual convention of the American Psychological Association, Toronto, Canada.

Okagaki, Lynn; & Frensch, Peter A. (1994). Effects of video game playing on measures of spatial performance: Gender effects in late adolescence. *Journal of Applied Developmental Psychology, 15,* 33–58.

Oliver, Mary Beth; & Hyde, Janet Shibley. (1993). Gender differences in sexuality: A meta-analysis. *Psychological Bulletin, 114,* 29–51.

Oliver, Mary Beth; Sargent, Stephanie Lee; & Weaver, James B., III. (1998). The impact of sex and gender role self-perception on affective reactions to different types of film. *Sex Roles, 38,* 45–62.

Olson, Cheryl B. (1994, August). *Hostile environment: Gender, self-esteem and perception of sexual harassment.* Paper presented at the 102nd annual convention of the American Psychological Association, Los Angeles, CA.

O'Neil, James M. (1981). Patterns of gender role conflict and strain: Sexism and fear of femininity in men's lives. *Personnel and Guidance Journal, 60,* 203–210.

Orlofsky, Jacob L.; & O'Heron, Connie A. (1987). Stereotypic and nonstereotypic sex role trait and behavior orientations: Implications for personal adjustment. *Journal of Personality and Social Psychology, 52,* 1034–1042.

Osgood, D. Wayne; O'Malley, Patrick M.; Bachman, Jerald G.; Johnston, Lloyd D. (1989). Time trends and age trends in arrests and self-reported illegal behavior. *Criminology, 27,* 389–417.

Page, Jessica R.; Stevens, Heather B.; & Galvin, Shelley L. (1996). Relationships between depression, self-esteem, and self-silencing behavior. *Journal of Social and Clinical Psychology, 15,* 381–396.

Paludi, Michele A. (1984). Psychometric properties and underlying assumptions of four objective measures of fear of success. *Sex Roles, 10,* 765–781.

Paludi, Michele. (1997). Sexual harassment in schools. In William O'Donohoue (Ed.), *Sexual harassment: Theory, research, and treatment* (pp. 225–240). Boston: Allyn and Bacon.

Parker, Louise. (1997). Causes of testicular cancer. *Lancet, 350,* 827–828.

Parlee, Mary Brown. (1973). The premenstrual syndrome. *Psychological Bulletin, 83,* 454–465.

Paskette, Electra D.; & Michielutte, Robert. (1997). Psychosocial factors associated with gynecological cancers. In Sheryle J. Gallant, Gwendolyn Puryear Keita, & Reneé Royak-Schaler (Eds.), *Health care for women: Psychological, social, and behavioral influences* (pp. 315–331). Washington, DC: American Psychological Association.

Patterson, Charlotte J.; & Chan, Raymond W. (1997). Gay fathers. In Michael E. Lamb (Ed.), *The role of the father in child development* (3rd ed., pp. 245–260). New York: Wiley.

Pearcey, Sharon M.; Docherty, Karen J.; & Dabbs, James M., Jr. (1996). Testosterone and sex role identification in lesbian couples. *Physiology & Behavior, 60,* 1033–1035.

Pennebaker, James W. (1982). *The psychology of physical symptoms.* New York: Springer-Verlag.

Pennebaker, James W.; & Roberts, Tomi-Ann. (1992). Toward a his and hers theory of emotion: Gender differences in visceral perception. *Journal of Social and Clinical Psychology, 11,* 199–212.

Peplau, Letitia Anne; & Campbell, Susan Miller. (1989). The balance of power in dating and marriage. In Jo Freeman (Ed.), *Women: A feminist perspective* (4th ed., pp. 121–137). Mountain View, CA: Mayfield.

Peplau, Letitia Anne; Cochran, Susan; Rook, Karen; & Padesky, Christine. (1978). Loving women: Attachment and autonomy in lesbian relationships. *Journal of Social Issues, 34*(3), 7–27.

Peplau, Letitia Anne; & Conrad, Eva. (1989). Beyond nonsexist research: The perils of feminist methods in psychology. *Psychology of Women Quarterly, 13,* 379–400.

Peplau, Letitia Anne; & Gordon, Steven L. (1985). Women and men in love: Gender differences in close heterosexual relationships. In Virginia E. O'Leary, Rhoda Kesler Unger, & Barbara Strudler Wallston (Eds.), *Women, gender, and social psychology* (pp. 257–291). Hillsdale, NJ: Erlbaum.

Peplau, Letitia Anne; Hill, Charles T.; & Rubin, Zick. (1993). Sex role attitudes in dating and marriage: A 15-year follow-up of the Boston couples study. *Journal of Social Issues, 49*(3), 31–52.

Perlick, Deborah; & Silverstein, Brett. (1994). Faces of female discontent: Depression, disordered eating, and changing gender roles. In Patricia Fallon, Melanie A. Katzman, & Susan C. Wooley (Eds.), *Feminist perspectives on eating disorders* (pp. 77–93). New York: Guilford.

Perls, Frederick S. (1969). *Gestalt therapy verbatim.* Lafayette, CA: Real People Press.

Perry, David G.; Perry, Louise C.; & Weiss, Robert J. (1989). Sex differences in the consequences that children anticipate for aggression. *Developmental Psychology, 25,* 312–319.

Phillips, Roger D.; & Gilroy, Faith D. (1985). Sex-role stereotypes and clinical judgments of mental health: The Brovermans' findings reexamined. *Sex Roles, 12,* 179–193.

Phillips, Susan D.; & Imhoff, Anne R. (1997). Women and career development: A decade of research. *Annual Review of Psychology, 48,* 31–59.

Piirto, Jane. (1991). Why are there so few: (Creative women: Visual artists, mathematicians, musicians). *Roeper Review, 13,* 142–147.

Pinel, John P. J. (2000). *Biopsychology* (4th ed.). Boston: Allyn and Bacon.

Pino, Nathan W.; & Meier, Robert F. (1999). Gender differences in rape reporting. *Sex Roles, 40,* 979–990.

Pittman, Frank. (1992, January/February). Why the men's movement isn't so funny. *Psychology Today,* p. 84.

Plant, E. Ashby; Hyde, Janet Shibley; Keltner, Dacher; & Devine, Patricia G. (2000). The gender stereotyping of emotions. *Psychology of Women Quarterly, 24,* 81–92.

Pleck, Elizabeth H.; & Pleck, Joseph H. (1997). Fatherhood ideals in the United States: Historical dimensions. In Michael E. Lamb (Ed.), *The role of the father in child development* (3rd ed., pp. 33–48). New York: Wiley.

Pleck, Joseph H. (1981). *The myth of masculinity.* Cambridge, MA: MIT Press.

Pleck, Joseph H. (1984). The theory of male sex role identity: Its rise and fall, 1936 to the present. In Miriam Lewin (Ed.), *In the shadow of the past: Psychology portrays the sexes* (pp. 205–225). New York: Columbia University Press.

Pleck, Joseph H. (1995). The Gender Role Strain paradigm: An update. In Ronald F. Levant & William S. Pollack (Eds.), *A new psychology of men* (pp. 11–32). New York: Basic Books.

Pleck, Joseph H. (1997). Parental involvement: Levels, sources, and consequences. In Michael E. Lamb (Ed.), *The role of the father in child development* (3rd ed., pp. 66–103). New York: Wiley.

Pleck, Joseph H.; Sonenstein, Freya L.; & Ku, Leighton C. (1993). Masculinity ideology: Its impact on adolescent males' heterosexual relationships. *Journal of Social Issues, 49*(3), 11–29.

Pliner, Patricia; & Chaiken, Shelly. (1990). Eating, social motives, and self-presentation in women and men. *Journal of Experimental Social Psychology, 26,* 240–254.

Plutchik, Robert. (1984). Emotions: A general psychoevolutionary theory. In Klaus R. Scherer & Paul Ekman (Eds.), *Approaches to emotion* (pp. 197–219). Hillsdale, NJ: Erlbaum.

Polivy, Janet; & Herman, C. Peter. (1983). *Breaking the diet habit: The natural weight alternative.* New York: Basic Books.

Polivy, Janet; & Thomsen, Linda. (1988). Dieting and other eating disorders. In Elaine A. Blechman & Kelly D. Brownell (Eds.), *Handbook of behavioral medicine for women* (pp. 345–355). New York: Pergamon Press.

Pollack, William. (1998). *Real boys.* New York: Holt.

Pollitt, Katha. (1992, December 28). Are women morally superior to men? *Nation,* pp. 799–807.

Pollitt, Katha. (1995). Marooned on Gilligan's island: Are women morally superior to men? In Katha Pollitt, *Reasonable creatures: Essays on women and feminism* (pp. 42–62). New York: Knopf.

Pontius, Anneliese A. (1997). No gender difference in spatial representation by schoolchildren in northwest Pakistan. *Journal of Cross-Cultural Psychology, 28,* 779–786.

Pope, Harrison G.; Kouri, Elena M.; & Hudson, James I. (2000). Effects of supraphysiologic doses of testosterone on mood and aggression in normal men. *Archives of General Psychiatry, 57,* 133–140.

Pope, Kenneth S. (1988). How clients are harmed by sexual contact with mental health professionals: The syndrome and its prevalence. *Journal of Counseling and Development, 67,* 222–226.

Pope, Kenneth S. (2000). Therapists' sexual feelings and behaviors: Research, trends, and quandaries. In Lenore T. Szuchman and Frank Muscarella (Eds.), *Psychological perspectives on human sexuality* (pp. 603–658). New York: Wiley.

Postman, Andrew. (1996, August). Big fat lies about men. *Mademoiselle, 102,* 152–155, 187.

Powlishta, Kimberly K. (1995). Gender bias in children's perceptions of personality traits. *Sex Roles, 32,* 17–28.

Powlishta, Kimberly K. (2000). The effect of target age on the activation of gender stereotypes. *Sex Roles, 42,* 271–282.

Powlishta, Kimberly K.; Serbin, Lisa A.; & Moller, Lora C. (1993). The stability of individual differences in gender typing: Implications for understanding gender segregation. *Sex Roles, 29,* 723–744.

President's Council on Physical Fitness and Sports. (1997). *Physical activity and sport in the lives of girls.* Minneapolis, MN: Center for Research on Girls and Women in Sport, University of Minnesota.

Pryor, John B.; & Whalen, Nora J. (1997). A typology of sexual harassment: Characteristics of harassers and the social circumstances under which sexual harassment occurs. In William O'Donohue (Ed.), *Sexual harassment: Theory, research, and treatment* (pp. 129–151), Boston: Allyn and Bacon.

Ptacek, J. T.; Smith, Ronald E.; & Zanas, John. (1992). Gender, appraisal, and coping: A longitudinal analysis. *Journal of Personality, 60,* 747–770.

Purifoy, Frances E.; & Koopmans, Lambert H. (1979). Androstenedione, testosterone, and free testosterone concentration in women of various occupations. *Social Biology, 26,* 179–188.

Quinn, Susan. (1987). *A mind of her own: The life of Karen Horney.* New York: Summit Books.

Raag, Tarja; & Rackliff, Christine L. (1998). Preschoolers' awareness of social expectations of gender: Relationships to toy choices. *Sex Roles, 38,* 685–700.

Ragaza, Angelo. (1999, February 8). I don't count as 'diversity.' *Newsweek, 133*(6), 13.

Ragins, Belle Rose; & Sundstrom, Eric. (1989). Gender and power in organizations: A longitudinal perspective. *Psychological Bulletin, 105,* 51–88.

Raichle, Marcus E. (1994, April). Visualizing the mind. *Scientific American, 270,* pp. 58–64.

Raja, Sheela. (1998). Culturally sensitive therapy for women of color. *Women & Therapy, 21,* 67.

Rapping, Elayne. (1994, May). Women are from Venus, men are from Mars. *The Progressive, 58,* 40–42.

Raudenbush, Bryan; & Zellner, Debra A. (1997). Nobody's satisfied: Effects of abnormal eating behaviors and actual and perceived weight status on body image satisfaction in males and females. *Journal of Social and Clinical Psychology, 16,* 95–110.

Rawlings, Edna I. (1993). Reflections on "Twenty years of feminist counseling and therapy." *Counseling Psychologist, 21,* 88–91.

Ray, William J. (1993). *Methods toward a science of behavior and experience* (4th ed.). Belmont, CA: Wadsworth.

Redman, Selina; Webb, Gloria R.; Hennrikus, Deborah J.; Gordon, Jill J.; & Sanson-Fisher, Robert W. (1991). The effects of gender upon diagnosis of psychological disturbance. *Journal of Behavioral Medicine, 14,* 527–540.

Regier, Darrel A.; Narrow, William E.; & Rae, Donald S. (1990). The epidemiology of anxiety disorders: The Epidemiologic Catchment Area (ECA) experience. *Journal of Psychiatric Research, 24* (Suppl. 2), 3–14.

Rehman, Jamil; Lazer, Simcha; Benet, Alexandru E.; Schaefer, Leah C.; & Melman, Arnold. (1999). The reported sex and surgery satisfactions of 28 postoperative male-to-female transsexual patients. *Archives of Sexual Behavior, 28,* 71–90.

Reid, Helen M.; & Fine, Gary Alan. (1992). Self-disclosure in men's friendships: Variations associated with intimate relations. In Peter M. Nardi (Ed.), *Men's friendships* (pp. 132–152). Newbury Park, CA: Sage.

Reid, Pamela Trotman. (1993). Poor women in psychology research: Shut up and shut out. *Psychology of Women Quarterly, 17,* 133–150.

Reid, Pamela T.; Tate, Carol S.; & Berman, Phyllis W. (1989). Preschool children's self-presentations in situations with infants: Effects of sex and race. *Child Development, 60,* 710–714.

Rejskind, F. Gillian; Rapagna, Socrates O.; & Gold, Dolores. (1992). Gender differences in children's divergent thinking. *Creativity Research Journal, 5,* 165–174.

Renzetti, Claire M.; & Curran, Daniel J. (1992). *Women, men, and society* (2nd ed.). Boston: Allyn and Bacon.

Resnick, Heidi S.; Kilpatrick, Dean G.; Best, Connie L.; & Kramer, Teresa L. (1992). Vulnerability-stress factors in development of posttraumatic stress disorder. *Journal of Nervous and Mental Disease, 180,* 424–430.

Resnick, Heidi S.; Kilpatrick, Dean G.; Dansky, Bonnie S.; Saunders, Benjamin E.; & Best, Connie L. (1993). Prevalence of victim trauma and posttraumatic stress disorder in a representative national sample of women. *Journal of Consulting and Clinical Psychology, 61,* 984–991.

Ribalow, M. Z. (1998). Script doctors. *The Sciences, 38*(6), 26–31.

Ricciardelli, Lina A.; & Williams, Robert J. (1995). Desirable and undesirable gender traits in three behavioral domains. *Sex Roles, 33,* 637–655.

Riessman, Catherine Kohler. (1990). *Divorce talk: Women and men make sense of personal relationships.* New Brunswick: Rutgers University Press.

Riger, Stephanie. (1991). Gender dilemmas in sexual harassment policies and procedures. *American Psychologist, 46,* 497–505.

Riger, Stephanie. (1992). Epistemological debates, feminist voices: Science, social values, and the study of women. *American Psychologist, 47,* 730–740.

Riggs, Janet Morgan. (1997). Mandates for mothers and fathers: Perceptions of breadwinners and care givers. *Sex Roles, 37,* 565–580.

Risman, Barbara J. (1989). Can men "mother"? Life as a single father. In Barbara J. Risman & Pepper Schwartz (Eds.), *Gender in intimate relationships: A microstructural approach* (pp. 155–164). Belmont, CA: Wadsworth.

Riter, Robert N. (1997). I have breast cancer. *Newsweek, 130*(2), 14.

Roberts, Tomi-Ann. (1991). Gender and the influence of evaluations on self-assessments in achievement settings. *Psychological Bulletin, 109,* 297–308.

Roberts, Tomi-Ann; & Nolen-Hoeksema, Susan. (1994). Gender comparisons in responsiveness to others' evaluations in achievement settings. *Psychology of Women Quarterly, 18,* 221–240.

Robertson, John; & Fitzgerald, Louise F. (1990). The (mis)treatment of men: Effects of client gender role and life-style on diagnosis and attribution of pathology. *Journal of Counseling Psychology, 37,* 3–9.

Robertson, John; & Fitzgerald, Louise F. (1992). Overcoming the masculine mystique: Preferences for alternative form of assistance among men who avoid counseling. *Journal of Counseling Psychology, 39,* 240–246.

Robine, Jean-Marie; & Ritchie, Karen. (1991). Healthy life expectancy: Evaluation of global indicator of change in population health. *British Medical Journal, 302,* 457–460.

Robinson, David. (1979). *Talking out of alcoholism: The self-help process of Alcoholics Anonymous.* Baltimore: University Park Press.

Robinson, Kelly A.; Obler, Loraine K.; Boone, R. Thomas; Shane, Howard; Adamjee, Riaz; & Anderson, John. (1998). Gender and truthfulness in daily life situations. *Sex Roles, 38,* 821–831.

Rodin, Judith. (1991). Foreword. In Marianne Frankenhaeuser, Ulf Lundberg, & Margaret Chesney (Eds.), *Women, work, and health: Stress and opportunities* (pp. vii–xi). New York: Plenum Press.

Rodin, Judith; & Ickovics, Jeannette R. (1990). Women's health: Review and research agenda as we approach the 21st century. *American Psychologist, 45,* 1018–1034.

Rogers, Carl R. (1951). *Client-centered therapy: Its current practice, implications, and theory.* Boston: Houghton Mifflin.

Rogers, Carl R. (1961). *On becoming a person: A therapist's view of psychotherapy.* Boston: Houghton Mifflin.

Rogers, Carl R. (1980). *A way of being.* Boston: Houghton Mifflin.

Rolls, Barbara J.; Fedoroff, Ingrid C.; & Guthrie, Joanne F. (1991). Gender differences in eating behavior and body weight regulation. *Health Psychology, 10,* 133–142.

Ronan, Colin A. (1982). *Science: Its history and development among the world's cultures.* New York: Facts On File Publications.

Roscoe, Bruce; Diana, Mark S.; & Brooks, Richard H., II. (1987). Early, middle, and late adolescents' views on dating and factors influencing partner selection. *Adolescence, 22,* 59–68.

Roscoe, Will. (1993). How to become a berdache: Toward a unified analysis of gender diversity. In Gilbert Herdt (Ed.), *Third sex, third gender: Beyond sexual dimorphism in culture and history* (pp. 329–372). New York: Zone Books.

Rose, Suzanna; & Frieze, Irene Hanson. (1993). Young singles' contemporary dating scripts. *Sex Roles, 28,* 499–509.

Rosenfeld, Megan. (1998, March 26). Little boys blue: Reexamining the plight of young males. *Washington Post,* A1.

Rosenfield, David; & Stephan, Walter G. (1978). Sex differences in attributions for sex-typed tasks. *Journal of Personality, 46,* 244–259.

Rosenfield, Sarah. (1982). Sex roles and societal reactions to mental illness: The labeling of "deviant deviance." *Journal of Health and Social Behavior, 23,* 18–24.

Rosenfield, Sarah. (1989). The effects of women's employment: Personal control and sex differences in mental health. *Journal of Health and Social Behavior, 30,* 77–91.

Rosenfield, Sarah. (1992). The costs of sharing: Wives' employment and husbands' mental health. *Journal of Health and Social Behavior, 33,* 213–225.

Rosenkrantz, Paul; Vogel, Susan; Bee, Helen; Broverman, Inge; & Broverman, Donald M. (1968). Sex-role stereotypes and self-concepts in college students. *Journal of Consulting and Clinical Psychology, 32,* 287–295.

Rosenthal, Patrice. (1996). Gender and managers' causal attributions for subordinate performance: A field story. *Sex Roles, 34,* 1–14.

Rothstein, Donna S. (1995). Do female faculty influence female students' educational and labor market attainments? *Industrial and Labor Relations Review, 48,* 515–530.

Rothstein, Edward. (1997, February 17). Software for girls: Glaring gender differences. *New York Times CyberTimes* (http://search.nytimes.com/search/daily).

Roy, Rosanne; Benenson, Joyce F.; & Lilly, Frank. (2000). Beyond intimacy: Conceptualizing sex differences in same-sex friendships. *Journal of Psychology, 134,* 93–102.

Rubin, Robert T.; Reinisch, June M.; & Haskett, Roger F. (1981). Postnatal gonadal steroid effects on human behavior. *Science, 211,* 1318–1324.

Ruble, Diane N.; & Martin, Carol Lynn. (1998). Gender development. In Nancy Eisenberg (Ed.), *Handbook of child psychology, Vol. 3: Social, emotional, and personality development* (5th ed., pp. 933–1016). New York: Wiley.

Rush, Florence. (1977). The Freudian cover-up. *Chrysalis,* 1, 31–45. (Reprinted in *Feminism & Psychology,* 1996, *6,* 261–276.)

Russell, Denise. (1995). *Women, madness and medicine.* Cambridge, UK: Polity Press.

Russell, Diana E. H. (1986). *The secret trauma: Incest in the lives of girls and women.* New York: Basic Books.

Russell, James A. (1991). Culture and the categorization of emotions. *Psychological Bulletin, 110,* 426–450.

Russell, James A. (1994). Is there universal recognition of emotion from facial expression: A review of the cross-cultural studies. *Psychological Bulletin, 115,* 102–141.

Russo, Nancy Felipe. (1990). Overview: Forging research priorities for women's mental health. *American Psychologist, 45,* 368–373.

Russo, Nancy Felipe. (1998). Editorial: Teaching about gender and ethnicity: Goals and challenges. *Psychology of Women Quarterly, 22,* i–vi.

Saal, Frank E.; Johnson, Catherine B.; & Weber, Nancy. (1989). Friendly or sexy? It may depend on whom you ask. *Psychology of Women Quarterly, 13,* 263–276.

Sadker, David; & Sadker, Myra. (1985). The treatment of sex equity in teacher education. In Susan S. Klein (Ed.), *Handbook for achieving sex equity through education* (pp. 145–161). Baltimore: The Johns Hopkins University Press.

Sadker, Myra P.; & Sadker, David M. (1980). Sexism in teacher-education texts. *Harvard Educational Review, 50,* 36–46.

Sadker, Myra; Sadker, David; & Steindam, Sharon. (1989). Gender equity and educational reform. *Educational Leadership, 46,* 44–47.

Samuel, Steven E.; & Gorton, Gregg E. (1998). National survey of psychology internship directors regarding education for prevention of psychologist-patient sexual exploitation. *Professional Psychology: Research and Practice, 29,* 86–90.

Sandnabba, N. Kenneth; & Ahlberg, Christian. (1999). Parents' attitudes and expectations about children's cross-gender behavior. *Sex Roles, 40,* 249–264.

Sandomir, Richard. (1997, April 23). Prospects for Title IX expected to improve. *New York Times.* Retrieved July, 1997, from the World Wide Web http://search.nytimes.com/search/daily.

Santrock, John W. (1993). *Adolescence: An introduction* (5th ed.). Madison, WI: Brown & Benchmark.

Sapolsky, Robert. (1997, March). Testosterone rules: It takes more than just a hormone to make a fellow's trigger finger itch. *Discover, 18,* 44–48.

Saragovi, Carina; Koestner, Richard; Di Dio, Lina; & Aubé, Jennifer. (1997). Agency, communion, and well-being: Extending Helgeson's (1994) model. *Journal of Personality and Social Psychology, 73,* 593–609.

Sarason, Irwin G.; & Sarason, Barbara R. (1993). *Abnormal psychology: The problem of maladaptive behavior* (7th ed.). Englewood Cliffs, NJ: Prentice Hall.

Savage, Robert M.; & Gouvier, W. Drew. (1992). Rey Auditory-Verbal Learning Test: The effects of age and gender, and norms for delayed recall and story recognition trials. *Archives of Clinical Neuropsychology, 7,* 407–414.

Savin-Williams, Ritch C. (1995). Lesbian, gay male, and bisexual adolescents. In Anthony R. D'Augelli & Charlotte J. Patterson (Eds.), *Lesbian, gay, and bisexual identities over the lifespan: Psychological perspectives* (pp. 165–189). New York: Oxford University Press.

Schachter, Stanley; & Singer, Jerome E. (1962). Cognitive, social, and psychological determinants of emotional state. *Psychological Review, 69,* 379–399.

Scheibe, Gabriele; & Albus, Margot. (1992). Age at onset, precipitating events, sex distribution, and co-occurrence of anxiety disorders. *Psychopathology, 25,* 11–18.

Scher, Murray. (1981). Men in hiding: A challenge for the counselor. *Personnel and Guidance Journal, 60,* 199–202.

Scherer, Klaus R.; Wallbott, Harald G.; & Summerfield, Angela B. (Eds.) (1986). *Experiencing emotion: A cross-cultural study.* Cambridge, England: Cambridge University Press.

Schiebinger, Londa. (1999). *Has feminism changed science?* Cambridge, MA: Harvard University Press.

Schlenker, Jennifer A.; Caron, Sandra L.; & Halteman, William A. (1998). A feminist analysis of Seventeen magazine: Content analysis from 1945 to 1995. *Sex Roles, 38,* 135–149.

Schmitz, Sigrid. (1999). Gender differences in acquisition of environmental knowledge related to wayfinding ability, spatial anxiety and self-estimated environmental competencies. *Sex Roles, 41,* 71–94.

Schneer, Joy A.; & Reitman, Freida. (1990). Effects of employment gaps on the careers of M.B.A.'s: More damaging for men than for women? *Academy of Management Journal, 33,* 391–406.

Schneider, Irving. (1987). The theory and practice of movie psychiatry. *American Journal of Psychiatry, 144,* 996–1002.

Schofield, Janet Ward. (1981). Complementary and conflicting identities: Images and interaction in an interracial school. In Steven R. Asher & John M. Gottman (Eds.), *The development of children's friendships* (pp. 53–90). Cambridge, England: Cambridge University Press.

Schofield, Toni; Connell, R. W.; Walker, Linley; Wood, Julian F.; & Butland, Dianne L. (2000). Understanding men's helath and illness: A gender-relations approach to policy, research, and practice. *Journal of American College Health, 48,* 247–256.

Schratz, Marjorie M. (1978). A developmental investigation of sex differences in spatial (visual-analytic) and mathematical skills in three ethnic groups. *Development Psychology, 14,* 263–267.

Schroeder, Debra S.; & Mynatt, Clifford R. (1999). Graduate students' relationship with their male and female major professors. *Sex Roles, 40,* 393–420.

Schultz, Duane P.; & Schultz, Sidney Ellen. (1992). *A history of modern psychology* (5th ed.). Fort Worth: Harcourt Brace Jovanovich.

Schutte, Nicola; Malouff, John; Curtis, Donna; Lowry, Manya; & Luis, Cheryl. (1996, August). *Women's acceptance of traditional roles and their career choice.* Paper presented at the 104th annual convention of the American Psychological Association, Toronto, Canada.

Schwartz, Pepper. (1994). *Peer marriage: How love between equals really works.* New York: Free Press.

Scott, Jacqueline. (1998). Changing attitudes to sexual morality: A cross-national comparison. *Sociology, 32,* 815–818.

Scully, Diana. (1990). *Understanding sexual violence: A study of convicted rapists.* London: HarperCollins Academic.

Segal, Julius; & Segal, Zelda. (1993, May). What five-year-olds think about sex: And when and how to give them the answers that they need to hear. *Parents' Magazine,* pp. 130–132.

Seid, Roberta P. (1994). Too "close to the bone": The historical context of women's obsession with slenderness. In Patricia Fallon, Melanie A. Katzman, & Susan C. Wooley (Eds.), *Feminist perspectives on eating disorders* (pp. 3–16). New York: Guilford.

Seidman, Steven A. (1999). Revisiting sex-role stereotyping in MTV videos. *International Journal of Instructional Media, 26,* 11–22.

Seligmann, Jean (with Rogers, Patrick; & Annin, Peter). (1994, May 2). The pressure to lose. *Newsweek, 123*(18), 60–61.

Sell, Randall L.; Wells, James A.; & Wypij, David. (1995). The prevalence of homosexual behavior and attraction in the United States, the United Kingdom and France: Results of national population-based samples. *Archives of Sexual Behavior, 24,* 235–248.

Sells, Lucy W. (1980). The mathematics filter and the education of women and minorities. In Lynn H. Fox, Linda Brody, & Dianne Tobin (Eds.), *Women and the mathematical mystique* (pp. 66–75). Baltimore: Johns Hopkins University Press.

Serbin, Lisa A.; Zelkowitz, Phyllis; Doyle, Anna-Beth; Gold, Dolores; & Wheaton, Blair. (1990). The socialization of sex-differentiated skills and academic performance: A mediational model. *Sex Roles, 23,* 613–628.

Serdula, Mary K.; Collins, Elizabeth; Williamson, David F.; Anda, Robert F.; Pamuk, Elsie; & Byers, Tim E. (1993). Weight control practices of U.S. adolescents and adults. *Annals of Internal Medicine, 119,* 667–671.

Sharpe, Mark J.; Heppner, Paul; & Dixon, Wayne A. (1995). Gender role conflict, instrumentality, expressiveness, and well-being in adult men. *Sex Roles, 33,* 1–17.

Sharps, Matthew J.; Price, Jana L.; & Williams, John K. (1994). Spatial cognition and gender: Instructional and stimulus influences on mental image rotation performance. *Psychology of Women Quarterly, 18,* 413–425.

Sharps, Matthew J.; Welton, Angela L.; & Price, Jana L. (1993). Gender and task in the determination of spatial cognitive performance. *Psychology of Women Quarterly, 17,* 71–83.

Shaywitz, Bennett A.; Shaywitz, Sally E.; Pugh, Kenneth R.; Constable, R. Todd; Skudlarski, Pawel; Fulbright, Robert K.; Bronen, Richard A.; Fletcher, Jac M.; Shankweiler, Donald P.; Katz, Leonard; & Gore, John C. (1995). Sex differences in the functional organization of the brain for language. *Nature, 373,* 607–609.

Shepela, Sharon Toffey; & Levesque, Laurie L. (1998). Poisoned waters: Sexual harassment and the college climate. *Sex Roles, 38,* 589–611.

Sherif, Carolyn W. (1982). Needed concepts in the study of gender identity. *Psychology of Women Quarterly, 6,* 375–398.

Sherman, Julia. (1978). *Sex-related cognitive differences: An essay on theory and evidence.* Springfield, IL: Charles C. Thomas.

Shields, Stephanie A. (1975a). Functionalism, Darwinism, and the psychology of women: A study in social myth. *American Psychologist, 30,* 739–754.

Shields, Stephanie A. (1975b). Ms. Pilgrim's progress: The contributions of Leta Stetter Hollingworth to the psychology of women. *American Psychologist, 30,* 852–857.

Shields, Stephanie A. (1984). "To pet, coddle, and 'do for'": Caretaking and the concept of maternal instinct. In Miriam Lewin (Ed.), *In the shadow of the past: Psychology portrays the sexes* (pp. 256–273). New York: Columbia University Press.

Shields, Stephanie A. (1994, August). *Practicing social constructionism—Confessions of a feminist empiricist.* Paper presented at the 102nd annual convention of the American Psychological Association, Los Angeles, CA.

Sibisi, Charles D. (1990). Sex differences in the age of onset of bipolar affective illness. *British Journal of Psychiatry, 156,* 842–845.

Sigel, Roberta S. (1996). *Ambition and accommodation: How women view gender relations.* Chicago: University of Chicago Press.

Signorella, Margaret L.; Bigler, Rebecca L.; & Liben, Lynn S. (1993). Developmental differences in children's gender schemata about others: A meta-analytic review. *Developmental Review, 13,* 147–183.

Signorella, Margaret L.; Frieze, Irene Hanson; & Hershey, Susanne W. (1996). Single-sex versus mixed-sex classes and gender schemata in children and adolescents: A longitudinal comparison. *Psychology of Women Quarterly, 20,* 599–607.

Signorielli, Nancy; & Bacue, Aaron. (1999). Recognition and respect: A content analysis of prime-time television characters across three decades. *Sex Roles, 40,* 527–544.

Silverstein, Brett; Carpman, Shari; Perlick, Deborah; & Perdue, Lauren. (1990). Nontraditional sex role aspirations, gender identity conflict, and disordered eating among college women. *Sex Roles, 23,* 687–695.

Silverstein, Brett; Perdue, Lauren; Wolk, Cordulla; & Pizzolo, Cecelia. (1988). Bingeing, purging, and estimates of parental attitudes regarding female achievement. *Sex Roles, 19,* 723–733.

Silverstein, Brett; & Perlick, Deborah. (1995). *The cost of competence: Why inequality causes depression, eating disorders, and illness in women.* New York: Oxford University Press.

Silverstein, Louise B. (1993). Primate research, family politics, and social policy: Transforming "cads" into "dads." *Journal of Family Psychology, 7,* 267–282.

Silverstein, Louise B. (1996). Fathering is a feminist issue. *Psychology of Women Quarterly, 20,* 3–37.

Silverstein, Louise B.; & Auerbach, Carl F. (1999). Deconstructing the essential father. *American Psychologist, 54,* 397–407.

Silverstein, Louise B.; Auerbach, Carl F.; Grieco, Loretta; & Dunk, Faith. (1999). Do Promise Keepers dream of feminist sheep? *Sex Roles, 40,* 665–688.

Simi, Nicole L.; & Mahalik, James R. (1997). Comparison of feminist versus psychoanalytic/dynamic and other therapists on self-disclosure. *Psychology of Women Quarterly, 21,* 465–483.

Simon, Rita J.; Scherer, Jennifer; & Rau, William. (1999). Sexual harassment in the heartland? Community opinion on the EEOC suit Mitsubishi Motor Manufacturing of America. *Social Science Journal, 36,* 485–496.

Simon, Robert I. (1999). Therapist-patient sex: From boundary violations to sexual misconduct. *Psychiatric Clinics of North America, 22,* 31–47.

Simon, William; & Gagnon, John H. (1986). Sexual scripts: Permanence and change. *Archives of Sexual Behavior, 15,* 97–119.

Simoni-Wastila, Linda. (2000). The use of abusable prescription drugs: The role of gender. *Journal of Women's Health and Gender-Based Medicine, 9,* 289–297.

Skovholt, Thomas M. (1978). Feminism and men's lives. *The Counseling Psychologist, 7*(4), 3–10.

Slade, Pauline. (1984). Premenstrual emotional changes in normal women: Fact or fiction? *Journal of Psychosomatic Research, 28,* 1–7.

Sleek, Scott. (1994, January). Girls who've been molested can later become molesters. *APA Monitor,* pp. 34–35.

Smith, Page Hall; Smith, Jason R.; & Earp, Jo Anne L. (1999). Beyond the measurement trap: A reconstructed conceptualization and measurement of woman battering. *Psychology of Women Quarterly, 23,* 177–193.

Smith, Thomas Ewin. (1997). Adolescent gender differences in time alone and time devoted to conversation. *Adolescence, 32,* 483–496.

Snodgrass, Sara E. (1985). Women's intuition: The effect of subordinate role on interpersonal sensitivity. *Journal of Personality and Social Psychology, 49,* 146–155.

Snodgrass, Sara E. (1992). Further effects of role versus gender on interpersonal sensitivity. *Journal of Personality and Social Psychology, 62,* 154–158.

Solomon, Alison. (1992). Clinical diagnosis among diverse populations: A multicultural perspective. *Families in Society, 73,* 371–377.

Somer, Eli.; & Saadon, Meir. (1999). Therapist-client sex: Clients' retrospective reports. *Professional Psychology: Research and Practice, 30,* 504–509.

Sommers, Christina Hoff. (2000, May). The war against boys. *Atlantic Monthly, 285,* 59–74.

Spence, Janet T. (1985). Gender identity and its implications for the concepts of masculinity and femininity. In Theo B. Sonderegger (Ed.), *Nebraska Symposium on Motivation, 1984: Psychology and gender* (Vol. 32; pp. 59–95). Lincoln: University of Nebraska Press.

Spence, Janet T.; & Buckner, Camille E. (2000). Instrumental and expressive traits, trait stereotypes, and sexist attitudes: What do they signify? *Psychology of Women Quarterly, 24,* 44–62.

Spence, Janet T.; & Hahn, Eugene D. (1997). The Attitudes Toward Women Scale and attitude change in college students. *Psychology of Women Quarterly, 21,* 17–34.

Spence, Janet T.; & Helmreich, Robert. (1978). *Masculinity and femininity: The psychological dimensions, correlates, and antecedents.* Austin: University of Texas Press.

Spence, Janet T.; Helmreich, Robert; & Stapp, Joy. (1974). The Personal Attributes Questionnaire: A measure of sex-role stereotypes and masculinity-femininity. *JSAS Catalog of Selected Documents in Psychology, 4,* 43 (Ms. no. 617).

Spitzer, Brenda L.; Henderson, Katherine A.; & Zivian, Marilyn T. (1999). Gender differences in population versus media body sizes: A comparison over four decades. *Sex Roles, 40,* 545–566.

Sprecher, Susan; & Felmlee, Diane. (1997). The balance of power in romantic heterosexual couples over time from "his" and "her" perspectives. *Sex Roles, 37,* 361–379.

Sprecher, Susan; Hatfield, Elaine; Cortese, Anthony; Potapova, Elena; & Levitskaya, Anna. (1994). Token resistance to sexual intercourse and consent to unwanted sexual intercourse: College students' dating experiences in three countries. *Journal of Sex Research, 31,* 125–132.

Sprecher, Susan; Regan, Pamela C.; & McKinney, Kathleen. (1998). Beliefs about the outcomes of extramarital sexual relationships as a function of the gender of the "cheating spouse." *Sex Roles, 38,* 301–311.

Sprecher, Susan; Regan, Pamela C.; McKinney, Kathleen; Maxwell, Kellye; & Wazienski, Robert. (1997). Preferred level of sexual experience in date or mate: The merger of two methodologies. *Journal of Sex Research, 34,* 327–337.

Springer, Sally P.; & Deutsch, Georg. (1998). *Left brain, right brain* (5th ed.). New York: Freeman.

Sroufe, L. Alan; Bennett, Christopher; Englund, Michelle; & Urban, Joan. (1993). The significance of gender boundaries in preadolescence: Contemporary correlates and antecedents of boundary violation and maintenance. *Child Development, 64,* 455–466.

Stack, Carol B. (1997). Different voices, different visions: Gender, culture, and moral reasoning. In Maxine Baca Zinn, Pierrette Hondagneu-Sotelo, & Michael A. Messner (Eds.), *Through the prism of difference: Readings on sex and gender* (pp. 51–57). Boston: Allyn and Bacon.

Stangor, Charles; & Ruble, Diane N. (1987). Development of gender role knowledge and gender constancy. In Lynn S. Liben & Margaret L. Signorella (Eds.), *Children's gender schemata* (pp. 5–22). San Francisco: Jossey-Bass.

Stark, Ellen. (1989, May). Teen sex: Not for love. *Psychology Today,* pp. 10–12.

Steele, Claude M. (1997). A threat in the air: How stereotypes shape intellectual identity and performance. *American Psychologist, 52,* 613–629.

Steele, Claude M.; & Aronson, Joshua. (1995). Stereotype threat and the intellectual test performance of African Americans. *Journal of Personality and Social Psychology, 69,* 797–811.

Steil, Janice M. (1989). Marital relationships and mental health: The psychic costs of equality. In Jo Freeman (Ed.), *Women: A feminist perspective* (pp. 138–148). Mountain View, CA: Mayfield.

Steil, Janice M. (1995). Supermoms and second shifts: Marital inequality in the 1990s. In Jo Freeman (Ed.), *Women: A feminist perspective* (5th ed.; pp. 149–181). Mountain View, CA: Mayfield.

Stein, Murray B.; Walker, John R.; & Forde, David R. (2000). Gender differences in susceptibility to posttraumatic stress disorder. *Behavior Research and Therapy, 38,* 619–628.

Steinberg, Karen K.; Thacker, Stephen B.; Smith, Jay; Stroup, Donna F.; Zack, Matthew M.; Flanders, Dana; & Berkelmen, Ruth L. (1991). A meta-analysis of the effect of estrogen replacement therapy on the risk of breast cancer. *Journal of the American Medical Association, 265,* 1985–1990.

Steingart, Richard M.; Packer, Milton; Hamm, Peggy; Coglianese, Mary Ellen; Gersh, Bernard; Geltman, Edward M.; Sollano, Josephie; Katz, Stanley; Moyé, Lem; Basta, Lofty L.; Lewis, Sandra J.; Gottlieb, Stephen S.; Bernstein, Victoria; McEwan, Patricia; Jacobson, Kirk; Brown, Edward J.; Kukin, Marrick L.; Kantrowitz, Niki E.; & Pfeffer, Marc A. (1991). Sex differences in the management of coronary artery disease. *New England Journal of Medicine, 325,* 226–230.

Steinke, Jocelyn; & Long, M. (1996). A lab of her own?: Portrayals of female characters on children's educational science programs. *Science Communication, 18,* 91–115.

Steinpreis, Rhea E.; Ritzke, Dawn; & Anders, Katie A. (1999). The impact of gender on the review of the curricula vitae of job applicants and tenure candidates: A national empirical study. *Sex Roles, 41,* 509–528.

Stephan, Cookie White; Stephan, Walter C.; Demitrakis, Katherine M.; Yamada, Ann Marie; & Clason, Dennis L. (2000). Women's attitudes toward men: An integrated threat theory approach. *Psychology of Women Quarterly, 24,* 63–73.

Stephens, Julie. (1999, June). The gendering of depression in children's films. *Arena Magazine,* 69.

Stephenson, P. Susan; & Walker, Gillian A. (1979). The psychiatrist-woman patient relationship. *Canadian Journal of Psychiatry, 24,* 5–16.

Sternberg, Robert J. (1986). A triangular theory of love. *Psychological Review, 93,* 119–135.

Sternberg, Robert J. (1987). Liking versus loving: A comparative evaluation of theories. *Psychological Bulletin, 102,* 331–345.

Sternberg, Robert J. (1998). *Love is a story: A new theory of relationships.* New York: Oxford University Press.

Stipp, David. (1996, May 13). The gender gap in cancer research. *Fortune, 133*(9), 74–76.

St. Lawrence, Janet S.; & McFarlane, Mary. (1999). Research methods in the study of sexual behavior. In Philip C. Kendall, James N. Butcher, & Grayson N. Holmbeck (Eds.), *Handbook of research methods in clinical psychology* (2nd ed.; pp. 584–615). New York: Wiley.

Stohs, Joanne Hoven. (2000). Multicultural women's experience of household labor, conflicts, and equity. *Sex Roles, 42,* 339–362.

Stokes, Joseph; Riger, Stephanie; & Sullivan, Megan. (1995). Measuring perceptions of the working environment for women in corporate settings. *Psychology of Women Quarterly, 19,* 533–549.

Straus, Murray A.; & Gelles, Richard J. (1986). Societal change and change in family violence from 1975 to 1985 as revealed by two national surveys. *Journal of Marriage and the Family, 48,* 465–479.

Straus, Murray A.; Gelles, Richard J.; & Steinmetz, Suzanne K. (1980). *Behind closed doors: Violence in the American family.* Garden City, NY: Anchor.

Stroh, Linda K.; Brett, Jeanne M.; & Reilly, Anne H. (1992). All the right stuff: A comparison of female and male managers' career progression. *Journal of Applied Psychology, 77,* 251–260.

Struckman-Johnson, Cindy. (1988). Forced sex on dates: It happens to men, too. *Journal of Sex Research, 24,* 234–241.

Struckman-Johnson, Cindy; & Struckman-Johnson, David. (1993). College men's and women's reactions to hypothetical sexual touch varied by initiator gender and coercion level. *Sex Roles, 29,* 317–385.

Struckman-Johnson, Cindy; & Struckman-Johnson, David. (1994). Men pressured and forced into sexual experience. *Archives of Sexual Behavior, 23,* 93–114.

Stumpf, Heinrich. (1993). Performance factors and gender-related differences in spatial ability: Another assessment. *Memory & Cognition, 21,* 828–836.

Subrahmanyam, Kaveri; & Greenfield, Patricia M. (1994). Effect of video game practice on spatial skills in girls and boys. *Journal of Applied Developmental Psychology, 15,* 13–32.

Suggs, Welch. (1999, May 21). More women participate in intercollegiate athletics. *Chronicle of Higher Education,* A44.

Suitor, J. Jill; & Carter, Rebecca S. (1999). Jocks, nerds, babes and thugs: A research note on regional differences in adolescent gender norms. *Gender Issues, 17,* 88–101.

Suitor, J. Jill; & Reavis, Rebel. (1995). Football, fast cars, and cheerleading: Adolescent gender norms. *Adolescence, 30,* 265–272.

Swaab, D. F.; & Fliers, E. (1985). A sexually dimorphic nucleus in the human brain. *Science, 228,* 1112–1115.

Swaab, D. F.; Gooren, L. J. G.; & Hofman, M. A. (1995). Brain research, gender, and sexual orientation. *Journal of Homosexuality, 28,* 283–301.

Swain, Scott O. (1992). Men's friendships with women: Intimacy, sexual boundaries, and the informant role. In Peter M. Nardi (Ed.), *Men's friendships* (pp. 153–171). Newbury Park, CA: Sage.

Swim, Janet K. (1994). Perceived versus meta-analytic effect sizes: An assessment of the accuracy of gender stereotypes. *Journal of Personality and Social Psychology, 66,* 21–36.

Tannen, Deborah. (1990). *You just don't understand: Women and men in conversation.* New York: William Morrow.

Tarkan, Laurie. (1995). Unequal opportunity. *Women's Sports and Fitness, 17,* 25–27.

Tavris, Carol. (1982). *Anger: The misunderstood emotion.* New York: Touchstone.

Tavris, Carol. (1992). *The mismeasure of woman.* New York: Simon & Schuster.

Tavris, Carol. (1994). Reply to Brown and Gilligan. *Feminism & Psychology, 4,* 350–352.

Tavris, Carol; & Wade, Carole. (1984). *The longest war: Sex differences in perspective* (2nd ed.). New York: Harcourt Brace Jovanovich.

Taylor, Shelley E.; Klein, Laura Cousino; Lewis, Brian P.; Gruenewald, Tara L.; Gurung, Regan A. R.; & Updegraff, John A. (2000). Biobehavioral responses to stress in females tend-and-befriend, not fight-or-flight. *Psychological Review, 107,* 411–429.

Terman, Lewis M.; & Merrill, Maud A. (1937). *Measuring intelligence.* Boston: Houghton Mifflin.

Theberge, Nancy. (1991). A content analysis of print media coverage of gender, women, and physical activity. *Journal of Applied Sport Psychology, 3,* 36–48.

Thompson, Becky Wangsgaard. (1999). "A way outa no way": Eating problems among African-American, Latina, and White women. In Carie Forden, Anne E. Hunter, & Beverly Birns (Eds.), *Readings in the psychology of women: Dimensions of the female experience* (pp. 340–351). Boston: Allyn and Bacon.

Thompson, Linda; & Walker, Alexis J. (1989). Gender in families: Women and men in marriage, work, and parenthood. *Journal of Marriage and the Family, 51,* 845–871.

Thompson, Sharon. (1999). Putting a big thing into a little hold: Teenage girls' accounts of sexual initiation. In Carie Forden, Anne E. Hunter, & Beverly Birns (Eds.), *Readings in the psychology of women: Dimensions of the female experience* (pp. 93–108). Boston: Allyn and Bacon.

Thompson, Teresa L.; & Zerbinos, Eugenia. (1995). Gender roles in animated cartoons: Has the picture changed in 20 years? *Sex Roles, 32,* 651–674.

Thompson, Teresa. L.; & Zerbinos, E. (1997). Television cartoons: Do children notice it's a boy's world. *Sex Roles, 37,* 415–432.

Thorne, Barrie. (1993). *Gender play: Girls and boys in school.* New Brunswick, NJ: Rutgers University Press.

Thornhill, Randy; & Palmer, Craig. (2000). *A natural history of rape: Biological bases of sexual coercion.* Cambridge, MA: MIT Press.

Tiefer, Lenore. (1995). *Sex is not a natural act and other essays.* Boulder, CO: Westview Press.

Tiger, Lionel. (2000). The decline of males. *Society, 37*(2), 6–9.

Tittle, Carol Kehr. (1986). Gender research and education. *American Psychologist, 41,* 1161–1168.

Titus, Jordan J. (1993). Gender messages in education foundations textbooks. *Journal of Teacher Education, 44,* 38–43.

Tjaden, Patricia; & Thoennes, Nancy. (2000). *Extent, nature and consequences of intimate partner violence: Findings from the National Violence Against Women Survey.* Washington, DC: U.S. Department of Justice.

Tjaden, Patricia Godeke; & Tjaden, Claus D. (1981). Differential treatment of the female felon: Myth or reality? In Marguerite O. Warren (Ed.), *Comparing female and male offenders* (pp. 73–88). Beverly Hills, CA: Sage.

Tobin-Richards, Maryse H.; Boxer, Andrew M.; & Petersen, Anne C. (1983). The psychological significance of pubertal change sex differences in perceptions of self during early adolescence. In Jeanne Brooks-Gunn & Anne C. Petersen (Eds.), *Girls at puberty: Biological and psychosocial perspectives* (pp. 127–154). New York: Plenum Press.

Tomasson, Kristinn; Kent, D.; & Coryell, W. (1991). Somatization and conversion disorders: Comorbidity and demographics at presentation. *Acta Psychiatrica Scandinavica, 84,* 288–293.

Travis, Cheryl Brown. (1988a). *Women and health psychology: Biomedical issues.* Hillsdale, NJ: Erlbaum.

Travis, Cheryl Brown. (1988b). *Women and health psychology: Mental health issues.* Hillsdale, NJ: Erlbaum.

Trentham, Susan; & Larwood, Laurie. (1998). Gender discrimination and the workplace: An examination of rational bias theory. *Sex Roles, 38,* 1–28.

Turner-Bowker, Diane M. (1996). Gender stereotyped descriptors in children's picture books: Does "Curious Jane" exist in the literature? *Sex Roles, 35,* 461–488.

Twenge, Jean M. (1997). Attitudes toward women, 1970–1995. *Psychology of Women Quarterly, 21,* 35–51.

Unger, Rhoda K. (1979). Toward a redefinition of sex and gender. *American Psychologist, 34,* 1085–1094.

Unger, Rhoda K. (1995). Conclusion: Cultural diversity and the future of feminist psychology. In Hope Landrine (Ed.), *Bringing cultural diversity to feminist psychology* (pp. 413–431). Washington, DC: American Psychological Association.

Unger, Rhoda K.; & Crawford, Mary. (1993). Commentary: Sex and gender—The troubled relationship between terms and concepts. *Psychological Science, 4,* 122–124.

Upchurch, Dawn M.; Levy-Storms, Lene; Sucoff, Clea A.; & Aneshensel, Carol S. (1998). Gender and ethnic differences in the timing of first sexual intercourse. *Family Planning Perspectives, 30,* 121–127.

Urberg, Katheryn A. (1979). Sex role conceptualizations in adolescents and adults. *Developmental Psychology, 15,* 90–92.

U.S. Bureau of the Census. (1975). *Historical Statistics of the United States, Colonial Times to 1970.* Washington, DC: U.S. Government Printing Office.

U.S. Bureau of the Census. (1999). *Statistical abstracts of the United States, 1999* (119th ed.). Washington, DC: U.S. Government Printing Office.

U.S. Bureau of Labor Statistics. (2000). Annual average tables from the January 2000 issue of Employment and Earnings. http://stats.bls.gov/cpsaatab.htm.

U.S. Department of Education (USDE), National Center for Education Statistics. (1999). *The condition of education 1999.* (NCES 1999-0220). Washington, DC: U.S. Government Printing Office.

U.S. Department of Education, National Center for Education Statistics. (2000). *The condition of education 2000* (NCES 2000-602). Washington, DC: U.S. Government Printing Office.

U.S. Department of Health and Human Services. (1989). *Reducing the health consequences of smoking: Nicotine addiction. A report of the Surgeon General, 1988* (DHHS Publication no. DC 88-8406). Washington, DC: U.S. Government Printing Office.

U.S. Department of Health and Human Services. (1990). *Alcohol and health: Seventh special report to the U.S. Congress.* (DHHS Publication no. ADM 90-1656). Washington, DC: U.S. Government Printing Office.

U.S. Department of Health and Human Services. (1997). *Child maltreatment 1995: Reports from the states to the National Child Abuse and Neglect data system.* Washington, DC: U.S. Government Printing Office.

U.S. Department of Health and Human Services (USDHHS). (1999a). *Healthy People, 2010.* Washington, DC: U.S. Government Printing Office.

U.S. Department of Health and Human Services (USDHHS). (1999b). *Mental health: A report of the surgeon general.* Washington, DC: U.S. Government Printing Office.

U.S. Department of Health and Human Services (USDHHS). (2000). *Health, United States, 2000.* Washington, DC: U.S. Government Printing Office.

U.S. Department of Justice. (1999a). *Sourcebook of criminal justice statistics 1998.* Washington, DC: U.S. Government Printing Office.

U.S. Department of Justice. (1999b). *Uniform crime reports: Crime in the United States 1998.* Washington, DC: U.S. Government Printing Office.

Vance, Carole S. (1984). Pleasure and danger: Toward a politics of sexuality. In Carole S. Vance (Ed.), *Pleasure and danger: Exploring female sexuality* (pp. 1–27). Boston: Routledge & Kegan Paul.

Vandervoort, Debra. (1999). Quality of social support in mental and physical health. *Current Psychology, 18,* 205–222.

Vasquez, Melba J. T. (1994). Latinas. In Lillian Comas-Díaz & Beverly Greene (Eds.), *Women of color: Integrating ethnic and gender identities in psychotherapy* (pp. 114–138). New York: Guilford Press.

Vasquez, Melba J. T.; & Kitchener, Karen Strohm. (1988). Introduction to special feature: Ethics in counseling: Sexual intimacy between counselor and client. *Journal of Counseling and Development, 67,* 214–217.

Vasta, Ross; Knott, Jill A.; & Gaze, Christine E. (1996). Can spatial training erase the gender differences on the water-level task? *Psychology of Women Quarterly, 20,* 549–567.

Vazquez-Nuttall, Ena; Romero-Garcia, Ivonne; & De Leon, Brunilda. (1987). Sex roles and perceptions of femininity and masculinity of Hispanic women. *Psychology of Women Quarterly, 11,* 409–425.

Verbrugge, Lois M. (1985). Gender and health: An update on hypotheses and evidence. *Journal of Health and Social Behavior, 26,* 156–182.

Verbrugge, Lois M. (1989). The twain meet: Emprical explanations of sex differences in health and mortality. *Journal of Health and Social Behavior, 30,* 282–304.

Voyer, Daniel; Voyer, Susan; & Bryden, M. Philip. (1995). Magnitude of sex differences in spatial abilities: A meta-analysis and consideration of critical variables. *Psychological Bulletin, 117,* 250–270.

Wainryb, Cecilia. (1993). The application of moral judgments to other cultures: Relativism and universality. *Child Development, 64,* 924–933.

Waldron, Ingrid. (1991). Effects of labor force participation on sex differences in mortality and morbidity. In Marianne Frankenhaeuser, Ulf Lundberg, & Margaret Chesney (Eds.), *Women, work, and health: Stress and opportunities* (pp. 17–38). New York: Plenum Press.

Walker, Betty A.; Reis, Sally M.; & Leonard, Janet S. (1992). A developmental investigation of the lives of gifted women. *Gifted Child Quarterly, 36,* 201–206.

Walker, Lenore E. (1989). Psychology and violence against women. *American Psychologist, 44,* 695–702.

Walker, William D.; Rowe, Robert C.; & Quinsey, Vernon L. (1993). Authoritarianism and sexual aggression. *Journal of Personality and Social Psychology, 65,* 1036–1045.

Wallace, Julia E. (1996). Gender differences in beliefs of why women live longer than men. *Psychological Reports, 79,* 587–591.

Wallston, Barbara Strudler. (1981). What are the questions in psychology of women? A feminist approach to research. *Psychology of Women Quarterly, 5,* 597–617.

Walsh, Mary Roth. (1985). Academic professional women organizing for change: The struggle in psychology. *Journal of Social Issues, 41*(4), 17–28.

Warin, Jo. (2000). The attainment of self-consistency through gender in young children. *Sex Roles, 42,* 209–232.

Wark, Gillian R.; & Krebs, Dennis L. (1996). Gender and dilemma differences in real-life moral judgment. *Developmental Psychology, 32,* 220–230.

Warr, Mark. (1985). Fear of rape among urban women. *Social Problems, 32,* 238–250.

Warren, Marguerite O. (1981). Gender comparisons in crime and delinquency. In Marguerite O. Warren

(Ed.), *Comparing female and male offenders* (pp. 7–16). Beverly Hills. CA: Sage.

Waterhouse, Ruth L. (1993). "Wild women don't have the blues": A feminist critique of "person-centered" counselling and therapy. *Feminism & Psychology, 3,* 55–71.

Way, Niobe. (1997). Using feminist research methods to understand the friendships of adolescent boys. *Journal of Social Issues, 53*(4), 703–723.

Weber, Lynn. (1998). A conceptual framework for understanding race, class, gender, and sexuality. *Psychology of Women Quarterly, 22,* 13–32.

Weidner, Gerdi. (2000). Why do men get more heart disease than women? An international perspective. *Journal of American College Health, 48,* 291–294.

Weinberg, Nancy; Uken, Janet S.; Schmale, John; & Adamek, Margaret. (1995). Therapeutic factors: Their presence in a computer-mediated support group. *Social Work with Groups, 18*(4), 57–69.

Weinburgh, Molly. (1995). Gender differences in student attitudes toward science: A meta-analysis of the literature from 1970 to 1991. *Journal of Research in Science Teaching, 32,* 387–398.

Weisman, Claire V.; Gray, James J.; Mosimann, James E.; & Ahrens, Anthony H. (1992). Cultural expectations of thinness in women: An update. *International Journal of Eating Disorders, 11,* 85–89.

Weisner, Thomas S.; & Wilson-Mitchell, Jane E. (1990). Nonconventional family life-styles and sex typing in six-year-olds. *Child Development, 61,* 1915–1933.

Weiss, Maureen R.; & Barber, Heather. (1995). Socialization influences of collegiate male athletes: A tale of two decades. *Sex Roles, 33,* 129–140.

Weisstein, Naomi. (1970). "Kinde, küche, kirche" as scientific law: Psychology constructs the female. In Robin Morgan (Ed.), *Sisterhood is powerful: An anthology of writings from the women's liberation movement* (pp. 228–245). New York: Vintage Books.

Weisstein, Naomi. (1982, November). Tired of arguing about biological inferiority? *Ms.,* pp. 41–46, 85.

Weitz, Rose. (2001). *The sociology of health, illness, and health care: A critical approach* (2nd ed.). Belmont, CA: Wadsworth.

Weitzman, Lenore. (1985). *The divorce revolution: The unexpected social and economic consequences for women and children in America.* New York: Free Press.

Welch-Ross, Melissa K.; Schmidt, Constance R. (1996). Gender-schema development and children's constructive story memory: Evidence or a developmental model. *Child Development, 67,* 820–835.

Wellman, Barry. (1992). Men in networks: Private communities, domestic friendships. In Peter M. Nardi (Ed.), *Men's friendships* (pp. 74–114). Newbury Park, CA: Sage.

Welter, Barbara. (1978). The cult of true womanhood: 1820–1860. In Michael Gordon (Ed.), *The American family in social-historical perspective* (2nd ed.; pp. 313–333). New York: St. Martin's Press.

West, Candace; & Zimmerman, Don H. (1987). Doing gender. *Gender and Society, 1,* 125–151.

Westkott, Marcia C. (1997). On the new psychology of women: A cautionary view. In Mary Roth Walsh (Ed.), *Women, men, and gender: Ongoing debates* (pp. 362–372). New Haven, CT: Yale University Press.

Wharton, Amy S.; & Baron, James N. (1987). So happy together? The impact of gender segregation on men at work. *American Sociological Review, 52,* 574–587.

Wharton, Amy S.; & Baron, James N. (1991). Satisfaction? The psychological impact of gender segregation on women at work. *Sociological Quarterly, 32,* 365–387.

Whatley, Marianne H. (1990). Sex equity in sex education. *Education Digest, 55*(5), 46–49.

White, Mark B.; Tyson-Rawson, Kirsten J. (1996, March/April). A peace plan for the gender wars. *Psychology Today, 29*(2), 51–54, 74, 76, 78, 80, 85.

Whiting, Beatrice Blyth; & Edwards, Carolyn Pope. (1988). *Children of different worlds: The formation of social behavior.* Cambridge, MA: Harvard University Press.

WHO International Consortium in Psychiatric Epidemiology. (2000). Cross-national comparisons of the prevalences and correlates of mental disorders. *Bulletin of the World Health Organization, 78,* 413–426.

Widiger, Thomas A.; & Settle, Shirley A. (1987). Broverman et al. revisited: An artifactual sex bias. *Journal of Personality and Social Psychology, 53,* 463–469.

Wieringa, Saskia E. (1994). The Zuni man-woman. *Archives of Sexual Behavior, 23,* 348–351.

Wilbur, Jerry. (1987). Does mentoring breed success? *Training & Development Journal, 41*(11), 38–41.

Wiley, Mary Glenn; & Eskilson, Arlene. (1985). Speech style, gender stereotypes, and corporate success: What if women talk more like men? *Sex Roles, 12,* 993–1007.

Wilkinson, Sue. (1999). Focus groups: A feminist method. *Psychology of Women Quarterly, 23,* 221–244.

Willemsen, Tineke M. (1998). Widening the gender gap: teenage magazines for girls and boys. *Sex Roles, 38,* 851–861.

Willett, Walter C. (1999). Goals for nutrition in the year 2000. *Ca, 49,* 3–21.

Williams, Christine L. (1992). The glass escalator: Hidden advantages for men in the "female" professions. *Social Problems, 39,* 253–267.

Williams, David R.; Takeuchi, David T.; & Adair, Russell K. (1992). Socioeconomic status and psychiatric disorder among Blacks and Whites. *Social Forces, 71,* 179–194.

Williams, Janet B. W.; & Spitzer, Robert L. (1983). The issue of sex bias in DSM-III: A critique of "A woman's view of DSM-III" by Marcie Kaplan. *American Psychologist, 38,* 793–801.

Williams, Joan. (2000). *Unbending gender: Why family and work conflict and what to do about it.* New York: Oxford University Press.

Williams, John E.; & Best, Deborah L. (1990). *Measuring sex stereotypes: A multination study* (Rev. ed.). Newbury Park, CA: Sage.

Williams, Juanita H. (1983). *Psychology of women: Behavior in a biosocial context.* (2nd ed.). New York: Norton.

Willingham, Warren W.; & Cole, Nancy S. (1997). *Gender and fair assessment.* Mahwah, NJ: Erlbaum.

Willingham, Warren W.; Cole, Nancy S.; Lewis, Charles.; & Leung, Susan Wilson. (1997). Test performance. In Warren W. Willingham & Nancy S. Cole, *Gender and fair assessment* (pp. 55–126). Mahwah, NJ: Erlbaum.

Wilson, Robert A. (1966). *Feminine forever.* New York: M. Evans.

Wisch, Andrew F.; Mahalik, James R.; Hayes, Jeffrey A.; & Nutt, Elizabeth A. (1995). The impact of gender role conflict and counseling techniques on psychological help seeking in men. *Sex Roles, 33,* 77–89.

Wiseman, Claire V.; Gray, James J.; Mosimann, James E.; & Ahrens, Anthony H. (1992). Cultural expectations of thinness in women: An update. *International Journal of Eating Disorders, 11,* 85–89.

Witkin, Herman A.; Mednick, Sarnoff A.; Schulsinger, Fini; Bakkestrøm, Eskild; Christiansen, Karlo O.; Goodenough, Donald R.; Hirschhorn, Kurt; Lundesteen, Claes; Owen, David R.; Philip, John; Rubin, Donald B.; & Stocking, Martha. (1976). Criminality in XYY and XXY men. *Science, 193,* 547–555.

Wituk, Scott; Shepherd, Matthew D.; Slavich, Susan; Warren, Mary L.; & Meissen, Greg. (2000). A topography of self-help groups: An empirical analysis. *Social Work, 45,* 157–165.

Women's International Network. (2000). Europe: Domestic violence—Some facts and figures. *WIN News, 26*(1), 47.

Wooley, O. Wayne. (1994). ...And man created "woman": Representations of women's bodies in Western culture. In Patricia Fallon, Melanie A. Katzman, & Susan C. Wooley (Eds.), *Feminist perspectives on eating disorders* (pp. 17–52). New York: Guilford.

Worell, Judith. (1996). Opening doors to feminist research. *Psychology of Women Quarterly, 20,* 469–485.

Worell, Judith; & Etaugh, Claire. (1994). Transforming theory and research with women: Themes and variations. *Psychology of Women Quarterly, 18,* 443–450.

Wyatt, Gail E. (1985). The sexual abuse of Afro-American and White-American women in childhood. *Child Abuse and Neglect, 9,* 507–519.

Wyatt, Gail Elizabeth. (1992). The sociocultural context of African American and White American women's rape. *Journal of Social Issues, 48*(1), 77–91.

Wyatt, Gail Elizabeth. (1994). The sociocultural relevance of sex research: Challenges for the 1990s and beyond. *American Psychologist, 49,* 748–754.

Xinhua News Agency. (2000, April 5). Local regulations issued to prevent domestic violence. Author, p. 1008096h1161.

Yama, Mark F.; Tovey, Stephanie L.; & Fogas, Bruce S. (1993). Childhood family environment and sexual abuse as predictors of anxiety and depression in adult women. *American Journal of Orthopsychiatry, 63,* 136–141.

Yeoman, Barry. (1999, November). Bad girls. *Psychology Today, 32,* 54–57, 71.

Yoder, Janice D.; & Kahn, Arnold S. (1993). Working toward an inclusive psychology of women. *American Psychologist, 48,* 846–850.

Yoder, Janice D.; & Schleicher, Thomas L. (1996). Undergraduates regard deviation from occupational gender stereotypes as costly for women. *Sex Roles, 34,* 171–188.

Zajonc, R. C. (1984). On the primacy of affect. *American Psychologist, 39,* 117–123.

Zera, Deborah. (1992). Coming of age in a heterosexist world: The development of gay and lesbian adolescents. *Adolescence, 27,* 849–854.

Zimmer-Schur, Lori A.; & Newcomb, Michael D. (1994, August). *Dieting and exercise behaviors:*

Subscale development gender differences and depression. Paper presented at the 102nd annual convention of the American Psychological Association, Los Angeles, CA.

Zinik, Cary. (1985). Identity conflict or adaptive flexibility? Bisexuality reconsidered. *Journal of Homosexuality, 11,* 7–19.

Zucker, Kenneth J.; & Bradley, Susan J. (1995). *Gender identity disorder and psychosexual problems in children and adolescents.* New York: Guilford.

Zucker, Kenneth J.; Bradley, Susan J.; & Sanikhani, Mohammad. (1997). Sex differences in referral rates of children with gender identity disorder: Some hypotheses. *Journal of Abnormal Child Psychology, 25,* 217–227.

Zucker, Kenneth J.; Wilson-Smith, Debra N.; Kurita, Janice A.; & Stern, Anita. (1995). Children's appraisals of sex-typed behavior in their peers. *Sex Roles, 33,* 703–725.

Name Index

Subject Index